The Insider/Outsider Debate

The Insider/Outsider Debate
New Perspectives in the Study of Religion

Edited by
George D. Chryssides and Stephen E. Gregg

SHEFFIELD UK   BRISTOL CT

Published by Equinox Publishing Ltd.

UK: Office 415, The Workstation, 15 Paternoster Row, Sheffield, South Yorkshire S1 2BX

USA: ISD, 70 Enterprise Drive, Bristol, CT 06010

www.equinoxpub.com

First published 2019

© George D. Chryssides, Stephen E. Gregg and contributors 2019

All rights reserved. No part of this publication may be reproduced or transmitted in any form or by any means, electronic or mechanical, including photocopying, recording or any information storage or retrieval system, without prior permission in writing from the publishers.

ISBN 978 1 78179 343 5 (hardback)
     978 1 78179 344 2 (paperback)
     978 1 78179 852 2 (ePDF)

British Library Cataloguing-in-Publication Data

A catalogue record for this book is available from the British Library.

Library of Congress Cataloging-in-Publication Data

Names: Chryssides, George D., 1945– editor.
Title: The insider-outsider debate : new perspectives in the study of
  religion / edited by George D. Chryssides and Stephen E. Gregg.
Description: Bristol : Equinox Publishing Ltd., 2019. | Includes
  bibliographical references and index.
Identifiers: LCCN 2018049704 (print) | LCCN 2019015961 (ebook) | ISBN
  9781781798522 (ePDF) | ISBN 9781781793435 (hb) | ISBN 9781781793442 (pb)
Subjects: LCSH: Religion–Study and teaching.
Classification: LCC BL41 (ebook) | LCC BL41 .I455 2019 (print) | DDC
  200.72–dc23
LC record available at https://lccn.loc.gov/2018049704

Typeset by JS Typesetting Ltd, Porthcawl, Mid Glamorgan

Contents

Preface   vii

Part I: New methodological approaches in the study of religion

1. Relational religious lives: beyond insider/outsider binaries in the study of religion
   Stephen E. Gregg and George D. Chryssides   3

2. The emics and etics of religion: what we know, how we know it and why this matters
   Steven J. Sutcliffe   30

3. The death pangs of the insider/outsider dichotomy in the study of religion
   Ron Geaves   53

4. Research ethics beyond the binaries of right and wrong
   Marie W. Dallam   70

5. Taking the body seriously, taking relationalities seriously: an embodied and relational approach to ethnographic research in the study of (lived) religion
   Nina Hoel   88

6. Negotiating blurred boundaries: ethnographic and methodological considerations
   Fiona Bowie   110

7. "On the edge of the inside": a contemplative approach to the study of religion
   Lynne Scholefield   130

8. Taking sides: on the (im)possibility of participant observation
   Rebecca Moore   151

9. Who researches? Who changes? Christian autoethnography and Muslim pupil identity in a Church of England primary school
   Tom Wilson   171

10. Imported insider/outsider boundaries: the case of contemporary Chinese Christianity researchers
    Naomi E. Thurston   190

Part II: Contested identities in the study of religion

11 Close encounters of a guru kind: ethnographic research as encounters with the cognitive worlds of others
    Stephen Jacobs — 213

12 Who is a Jew? New approaches to an old question
    Dan Cohn-Sherbok — 236

13 Between institutional oppression and spiritual liberation: the female ordination movement in the Catholic Church and its utilization of social media
    Lyndel Spence — 249

14 Navigating multiplicity in a binary world: a Javanese example of complex religious identity
    Katherine C. Rand — 270

15 When it gets crowded under the umbrella: an examination of scholarly categorization of Buddhist communities in the United States
    Claire Miller Skriletz — 291

16 Being Catholic since Vatican II: challenges and opportunities in secular times
    Andrew P. Lynch — 310

17 Reflexive and holistic switchers: older women/newer commitments
    Janet B. Eccles — 330

18 Scientology inside out: complex religious belonging in the Church of Scientology and the Free Zone
    Stephen E. Gregg and Aled J. L. Thomas — 350

19 Moving out: disengagement and ex-membership in new religious movements
    George D. Chryssides — 371

20 Both outside and inside: "ex-members" of new religions and spiritualities and the maintenance of community and identity on the internet
    Carole M. Cusack — 393

Index — 417

Preface

When the editors first contemplated a new volume on the insider/outsider debate, we decided to use a number of electronic lists to invite proposals. We expected only a small handful, but were quite overwhelmed with the response. Over forty colleagues from different cultural and geographic contexts sent in proposals, the vast majority of which were of a highly promising standard, and the end result is, we very much hope, a substantial volume which is testament to the keen interest that remains in this topic within the academic study of religion.

The classic text on the topic is still Russell McCutcheon's celebrated anthology *The Insider/Outsider Problem in the Study of Religion*, published in 1999. The book has a number of prevailing premises, which have come to be accepted by scholars of religion. First, those who have written about religion have tended to assume a binary distinction between "insider" and "outsider": either the researcher is a member of the religion under study or, perhaps more usually in this field, he or she is studying an unfamiliar worldview and lifestyle. The maxim that the scholar "makes the strange familiar, and the familiar strange" reinforces this dichotomy: we are either "at home" with the religion that we are researching, or it is "foreign" to us, and we use metaphors such as "positioning" oneself in relation to the subject matter. All this suggests boundaries and locations within them. Second, the problem tends to be defined as how the unfamiliar can be understood by the outsider, how the outsider researcher can find the essence of a religion, or indeed religion itself. A third issue concerns neutrality. To what extent can the scholar be neutral, and is neutrality – sometimes named methodological agnosticism – even desirable? Or should we just accept that there is no ideal vantage point or approach but, as the post-modernist would contend, simply a range of subjective perspectives, which we can only acknowledge?

The main thrust of the contributions in this anthology is that the issues are in reality much more complex. There are not merely insiders and outsiders, but a whole range of positions that those who belong or do not belong to religious communities find themselves in. The various authors explore the complexities of affiliation(s), non-affiliation(s) and disaffiliation(s), acknowledging different modes of accepting and rejecting various forms of religious life. We begin the volume with some methodological reflections. In the first chapter Stephen E. Gregg and George D. Chryssides explore inherited approaches to the debate within the academic study of religion, demonstrating the non-binary complexity of the issue, and the requirement for a new relational understanding of "insideness" and "outsideness" within emerging academic approaches subsequent to the dominance of the World Religions paradigm. In Chapter 2, Steven J. Sutcliffe analyses the use of the alternative terms emic and etic, applying them to the nebulous nature of the concept of New Age, making it problematic to define insiders and outsiders. This is followed by Ron Geaves's discussion of the contrast between seekers and scholars (Chapter 3), and why any such distinction cannot equate with any insider/outsider dichotomy.

Where one is researching a religious group to which one does not belong, how far inside should the researcher go? Marie W. Dallam raises this question in Chapter 4, asking the extent to which the researcher should participate, and how much he or she should disclose about identity and circumstances. If being an outsider is a barrier, engaging in covert research makes the outsider appear to be an insider – but what about the ethics of covert research? Nina Hoel (Chapter 5) likewise comments on the blurring of distinctions between the researcher and the subject and suggests that the relationship should not be defined starkly as insider/outsider, but rather as intersectional, and dependent on bodily characteristics such as gender, sexual orientation, age, ableness, race and class. The researcher "walks about with" her subjects, rather than observes them as objects. This focus upon relational approaches to insider-outsider issues is continued in Fiona Bowie's contribution (Chapter 6) which explores anthropological method in the study of religion, analysing how researchers are affected by their interaction with their subjects of research. Examining communities as diverse as British Spiritualist Mediums, Amerindian cosmology and French witches, Bowie argues that researchers are 'professional blurrer[s] of boundaries' in their role as ethnographers.

Chapters 7–11 deal with the role of participation in research. In Chapter 7 Lynne Scholefield explores the "edges of inside", referring to those who claim to be "spiritual but not religious", and the convert to a religious community, who therefore typically do not share all the characteristics of those who belong. Scholefield contends that some degree of religious practice – notably contemplative meditation - can open up an intersubjectivity which blurs the boundaries between insider and outsider. Rebecca Moore (Chapter 8) writes about Jim Jones's Peoples Temple from a unique stance: her two sisters died among the mass deaths, and she has participated in some of the survivors' gatherings, thus placing herself in a role that is neither inside nor outside, but which enables her to write a thought-provoking personal academic account here. Writing as an Anglican priest and academic, researching Muslim children in an Anglican primary school, Tom Wilson (Chapter 9) reflects on the issue of one's own identity as a researcher and the amount of forthrightness that is desirable. Wilson argues that divulging one's position in itself sets relational boundaries, but that this can also alter the boundaries surrounding one's own faith and one's own spiritual practices.

The relationship between one's own faith (where the researcher has one) and its academic study raises questions about the role of theology in academia. Focusing on Chinese academic life in Chapter 10, Naomi E. Thurston explores the question of whether theology is something that is done in the service of the Church, or whether Sino-Christian Studies more comfortably has a wider agenda, including history, translation of classical texts, and so on. The discussion raises questions of boundaries, both within academia, and with the Church. Stephen Jacobs (Chapter 11) raises issues about how the outsider penetrates – fails to penetrate – the world of the insider, with particular reference to the Hindu gurus Swami Divyananda Saraswati and Sri Sri Ravi Shankar. He argues that gaining access is not a simple matter of finding a "gatekeeper", but is rather a reflexive process, in which one reconciles and accommodates one's own view of reality with that of the community being researched.

In Chapters 12–16, contributors comment on a variety of forms of identity associated with religion. Dan Cohn-Sherbok raises the familiar question of "What is a Jew?" (Chapter 12), demonstrating a wide variety of forms that a Jewish identity can take, taking the reader far beyond the simplistic definition that a Jew as someone who is born of a Jewish mother. In Chapter 13 Lyndel Spence raises the question of who or what is a Roman Catholic, highlighting the variety of strands within one particular tradition – Roman Catholicism – and discusses a number of organizations committed to the ordination of women. The women's ordination movement illustrates the point that "insiderness" causes limitations for certain categories of adherence, in this case women. Katherine C. Rand, focusing on religion in Indonesia (Chapter 14), demonstrates that religious identity and diversity is not always found by belonging to a single tradition, but is complex, entailing that one can be "inside" in varying degrees to what have traditionally been identified as different faiths: Buddhism, Hinduism and Islam. Claire Miller Skriletz (Chapter 15) comments on the variety of identities that pertain to Buddhism, with special reference to Buddhist Churches of America. Identifying two main strands – "White Buddhism" and the type of Buddhism that has come to the West through immigration, she argues the importance of acknowledging one's own location as a scholar (in her case as a white non-Buddhist woman) in researching her subject matter. Discussion of the Roman Catholic tradition returns in Chapter 16, where Andrew P. Lynch discusses the Church in the wake of Vatican II, arguing that the distinction between insider and outsider is contested in the wake of modernity and the changing religious and cultural landscape. The phenomenon of the traditionalist Society of Saint Pius X (SSPX) highlights an interesting phenomenon of excommunication being revoked, while the schismatics do not become insiders to the Church's institutional structures.

Insider and outsider status is not static, but fluid, and the final four essays deal with ways in which people move away from their faiths. Janet B. Eccles (Chapter 17) uses a number of case studies of women whom she classifies as "reflexive switchers" and "holistic switchers". The former have sought more liberal ways of expressing their spirituality – sometimes to "New Age" ideas – while the latter have disaffiliated. The phenomenon of reflexive switching, she argues, should not be disparaged as picking and mixing, but a change in spiritual perception that blurs the boundaries between the sacred and the secular. The three subsequent chapters focus on new religions. Stephen E. Gregg and Aled J. L. Thomas (Chapter 18) focus on ways in which some Scientologists have moved away from the original Church of Scientology to practise the Religious Technology of L. Ron Hubbard, offering services based on a shared provenance, but outside the organization, thus also blurring boundaries between insider and outsider status. George D. Chryssides looks more generally at ex-members of new religious movements in Chapter 19, examining various typologies of leave-taker, the reliability of their testimony, and the different ways in which exiting can take place. In the final Chapter 20, Carole M. Cusack considers ex-members of two new religious groups – Kerista, which is now defunct as a commune, and the School of Economic Science. Both sets of ex-members have taken their former membership online, and continue to exchange reflections. Such forms of ex-membership, of course, maintain an interest in the form of organization, again the blurring insider/outsider distinctions.

About the authors

Stephen E. Gregg is senior lecturer in religious studies at the University of Wolverhampton, and honorary secretary of the British Association for the Study of Religions. He studied at the University of Wales, Lampeter, and has previously taught at the University of Wales, and Liverpool Hope University. His work focuses upon minority communities and muted voices in contemporary religion, and method and theory in the Study of Religion. Recent and in-press books include *Jesus Beyond Christianity* (Oxford University Press, 2010, with Gregory A. Barker) *Engaging with Living Religion* (Routledge, 2015, with Lynne Scholefield), *A Universal Advaita: Swami Vivekananda and Non-Hindu Traditions* (Routledge, 2019) and *The Bloomsbury Handbook to Studying Christians* (Bloomsbury, 2019, with George D. Chryssides).

George D. Chryssides studied philosophy and theology at the University of Glasgow, and gained his doctorate from the University of Oxford. He taught philosophy and religious studies at various British universities, and was head of religious studies at the University of Wolverhampton, England from 2001 to 2008. He is currently honorary research fellow at York St John University. He has published extensively, principally on new religious movements, and recent publications include *The A to Z of Jehovah's Witnesses* (2009); *Heaven's Gate: Postmodernity and Popular Culture in a Suicide Group* (2011); *Christians in the Twenty-First Century* (with Margaret Z. Wilkins, 2011); *Historical Dictionary of New Religious Movements* (2012) and *Jehovah's Witnesses: Continuity and Change* (2016). He has co-edited (with Benjamin E. Zeller) *The Bloomsbury Companion to New Religious Movements* (2014), and *The Bloomsbury Handbook to Studying Christians* (2019), edited with Stephen E. Gregg.

PART I
NEW METHODOLOGICAL APPROACHES IN THE STUDY OF RELIGION

1

Relational religious lives

Beyond insider/outsider binaries in the study of religion

Stephen E. Gregg and George D. Chryssides

The insider/outsider debate is frequently described as the "insider/outsider problem". There would appear superficially to be few problems relating to belonging. Surely people belong to a religion or they do not? When asked their affiliation, they can usually give a reply with little difficulty. When a question about religious affiliation is asked in a national census, few, if any, have difficulty in responding, although of course some may decline to answer, or find that the specific category into which they fit is not provided.

There is a cluster of questions that pertain to belonging to religions. In England and Wales some 59 per cent of the population defined themselves as Christian in the 2011 census, yet that proportion in no way was reflected in church attendance, which is around 4.7 per cent (Office of National Statistics 2012; Faith Survey 2018). So, if we are studying "the Christian faith", who are the Christians that we are supposed to be studying? Should our subject matter be identified by people's self-definition, or should we exclusively be interested in those who are sufficiently involved to be part of a congregation? Is there a phenomenon of "believing without belonging", or should the study of a religion be focused on those who belong? There are other measures than self-definition and attendance, however: there are ways in which one can make belonging explicit, such as baptism, confirmation, or placing oneself on a membership roll. But again, not all religious organizations have such visible signs, and those who undergo rites of passage such as baptism may show no further commitment.

There is a wider issue about belonging. If we are considering religions in terms of the broad "world religion" categories, then who should we regard as inside, and who is outside? Are Jehovah's Witnesses or members of Sun Myung Moon's Unification Church Christian, or are they outside the true Church? Many mainstream Christians would regard them as outsiders, using descriptors like "cult", "sect", or "Christian deviations". To what extent is it permissible to use such categories to describe those who appear to be on the fringes of a faith? Scholars have tended to avoid such terms on the ground that they are pejorative, and that the study of religion ought to be as objective as possible.

This raises the question of objectivity. Is it possible – or even desirable – to be objective in studying a religious community? Might this depend on whether the scholar belongs to the faith under study, or whether he or she is a nonbeliever, an outsider? The most obvious issue here is who is in a better position to understand a religion – is it the believer, who has inside knowledge, and who can be regarded as sufficiently sympathetic to have joined in the first place (or at least not left, if he or she has been a member from birth), or is it the outsider, who may arguably be best placed to maintain a critical distance, and not conflate making spiritual progress with academic understanding? In any case, it is not necessary true that insiders know more about their faith and outsiders; in researching religious communities, both authors have encountered the comment from insiders that we know more about a faith than they do.

In the history of the study of religion in the West, the pattern in previous years was for scholars to be predominantly Christian, and hence Christianity was studied by insiders, whereas other religions were studied by the Christian outsider. Indeed, much of the early study of religions such as Hinduism and Buddhism were done by Christian missionaries. This rather sharp division between believer and non-believer has been encouraged by the missionary tradition within Christianity. The Gospel accounts of the beginning of Jesus' ministry might be taken to portray Jesus as commissioning the early disciples to be "fishers of men", winning them from their own forms of spirituality to accept the message of salvation, which can only be found through faith in Christ. Statements like "No one comes to the Father except through me" (John 14:6) and "Salvation is found in no one else" (Acts 4:12) suggest an exclusivity. Either a person has come to the Father and the found salvation or they have not; there is no middle way. Particularly in the Protestant evangelical tradition, believers are encouraged to locate a decisive moment in their lives when they have "seen the light", "asked Christ into their hearts", or gone forward at some evangelical rally, marking a transition from being a sinner to being redeemed. The Christian faith has traditionally taught that there are only two eternal destinies – heaven and hell – and the Bible teaches that no one who is impure can enter the heavenly city, but "but only those whose names are written in the Lamb's book of life" (Revelation 21:27). It appears to be an all-or-nothing matter: either one is in or out.

The phenomenological background

The scholars who sought to study religions as they are practised were principally anthropologists, who sought to bridge the gap between the outsider researcher and the insider practitioner, and one model that was considered appropriate was a phenomenological one, derived from the German scholar Edmund Husserl (1859–1938). Essentially, a phenomenological approach to the study of religion involved three steps: first, "epoché" – the bracketing of one's preconceptions; second, building a "bridge of understanding" between the scholar and the believer; and third, achieving "eidetic vision" – meaning experiencing the form or essence of the religion under study.

Much has been written about phenomenology, and it is not appropriate to go into extensive exposition or critique here. For our present purposes the notion of the bridge of understanding suggests that there is a chasm between the scholar and the believer, with the scholar standing outside the religious community under study and the community as something that has to be understood through entering in to its way of life and ways of thinking. Ninian Smart (1927–2001), sometimes regarded as the last of the phenomenologists, characterized the building of this bridge of understanding as "moccasin-walking" (Smart 1995: 14), drawing on an ancient Native American proverb that you cannot understand a person until you have walked a mile in his or her moccasins. Smart's reference to moccasins rather than shoes is intended to reinforce the idea that the believer under study has donned a worldview that is alien to the scholar.

This view of the study of religion has a superficial appeal, particularly to students who are initially unfamiliar with most of the religions that they will study, and who find this model appropriate and easy to grasp. For scholars of religion, the phenomenologists presented a methodology that was an advance on previous practices of Christian scholars adopting confessional approaches, imposing inappropriate vocabulary to explain other faiths, for example speaking of the Buddhist Sangha as the "Church", or "idols" to describe statues and images. In seeking to traverse the bridge of understanding, the scholar therefore endeavoured to expound the worldview and the practices of the believer by noting how those practices are described and explained from within. As the scholar Wilfred Cantwell Smith wrote, "no statement about a religion is valid unless it can be acknowledged by that religion's believers" (Smith 1959: 42). The phenomenological approach thus contrasts with a confessional one which privileges the researcher's religion (if he or she has one): for the phenomenologist the believer's version of his or her faith community is privileged. Eric J. Sharpe encapsulated the phenomenologist's position as entailing that "the believer is always right" (Sharpe 1977: 81).

The phenomenological model presupposes the academic researcher's role as that of the outsider. The "bridge of understanding" presupposes two sides – the scholar on one, and the religious practitioners on the other. Particularly in the early days of acquaintance with unfamiliar religions, there was a marked difference between the worldview of the researcher – often a Christian missionary in the early years of acquaintance – and that of the communities being studied. The idea of a bridge linking the scholar to his or her subject matter is problematic for a number of reasons. Practising *epoché* is more easily said than done, and is probably an impossible task. We are not always aware of our preconceptions and, even when we are, we can persuade ourselves that they are legitimate. Much of the early scholarship on the so-called "world religions" had a distinctively Western, ethnocentric, and Christian bias. Carried out at a time when the societies under study were subject to colonial rule, Western scholarship has come under the criticism for being "colonialist". This criticism is multifaceted. A substantial amount of early scholarship blatantly presupposed the superiority of Christianity: evolutionary approaches to religion invariably placed the Christian faith at the top of the evolutionary scale and, particularly, forms of animism and religions with oral rather than written traditions could find themselves described as "primitive", or even "savage". The very fact that Western scholars were studying and writing about Eastern religions placed them in a position of power: the author determines how religions are categorized, which forms are definitive, what are the salient aspects of the religion under study, what material to select, and how the religious communities under discussion are portrayed.

Such bias, of course, is not necessarily deliberate or malicious. A Western scholar may not realize that what he or she sees is not necessarily typical of that religion across the board, but is inevitably only acquainted with those communities with which he or she has come into contact. This is evident, for example, in the study of the Hindu religions, where North Indian religion has tended to be the focus for Western textbooks, with little discussion about differing forms of spirituality in the South. The textbook versions of the Sikh faith continue to promote the khalsa Sikh as the authentic practitioner, perhaps because the wearing of the five Ks and the turban make him more visible than Sikhs who cut their hair. Likewise, Islam is typically portrayed in terms of the five pillars, overshadowing the Sufi tradition, in which there are many sacred shrines venerating their saints. Thus the West has come to stereotype or "essentialize" the religions under study. The phenomenon of essentialism not only has the effect of oversimplifying and ignoring the variety of forms of spirituality: it can lead to an inadvertent ranking of its adherents. The non-Khalsa Sikh is thus portrayed as being lax and guilty of making concessions to Western culture, perhaps for pragmatic rather than spiritual reasons. Not all the blame for decentralizing, however, rests with Western scholars. A religion's practitioners, and particularly its recognized authorities, can help to define its supposedly authentic forms and its retrograde versions; for example, in Islam the conservative Wahhabi movement can insist that the veneration of saints is a debased form of Islam and, because Islam's five pillars serve as a common denominator for Muslims, these alone can be defined as its essence, and the veneration of saints becomes regarded as a debased and unwelcome form of the religion.

Because Western scholars have been accustomed to studying the Christian faith, a number of Christian-centred assumptions and approaches have found their way into the study of other faiths. For example, Christians (as well as their parent religionists, the Jews) have attached great value to their scriptures and to the study of them, and the training in theological seminaries tends to be predominantly text-based. It was therefore an understandable preconception that, if one wanted to understand another form of religion, one should find their scriptures and subject them to translation and scholarly exegesis. Thus, nineteenth-century Western scholarship saw the proliferation of translations of Indian scriptures belonging to both the Hindu and Buddhist traditions, and thus these religious traditions can only too readily be defined in terms of their written texts. Of course, where literacy rates are low, and poverty prevents the purchase of literature or the education to access texts, the written versions of a religion are unlikely to be definitive. Followers may be aware of some of the basic stories – such as the Mahabharata and the Ramayana in the Hindu faiths, and the life of the Buddha in the Buddhist tradition – but such acquaintance is not mediated directly through literature, but rather from teachings given in temples, and from pictorial representations of scenes from such legends.

Wittgensteinian fideism

A more extreme view which privileged the insider's status was one which gained some currency in the philosophy of religion in the 1960s, and which asserted that not only was the believer's account superior to that of the non-believer, but that the believer's account could only be understood by the believer, and never by the non-believer. This position came to be known as Wittgensteinian fideism, one of the principal exponents of which was the philosopher of religion D. Z. Phillips (1934–2006). The position is based on

Wittgenstein's notion of a "language game", and draws largely on a set of three lectures and conversations on religious belief between Wittgenstein and some of his disciples (Phillips 1967; Wittgenstein 1966).

Phillips develops this notion by using the example of the Ontological Argument for God's existence. Simply put, the Ontological Argument regards God as having "necessary existence" as a divine attribute, and hence as part of the meaning of the concept of God. An opponent who denies God's existence appears to be asserting that a being who necessarily exists does not exist – which is a contradiction, unless of course the non-believer is using the word "God" in a different sense from the believer, failing to understand the concept of God, as espoused by the believer. A non-believer might suppose that the Christian regards the Last Judgement as a future event, akin to a cosmic court trial, following which humankind will be rewarded or punished according to their faith and deeds. According to Phillips, this is a misunderstanding, and the true meaning of the doctrine can only be rightly understood from the standpoint of faith: for the believer, the Last Judgement involves living one's life as being under the constant sight and scrutiny of God. Religious beliefs are thus *sui generis*, and can only be understood by the insider, who is acquainted with the rules of the language game. The only way, therefore, to understand a religion is to convert to it, and to become the insider.

This account of the relationship between the believer and the non-believer encounters some fairly obvious problems. How could outsiders convert to a religion, unless they first understood at least something about its beliefs and practices? Indeed, Phillips already contradicts himself by offering an explanation of the Last Judgement which can apparently be well understood by believer and non-believer alike. But what is one to say about the apostate? Does someone who abandons a faith cease to understand it, or have such persons never understood it in the first place? How does one account for the contested nature of religious doctrines? Many religious believers hold concepts of the Last Judgement in precisely the way in which Wittgenstein and Phillips reject, and which Phillips labels as a "superstition". Both Wittgenstein and Phillips were writing at a time before the variety of the world's religions were commonly studied, and hence the dichotomy between believer and non-believer was regarded as an irreconcilable difference between the Christian and the atheist or agnostic. The increased prevalence of a multifaith society would at best require a more complex definition of a fideist position. Does the Christian not understand the Buddhist, and has the Hindu failed to understand the Muslim? Do different faiths believe in different gods, and do they share nothing in common? To regard them as totally separate language games would seem strange, particularly since the Jewish Tanakh,

Christianity's Old and New Testaments, and the Qur'an have obvious overlaps and contain many of the same characters.

Deconstructing religion

These issues relate to a further problem that has come to the fore recently in the study of religion, namely the questioning of the category of religion itself. What precisely is the insider inside? Traditionally, textbooks on the so-called world religions identify the major traditions as what is sometimes called the "big six": Buddhism, Christianity, Hinduism, Islam, Judaism, and Sikhism. It is not altogether obvious why these six religions receive privileged treatment in academic literature. The possible reasons might include missionary encounter and the availability of scriptures. However, if one were to arrange the world's religions in order of size, one website provides the following rank order: Christianity (2.2 billion), Islam (1.5 billion), non-religious (1.1 billion), Hinduism (900 million), Chinese religions (394 million), primal/indigenous (300 million), African (traditional and diasporic) (100 million), Sikhism (23 million) and Juche (19 million) (Adherents.com 2007).

Even a cursory reflection on these lists will reveal the problems of determining who are insiders and outsiders. The name Juche may be unfamiliar to some readers: it is sometimes described as the state religion of North Korea, but it could be argued that it is more of a political ideology than a religion. Other categories above (non-religion, Chinese religions, primal-indigenous and African religions) are groupings rather than discrete religious organizations. To be "inside" an indigenous religion could mean anything from being an Australian aboriginal to a Native American. Arguably too, Hinduism is not a single religion, but an array of Indian religions, focusing on different forms of deity, but possibly deriving historically from the Aryans and the Vedic scriptures. To claim a distinction between Hinduism and Buddhism is also problematic: many Buddhist temples in the East incorporate large images of Ganesha; the Buddha is frequently portrayed as one of Vishnu's avatars; and many Buddhist temples in Sri Lanka depict scenes from the Hindu epic, the Ramayana.

Christianity may seem to be more clearly defined. However, quite apart from some Protestant evangelicals' exclusivist ideas on who is a Christian, different traditions and denominations have frequently asserted their own claims to Christian uniqueness. Traditionally, the Roman Catholic Church has claimed to be the only true Church, and most forms of Eastern Orthodoxy regard those traditions (in fact the majority who would self-define as Christians) that emerged on the other side of the 1054 Great Schism as being outside the true Church. Typically, the rite of baptism has served as the mark of entry to the Church, but some denominations do not practise baptism – notably the Quakers and the Salvation Army – while others refuse to recognize the baptism administered in other traditions. Further, baptism is often sought for social or family rather than explicitly theological or spiritual reasons, and many who have been baptized have ceased practising – if indeed they ever practised in the first place. With the exception of Baptist and Pentecostal denominations, baptism is not the expression of commitment to Christianity, and hence many denominations have devised confirmation or joining ceremonies to admit candidates into full membership. Again, expression of commitment is problematic in defining who is within the Christian fellowship and who is not: in Anglicanism and Roman Catholicism confirmation is often carried out at a relatively young age, often reflecting the wishes of the parents or wider family, and does not guarantee lifelong commitment. On the other hand, it is arguable that children are an important part of Christian congregations, even though they might not have reached the age of undergoing formal commitment through adult baptism or confirmation.

In contrast with the 59 per cent who self-defined as Christian in England and Wales, and the 4.7 per cent who attend church on a Sunday, a greater proportion of the British population might be counted as "cultural Christians": that is to say, they celebrate Christian festivals such as Christmas and Easter, exchanging presents, erecting a Christmas tree, buying Easter eggs, or maybe even attending a carol service. According to a survey in 2001, 94 per cent of the British population exchange presents; 49 per cent buy a Christmas tree; and 35 per cent attend a Christmas service in a church (Thomas 2003: 20). Should these count as insiders? One should bear in mind that adherents to other faiths also celebrate Christmas. The authors have taught in a multifaith, multicultural environment, and have at times received Christmas cards from Muslim, Sikh, Atheist and Hindu students, some of whom confirm that they have Christmas trees and receive presents at the festival, like their Christian counterparts. Jesus is a prophet of Islam, and hence Muslims will venerate him as such, and many see no problem in observing a Christian festival, while not claiming any kind of Christian identity.

To speak of insiders and outsiders invites the question of what it is that the scholar or believer is meant to be inside or outside. One may be inside religion in general, in the sense of being a believer in some form of spirituality rather than an atheist or an agnostic. More specifically, one might be deemed to be an insider to a specific religious tradition, such as Christianity, Judaism, Islam, or whatever – assuming one accepts such categories. Even more specifically, one's insider status might refer to a particular form of religion, such as being a Sunni or Shi'a Muslim, or a Roman Catholic, an Eastern Orthodox Christian, or a Protestant – and of course each of these has its own sub-categories. When one reflects on specific religious organizations and communities, there can again be different opinions about belonging. Are Mormons, Jehovah's Witnesses, or members of the Ku Klux Klan Christians? Is ISIS a form of Islam? Are the Niramkaris and Ravadassis Sikhs? Such questions may be determined by whether such groups belong to umbrella organizations, such as the World Council of Churches (WCC) in the case of Christianity. However, not all organizations that are unarguably Christian have sought membership, and at times there are organizations whose right to membership is questionable, for example the Kimbanguists' presence in the WCC.

The thrust of our argument is that there are no clear definitions of insider and outsider, and that at best classifications that are based on belonging or not belonging need to be much more nuanced. Because inside and outside are frequently unclear, it follows that there can be no clear answer to the question of whose account of a religion should be privileged when it comes to seeking understanding. If it were contended that Christians understood the Christian traditions better than non-Christians, such a claim would be seriously problematic. A Christian might lack knowledge of his or her own tradition, or more likely other divergent traditions also labelled Christian by scholars; the student who once sought exemption from a module on Christianity on the grounds that she was a Sunday School teacher may have been a reliable informant about her own experiences of introducing her pupils to her understanding of Christianity, but it was unlikely that she would be conversant with Christian history, biblical exegesis, or the variety of expressions of the Christianity that academic study would cover. It is even less likely that this Sunday school teacher – who was a Protestant – would be able to tell us much about Roman Catholicism or, less still, Eastern Orthodoxy. When it comes to practising one's faith, a follower may know the teachings, but fail to put them into practice: most Roman Catholics are aware of the Church's teachings on contraception, but more than half of them ignore the Pope's ruling. Does this make them less of an insider?

The role of the academic researcher

A further preconception that impinges on the insider/outsider debate, and which derives from Christianity (and which is common to the Abrahamic faiths more widely) is the requirement of exclusive allegiance. The Ten

Commandments include the injunction, "You shall have no other gods before me", and Yahweh is described as a "jealous god" who can tolerate no rival. Although the Christian may study other faiths, he or she may not espouse them, and indeed some Christian evangelicals are highly intolerant of importing any elements that may derive from other faiths – which can often include having yoga groups using church premises, or using alternative therapies that may come from Eastern traditions. However, one does not need fanatically to avoid such practices to presuppose a Christian-centred approach. The notion that one exclusively follows a single religion is an assumption that can readily be superimposed on other religions that are being studied. Because the Christian, Jewish and Islamic faiths tend to presuppose exclusive allegiance, it can be readily assumed that Hinduism, Buddhism, Taoism and other Eastern forms of spirituality are discrete entities. Such an assumption is not only at odds with what one finds in daily practice; it also leads to assumptions that practitioners of the so-called "major traditions" combine their faith with debased forms of spirituality, or can be guilty of "syncretism". Thus, the presence of small shrines with food offerings, which are often found at roadsides in Buddhist countries, can be attributed to forms of animism, which practising Buddhists combine with their own principal faith. Similarly, it is sometimes observed that temples in Eastern countries, and in some major UK cities, combine elements of Buddhism, Taoism, Confucianism, or that Hinduism and Buddhism "blend" in countries like Sri Lanka. These are often portrayed as examples of religious syncretism, but syncretism implies the combining of different systems, thus supposing that they were once separate.

Of course, the assumption that there were once "pure" versions of these religions, which merged together at some later stage, seems unlikely. Certainly there once existed figures like Gautama the Buddha, Confucius and Lao Tzu, but it is unlikely that their early supporters gave them exclusive allegiance – whatever that might mean. It is not altogether clear how we should replace the traditional mode of teaching these apparently discrete religions, but one way of thinking about the phenomenon might be to consider different interacting currents. No one would wish to assert that some Protestant congregation was "syncretistic" on the grounds that it allegedly combined Augustinianism, Lutheranism, Calvinism, consumerism and capitalism. (Yes, churches do sell things, and they must comply with the legal requirements of a capitalist system.) All the strands – and others – may well be found within the Protestant tradition, "combined" with the teachings of Jesus and Paul, but it would be absurd to suggest that these had an independent existence before somehow being drawn together.

The phenomenon of Western hegemony becomes more complicated when we consider Westerners who convert to Eastern religions – where the "outsider" decides to become the "insider". The transition of Westerners to Buddhism is a good example. Unlike those who have been brought up in a Buddhist country, Westerners tend to discover Buddhism either by reading a book, or by attending a class – often a meditation session – led by a Buddhist teacher, who is frequently a Western convert. The consequence for Western converts to Buddhism is that they tend to espouse the version of Buddhism that is intellectualized, transmitted by texts, and is, in Melford Spiro's terminology, "nibbanic" (Spiro 1971: 12). In other words, it focuses on making spiritual progress towards the final goal of nirvana, and emphasizes spiritual practices such as meditation – something that is only practised by a minority of Buddhist monks, and seldom by laity. There tends to be disagreement among Western Buddhists as to whether their espoused form of Buddhism may be practised alongside another religion, but Western Buddhists tend to distinguish their faith clearly from other forms of spirituality such as Hinduism and animism, as well as from folk practice.

One of the authors recalls recounting to a practising Western Buddhist his own experiences of seeing Asian Buddhists making offerings for ghosts, the prevalent presence of fortune-telling devices in temples, facilities for exorcism, and the widespread selling of amulets. Her response was that these were simply not part of Buddhism – notwithstanding the fact that in the East it would be hard to find a temple that did not offer at least some of these facilities. On another occasion this author attended a Wesak celebration in England, which was attended by several Buddhist monks, including one or two Western members of the Sangha. The lay members had provided tea and cakes, and the children performed some dances. When it was time for speeches, one Western monk mounted the platform and reprimanded the audience, saying that it was all very well to provide refreshments and entertainment, but that this would not help their spiritual attainment, to which they should pay more attention. These Westerners' attitudes raise a number of issues. First, they seem to privilege the Western interpretation of the Buddhist religion to that of its indigenous supporters, thus reinforcing accusations of Western imperialism when it comes to deciding on the authenticity of religious practices. Second, it indicates that there are different boundaries to be drawn to mark out the limits and the periphery of a religious system: for many Western converts the limits of Buddhism are confined to its "nibbanic" elements, while the Asian Buddhist tends to view the religion as much broader, serving a wide variety of pragmatic and social purposes.

The incidents we have highlighted indicate a further problem for the phenomenologist's model of the study of religion. If the phenomenologist suggests that there is some "thing in itself" which can be penetrated once we have practised epoché by shaking off our preconceptions, it is not clear what this "eidetic vision" would consist of. What does it mean to see Buddhism as it is? Is it the Westerners' nibbanic notion, or is it the Asian practitioner's wider concept, which encompasses other elements such as gaining merit, attaining a good rebirth, obtaining health, good luck and longevity, and fending off evil? Or might it somehow be all of these?

The role of the researcher

The phenomenological model which we have discussed places the researcher in the position of the outsider. However, this is not always the case, and the model leaves out the practice of reflexive ethnography, in which the researcher already belongs to the community under study. Indeed, the study of Christianity historically has largely been done by those who belong to the Christian faith. In the case of other religions, it is becoming increasingly common for a researcher to be part of the religion that is being studied. This may be because the researcher has already espoused that religion and wants to study it in more detail; in other instances a student has been captivated by a religion, and has decided to move from outsider to insider status.

At what point does a sympathetic researcher become an insider? Particularly in the case of religions that lack clear boundaries of belonging, and which are non-salvific, the researcher might plausibly be regarded as indistinguishable from the supporter. One case in point might be Druidry, with attendees at gatherings simply liking the pageantry – a liking which can equally be shared by researchers. So what is the difference between the insider and the outsider in this example? By virtue of engaging in participant observation the researcher, even in a small degree, becomes part of the phenomenon and makes some degree of difference, however small, to it, even if it is no more than adding one extra statistic if attendance is counted, or making a donation if contributions are sought.

The participant observer goes "inside", taking part in at least some of the activities of the group under study. Exactly how far inside the researcher can penetrate relies on a number of factors. The most obvious are time, finance and opportunity. There is also the group's willingness and ability to accept visitors: if one's fieldwork involves "living in" a community, where being "inside" entails physically being an insider, there can be physical limits to the number of people who can be accommodated on its premises. There may also be events from which outsiders are barred: obvious examples are the "ordinances" that take place inside a Mormon temple.

The extent to which one can penetrate the inside of a religious community does not merely rely on the group; it can equally depend on the researcher's characteristics. One's gender or skin colour can either exclude a researcher completely, or at least make access more difficult. There are also personal qualities that the researcher may have chosen. If the researcher is vegetarian, but the group being researched is not, should one's dietary convictions be set aside in the name of research, or should the researcher maintain his or her principles? A striking example of "going native", as it is sometimes called, is Karen McCarthy Brown's research on Haitan Vodou. Her book *Mama Lola: A Vodou Priestess in Brooklyn* (1991) is an autobiographical account of the author's experiences with a Vodou priestess, commonly known as Mama Lola. Brown describes how she first met Mama Lola, her conversations with the practitioner, and her participation in various Vodou rituals. She describes Mama Lola's invocation of spirits as if the spirits had real independent existence, and without raising any ontological questions about their reality. She comes to regard Mama Lola as a kind of confidante, discussing her personal life in the context of the Vodou religion. At one point she goes so far as to accept Mama Lola's recommendation that she should participate in a marriage ritual, in which she becomes spiritually wedded to Papa Ogou, who is Mama Lola's principal counsellor in the spirit world. Brown's story is a fascinating one, but it raises the question of whether the author goes beyond the boundaries of acceptable fieldwork in religion. Has she effectively converted to Vodou? Autoethnography is at best controversial, and Brown might justly be accused of failing to maintain a critical distance from the subject matter. Whether the researcher has remained the outsider, or become an insider, it is important to be able to raise critical questions, and not to confuse seekership with scholarly research.

These examples suggest a blurring of the relationship between the researcher, who is usually (although not always) the outsider, and the insiders within the religious community. To this end, Graham Harvey has suggested a new model of the researcher–subject relationship which purports to surmount at least some of the problems discussed above. His suggestion is that the field worker might be considered as the community's "guest". This idea is based on Harvey's own fieldwork with Maori communities, where, in order to gain access to their religious rites one must be invited and formally welcomed. The notion of the researcher as guest is productive for a variety of reasons. First of all, the researcher must gain access to the community by getting past the gatekeepers – the equivalent of the householder. The guest is, at least temporarily, part of the household, and participates in the family's activities.

He or she is no mere observer, but is interacting with the host, living the same lifestyle, and being temporarily the insider. The host's discretion determines what the guest may have access to, and what is out of bounds, and of course it is inappropriate for a guest to transgress the host's expectations.

New approaches to religious belonging

As methodology within the study of religion – and particularly the study of everyday religion – has developed in the last decade, we argue that a more nuanced understanding of what it means to be an outsider is needed. Relating especially to the conversation started by Primiano (1995, 2012), and developed by Ammerman (2007), McGuire (2008) and Harvey (2003, 2009, 2013), the re-evaluation of "what religion is" within the performance of everyday religious lives has been complicated. In so doing, we complicate the associated narratives.

Quite simply, when we re-negotiate "what religion is" and "what religious people do", with the subsequent challenging of sacred/profane dichotomies, we create a landscape where structured and restrictive notions of "insideness" and "outsideness" may no longer apply. If this is indeed the case, we need to re-focus upon performed everyday narratives and malleable, often complicated and contested, religious identities at the overlaps and edges between individuals and religious hierarchies, communities and worldviews.

Primiano's seminal work on vernacular religion remains foundational to new approaches, and yet, over twenty years after this publication, (Primiano 1995) the study of lived, vernacular or everyday religion remains at the edge of much scholarly debate, and almost all public discourse, on religion. While Primiano reminds us that all religion is vernacular religion, it is clear that large tranches of scholarship still construe authority in paradigms of top-down institutional, monoglotic authority. By understanding religion as everyday (Ammerman 2007), relational (Harvey 2013) and, above all, embodied (Gregg and Scholefield 2015) and socially contextualized (Bowman and Valk 2012), we change what we mean by religion. Despite this, much discourse on religion continues to privilege essentialized paradigms of religion, often with a focus on belief and "religion" as a unilateral category of participation separate from culture (Sharma 2008). We argue that this is a major issue in our discipline.

The reasons for this are well known – a thousand-year theological inheritance in our universities which has created a World Religions Paradigm that woefully misrepresents our subjects of study, usefully critiqued by Owen (2011) and others (Gregg and Scholefield 2015; Cotter and Robertson 2016).

The colonial inheritance of monolithic religious identity boundaries from the British administration's censuses in the Punjab (Barrier 1981), through to the invention of "World Religions" via the Chicago Platforms of 1893 (Masuzawa 2005) right up to contemporary xenophobic anti-migration parties in Europe. All of these approaches formulate a category of religion and a view of religious participation that mislocates authority in religion. Of course, there has been much response to this in recent years. Works by Ammerman (2007), McGuire (2008), Orsi (2003, 1997), Bowman and Valk (2012), Harvey (2009, 2013), Barker (1984) and Hall (1997) all question top-down authority and prioritize the everyday, relational, embodied and living nature of religion as a category and of the identity construction of religious actors and religious communities.

At the start of the century, Robert Orsi asked the question "Is the Study of Lived Religion Irrelevant to the World We Live in?" in his address and article of the same name (Orsi 2003). In this work, Orsi responds to the challenge in the title by arguing, like Primiano, that "Religion is always religion-in-action, religion-in-relationships between people, between the ways the world is and the way people imagine or want it to be" (ibid.: 172). He goes on to state that: "The interpretive challenge of the study of lived religion is to develop the practice of disciplined attention to people's signs and practices as they describe, understand, and use them, in the circumstances of their experiences, and to the structures and conditions within which these signs and practices emerge" (ibid.: 172).

One way of doing this is to encompass alternative hermeneutical approaches when, by focusing on performative, vernacular and living religion, we redefine what religion is. Sharma, using the example of Hindu traditions, argues that "Western hermeneutics functions under a definition of religion which has been uncritically applied to Hinduism" (Sharma 2008: 11). Sharma's approach is helpful, not just in rescuing Indian conceptions of religion from colonial and post-empire academic lenses, but can also helpfully contribute to an analysis of "what religion is" (and therefore how we relate to it or are "inside" or "outside" it) in an academic world which is adopting paradigms of religion and religious studies beyond the World Religions Paradigm-dominated methodologies of previous generations, which can be seen to have been moulded by mid-twentieth-century liberal Protestant theological responses to religious pluralism.

This examination of "non-Western" approaches to religion also highlights the importance of voices beyond the mainstream discourse that has dominated previous generations of scholarship about religious identity and belonging. One such voice, from which post-World Religions Paradigm approaches to religion can learn, is that of theoretical approaches to gender and sexuality. In recent decades, in both academic and political discourse, understandings of gender and sexuality have moved beyond binary understandings of male/female or homo/heteronormativity (see, for example, Lorber 1996; Russell and Consolacion 2003). We think this is a useful model for religious identity – indeed, as Yip Tuck has noted, queer theory can be seen as "turning theology upside down" and as a process which "prioritises embodiment and experience" (Yip Tuck 2010: 40). This turn away from binary essentialism towards embodied and performative identities is very closely aligned to the current academic rejection of previous generations' focus on "belief", "doctrine" or "tradition", and is directly relevant to understanding religious identity as nuanced, relational and dynamic; especially when understood from the everyday practitioner upwards, rather than from essentialized or hierarchical institutions of authority downwards. To this end, Jenzen and Munt have argued that the act of queering religious studies may be "productive in undoing the 'assemblages' of both the homo-norm and religious other" (Jenzen and Munt 2012: 50) and no more so is it necessary to understand this than with regard to conceptions of being "inside" or "outside" a religious community or identity, as this of course creates implicit and explicit senses of the religious "other".

Perhaps, then, in addition to possible helpful links to emergent approaches to gender and sexuality, we should also turn to what Hardman has previously called "muted voices" (Hardman 1973). In a generation past, this was applied to gender, but perhaps we may now examine new muted voices at the edges which help us to queer issues of relational religious identity – particularly with regard to embodied understandings of religious practice and beliefs-in-action. Perhaps we can learn from artists such as Claire Cunningham, whose "Guide Gods" was an audience-interactive show created in 2014 and performed in the UK and Australia, which fused dance, audience interview, academic commentary, and cups of tea to analyse the ways in which a disabled person may relate to – and thus consider themselves inside, outside or liminal to, different religious communities' views on physical impairment. As scholarship focuses upon the embodiment of belief-in-action, and religion is understood as a performative embodied way of everyday living, what does it mean to have one's "soul" accepted, but not one's body? From performing flagellation in medieval Catholicism, to climbing mountains as a contemporary member of the Aetherius Society, what does being disabled mean for differently enacting and performing beliefs in the corporeal world? Beyond questions of gender, sex or sexuality, how do different forms of embodiment affect the continuums of relational positionality with regard to religious participation and belonging?

One conclusion may be to suggest that to think simply in categories of "insider" and "outsider" is unduly simplistic and unrepresentative of the relational constructed religious lives that we are examining. There is a complex spectrum of religious affiliation, rejection and relation, and to ignore it would be to do our subject a gross disservice. Indeed, if we are to link new understandings of "outsideness" to developing theories on methodology in the study of religion, a failure to engage with the nuanced discourse would misrepresent the very subject matter we are seeking to understand.

Perhaps, then, an understanding of the performance of religious lives beyond insider-outsider binaries is important for the development of our understanding of contemporary religion. As religion changes, so our relationship to communities and worldviews changes. Importantly, we must recognize that this happens for people "inside" communities as well as to those who are "outside" them. Anglicans who grew up in the Church of England in the 1980s or 1990s now face relating to a radically different Church subsequent to the "Mission-shaped Church" policy of the early 2000s. Similarly, religious adherents who identify as insiders to Anglican Christianity but who are opposed to women bishops or who are strongly behind church marriages for same sex couples may find themselves no longer identifying with public declarations of the leadership of religious community to which they belong as "insiders". This necessarily means that we also need to examine how practitioners move *through* identities and communities to remind us that we are dealing with fluid and evolving dynamics, which again contest whether one can simply be an "insider" or "outsider". Additionally, muted voices, which are often contradictory and complex, and the permeable boundaries which sit between an individual and their performed religious life are more and more in opposition to the textbook boundaries which suggest the possibility of a neat and tidy notion of belonging or not belonging to a categorized and set religious worldview or community.

This is particularly the case when it comes to conceptions of "belief" – noted as a problematical term in the study of religion from as far back as Wilfred Cantwell Smith (1979), through Ruel (1997) to contemporary contributions from Harvey (2013), as it has so often been prioritized above other aspects of religious identity or performance to the detriment of our understanding of lived and everyday religion. This is important to the current discussion, as belief has consistently, particularly in the Anglo-American university system of studying religion, been understood as a barometer of belonging; a safe measure by which one's orthodoxy or heresy could be tested. Of course, we reject such an approach, and here purposefully suggest that belief (that is, belief-in-action, or embodied, performed everyday belief) may itself be a useful example of the negotiated and relational understanding of religious belonging we wish to propose.

When a seemingly simple question such as asking what Catholics believe about a certain issue is posed, the traditional response has often been to revert to authority, institution, or hierarchy. The preferencing of popes, catechisms and doctrines is, indeed, one way of responding to this question. However, when we purposefully subvert outdated paradigms of religion which rest too much upon the theological assumptions and confessional approaches of the past, and seek to understand the lived realities of everyday Catholics – the church cleaners, the choristers, the intermittent attendees – we often see views, opinions and actions that seemingly sit at odds to the official church teachings. In generations past, debates may have centred on why such religious actors "weren't being good Catholics". However, such an approach suggests that there is one way of being a Catholic, an essentializing of a worldview which betrays monolithic or static conceptions of religion and religious identity. We suggest that this woefully misrepresents the complexity of religious belonging. In recent years, much public and media attention has been placed on Catholic attitudes towards ethical family issues. When we analyse recent surveys, it is clear that there is a dissonance between official teachings of the Church and views, opinions and practices of everyday Catholics. In the Pew Research Centre (2015) survey of US Catholics and Family Life, we can clearly see that an overwhelming number of Catholics believe that non-traditional forms of family are perfectly acceptable ways of living. Eighty-four per cent surveyed considered unmarried parents to be an acceptable arrangement, 87 per cent thought single parenting to be acceptable, and perhaps most interestingly, two thirds believed that gay or lesbian couples raising children to be an acceptable way of living. When children are taken out of the equation, the figures for cohabiting different-sex couples and same-sex couples both increase further. Such people, who may have been dismissed in previous generations as somehow not counting or fitting in due to their not toeing the party line, rather than being understood as somehow deficient, must instead be understood as representative of what it means to be a Catholic in the contemporary world. Similarly, Roman Catholics who disagree with the Vatican's position on women priests do not leave the Roman Church to seek membership of other denominations which do ordain women, but choose to actively pursue a different type and understanding of Catholicism from within the Catholic Church. Beyond the unhelpful labels of "heretics" which may have been used in the past, such people are instead better understood as discordant insiders, with as much right to be called Catholics as the cardinals with whom they may be arguing.

Similarly, to give an example from Muslim traditions, within contemporary society, perhaps the most complex issue for Muslim religious identities, is that of Muslim atheists. Indeed, the very phrase "Muslim atheist" is, to many scholars, an oxymoron, as Islam is often viewed solely within theological constraints, which misrepresents the huge diversity of Muslim communities as one idealized or essentialized worldview based on belief and textual authority, rather than practice, discourse and performance. In an important recent work in an under-studied area of scholarship, Cottee (2015) has examined apostasy within Islam, not as a theological phenomenon, but as a social dynamic. Crucially, the research did not focus on what the Qur'an or hadith may or may not say on a subject, but on what real Muslims actually do. Looking specifically at Muslims within the UK and Canada, the work notes that apostates are both open and hidden, meaning that many atheist Muslims continue to live within religiously adhering families and societies, and continue to participate within life-cycle and community calendar events. Likewise, the self-defined atheist Muslim Ali Rizvi has noted his continued association with cultural and ethnic celebrations, activities and social mores, as an important part of his non-supernatural, post-theological worldview (Rizvi 2013). It is uncontroversial to describe someone as a Jewish atheist – Woody Allen, Albert Einstein, Stephen Fry, and indeed even Christopher Hitchens, all fit into this category – and yet public discourse on Islam seems only capable of understanding a monolithic theological definition of the manifestly diverse, complex and fascinating group of religious communities we label as Muslim. We suggest that a relational, rather than essentializing, understanding of religious identity, may go some way to better understand the worldviews of such self-defining atheist Muslims.

A new framework of religious identity?

In a recent work (Gregg and Chryssides 2017) the authors have focused upon a new framework of religious identity beyond insider/outsider binaries. In this chapter, we have sought to build on this, and develop this approach in light of the realities of lived everyday religion, and new approaches to the study of religion. Our previous work suggested new ways of understanding the relational framework of religious actors' identity by nuancing different types of outsiders and insiders. These are summarized in Figures 1.1 and 1.2 (below). These models, which are indicative rather than definitive, suggest that the relationship actors have to their religious institution or fellow members sits at the heart of their sense of identity. Crucially, this is not a simple binary matter of being "inside" or "outside", but is a fragmented, contextualized, and sometimes contradictory, set of dynamics which build up a bricolage of identity factors which create an individual, relational form of religious identity which is performed in the negotiation of everyday etiquette (Harvey 2013). Desmond Tutu, Archbishop emeritus of Johannesburg, has previously spoken (Tutu 2010) about the spirit of Ubuntu – a philosophical understanding of personhood taken from the Nguni language, which represents a concept not wholly translatable into English. In short it means that my humanity is bound up in your humanity. I am a person because of my relationship with other people. Put simply, we make no sense as individuals but are inherently social, communicative and relational creatures. The anthropologist Clifford Geertz similarly stated, "whatever God may or may not be … religion is a social institution, worship a social activity, and faith a social force" (Geertz 1968: 19). This has implications for understanding both "insideness" and "outsideness".

What we seek to highlight here is that it is too simplistic to talk of someone as a Christian, or not a Christian, a Muslim, or not a Muslim, and so on. While this may seem an uncontroversial statement, in practical use, both inside academia, and also in public discourse, it is abundantly clear that such nuances are not part of mainstream discourse. It is a simple fact that umbrella terms seeking to define and describe a group of people will be tested and contested when such groups are understood within their everyday lives. For example, a notion of religious identity may be inextricably linked with ethnic

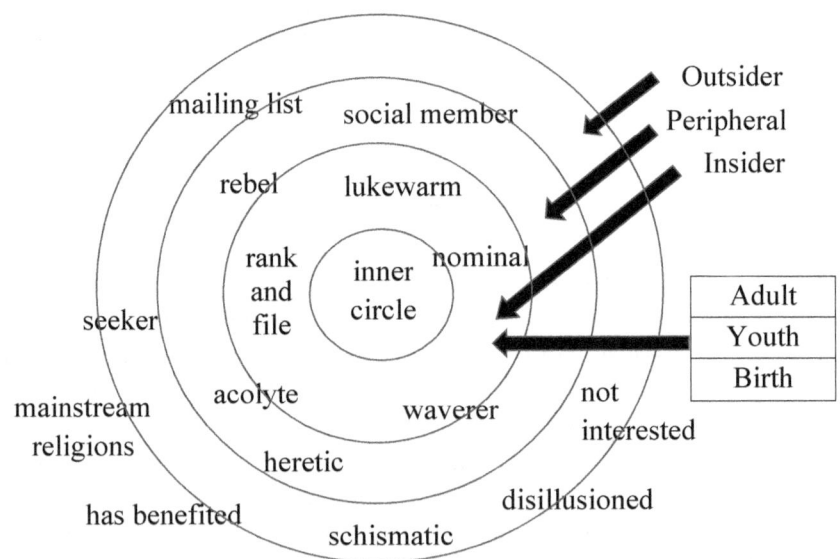

Figure 1.1 Varieties of insider/outsider positionality.

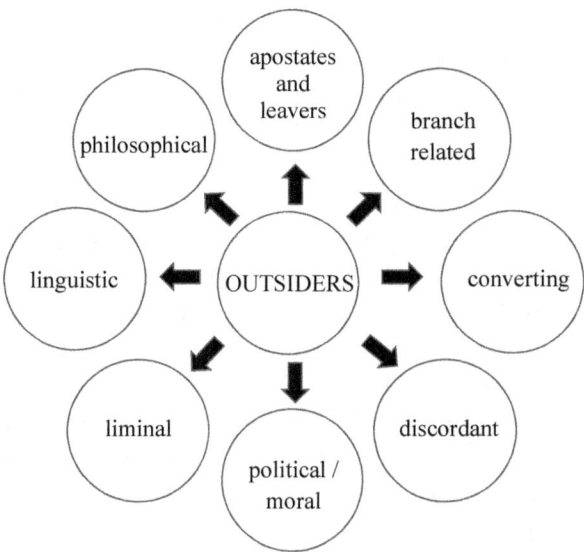

Figure 1.2 Relational categories of outsideness.

or linguistic forms of identity if one is born into a tradition and chooses to perpetuate that tradition within a family setting. Such a person, who may equally identify as an Orthodox Jew, a Protestant Christian, or Vaishnava Hindu, would clearly have an identity different from a convert into any of these traditions, who does not share their background. Similarly, the point at which a person converts – be that as an adolescent, or as an adult – will affect their relationship to their chosen community and their individual identity within this. The dynamic will be different again for someone born into a tradition – what we have called a "birth insider". Similarly, active engagement, or proactive disengagement, from the life cycle of communities – for example, Friday prayers or Sunday morning services, will both reflect and inform us of individuals' understanding of their own identity and relationship to their community – different patterns of engagement will lead to different understandings of relational identity, which we must be careful not to interpret unequally. Likewise, formal and informal roles taken within the community by different adherents mean that multiple voices will speak for the same umbrella term defined traditions.

Of course, any relational form of identity which seeks to understand insiders to religious traditions in a new way, such as discordant Catholics or Muslims, must necessarily reinterpret outsiders as well. In this simple model, we are suggesting a new way in which people can be types of outsiders, to challenge and nuance the old-fashioned binary inside/outside approach to religious belonging. In short, we aim to highlight the relational aspects of outsideness, which will necessarily impact upon the construction of religious identity and the way in which such identities are performed and embodied in everyday living. For example, the notion of a philosophical outsider refers to the fact that while a person may be an outsider to, say, a Muslim religious community, a non-Muslim monotheistic outsider may have a more overlapping worldview or experience than an animist or humanist outsider. Likewise, with regard to branch-related outsiders, the relational understanding of "outsideness" will be complicated if a person is a Trinitarian Anglican who approaches a Christian-based community such as the Latter-day Saints, for, while there may well be "insider discourse" with regard to the person of Jesus, there is likely to be "outsider discourse" with regard to understandings of deity and afterlife. Similarly, both Desmond Tutu and the Westboro Baptist Church will share some overlap in having a supernatural worldview, preferencing the person of Christ and seeing their work as a form of Christian social action, but it would be nonsensical to label them as sharing a moral or political worldview in categorizing notions of "insideness". Each of these categories suggests how notions of "insideness" and "outsideness" are necessarily relational and often liminal.

Interestingly, this liminality also applies to critics, political opponents and protestors of religions – protestors that on the previous binary models of religious belonging would very clearly be categorized as "outsiders". We suggest that this can no longer be understood to be the case under a new relational approach to religious identity. Intriguingly, examples can be found both within and outside religious worldviews. The former can be exampled by the International Raelian Movement, where several studies have shown the clear link between French Roman Catholicism and Raelian religious identity (Brown 2005; Gregg 2012, 2014) with particular reference to cosmology, ethical views and ritual practice within their public protests against the Vatican with regard to diverse adult sexualities, abuse scandals and rights for apostates. The latter can be seen within recent protest movements against some minority religions – particularly the Anonymous campaigns against the Church of Scientology, more fully explored in Chapter 18, which create the somewhat bizarre situation of people on the outside of an organization having greater access to mythic or ritual knowledge than those inside, against whom they are protesting, due to the hierarchical revelation of knowledge through which insiders must journey, but which is freely available to outsiders since the advent of the internet. Here, again, identities are being formed in relation to religious worldviews for both insiders and outsiders of that tradition, but we are arguing that what is happening explicitly in these two examples happens implicitly in all forms of religious identity; we define ourselves as much by what we are not as what we are – identity is also relational, never binary.

In this regard, therefore, our previously suggested models for new approaches to conceptions of insideness and outsideness need to be further nuanced. For example, the models presume that it is the individual that moves through the tradition, but often traditions move; the examples given above regarding changes of policy on ethical issues from the leadership of organizations serve as examples of this; the result for members who do not share these new approaches is that they are left standing on ground no longer occupied by their sisters and brothers within the fold. Crucially, hierarchy often moves in both directions – outsiders are brought within the fold, and insiders are left standing "outside on the inside". The reality is one of negotiated, fluid relationships where change, rather than stasis, is the norm. To this end, we argue that we need to speak of religious identity, and specifically notions of insideness and outsideness as a relational continuum. Returning to the example of recent methodological approaches to sexuality and gender, beyond the binary approaches of the past, which saw identity as a fixed and binary choice (straight or gay, male or female) but which now have developed to understand identities in non-binary terms to include "new" categories such as pan-sexual or inter-sex, we argue that a similar change of approach could benefit understandings of religious identity. Beyond binary notions of insideness and outsideness lies the reality of the lived situation of the everyday lives of religious actors; identities that are negotiated and, crucially, re-negotiated on an on-going basis in relation to the social dynamics of their "host" tradition, which in turn are dynamically being re-negotiated by those other religious actors that make up that tradition in relation to all other identities with which they interact. The lived reality is complex.

In arguing that the insider/outsider binary is an oversimplification, we have presented a more complex and more realistic way of understanding types of belonging as a series of concentric circles within which and out of which the individual can move. However, even that is still an oversimplification. As we have argued above, there can be different circles, such as a single congregation, a denomination, a tradition, a religion – and, as we have also argued, the last of these has increasingly come to be regarded as problematic. Not only can the individual move, but so can the circle. The religious community to which a person belongs is in all likelihood importantly different from its identity even two decades ago, and as the circle moves the inhabitant can decide whether to move with it, to position himself or herself differently within it, or to move outside it. Also, it should be noted that the use of spatial metaphors is not without its problems – notions of insideness are not limited to physical location within or without a given community, but are often predicated upon the performance or non-performance of rituals or practices, the believing or not-believing of particular world-views, both of which often occur within spaces demarcated as belonging to religious practitioners "belonging" to a tradition or a community, but which will also relate to the contested identities of the individuals present or not present in these spaces.

Finally, it must be asked whether our discussion shows the inappropriateness of the insider/outsider distinction and whether, in the light of our analysis it should simply be abandoned. If our spatial metaphors are also flawed, is even our more sophisticated analysis of insiders and outsiders of limited value? However, no schemata can ever totally encompass all possible scenarios. There will always be awkward cases and exceptions, and their existence does not invalidate our model, but merely serves to make us aware that – like every theory – it has its scope and limitations. We would suggest that the various scenarios we have outlined in this discussion help the student of religion to understand the various positions that can exist for religious affiliates and non-affiliates, and the various positions that the scholar can have in researching them. Until someone can suggest a better model, we offer ours as a contribution for more nuanced understanding of so-called "insiders" and "outsiders".

About the authors

Stephen E. Gregg is senior lecturer in religious studies at the University of Wolverhampton, and honorary secretary of the British Association for the Study of Religions. He studied at the University of Wales, Lampeter, and has previously taught at the University of Wales, and Liverpool Hope University. His work focuses upon minority communities and muted voices in contemporary religion, and method and theory in the Study of Religion. Recent and in-press books include *Jesus Beyond Christianity* (Oxford University Press, 2010, with Gregory A. Barker) *Engaging with Living Religion* (Routledge, 2015, with Lynne Scholefield), *A Universal Advaita: Swami Vivekananda and Non-Hindu Traditions* (Routledge, 2019) and *The Bloomsbury Handbook to Studying Christians* (Bloomsbury, 2019, with George D. Chryssides).

George D. Chryssides studied philosophy and theology at the University of Glasgow, and gained his doctorate from the University of Oxford. He taught philosophy and religious studies at various British universities, and was head of religious studies at the University of Wolverhampton, England from 2001 to 2008. He is currently honorary research fellow at York St John University. He has published extensively, principally on new religious movements, and recent publications include *The A to Z of Jehovah's Witnesses* (2009); *Heaven's Gate: Postmodernity and Popular Culture in a Suicide*

Group (2011); *Christians in the Twenty-First Century* (with Margaret Z. Wilkins, 2011); *Historical Dictionary of New Religious Movements* (2012) and *Jehovah's Witnesses: Continuity and Change* (2016). He has co-edited (with Benjamin E. Zeller) *The Bloomsbury Companion to New Religious Movements* (2014), and *The Bloomsbury Handbook to Studying Christians* (2019), edited with Stephen E. Gregg.

References

Adherents.com. (2007). Major Religions of the World Ranked by Number of Adherents. Retrieved from www.adherents.com/Religions_By_Adherents.html (accessed 4 October 2018).

Ammerman, N. T. (2007). *Everyday Religion: Observing Modern Religious Lives*. New York: Oxford University Press USA. https://doi.org/10.1093/acprof:oso/9780195305418.001.0001

Barker, E. (1984). *The Making of a Moonie: Brainwashing or Choice?* Oxford: Blackwell.

Barrier, N. G. (1981). *The British Census in India: New Perspectives*. New Delhi: Manohar.

Bowman, M. and Valk, Ü. (eds). (2012). *Vernacular Religion in Everyday Life: Expressions of Belief*. Durham: Acumen.

Brown, Karen McCarthy (1991). *Mama Lola: A Vodou Priestess in Brooklyn*. Berkeley, CA: University of California Press.

Brown, Robert E. (2005). Review: Aliens Adored: Rael's UFO Religion. *Journal of Religion and Popular Culture* 11(1): 6.

Cottee, S. (2015). *The Apostates: When Muslims Leave Islam*. London: C. Hurst & Co.

Cotter, C. R. and Robertson, D. G. (eds). (2016). *After World Religions: Reconstructing Religious Studies*. Abingdon: Routledge. https://doi.org/10.4324/9781315688046

Faith Survey (2018). Christianity in the UK. Retrieved from https://faithsurvey.co.uk/uk-christianity.html (accessed 4 October 2018).

Geertz, C. (1968). *Islam Observed: Religious Development in Morocco and Indonesia*. Chicago, IL: University of Chicago Press.

Gregg, S. E. (2012). Poking Fun at the Pope: Anti-Catholic Dialogue, Performance and the "Symbolic Construction" of Identity in the International Raelian Movement. *International Journal for the Study of New Religions* 3(1): 71–91. https://doi.org/10.1558/ijsnr.v3i1.71

Gregg, S. E. (2014). Queer Jesus, Straight Angels: Complicating "Sexuality" and "Religion" in the International Raelian Movement. *Sexualities* 17(5/6): 565–582. https://doi.org/10.1177/1363460714526129

Gregg, S. E. and Chryssides, G. D. (2017). "The Silent Majority?" Understanding Apostate Testimony Beyond "Insider / Outsider" Binaries in the Study of New Religions. In E. V. Gallagher (ed.), *Visioning New and Minority Religions: Projecting the Future*, 20–32. Abingdon: Routledge.

Gregg, S. E. and Scholefield, L. (2015). *Engaging with Living Religion: A Guide to Fieldwork in the Study of Religion*. Abingdon: Routledge. https://doi.org/10.4324/9781315716671

Hall, David D. (ed.) (1997). *Lived Religion in America: Toward a History of Practice*. Princeton, NJ: Princeton University Press.

Hardman, C. (1973). Can there be an Anthropology of Children? *Journal of the Anthropology Society of Oxford* 4(2): 85–99.

Harvey, G. (2003). Guesthood as Ethical Decolonising Research Method. *Numen: International Review for the History of Religions* 50(2): 125–146. https://doi.org/10.1163/156852703321506132

Harvey, G. (ed.) (2009). *Religions in Focus*. London: Equinox.

Harvey, G. (2013). *Food, Sex and Strangers: Understanding Religion as Everyday Life*. Durham: Acumen. https://doi.org/10.4324/9781315729572

Jenzen, O. and Munt, S. R. (2012). Queer Theory, Sexuality and Religion. In S. J. Hunt and A. Yip (eds), *The Ashgate Research Companion to Contemporary Religion and Sexuality*. Farnham: Ashgate.

Lorber, J. (1996). Beyond the Binaries: Depolarizing the Categories of Sex, Sexuality, and Gender. *Sociological Inquiry* 66(2): 143–160. https://doi.org/10.1111/j.1475-682X.1996.tb00214.x

Masuzawa, T. (2005). *The Invention of World Religions*. Chicago, IL: University of Chicago Press. https://doi.org/10.7208/chicago/9780226922621.001.0001

McGuire, M. B. (2008). *Lived Religion: Faith and Practice in Everyday Life*. Oxford: Oxford University Press. https://doi.org/10.1093/acprof:oso/9780195172621.001.0001

Office for National Statistics. (2012). Religion in England and Wales 2011. Retrieved from www.ons.gov.uk/peoplepopulationandcommunity/culturalidentity/religion/articles/religioninenglandandwales2011/2012-12-11 (accessed 4 October 2018).

Orsi, R. (1997). Everyday Miracles. In David A. Hall (ed.), *Lived Religion in America: Toward a History of Practice*. Princeton, NJ: Princeton University Press.

Orsi, R. (2003). Is the Study of Lived Religion Irrelevant to the World We Live in? Special Presidential Plenary Address, Society for the Scientific Study of Religion, Salt Lake City, 2 November 2002. *Journal for the Scientific Study of Religion* 42(2): 169–174. https://doi.org/10.1111/1468-5906.t01-1-00170

Owen, S. (2011). The World Religions Paradigm: Time for a Change. *Arts and Humanities in Higher Education* 10(3): 253–268. https://doi.org/10.1177/1474022211408038

Pew Research Center (2015). US Catholics Open to Non-Traditional Families. 2 September. Retrieved from www.pewforum.org/2015/09/02/u-s-catholics-open-to-non-traditional-families (accessed 4 October 2018).

Phillips, D. Z. (1965). *The Concept of Prayer*. London: Routledge and Kegan Paul.

Primiano, L. N. (1995). Vernacular Religion and the Search for Method in Religious Folklife. *Western Folklore* 54(1): 37–56.

Primiano, L. N. (2012). Afterword – Manifestations of the Religious Vernacular: Ambiguity, Power and Creativity. In M. Bowman and U. Valk (eds), *Vernacular Religion in Everyday Life: Expressions of Belief*. Durham: Acumen. https://doi.org/10.2307/1499910

Rizvi, Ali A. (2013). Why I Call Myself an "Atheist Muslim". *Huffington Post*, 13 April. Retrieved from www.huffingtonpost.com/ali-a-rizvi/why-i-decided-to-call-myself-an-atheist-muslim_b_3261226.html (accessed 4 October 2018).

Ruel, M. (1997). *Belief, Ritual and the Securing of Life: Reflexive Essays on a Bantu Religion.* Leiden: Brill.

Russell, S. T. and Consolacion, T. B. (2003). Adolescent Romance and Emotional Health in the United States: Beyond Binaries. *Journal of Clinical Child and Adolescent Psychology* 32(4): 499-508. https://doi.org/10.1207/S15374424JCCP3204_2

Sharma, A. (2008). The Hermeneutics of the Word "Religion" and Its Implications. In R. D. Sherma and A. Sharma (eds), *Hermeneutics and Hindu Thought: Toward a Fusion of Horizons.* London: Springer. https://doi.org/10.1007/978-1-4020-8192-7

Sharpe, Eric J. (1977). Some Modern Approaches to the Study of Religion. In Open University, AD208, *Seekers and Scholars*, 48-83. Maidenhead: Open University Press.

Smith, Wilfred Cantwell (1959). Comparative Religion: Whither – and Why? In Mircea Eliade and Joseph M. Kitagawa (eds), *The History of Religions: Essays in Methodology.* Chicago, IL: University of Chicago Press.

Smith, William Cantwell (1979). *Faith and Belief.* Princeton NJ: Princeton University Press.

Spiro, Melford E. (1971). *Buddhism and Society: A Great Tradition and its Burmese Vicissitudes.* London: George Allen & Unwin.

Thomas, Richard (2003). *Counting People In: Changing the Way we Think about Membership and the Church.* London: SPCK.

Tutu, D. M. (2010). Foreword. In G. A. Barker and S. E. Gregg (eds), *Jesus Beyond Christianity: The Classic Texts.* Oxford: Oxford University Press.

Wittgenstein, Ludwig (1966). *Lectures and Conversations on Aesthetics, Psychology and Religious Belief.* Oxford: Blackwell.

Yip Tuck, A. (2010) Coming Home from the Wilderness: An Overview of Recent Scholarly Research on LGBTQI Religiosity/Spirituality in the West. In K. Browne, S. R. Munt and A. Yip Tuck (eds), *Queer Spiritual Spaces: Sexuality and Sacred Places*, 35-50. Farnham: Ashgate.

2

The emics and etics of religion

What we know, how we know it and why this matters

Steven J. Sutcliffe

> The cognitive power of any translation, model, map, generalization or redescription – as for example in the imagination of "religion" – is, by this understanding, a result of its *difference* from the subject matter in question and not its congruence. This conclusion has, by and large, been resisted throughout the history of the history of religions. But this resistance has carried a price. Too much work by scholars of religion takes the form of a paraphrase ... which is a particularly weak mode of translation, insufficiently different from its subject matter for purposes of thought. (Smith 2001: 145)

The emic/etic distinction in relation to insider/outsider discourse

I want to argue that an approach to the study of religion/s which generates both "emic" and "etic" knowledge of beliefs and practices, based on a principle of "difference" rather than "congruence" as outlined above by J. Z. Smith, provides a powerful epistemic tool which has been unjustly neglected in the study of religion/s. By revisiting the classic debate between linguist Kenneth Pike and anthropologist Marvin Harris in the 1970s and 1980s, I argue for the restitution of the emic/etic distinction in our analyses to renew enquiry into the epistemic status of religious representations, by which I mean the question of *how*, rather than *by whom*, the object of knowledge is constructed. The emic/etic distinction provides "cognitive power" to tease out the epistemological basis (the question of *how*, or on what ground or premise the claim is made) which has become obscured by the cultural-political interests mobilized by "insider" and "outsider" discourse (the question of *who*, or the identity of the claimant). While it may be important for particular research projects to identify and analyse the politics of insider/outsider claims and the interests this discourse advances, I assume for the purposes of this chapter that knowledge claims and identity claims are sufficiently different to warrant separate analysis. There has been a tendency either to neglect the emic/etic distinction altogether or, worse, to conflate the two terminologies by implying that the epistemology of emics/etics is simply another term for the politics of insider/outsider. However, even casual reference to a distinction between "insiders" and "outsiders" risks at best legitimating the normative and strategic discourses of certain actors in the field and at worst may be read as supporting an uncritical politics of identity in which legitimate knowledge (epistemology) can only be a function of existence or being (ontology). I therefore begin with a brief critique of insider/outsider discourse before shifting my attention to the emic/etic distinction, initially as articulated in the debate between Kenneth Pike and Marvin Harris. I will argue that emics/etics affords a level of epistemological subtlety which is obscured by the more discursive terminology of insider/outsider. In fact the emic/etic level of analysis reveals insider/outsider to be an emic distinction: *explanandum* rather than *explanans*. I provide three brief examples from my own research to support the recovery of emics/etics in the study of religion/s and conclude that we cannot afford to neglect its cognitive power if we wish to retain scientific (theoretical and comparative) status for our field. As Headland (1990: 17) puts it: "anthropologists ... if not other social scientists ... owe their jobs to their ability to make the distinction between *emic* and *etic*".

Despite poststructuralist critique, binary constructions appear to be psychologically and sociologically entrenched in many societies, as seen in the prevalence of everyday tropes of relational identity and positionality such as me and you, us and them, here and there, in and out. In the human sciences this essentially folk construction of difference is reproduced (and politicized) in the discourse on "insiders" and "outsiders". The study of religion/s is no exception, as seen in Russell McCutcheon's widely cited reader *The Insider/Outsider Problem in the Study of Religion* (1999). The methodological "problem" raised in the title is largely confined to the philosophical level of adjudicating rival truth claims between different scholars and practitioners, with relatively limited attention being paid to ethnographic or social historical case studies where informants are typically making more strategic and political claims, although inclusion of an extract on emic/etic terminology (Pike 1999) opens up a different analytical seam.[1] The presentation of the collection as a whole may even inadvertently legitimize a folk meta-discourse, namely that "there is something specific about religion that makes the question of whether the researcher is an insider or an outsider fundamentally important", as Martin Stringer (2002: 4) puts it in his introduction to *Theorizing Faith: the Insider/*

Outsider Problem in the Study of Ritual (Arweck and Stringer 2002). This is really a theological (or better, confessional) hermeneutic, which is unfortunately regularly triggered due to widespread public conflation of the categories theology (or faith) and religion, as Stringer implies. A stronger ethnographic dimension is provided in contributions to Stringer's volume, which points to the role of environmental factors in the production of knowledge claims, but frustratingly there is no mention of emics/etics.

A cogent critique of insider/outsider discourse is provided by Jeppe Jensen (2011) who argues that the presentation of an ontology of "insides" and "outsides" imputes a superior authority to what "insiders" know, since "in" is invariably coded more positively than "out". A "mystique" consequently arises: that "'insiders' have special kinds or privileged modes of access to experience, information and knowledge that 'outsiders' do not and cannot have" (ibid.: 31). Similarly the sociologist Robert Merton describes the operation of an "insider doctrine" within many social and political movements, the logic of which can be reduced to the expression "you have to be one in order to understand one" (Merton 1996: 246). The "extended version of the Insider doctrine", argues Merton, goes further: "one must be one *in order to understand what is most worth understanding*" (ibid.: 248; emphasis added). But since it is in the nature of the "mystique" that these "privileged modes of access" are themselves not fully communicable, it follows that one "insider" could have as much difficulty communicating what they know to another "insider" as to an "outsider". Clearly there must be multiple "insiders" within any designated group, a fact that can be amply confirmed by studying debates within groups and lineages on where authority is deemed to lie.[2]

The insider/outsider trope also draws on an appealing spatialization of the subject-as-knower. This is made explicit in J. M. Yinger's metaphor of "religion" as a stained-glass window in a church, as viewed by the perambulating subject, in his seminal textbook *The Scientific Study of Religion* (Yinger 1970). The advantage of this metaphor, Yinger suggests, is that it shows that there is what he calls a "whole meaning" to the stained glass window (although "rounded" might be less ambiguous than "whole") which "is apparent only as the light shines through, just as the true meaning of religion is visible only to one on the inside" (ibid.: 1–2). He dynamizes the metaphor by modelling of a mobile subject-as-knower:

> It's only a part truth to say that one can see a stained-glass window only from the inside. One can see the *inside* of the window only from the inside. From the outside we can see the outside, and one can find out who built it, who put it in, who keeps it in repair, and who goes inside to see it from that perspective. (Yinger 1970: 1–2)

In this way Yinger partly rescues his metaphor by developing the idea of multiple vantage points on the object of knowledge enjoyed by an itinerant subject-as-knower moving in and out and to and fro. In 1970 both the fact of the pluralization of religious formations as objects of study and the idea of combining different methodological perspectives, implicitly "positioned", marked significant disciplinary advances. But Yinger's metaphor remains unsatisfactory insofar as it requires the subject to be spatialized – to be topographically located either "in" or "out" of a building, group, location, or territory – as a condition of available knowledge.

A final problem with insider/outsider discourse is that it presupposes a unified subject in the sense that a person's thoughts, desires and motives are deemed to be coherent, consistent and transparent. There is ample evidence to the contrary from real-life settings, in the form of fractionated and/or tactical selves: for example, the "conflictual actor" in New Age networks, who is formed by "conflict towards their socialization" whatever its substantive content (Possamai 2005: 21–23); the "dual belonging" to Buddhist and Christian traditions following exposure to religious pluralization, as described by Drew (2011); and the "quest for composure" displayed by members of the middle classes in Scotland as they are interpellated by multiple religious authorities (Sutcliffe 2010). There is support for a more psychologically distracted anthropological model of the subject from the cognitivist argument made by Barrett (1999) that how subjects think in the heat of the moment undercuts the normative "theological correctness" promulgated by priestly and scholastic cadres. Similarly, ethnography has shown that popular rituals, discourses and identities are typically *ad hoc* and strategic performances which vary in intensity and duration according to context and audience.[3] In short, everyday and metaphorically "on-line" behaviour tends to articulate more proximate, quotidian and tactical concerns than the (Paul) Tillichian philosophy of "ultimate concern" which appears to shape the insider/outsider trope.

In sum, as Jensen argues, the distinction between insider and outsider is normative rather than empirical: it is "a politically expedient construction" which at best indicates "the plain reality that knowledge is unevenly distributed among subjects" (Jensen 2011: 30). It is clear that we do not need to be axiologically or emotionally committed to each thing that we know in order for our knowledge to be contingently valid and useful. What the study of religion/s requires is not an at best naïve and at worst politicized representation of "us" and "them" in which "the Other" becomes fundamentally unknowable – a tendency which "insider/outsider" discourse can serve to legitimize – but an epistemological tool capable of identifying, assessing and comparing the status of representations made by all parties to an event or a debate.[4]

The emic/etic distinction, while no magic bullet, is serviceable for this task. This is not a new claim, but it has been neglected for disciplinary reasons within the study of religion/s which I cannot address here. In what follows I revisit the classic debate between Kenneth Pike and Marvin Harris, beginning with the terms "emic" and "etic" developed by Pike from his work in linguistics in the 1950s and 1960s, followed by the critique of Pike's model in Harris's anthropology from the 1960s, and then the interaction of both scholars (and others) in a symposium between anthropologists, psychologists and linguists published as *Emics and Etics: The Insider/Outsider Debate* (Headland 1990). I then briefly indicate how emics/etics might be used as a tool in the Study of Religion/s with reference to my own research. I argue that the pay-off from making controlled emic/etic comparisons is threefold: to be able to tease apart the behavioural stream of events (what people *actually* do) from normative ideals (what they *intend* or *ideally wish* to do); to be able to identify salient differences between various religious and cultural representations; and finally, but no less importantly, to be able to identify salient similarities *across* the same.[5]

The debate on emics/etics in linguistics and anthropology

The linguist Kenneth Pike (1912–2000) coined the terms "emic" and "etic" in 1954 from the suffixes of the words phonemic and phonetic.[6] The latter terms refer respectively to the smallest meaningful sound unit recognized "phonologically" in their own speech by indigenous language speakers, and to a synthetic comparative sound unit operationalized by trained linguists to identify similarities and differences in and across languages. Pike wanted to extend the implications of this linguistic difference to his larger project, described in the title of his book as no less than "a unified theory of the structure of human behavior" (Pike 1967). To this end Pike detached the suffixes -emic and -etic from phonemic and phonetic to convert them into putatively free-standing terms which provided parsimonious descriptions of "units" of cultural behaviour. By analogy with a sound unit (phoneme) recognized as salient and meaningful by a particular language speaker, Pike proposed "emic" to refer to a cultural representation – an idea, practice, object or event – as it is cognized and articulated in a form recognized and endorsed by the practitioner. By analogy with the International Phonetic Alphabet (IPA) – a cross-cultural taxonomy of synthetic comparative sound units written in a specialist orthography[7] – Pike proposed "etic" to refer to the same cultural representation, now as cognized and articulated through a synthetic cross-cultural terminology.

The nature of the relationship between emics and etics is clearly crucial. McCutcheon develops a key difference implicit in Pike's early discussion: that "phonetics scholars develop a comparative basis which is itself outside the language systems they are studying (after all, no language users write in the Phonetic Alphabet) to study not simply one language but *the phenomenon of human language* itself" (McCutcheon 1999: 16). In other words, the etic account operates within the framework of a general and systematic theory – of religion/s, for example. At this level of analysis it supervenes the emic account just as the phonetic alphabet for the purpose of linguistic analysis supervenes the kind of tacit phonemic and morphemic knowledge which is specific, for example, to French, Russian or Arabic speakers. As Pike puts it:

> The *etic view is cross-cultural* in that its units are derived by comparing many systems and by abstracting from them units which are synthesized into a single scheme which is then analytically applied as a single system. The *emic view is monocultural* with its units derived from the internal relations of only one individual or culture at a time. (Pike 1962: 37; emphasis added)

This meta-analysis can be translated into disciplinary terms. A concern with understanding and fine-tuning emic representations is arguably consistent with the projects of Buddhist studies, Jewish studies, Islamic studies or Pagan studies, for example, each of which by definition pursues questions about, or articulated within, the "tradition" in question, and none of which requires systematic comparison with other formations to fulfil its aim, either using the etic genus "religion", or similar etic terms in the comparativist's lexicon such as "text", "ritual", "myth", "class", "gender" or "sexuality". The inverse is the case for the study of religion/s which is, by definition, a theoretical and comparative analysis of similarities and differences within and across formations, for which etic knowledge is essential.

In Pike's original presentation, emic knowledge is organic and holistic and has the primary aim of specifying and affirming indigenous representations. In contrast, etic knowledge is parts-oriented and reductive, with the primary aim of generating comparison and analysis of whole formations or their constituent parts. Despite this epistemic difference, Pike allows for co-existence, even for a kind of dialectic, between emic and etic. As an analogy for their interaction he describes how the operational unity of an integrated object such as a car can be cognized both emically and etically:

> In an emic approach, the analyst might describe the structural functioning of a particular car as a whole, and might include charts showing the parts of the whole car as they function in relation to one another; in an etic approach he might describe the elements one at a time as they are found in a stock room,

where bolts, screws, rims, fenders and complex parts, such as generators and motors from various models and makes of cars, have been systematically "filed" according to general criteria. (Pike 1999: 30)

In this way Pike presents emics/etics as a kind of "Haynes manual"[8] in which emic know-how assembles its theoretical object while etic analysis takes it apart to see how it works and to make repairs. Pike argues that, taken together, the pair provide a "stereoscopic window on the world" (Pike 1962: 35ff) in the sense that "emic and etic data do not constitute a rigid dichotomy … but often present the same data from two points of view" (Pike 1967: 41).

This "binocular" perspective is analogous to holding in tension the general and the particular or the nomothetic and idiographic:

> Through the etic "lens" the analyst views the data in tacit reference to a perspective oriented to all comparable events (whether sounds, ceremonies, activities), of all peoples, of all parts of the earth; through the other lens, the emic one, he views the same events, at the same time, in the same context, in reference to a perspective oriented to the particular function of those particular events in that particular culture, as it and it alone is structured. (Pike 1999: 32–33)

Although he values "stereoscopic" effect, Pike explicitly prefers the emic lens insofar as it provides knowledge of "that particular culture, as it and it alone is structured" and treats the emic unit "as the same emic unit in spite of etic variability" (ibid.). In contrast, the etic approach serves the interests of an "*outside* disciplinary system" (Pike 1990: 28; emphasis added). It follows that for cultural units to be properly understood, in Pike's view, they must be treated holistically and in series (one after the other, reinforcing incomparability) rather than componentially and synchronically (which would privilege components and generic characteristics). For Pike, the chief purpose of etic knowledge is to facilitate the identification of, and subsequent entry into, new or imperfectly understood cultural systems. Once entered, the unfamiliar system is treated as an organic whole and subsequently can (and should) be treated on its own terms. Pike encapsulates his understanding of the proper relationship between emics and etics in a short poem with the title of "emic circle", which describes what he calls "the involved nature of emics leading to etics, and etics leading to emics":

> See, and know.
> Know, and be.
> Be, and do.
> Do, and see.
> See, and know. (Pike 1990: 45)

To recap, Pike developed the emic/etic distinction from linguistics as shorthand for an analysis of the epistemic status of knowledge about wider cultural practices: that is, the question of how (by means of what cognitive operations) subjects know what they know. In the process Pike indicated his settlement of their relationship by claiming a higher status for emic knowledge, thereby subordinating etics to emics in the final analysis, as can be seen in the key line in his "emic circle" poem which conflates knowledge and being: "Know, and be".

Pike's pioneering work on emics/etics was engaged in the late 1960s by the anthropologist Marvin Harris (1927–2001), who took a very different epistemological position. In *The Rise of Anthropological Theory* (Harris 2001a), first published in 1968, Harris argued that an "emicized" episteme had come to dominate the social sciences whereby the concepts and symbols of the cultures studied had become absorbed into and blended indiscriminately with scholarly categories and analysis. This had come about, Harris argued, through an idealization of the "other" in comparison with the perceived failings (scientific and political) of modern Western societies, coupled with guilt in the face of the complicity of anthropological science with colonial history. The result was that "emicized" anthropologists tended to privilege the norms and intentions (emics) of subjects over analysis of their historical behaviour within the environment (etics).

Harris's proposal was to use emics/etics to tease out different representations of events: both one and the same event, and to compare events (cross-culturally) in order to test for similarities and differences at both emic and etic levels. In particular, Harris became interested in the question of whether there was congruence between the (mental) intentions of subjects and their (historical) behaviour and between their ideals (norms) and practices ("outputs"), and how subjects and observers explained any differences that might be identified. Where Pike's aim was methodologically to induce emic uniqueness through etic comparison, Harris's aim was to juxtapose the emics of a culture – the aggregate of exponents' ideals, aspirations and intentions – with an etics of that same culture's social-historical practices: the behavioural "output" of the group concerned. In Harris's case outcomes were to be assessed according to his theoretical programme of cultural materialism in which technological development and economic organization form the causal infrastructure for the development of cultural systems (Harris 2001b; Kuznar and Sanderson 2007).[9]

Despite their differing metatheoretical commitments – materialist and idealist respectively – Harris and Pike were agreed that emic statements referred to "phenomenal distinctions ... built up out of contrasts and discriminations significant, meaningful, real, accurate or in some other fashion regarded as appropriate by the actors themselves' (Harris 2001a: 571). In other words, practitioners' assessment of the appropriateness of any given term, taxon or discursive description, is the hallmark of emics. Harris introduced a principle of falsification to strengthen this criterion:

> An emic statement can be falsified if it can be shown that it contradicts the cognitive calculus by which relevant actors judge that entities are similar or different, real, meaningful, significant, or in some other sense "appropriate" or "acceptable". (Harris 2001a: 571)

Harris means that only reference to actors' acts or statements can tell us what is or is not important to the emic frame. His definition of etic also does not differ in key respects to Pike's: "Etic statements depend upon phenomenal distinctions judged appropriate by the community of scientific observers" (Harris 2001a: 575). However, Harris's defence of the independence or autonomy of etic statements introduces clear water:

> Etic statements cannot be falsified if they do not conform to the actor's notion of what is significant, real, meaningful, or appropriate. Etic statements are verified when independent observers using similar operations agree that a given event has occurred. An ethnography carried out according to etic principles is thus a corpus of predictions about the behavior of classes of people. (Harris 2001a: 575)

In other words, Harris is claiming that etic distinctions are by definition not open to dispute simply because they differ from what actors say, but only if they contravene the methodological principles of the research programme within which they are deployed.

Because of the differential status of emic and etic representations, the researcher needs both for a rounded account. Moreover clearly etic analysis cannot proceed until emic data have been gathered. This is not as simple as it might appear. Harris offers two examples in support of his claim that "actual behavior can be treated in both an emic and an etic fashion" (Harris 2001a: 580–581). In *The Rise of Anthropological Theory* Harris describes the process of validation of the skills of captains of fishing boats in the Brazilian state of Bahia according to emic and etic categories. He begins by describing what he calls the "ideal behaviour" required of participants to explain how captains are able to find the "proper spot" to fish. This emic account stipulates factors such as lining up the correct landmarks from the boat in order to cross-reference the location of this "proper spot". The captain's eyesight and memory is judged to be a key skill. His ability to find "the spot" can be retrodicted by the size of the catch: a large haul confirms his reputation and enhances crew retention in a competitive labour market. Harris argues that this emic account is constructed proactively and persuasively by participants in real time, such that "one can *actually* see and hear the captain look for the landmarks, manoeuvre the boat into position, order the sails down and the anchor dropped; and one can actually watch the fishing commence over the 'spot'" (ibid.: 581). As he says: "*actual* culture here corresponds to a large degree to *ideal* accounts of it" (ibid.: 581; emphasis added). Harris then shifts to an etic account of the same event. This time he notes that "when the captain locates the spot and the men start to fish, they not infrequently fail to catch a single fish. On such occasions the captain explains that the fish are not at home … and he orders the boat off to another spot" (ibid.). As Harris puts it: "the etics of the matter do not commit us to a description of this behavior in terms of the captain's emically appreciated skills" (ibid.); instead, the etic account "observes the constant use of a plumb line, and … widespread knowledge of the relationship between type of bottom, water depth, and type of fish likely to be found in broad zones as opposed to 'spots'" (ibid.). In this way, as Harris puts it, "etic categorizations open quite a different ethnographic trail":

> An analysis of the relationship between age of captain, size of catch, and stability of crew reveals that younger, more active and vigorous men who do not drink, who work hard, and who manifest a "protestant" type of behavior (an eminently etic category since they are all "Catholics") are the ones who are likely to be successful captains around whom the reputation for keen landmark sighting and good "spot memory" will develop. (Harris 2001a: 581–582)[10]

In these different causalities, the emic account foregrounds the mystique and charisma of the authority figure (the captain) and the overall "providence" guiding the boat, while the etic account emphasizes the impact of technical training, leadership and labour. Explaining the relative success of the fishing is the goal, but there is a sharp difference in how this is done. Emics gives a holistic representation of the fate of this singular Bahian crew, while etics gives a more reductive causal model which could be applied to the performance of another boat, or to the relative fortunes of a fleet.

Moving to Kerala, South India, Harris's second example is based on his interviews with farmers by means of which he seeks to account for the differential cause of death of cattle in a situation where the local mortality rate of male calves is statistically almost double that of females. On the basis of interview data, Harris states that "every farmer insisted that he would never deliberately shorten the life of one of his animals" and "ardently affirmed the legitimacy of the standard Hindu prohibition against the slaughter of domestic bovines" (Harris 2001b: 32–33). He claims that the farmers themselves attributed the mortality differential to "the relative "weakness" of the males: '"The males get sick more often', they say" (ibid.: 33). Harris lists a number of emic reasons adduced for this differential mortality and emphasizes that "again and again I was told that every calf has the right to life regardless of its sex" (ibid.: 33). He then shifts to an etic analysis in which environmental factors come to the fore:

> [N]o one would say that since there is little demand for traction animals in Kerala, males are culled and females reared ... [T]he etics of the situation are that cattle sex ratios are systematically adjusted to the needs of the local ecology and economy through preferential male "bovicide". Although the unwanted calves are not slaughtered, they are more or less rapidly starved to death. (Harris 2001b: 33)

According to the emic view, in contrast, "the systemic relationship between Kerala's cattle sex ratios and local ecological and economic conditions simply does not exist" (ibid.: 33). Harris compares the situation in Kerala with bovine farming in Uttar Pradesh where, in a very different ecological environment, he finds that "preferential etic bovicide is practised against *female* rather than *male* cattle" (ibid.: 33; emphasis added). In other words, by comparing emic and etic accounts across multiple contexts, Harris argues that the relationship between human behaviour and its ecological-economic environment is systemic and predictable rather than idiosyncratic and variable.

Harris's examples arguably could be more nuanced ethnographically[11] and he is also rhetorically prone to hyperbole and irony as indicated in his "protestant" quip about the Bahian fishermen.[12] Nevertheless his theoretical contribution is to reintroduce the concept of epistemic difference as a systematic variable in explaining behaviour cross-culturally. The epistemic difference in the Bahian example lies between the (emic) interpretation of the captain's charismatic gift which is contrasted with the (etic) analysis of the instrumental rationality underpinning the boat's operation. The case of the Keralan "bovicide" raises questions about the application of etics as a potentially beneficial material intervention in peasant livelihoods in a situation where emic ideals, supported by religious taboo, hold sway. Both examples also suggest that juxtaposing etics against emics, either in relation to the same event, or comparatively across different events, can be politically sensitive. At the same time Harris claims that his approach is not a zero sum option: "to insist upon the separateness of emic and etic phenomena and research strategies is not to affirm a greater or lesser 'reality' or a higher or lower scientific status for either of them" (Harris 2001a: 579). Nevertheless he holds that it is the capacity to generate an etic perspective that "makes the social sciences possible" through the deployment of "trained comparative knowledge" (Harris 1990: 49). He is therefore correct that "it is the status of etics, not emics, that lies at the heart of our [Pike's and Harris's] disagreement" (*ibid*). In the final analysis Harris wants to be able to test for tension between the ideal and the intentional and the historical and behavioural on the grounds that there is "little indication that the normal condition of social life is one in which conformity to emic norms predominates" (Harris 2001a: 592). There is also a provocative moral agenda: working the "seam" of the emic/etic distinction can probe "the human capacity to lie, obfuscate, forget, and disguise our inner lives; to say one thing and do another; and to produce in the aggregate effects that were not intended by any individual" (Harris 1990: 55).[13]

Applying emics/etics in the study of religion/s: three examples

Now that we have some historical and theoretical background, I would like to indicate how the emic/etic distinction can be used in the study of religion/s via three brief examples from my own research in the ethnographic history of alternative religion/s.

My first example is the question of the existence of a "New Age movement". This supposedly robust etic term – a "New Age movement" – has been widely utilized as a category to designate relatively diffuse and amorphous data. Unfortunately it has obscured the history of emic discourse on the coming "New Age" which does not coincide either substantively or chronologically with the sociological concept of the "New Age movement" (Sutcliffe 2003: 9–30). The latter term is almost impossible to falsify since it sucks up more or less anything "alternative", "esoteric" or "spiritual" in Weber's world-affirming sense. In contrast, the emic term "New Age", as used for example by Alice Bailey in New York in the 1930s, by the Heralds of the New Age in New Zealand in the 1950s, and by the early Findhorn community in Scotland in the mid–1960s, was strongly millennialistic and in Weberian terms world-denying: Christ, or Space People, or UFOs were expected to appear imminently to announce the end of the world and to deliver the salvation of the elite group in question. In other words, whether "New Age" is understood *emically or etically* significantly impacts the finer grain of our historical and sociological knowledge. One example of the potential mischief that can result is the substantial conservative Christian literature published in the 1980s, most notoriously Constance Cumbey's *The Hidden Dangers of the*

Rainbow: the New Age Movement and our Coming Age of Barbarism (1983) and Texe Marrs's *Dark Secrets of the New Age: Satan's Plan for a One World Religion* (1987), which claimed to expose the existence of clandestine forces underpinning this "New Age Movement" (Saliba 1999: ch. 2). At that time (the mid-1980s) there was no adequate social history of the phenomenon, with the result that, even as the more lurid or conspiratorial features described by Cumbey and Marrs were rejected, the idea that there was nevertheless an empirical phenomenon that could be identified (for purposes of evangelizing) as "the New Age movement" was convenient for polemicists and sociologists alike. This notion was reinforced in the mid-1990s by the "first wave" of scholarly monographs (Sutcliffe 2014: 43-44) which despite ascribing different genealogies (varying from post-1960s counterculture, to Western esotericism, to philosophical vitalism) agreed that there existed a quantifiable and falsifiable "New Age movement". Yet during the 1970s and 1980s, the core period treated by these monographs, use of the term "New Age" by practitioners –its emic status – declined significantly. In other words, increasing disinterest in using the term or identifying with it in the 1970s and 1980s, in preference for signifiers like "holistic" or "spiritual", can be contrasted with vigorous debate on the millennialistic dawning of a "New Age" between the 1930s and 1960s. In this way the pseudo-etic category "New Age movement" has displaced the evidence-based history of emic use of the term "New Age". When scholars began to study the "New Age movement" in the 1990s, widespread identification with the term by practitioners – the emic hallmark – was already over. It is the confusion of the emic and etic status of a term, rather than "amorphous" data, which has produced the "pseudo-problem" (Jensen 2011) of defining the "New Age movement".

My first example shows the importance of attending to the fine grain of emics – those "phenomenal distinctions" deemed "significant, meaningful, real, accurate" to practitioners (Harris 2001a: 571) – in order to be able to do justice to the historical record as well as to generate reliable data for etic (comparative) analysis. My second example, the category "spirituality", reveals a similar epistemic confusion of status, but spreading in relation to a contemporary object of study. Primary sources embrace the term emically, but scholarly sources are often unclear. Historically there has been a variety of emic uses which continues into the present. Christian inflections have been documented by scholars such as Jones et al. (1986) in *The Study of Spirituality* and by Sheldrake (2013) in *Spirituality: A Brief History*. There is also a lively "occult" genealogy. For example, the Theosophist G. R. S. Mead (1863-1933) published an essay in 1910 called "On the Track of Spirituality" in which he wrote that "the terms "spirit", "spiritual" and "spirituality" occur perhaps more frequently than any others in mystical, religious and philosophical literature"; he also noted that "there is no consensus of opinion as to their definite meaning" (Mead 1910: 149). That little has changed almost one hundred years later can be seen when journalist Mick Brown (1998: 1) in *The Spiritual Tourist* describes spirituality as a "buzz-word of the age". The category is evidently meaningful for many different contemporary audiences as suggested by publications such as *Integral Spirituality: Resources for Community, Justice, Peace and the Earth* (Dorr 1990), *The Lost Art of Being Happy: Spirituality for Sceptics* (Wilkinson 2007), and *The Book of Atheist Spirituality* (Comte-Sponville 2008) in which the term is deployed enthusiastically to serve very different interests. Clinicians and person-centred professions in the UK and US, including psychiatrists, counsellors, nurses and social workers, have also developed a strong stake in the concept. Religious Studies scholars have followed suit, from advocating the development of a "progressive spirituality" (Lynch 2007) to critiquing expressions of "capitalist spirituality" (Carrette and King 2004). It is perhaps not surprising that Rose (2001) should ask: "Is the Term 'Spirituality' a Word that Everyone Uses, But Nobody Knows What Anyone Means by it?".

If the hallmark of emics is the capacity to represent (multiple) "contrasts and discriminations" appropriate and meaningful to practitioners (Harris 2001a: 571), "spirituality" is clearly a vital emic term. The analytical problem arises when it is uncritically translated into an etic register. For example, between 2007 and 2017 Sara Mackian's UK-based Open University blog, "Everyday Spirituality", described itself as a medium in which to explore "what 'spirituality' means in modern society, and how and why people use spirituality in their daily lives. We are not talking here of religion as an organized, institutional way of understanding ... but as the idiosyncratic and unique ways that individuals seek meaning in their lives."[14] Mackian's blog provides a rich repository of popular understandings of "spirituality" as something "idiosyncratic" and "unique" pursued by the autonomous individual. However the existence of social and historical conditions of subject formation which might qualify the self-evident authority of emic spirituality are not addressed on this university platform. As a result the blog serves to endorse popular narratives of individual spiritual experience which are said to oppose "organized, institutional" religion. It therefore provides a rich repository of emic understandings but endorses an ideology of "spirituality" rather than subjecting the term to etic analysis.[15]

My third and final example of the salience of emics/etics to the theoretical enterprise of the Study of Religion/s is the trend of self-identification as a "seeker". For this example I begin with the etic model in order to emphasize the impinging reality of the social structure within which the emic discourse of the autonomous "seeker" is articulated. An etic model of "seekership" was developed by Colin Campbell in his famous essay on the environment in which seekers operate, which he calls the "cultic milieu". Campbell argues that seekers form a key constituency in this environment, because they have "adopted a problem-solving perspective while defining conventional religious institutions and beliefs as inadequate. Such persons are defined as 'searching for some satisfactory system of religious meaning to resolve their discontents'" (Campbell 1972: 123).[16]

Seekers are defined as persons dissatisfied with traditional religion(s) who are looking for answers among the multiple authorities operating within the cultic milieu. The determinative impact of social structure on the seeker's search is suggested by Campbell's etic description of the "milieu" as being "united and identified by the existence of an ideology of seekership and by seekership institutions" (Campbell 1972: 135). In this analysis, practices of "seeking" are represented as being as much an effect of wider structural conditions as their cause. The neophyte seeker is socialized into a collective disposition or *habitus* "which both arises from and reinforces the ... receptive and syncretistic orientation, and the interpenetrative communication structure" of the wider milieu (ibid.: 123). The seeker cannot be separated from their environment: put more strongly, their behaviour is as much an effect as a cause.

The emic understanding of what is going on is (of course) rather different. At this level, actors' self-descriptions of "seeking" and "seeker", and of their "quests" and "journeys", are understood to be autonomous, inspired choices. The typical emic seeker story describes a self-directed individual following their "path" which is reminiscent of testimonies on MacKian's blog. For example, an Australian seeker, Julian, describes the stages in his "search for spiritual truth":

> Be a student but not to any self-proclaimed guru
> Have teachers but not one teacher
> Partake of group activities but be not bound to only one group for this may limit your growth.
> At the same time, do not wantonly hasten down every spiritual path that is presented to you;
> Rather, use discernment.
> Have the confidence to trust your intuition for your intuition is your higher genius
> It is the guidance of your guardian angel (cited in Possamai 2005: 21–22)

In this testimony Julian constructs an idealized autonomous self, legitimated by an individualized source of illumination only minimally differentiated from himself as subject. The emics are strong and vivid. But Julian's account is implausible – or at best incomplete – once the ideology of seekership and the social institutions of the cultic milieu are taken into account. These take the form of the "gurus", "teachers", "group activities" and other "students" which structure Julian's search (we know this because he tells us) and which inevitably form his behaviour. As with the discourse on "spirituality", the emics of seeking give rich data but should not be mistaken for (etic) explanation. That is, to understand Julian's search as a response to an environment of multiple competing authorities is an etic explanation of his emic account of expressing his 'higher genius'.

An autobiography by the English goddess priestess Kathy Jones (b. 1947), evinces a similar tension between emic self-representation (as an autonomous "seeker") and etic contextual evidence (that the cultic milieu forms her "seekership"). Jones was born in 1947 in North East England, grew up in a secularized Methodist background, studied psychology at university, entered the 1960s counterculture, visited Morocco on the "hippy trail", and then moved to rural west Wales where she read about "Taoism, Buddhism, those sorts of things" (Jones 2001: 240–242). Later she visited Findhorn and practised Alice Bailey full moon meditations (ibid.: 243) before settling in Glastonbury to establish a goddess conference and a goddess temple (ibid.: 249).[17] Jones's story, like others during this period, is narrated as a process of pure self-realization: for example, the section in which she describes her visit to Morocco, her residency in rural Wales, and her eclectic reading is subtitled "a lone development of spirituality" (ibid.: 241–242). This is in despite of the list of the company Jones keeps, the places she visits and the texts she consumes (again, we know this because she tells us). Each stage in her story can be cross-referenced to prominent sites, sources or signifiers of collective membership in the cultic milieu in the UK in the second half of the twentieth century, and can be correlated with other biographical testimonies by seekers containing the same or similar ingredients (e.g. Boice 1990; Losada 2001). This point could also be made negatively by noting what Jones *did not* read, what she *did not* do, and where she *did not* reside. In short, seeking as self-realization, described emically by Julian in Australia and by Kathy Jones in the UK, can be explained etically by seekership as a socially structured practice.

Conclusion: the cognitive power of emics/etics in the study of religion/s

The sociology of democracy may be an interesting exercise, but the sociology of democratic societies is a far more important task. So it is with the study of religion. We must be alert to the distinction between what a religion, ideally or culturally conceived, *might* do and what religious systems, embedded in societies and in individuals, *actually* do. (Yinger 1970: 22)

By revisiting the debate between Pike and Harris followed by consideration of examples from my own research, I have argued that emics/etics provides a robust tool to analyse how we know what we know about religion/s. Emics/etics yields a more productive level of analysis than the insider/outsider distinction, with which it is often conflated, because the latter can only at best describe a position in which knowledge is a function of being rather than a cognitive operation which at worse can legitimize forms of identity politics. Emics/etics promotes clarity and transparency by keeping two orders of epistemology in play while simultaneously preventing their indiscriminate blending. Attention to both orders is required for scholarly work: as Jardine (2004: 275) puts it: "etics without emics is empty, emics without etics blind". Analysing the relationship between emics and etics should be core business in the study of religion/s: otherwise, as Smith warns, our account will become merely "a paraphrase", a genre of descriptive writing which is "insufficiently different from its subject matter for purposes of thought" (Smith 2001: 145). The zero point of the paraphrase is the statement made by the nascent History of Religions department at the University of Chicago in 1961, namely that "a valid case can be made for the interpretation of transcendence as transcendence". Such a position, Smith argues, "denies the legitimacy of translation, and the cognitive value of difference" and carries the absurd implication that "a word can only be translated by itself" (ibid.: 145–146). Or, in Yinger's terms above, that what "religious systems ... *actually* do" is identical to "what a religion, ideally or culturally conceived, *might* do".

An important discussion has developed in the human sciences on the value of otherness and alterity as a moral and political responsibility in representing marginalized identities (e.g. Guzy and Kapaló 2017). The study of religion/s has embraced this position, in part due to attention to its own imperialist history, in part through its espousal of liberal-progressive political values. Recovery of the emic/etic distinction can enhance alterity and difference in representations, enabling scholars to compare and translate divergent knowledge claims as part of systematic study without losing either specificity or the ability to generate comparison. The caveat is that if, as Harris claims, there is "little indication that the normal condition of social life is one in which conformity to emic norms predominates" (Harris 2001a: 592), etic analysis will not always be welcomed. Yet it is essential because "a theory, a model, a conceptual category, a generalization cannot be simply the data writ large"

(Smith 2001: 145).[18] This is why how we know what we know matters, whether about religion or indeed any other social practice.

About the author

Steven J. Sutcliffe is senior lecturer in the study of religion in the School of Divinity at the University of Edinburgh and was, from 2015 to 2018, the president of the British Association for the Study of Religions. His main research interests are the history and ethnography of alternative religion in the twentieth century, and the history of the study of religion since 1950, but he is also interested in atheism, humanism and the rejection of religion. He is the author of *Children of the New Age: A History of Spiritual Practices* (2003), editor of *Religion: Empirical Studies* (2004) and co-editor (with Ingvild Gilhus) of *New Age Spirituality: Rethinking Religion* (2013).

Acknowledgements

My thanks to Carole Cusack, Arko Longkumer, Jo Miller and Bjørn Ola Tafjord for their feedback on earlier versions of this chapter.

Notes

1. McCutcheon (2004) subsequently develops a critique of the political function of insider/outsider discourse which is closer to my understanding of it as *explanandum* rather than *explanans*, following Jensen (2011).
2. See for example the analysis by Waterhouse (1999) of the contested process of identification of the rightful leader of the Tibetan Kagyu lineage.
3. See for example the classic studies by Fuller (2004) on Hindu practices in South Asia and by Stringer (2008) on Christian practices in England.
4. Geertz's classic discussion of the merits of understanding "the native's point of view" helpfully stresses both the epistemological nature of the issue and the matter of "degree, not polar opposition" involved in moving between what he calls "experience-near" and "experience-distant" concepts (Geertz 1999: 51). Geertz's account is close to Jensen's view of the uneven distribution of knowledge among subjects which is better represented as a continuum rather than a divide; however, in using the language of experience, Geertz espouses the kind of subjectivist hermeneutic also critiqued by Jensen (2011: 44–45) for supporting an "ontological" basis of knowledge.
5. Discussion of the emic/etic distinction in Religious Studies is relatively rare. In four handbooks between 2005 and 2012 (Hinnells 2005; Segal 2009; Stausberg and

Engler 2011; Orsi 2012) there is passing mention in only one contribution (Knott 2005). Six papers by continental European scholars, derived from a symposium in Bern in May 2014, were published in *Method and Theory in the Study of Religion* (volume 28, issue 4–5). For an overview of contents, plus a discussion of the centrality of this debate to the Study of Religion/s and a critique of the entanglement of emic/etic and insider/outsider consonant with the position advanced here, see Mostowlansky and Rota (2016). In addition to the core disciplines of linguistics (Pike 1967) and anthropology (Barnard 2009), emics/etics has been debated in folklore (Dundes 2007), ethnomusicology (Alvarez-Pereyre and Arom 1993), psychology (Dasen 2012) and history of science (Jardine 2004), among other disciplines. This is why how we know what we know matters, whether about religion or indeed any other social practice.

6 The revised edition of his text (Pike 1967) is usually cited.
7 Systematized in 1888 but periodically revised: see www.internationalphoneticassociation.org/content/ipa-chart (last accessed 2 February 2019).
8 A series of "how to" guides for maintenance and repair of automobiles begun in 1960 but which now includes "practical lifestyle" topics: https://haynes.com/en-gb (accessed 29 August 2018)
9 The philosophical basis of the research programme is arguably less important than the requirement to practice emic/etic analysis within a coherent theoretical framework; nevertheless Harris's preference is clear and he compares structuralism and psychoanalysis unfavourably in its light (Harris 1990: 52–53).
10 Harris muddies the status of his concepts by describing "protestant" as an etic category when it is clearly another emic category (although his use of inverted commas may be ironic).
11 See Sebring's (1987) critique and Harris's (1987) response.
12 Compare his polemics on the counterculture in Harris (1977) and on postmodernism in Harris (1999).
13 This statement points to a moral-ideological subtext to both scholars, as Murray (1990) has shown. Pike developed his original model "while analysing languages for Bible translation purposes", claiming in his memoir (Pike 1962) that "emic analyses of broader cultural systems could be useful to the Christian missionary cause" (Murray 1990: 143). In contrast Harris "laments the murders caused and the emic cover-up perpetrated by those withholding abortion from Third World women" (*ibid*; for this, see Harris 1990: 58–59). Macagno (2016: 3) describes how publications by Harris in the late 1950s on migration and education among Mozambican workers led to "the elaboration of the first organized critique of Portugal's colonial policies on African labor and the Regime de Indigenato".
14 Opening post, 5 October 2007: see archive at www.open.ac.uk/blogs/Everyday Spirituality/ (last accessed 30 August 2018). In this post MacKian invited responses "if you have an interest in 'the spiritual' but do not necessarily consider yourself 'religious'" (see also MacKian 2012). At the time of writing, Mackian was working within the School of Health, Wellbeing and Social Care (see www.open.ac.uk/people/scm374).

15 Compare a similar blurring of emics and etics in *The Spiritual Revolution* (Heelas and Woodhead 2005) in which their putatively etic model of "subjective-life spirituality" versus "life-as religion" reproduces the dichotomies of emic discourse without qualification. For a critique of "sociology of spirituality" as an "emicized" enterprise, see Wood (2010).
16 The internal quotation is from an earlier paper on seekers by Lofland and Stark (1965: 868).
17 For further information see https://goddessconference.com and www.goddesstemple.co.uk (last accessed 30 August 2016). On the significance of Alice Bailey, Findhorn and Glastonbury in UK networks of "New Age" discourse, see chapters two to seven in Sutcliffe (2003).
18 I have focused in this chapter on the role of emics/etics in the elucidation of differences in religious representations, but its cognitive power can (of course) also be used to investigate similarities. This must await another occasion.

References

Alvarez-Pereyre, F. and S. Arom (1993). Ethnomusicology and the Emic/Etic Issue. *The World of Music* 35(1): 7–33.

Arweck, E and M. Stringer (eds). (2002). *Theorising Faith: The Insider/Outsider Problem in the Study of Ritual.* Birmingham: University of Birmingham Press.

Barnard, A. (2009). Emic and etic. In A. Barnard and J. Spencer (eds), *The Routledge Encyclopedia of Social and Cultural Anthropology*, 220–223. London: Routledge. https://doi.org/10.4324/9780203866474

Barrett, J. L. (1999). Theological Correctness: Cognitive Constraint and the Study of Religion. *Method & Theory in the Study of Religion* 11(4): 325–339. https://doi.org/10.1163/157006899X00078

Boice, J. (1990). *At One with All Life: A Personal Journey in Gaian Communities.* Forres: Findhorn Press.

Brown, M. (1998). *The Spiritual Tourist: A Personal Odyssey through the Outer Reaches of Belief.* London: Bloomsbury.

Campbell, C. (1972). The Cult, the Cultic Milieu and Secularization. In M. Hill (ed.), *A Sociological Yearbook of Religion in Britain 5*, 119–136. London: SCM.

Carrette, J. and R. King (2004). *Selling Spirituality: The Silent Takeover of Religion.* London: Routledge. https://doi.org/10.4324/9780203494875

Comte-Sponville, A. (2008). *The Book of Atheist Spirituality.* London: Bantam.

Cumbey, C. (1983). *The Hidden Dangers of the Rainbow: The New Age Movement and our Coming Age of Barbarism.* Lafayette, LA: Huntington House.

Dasen, P. (2012). Emics and Etics in Cross-Cultural Psychology: Towards a Convergence in the Study of Cognitive Styles. In T. Tchombe, A. Nsamenang, H. Keller and M. Fülöp (eds), *Cross-Cultural Psychology: An Africentric Perspective*, 55–73. Limbe: Design House.

Dorr, D. (1990). *Integral Spirituality: Resources for Community, Justice, Peace and the Earth*. Dublin: Gill and MacMillan.

Drew, R. (2011). *Buddhist and Christian? An Exploration of Dual Belonging*. London: Routledge.

Dundes, A. (2007). From Etic to Emic Units in the Structural Study of Folktales. In S. Bronner (ed.), *The Meaning of Folklore: The Analytical Essays of Alan Dundes*. Logan, UT: University of Utah Press.

Fuller, C. (2004). *The Camphor Flame: Popular Hinduism and Society in India* (revised and expanded edition). Princeton, NJ: Princeton University Press. https://doi.org/10.1515/9780691186412

Geertz, C. (1999). From the Native's Point of View: On the Nature of Anthropological Understanding. In R. McCutcheon (ed.), *The Insider/Outsider Problem in the Study of Religion: A Reader*, 50–63. London: Cassell.

Guzy, L. and J. Kapaló (eds) (2017). *Marginalised and Endangered Worldviews: Comparative Studies on Contemporary Eurasia, India and South America*. Berlin: Lit Verlag.

Harris, M. (1977). Return of the Witch. In his *Cows, Pigs, Wars and Witches: the Riddles of Culture*, 169–185. Glasgow: Fontana.

Harris, M. (1987). Response to Sebring. *Journal of Anthropological Rsearch* 43(4): 320–322. https://doi.org/10.1086/jar.43.4.3630539

Harris, M. (1990). Emics and Etics Revisited. In T. N. Headland, K. L. Pike and M. Harris (eds), *Emics and Etics: The Insider/Outsider Debate*, 48–61. London: Sage.

Harris, M. (1999). *Theories of Culture in Postmodern Times*. Walnut Creek, CA: AltaMira Press.

Harris, M. (2001a). *The Rise of Anthropological Theory: A History of Theories of Culture* (updated edition). Walnut Creek, CA: AltaMira Press.

Harris, M. (2001b). *Cultural Materialism: The Struggle for a Science of Culture* (updated edition). Walnut Creek, CA: AltaMira Press.

Headland, T. N. (1990). Introduction: A Dialogue between Kenneth Pike and Marvin Harris on Emics and Etics. In T. N. Headland, K. L. Pike and M. Harris (eds), *Emics and Etics: The Insider/Outsider Debate*, 13–27. London: Sage.

Heelas, P. and L. Woodhead (2005). *The Spiritual Revolution: Why Religion is Giving Way to Spirituality*. Oxford: Blackwell.

Hinnells, J. (ed.) (2005). *The Routledge Companion to the Study of Religion*. London: Routledge. https://doi.org/10.4324/9780203412695

Jardine, N. (2004). Etics and Emics (Not to Mention Anemics and Emetics) in the History of the Sciences. *History of Science* 40: 261–278. https://doi.org/10.1177/007327530404200301

Jensen, J. S. (2011). Revisiting the Insider–Outsider Debate: Dismantling a Pseudo-problem in the Study of Religion. *Method & Theory in the Study of Religion* 23: 29–47. https://doi.org/10.1163/157006811X549689

Jones, C., G. Wainwright and E. Yarnold (eds). (1986). *The Study of Spirituality*. Oxford: Oxford University Press.

Jones, K. (2001). Embodying the Goddess. In A. Leonard (ed.), *Living in Godless Times: Tales of Spiritual Travellers*, 239–252. Edinburgh: Floris Books.

Knott, K. (2005). Insider/Outsider Perspectives. In J. Hinnells (ed.), *The Routledge Guide to the Study of Religion*, 243–258. Abingdon: Routledge.

Kuznar, L. A. and S. K. Sanderson (eds). (2007). *Studying Societies and Cultures: Marvin Harris's Cultural Materialism and its Legacy*. Boulder, CO: Paradigm Publishers.

Lofland, J. and R. Stark (1965). Becoming a World-Saver: A Theory of Conversion to a Deviant Perspective. *American Sociological Review* 30: 862–875. https://doi.org/10.2307/2090965

Losada, I. (2001). *The Battersea Park Road to Enlightenment*. London: Bloomsbury.

Lynch, G. (2007). *The New Spirituality: An Introduction to Progressive Belief in the Twenty-First Century*. London: I. B. Taurus.

Macagno, L. (2016). The Birth of Cultural Materialism? A Debate between Marvin Harris and António Rita-Ferreira. *Vibrant: Virtual Brazilian Anthropology* 13(1): 1–21. https://doi.org/10.1590/1809-43412016v13n1p001

McCutcheon, R. (ed.) (1999). *The Insider/Outsider Problem in the Study of Religion: A Reader*. London: Cassell.

McCutcheon, R. (2004). The Ideology of Closure and the Problem of the Insider/Outsider Problem in the Study of Religion. *Studies in Religion/Sciences Religieuses* 2004: 337–352. https://doi.org/10.1177/000842980303200306

MacKian, S. (2012). *Everyday Spirituality: Social and Spatial Worlds of Enchantment*. Basingstoke: Palgrave. https://doi.org/10.1057/9780230365308

Marrs, T. (1987). *Dark Secrets of the New Age: Satan's Plan for a One World Religion*. Westchester IL: Crossway Books.

Mead, G. R. S. (1910). On the Track of Spirituality. In his *Some Mystical Adventures*. London: John M. Watkins.

Merton, R. K. (1996). Insiders and Outsiders. In his *On Social Structure and Science*, 241–263. Chicago, IL: University of Chicago Press.

Mostowlansky, T. and A. Rota. (2016). A Matter of Perspective? Disentangling the Emic-Etic Debate in the Scientific Study of Religion\s. *Method and Theory in the Study of Religion* 28: 317–336. https://doi.org/10.1163/15700682-12341367

Murray, G. (1990). Anthropology, Evangelization, and Abortion: Applications of Emics and Etics. In T. N. Headland, K. L. Pike and M. Harris (eds), *Emics and Etics: The Insider/Outsider Debate*, 143–163. London: Sage.

Orsi, R. (ed.) (2012). *The Cambridge Companion to the Study of Religion*. Cambridge: Cambridge University Press.

Pike, K. L. (1962). *With Heart and Mind: a Personal Synthesis of Scholarship and Devotion*. Grand Rapids, MI: Eerdmans.

Pike, K. L. (1967). *Language in Relation to a Unified Theory of the Structure of Human Behavior*. The Hague: Mouton. https://doi.org/10.1515/9783111657158

Pike, K. L. (1990). On the Emics and Etics of Pike and Harris. In T. N. Headland, K. L. Pike and M. Harris (eds), *Emics and Etics: The Insider/Outsider Debate*, 28–47. London: Sage.

Pike, K. L. (1999). Etic and Emic Standpoints for the Description of Behavior. In R. McCutcheon (ed.), *The Insider/Outsider Problem in the Study of Religion*, 28–36. London: Cassell.

Possamai, A. (2005). *In Search of New Age Spiritualities*. Aldershot: Ashgate.
Rose, S. (2001). Is the Term "Spirituality" a Word that Everyone Uses, But Nobody Knows What Anyone Means by it? *Journal of Contemporary Religion* 16(2): 193–207. https://doi.org/10.1080/13537900120040663
Saliba, J. (1999). *Christian Responses to the New Age Movement*. London: Chapman/Cassell.
Sebring, J. (1987). Bovidicy. *Journal of Anthropological Research* 43(4): 309–319. https://doi.org/10.1086/jar.43.4.3630538
Segal, R. (ed.) (2009). *The Blackwell Companion to the Study of Religion*. Oxford: Wiley-Blackwell.
Sheldrake, P. (2013). *Spirituality: A Brief History*. Oxford: Blackwell/Wiley.
Smith, J. Z. (2001). A Twice-told Tale: the History of the History of Religions' History. *Numen* 48: 131–146. https://doi.org/10.1163/156852701750152636
Stausberg, M. and S. Engler (eds). (2011). *Routledge Handbook of Research Methods in the Study of Religion*. Abingdon: Routledge.
Stringer, M. (2002). Introduction: Theorizing Faith. In E. Arweck and M. Stringer (eds), *Theorizing Faith: the Insider/Outsider Problem in the Study of Ritual*, 1–20. Birmingham: University of Birmingham Press.
Stringer, M. (2008). *Contemporary Western Ethnography and the Definition of Religion*. London: Bloomsbury.
Sutcliffe, S. (2003). *Children of the New Age: A History of Spiritual Practices*. London: Routledge.
Sutcliffe, S. (2010). After "the Religion of My Fathers": The Quest for Composure in the "Post-presbyterian" Self. In L. Abrams and C. Brown (eds), *A History of Everyday Life in Twentieth Century Scotland*, 181–205 Edinburgh: Edinburgh University Press.
Sutcliffe, S. (2014). New Age. In G. D. Chryssides and B. E. Zeller (eds), *The Bloomsbury Companion to New Religious Movements*, 41–46. London: Bloomsbury.
Waterhouse, H. (1999). Who Says So? Legitimacy and Authenticity in British Buddhism. *Scottish Journal of Religious Studies* 20(1): 19–36.
Wilkinson, T. (2007). *The Lost Art of Being Happy: Spirituality for Sceptics*. Findhorn: Findhorn Press.
Wood, M. (2010). The Sociology of Spirituality: Reflections on a Problematic Endeavour. In B. Turner (ed), *The New Blackwell Companion to the Sociology of Religion*, 267–285. Oxford: Wiley-Blackwell. https://doi.org/10.1002/9781444320787.ch12
Yinger, J. M. (1970). *The Scientific Study of Religion*. London: Macmillan.

3

The death pangs of the insider/outsider dichotomy in the study of religion

Ron Geaves

The chapter will explore how the insider/outsider dichotomy in the study of religions has become increasingly untenable as "objectivity" was increasingly challenged by post-modernist theory, the advent of reflexivity and the collapse of primordial theories of identity construction as they were supplanted by newer understandings. On route, the paper will argue that the study of religion is uniquely placed to revolutionize both scientific methodological paradigms and the ethics of research that currently prevail in the social sciences. In particular, the arguments will be offered that the humanities as a field of studies must be careful not to be subsumed under the social science paradigm with regard to methodologies of fieldwork, and, in particular, the study of lived religions. It will show how the insider/outsider framework has a particular applicability within the study of religion and the degree to which the "classic" understanding of this model has come under challenge in recent decades, especially with the focus on Islam and Muslim studies, that has captivated policy makers, media and academics and provided a sharp forum for the examination of field ethics, insider/outsider categories and the framing of "objectivity" in traditional social science paradigms. Through an exploration of the growth of the Muslims in Britain Research Network as a case study, the chapter will argue that the euro-centricity of current paradigms of methodology and field ethics can be challenged creatively by the many Muslims now studying their own communities and lived religious experience within those communities by drawing upon the subjectivities of religious traditions to develop new paradigms of research ethics and methodologies that can result from further deconstructing models of insider/outsider belonging.

The arguments put forward in this chapter were first presented in embryonic form at Cardiff University at the postgraduate seminar entitled "Inside Out: Reflexivity and Methodology in Research with British Muslims" organized by the Centre for the Study of Islam in the UK based in the School of History, Archaeology and Religion at Cardiff in association with the Muslims in Britain Research Network (MBRN). According to its website, the MBRN was "established to encourage and promote the study of Muslims and Islam in Britain. It brings together academics, professionals, teachers, students, researchers and journalists" (see www.mbrn.org). In short, an ideal field to assess the changing relations between the etic and the emic, at least in the study of one religion. The Network was created by Jorgen Nielsen in the mid-1980s when he taught at Selly Oak Colleges in Birmingham. Significantly the Network was established in, more or less, the same time frame as the Community Religions Project based in the Theology and Religious Studies department at the University of Leeds. The significance of the Leeds project is that it encouraged the study of lived religions as they were arriving in Britain after the post-Second World War mass migrations from the new commonwealth. In addition to new forms of Christianity and Rastafari arriving with the Afro-Caribbean communities, significant populations of Hindus, Muslims, Sikhs, Jains and Parsees were arriving to supplement very small presences that had existed in some cases back into the nineteenth century. The demographic of British religious life was to change dramatically with Islam becoming the second largest faith-based allegiance in the nation sometime in the second half of the twentieth century. These new religious constituencies on British soil would transform the landscape of the academic study of religion, with many more postgraduates and researchers becoming excited by the possibility of field studies involving lived religious communities. The study of Islam and Muslims in Britain would not only be fed by this new-found research terrain, but also in the growing interest in their own history in Britain among British-born second and third generation Muslims. All of this was, of course, vastly accelerated by the troubled relationship developing in the twenty-first century, as Muslims and non-Muslims tried to come to grips with religious and political extremism, issues of identity, Muslim education, dress codes, religious leadership and Islamophobia. A number of university faculties were to create centres that would focus on the study of Muslims and Islam in Britain, some were to benefit from substantial bursaries originating in the Middle East from well-meaning benefactors. By the first decade of the twenty-first century the membership of the Muslims in Britain Research Network was over two hundred and dominated by young Muslim scholars. The same could be said of the new centres established to study various aspects of Muslim presence in Britain. As postgraduate and post-doctoral Muslim researchers sought for funding and publication outlets they were forced to consider methodology and look at the challenges presented by their emic identities and social science disciplines that historically have favoured the etic.

"Insiders" and "outsiders"

When I first engaged with the study of religion as an Open University student between 1983 and 1988 the issue of "insiders" and "outsiders" was outlined as advantages and disadvantages of "seekers" and "scholars". These were listed as follows:

Seekers

- are committed to understand or to enable themselves to practise their own faith better;
- study religion using the criteria provided by a particular tradition;
- are students who start with the belief that God (or equivalent) exists and can be known;
- require a measure of commitment;
- are believers have predetermined position so approach must be distorted; and
- find religious commitment to be an advantage since they can appreciate the nature of religious experience, and what it means in the life of the believer.

Scholars

- are non-denominational and non-confessional, and allow each religion to speak for itself;
- have their criteria provided by what is commonly called "scientific method" or "methodological agnosticism" (religious data are studied and evaluated in an objective and unprejudiced way);
- are students who start by recognizing only that there is something there to be studied (beliefs may true or false, rational or irrational);
- require a measure of detachment;
- lack experience of religion so can never appreciate what it is about (so their results must contain a measure of distortion);
- regard commitment as a disadvantage since to accept one's view of religion as "true" may mean that one has to disown other's view of religion as "false" (religious commitment can blind the believer in regard to understanding a religious phenomenon; Open University 1977).

The polarization of seekers and scholars was useful in that it placed the emic/etic arguments into the framework of the study of religion and provided a basic model for students to work with; even today it is possible to hear some of these dichotomies still being discussed in the methodology chapters of various postgraduate theses where the researcher has engaged in the field. The claim that it was possible to study religion adequately from a disinterested position was hotly debated within the study of the religion throughout the 1990s and the first decade of the twentieth century and occurred repeatedly in the British Association for the Study of Religions as part of a contested discourse between scholars of religion and theologians, where the former were often influenced by Ninian Smart and the Lancaster department for the study of religions where Smart's version of phenomenology was put into practice. The debates in the latter half of the twentieth century would produce a number of influential texts and some significant discussions between upholders of polarized key positions (Reat 1983; McCutcheon 1998). Within the study of religion these debates would express themselves between academics who maintained that religion is a sui generis entity and those such as Timothy Fitzgerald and Robert Segal who held to a reductionist position in which any scholar who utilizes a sui generis definition of religion is negatively labelled as a "theologian" or a "religionist". In this position, scholars who held that religion was a sui generis entity were implicitly labelled as a kind of "insider". The debate owes its origins to the attempt to categorize religion in either functional or substantive definitions.

The official Bulletin of the British Association of the Study of Religions picked up the debates in 2003. In the November 2003 edition of *the BASR Bulletin*, the two sides of the debate were picked up by Robert Segal and Frank Whaling (2003: 57–59). In response to Robert Segal's argument that the aim of the scholar of religion is to "develop methods for uncovering the *unrecognized* believer's point of view and theories to *account* for that point of view" (ibid.: 58), Whaling provides a defence for those that maintain religion is a sui generis entity. There is nothing particularly new in Whaling's argument, although it is interesting to note that both sides accuse the other of indulging in metaphysics. Whaling's understanding of metaphysics in this context is described by him thus: "Humanities and Social Science approaches are needful and necessary. The dilemma comes when methods are transformed into metaphysics which explain religion and even explain away religion and reduce it to something else. They become ends rather than means." (ibid.: 59).

In the June 2004 edition, Robert Segal's piece on Freud's *Totem and Taboo* notes that he has added Otto, Eliade and Schleiermacher to his course on the study of religion "as a concession to the 'religionists'". He complains that each "deciphers religion only as taking it as unlike anything else" (Segal 2004a: 39). In a series of responses to the piece by Segal, Paul-François Tremlett (2004) argues that reductionist studies of religion function in modernity to signify a pre-modernist past whose mentalities in the form of "erroneous religious beliefs" require correction. Segal answers with eight criticisms of Tremlett's position (Segal 2004b). The argument was to rumble on until November 2004 when the editor called a halt.

The reductionist argument that religion is merely a sub-set of cultural phenomena, taken to its logical conclusion, would see the study of religion removed to cultural studies or social science faculties. Indeed, Timothy Fitzgerald, arguably the main proponent of the reductionist position not only suggests that "work of outstanding originality" is only produced by such scholars but goes on to add that such scholars might "legitimately be in departments of history, anthropology, cultural studies or areas studies instead" (Fitzgerald 2000: 4). Although Fitzgerald does not actually say so, the implication is that any worthwhile study of religion cannot be achieved by scholars who consider religion a sui generic entity. The suggestion is that University departments founded in the strategic partnership between theology, comparative religion and phenomenology compound a sui generic understanding of religion and that the study of religion as influenced by Ninian Smart and the Lancaster model is really a contemporary form of theology which Fitzgerald (ibid.: 5) labels "liberal ecumenical theology", disguised by affirming that religion is a natural category that all human beings have an innate capacity to experience. The argument between the camps of sui generis and reductionist supporters appeared in two important conferences during the same period. In December 2003, it dominated the questions and answers during the Religious Studies: What is the Point? conference at Lancaster University organized in conjunction with the PRS-LTSN Learning Centre, whose title indicated the implications for the subject area, and then appeared again in the opening keynote lecture entitled "The Contentious Term Religion" at the 50th Annual Conference of the British Association of the Study of Religion held at Manchester College, Oxford in September 2004. The keynote lecture was given by James Cox and originated from fieldwork undertaken in Zimbabwe which explored the relationship between the spirit world and the hierarchical ordering of society among the Shona. Cox concludes that "indigenous groups in Zimbabwe have passed on their traditions and customs authoritatively from generation to generation" (Cox 2007: 157) but significantly asserts that his research endorses the view of religions as social and cultural expressions, but without carrying forward the essentialist notion of religion as transcendentally focused (Kunin and Watson 2006: 3). Thus substantive definitions of religion should be avoided as they tend to maintain "religion" as an ontological category, which, as argued by Fitzgerald (2000: 6), is a surreptitious form of theology.

The counter-argument is that "religion" refers to a totally distinct and unique category of human experience which is beyond the comprehension of those who have not shared this experience. A technical way of referring to this is to speak of religion as autonomous (subject to its own laws) or as being sui generis. The implications of this view for the student have been spelled out in no uncertain terms:

> The reader is invited to direct his mind to a moment of deeply-felt religious experience, as little as possible qualified by other forms of consciousness. Whoever cannot do this, whoever knows no such moments in his experience, is requested to read no further; for it is not easy to discuss questions of religious psychology with one who can recollect the emotions of his adolescence, the discomforts of indigestion, or, say, social feelings, but cannot recall any intrinsically religious feelings. (Otto 1958: 8)

According to this view there are severe limits to the extent to which religion can be understood by the "outsider" who has not known "intrinsically religious feelings".

Yet, we should be aware of the implications of rejecting the sui generis argument. In so doing we *have* made a statement about the nature of religion: that, for the purposes of study, we are assuming that it is possible to study religion in much the same way as we study other aspects of human experience. On the other hand, those who view religion as sui generis face the problems of identifying what makes it so (which, given the varied forms of religion, is not easy), and also of convincing us that a person who has experienced one form of religion may apply this experience in the analysis of another.

Reflexivity

Arguably these debates within the field of the study of religion were merely a prolonging of the classic insider/outsider dichotomy and the "death knells" had already commenced. They were to come initially from within the social sciences. While the scholars of religion from within the social sciences were arguing for a more empirical approach that privileged reductionism, postmodernist theory was beginning to unsettle the claims of objectivity and neutrality that accompanied empiricism. The rapidly changing terrain of the social sciences was beginning to reassess classic theories of methodology, challenged by new ideas concerning subjectivity and objectivity. For the scholars of religion, this would result in an important question: "Can anyone really be disinterested?" and with regard to whether the understanding of the observer can achieve the same level of insight and authority as the participant in a religion, the empiricism of the scientist was challenged by the postmodern view that scientific objectivity is no less a construct than religious conviction.

Fiona Bowie (2000) reminds us that any account of a religion is a translation of one language to another, from one symbolic system to another and that there is a three way encounter between people studied, the scholar and the intended audience. In her view this process involves a problem of translation and no account of another's cultural experience can be value free or objective. All such accounts reflect the agenda of the observer and the quality of access to other people's ways of thinking and being, filtered through life history, prior experience, conscious or unconscious intention (ibid.).

Reflexive anthropology becomes one solution to this challenge. The "fly on the wall" approach is undermined and it is understood that the observer's position will direct and delimit what is observed. A homogenous "other" will interfere with the encounter. It is therefore desirable to break down the emic and etic boundaries and provide a more holistic approach where reflexivity becomes the modus operandi of the student of religion. As explained by Helen Callaway (2005: 43) "a dialogical methodology which rejects the division between subject and object, places the self within the field of investigation, evaluates positionality and power relations, and creates an intersubjective matrix for knowledge".

In addition, but not disconnected, new theories of identity formation were arguing that identity itself is "situational" and complex rather than a rigid compartmentalization of being. Situational theories attempt to explain how certain circumstances lead to the rational, strategic selection of ethnic identity (Scott 1990). The old primordialist theory of identity that can feed into racist discourse and the language of "othering" was under challenge. Under these sustained attacks the dichotomy of "insider" and "outsider" begins to dissolve into a series of questions such as:

- When I am an "insider" (and is it relevant)?
- When am I an outsider (and is it relevant)?
- Which identity construct is operating at any one time?
- Who am I?

Later I will discuss how these would impact upon young Muslim scholars engaged in the field in particular. My own thoughts have been influenced by such deliberations but also by concerns not to essentialize in the study of religion. This is crucial in the study of Islam. It would seem to me that "insider" and "outsider" are in themselves essentialized categories of identity and neither takes us very far in understanding how Islamic identity is constructed. In the field this may be relevant to our analysis in the form of these two questions:

- How is Muslim identity constructed?
- How is non-Muslim identity constructed?

The changing face of the Study of Religion

Arguably the Open University's useful dichotomy of "seekers and scholars" was devised at a time when the overwhelming mode of study undertaken by scholars of religion was textual. The hermeneutical study of sacred texts by scholars of religion had aroused crises of faith and debates with insiders at least since the nineteenth century had heralded advance in Biblical scholarship. Christianity was not only the religion to feel the impact of this conflict. Sikhism was to become embroiled in a "tradition versus history" conflict as challenging insights from W. H. McLeod (1984, 1989) and his research students which, in turn led to the creation of Sikh Studies at Punjab University, Chandigarh that maintained a more traditionalist approach to Sikh text. Muslim Islamic scholars have long been aware of the dangers to the integrity of the truth-claims of the Qur'an and Hadith if the methodology used to deconstruct the Bible was replicated. In particular, John Wansbrough (1977, 1978) and his students were raise challenging questions concerning the origins of the Qur'an.

By the 1980s the terrain of studying religion in Britain was beginning to shift. Increasingly a number of scholars of religion would begin to argue that lived religion needed to be explored through the means of field studies. In the 1970s, the sociological debates concerning the decline of religion would result in a number of field studies carried out on new religious movements and the phenomena of New Age. These religions could be studied in localities not far away from university campus. From the 1980s scholars of religion would be become aware that the same applied to Hinduism, Sikhism, Jainism, Buddhism and Islam. As temples, gurdwaras and mosques sprung up in many of Britain's inner cities, scholars of these religions realized that they did not have to travel far to challenge existing theories or study adaptation. Nowhere was this growth in local field studies felt more than among those who chose Islam in Britain. However, a number of high profile incidents beginning with the Salman Rushdie protests, 9/11, 7/7 and continuing through to the present would place the study of Muslims in Britain under a spotlight of media and policy making interest. Simultaneously, identity formation processes among second and third generation British Muslims would interest hundreds of both genders in the study of their own presence in Britain. As young Muslim scholars began to engage with the field from across a variety of disciplines, first undertaking postgraduate and then postdoctoral study, the question of insider/outsider status and its fluid borders began to concern them.

The field was always going to be a challenging terrain for a generation brought up to question primordial theories of identity construction. In a three-way dynamic between British. ethnic and religious identity, young Muslims scholars were used to shifting on a daily basis to negotiate life possibilities and resolve conflicts. These skilful players of identity would challenge the simple dichotomy of insider/outsider. It was never going to be a simple religious construction of insider status that would determine access, privileged knowledge, methodology, or insights. Gender would also play a significant role. Sophie Gilliat-Ray (2005) would write an influential article on her failure to access a *dar al-ulum* (traditional Muslim seminary) in northern England. Gilliat-Ray notes three previous examples of failed access to similar institutions in Britain. The first example was my own attempt in 1994. In my case I was a non-Muslim male. The second example was a request by a group of Bradford Christian clergy. This met with a flat refusal. Although linked by their shared status as religious professionals, again this group were non-Muslim males. So far, it is arguable that insider/outsider dynamics were coming into play. In the final example, a fellow imam from a similar institution was refused. Clearly, in this latter case simplistic dichotomies of insider/outsider fail to explain the refusal. In every way, the final example shared "insiderness" with the group to be accessed except one (ibid.: 15–16). He was from another (possible rival) institution. Gilliat-Ray was also refused access despite being Muslim. Arguably in this case, traditional Islamic gender roles would play a more significant role than religious identity. Interestingly, Gilliat-Ray notes that the only successful attempt to gain access was achieved by Philip Lewis, a non-Muslim male clergyman. Gilliat-Ray states "Lewis' success in gaining some access to Deobandi *dar al-uloom* in the early 1990s rested upon this ability to draw upon an identity that would have had meaning and salience in the Deobandi worldview, namely fellow 'man of God'" (ibid.: 25). In this case, Lewis was able to achieve access when the clergymen in the second example failed. However, it needs to be noted that Lewis spoke fluent Urdu and had lived in Pakistan for several years, arguably providing him with a shared "insiderness" in addition to being a "man of God". Gilliat-Ray seems to be suggesting that sharing language, religious professional status and cultural literacy resulting from living in the same habitus were enough to overcome Lewis's whiteness and belonging to another religion. Certainly these examples will cause us to reflect on the impact of multiple identities in the field.

Strategic identity matches

Gilliat-Ray (2005: 25) concludes that her gender was a major obstacle and states "It is clear that I was not able to achieve any kind of strategic identity 'match' in relation to Deobandi dar al-uloom." She goes on to argue that researchers need to "do something" to show their "appreciation of the identity of potential participants" (ibid.: 25–26). She cites the example of Whyte's Street Corner Society, where the researcher learned Italian to bridge the gap between himself (white Anglo-Saxon Protestant) and his research cohort (Italian-speaking Roman Catholic working class; ibid.: 26). Whyte's learning of Italian may appear to be a strategic device to ensure the success of his research but others have argued that field work needs to be a relational activity. Drawing upon feminist studies, Rosaldo notes that it is necessary to escape "the tendency for the self-absorbed Self to lose sight altogether of the culturally different Other" (Rosaldo 1989: 7). Returning to the anthropological notion of reflexivity, David Hufford argues that it acknowledges the fact that qualitative research is based on an interaction between researcher and informant.

> Reflexivity is a metaphor from grammar indicating a relationship of identity between subject and object, thus meaning the inclusion of the actor (scholar, author, observer) in the account of the act and/or its outcomes. In this sense reflexivity shows that all knowledge is "subjective". (Hufford 1995: 57)

Graham Harvey also sees fieldwork as relational and develops the notion of "methodological guesthood" in which the researcher perceives herself as a "guest-researcher" (Harvey 2003: 126). He considers this method to go beyond the colonial mindset of "us" versus "them" as it allows hosts and guests to think in terms of "us". He states: "This third position that is neither 'subjective native' nor 'objective outsider' has always been a possibility and, indeed, has often been offered" (ibid.: 142–143). Robert Orsi (2005: 2) also argues that research should acknowledge the "intersubjective nature of particular social, cultural, and religious identities and indeed of reality itself", and should appreciate that the researcher becomes part of this network of connections and that therefore research also has an essentially intersubjective nature. "Once religion is understood as a web not of meanings but of relationships between heaven and earth, then scholars of religion take their place as participants in these networks too, together with saints and in the company of practitioners" (ibid.: 5). Bowman and Valk acknowledge this, stating that contemporary scholars of religion are increasingly to be seen as "partners in communication, participants in a heteroglot dialogue of indefinite numbers of voices and points of view" (Bowman and Valk 2012: 2).

Harvey's relational model of "guesthood" involves a reciprocal relationship in which the guest has to enter the worldview of the religious to the degree that particular ethical understandings of guesthood are comprehended. In Islam the ethics of host and guest are very strong and form part of the divinely sanctioned relations between human beings. To engage with guesthood with Muslims requires cultural literacy and a subsequent breaking down of the borders between "insider" and "outsider". In my own experience of Muslim hospitality when researching in Deoband, northern India, it was deemed necessary for me to have a more secure "insider" status to circumnavigate the restrictions of guesthood. On arriving in Deoband unannounced, for fear that letters requesting access from a total stranger would lead to an institutional refusal, I found myself literally a "guest" occupying a room in the *dar al-ulum*'s guesthouse. In order to prolong my stay I was taken by two students to the Shaikh al-Hadith, who was the most senior figure underneath the principal of the college. The Shaikh was considered more approachable by the two students and therefore more likely to allow me to stay. The Shaikh's approach was novel. He questioned me on my personal beliefs and was content to discover that I was, at least, a theist, even if not affiliated to a particular faith tradition. He asked me two questions: did I accept that the Qur'an contained within it divine truths? And did I accept that Muhammad was a messenger able to communicate those truths to human beings? I had no problem answering in the affirmative. The Shaykh declared:

> Then you are a Muslim. In which case, you can remain here longer than the three days allocated to guests. You will need to follow all the requirements expected of a student here. I can now take you to the Principal and confirm my invitation extended to you.

Deoband is a very conservative tradition and my stay involved living every day as a seminary student, Islamic prayer, dress codes, the timetable were all observed meticulously. The Shaykh had effectively allowed me to become a Muslim for the duration of my stay. Insider and outsider walls began to dissolve. I have utilized the temporary status of "Muslim" in all my future stays in Islamic religious institutions. It serves a dual purpose. I am able to be a participant "observer" but I can transcend the relationship of "observed" and "observer" and find benefits that transcend the research environment and impact upon my religious life. It is strategic but it is also relational and to this degree I have labelled it "strategic temporary insider".

Reflections

As the above examples demonstrate varying attempts to delimit insider/outsider constructions, have been made, and others in the field become aware that there is no escaping the fact that this type of research is likely to transform both the researcher and the researched. Both will engage in a common journey with each other. In a collection of essays edited by Hillary K. Crane and Deana L. Weibe (2013), the overall consideration is the way that the researcher "self" is, in the words of Riyaz Timol, "reconfigured and reconstituted, even 'bent out of shape', in our unremitting quest to penetrate the inner life-worlds of others" (Timol 2014: 496). Timol, however, has two criticisms to make that are highly pertinent to this article. He notes that:

> The collective field stance, rather, is one of stoical agnosticism – described variously as "partially in / partially out", "betwixt and between" or "walking between worlds" – which does nothing to dispel the positivist image of an objective, rational Westerner studying natives...If religion, as scholars such as Frank Whaling or Ron Geaves aver, is not simply a function of culture but an entity sui generis then how can it be adequately accounted for within the parameters of a discipline whose foundational epistemologies, operational methodologies and living exemplars are overwhelmingly secular in nature? (Timol 2014: 495–496)

Reflexivity, "methodological guesthood", "strategic temporary insider" may all function as devices to bridge the gap but can they do enough to dispel completely the implicit superiority of the "rational Westerner studying natives"? Harvey is aware of this challenge and argues that it is solely the "compromising entanglement of academia in colonial power dynamics" which has stopped us knowing the benefits of being guests among or with those we research (Harvey 2003: 142–143). Harvey appears to be satisfied that "methodological guesthood" based on his research in the field with Maori communities functions as an "ethical decolonising research method" (ibid.: 143). But is it enough to resolve his pertinent observations regarding inequalities in the field? Partly, the problem is that Harvey's useful contribution still maintains the insider/outsider dichotomy even as it offers the opportunity to explore the "other" relationally.

Much as I appreciate Harvey's contribution I am not convinced that it goes far enough to resolve Timol's critique. Perhaps the category "religion" through the lens of the social sciences can never resolve either question posed by Timol, but religion studied within the realm of the humanities acknowledging the creative imagination of the human endeavour to understand its existential dilemma may find answers that transcend the Western bias in methodology that appears to have no choice but maintain the insider/outsider dichotomy, and which at best seeks benign or paternalistic ways to make the relationship more equal. If we tacitly accept that being religious by itself is not a necessary qualification for a scholar of religion, and that someone standing outside all religions, but interested in their study, may or may not bring an openness and sympathy that a person with a particular religious commitment would find hard to match then the "insider"/outsider dichotomy begins to collapse in on itself. In such a scenario it will depend upon the skill and sensitivity of each researcher and the receptivity of the researched. However, the transformation of the British terrain for the scholar of religion, that is the arrival of a pluralist, multi-faith landscape as a result of migration and religious choice post second world war, did more than only turning the UK into an ideal locality for studying religions as "lived" realities as opposed to textual constructs. It also brought into the field hundreds of Muslim scholars studying their own religious and cultural landscapes, and to a lesser extent, Hindus, Sikhs and others who have been part of changing the very landscapes they are now studying. The increasing awareness of "lived religion" that this has engendered has also brought Christian theologians to the field and led them to speculate on how to "do theology" in the field and the relationship between ethnography and theological discourse (Swinton and Mowatt 2006; Scharen and Vigen 2011; Scharen 2012; Scharen and Smith 2015). It would seem that these authors have recognized that ethnographic studies of lived religions can make a significant impact upon theological and ethical thinking. As scholars of religion have recognized, it is one thing to state what religious traditions believe and hold as truth claims but it is another thing to uncover and to describe the daily workings out of these beliefs in specific faith communities. The theologians adopting ethnography have realized that theology is worked out in the gap between normative accounts of doctrines and detailed descriptions of actual practices. The motives of these "insider" ethnographers may be different. They are attempting to comprehend patterns of discourse about God, the world and believers' lives in order to develop "truth" narratives that reflect the reality on the ground. These scholars have recognized that Christian beliefs and practices in the West may also be impacted by the new field of diasporic and hybrid communities as much as Muslim or other religious presences.

However, as much as anthropology has influenced both scholars of religion and some theologians to recognize that "lived" religion can often undermine what is recorded or prescribed in sacred texts and discourses, the entry of "insiders" into the field of ethnography has not attracted the correspondent field of anthropological literature. Timol (2014) complains that none of the essays in the collection he reviewed provided the opportunity for the "insider" to reflect upon the challenges of studying their own religion in the field. On the surface these debates among "insider" ethnographers may appear to be keeping the "insider/outsider" dichotomy alive, but I would argue that is the realities of the field for "insiders" studying "insiders" that challenges simplistic understanding of "insider", such as Muslims studying Muslims or Christians studying Muslims. Most British Muslim scholars have dutifully prescribed to standard social science methodologies, even though their work is predominantly qualitative and they have not followed Christian ethnography down the path of renewing theological thinking. But they have quickly been drawn into reflective thinking concerning "insider" and "outsider" status. Gender, class, social and economic status, education and ethnicity can all over-ride religious identity in the field and it is a shifting landscape. I am increasingly aware, for example, that I am more at ease in the South Asian mosque and the conservative *dar al-ulum* environment than many of the young Muslim researchers that I speak to or examine. I am either more culturally literate or empathetic/sympathetic with these environments than middle-class educated young British Muslims. Young Muslim women may not get access to the place that I can enter, I may be prepared to join in prayer with fellow theists; some of them may not. Ethnicity may be as much a stumbling block for them as with me or even more so. A British Muslim of Turkish or Iraqi family origin may find access to South Asian institutions difficult and intimidating and fail to recognize some of the Islamic practices as normative.

The disciplines of the social sciences may insist a common set of methodological tools for everyone, but the Humanities may be able to be innovative. There is an argument to be put forward that if we are to be truly inclusive and ethical in our research, fully bridging the "othering" implicit in outsider/insider dichotomies, that the religions themselves may offer avenues for research methodology to be pioneered by those with an interest in truth claims.

There are signs of this taking place. For example, Farah Ahmed, a Muslim educationist and activist involved in setting up the Centre for Research and Evaluation of Muslim Education at the Institute of Education, University of London, has been studying how to develop "a culturally coherent pedagogy" for Muslim children in Britain (Ahmed 2012). Not only is her work significant in cross-cultural education but her field methodology borrowed from classical Islamic practice. Ahmed used Islamic study circles or *halaqahs* as a research method (Ahmed 2013). *Halaqah* means "circle" in Arabic. Usually a *halaqah* is a religious gathering, a kind of sanctified space for the study of Islam or the remembrance of God. Such circles are often favoured by women and ideal for research gathering from Muslim children and their mothers.

It is a beginning. I have long used the Qur'an's injunction: "O mankind! Lo! We have created you male and female, and have made you nations and tribes that ye may know one another" (Qur'an 49:13) as my primary motivation for studying religion and engaging in fieldwork. This is both a personal and humanistic approach to fieldwork and I also would prefer the central concept upon which Islam is built, that is *tawhid* (unity) as both a framework for research with fellow human beings to the dualistic insider/outsider model and to the formation of research ethics. To *tawhid*, I would also add *adl* (justice) and *adab* (manners) into the mix for developing a genuine robust but flexible model for research ethics than the Quality assurance focus which primarily protect the institutions that support our research as opposed to the researched. For example, a researcher (a fellow *dalit* woman) was asked by a university research committee to provide consent forms to her cohort (rural *dalit* women in India). It was clear to the researcher applying her shared world knowledge with her cohort that such forms could only intimidate an already oppressed and frightened subaltern community. I find an easy and natural fit between Islamic concepts such as *tawhid*, *adl* and *adab* to my own theistic and humanistic worldview without becoming a convert to Islam. I leave it to the many Muslim inheritors of the field in Britain to consider building upon the work of Ahmed and to seek Islamic alternatives to field practices developed by the objectivist model of social science rooted in secular or even atheist paradigms of knowledge. Only then can Timol's dilemma be resolved and Harvey's concerns be fully addressed.

About the author

Ron Geaves (2014). Ron Geaves is currently visiting professor in the Department of History, Archaeology and Religion, based in the Centre of the Study of Muslims in Britain at Cardiff University, previously holding chairs in religious studies at the University of Chester (2001–2007) and in the comparative study of religion at Liverpool Hope University (2007–2013). Professor Geaves remains active in research. Usually, his research is contemporary in focus and involves ethnographic study, although recently he has embarked on the historical study of the Muslim presence in Britain. He has written and edited nineteen books and contributed to around twenty-five edited collections and numerous journal articles. His works include *Sectarian Influences in Islam in Britain* (1994), *Sufis in Britain* (2000), *Islam and the West Post 9/11* (2004), *Aspects of Islam* (2005), *Islam Today* (2010), *Islam in Victorian Britain: The Life and Times of Abdullah Quilliam* (2010), *Sufis of Britain* (2014) and *Islam and Britain: Muslim Mission in an Age of Empire* (2017). He is currently working on *Glastonbury and the Making of New Age Spirituality: An Indian Guru and Esotericism in 1971* (Bloomsbury).

References

Ahmed, Farah (2012). Tarbiyah for Shakhsiyah (Educating for Identity): Seeking Out Culturally Coherent Pedagogy for Muslim Children in Britain. *Compare: A Journal of Comparative and International Education* 42(5): 725–749. https://doi.org/10.1080/03057925.2012.706452

Ahmed, Farah (2013). Using Islamic Study Circles (Halaqahs) as a Research Method. Retrieved from http://sites.cardiff.ac.uk/islamukcentre/virtual-centre/public-lectures/2013-public-lectures/farah-ahmed (accessed 25 August 2018).

Bowie, Fiona (2000). *The Anthropology of Religion*. Oxford: Blackwell.

Bowman, Marion, and Valk, Ulo.(2012). Introduction: Vernacular Religion, Generic Expressions and the Dynamics of Belief. In Marion Bowman and Ülo Valk (eds), *Vernacular Religion in Everyday Life : Expressions of Belief*, 1–19. Sheffield: Equinox.

Callaway, Helen (2005). Ethnography and Experience: Gender Implications in Fieldwork and Texts. In Judith Oakley and Helen Calloway (eds), *Anthropology and Autobiography*, 2nd edition, 29–48. London: Routledge. https://doi.org/10.4324/9780203450536_chapter_2

Cox, James, Leland (2007). *From Primitive to Indigenous: The Academic Study of Indigenous Religions*. Aldershot: Ashgate.

Crane, Hillary and Deana L. Weibel, Deana (eds) (2013). *Missionary Impositions: Conversion, Resistance and Other Challenges to Objectivity in Religious Ethnography*. Plymouth: Lexington Books.

Fitzgerald, Timothy (2000). *The Ideology of Religious Studies*. Oxford: Oxford University Press.

Gilliat-Ray, Sophie (2005). Closed Worlds: [Not] Accessing Deobandi dar al-uloom in Britain. *Fieldwork in Religion* 1(1): 7–33. https://doi.org/10.1558/firn.v1i1.7

Harvey, Graham (2003). Guesthood as Ethical Decolonising Research Method. *Numen* 50(2): 125–146. https://doi.org/10.1163/156852703321506132

Hufford, David (1995). The Scholarly Voice and the Personal Voice: Reflexivity in Belief Studies. *Western Folklore* 54(1): 57–76. https://doi.org/10.2307/1499911

Kunin, Seth and Watson, James (eds) (2006). Introduction. In Seth Kunin and James Watson (eds), *Theories of Religion: A Reader*. Edinburgh: Edinburgh University Press.

McCutcheon, Russell (ed.) (1998). *Insider/Outsider Problem in the Study of Religion: A Reader*. London: Continuum.

McLeod, W. H (1984). *Textual Sources for the Study of Sikhism*. Manchester: Manchester University Press.

McLeod, W. H. (1989). *The Sikhs: History, Religion and Society*. New York: Columbia University Press.

Open University (1977). *Seekers and Scholars*. Milton Keynes: Open University Press.

Orsi, Robert (2005). *Between Heaven and Earth: The Religious Worlds People Make and the Scholars Who Study Them*. Princeton, NJ: Princeton University Press.

Otto, Rudolf (1958). *The Idea of the Holy*. Oxford: Oxford University Press.

Reat, Ross, N. (1983). Insiders and Outsiders in the Study of Religious Traditions. *Journal of the American Academy of Religion* 51(3): 459–476. https://doi.org/10.1093/jaarel/LI.3.459

Rosaldo, Renata (1989). *Culture and Truth: the Remaking of Social Analysis*. Boston, MA: Beacon Press.

Scharen, Christian (2012). *Explorations in Ecclesiology and Ethnography*. Grand Rapids, MI: William Eerdmans.

Scharen, Christian and Smith, James (eds) (2015). *Fieldwork in Theology: Exploring the Social Context of God's Work in the World (The Church and Postmodern Culture)*. Ada, MI: Baker Academic.

Scharen, Christian and Vigen, Aana (eds) (2011). *Ethnography as Christian Theology and Ethics*. London: Continuum.

Scott, George (1990). A Resynthesis of the Primordial and Circumstantial Approaches to Ethnic Group Solidarity: Towards an Explanatory Model. *Ethnic and Racial Studies* 13(2): 147–171. https://doi.org/10.1080/01419870.1990.9993667

Segal, Robert (2004a). Turning Point: Sigmund Freud *Totem and Taboo*. *British Association for the Study of Religions Bulletin*102 (June): 35–37

Segal, Robert (2004b). Robert Segal Responds. *British Association for the Study of Religions Bulletin* 103 (November): 51–53.

Segal, Robert and Whaling, Frank (2003). Empathy or Diagnosis. *British Association for the Study of Religions Bulletin* 100 (November): 56–57.

Swinton, John and Mowatt, Harriet (2006). *Practical Theology and Qualitative Research*. Norwich: SCM Press.

Timol, Riyaz (2014). Book Review: Missionary Impositions: Conversion, Resistance and Other Challenges to Objectivity in Religious Ethnography. *Culture and Religion: An Interdisciplinary Journal* 15(4): 494–500. https://doi.org/10.1080/14755610.2014.972089

Tremlett, Paul-François (2004). Turning Point: A Reply to Robert Segal. *British Association for the Study of Religion Bulletin* 103: 50–51.

Wansbrough, John (1977). *Quranic Studies: Sources and Methods of Scriptural Interpretation*. Oxford: Oxford University Press.

Wansbrough, John (1978). *The Sectarian Milieu: Content and Composition of Islamic Salvation History*. Oxford: Oxford University Press.

4
Research ethics beyond the binaries of right and wrong

Marie W. Dallam

In recent decades, the professional associations of many fields as well as university review boards have assumed increasing amounts of influence and control over research that involves human subjects. The overarching goal of such oversight is to protect people from harm that could be caused by a researcher's actions, either deliberately or inadvertently. This institutional oversight can come as a surprise to the scholar of religion, who may not be accustomed to going through a lengthy clearance process before attending a religious service or speaking with an officiant. There are times when layers of clearance, including ethics training and methodological review, results in a carefully thought out research plan and an investigator who is well prepared for contingencies. However there are also many times when these preparations cannot predict the realities of the field, especially if one's research involves religious people who lie outside of mainstream social codes. Furthermore, regardless of preparation, it is not unusual for scholars to confront unforeseen questions of ethical procedure in the midst of their research and find that no viable course of action feels precisely "right". As Bromley and Carter (2001) have observed, such situations have often taken the researcher by surprise, and in the moment he or she becomes "caught up in rapidly developing and sometimes tumultuous events, complex and opaque relationships, and situations that produced strong personal reactions which they tried simply to cope with at the time" (ibid.: 3). After the fact, scholars can be understandably reluctant to discuss conundrums they have faced, because they may doubt the appropriateness of their own actions and fear that too much transparency could negatively impact the reception of their work.

What this means is that there is often a certain degree of silence for religious studies scholars around difficult fieldwork situations.[1] This silence is unnecessary, because the more we openly discuss our challenges the more we are likely to find common ground. As a starting point, this essay pulls together a wide range of examples from scholars who have been willing to write about problems that arose during research on religious groups. In some cases, they experienced ethical questions in the field and felt there were no clear right and wrong answers, only a range of choices with varying consequences. In others, the questionable nature of a research choice only became evident to them long after the fact. Exploring the puzzles that such examples provide makes it all the more clear that the ethical binary of right and wrong, as dictated to us by review boards, is not always helpful. Just as we acknowledge the interstice between "ideal" religion and "lived" religion, perhaps it would behove us to also do this in fieldwork ethics, admitting that the protocols built into our ideal fieldwork plans are often transgressed. The ideal may be overt research in which a scholar is entirely honest with subjects about who she is and what she is doing. Her presence never affects the tone of what occurs in her subject community, and she never participates in any way that is disruptive to the norm. When she leaves and publishes her findings, these actions have no negative effect either on individuals or the community as a whole. And just like ideal religion, living up to such stringent standards is utterly impossible. The reality is that we are rarely neutral figures in our own research, and distinguishing correct practices from errors can be a murky business.

As a basic example of what I mean, a typical ethical rule of thumb states that the researcher should not taint what she studies. Maintaining a level of distance and detachment prevents her from upsetting the natural balance of the community, such as by introducing new ideas or behaviours. But as Wilcox (2002) astutely notes about her own research on LGBTQ Christians, who were often struggling with anti-gay Christian teachings, "the process of observation itself alters that which we observe" (ibid.: 54). Wilcox found that in conversational interviews she sometimes suggested an alternate perspective on a religious idea; technically this was an ethical transgression, but because it brought solace to her interviewee, contextually it felt like the most ethical choice. But actions even smaller than Wilcox's can alter the circumstances. Realistically, any time a single human is added to a group situation, that person's presence changes what unfolds, and this applies even to participant observers. In the course of my own field research I have attended several training seminars for leaders within an alternative Christian church in the United States. By remaining quiet during the training sessions, taking notes rather than participating in discussion, my intention was to keep a safe distance and not affect any of the natural dynamics or topics of conversation. But in time I came to realize that the mere fact that I was taking notes made some people uncomfortable and perhaps more guarded in what they said, and in other instances caused people to seek me out and offer a barrage of opinions.[2] Either way, I failed in my attempts to be unobtrusive, and my presence certainly changed some of the conversations. When it is this easy to alter that which you are studying, it should not be surprising that it becomes even more complicated when the issue is not whether to mention an idea or take a few notes, but larger questions such as identity disclosure, relationships with subjects, or participation in the religious rituals.

Overt and covert research

One of the first questions a researcher must tackle is whether their fieldwork will be conducted overtly or covertly; more often than not, the former is deemed the most ethical choice and is therefore the preferred method. However, this was not always the case; research on religious communities in the past was often carried out as an undercover operation, based on the premise that a researcher might be unwelcome in an intimate religious setting. In thinking through the overt/covert dichotomy, Spicker (2011) makes the astute point that "covert" should not be automatically equated with "deceptive". Rather, covert simply suggests that the subject is not aware that research is taking place, whereas deceptive research occurs when a subject is misled about the nature of the research, and this latter type is typically considered unethical. But in reality, deception and covert work may take place in combination or independently; thus, overt work could be deceptive, and covert work might not be. Similarly, Gordon (1987) argues that there are four positional variations in fieldwork on religious groups: covert research in which the researcher feigns deep interest in the subject's religious ideas, possibly even converting; overt research in which the researcher is forthright about holding different religious views; overt research in which the researcher keeps his religious views entirely private and off the table for discussion; and research on one's own religious group. Surely there are other variations, including a research identity that evolves over time, or an identity that varies with different members, or even overt research in which the researcher is deceitful about his own religious views.[3] Prior to engaging with a subject community, it is wise to think through the advantages and possible consequences of each position given what is known about the group in question. The decision should take into account how the religious group may respond to a researcher in their midst, but it should also consider the researcher's comfort level with self-disclosure.

Exemplifying a mutable identity, sociologist Ken Pryce (1979), researching West Indian Pentecostals in Bristol, found that the austere and world-renouncing church members were not especially welcoming to the university student who suddenly began attending services. Pryce's experience was by no means unique; in religious groups that have marginal social status, newcomers are commonly regarded with heightened suspicion, making it difficult to fit in. Pryce had to sell himself as a lapsed religious person seeking to reconnect with a church community, and his Jamaican heritage created a degree of social common ground with members. However, his work stalled without further religious commitment. Pryce took the dramatic step of getting baptized into the church, after which he found that members warmed to him, invited him into their homes, and engaged in rich conversations about their life struggles. Though Pryce's choices led to successful research he was never comfortable with presenting a false identity, later reflecting that he was "highly conscious of the ethical implications of [his] approach" (Pryce 1979: 284), and always on the lookout for opportunities to confess the real nature of his church involvement.

If the subject community is willing to accept a researcher in its midst, then explicitly overt research is usually considered the best way to go. However, the researcher should not fool himself into thinking that overt research means being entirely up front about everything, nor that overt status will preclude any sticky situations involving ethical choices. Many people have found that despite their intention of being forthright, subjects misconstrue aspects of their research; with religious groups it is very common for the researcher to be regarded as a potential convert, especially because subjects may equate "research" with "seekership".

Perhaps surprisingly, covert research in religion used to be something of a norm. Just a few decades ago it was common practice for researchers in various fields to go undercover in order to study religion, and rarely did they indicate that they gave such deception a second thought. As mentioned previously, the assumption was that religious groups that were somewhat askew from mainstream traditions would not be friendly toward a researcher in their midst, and therefore high quality research could only be done by going in undercover. This approach led to some publications that remain relevant today, including Festinger et al.'s (1956) study of a UFO group in which prophecy failed, and Balch and Taylor's (1977) early work on the group that came to be known as Heaven's Gate. Malcolm Calley (1965), who conducted covert work in several Pentecostal churches, has stated that when dealing with groups that place little value on secular academics and intellectual inquiry, inroads are best made by aligning oneself with the community's worldview. By appearing to be a seeker Calley had a logical reason for asking questions, and the religious believers had a desire to answer them, whereas their reception may have been chilly had they known he was conducting academic research. Calley's point is worthy of consideration even though his stance may not be readily accepted today. In a similar – though more vivid – assessment of subject resistance to scholarly research, Palmer recalled that, "Grossed out by the social-scientific method and sick of a sociologist's depressingly secular scrutiny, leaders have denounced me to their disciples as a hireling of a corrupt society" (Palmer 2001: 102). A religious group that holds strong opinions on intellectual inquiry may be difficult to approach, but this will not always be the case. Variations are made evident by the work of Shaffir (1998), who conducted both overt and covert studies of Hasidic communities.[4] He found that members' familiarity with academic research translated into very clear responses to him of both the positive and negative varieties, whereas those members who were unfamiliar with it typically had little interest in or concern about what he was doing, treating him as just another member in the crowd.

Among those who have argued in favour of the covert approach to marginalized groups were Walker and Atherton (1971), who asserted that, "The outsider is at a peculiar disadvantage in Pentecostal circles. He is treated either as an object of distrust or more likely as one in need of salvation" (ibid.: 385). Echoing Calley, the Walker and Atherton study, which involved a team of researchers, showed that those who adopted the role of "committed believer" gained greater access to different kinds of gatherings than did those who identified themselves as "potential converts". But ultimately the "believers" did not have all of the advantages: although they could attend more functions, they had less ability to ask questions because that was simply not acceptable behaviour among inner circles. Even today, when Pentecostals are far less stigmatized than they were just a few decades ago, this assessment of their reception still rings true in some cases. In my own experiences with a Pentecostal church – which was not covert work – several members expressed that I needed permission from the church hierarchy in order to conduct research, and unless I had it my visits and questions were regarded as intrusive. This was particularly frustrating because by that time I had already published a book about the church (Dallam 2007), and I was attending services by invitation, rather than as part of any planned study, and my questions were merely conversational.

Some scholars continue to speak in favour of covert research, and in situations involving religious groups that are secretive or socially isolated it may be the best option.[5] Lauder (2003) has pointed out that work on groups with high potential for violence may more appropriately call for covert work, in part so that the researcher might be able to thwart violent actions. In Lauder's specific project, the religious group's *us versus them* mentality prevented any outsider from participating as a neutral observer, so feigning conversion was the only way for him to move forward. However there are also many less dramatic, even mundane, reasons for not revealing one's identity. It is easy to imagine situations in which the moment research officially begins, and therefore when one's identity should be made known, could be rather unclear. Palmer (2001) rightly notes most research begins with initial scouting visits, if not chance encounters with a person or group that gradually becomes of interest. During this time, when it is unclear whether any further study will even occur, revealing one's identity would be superfluous. Certainly, in our "regular" lives we humans have different behaviours and agendas when interacting with different people, sometimes slight and other times quite marked. Yet we do not typically think of ourselves as living "undercover". Barker (1984) expressed it well by saying that she developed a new side of her personality through her fieldwork, and although it was a side that only existed with members of the subject community, it was no less genuine than other roles she adopted in life such as "mother" or "writer".

With all of these nuances to consider, it is still that case that today most professional associations advise against conducting covert research, not only to maintain ethical standards but also because in the long run such work may damage a group's trust of outsiders. This latter point elides the fact that trust would be disrupted by any publication with which the group disagreed, regardless of the manner in which the research had been conducted. The overall tide has turned to favour overt research under most circumstances, and while this is generally a good thing, many individual research stories indicate that the binary of right and wrong is something of a false dichotomy. Anyone weighing the options of covert and overt research would be well advised to read examples from people who have fieldwork experience either with that particular religious group or one that is theologically and/or structurally similar.

Relationships with subjects

Another question that readily emerges when engaging in field research is the extent to which one can and should befriend members of the subject community. For most of us, it is natural to make genuine connections when meeting new people: discovering common interests, sharing jokes, or otherwise engaging in interesting conversations. The potential for developing friendships increases if the study requires repeat visits or extended stays. But losing oneself in such interactions may give the researcher pause later on. Friendly connections can in some cases enhance the research by making the subject more open, but the subject may feel deceived if the information is later used in a negative way. Keeping subjects at a distance to ensure this does not happen can feel equally unnatural.

There does not appear to be a clear consensus about the best approach to friendship and socializing with members of subject communities, although numerous writers have addressed its complexity. Some examples suggest that firm social limits can be helpful. Palmer (2001) felt conflicted about subjects taking advantage of her research time by using it as an opportunity to break normal religious rules; she appreciated their ingenuity but did not want to be their facilitating agent. She found it was best to set social boundaries, especially when members tried to manipulate her into supporting their own agenda of partying. But others have made fine friends among subject communities: Barker, for instance, wrote of being "genuinely fond" of some members of the Unification Church, even going on a short holiday with one person, despite the fact that the Moonies' worldview was quite different from her own (Barker 1984: 21).

There are also cases when friendships with subjects have caused the researcher to feel regret, a sense of loss, or even serious doubt about the future of a project. This is particularly true when a seemingly good relationship suddenly becomes fraught. For instance, Tayfun Atay (2008) became deeply involved with a Sufi group in London for his dissertation research and felt he had made some true friends in the subject community; he admitted that at times he felt more at home with them than with people from his outside life. On one occasion he was invited to a special meeting with the sheikh to discuss his work, which several disciple friends also attended. After explaining the academic approach of his research, a surprised Atay was publicly shamed by the sheikh, who insulted his skills and mocked him in ways that felt quite personal. His embarrassment, as well as his sense that he had lost his friends' respect, was so crushing that he came close to abandoning the research altogether. As Atay wrote, "It was the worst and most painful experience of my fieldwork and, without exaggeration, of my life" (ibid.: 53). No one wants the subject community to reject their work, especially in such a public way, but this is not always within our control. Atay's story is a good reminder that even with strong personal boundaries, self-preservation is not always full-proof. Others suggest that friendship with subjects should best be limited to certain realms of interaction. DeWalt and DeWalt (2011), researching the people of Temascalcingo, accepted the invitation to become godparents of a child in their subject community.[6] However, once their study ended and they moved on to new research projects, it was difficult to maintain social connections. They regretted having made a commitment that was meant for the long term when they knew from the start that their presence in the community had a point of termination. "Transience may not be the expectation of those individuals who become our informants" (ibid.: 224), they cautioned, but because it is more normal for the researcher, one should think carefully about the long-term consequences of new relationships.

In contrast with the above, there are also times when a researcher experiences a stumbling block because he strongly dislikes participating in the subject community. Wallis (1977), researching Scientologists for his doctoral thesis, set out to conduct three weeks of covert study by enrolling in a Scientology Communications course. After living in a community home for just a few days, the combined pressures of studying material he disagreed with, spending all of his social time with committed members, and the need to appear interested in the teachings felt like more of a burden than it was worth. Wallis packed up and snuck out one evening, abandoning the participant observation leg of his research project. For similar reasons, Van Zandt (1991) was unable to sustain covert work on the Children of God. He found his stress level was elevated by spending intense amounts of time with members of the subject community. Though he tried to feign friendship, he actually regarded aspects of their behaviour "unattractive" and considered their overall religious message "unacceptable" (ibid.: 15, 17). Because the only way to complete his project was to persevere and increase the amount of time he spent with them, Van Zandt stepped away for a period of time and later returned in an overt research capacity, which allowed him to take more frequent social breaks even when living with them.

For anyone who may consider becoming deeply, personally involved with their subject religious community, two authors provide cautionary tales. Karen McCarthy Brown spent many years engaged in research on Vodou practitioners in New York City, and was ultimately initiated. Following the publication of her book, she openly addressed tough questions about her close friendship with the main subject, the financial arrangements between the two of them, her participation in Vodou religious rituals, and her transformation from researcher to initiate. Brown concludes that in fieldwork there is always a component of "moral and intellectual ambiguity", because it is in reality a "social art form" (Brown 2002: 133) rather than a rigid and methodical practice. Coming to similar conclusions, James Wafer (1996) found his research on Candomble was greatly enhanced after he became romantically involved with a person attached to his subject community. The relationship automatically created new bridges of trust and he became a part of the informal kinship system, all of which his academic training had taught him to avoid. Once the boundaries between his work and his personal life blurred, he found it extremely difficult to write an academic ethnography that bracketed and compartmentalized his own experiences. Both Brown and Wafer each regarded themselves as having crossed traditional ethical boundaries when it came to personal involvement, and experienced some criticism for doing so. But, reflecting on it years later, they both stood by their choices as having been the correct ones for the circumstances.

Religious identity

In any research project involving a religious group, the question arises of how honest a researcher should be about his own religious identity. If his beliefs are known to be quite different from those of the subject group, members might avoid or reject him; conversely, some might target him for proselytization and conversion. Does it make more sense for the researcher to be up front about his own religious beliefs, thus lessening the attempts at conversion? Or will revealing different beliefs actually cause greater strain? Either way, the researcher's job is made more difficult when his own religious identity becomes the focal point of interactions. Across the board, most accounts attest that members of the subject community will regard the researcher as a potential convert regardless of what he does or does not say about his own religious beliefs and membership. However, subjects' attempts to religiously engage him can range from being a mild nuisance to an extreme intrusion, depending on the circumstances. Gordon (1987) sums up the typical spectrum of feelings of the researcher who is constantly trying to be converted: "fear, discomfort, annoyance, and guilt" (ibid.: 268), and in extremes these can cause significant psychological strain. Because there is rarely an established and accepted role in religious communities for people who regularly attend but are neither believers nor working toward conversion, sooner or later the researcher's inability to fit in will become evident and may even rupture the research process.

For the above reasons, some people have chosen a strict policy of non-disclosure about their own religious identity. In theory this creates a clear boundary and prevents subjects from developing religious bias toward (or against) the scholar, but this approach does not always function optimally. Dick Anthony (Robbins et al. 1973), for example, developed a particularly positive relationship with many of the Jesus Freaks he studied. His empathy and rapport with them, in combination with their religious expectations, implied to them that he would convert. Eventually his failure to convert became a point of tension for subjects, and to keep the focus on them he refused to discuss his own religious beliefs when asked. This only elevated the tension, because as they tried to figure out what the "problem" was, it continued to keep the focus on the researcher. Anthony, likewise, became increasingly unhappy conducting commune visits and interviews, because he was met with aggressive proselytism and prayers for his salvation. Towards the end of his study, Anthony "felt tense and inhibited and decreased his frequency of interaction" (ibid.: 268), making it a struggle to complete.[7]

As a different approach, some scholars have converted during the course of their study; at times this has been a personal religious choice, whereas with others it was a deliberate move to advance the research.[8] And there are also instances in which a conversion doesn't quite fit either mould. Atay (2008), for instance, found that the longer he stayed involved with his subject Sufi community, the more he was urged to join. They insisted he could only truly understand by being a part of it, and with his continued refusal to do so some members distanced themselves from him. One day, seemingly at random, a ceremony leader offered to perform an oath rite for Atay, and all of his friends in the room responded enthusiastically. Caught up in the moment, Atay felt unable to decline, and before he knew it he had been initiated. It was not long before he realized that his membership caused members of the group to have greater trust in him, and they were more willing to assist his research. His conversion worked to advance the study even though he did not genuinely share their religious views.

In other cases, the scholar prefers to cloak her religious identity only as much as necessary. My own experience with this approach leads me to conclude that consistency is important. When overtly studying an evangelical Christian community I was often asked about my own religion, and depending on the phrasing I usually gave an answer that allowed me to be deceptively evasive without lying outright. For instance, I would say: "I was raised Presbyterian, but I have not been involved with any particular church recently." This answer was not untrue, and it allowed the asker to hear what he or she wanted to hear, yet it also did not accurately describe my long-standing atheist identity. Once I became more comfortable in the community, I began to think that it might not hurt my research to be more up front with interviewees. And so, when randomly speaking with an elder at one church, I said that I was not a believer. This proved to be a painful error, leading to an aggressive attempt by the pastor, his wife, and the elder to convert me. Rather than being cooperative with my appointment for an interview, they determined that Jesus had sent me to them so that my heart could be changed that very day. In the hour that followed we talked at cross-purposes: me attempting to ask questions and the pastor attempting to sway me with sad stories, tears, and passive theological threats. With each moment that ticked by I felt unsure about what to do. I had driven six hours specifically for the interview, and to abruptly leave would have felt like a failure. But the entire experience was increasingly annoying. I stuck it out, keeping stone-faced at the pastor's weeping and appeals to my conscience, and turning the conversation back to practical matters at every opportunity.[9] Only when I pulled out of the parking lot did I give in to my own angry tears. I felt emotionally battered. In the weeks that followed, the memory of the incident made me feel ill, and I began to sour on the entire research project. I regretted failing to maintain a consistent position that had already proven successful in that religious context. To my chagrin, deliberately lying about my religious beliefs became much more attractive after that experience.

There are also those who share partial religious overlap with their subject community and try to use that to their advantage, downplaying potential points of conflict. Leatham (2001), for instance, was welcomed in to research a sectarian Catholic community in Mexico, partly because he was Catholic himself. Most members regarded him as an atypical seeker – one who had both religious and intellectual interest in the teachings – and though he was uncomfortable with this label he felt it was better than being regarded as a complete outsider. In time, community leaders became unhappy with his presence. His failure to convert was interpreted as spiritually problematic and caused enough tension that he felt obliged to leave. Leatham's larger conclusion was that it can be extremely beneficial when the researcher shares a degree of religious commonality with the group he studies, but that, particularly with extremist groups, this scenario will also inevitably lead to conflict because of member expectations for conversion or viewpoint change in the researcher.

Perhaps scholars should take a cue from the optimistic perspective of Mary Jo Neitz (2002), who acknowledges that she is always concerned with the question of overlap between her personal faith and that of her subjects. However, rather than seeing religious differences as a point of tension, she is comfortable observing that commonalities between their perspectives will coincide more or less at various points of her research process. For instance, although she found much personal alignment with Wiccan understandings of earth and nature, she recoiled during conversations that treated fairies as material realities. She similarly experienced both alignment and dissonance when involved in research on conservative Christian churches in rural Missouri. Neitz advises accepting that, as researchers, we occupy a fluid place in the subject community; a place that will shift around on a spectrum of insider/outsider status. Spending extensive time worrying about what believers think about our own religious beliefs, and trying to address that difference in a way that controls the situation, will always be a losing battle.[10]

Religious participation

Closely related to issues of religious identity disclosure is the question of how much a researcher should participate in the life of a religious community, which might include taking part in rituals or ceremonies, attending study groups, business meetings, and social activities, or even accepting leadership roles. In many places, it would be unacceptable for a guest to take an active part in ritual events, whereas in others the opposite is true, and abstention would be considered rude. Homan has pointed out that in religious spaces, people "display private behaviours in public" (Homan 1991: 45), thus the religious environment presents unusual conundrums to the researcher who is trying to be unobtrusive. Even something as mundane as watching people pray might be "invasive" (ibid.), for instance, because the person would not expect to be observed. Appropriate answers to questions of participation should be influenced not only by the particular religious context, but also by the design and goals of the study. More often than not, answers will be both easy and obvious: yes, a researcher can attend a religious study group, but no, a researcher should not accept a position of influential leadership within the organization. And yet, over the years as researchers have tried to chart ethical courses of action, even things as small and large as these examples have become points of confusion, demonstrating again that there is a vast grey area between correct and incorrect fieldwork practice.

As a starting point, the issue of covert or overt research influences questions of participation. Overt work gives one more leeway to excuse herself from certain types of activities. Covert work clearly creates a much higher expectation for participation, which is a part of why it strains the bounds of ethical appropriateness. For instance, covertly working among the Pentecostals, Calley (1965) led prayers, participated in business meetings, and even preached, yet he drew the line at speaking in tongues. At first this abstention appears to be a random ethical choice, out of sync with his other decisions regarding participation, but in fact he did not relate it to ethics at all; instead, Calley chose not to speak in tongues because that would have created an expectation for him to officially join the church, which he did not want to do. But many would take issue with his other active moves, especially preaching. In a similarly questionable series of participation decisions, sociologist Randall Alfred (1976) became not merely a member of the Church of Satan but a part of the local ruling body during his long-term covert research project. This meant he had to be particularly careful about what activities and ideas he endorsed, because as a leader he had the capacity to influence the behaviour and ideas of members of his subject community. Sometime later, Alfred felt that his covert work had been unethical, and thus he returned and confessed his role. He was surprised to discover that church members were not angry; instead, they viewed his deception and manipulation as a form of "lesser magic" (ibid.: 185) that is recognized within the satanic milieu. Making a different choice in a similar situation, Lauder (2003) found that covert work on a white supremacist group inevitably led him to engage in activities that were distasteful (and potentially illegal) in order to protect his cover. Ultimately the strain of active participation became too much for him, and he abruptly disengaged from the group.

Overt work, even with careful participation boundaries, does not automatically eliminate awkward moments; in fact abstention itself can cause problems and/or be misinterpreted. For instance, Shaffir's (1998) attempt to be respectful at a subject synagogue was interpreted as rudeness. Wanting to distinguish himself as a researcher and not get overly involved, during services Shaffir sat in the back, away from regular members. It was only when he began sitting in the centre of the crowd that people's attitude toward him became more welcoming, because he was no longer considered standoffish. Situational mistakes such as this are difficult to avoid because each researcher enters new spaces with a unique set of experiences and assumptions, and what is appropriate in one setting may be offensive in another. Similarly, I once observed a religious service during which the leader called forth everyone in the congregation, urging us to huddle close together in a corner of the room to engage in a charismatic prayer activity. Initially, it felt inappropriate for me to participate since I was neither a member or a believer, and because I had identified myself as a researcher I felt comfortable staying seated in the pews. But as others were gradually enticed to rise and come forward, my resistance became increasingly awkward; the preacher was determined to get every person involved. Two women behind me also chose not to participate, and in the end we were the only three in the room who did not do so. From my subsequent interactions with members it was clear I had committed a spiritual affront even though that was the very thing I had sought to avoid. But even from my own perspective, I lost track of whether I was resisting the activity out of respect, or because I simply resented the attempt at peer pressure. No choice had seemed "right".

Manipulation

Finally, one other ethically grey area is that of subject manipulation. It is normal human behaviour to attempt to direct situations so that they become more favourable for ourselves, and often this happens in tiny, subconscious ways. However in research situations, scholars sometimes have the opportunity to do this more directly. We may manipulate subjects into situations that are favourable for the research, and then feel guilty about it. Some of us have even missed valuable research opportunities because we paused to question our own deliberate, possibly unethical, behaviour. For instance, while Shaffir (1985) was working undercover as a clerk in a potential subject community, several members, Hasidic Jews, suggested he should write about their group for his graduate thesis. Shaffir knew very well that he had planted this idea in their heads, but he wanted to make it appear as though the thought had not previously occurred to him. Secretly gleeful, he commented that it was an interesting proposition, but he needed time to think it over. Within a day, his subjects had changed their minds and retracted the offer, and Shaffir had to abandon that particular project until some years later. He considered the situation a missed opportunity, rather than a questionable move on his part. In contrast, I regarded my own similar actions as ethically dubious. I had determined that I would get myself invited to a Peace Mission banquet, which is the central religious ritual in a dwindling alternative community. I chose to make my "tourist" visit to the Gladwyne, Pennsylvania headquarters late in the afternoon on banquet Sunday. As cars rolled in and members began to arrive, the elderly Mother Divine descended the grand staircase and greeted me, as she often does with visitors. My tour guide/host seemed nervous about us having a conversation, most likely because the elderly leader was alleged to have serious memory issues. Then the magic happened: Mother Divine said they were about to have a banquet, and I was welcome to join them. I adopted a look of surprise. "Well, I didn't expect that, but maybe I could ..." I began to say, and then suddenly I felt a punch of guilt. I had just selfishly manipulated an invitation from a woman with possible dementia, and if I followed through I would have to carry the ruse much further with a number of other guests. This did not feel right to me. I glanced at my host with concern and she jumped in, telling Mother Divine that I would not be able to join them that day. I forever kicked myself for missing the opportunity to attend a banquet with Mother Divine, even though I am also confident that I made the ethically appropriate decision.

Conclusion

Though some would disagree, I hold that ethics are frequently fluid and situational. Just as a scholar's personal ethical norms may differ from those of their subject community, they may also differ from institutional standards. What these many examples show is that sometimes in fieldwork situations, we only have a vast grey area of behaviour to choose from when a question arises. Calling a given decision "ethical" or "unethical" is often more about political justification rather than a matter of timeless absolutes. When we insist that firm categories exist, it has the potential to isolate scholars from one another, rather than helping us toward collaborative knowledge based on collective experience. As a parallel point, Ann Gleig has astutely written, "One limitation of the insider-outsider framing is that it often constructs two ideal categories and implies within each a false uniformity. Often, however, there is no single insider but a multiplicity of different and conflicting insiders" (Gleig 2012: 97-98). The category we call "fieldwork ethics" is hampered by this same set of limitations.

As the above has been merely a sketch, there remain many other areas of religious studies fieldwork that can lead to conundrums. These include gaining entrance to a community and permission to study it, how the presence of a researcher can cause members to act out, potential distortion of information provided to researchers, potential harm to both the subject and researcher, subjects turning against the researcher in the middle of the project, concluding a study and leaving the community, revelling secretive or damaging information in publication, allowing potential responses shape your work, and speaking publicly as an authority about a given group, such as to the media or even as an expert witness. Based on his own experiences, Snow (1980) tells us that there is no easy solution or perfect guideline for every question we will confront, and thus even after a project is completed and the work is published, we are "likely to be haunted by various ethical issues and decisions" (ibid.: 117). Hopefully, Snow is incorrect about this. Instead of being "haunted", we should learn to live with the fact that many decisions are made in the liminal space between ideal categories, which is the space of lived fieldwork ethics.

About the author

Marie W. Dallam is associate professor of American religion and culture at the University of Oklahoma Honors College. Her publications include *Cowboy Christians* (2018), *Daddy Grace: A Celebrity Preacher and His House of Prayer* (2007) and the co-edited volume *Religion, Food, and Eating in North America* (2014). She is also co-general editor of *Nova Religio: The Journal of Alternative and Emergent Religions*.

Notes

1 This is not to suggest that scholars are afraid to discuss such issues in person; however the record suggests they are more hesitant to put them into writing.
2 Note-taking itself can present particular challenges in religious settings. For contrasting examples of how a researcher handled note-taking, see Calley (1965: 148) and (Warner 1988: 73–75).
3 For further exploration of covert research, see Homan's discussion of "types of covertness" (Homan 1991: 104–108). For examples of scholars who have made the tricky transition from covert to overt research, see Van Zandt (1991) and Lauder (2003). Also noteworthy are Pryce (1979) and Shaffir (1985), who each discuss blended identity types that are the messy result of having tried to move from one to the other with only mixed success. For more extensive discussion of ethical project design, see Dallam (2011a).
4 I revert to the most common spelling of this word, though Shaffir prefers the less common "Hassidic".
5 Spicker (2011) argues in favour of covert research and also parses the ethical sub-issues at great length.
6 The work of the DeWalts is somewhat different from that of others discussed in this chapter. The DeWalts were studying a geographically defined community, rather than a religious group. However their willingness to enter into a covenantal religious relationship is surely instructive for other researchers, who may be invited to do the same by virtue of spending extensive time in religious communities as participant observers.
7 See examples of other similar experiences in Ayella (1990).
8 See examples in Brown (2002) and Alfred (1976), respectively.
9 I realize my bias in this statement: to them, there is nothing more urgent and practical than a person's salvation.
10 Further discussion of issues related to a researcher's religious identity is found in Dallam (2011b).

References

Alfred, R. H. (1976). The Church of Satan. In C. Y. Glock and R. N. Bellah (eds), *The New Religious Consciousness*: 180–204. Berkeley, CA: University of California Press.

Atay, T. (2008). Arriving in Nowhere Land: Studying an Islamic Sufi Order in London. In H. Armbruster and A. Laerke (eds), *Taking Sides: Ethics, Politics and Fieldwork in Anthropology*: 45–64. New York: Berghahn Books.

Ayella, M. (1990). "They Must Be Crazy": Some of the Difficulties in Researching "Cults". *American Behavioral Scientist* 33(5): 562–577. https://doi.org/10.1177/0002764290033005005

Balch, R. W. and Taylor, D. (1977) Seekers and Saucers: The Role of the Cultic Milieu in Joining a UFO Cult. *American Behavioral Scientist* 20(6): 839–860. https://doi.org/10.1177/000276427702000604

Barker, E. (1984). *The Making of a Moonie: Choice or Brainwashing?* New York: Basil Blackwell.

Bromley, D. G. and Carter, L. F. (2001). Re-envisioning Field Research and Ethnographic Narrative. In D. G. Bromley and L. F. Carter (eds), *Toward Reflexive Ethnography: Participating, Observing, Narrating*, 1–36. Amsterdam: Elsevier.

Brown, K. M. (2002). Writing about "The Other", Revisited. In J.V. Spickard, J. S Landres and M. B. McGuire (eds), *Personal Knowledge and Beyond: Reshaping the Ethnography of Religion*, 127–133. New York: NYU Press.

Calley, M. J. C. (1965). *God's People: West Indian Pentecostal Sects in England.* London: Oxford University Press.

Dallam, M. W. (2007). *Daddy Grace: A Celebrity Preacher and His House of Prayer.* New York: NYU Press.

Dallam, M. W. (2011a). Ethical Design of New Religion Field Projects. *Religion Compass* 5(9): 520–527. https://doi.org/10.1111/j.1749-8171.2011.00303.x

Dallam, M. W. (2011b). Ethical Problems in New Religion Field Research. *Religion Compass* 5(9): 528–535. https://doi.org/10.1111/j.1749-8171.2011.00302.x

DeWalt, K. M. and DeWalt, B. R. (2011). *Participant Observation: A Guide for Fieldworkers*, 2nd edition. Walnut Creek, CA: AltaMira Press.

Festinger, L., Riecken, H. W. and Schachter, S. (1956). *When Prophecy Fails.* New York: Harper & Row. https://doi.org/10.1037/10030-000

Gleig, A. (2012). Researching New Religious Movements from the Inside Out and the Outside In. *Nova Religio: The Journal of Alternative and Emergent Religions* 16(1): 83–103. https://doi.org/10.1525/nr.2012.16.1.88

Gordon, D. F. (1987). Getting Close by Staying Distant: Fieldwork with Proselytizing Groups. *Qualitative Sociology* 10(3): 267–287. https://doi.org/10.1007/BF00988990

Homan, R. (1991). *The Ethics of Social Research.* London: Longman Group.

Lauder, M. A. (2003). Covert Participant Observation of a Deviant Community: Justifying the Use of Deception. *Journal of Contemporary Religion* 18(2): 185–196. https://doi.org/10.1080/1353790032000067518

Leatham, M. C. (2001). Ambiguous Self-Identity and Conflict in Ethnological Fieldwork on a Mexican Millenarian Colony. In D. G. Bromley and L. F. Carter (eds), *Toward Reflexive Ethnography: Participating, Observing, Narrating*, 77–92. Amsterdam: Elsevier.

Neitz, M. J. (2002). Walking Between the Worlds. In J. V. Spickard, J. S Landres and M. B. McGuire (eds), *Personal Knowledge and Beyond: Reshaping the Ethnography of Religion*, 33–46. New York: NYU Press.

Palmer, S. J. (2001). Caught up in the Cult Wars: Confessions of a Canadian Researcher. In B. Zablocki and T. Robbins (eds), *Misunderstanding Cults: Searching for Objectivity*

in a Controversial Field, 99–122. Toronto: University of Toronto Press. https://doi.org/10.3138/9781442677302-006
Pryce, K. (1979). *Endless Pressure: A Study of West Indian Life-Styles in Bristol.* Harmondsworth: Penguin Books.
Robbins, T., Anthony, D. and Curtis, T. E. (1973). The Limits of Symbolic Realism: Problems of Empathic Field Observation in a Sectarian Context. *Journal for the Social Scientific Study of Religion* 12(3): 259–271. https://doi.org/10.2307/1384427
Shaffir, W. (1985). Some Reflections on Approaches to Fieldwork on Hassidic Communities. *The Jewish Journal of Sociology* 27(2): 115–134.
Shaffir, W. (1998). Doing Ethnographic Research in Jewish Orthodox Communities. In S. Grills (ed.), *Doing Ethnographic Research: Fieldwork Settings*, 48–64. Thousand Oaks, CA: Sage Publications.
Snow, D.A. (1980). The Disengagement Process. *Qualitative Sociology* 3(2): 100–122. https://doi.org/10.1007/BF00987266
Spicker, P. (2011). Ethical Covert Research. *Sociology* 45(1): 118–133. https://doi.org/10.1177/0038038510387195
Van Zandt, D. E. (1991). *Living in the Children of God.* Princeton: Princeton Univ. Press. https://doi.org/10.1515/9781400862153
Wafer, J. (1996). Out of the Closet and Into Print: Sexual Identity in the Textual Field. In E. Lewin and W. L. Leap (eds), *Out in the Field: Reflections of Lesbian and Gay Anthropologists*, 261–273. Urbana, IL: University of Illinois Press.
Walker, A. G. and Atherton, J. S. (1971). An Easter Pentecostal Convention: The Successful Management of a "Time of Blessing". *The Sociological Review* 19(3), 367–387. https://doi.org/10.1111/j.1467-954X.1971.tb00637.x
Wallis, R. (1977). The Moral Career of a Research Project. In C. Bell and H. Newby (eds), *Doing Sociological Research*, 149–167. New York: Free Press.
Warner, S. R. (1988). *New Wine in Old Wineskins: Evangelicals and Liberals in a Small-Town Church.* Berkeley, CA: University of California Press.
Wilcox, M. M. (2002). Dancing on the Fence. In J. V. Spickard, J. S Landres and M. B. McGuire (eds), *Personal Knowledge and Beyond: Reshaping the Ethnography of Religion*, 47–60. New York: NYU Press.

5

Taking the body seriously, taking relationalities seriously

An embodied and relational approach to ethnographic research in the study of (lived) religion

Nina Hoel

Remember to breathe. My sweaty palms are searching for solace and a calm place to rest. A noticeable pressure builds up in my chest, labouring for release. Remember to breathe. Toes twitching, knees are trembling slightly. Breathe. Excitement runs through my veins, awakening the cells and tissue that constitute my body. Breathe. I am here. The *whole* of me is here, in the vibrant and dynamic so-called "field". Remember, feel, sense, how life is lived here; the various ways in which bodies occupy this space, how they move, interact and relate to one another, and how my enfleshed self becomes enfolded in the intricate bodily tapestry that permeates this particular spatial location.

It is challenging to articulate our own bodily responses and reactions. Taking our bodies seriously, listening to it, being aware of its presence and movements. What is certain is that we never leave our bodies behind on our journey to the field. My body *is* where I go. We *are* matter and we *are* matter materializing, continuously and in process. Moving into the field, as researchers, we are always already embodied. Our bodies materialize in various ways in the space where research is undertaken, and our bodies relate to other bodies through our engagement with research participants (and, most of the time, also with multiple "non-participant" bodies as well).

The title of this chapter is reflective of what I perceive to be commonly ignored, or at least seldom transparent, in the study of (lived) religion: The body of the researcher and the relational dynamics that emerge between the body of the researcher and the body (bodies) of participants. Bodies and relationalities are constitutive and integral elements in knowledge production, theorizing and meaning-making. The body is the locus of experience and vital in how we perceive, understand and interact with the world around us. As the locus of experience, the body is also a vessel that carries with it multifaceted histories and dreams and "interferes", "responds" and "acts" through its very being in the field. I contend that increased attention to bodies and relationalities in "the field", in the field of lived religion, may contribute to the development of research methodologies that importantly are flexible and self-reflexive (that is, responsive to contextual demands, and thus, deliberately situated).

Notably, foregrounding the body and relationalities as analytical (embodied) categories, shift the research gaze from the content of research to the process of research – for example, research as a process that is lived, the field as enfleshed, and so on – and from the "object" of research to the interactive modes that constitute and facilitate complex and diverse research relationships. It is against this backdrop, of taking the body seriously and taking relationalities seriously, that I believe it is possible to unsettle and disrupt the insider/outsider binary, with all its positivist assumptions, which has marked not only various sub-disciplines in religious studies, but the development of religious studies as a particular field of study more broadly.

This chapter aims to provide a much needed methodological contribution to the study of (lived) religion, which may equip students and scholars in religious studies with a set of conceptual tools that bring to bear on the cultivation of self-reflexive research practices. As I have argued elsewhere (Hoel 2013), feminist methodologies and analytical categories open up a horizon of possibilities that help us complicate and move beyond the insider/outsider binary and problematize positivistic notions such as detachment and non-involvement. By foregrounding the researcher as an embodied being and by paying attention to the relational aspects of ethnographic research, feminist methodological engagements offer invaluable insights for the study of (lived) religion in contemporary contexts.

This chapter will introduce a selection of feminist theoretical and conceptual "interventions", which I argue are useful in thinking about bodies and relationalities in the field of lived religion. By underlining (feminist) commitments to take the body seriously, and, relatedly, to take relationalities seriously, this chapter outlines analytical categories that highlight the various ways in which the body of the researcher and her developing relationalities to research participants are important and composite enfleshed "lenses" through which to understand, analyse and theorize about lived religion. In particular, this chapter engages "feminist standpoint epistemology", as developed by Dorothy Smith (1992), Patricia Hill Collins (1989, 1990), Nancy Hartsock (1996, 1998), Allison Jaggar (2000) and Sandra Harding (1991);

"intersectionality", coined and theorized by Kimberlé Crenshaw (1989, 1991, 2011); and, lastly, "reflexivity", as problematized by DeVault (1999) and Oakley (1981), among others. These analytical categories, I contend, do not only offer a poignant critique toward "malestream" methodologies in the social sciences, nor do they solely suggest new, perhaps more inclusive (and some would argue more objective, see Harding 1991, 1993), ways of theorizing. These analytical categories attempt to provide critical insights pertaining to the discursive and corporeal functioning of real bodies in temporal spaces *and* these bodies' interactions with differently situated bodies. "Feminist standpoint epistemology", "intersectionality" and "reflexivity", may prove fruitful analytical categories when engaging the wonderful messiness that saturates "the field" of lived religion. Being fully present in the field, accepting that the topographical texture of the field informs one's own bodily performance and movements, as well as the dynamism of research encounters – wherein the affective formation of relationalities find expression – I believe, is a productive place to start.

Employing feminist analytical categories to move beyond the insider/outsider binary in the study of (lived) religion

Feminist theorists perceive the body, and women's bodies in particular, as central to knowledge production and meaning-making (see Moi 2005; Grosz 1994; Butler 1993). As such, feminist approaches to research challenge and destabilize objectifying and objectivist research paradigms by taking seriously the embodied situatedness of research participants – perceived as research *subjects* – and the researcher's own embodied being as centrally involved in the relational production of knowledge and meaning-making. Hence, ideals such as detachment, non-participation and objective accounts of lived realities (although still cherished by many scholars in religious studies, see Lukens-Bull 2007) are perceived to be archaic, outdated and, more importantly, artificial and deceptive approaches to research (see Trinh 1989). Problematizing inherited preconceived assumptions of neutrality and the "rational" dis-embodied researcher, feminist researchers suggest that doing fieldwork includes partaking in complex, at times, asymmetrical constellations of power as expressed and performed by researchers *and* participants.

Going into the field also includes being aware of the politics of positioning, wherein a researcher explicitly discern and make transparent the multiple and fluid positionings that animate encounters between researcher and participant (see Alcoff 1995; Best 2003; Hellawell 2006; Jaschok and Jingjun 2000; Naples 2003; Sherif 2001). In other words, there is *never* just *one* way of positioning oneself – which has been a confining implication of trailing the problematic construction of the insider/outsider binary. Employing the insider/outsider binary, as a static or rigid frame of reference, essentialize researchers (as either insiders or outsiders), conceal their diversity and multifacetedness, and often uphold particular "I"/"Other" dualisms and objective distance in research encounters. Nonetheless, if one continues to find *the language* of the insider/outsider binary useful, as the binary pair does indicate something about positioning and, perhaps, a researcher's reflection upon her or his positioning in the field, I suggest, as I have suggested elsewhere (Hoel 2013: 32) that the binary can be used to identify the multiple movements that take place along an "insider/outsider continuum":

> a researcher is never fully an insider, nor, never fully an outsider. By moving like a pendulum along the insider/outsider continuum, a shifting interactional process in which the relationship between the researcher and the respondent is formed, there is an opportunity to explore the multiple subjectivities of both researcher and respondent. Consequently, by exploring what is unfamiliar to us, in the words of Julia Kristeva (1991), we also encounter the "stranger within." Hence, research encounters have the potential to be co-constructions in which redefinitions of the insider/outsider binary can take place in ways that are more meaningful and inclusive than an "either/or" paradigm. (Hoel 2013: 32)

For feminist researchers, dualisms and binaries are always met with a sense of suspicion as such constructions, to a large degree, are foundational for patriarchal discourses – wherein women have ended up with the short end of the stick, being rendered qualitatively "Other" and "othered" by such discursive constructions (see de Beauvoir 1993). Hence, the move to the analytical category of "positioning" or "positionality" can be seen both as a recognition and a critique of binaries as distinctive patriarchal inventions, as well as the introduction of a new analytical "lens" that captures the complex and multiple positionings we inhabit and corporeally embody in real life, and consequently, also in the field.

Also taking into account, and being reflexive about, the workings of power, and relations of power in the field (including a researcher's multiple positioning vis-à-vis participants), ultimately interrupt and complicate modernist (mis)conceptions and fallacies regarding the primacy of dis-interested and "clinical" research practices (see Wolf 1996). Questions of researcher positionality, partiality and accountability in the field constitute important epistemological keys and relate to what Donna Haraway has called the production of "situated knowledges" (see Haraway 1988, 1991; see also Hoel 2013, where these concepts are put into conversation with the experienced ethical quandaries emerging when doing fieldwork on lived religion). Haraway's "situated knowledges" concept illuminates that knowledge production always is situated, that is, contextual and located in time and space and thus dependent or contingent on particular frames of reference. Knowledge is also produced through relational modes, practices and encounters, which are deeply experiential in nature. Acknowledging the mechanisms of "situated knowledges" allow the researcher to begin to address, or at least offer some thoughts on how the "researcher body" relates to participants' bodies, and how this interaction inform the (embodied) theorization of lived religion.

The feminist analytical categories employed and explored in this chapter – "feminist standpoint epistemology", "intersectionality" and "reflexivity" – are situated in and follow this feminist methodological lineage. The ensuing sections of this chapter outline the meaning of these categories, their usefulness in taking seriously the body and relationalities in the field, and engage the categories' implications, and hopefully, value for the study of lived religion in complex contemporary contexts.

Feminist standpoint epistemology

Feminist standpoint epistemology traces its intellectual genealogy and theoretical beginnings to Hegel's master/slave dialectic (Harding 1993), wherein the oppressed slave finds liberation (or freedom of consciousness) once she or he become conscious of her or his asymmetrical relationality to the master. By recognizing and becoming conscious of the everyday struggles and relations of power that inform slave-life vis-à-vis the master, the slave is enabled to embody and act in the world in different ways. Hegel's theorizations of the master/slave dialectic engendered a shift in thinking about what lenses through which to analyse systems of oppression and injustice. A new discursive engagement emerged where the "standpoint" of the slave was seen as a better suited perspective to understand and theorize structures of oppression and injustice.

In feminist standpoint theory, it is the "standpoint" (that is, the lifeworlds, experiences and perspectives) of women that constitutes the central focus. The focus on women – perceived to be an oppressed group, who is, and has been, ignored, deliberately excluded, marginalized, misconstrued, and so on, by patriarchal discourses – and women's epistemologies, present to the world "new" ways of being, knowing and relating. Employing feminist standpoint in research means that the researcher solicits women participants, listens to and engages women's stories, takes seriously women's experiences and embodied understandings of reality, and as such partakes in the development of women's epistemologies as valid and invaluable sources of knowledge. Women's epistemologies can be said to constitute an important corrective to "normative" epistemologies, which may present themselves as universal dis-embodied "truths", but, in fact, are steeped in male experiences and understandings of reality.

Taking seriously the politics of location and positioning, feminist standpoint imagines the research relationship between researcher and participant as horizontally aligned; rendering the researcher someone who *partakes* in the research process rather than someone who possesses authoritative or expert knowledge (and thus inhabit a higher position in the research-participant relationship). Feminist standpoint attempts to subvert hierarchical research relationalities (such as powerful/powerless or dominant/dominating), and also recognizes, through employing horizontal research practices, the exclusionary effects of authoritative research for/on women. Researchers employing feminist standpoint are acutely aware of the "othering" mechanisms and universalizing accounts researching have led to (see Opie 1992; Fawcett 2000), and aims to destabilize such objectifying implications by emphasizing diversity of experience, contextual specificity and situatedness of researcher and participant(s).

Research undertaken from feminist standpoint aims to challenge asymmetrical power relations and systems of oppression, which continue to marginalize and exclude women. As such, feminist standpoint research has an overtly liberatory agenda. Such an emancipatory project, with its implicit claims to a normative "women's plight", has been problematized by Maynard (1994), Hartsock (1996, 1998) and Flax (1983, 1992), among others, who highlight the existence of different and diverse standpoints (e.g. Womanist standpoints, lesbian feminist standpoints, radical feminist standpoints, Marxist feminist standpoints, eco-feminist standpoints, and so on). In other words, women – as a group – occupy multiple standpoints, and at times, these standpoints can be in tension with one another. Recognizing the plurality of existing standpoints – rather than *a* feminist standpoint perceived to represent the relations of power that render women oppressed *as a group* – is reflective of the diverse historical trajectories (e.g. histories of colonialism, imperialism and empire) that women are situated within and that inform women's epistemological "truths" and empancipatory agendas.

Turning the research gaze inwards, toward the researcher who employs feminist standpoint in the field has underscored: first, that research "data" is collected by an enfleshed researcher (that is, "data" do not write themselves from a position of "nowhere"); second, the enfleshed researcher may occupy multiple positionings while in the field; third, this enfleshed researcher embodies and performs gender and sexuality in particular ways; and fourth, that because the researcher is enfleshed, gendered and sexed, the researcher may inhabit and experience the field differently than a differently embodied researcher. For instance, a black heterosexual woman is likely to experience the field differently to a white heterosexual man. Likewise, a white heterosexual woman is likely to experience the field differently to that of a Latina queer woman. Obviously, diverse experiences in and of the field are also contingent on what constitutes the field (where/what is it?); who are the participants?; and the subject of research, among other things (for works engaging factors that contribute to researchers' experiences of the field, see Abu-Lughod 1990; Bell et al. 1993; Kulick and Wilson 1995; Warren 1988; Whitehead and Conaway 1986; Wolf 1996). In other words, the experiences of researchers and participants are not "representative" or reflective of the experiences of *all* researchers and participants; rather experiences are particular, subjective, partial, situated and variously embodied.

Employing feminist standpoint to research on lived religion or religion *as* lived involves being attentive to the methodological biases of the discipline, and sub-disciplines, of religious studies, as well as to the underlying structural relations of power that inform the subject of research. In terms of research methodology, many feminist scholars of religion (e.g. Gross 1996, 2009; King 1995, 2004; Warne 2001; Christ 2001) have pointed out the "malestream" tendency to endorse the positivist ideals of neutrality, detachment and non-participation when undertaking research on religious discourses and religious persons. Likewise, the subject of research, such as religious myths, rituals and symbols, as well as religious experiences, are often engaged without any attention to the distinct gendered politics of inclusion/exclusion, rendering research on such subjects profoundly partial accounts of religious lifeworlds (although presented as "representative" or normative for particular religious communities).

Employing feminist standpoint in research on lived religion also means that power, and relations of power are foregrounded so as to render visible the various ways in which women's experiences of religious traditions and religious personhood (alternatively other "Others", such as queer or disabled religious subjects) often have been excluded or marginalized by "malestream" "official" or authoritative discourses. Employing feminist standpoint involves shifting the attention from "accepted truths" and claims to normativity to the workings of power that produce certain understandings of reality and conceal or suppress others. It also includes moving from "representatives" or powerfully positioned religious subjects to the experiential dimensions of ordinary people's lives. As such, feminist standpoint implies considering and taking seriously the opinions, concerns and experiences of people who are not in positions of authority, but whom are affected by dominant religious structures and decision-making.

Employing feminist standpoint also means being attentive to living religious communities and practices that commonly fall outside the dominant fold of a normative religious landscape, traditions that arguably also tend to be less visible in courses offered in departments of religious studies (for example, shamanism, paganism, African religious traditions). Feminist standpoint's emphasis on working from the standpoint of the disadvantaged and marginalized can, as such, also be used to consciously reflect on the asymmetrical foci of religious traditions/subjects in departments of religious studies, and lead the researcher to seek out religious communities and practices that are less known or that contributes to "multiply" the diversity that exist within locally situated religious traditions.

Employing feminist standpoint in research on lived religion may prompt the researcher to ask critical questions pertaining to *who* should participate, *why*, and *how* should they be approached? Reflecting on who, why and how, take into account the various ways in which knowledge about religious communities have been generated by partial accounts of religious experience (often represented by dominant or authoritative religious persons); it is attentive to the dynamics of power that render visible/invisible certain subjects of research, and it carefully considers the ways in which the field, and research subjects, should be approached so as to establish horizontal relationalities between researcher and participant. Furthermore, the ideal of horizontal relationalities, as opposed to research that objectifies or marginalizes participants through hierarchical modes of engagement, also aims to empower participants through the research process (see Smith 1992; Lynch 2004; Opie 1992; Scheyvens and Leslie 2000). Lastly, feminist standpoint also turn the gaze inwards, towards the enfleshed researcher, who is distinctly marked and inscribed by gender, sex, race, and so on, and, as such, embody the field in a particular way. Taking this important insight into the field of lived religion, a researcher needs to reflect upon the various ways in which her corporeality and markers of identity impact her experience of, and movement in, the field – while also being cognizant of the ways in which the enfleshed self informs the relational dynamics that emerge when interacting with research participants. This latter point brings us to the second feminist analytical category discussed in this chapter, intersectionality.

Intersectionality

The analytical category of intersectionality, coined and theorized by Kimberlé Crenshaw (1989, 1991), emerged as a Black feminist response to the theoretical hegemony configured by White feminists. The category of intersectionality was meant to illuminate the distinct experiential realities of African American women, which was seen as not only shaped by gender dynamics, but also compounded by particular assumptions related to race and class. In other words, African American women were not only affected by the structures of oppression that circumscribed their gendered positionalities, but also by racist and classist socio-economic paradigms. Hence, African American women's experiences were perceived to be enfolded in *multiple* systems of oppression and marginalization.

The analytical category of intersectionality importantly highlighted that subjects such as race and gender needed to be analysed *intersectionally*; that is, as intersecting components that in various ways inform subjective experiences (Hill-Collins 1990). As such, intersectionality studies became invaluable in theorizing difference and brought to the fore an understanding of social identities as deeply heterogeneous, interconnected and mutually constitutive, as opposed to homogeneous, rigid and mutually exclusive. The plasticity of the analytical category intersectionality has, of late, led to the inclusion of several social identity markers (such as, sexual orientation, age, religious belonging, ethnicity, geographical location, economic status, educational background, and so on), which are intersectionally employed, in various combinations, so as to understand and theorize various forms of structural oppression and discrimination (see Davis 2008; Jordan-Zachery 2007).

Locating the analytical category of intersectionality in the precarious ethnographic field, many researchers have employed the term to theorize the multiple structures of oppression that inform the lives of distinctly situated research participants, as well as the multifaceted social identities that mark and inscribe all persons – also those in positions of power and privilege (Christensen and Jensen 2012; Yuval-Davis 2011). Intersectional approaches are well-suited for empirical research that uses in-depth interviews as its primary method (Bowleg 2008; Bauer 2014). However, few studies have foregrounded the intersectional identities of the researcher and the implications these social markers have on research participants who are differently situated and embodied (Fournillier 2009; Turgo 2012). Traditionally, and similarly to research done within the discipline of religious studies, researchers have tended to identify themselves, often quite simplistically, within an insider/outsider paradigm (Kanuha 2000). In other words, is the researcher positioned as a "native" or a "stranger"? As noted earlier, the insider/outsider binary is limited and limit*ing* as it does not take into account the fluidity of real and enfleshed subjects and the multiple positionings that a researcher can embody in the field. The analytical category of intersectionality provides researchers with a more dynamic and *intersectional* frame of reference that may capture the complexity of social identity markers (a *both-and* approach, as opposed to *either/or*). An intersectional approach to participants and researchers' embodied inscriptions, as well as attentiveness to the dynamics that these inscriptions produce in the research relationship, is arguably better suited to capture the "in-betweenness" of enfleshed personhood than an insider/outsider paradigm.

Many researchers have noted the usefulness in approaching the field intersectionally, as opposed to as an insider or an outsider (Obasi 2014; Turgo 2012; Trahan 2011). An intersectional approach acknowledges that the researcher embodies diverse markers of identity, some of which can be completely different from that of participants and others that might be congruent or intersecting. Moreover, the researcher's (whole) intersectional identity is inextricably linked to and situated in the field where research is undertaken. The intersectional identity of the researcher affects the various ways in which she embodies the field, how she moves in the field, and how she experiences the field. The intersectional identity of the researcher also informs the ways in which she engages with participants, which effect the development of particular relational dynamics. And, the intersectional identity of the researcher also has consequences for how she is perceived by participants, and the implications these perceptions have for the research relationship.

Employing intersectionality as an expansive methodological lens in research on lived religion complicates and challenges the utility of the insider/outsider binary. First, an intersectional approach cultivates an awareness of the possibility of multiple positionings, that is, that the researcher is not only *either* an insider *or* an outsider; *either* a "native" *or* a "stranger". Rather, the researcher can share particular identity traits (for example, educational background, interests/hobbies, age and race), whereas other embodied inscriptions (for example, gender, religion, sexual orientation) are distinct. Note that particular intersectional relationalities between researcher and participant does not remove or render invisible the workings of power in this relation – as power, and relations of power *always* inform research relationships.

Second, bearing in mind that researchers' identities are complex and multiple, an intersectional approach can be valuable to analysing the relationship and relationalities that emerge between the researcher and participant. Reflections on positioning often begin before the researcher enters the field, as researchers outline possible (and expected) challenges and quandaries. However, it is exceedingly important that these reflections continue once the researcher embodies the field as this is when actual heterogeneous identities interact with one another. Likewise, is it important for the researcher to reflect on the various ways in which her intersectional identity becomes imbricated in facilitating or hindering particular relational dynamics *and* the various ways in which power relations are enfolded in these intersectional relationalities. As I have noted elsewhere (Hoel 2013), research relationalities can forge primary human relationalities that, at various times, are marked by moments of convergence, conflict and despondency – these "moments" also encompass the multi-directional workings of power between researcher and participant.

Employing intersectionality in research on lived religion also brings to the fore that religion only constitutes *one* category of participants' intersectional identities. In other words, the religious aspect of participants' identity is not the *only* inscription that informs their experience of religious discourses (or, life in general for that matter). Rather, their gender, sexual orientation, age, ableness, race, class, and so on, also intertwine with participants' understandings and embodiment of religious personhood and has implications for how they perceive or engage religious traditions. For example, the experience (or lack thereof) of particular religious ritual practices may be marked by the participants' genderedness. As we are acutely aware of, as students and scholars of religion, religious rituals are, at times, regulated by quite strict politics of gendered inclusion/exclusion. Similarly, the experience of being a queer Muslim, for example, may have consequences for how the participant experiences and relates to his or her religious community, which may be quite different to that of a heterosexual Muslim. Likewise, the racialized history in a country like South Africa, for example, possibly impact the various ways in which contemporary racialized subjects (be they white or black) engage their religious communities. An intersectional approach to research on lived religion, I argue, is thus invaluable as it takes into account the different, yet intersecting identity categories that mutually constitute participants experience of religion in contemporary locations.

Employing intersectionality in research on lived religion also involves taking the body and relationalities, perhaps, *more* seriously than an approach where the multiple identities of researcher and participant are less transparent, or concealed all together. Intersectional categories are not only "identitarian" characteristics of researcher and participant, but rather deeply embodied subjectivities that are enacted and performed in diverse and complex ways. Furthermore, intersectional embodied subjects do not only act or perform individually; rather intersectional subjects encounter one another and interact with one another, and, as such, materialize in their relation to one another. An intersectional approach to research on lived religion, then, opens a dynamic horizon to analyse and theorize the various ways in which both researcher and participant embody, enact and perform particular or multiple aspects of their identities in their research engagement, and the ways in which these inform both the knowledge production and meaning-making about lived religion. Developing self-reflexive modes that take seriously these processual and vibrant dynamics is the focus of the next section.

Reflexivity

Reflexivity is a key concept in feminist methodology and constitutes a primary lens through which the feminist researcher engages the field (Deutsch 2004; Finlay 2002). Reflexivity involves paying particular attention to self-positioning and workings of power, and attempts to document the various ways in which knowledge production always is a collaborative process – a co-construction – between researcher and participant(s) (Harrison and Lyon 1993; see also Hoel 2013). Haraway's notion of "situated knowledges" similarly presupposes reflexive moves that shift between turning the gaze inwards (self-reflexivity; researcher positionality) to reflexivity about researcher-participant dialectics (wherein shifting power relationalities form an intrinsic part) (see also Rose 1997, who engages Haraway's "situated knowledges"). Furthermore, reflexivity also involves bringing to the fore the particularities of the locatedness of research – illuminating how context also informs and mediates knowledge production and meaning-making (Ellis and Bochner 2005). As such, reflexivity can act as a powerful diagnostics to assess researcher-participant-context relationalities.

Being a reflexive researcher renders visible that doing fieldwork and engaging in conversations with participants involve various levels of intimacy, affect and vulnerability. Both researcher and participant engage in a primary *human* relationality, which may invite opportunities for mutual sharing and self-disclosure (see Hoel 2013). The horizontal research relationship that feminist researchers aim to establish (as opposed to reproducing hierarchical relationships of exploitation or marginalization), may, with its dialogical focus, make the research encounter an empowering experience for participants (see Scheyvens and Leslie 2000). Furthermore, research initiatives/projects that emerge from collaborative efforts – that is, research projects developed in conversation *with* communities – might possibly bring about research processes that are more akin to feminist participatory/empowering ideals than projects that are articulated from the position of doing research "on" particular communities (Lynch 2004; Jaggar 2000).

Reflexive research practices offer an important corrective to research that perpetuates knowledge as detached from the "knower" and posits self-knowledge, that is, an epistemic awareness/mode of being and becoming a particular kind of person, as deeply intertwined with the various ways in which relationalities with participants materialize. Simultaneously, it is important to acknowledge that self-knowledge does not necessarily lead to or encompass affirming or sympathetic insights (be it pertaining to self, or to participants). Rather, self-knowledge might equally be reflective of frictional, painful and uncomfortable insights (or assumptions) about self and/or participant. Pillow (2003: 188) has labelled this a "reflexivity of discomfort" – that is, a reflexivity that not only takes seriously the various ways in which the quest for knowledge and the act of know*ing* is subjective, but also the ways that situated knowledge and knowing can be fragile and tenuous. Attending to the discomfort, reflexively, according to Pillow, equally provide particular insights to the relationalities developing between researcher and participant, and to the (co-)production of knowledge in general.

Elsewhere I have engaged in great detail the importance of reflexivity for thinking about and making sense of the power dynamics that encompass the relationalities that find expression between researcher and participant (Hoel 2013). Here, I wish to focus on context as an important reflexive source for locating research as an embodied and relational activity. With the emergence of "mobile research", research takes into account that research journeys and encounters with participants takes place in *a* context (see Ross et al. 2009; Binnie et al. 2007). In other words, research contexts are contexts wherein the bodies of the researcher and participant are materially and experientially entangled (see Casey 2001, 2009). A context is experienced through the body, and inhabited by researcher and participant in diverse ways. Paying increased attention to the various ways in which knowledge production is made meaningful through "walking about" with participants, or how "movement" in a contextual location can bring about interesting dynamics between researcher and participant (for example, participant as "tour-guide", "mentor", protector), adds richness and fluidity to reflexively thinking about power and positionality.

Mobile interviewing opens up fertile avenues for getting to know participants' everyday lives – and thus adds an invaluable layer to understanding participants' lifeworlds. Mobile interviewing might also cultivate constructive bonds between researcher and participant as they share an experience of moving through space together. Furthermore, participants' narratives might become more meaningful, or, at least, more accessible to the researcher when the researcher's body becomes enfolded into the context that for participants constitute an important frame of reference. Narratives are often intricately connected to context or particular material places, hence, embodying those spaces may engender enriched and memorable research encounters Moreover, being bodily present together with participants in spaces that perhaps are unfamiliar, grants the researcher an opportunity to experience the messiness of the field.

"Walking about" with participants might also, however, invite unwanted attention. Many feminist researchers have pointed out concerns about their own safety as women's visibility in public spaces does not always go unnoticed (see Gurney 1985; Sampson and Thomas 2003; Moreno 1995). A researcher's gender or visible religiosity, for example, inform how she is perceived by people inhabiting the research site, and consequently, may have serious implications for how she moves, or performs her gender/religiosity in the field. As such, it is exceedingly important to critically reflect on one's own embodiment of the field, as, after all, ethnography is an embodied practice, and whether the potential challenges (for example, sexual harassment or surveillance) constitute "risks" that one simply is not willing to take. Self-reflexivity pertaining to the *contextual* social scripts (gendered, religious, racial etc.) of the field, then, emerges as necessary and responsible research praxis when taking the body and relationalities seriously in the field.

Employing the feminist principle of reflexivity in research on lived religion involves bringing to the fore the relationalities that emerge through the tripartite nexus of researcher-participant-context. In addition to providing critical insights on the relations of power that permeate the researcher-participant relationship, I argue that it is central in any analysis of lived religion to locate the subject of research, that is, to underscore the various ways in which a contextual location functions as one of the central mediating factors in producing knowledge about a particular subject, and making sense of it. For example, in researching religious persons use of and performance in a "religious site" (for example, mosque, synagogue, or pilgrimage site), what can the context wherein this "religious site" functions tell us about the politics and poetics of place? How does the site convey and configure meaning through its very location? Undoubtedly, the location of a mosque in a predominantly Christian/

secular context such as Norway or Denmark might reveal marked social frictions and/or participants tenuous relationships to performing religiosity at these religio-secular locations. Likewise, the lack of, or exclusion of women from entering certain religious sites, tell us something about the social scripts that inform spatial religious practices.

Reflexive research praxis pertaining to researcher's embodiment in the field of lived religion is further compounded by the possibility of the researcher's participation or refusal thereof to participate in religious practices. Coming back to the notion of how sharing experiences might develop increased levels of trust between researcher and participant, what might be at stake in moving through religious spaces together with participants? How might a "reflexivity of discomfort" (Pillow 2003) emerge in ways that offer the researcher important insights pertaining to the boundaries, symbolic or real, of research as embodied practice? And, how might such a reflexive practice (of discomfort) complicate the relationalities between researcher and participant and knowledge production as a collaborative project? Furthermore, a reflexive research practice in the ethnographic field of lived religion can highlight the various ways in which a researcher's gender or visible religiosity, for example, may preclude her from moving into certain spatial domains, or partaking in/observing particular gendered religious rituals. A researcher's gender or religiosity might also have very real implications for how her corporeality is regulated or "policed" by the religious community she aims to explore, or be decisive for how she performs her gender or religiosity in this space (for example, by de-feminizing her presence, rendering the religious space normatively male).

Employing reflexivity in research on lived religion also involves negotiating the perimeters of self-disclosure and attending to one's own bodily levels of comfort/discomfort. When deciding on a research topic, if you were asked the questions you seek to explore, what are you willing or prepared to share? Is your research articulated from the position of doing research "with" or "on" a particular religious community? Seeing horizontal relationalities as part of your research mandate, what are your responsibilities in the field to avoid perpetuating "othering" or marginalizing research relationships? Taking bodies and relationalities seriously in research on lived religion involve cultivating reflexive research practices that attend to the questions above (and many more not mentioned here). Taking bodies and relationalities seriously also implies locating research as an embodied and relational activity – and, thus, self-reflexively renders visible our embodied relationship to the field, to the research subject, and to the relationalities forged with participants.

Taking the body seriously, taking relationalities seriously: some concluding reflections

This chapter has outlined some methodological suggestions for an embodied and relational approach to ethnographic research in the study of lived religion. By drawing on feminist theoretical and methodological insights, which foreground the body as the locus of experience, this chapter has argued that bodies and relationalities need to occupy a more central place in the field of lived religion in order to complicate and destabilize, indeed to *move beyond* the insider/outsider binary. Bodies and relationalities are constitutive in all research on lived religion, as ethnography always involves the bodies of the researcher and participants, and their engagement with one another. Furthermore, bodies are always situated, enacted and inscribed in particular ways, which implies that knowledge production, theorizing and meaning-making are embodied activities that, through varying modes, are informed by these bodily scripts. The researcher body also "speaks" in the way that it moves through a research location together with participants, and engages in bodily negotiation, for example, by partaking in some activities and by refusing others. By engaging a selection of feminist (embodied) analytical categories, namely "feminist standpoint epistemology", "intersectionality" and "reflexivity", I hope to have shown some of the ways in which bodies and relationalities are compounded by real and symbolic discourses of power and relations of power – discourses that also pertains to bodies and relationalities in the field of lived religion. The three analytical categories here described are envisioned as enfleshed "lenses" through which to understand, analyse and theorize about lived religion – and situate bodies and relationalities as fundamental for its meaning-making.

Notably, feminist standpoint epistemology offers us insights pertaining to disciplinary biases, particularly as it relates to "malestream" methodologies, and suggests that attention to the gendered politics of (religious) lifeworlds, for example, can bring about "new" ways of knowing (that is, women's epistemologies). Such insights bring to bear on power and relations of power that may inform the development of religious personhood (for example religious authority vs. ordinary religious), with consequences for the varying ways in which relationalities between researcher and participant materializes. Also, feminist standpoint requires the researcher to critically reflect on *who* they involve in research on lived religion, and *how* these participants should be approached. In other words, employing feminist standpoint includes a heightened attention to the subjects that become entwined in research relationships and render visible the possibility of empowering participants through establishing horizontal research relationalities.

The feminist analytical category of intersectionality deeply unsettles and problematizes the insider/outsider binary as an intersectional approach acknowledges the possibility of multiple positionings. The analytical category of intersectionality can prompt the researcher to be attentive to the actual heterogeneous identities (of researcher and participant) that interact with one another during research encounters and the various ways in which intersectional identities becomes imbricated in enabling (or restricting) relational dynamics. Importantly, intersectionality is beneficial for research on lived religion in that it foregrounds religious identity as *one* aspect of participants embodied lives. In other words, intersectionality provide us with an invaluable enfleshed lens through which to take into account that participants' gender, sexual orientation, ethnicity and race, to name a few, intricately interweave with their understandings and embodiment of religious personhood – facets of participants' embodied being that also have implications for researcher-participant relationalities.

My attention to the importance of reflexivity has, in this chapter, focused on the significant insights that can be gleaned from paying attention to the researcher–participant–context nexus. By taking seriously what Donna Haraway has called "situated knowledges", the contextual location of research emerges as a crucial source for reflexive work. Reflexive research practices that take into account the contextual location of research do not only tell us something about the social scripts that delicately weave through religious communities, for example, but also the various ways in which the researcher's embodiment in the field of lived religion becomes entangled in the body politics of religious discourses in ways that may complicate the relationalities between researcher and participant (or with a religious community in general).

Taking bodies and relationalities seriously in ethnographic research on lived religion importantly fixes the research gaze on the enfleshed situated subjects that produce knowledge by their very being and interactions in the field. Incorporating feminist (embodied) analytical concepts in ethnographic research on lived religion, I argue, provide a rich methodological horizon for students and scholars of religion through which to approach research as a complexly embodied and deeply relational project.

About the author

Nina Hoel is associate professor in religion and society at the Faculty of Theology, University of Oslo, Norway. Her work uses feminist theory and methodology in the study of lived religion. She writes on issues pertaining to religion, bodies and sexualities and has conducted extensive research in the field of Islam, gender and sexuality in South Africa, using anthropological approaches as her main method. She is widely published in, among other journals, *Journal of Feminist Studies in Religion*, *Fieldwork in Religion*, *Journal for Islamic Studies* and *Journal for the Study of Religion*.

References

Abu-Lughod, L. (1990). Can there be a Feminist Ethnography? *Women and Performance* 5(1): 7–27. https://doi.org/10.1080/07407709008571138

Alcoff, Linda. (1995). The Problem of Speaking for Others. In J. Roof and R. Wiegman (eds), *Who Can Speak? Authority and Critical Identity*, 97–119. Urbana, IL: University of Illinois Press.

Bauer, G. R. (2014). Incorporating Intersectionality Theory into Population Health Research Methodology: Challenges and the Potential to Advance Health Equity. *Social Science & Medicine* 110: 10–7. https://doi.org/10.1016/j.socscimed.2014.03.022

Bell, D., Caplan, P., and Karim W. J. (eds) (1993). *Gendered Fields: Women, Men, and Ethnography*. New York: Routledge.

Best, Amy L. (2003). Doing Race in the Context of Feminist Interviewing: Constructing Whiteness through Talk. *Qualitative Inquiry* 9(6): 895–914. https://doi.org/10.1177/1077800403254891

Binnie, J., Edensor, T., Holloway, J., Millington, S. and Young, C. (2007). Mundane Mobilities, Banal Travels. *Social & Cultural Geography* 8(2): 165–174. https://doi.org/10.1080/14649360701360048

Bowleg, L. (2008). When Black + Lesbian + Woman ≠ Black Lesbian Woman: the Methodological Challenges of Qualitative and Quantitative Intersectionality Research. *Sex Roles* 59: 5–6. https://doi.org/10.1007/s11199-008-9400-z

Butler, Judith. (1993). *Bodies that Matter: On the Discursive Limits of "Sex"*. London: Routledge.

Casey, E. S. (2001). Between Geography and Philosophy: What Does it Mean to Be in the Place-world? *Annals of the Association of American Geographers* 91(4): 683–693. https://doi.org/10.1111/0004-5608.00266

Casey, E. S. (2009). *Getting Back into Place*. Bloomington, IN: Indiana University Press.

Christ, Carol P. 2001. Mircea Eliade and the Feminist Paradigm Shift. In Darlene M. Juschka (ed.), *Feminism in the Study of Religion: A Reader*, 571–590. London: Continuum.

Christensen, A. D. and Jensen, S. Q. (2012). Doing Intersectional Analysis: Methodological Implications for Qualitative Research. *Nora - Nordic Journal of Feminist and Gender Research* 20(2): 109–125. https://doi.org/10.1080/08038740.2012.673505

Crenshaw, K. (1989). Demarginalizing the Intersection of Race and Sex: A Black Feminist Critique of Antidiscrimination Doctrine, Feminist Theory, and Antiracist Politics. In K. T. Bartlett and R. Kennedy (eds), *Feminist Legal Theory: Readings in Law and Gender*. Boulder, CO: Westview Press.

Crenshaw, K. (1991). Mapping the Margins: Intersectionality, Identity Politics, and Violence against Women of Color. *Stanford Law Review* 43(6): 1241–1299. https://doi.org/10.2307/1229039

Crenshaw, K. (2011). Postscript. In H. Lutz, M. T. Herrera Vivar and L. Supik (eds), *Framing Intersectionality: Debates on a Multi-faceted Concept in Gender Studies*, 221–233. Burlington, VT: Ashgate.

Davis, K. (2008). Intersectionality as Buzzword: A Sociology of Science Perspective on what makes a Feminist Theory Successful. *Feminist Theory* 9(1): 67–85. https://doi.org/10.1177/1464700108086364

De Beauvoir, Simone. (1993). *The Second Sex* (translated and edited by H. M. Parshley; with an introduction by Margaret Crosland). New York: Alfred A. Knopf.

Deutsch, N. L. (2004). Positionality and the Pen: Reflections on the Process of Becoming a Feminist Researcher and Writer. *Qualitative Inquiry* 10(6): 885–902. https://doi.org/10.1177/1077800404265723

DeVault, M. (1999). *Liberating Methods: Feminism and Social Research*. Philadelphia, PA: Temple University Press.

Ellis, C. and A. P. Bochner. (2005). Autoethnography, Personal Narrative, Reflexivity: Researcher as Subject. In Denzin, N. K. and Y. S. Lincoln (eds), *The Sage Handbook of Qualitative Research* (3rd edition), 733–768. Thousand Oaks, CA: Sage.

Fawcett, B. (2000). *Feminist Perspectives on Disability*. London: Longman.

Finlay, L. (2002). "Outing" the Researcher: The Provenance, Process, and Practice of Reflexivity. *Qualitative Health Research* 12(4): 531–545. https://doi.org/10.1177/104973202129120052

Flax, J. (1983). Political Philosophy and the Patriarchal Unconscious: A Psychoanalytic Perspective on Epistemology and Metaphysics. In S. Harding and M. Hintikka (eds), *Discovering Reality: Feminist Perspectives on Epistemology, Metaphysics, Methodology and Philosophy of Science*. Dordrecht: Reidel.

Flax, J. (1992). The End of Innocence. In J. Butler and J. Scott (eds), *Feminists Theorize the Political*. London: Routledge.

Fournillier, J. B. (2009). Trying to Return Home: A Trinidadian's Experience of Becoming a "Native" Ethnographer. *Qualitative Inquiry* 15(4): 740–765. https://doi.org/10.1177/1077800408330344

Gross, Rita. (1996). *Feminism and Religion: An Introduction*. Boston, MA: Beacon Press.

Gross, Rita. (2009). *A Garland of Feminist Reflections: Forty Years of Religious Exploration*. Berkeley, CA: University of California Press. https://doi.org/10.1525/california/9780520255852.001.0001

Grosz, E. (1994). *Volatile Bodies: Towards a Corporeal Feminism*. Sydney: Allen & Unwin.

Gurney, J. N. (1985). Not one of the Guys: The Female Researcher in a Male-Dominated Setting. *Qualitative Sociology* 8(1): 42–62. https://doi.org/10.1007/BF00987013

Haraway, Donna. (1988). Situated Knowledges: The Science Question in Feminism and the Privilege of Partial Perspective. *Feminist Studies* 14(3): 575–599. https://doi.org/10.2307/3178066

Haraway, Donna. (1991). *Simians, Cyborgs, and Women: The Reinvention of Women*. London: Routledge.

Harding, S. (1991). *Whose Science? Whose Knowledge? Thinking from Women's Lives*. Milton Keynes: Open University Press.

Harding, S. (1993). Rethinking Standpoint Epistemology: What is "Strong Objectivity". In Linda Alcoff and Elizabeth Potter (eds), *Feminist Epistemologies*, 49–82. London: Routledge.

Harrison, B. and Lyon, E. S. (1993). A Note on the Ethical Issues in the Use of Autobiography in Social Research. *Sociology* 27: 101–109. https://doi.org/10.1177/003803859302700110

Hartsock, N. (1996). Postmodernism and Political Change: Issues for Feminist Theory. In S. J. Hekman (ed.), *Feminist Interpretations of Michel Foucault*. University Park, PA: Pennsylvania State University Press.

Hartsock, N. (1998). *The Feminist Standpoint Revisited and Other Essays*. Boulder, CO: Westview.

Hellawell, David. (2006). Inside-Out: Analysis of the Insider–Outsider Concept as a Heuristic Device to Develop Reflexivity in Students Doing Qualitative Research. *Teaching in Higher Education* 11(4): 483–494. https://doi.org/10.1080/13562510600874292

Hill Collins, P. (1989). The Social Construction of Black Feminist Thought. *Signs: Journal of Women in Culture and Society* 14(4): 745–773. https://doi.org/10.1086/494543

Hill Collins, P. (1990). *Black Feminist Thought: Knowledge, Consciousness, and the Politics of Empowerment*. Boston, MA: Unwin Hyman.

Hoel, Nina. (2013). Embodying the Field: A Researcher's Reflections on Power Dynamics, Positionality and the Nature of Research Relationships. *Fieldwork in Religion* 8(1): 27–49. https://doi.org/10.1558/firn.v8i1.27

Jaggar, A. (2000). Globalising Feminist Ethics. In U. Naranyan and S. Harding (eds), *Decentering the Centre: Philosophy for a Multicultural, Postcolonial and Feminist World*, 1–25. Bloomington, IN: Indiana University Press.

Jaschok, Maria, and Shui Jingjun. (2000). "Outside Within": Speaking to Excursions Across Cultures. *Feminist Theory* 1(1): 33–58. https://doi.org/10.1177/14647000022229056

Jordan-Zachery, J. S. (2007). Am I a Black Woman or a Woman who is Black? A few Thoughts on the meaning of Intersectionality. *Politics & Gender* 3(2): 254–263. https://doi.org/10.1017/S1743923X07000074

Kanuha, V. K. (2000). "Being" Native versus "Going Native": Conducting Social Work Research as an Insider. *Social Work* 45(5): 439–447. https://doi.org/10.1093/sw/45.5.439

King, Ursula (1995). Introduction: Gender and the Study of Religion. In Ursula King (ed.), *Religion and Gender*, 1–38. Oxford: Blackwell. https://doi.org/10.1177/135583589500300113

King, Ursula. (2004). General Introduction: Gender-Critical turns in the Study of Religion. In Ursula King and Tina Beattie (eds), *Gender, Religion and Diversity: Cross-Cultural Perspectives*, 1–10. London: Continuum.

Kristeva Julia. (1991). *Strangers to Ourselves*. New York: Columbia University Press.

Kulick, D. and Wilson, M. (1995). *Taboo: Sex, Identity, and Erotic Subjectivity in Anthropological Fieldwork*. New York: Routledge.

Lukens-Bull, Ronald. (2007). Lost in a Sea of Subjectivity: the Subject Position of the Researcher in the Anthropology of Islam. *Contemporary Islam* 1: 173–192. https://doi.org/10.1007/s11562-007-0014-y

Lynch, K. (2004). Emancipatory Research as a Tool of Change. In J. Baker, K. Lynch, S. Cantillon and J. Walsh (eds), *Equality: From Theory to Action*, 169–182. Basingstoke: Palgrave Macmillan. https://doi.org/10.1057/9780230508088_9

Maynard, M. (1994). Methods, Practice and Epistemology: The Debate about Feminism and Research. In M. Maynard and J. Purvis (eds), *Researching Women's Lives from a Feminist Perspective*. London: Taylor & Francis.

Moi, Toril. (2005). *Sex, Gender, and the Body: The Student Edition of What is a Woman?* Oxford: Oxford University Press.

Moreno, E. (1995). Rape in the Field: Reflections from a Survivor. In D. Kulick and M. Wilson (eds), *Taboo: Sex, Identity, and Erotic Subjectivity in Anthropological Fieldwork*, 219–250. New York: Routledge. https://doi.org/10.4324/9780203420379_chapter_8

Naples, Nancy A. (2003). *Feminism and Method: Ethnography, Discourse Analysis, and Activist Research*. New York: Routledge.

Oakley, A. (1981). Interviewing Women: A Contradiction in Terms. In H. Roberts (ed.), *Doing Feminist Research*. London: Routledge.

Obasi, C. (2014). Negotiating the Insider/Outsider Continua: A Black Female Hearing Perspective on Research with Deaf Women and Black Women. *Qualitative Research* 14(1): 61–78. https://doi.org/10.1177/1468794112465632

Opie, A. (1992). Qualitative Research: Appropriation of the "Other" and Empowerment. *Feminist Review* 40(1): 52–69. https://doi.org/10.1057/fr.1992.5

Pillow, W. (2003). Confession, Catharsis or Cure? Rethinking the Uses of Reflexivity as Methodological Power in Qualitative Research. *International Journal of Qualitative Studies in Education* 16(2): 175–196. https://doi.org/10.1080/0951839032000060635

Rose, G. (1997). Situating Knowledges: Positionality, Reflexivities and other Tactics. *Progress in Human Geography* 21(3): 305–320. https://doi.org/10.1191/030913297673302122

Ross, N. J., Renold, E., Holland, S. and Hillman, A. (2009). Moving Stories: Using Mobile Methods to Explore the Everyday Lives of Young People in Public Care. *Qualitative Research* 9(5): 605–623. https://doi.org/10.1177/1468794109343629

Sampson, H. and Thomas, M. (2003). Lone Researchers at Sea: Gender, Risk and Responsibility. *Qualitative Research* 3(2): 165–189. https://doi.org/10.1177/14687941030032002

Scheyvens, R. and H. Leslie (2000). Gender, Ethics and Empowerment: Dilemmas of Development Fieldwork. *Women's Studies International Forum* 23(1): 119–130. https://doi.org/10.1016/S0277-5395(99)00091-6

Sherif, B. (2001). The Ambiguity of Boundaries in the Fieldwork Experience: Establishing Rapport and Negotiating Insider/Outsider Status. *Qualitative Inquiry* 7(4): 436–447. https://doi.org/10.1177/107780040100700403
Smith, D. (1992). Sociology from Women's Experience. *Sociological Review* 10(1): 88–98. https://doi.org/10.2307/202020
Trahan, A. (2011). Qualitative Research and Intersectionality. *Critical Criminology* 19(1): 1–14. https://doi.org/10.1007/s10612-010-9101-0
Trinh, T. M. (1989). *Woman, Native, Other: Writing Postcoloniality and Feminism*. Bloomington, IN: Indiana University Press.
Turgo, N. (2012). "I know him so well": Contracting/tual "Insiderness", and Maintaining Access and Rapport in a Philippine Fishing Community. *Sociological Research Online* 17: 3. https://doi.org/10.5153/sro.2660
Warne, Randi R. (2001). (En)gendering Religious Studies. In Darlene M. Juschka (ed.), *Feminism in the Study of Religion: A Reader*, 147–156. London: Continuum.
Warren, K. (1988). *Gender Issues in Field Research*. London: Sage.
Whitehead, T. L. and Conaway, M. E. (1986). *Self, Sex, and Gender in Cross-Cultural Fieldwork*. Chicago, IL: University of Illinois Press.
Wolf, D. L. (1996). Situating Feminist Dilemmas in Fieldwork. In D. L. Wolf (ed.), *Feminist Dilemmas in Fieldwork*, 1–55. Boulder, CO: Westview Press. https://doi.org/10.4324/9780429493843-1
Yuval-Davis, N. (2011). *The Politics of Belonging: Intersectional Contestations*. Thousand Oaks, CA: Sage. https://doi.org/10.4135/9781446251041

6

Negotiating blurred boundaries
Ethnographic and methodological considerations

Fiona Bowie

As I sat in a darkened séance room, holding the hands of my neighbours and singing along to popular songs on a cassette recorder, I felt a mixture of foolishness and nervous expectation. Neither "believer" nor "sceptic", I was open to experience whatever the evening had in store. After a few moments a loud voice was heard from somewhere near the ceiling, clear and apparently independent of those sitting around the walls of the room, including the bound medium in the "cabinet". Over the next two hours we were treated to a series of voices identified as discarnate personalities, distinguished by their very different accents, tones, gender and speech content. There were also physical phenomena that appeared to manifest independent of human intervention, such as glowing "trumpets" moving around the room at high speed, the playing of musical instruments, the sound of loud footsteps and dancing, and an apparently levitated medium whose cardigan had been mysteriously reversed.

The physical/trance demonstration was part of my research into mediumship and afterlife phenomena. Spirit possession and mediumship are not unusual topics for an anthropologist of religion, but by studying paranormal phenomena in the UK I had crossed a disciplinary boundary of academic probity, and risked being seen as gullible and academically unsound. A second boundary crossing involved the body of the medium, who sat blindfolded, gagged and bound hand and foot to a chair. According to the narrative we had been given, the medium's body had been "borrowed" by a series of discarnate entities, who had made use of both the medium's energy and that of the "sitters" in order to materialize. The theory is that the entranced medium had somehow vacated part of his body, moving aside to enable other normally discarnate entities to enter. The discrete boundary we like to think unites our physical body with whatever other elements make us human (soul, spirit, consciousness, mind) was suddenly called into question. Assuming the séance was not simply an elaborate hoax, was it perhaps evidence that we live simultaneously on more than one plane of existence, and that direct communication between planes and their inhabitants is possible? This discussion is about boundary crossing, methodologically, in terms of subject matter, and ontologically, in seeking to understand how the world is constructed.

As an anthropologist there are some tried and tested ways of dealing with phenomena such as spirit possession and mediumship, the most popular involving a kind of mental gymnastics known as "methodological agnosticism". Attempts to integrate data gathered in the field and lived as first-hand experience are prevented from unsettling one's native categories – in this case the comfortable certainty that the dead don't *actually* dance about darkened rooms in Oxfordshire for the amusement of paying guests. Over the last decade or so dissatisfaction with both hegemonic Western, Enlightenment thinking, and with the so-called post-modernist paradigm, which came to be seen as another form of imperialism masquerading as extreme cultural relativism, has led to the search for new interpretive models. An Enlightenment thinker might well conclude that physical phenomena at trance séances are the result of fraud on the part of the medium and accomplices, and suggestibility on the part of the sitters. A post-modernist might conclude that the séance is an ironic performance, the meaning of which lies in its symbolic significance. The truth, or otherwise, of what is claimed is not an issue. The task of the anthropologist is then to interpret the semiotic language of the ritual. In both instances the privileged, knowing, observer performs his or her own magic trick, uncovering the structure of the event and its hidden meanings, even if these are far removed from the categories and language used by the "natives", as well as the embodied experience of the ethnographer – who really did see and hear things that defy rational scientific explanation. Whether exposing the fraudulent medium or, more generously, politely ignoring or explaining away insider or emic understandings of what is happening, perhaps looking for a sound functionalist or psychological explanation, the anthropologist reaffirms his or her own privileged (Western) epistemology.

The growing unease on the part of some, but by no means all, anthropologists, stems at least partly from ethical concerns and the conviction that previous models have not served us well. We face unprecedented environmental challenges, exacerbated by political expediency and unbridled capitalism, with its search for profit as the highest good. Religious, social and political systems seem unable to either rein in our rush to destruction or to help us get along with one another in an increasingly crowded world. There is an idealistic hope that if we can at last listen to and learn from other ways of understanding and being in the world, we might change before it is too late. Under the broad rubric of the "ontological turn", or an "anthropology of wonder" (Scott 2013, 2014), as well as my own methodological efforts in the form of "cognitive, empathetic engagement" (Bowie 2012, 2013), there have been various recent attempts to breach the boundary between insider and outsider, informant and ethnographer, and to allow or insist that these categories be allowed to challenge one another. They seek to hold open the possibility that the seemingly impossible in the native point of view with its alien ontology, might in fact be an equally valid response to the world, even if not framed in ways that "we", educated children of the Post-Enlightenment West, are familiar with.

It is important not to throw the baby out with the post-interpretive ontological new order, while privileging the "native point of view". There are forms of knowledge and interpretations that require a certain distance if one is to see the underlying cultural patterning. One need only think of Kate Fox's wonderful ethnographic insights in *Watching the English: The Hidden Rules of English Behaviour* (2004) to enjoy the frisson of recognizing oneself in the succession of apologies that hide our social awkwardness and smooth everyday interactions (such as apologizing when bumping into someone, or when encountering a stranger, as in "*I'm sorry*, but do I know you?"). The mark of successful ethnographic description is surely that the natives recognize themselves in the picture presented; the familiar is rendered strange enough to become visible, but not so strange as to be unrecognisable, or perhaps inadmissible. I suspect that most English people reading Fox will see themselves represented, but in a new light. However, it is because so much anthropological writing implicitly dismisses the ontological and cosmological understandings of others, rather than revealing them in a new light, that so many "natives", on encountering the anthropologist or professional outsider, engage in concealment. As Jeanne Favret-Saada discovered, Normandy peasants would only disclose an experience of witchcraft when confident that their interlocutor was not going to ridicule or dismiss them (Favret-Saada 2015: 13ff). People who have had (quite common) anomalous experiences report a similar reaction. When medical personnel fail to validate the intensely meaningful and transformative out of body encounters of patients who have had a near-death experience, for example, or seek to explain away encounters with deceased loved-ones in terms of wish-fulfilment, that person might well feel crushed and never speak of their potentially momentous and healing experience again.

I will look first at some ethnographic examples in which the boundaries between insider and outsider have become blurred and then at some of the methodological considerations that arise. My own position, while similar to many of those associated with the "ontological turn" in anthropology (which

I return to below), is not identical to it. My interests in the paranormal, mediumship and the afterlife have drawn me more towards parapsychology and the experiential source hypothesis (Hufford 1982), and in some ways have more in common with the critical realism proposed by Roy Bhaskar (1975) and David Graeber (2015). I note that refusing to bracket out certain tabooed phenomena in a typically Husserlian, phenomenological manner (practising methodological agnosticism), presents a particular challenge when studying in Western contexts. Engaging with entranced mediums in Singapore or in Brazil is exotic and exciting. To do so in England or Germany can be regarded as perverse and academically compromising. What I hope to achieve is to demonstrate or, less ambitiously, suggest, that we do have tools that enable us to tackle ontological questions in ways that open up the field, questioning the boundaries between self and other, insider and outsider, privileged versus hidden knowledge, religious belief and interpretation versus science and hard facts.

Does the insider/outsider boundary exist?

Before I go any further I will make a slight digression (which is nevertheless pertinent to the central theme of this volume) to state my understanding of how the insider/outsider dichotomy operates. First of all I don't believe that there is any essential, unified ontological core to any particular form of identity. Despite recent UK government calls for all schools to teach "British values" for instance, I don't think that we will ever discover a race called "the British" or be able to enunciate in other than very general and probably idealized what a British value might consist of. Whatever group we are studying, ethnicity or nationality will probably only form one of many aspects of an individual's identity. Whether someone with whom I communicate is an outsider or insider, somewhere in between, or moving from one to the other, will depend on how each of us is situated. These are often fluid, relational and negotiated positions. It is easy to essentialize others and to assume that all Christians/Muslims/Jews/atheists/members of a particular "cult" or sect, or whatever it might be, think and believe the same things and will react in the same way, but of course that is not the case. The closer one gets "into" a community, the more apparent the differences become, unless the boundaries are so closely policed that all dissent and difference is hidden.

Do we therefore conclude that the insider/outsider boundary is meaningless, as some commentators have suggested?[1] Anthropologists have long studied boundaries as a useful way of discovering who is and what it takes to be accepted as an insider, and to see how, and how strictly, these boundaries are formed and maintained. I am in no doubt that some types of knowledge are only accessible to those who are prepared to participate in certain activities, for a variety of reasons. When studying Welsh learners, for example, I could not have understood how the Welsh-speaking community reacted to and incorporated new Welsh-language speakers if I had limited myself to interviewing people in English. Neither would I have been able to observe the adroit switching of languages depending on who was present and their perceived language competence if I had not been classified as a Welsh-speaker (Bowie 1993). When studying a mission community in Cameroon I would not have been able to physically access or intellectually interpret, the community without a long previous association and practical and spiritual fellowship with the group. This did not mean that I could not simultaneously analyse and translate my findings into the language of academic social science. It did mean that if I had been or remained an outsider to the community I would have had a very limited knowledge of the motivations and experiences of its members. What matters is to reflect on and be aware of one's standpoint and both the limitations and advantages that any particular position or perspective affords. As a single female member of the mission I was not able to participate in overnight ceremonies in Cameroonian compounds. On other occasions, however, when older, married and the guest of Cameroonians rather than a mission employee, I could, and did. I learnt different things from each form of participation, but as they were mutually exclusive could not participate in and learn from both simultaneously (Bowie 2009).

Blurred boundaries: ethnographic examples

Amerindian perspectivism

One example of "blurred boundaries" concerns the work of Eduardo Viveiros de Castro on what he terms "Amerindian perspectivism" (Viveiros de Castro 1998, 2012). Western categories of nature and culture, mind and body are shown to be local constructs rather than universals – they are a way of dividing up the world that is very different from that commonly found in Amazonia. If we look at the body, for example, it is not a case of "culture" being added to something "natural" (physical) as it might be imagined from a Western perspective. As Vivieros de Castro (1998: 480) puts it: "Amerindian emphasis on the social construction of the body cannot be taken as the culturalization of a natural substrate [sic] but rather as the production of a distinctly human body, meaning *naturally* human." To understand this we need to know that for Amerindians bodies are made rather than given, and there is no spiritual change that is not also a bodily transformation. There is no discontinuity between body and soul: "As bundles of affects and sites of perspective, rather than material organisms, bodies 'are' souls, just, incidentally, as souls and spirits 'are' bodies" (ibid.: 481). The Amerindian plural conception of the human soul distinguishes between the site or carrier of an individual human history, memory and affect, and a "true soul" described as "pure, formal subjective singularity, the abstract mark of a person" (ibid.).[2] Discarnate spirits are not immaterial entities in Amerindian cosmology, but "types of bodies, endowed with properties – affects – *sui generis*" (ibid.).

Western Christian missionaries were concerned with the individuality of minds and souls – what a person believed was important if they were to convert him or her. For the early missionaries the Amerindians have human bodies but might in fact be without souls, or lost souls, and not therefore regarded as human at all. The Amerindian, on the other hand, is more concerned with bodies that have to differentiate themselves culturally in order to express their natural difference. On leaving the body, the soul maybe attracted to the body of an animal. This gives rise to the fear of "no longer being able to differentiate between the human and the animal, and, in particular, the fear of seeing the human who lurks within the body of the animal one eats" (Vivieros de Castro 1998: 481). This reminds one of the Arctic shaman's lament that the great sorrow of his people is that they are forced to "eat souls" (Rasmussen 1929 in Bowie 2006: 182). If the Westerner worries over whether the similarity of bodies "guarantees a real community of spirit" the Amerindian has the opposite problem. There is an ever-present danger of cannibalism as "the similarity of souls might prevail over the real differences of body and that all animals that are eaten might, despite the shamanistic efforts to de-subjectivize them, remain human" (ibid.).

In recent reflections on the "ontological turn" and role of Amerindian perspectivism, Vivieros de Castro (2014) frames his problem as being "how to create the conditions of the ontological self-determination of the other when all we have at our disposal are our own ontological presuppositions. He draws out what he terms a fundamental principle epistemological ethics, "always leave a way out for the people you are describing" (ibid.) by which I think he means, not to come to a (quick) determination about the reality or otherwise of what you hear. Rather than enter the world of another to either validate or explain it away, Vivieros de Castro takes inspiration from Deleuze's "Other" (*Autrui*) which he explains in terms of "freeze-framing" your description of the Other at the moment in which it is expressed. Vivieros de Castro goes onto explain this process as one of "refusing to actualize the possibilities expressed by indigenous thought – choosing to sustain them as possible *indefinitely*, neither dismissing them as the fantasies of others, nor by fantasizing ourselves that they may gain their reality for us" (ibid.). This looks like good old methodological agnosticism, and while it might sound seductive to multiply worlds of possibility, there comes a point at which one needs to come clean with oneself and others. Is something real, or true, or possible, or not? If it challenges one's world view, in what way, and how should one respond to that challenge? If one is genuinely perplexed and no-longer has a working model of what is real or true, or for whom, then that is also a valid perspective, but one that is actualized in time and space, and not rendered forever virtual and abstract.

Normandy witchcraft

In the 1970s a young French anthropologist, Jeanne Favret-Saada (1980, 1989), travelled a few miles from Paris to the hedge-country or *bocage* of Normandy to undertake fieldwork. Although it could reasonably have considered fieldwork "at home", the distance between the metropolitan life of the capital and rural Normandy meant that Favret-Saada was very much more of an outsider than insider within the community. In the 1970s the rural economy was still based on peasant family farms. One son (not necessarily the eldest) inherited the farm and lived with his parents helping out until they retired, leaving him the farm. Other children were largely disinherited in this process. A farmer as head of household, his family, land, goods and livestock were treated as a single unit, and in the world of Normandy witchcraft it was always this unit, rather than an individual, that was subject to attack.

Favret-Saada was interested in studying witchcraft but was unclear where to begin. Most previous studies of Normandy witchcraft had been carried out by folklorists, whose descriptions of unwitching rituals were lacking social context. The person performing the rituals and their social relationships were absent from these accounts. There was also the problem that, faced with an outsider, people would deny that witchcraft existed, or if it did, that they "believed in" it. Direct questions were met with denial and protestations of ignorance. Favret-Saada decided to start by carefully observing the words people used to describe misfortune, particularly aspects related to the biological life of the farm and family. The first thing she noticed was that one-off events were seen as natural, and were distinguished from a sequence of unfortunate events. If a cow died, an expensive tractor broke down, the wife had a miscarriage, the bread failed to rise, and so on, people begin to ask themselves what else might happen. They might consult the vet, mechanic and doctor to treat individual events, but they couldn't explain or prevent the continuing series. Even if the symptoms of misfortune had been addressed, the cause had not.

Sooner or later a friend, neighbour or family member would suggest that perhaps someone wishes them harm. The couple may approach the parish priest, particularly if he is a local and will not dismiss their concerns. The priest, if he does not regard the couple's anxiety as mere superstition, may carry out an exorcism of the house and farm, or call in the diocesan exorcist to perform one. In this capacity he acts as a small scale "dewitcher" (*désorcelleur*). His prayers and rituals might protect the family from a not very powerful spell, but won't send the curse back on the witch. If this doesn't work the family will seek out a more powerful dewitcher, generally someone from another town, recommended by the person who first suggested that witchcraft might be the cause of their problems. The dewitcher then embarks on a kind of therapy, questioning the family (in practice often the wife on behalf of the family unit) about what has happened, the story of how they came to take over the farm, their finances, relationships with neighbours and so on. These are matters that would normally be kept private, but over the course of the consultations the "victims" come to create a new narrative concerning their situation. It could be that the man did not have the aggression and toughness necessary to succeed as inheritor of the farm, but during the process of consultation the family are drawn together as a unit and begin to take control of their lives rather than seeing themselves as passive victims.

The dewitcher will eventually narrow down the choice of people who might wish the family harm, and usually name a neighbouring household head – someone not so close that a lack of cooperation would harm the family business, but as a witch needs some physical contact with the victims in order to cast his spells, not too distant. The family are then advised to "close up" all entry points to the farm and to avoid unnecessary social contact, especially with the person identified as the aggressor. They are given a time-consuming series of daily rituals to perform, such as reciting certain formulae and sprinkling salt around the boundaries of their landholding for protection. The boundaries around the family and farm are thus clearly re-established and visible to all. While the ritual policing of boundaries is a common reaction to perceived outside threats (Sanday 1981; Douglas 1966), Favret-Saada discovers that things are not always as they seem. As has been noted in cases of witchcraft in parts of Africa (Bowie 2000), victim and aggressor may be one and the same person. Favret-Saada came to believe that most, if not all, of those identified as victims of witchcraft had also at some time been accused of being witches.

One of the dewitcher's roles is to use his or her psychic powers to deflect the witch's spells so that they rebound on the witch. A series of misfortunes could therefore be interpreted as the attack of someone who wished to take the life force of the family in order to enhance their own power and fortune, or as the result of spells that had rebounded on the sender. In this zero-sum understanding of the world, all fortune is the result of someone else's misfortune. If someone is doing well and has more than their share, they must have taken it from someone else, who is suffering as a consequence. Casting an apotropaic spell is an aggressive act, not only rebalancing the harm done but taking the life-force of the witch, who will suffer harm as a consequence.

This world of bewitching and dewitching remained closed to Favret-Saada until she was the victim of minor accident, despite living at the time with a family who believed themselves to be bewitched. Her interest in the topic was known, but as an outsider she was not trusted sufficiently to gain access to the discourse and practices of witchcraft. After the accident, however, the situation changed. According to some local interpretations she was the victim of witchcraft, others thought the accident demonstrated that Favret-Saada herself was a witch, or perhaps a not very powerful dewitcher, whose efforts on the part of the family had backfired as the witch's power was stronger than her own. Favret-Saada was introduced to a powerful dewitcher who agreed to accept her as an apprentice. In this privileged position, Favret-Saada was able to sit in on numerous interviews with clients and to learn the prescriptions for dealing with witches first hand. This sort of data had never been recorded before, and led Favret-Saada to conclude that dewitching was above all a form of therapy. She claimed never to have met a witch and did not ultimately believe that witches existed, but witchcraft certainly did, in the sense that it was a belief and above all a practice that many of the people she met became enmeshed in and which came to dominate their lives.

Methodological considerations

"Affect" as a methodological tool

Methodologically, Favret-Saada wishes to restate the importance of somatic learning or *affect* (the state of being affected), and to move away from a philosophical preoccupation with what she refers to as "anthropology's parochial emphasis on the ideal aspects of the human experience, on the cultural production of 'understanding' [and] ... to rehabilitate old-fashioned 'sensibility'" (Favret-Saada 2015: 77). Favret-Saada sought to move from observation to participation, and she critiques "the disqualification of native speech and the promotion of that of the ethnographer – whose activity seems to consist of making a detour through Africa in order to verify that only he holds ... we're not sure what, a set of vaguely related notions that, for him, apparently equal the truth" (ibid.:78). Anthropologists generally regarded European witchcraft as having only historical relevance, while in Africa it was seen as lying outside the experience and understanding of the ethnographer. Favret-Saada refused to accept that a fascinating fieldwork experience could remain beyond her understanding, although aspects of that experience took years to process and distil into words. Like Kirsten Hastrup (1995) and many other participative ethnographers who have moved as far as possible from being outsiders to insiders, Favret-Saada found that the intensity of the dewitching séances rendered them all but untellable: "It was so complex that it defied memorization and, in any event, it affected me too much" (Favret-Saada 2015: 81). At first she tried to take notes, but was constantly put on the spot and ordered to intervene, so in the end just accepted her role and went with it, writing up what she could when she got home, as well as recording and later transcribing some of the séances. With refreshing honesty, Favret-Saada admits that, "I let situations unfold without second guessing anything, and from the first séance to the last, I understood practically nothing of what was happening" (ibid.).

This sort of participation is not, according to Favret-Saada, a technique "for the acquisition of knowledge via empathy" (ibid.: 82). She defines empathy as either an act of imagination, a distancing process by which one tries to imagine or represent how the other must feel, which is quite different from being in that place yourself, or as affective communion (*Einfühlung*). This form of empathy "emphasises the immediacy of communication, the interpersonal fusion one can reach via identification with another". It is a means by which one comes to "know the other's affective state" (ibid.: 82). What Favret-Saada is trying to express is that being there, and being affected, do not necessarily imply an act of imagination concerning the state of mind or state of being of the Other. When she took part in séances she did not know what the others were feeling, but was aware of the intensity of the emotion. She was able to connect with the state of being bewitched because she herself was affected by it. This is another way of expressing the reality of fieldwork that Johannes Fabian (1983) termed co-presence or coevalness. The ethnographer is not in some outside time and space, but embedded within a specific narrative and relationship, however they might choose to represent that reality when translating it into a text. In Favret-Saada's words:

> When two people are affected, things pass between them that are inaccessible to the ethnographer; people speak of things that ethnographers do not address; or they hold their tongues, but this too is a form of communication. By experiencing the intensities linked to such a position, it is in fact possible to notice that each one presents a specific type of objectivity; events can only occur in a certain order, one can only be affected in a certain way. As we can see, the fact that an ethnographer allows herself to be affected does not mean that she identifies with the indigenous point of view, nor that her fieldwork is little more than an "ego-trip." Allowing oneself to be affected does however mean that one risks seeing one's intellectual project disintegrate. For if this intellectual project is omnipresent, nothing happens. But if something happens and the intellectual project is somehow still afloat at the end of the journey, then ethnography is possible. (Favret-Saada 2015: 83)

Favret-Saada distinguishes four traits that characterize her fieldwork. Firstly, she resists the temptation to write her experience out of the text. Professional ethnographers are taught to disguise episodes of involuntary, affective, intense experience in the field as acts of "voluntary and intentional communication aimed at discovering the informant's system of representations" (ibid.: 83). This impoverished sort of communication often disguises the fact that the ethnographer is overwhelmed by the experience and doesn't know quite how to handle it (or perhaps hasn't really engaged at all). Rather, Favret-Saada suggests, as Edith Turner also insists, these experiences should be treated as ethnographic data (personal communication; see also Turner 2005). The second characteristic Favret-Saada notes is that the researcher has to be able to tolerate a degree of separation between the immersive act of engagement in the field and the distancing act of reflection and analysis. The third understanding she reached was of the patience needed over a sustained period of time. Experience, recounting the experience, and then being able to understand or analyse it are often mutually exclusive and may be spread over many years. Lastly, the intensity or density of the material gained in this way has the potential to yield new scientific insights. If Favret-Saada had not participated intensively in so many informal episodes of witchcraft, and have been caught up in the discourse of witchcraft through her own experience, she would never have understood the central importance of dewitching rituals and their role as therapy. If Favret-Saada had followed the extant literature and convention of undertaking symbolic analysis, she would not have contributed new insights to the field.

Having deconstructed Normandy witchcraft as a form of therapy, Favret-Saada ends her 2015 essay on a psychotherapeutic note with a dig at what she describes as "the implicit ontology of the discipline" of anthropology:

> Empiricist anthropology presupposes, among other things, the human subject's essential transparency to himself. Yet my experience in the field (because it allowed space for nonverbal, non-intentional, and involuntary communication, for the rise and free play of affective states devoid of representation) drove me to explore a thousand aspects of the subject's essential opacity to himself. This notion is in fact as old as tragedy itself, and has been at the heart of all therapeutic literature for a century or more. It matters little what name is given to this opacity (e.g. the "unconscious"): what is important, in particular for an anthropology of therapies, is to be able to posit it, and place it at the heart of our analysis. (Favret-Saada 2015: 84)

Experience as a source of religious imagination

The recurrence of certain themes, often quite specific in detail, across time and geographical location suggests that direct experience may sometimes be a source for religious imagination. Experience may give rise to formal belief structures and practices, or produce insights that remain largely private or hidden. Those who share an intense experience may all be considered "Insiders", although interpretations of that experience may vary widely across and within cultures. One example of this is sleep paralysis, described here by David Hufford:

> In December of 1963 I was a college sophomore. One night I went to bed early in my off campus room. I had just completed the last of my final exams for the term, and I was tired. I went to bed about 6 o'clock, looking forward confidently to a long and uninterrupted night's sleep. In that I was mistaken. About 2 hours later I was awakened by the sound of my door being opened, and footsteps approached the bed. I was lying on my back and the door was straight ahead of me. But the room was pitch dark, so when I opened my eyes I could see nothing. I tried to turn on the light beside my bed, but I couldn't move or speak. I was paralyzed. The footsteps came to the side of my bed, and I felt the mattress go down as someone climbed onto the bed, knelt on my chest and began to strangle me. I thought that I was dying. But far worse than the feelings of being strangled were the sensations associated with what was on top of me. I had an overwhelming impression of *evil*, and my reaction was primarily revulsion. Whatever was on my chest was not just destructive; it was disgusting and I shrank from it. I struggled to move, but it was as though I could not find the "controls." Somehow I no longer knew how to move. And then I did move, first my hand and then my whole body. I leaped out of bed, heart racing, and turned on the light to find the room empty. I ran downstairs where my landlord sat watching TV. "Did someone go past you just now?" He looked at me like I was crazy and said "no." I never forgot that experience, but I told no one about it for the next eight years. (Hufford 2013: 4)

Hufford, an American folklorist, went on to do fieldwork in Newfoundland, where he discovered that what he had assumed was a unique experience was not only common but thematized in the "old hag" tradition. Subsequent research around the world confirmed that sleep paralysis is universal and shares the frighteningly specific features Hufford himself experienced. It is often associated with witchcraft and possession and is, for the sufferer, terrifyingly real.

Hufford came up with the term "experiential source hypothesis" to describe aspects of belief and practice that arise from direct personal experience. A characteristic of such experiences is their similarity, despite different interpretations and varying degrees of recognition and acceptance. Hufford did not conclude that there was an evil spirit attacking him, and remains somewhat agnostic as to the source of sleep paralysis.

Another example of experience giving rise to beliefs and practices is the so-called near-death experience (NDE), in which evidential information[3] points to the non-local nature of consciousness, perhaps giving rise to descriptions of the afterlife and discarnate beings.[4] The core features of an NDE recur in ancient as well as modern societies in circumstances in which diffusion is unlikely. These include the sensation of looking down on one's body, often noting who is around or what is happening to it, followed by the sensation of travelling through a constricted space such as a cave or tunnel towards a light. People then record being met by loving beings or presences and deceased friends and relatives who are able to communicate telepathically. There is a sense of being known, understood and loved, of "coming home". There may be some form of rapid life review and a visit to other planes of existence, but sooner or later the person is told that they should return to their bodies. They may be told that they still have a task to complete, or that their time has not come to cross over. The person then finds themselves back in their body, which at that moment shows renewed signs of life. The experience remains vivid, whether or not it is communicated, and removes the fear of death. People report not that they *believe* they will survive the death of their bodies, but that they *know* they will. The extent to which such stories are shared depends to a large extent on the degree of understanding and social acceptance they encounter. A Native American traveller to other realms may be validated and honoured, an African revenant may be feared and treated as a zombie (Shushan 2009). With NDEs that occur in controlled medical settings we have the possibility to examine both the narrative and scientific dimensions of event, and to come to some understanding of the ontological and epistemological processes involved (Van Lommel 2007; Shushan 2009).

Cognitive, empathetic engagement, critical realism and the "ontological turn"

I find many echoes of my own approach to studying phenomena such as spirit possession, witchcraft, psychic powers and cosmologies of the afterlife in the work of David Hufford, Jeanne Favret-Saada and Eduardo Vivieros de Castro. I am certainly interested in ontology, understood as a discourse about the nature of being and epistemology, defined as the possibility of knowledge about the world (Graeber 2015: 15). If there is a danger in the some of the positions adopted by those espousing the so-called "ontological turn" in anthropology, it is that it can remain at the level of abstract theory. One can endlessly hold open the possibility of other worlds without engaging with the specificity and materiality of an idea, event or cosmology, let alone demonstrate the ways in which this engagement has practically affected previously held positions.[5] This is one of David Graeber's critiques of the ontological turn. He points out that, "the moment one decides one cannot stand in judgment over the views of someone residing in a different cultural universe ... one immediately develops the need for a special supercategory – such as 'modern' or 'Western' – in which to include those views one feels one should be allowed to disagree with or condemn" (Graeber 2015: 33).

There are claims that the ontological turn represents a radical political movement, and not just a methodology (Holbraad, Pedersen and Viveiros de Castro 2014), but in practice it can look rather safe and end up perpetuating the academic *status quo*.[6] I find myself in agreement with Graeber that it is more radical to weigh up the statements of one's informants and come to some sort of judgment concerning them (which is what we do in normal human interactions, after all). Referring to his own fieldwork in Madagascar, Graeber asks what would happen if charms really could prevent hail falling on people's crops? He finds this proposition unlikely but nevertheless asks:

> But maybe, just possibly, I was wrong. Still, of one thing I am certain: we'll never have any chance of finding out if we commit ourselves to treating every statement our informants make that seems to fly in the face of accepted ideas of physical possibility *as if* it were the gate to some alternative reality we will never comprehend. Engaging in such thought experiments does not *really* open us to unsettling possibilities. Or, anyway, not the kind of unsettling possibilities that are likely to get anyone fired from their jobs. To the contrary, it ultimately protects us from those possibilities. (Graeber 2015: 35)

In my own work I do refer to conducting an *as if* thought experiment (Bowie 2013) but crucially not to hold open endless possibilities without ultimately coming to judgment. This is where the "cognitive" part of my methodology comes into play. We should be prepared to subject the ontological statements and actions of others to our own growing, developing, open-minded but nevertheless honestly held view of how the world actually works.

Graeber cites the influence of Roy Bhaskar's critical realism on his own thinking (see for instance, Bhaskar 1975, 1989).[7] I think that the following statement well illustrates both the influence of Bhaskar's philosophy of social science and my own approach to ontology when studying the Other:

> I remarked earlier that an ontological realism that makes it possible to say some scientific statements are true also makes it possible to say other ones are false. Let me turn this around for a moment – even if it means violating a kind of unspoken taboo in anthropological writing (I'm aware that saying what I'm about to say could potentially get me into far more trouble than advocacy of any sort of "radical social theory" ever could): being able to say that certain forms of magic don't really work is what makes it possible to say that other forms of magic do. (Graeber 2015: 34)

Like Graeber, I often return to the work of Evans-Pritchard and the kind of open dialogue he had with his Azande informants concerning the nature of witchcraft, oracles and magic (Evans-Pritchard 1937). Evans-Pritchard was an outsider who was also a participating practitioner during his stay in Central Africa. While he provided a rational explanation for witchcraft, he nevertheless held open the possibility that some events defy rational explanation. As Graeber (2015: 36) remarks, "If someone *that* no-nonsense tells you there might be something happening that science can't account for, one has to confront the possibility that he might actually be right."

Favret-Saada chooses to emphasize *affect* rather than empathy. Evans-Prichard was clearly affected by his brush with what might have been a Zande witch, or he would not have remembered and recorded the incident. Not all fieldwork situations, however, provide possibilities for the degree of immersion experienced by Favret-Saada in the world of Normandy witchcraft, or Evans-Pritchard with the Azande. As a tool, empathy – an imaginative act that goes some way towards entering the life-world of another – is preferable to intentional distancing and its opposite – a lack of empathy, which is almost certain to constrain the quality of relationship and type of information that can be communicated. This is in part a matter of semantics, as I contend that the communicative co-presence described by Favret-Saada is a form of empathetic engagement, and that one does not have to actually "get inside the head of" the Other or guess what they are thinking and feeling to practice empathy.

Whereas Favret-Saada never met someone who admitted to or claimed to have been a witch, and therefore concluded that actual Normandy witches did not exist, my own fieldwork with mediums in the UK has drawn me in other directions. My interlocutors in disciplinary terms are not folklorists and historians but parapsychologists, who for over a century have collected data, tested mediums, and recorded anomalous events in the name of science. Proof, validity, reality, and their opposites, lack of evidence, chicanery and imagination, are the currency of many of the debates. As Graeber noted above, this is uncomfortable territory for anthropologists used to the phenomenological method, bracketing out anything that touches on questions of truth and validity (Caswell, Hunter and Tessaro 2014; Bowie 2014, 2016).

Cognition, by which I mean examination of the data, by whatever method it is gained, and reaching a conclusion, albeit one that is likely to be provisional, suspended or tentative is, I believe important. It is important for the ethnographer because it is important for her informants. Trance mediums train for years to give their bodies over to the spirit world, usually, it is claimed, because the spirits wish to prove that the physical death of the body is not the end of individual existence. Proof is not proof at all if belief is endlessly suspended. The effort is wasted if, out of a claimed respect for the Other, the work of the medium and spirits is described in terms of theoretical possibilities. Unlike a scientifically motivated parapsychologist I am not out to find scientific proof of paranormal phenomena, but I am out to engage seriously with a world in which strange things might, and quite probably do, exist and happen. It matters to me that such evidence of the reality or otherwise of phenomena exists. Where it does not exist, this too should be stated as part of the data. This may be a step too far for some, a deliberate blurring of the boundaries between academic credibility and pseudoscience, between objectivity and "going native". In reality it is another form of holding open the possibility that we do not have a monopoly in our understanding of the world, that the Other, whether a Western medium or Amerindian shaman, might actually be onto something, or equally might not. If they have insights that are reasonable descriptions of reality (whatever that is), particularly when there seems to be an experiential, consistent core to many ideas, beliefs and practices concerning the spirit world, this should be explored rather than ignored.

Insider and Outsider are relative terms. If we are to understand them as a series of relationships, moving along continua from distant to close, experience far to experience near, one minute opening up possibilities and in another unsettling, confusing or rejecting them, we might come close to the messy reality of fieldwork. As Favret-Saada so eloquently put it, the possibility of ethnography emerges from the experience of loss of oneself as an outside observer. It is a risky business, but if we are to continue our role as professional blurrers of boundaries and translators of other worlds we need to be true to our own experience – have the courage to be affected by it and then emerge on the other side.

About the author

Fiona Bowie is a research affiliate in the School of Anthropology and Museum Ethnography, Oxford. She studied anthropology at the universities of Durham and Oxford, specializing in the anthropology of religion, with regional interests in Cameroon, and Wales. Fiona has taught at several universities in the UK and overseas, including the University of Wales, Bristol University, and the University of Virginia, in areas related to religion, gender, spirituality, kinship, ethnography and the afterlife. She is widely published, including recent chapters in *The Study of Religious Experience* (Equinox, 2016), *Talking with the Spirits: Ethnographies from between the Worlds* (Daily Grail Publishing 2014) and *The Cambridge Companion to Miracles* (Cambridge University Press, 2011).

Notes

1 See, for instance, Jensen (2011) who reacts against the view that only someone defined as an insider to a particular religion can validly teach or understand it. While I have some sympathy with certain expressions of Jensen's argument that the insider is often essentialized and mythologized, Jensen fails to give adequate attention to the ways in which embodied, experiential learning (habitus), as well as language, can and does lead to a deeper and different understanding of a community or group than can be obtained by less experience-near methods of observation. Of course translation can take place, but every position and standpoint will yield different data, and be useful for different purposes.

2 This sounds remarkably like Theosophical and Spiritist notions of a soul or spirit (individual human life, carrying emotion and memory) and Higher Self or Spirit (incorporating the former but carrying a unique vibratory note that characterizes the soul beyond our embodied time and space).

3 Evidential information is accurate information gathered by non-physical means. In this case the consciousness of the patient appears to be non-local, with a viewpoint outside the physical body. See, for example, van Lommel (2007) and Carter (2010).

4 Non-local consciousness is also a feature of some types of dreaming and out of body experiences.

5   In what amounted to a founding mission statement for this approach, Henare, Holbraad and Wastell (2007: 1) wrote that: "Rather than dismiss informants" accounts as imaginative "interpretations" – elaborate metaphorical accounts of a "reality" that is already given – anthropologists might instead seize on these engagements as opportunities from which novel theoretical understandings can emerge." This is admirable as far as it goes, but sidesteps how such novel theoretical understandings might actually influence and change dominant Western epistemologies, and what these changes might actually consist of.
6   More recently the term "ontological turn" has been used to refer to "sociocosmological transformation", by Vilaça (2015), who explores the conversion of the Amazonian Wari to Christianity. Vilaça claims to take her inspiration from Philippe Descola (2013) and his "four ontologies" to describe the ways in which human beings relate to nature (animism, totemism, naturalism and analogism). Descola, like Vivieros de Castro, sees the Western nature/culture divide as both recent and culturally specific. It is apparent from these various works that the terms "ontology" and "ontological turn" are being used in rather different ways, with different political agendas.
7   The term "critical realism" is attributed to Roy Wood Sellars (1880–1968) in 1915. It was a form of scientific materialism that sought to distinguish itself from Idealism, Pragmatism and Realism. In Bhaskar's philosophy of science there is an emphasis on process and not just the observation of cause and effect, openness to the transcendental and recognition that a strict adherence to the rule that only something that can be falsified can be tested empirically is inadequate. He pointed out that a causative mechanism may not be activated, be activated but not perceived, or be activated but countered by other mechanisms that alter its effects. This opens the door to many phenomena that are observed in practice (such as magic or the effects of physical mediumship) but denied in positivistic science. According to Bhaskar, when studying human beings the variability and fluidity of human agency needs to be factored into our models, and social science needs to be able to take into account the degree to which those inhabiting social structures can reflect upon and change them.

References

Bhaskar, Roy (1975). *A Realist Theory of Social Science*. Leeds: Leeds Books.
Bhaskar, Roy (1989). *Reclaiming Reality: A Critical Introduction to Contemporary Philosophy*. London: Verso.
Bowie, Fiona (1993). Wales from Within: Conflicting Interpretations of Welsh Identity. In Sharon Macdonald (ed.), *Inside European Identities: Ethnography in Western Europe*, 167–193. Oxford: Berg.
Bowie, Fiona (2000). Witchcraft and Healing among the Bangwa of Cameroon. In Graham Harvey (ed.) *Indigenous Religions: A Companion*, 68–79. London: Cassell.

Bowie, Fiona (2006). *The Anthropology of Religion* (2nd edition). Oxford: Blackwell.
Bowie, Fiona (2009). The Challenge of Multi-sited Ethnography. In Ian Fowler and Verkijika G. Fanso (eds), *Encounter, Transformation, and Identity: Peoples of the Western Cameroon Borderlands, 1891-2000*, 184–198. Oxford: Berghahn.
Bowie, Fiona (2012). Devising Methods for the Ethnographic Study of the Afterlife: Cognition, Empathy and Engagement. In Jack Hunter (ed.), *Paranthropology*, 99–106. Bristol: Paranthropology.
Bowie, Fiona (2013). Building Bridges, Dissolving Boundaries: Towards a Methodology for the Ethnographic Study of the Afterlife, Mediumship and Spiritual Beings. *Journal of the American Academy of Religion* 81(3): 698–733. https://doi.org/10.1093/jaarel/lft023
Bowie, Fiona (2014). Believing Impossible Things: Scepticism and Scientific Enquiry. In Jack Hunter and David Luke (eds), *Talking with the Spirits: Ethnographies from between the Worlds*, 19–56. Brisbane, Australia: Daily Grail Publishing.
Bowie, Fiona (2016). How to Study Religious Experience: Historical and Methodological Reflections on the Study of the Paranormal. In Bettina Schmidt (ed.) *The Study of Religious Experience*. Sheffield: Equinox.
Carter, Chris (2010). *Science and the Near-Death Experience: How Consciousness Survives Death*. Rochester, VT: Inner Traditions.
Caswell, Joey M., Hunter, Jack, and Tessaro, Lucas W. E. (2014). Phenomenological Convergence between Major Paradigms of Classic Parapsychology and Cross-Cultural Practices: An Exploration of Paranthropology. *Journal of Consciousness Exploration and Research* 5(5): 467–482.
Descola, Philippe (2013). *Beyond Nature and Culture*. Chicago, IL: University of Chicago Press. https://doi.org/10.7208/chicago/9780226145006.001.0001
Douglas, Mary (1966). *Purity and Danger:* London: Routledge & Kegan Paul.
Evans-Pritchard, E. E. (1937). *Witchcraft, Oracles and Magic among the Azande*. Oxford: Clarendon Press.
Fabian, Johannes (1983). *Time and the Other: How Anthropology Makes its Object*. New York: Columbia University Press.
Favret-Saada, Jeanne (1980). *Deadly Words: Witchcraft in the Bocage*. Cambridge: Cambridge University Press.
Favret-Saada, Jeanne (1989). Unwitching as Therapy. *American Ethnologist* 16(1): 40–56. https://doi.org/10.1525/ae.1989.16.1.02a00030
Favret-Saada, Jeanne (2015). *The Anti-witch*. Chicago, IL: Hau Books.
Fox, Kate (2004). *Watching the English: The Hidden Rules of English Behaviour*. London: Hodder.
Graeber, David (2015). Radical Alterity is Just Another Way of Saying "Reality": A Reply to Eduardo Vivieros de Castro. *Hau: Journal of Ethnographic Theory* 5(2): 1–41.
Hastrup, Kirsten (1995). *A Passage to Anthropology: Between Experience and Theory*. London: Routledge. https://doi.org/10.14318/hau5.2.003
Henara, Amiria, Holbraad, Martin and Wastell, Sari (2007). Introduction: Thinking through Things. In Amiria Henare, Martin Holbraad and Sari Wastell (eds), *Thinking Through Things: Theorising Artefacts Ethnographically*, 1–31. Abingdon: Routledge.

Holbraad, Martin, Pedersen, Morten Axel and Viveiros de Castro, Eduardo (2014). The Politics of Ontology: Anthropological Positions. *Cultural Anthropology Online*, January 13. Retrieved from www.culanth.org/fieldsights/462-the-politics-of-ontology-anthropological-positions (accessed 20 December 2015).

Hufford, David (1982). *The Terror that Comes in the Night*. Philadelphia, PA: University of Pennsylvania Press.

Hufford, David (2013). Modernity's Defences. Presentation at Symposium on the Anthropology of the Paranormal. Centre for Theory and Research, Esalen Institute, Big Sur, CA, October.

Jensen, Jeppe Sinding (2011). Revisiting the Insider–Outsider Debate: Dismantling a Pseudo-Problem in the Study of Religion. *Method and Theory in the Study of Religion* 23: 29–47. https://doi.org/10.1163/157006811X549689

Rasmussen, Knud (1929). *Intellectual Culture of the Iglulik Eskimos*. Report of the Fifth Thule Expedition. Copenhagen: Gyldendalske Boghandel, Nordisk Forlag.

Sanday, Peggy Reeves (1981). *Female Power and Male Dominance*. Cambridge: Cambridge University Press.

Scott, Michael W. (2013). The Anthropology of Ontology (Religious Science?). *Journal of the Royal Anthropological Institute* 19(4): 859–872. https://doi.org/10.1111/1467-9655.12067

Scott, Michael W. (2014). To Be a Wonder: Anthropology, Cosmology, and Alterity. In Allen Abramson and Martin Holbraad (eds), *Framing Cosmologies: The Anthropology of Worlds*. Manchester: Manchester University Press.

Shushan, Gregory (2009). Rehabilitating the Neglected "Similar": Confronting the Issue of Cross-cultural Similarities in the Study of Religions. In M. Ivar (ed.), *Comparative Religion: From Subject to Problem*. Moscow: Moscow State University. (Reprinted in *Paranthropology: Journal of Anthropological Approaches to the Paranormal* 4(2), Spring 2013.)

Turner, Edith (2005). *Heart of Lightness: The Life Story of an Anthropologist*. Oxford: Berghahn.

Van Lommel, Pim (2007). *Consciousness beyond Life: The Science of the Near-Death Experience*. New York: HarperCollins.

Vilaça, Aparecida (2015). Do Animists Become Naturalists when Converting to Christianity? Discussing and Ontological Turn. *Cambridge Journal of Anthropology* 33(2): 3–19. https://doi.org/10.3167/ca.2015.330202

Viveiros de Castro, Eduardo (1998). Cosmological Deixis and Amerindian Perspectivism. *Journal of the Royal Anthropological Institute* 4(3): 469–488. https://doi.org/10.2307/3034157

Viveiros de Castro, Eduardo (2012). Cosmological Perspectivism in Amazonia and Elsewhere. Four lectures delivered at the Department of Social Anthropology, University of Cambridge, February–March 1998. Retrieved from www.haujournal.org/index.php/masterclass/issue/view/Masterclass%20Volume%201 (accessed 20 December 2015). https://doi.org/10.1016/S1361-3723(98)90278-0

7
"On the edge of the inside"
A contemplative approach to the study of religion

Lynne Scholefield

Introduction

"Who are 'we'?", I have written on the essays of countless students who use the term "we" in the study of religion without any awareness of its problematic nature. They assume an unarticulated set of shared characteristics between themselves, other students in the cohort and in the wider university, and me, their tutor. These characteristics include religion, nationality, a London focus which ignores much of the experience of the rest of England, Wales and Scotland, gender, sexuality, age. This approach may lead to the "demonizing" of those who are not like "us" in some of these ways.[1] This is one form of an over-strict separation of insider and outsider in the study of religion. Unreflective use of "we" may also lead to the conclusion that everyone is really the same, an a priori assumption which decides in advance that "our" experience has universal value.

Reflexive knowing

In contrast with this, recent epistemology in qualitative research encourages us to practise "situated knowing" which means being reflectively aware of where we see from, the particularity of our own, inside experience. As Lynn Davidman writes:

> By becoming self-reflexive about my own "sacred" spaces and practices, I was better able to see the many symbolic practices by which my respondents are comforted ... *Tradition*, in contrast, focused on women who had made major life choices that were the opposite of mine ... Here I found that although my emotions did not provide me with access to others' similar feelings, sometimes they actually afforded me insights into how my very different stance might be impeding my full understanding. (Davidman 2002: 21, 23–24)

At its best, this inter-subjective epistemology enables us to begin to know the "other" without collapsing the differences between us, although this is a challenge. It is not difficult to find plenty of examples where religious people and institutions do not act like that – they judge and may well punish the "other", the "outsider". Scholars (of religion) may also do this. Charlene Spretnak notes how the author of an interesting and pioneering example of the archaeology of goddess worship was "relentlessly misrepresented in the extreme, pilloried for holding positions that she repeatedly argued against, and demeaned and dismissed – beginning first with a small group of professors and spreading to such an extent that her work is no longer read, assigned, or cited in the classes of many Anglo-American professors of European archaeology" (Spretnak 2011: 25). This punishing of the outsider is a form of tribal consciousness. The rest of the chapter explores some recent ideas about levels of consciousness including contemplative awareness and then uses this as an approach to the analysis of religions and to the study of religion, as a way to question the boundaries of the insider/outsider categories.

Ken Wilber and integral theory

The chapter will firstly examine the thinking about levels of consciousness in Ken Wilber's work on integral theory and then how these ideas are being used. His approach reflects a deliberate attempt to harmonize insights from within religions, particularly about contemplation, with contemporary scientific research.

Wilber is described by Paul Smith, in his book *Integral Christianity*, as "the most widely translated academic writer in America. He is also the most famous contemporary philosopher and mystic you have never heard of" (Smith 2011: xx–xxi). I don't know if that is true but his ideas are being applied in a number of different fields such as ecology, sustainability, psychotherapy, psychiatry, education, business, medicine, politics, sports, and art as well as religion.

Integral theory attempts to provide a "theory of everything" reflected in the term AQAL (pronounced *ah-qwul*) which is short for, in Wilber's terminology "all quadrants, all levels, all lines, all states, all types" (Wilber 2006: 18). The theory of the quadrants is complex and there is no attempt to cover it in detail here. What follows is the basic pattern – pictorially represented in Figure 7.1. Imagine a square divided by a vertical and a horizontal line into quarters. The upper left quadrant is labelled "interior individual – I", the upper right is "exterior individual – it", the lower left is "interior collective – we" and the lower right is "exterior collective – its". There is "I", "we",

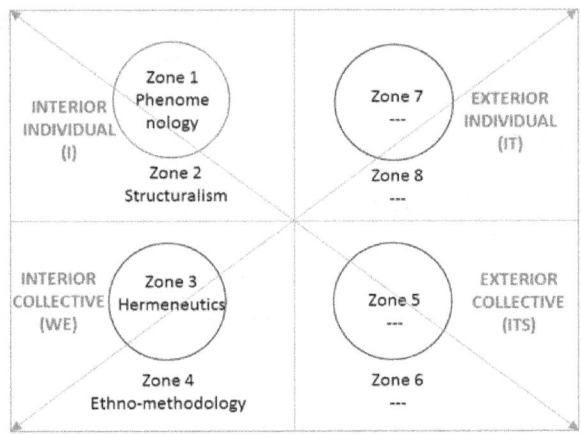

Figure 7.1 Wilber's quadrant approach.

"it" and "its" but no "you" because if you and I are communicating this is "we".

Now, imagine a diagonal cross added to the diagram. Where it crosses in the middle is the lowest level of phenomena and as the lines move out so we go up the levels in each quadrant. This shows growth, development or evolution. Any phenomena can be mapped onto the four quadrants and, in addition, within each quadrant, it is possible to experience or consider the phenomena from the inside and from the outside. Upper left (UL) inside perspective, zone 1, is called phenomenology; UL, outside perspective, zone 2 is "structuralism". Lower left (LL), inside perspective, zone 3, is "hermeneutics" and LL, outside perspective, zone 4 is "ethnomethodology". There are also inside and outside perspectives in the right hand quadrants (zones 5–8) but these will not particularly feature in the analysis that follows. Wilber says that "This is an example of how a map – in this case, the IOS or Integral Map – can help you look for territory you might not have even suspected was there, and then give you tools to navigate it" (Wilber 2007: 30).

The levels or stages are hierarchical – the higher levels include and transcend the lower ones. This is what is meant by "holons". For example, in the upper right quadrant, a molecule is a holon that contains whole atoms and is contained by whole cells. Zone 2, the upper left outside perspective, maps levels or stages of personal development. Structuring and understanding human experience in this way is not new, of course, and there have been many attempts to articulate levels of consciousness in the fields of moral development or cognitive awareness or values or spiritual growth and so on. Different scholars have differing numbers of stages and they call them by differing names, and also sometimes give them colours (see, for example, Beck and Cowan 1996; Fowler 1981; Gilligan 1990; Piaget 2001). Ken Wilber names the stages in different ways at times but when he is talking about religion and spirituality he regularly uses the following: archaic, magic, mythic, rational, pluralistic, integral, super integral (Wilber 2006: 90).

Not only do individuals develop or evolve over time, but, according to the theory, so do cultures (LL) and societies (LR). Of course a society will have individual members and groups at differing stages but the overall level determines how the world is understood, the ways in which people are treated and so on. Wilber argues that early foraging groups were at the archaic level, much of early recorded settled history was magic and both these are "egocentric" stages. The mythic stage is tribal or "ethnocentric", and still widely found. This stage is "premodern". Although there are many examples of more universal, and individual thinking from what is sometimes understood as the first axial age in the second half of the first millennium BCE, Wilber views societies as only shifted fully towards the rational in the enlightenment. This is the time of "modernity" and industrialization, and begins a shift towards "worldcentrism". We are now living in the "postmodern", informational, and pluralistic world and may be moving towards the integral stage.

There are two more elements of integral theory to consider before we begin to see how all this might offer an approach to the study of religion. One of Wilber's most important insights is the distinction between *stages* (zone 2) (which we have been discussing) and *states* (zone 1). All the states of consciousness, whether ordinary ones such as waking, dreaming or sleeping, or non-ordinary ones including heightened, spiritual and meditative states, are available to people in all the stages but *they are interpreted differently according to the stage*. I will give an extended example of this below.

Finally, there is the "pre/trans" fallacy. The mythic, and lower stages are pre rational. They do not use the kind of logical, objective and abstract thinking, often associated with the left side of the brain, which we can understand as "modern". However, the postmodern does not depend on this kind of thinking either – in fact, it critiques and transcends it. It is definitely not the same as mythic thinking and Wilber argues that to confuse the two is fallacious. For example, the mythic world could be described as "enchanted" – someone religious might seek a miracle of healing from the shrine of a holy person. Rationality disenchants the world, explains (away) miracles and relies on operations, drugs and hospitals. The postmodern person may live in a "re-enchanted" world where a holistic approach to healing includes energy practices and a combined awareness of body, mind and spirit.

Using levels of consciousness to analyse religious phenomena

Within this framework, it can be seen that the study of religion is often interested in contemplative states (zone 1) and the religious texts, beliefs and practices that relate to contemplation (zone 3). I will come back, explicitly, to these insider perspectives several times in the chapter but I want to consider now how integral theory can offer a way of analysing religions, religious institutions and religious people in terms of stages or levels. I have spent my teaching life explaining to students that there is diversity within religions, and I have helped them to see the historical and geographical aspects of that – the change over time and in different parts of the world in the ways in which a religion is constructed. This could be referred to as aspects of cultural diversity (zone 4). What I now want to add to this model are the explicit evolutionary stages used in integral theory which give some new perspectives on understanding religions.

What follows is an extended extract from Ken Wilber which will give a taste of the kind of analysis that his approach offers. He uses colours to distinguish the stages and I have added in brackets the names for the levels which we have been using so far:

> Let's say a person has a peak experience of seeing a cloud of radiant white luminosity, which at times appears to be a person or being of light, and then has a sense of merging into that light, feeling a sense of infinite love and unbounded bliss. Let's say that this person is a Protestant, whose Lower-Left quadrant has predisposed his interpretations to see and clothe this experience in Christian terms. What will this person see?
>
> If he's at red altitude [magic], he might see this as a magical Jesus who can walk on water, resurrect the dead, turn water into wine, multiply loaves and fishes, and so on. At amber [mythic], he might see Jesus as the eternal lawgiver, the bringer of complete salvation if one believes the myths and dogmas and follows the codes, commandments, and covenants given to the chosen people and found in the one and only true Book [the Bible]. At orange [rational], this person might see Jesus as a universal humanist, yet also divine, teaching worldcentric love and morality, and who can bring salvation not just in heaven but to some degree on this earth, in this life. At green [pluralistic], this person might see Jesus as one of many, equally valid spiritual teachers, and hence embracing Jesus might give complete salvation for me, which is why I passionately do so, but other individuals and cultures might find other spiritual paths to be better for them, knowing that all genuine spiritual paths, if they go deep enough, can offer an equal salvation or liberation. If this

person is flying at turquoise [integral], he might see Jesus as a manifestation of the same Christ-consciousness that everybody, including you and me, can have complete access to, and thus Jesus is emblematic of a transformative consciousness that shows each person to be part of a vast system of dynamic, flowing, and mutually interpenetrating processes that includes all of us in its radiant sweep. At violet and ultraviolet [super integral], Christ-consciousness might be seen as emblematic of the transcendental, infinite, selfless Self, the divine consciousness that was in Jesus and is in you and in me, a radically all-inclusive consciousness of Light, Love, and Life that is resurrected from the stream of time upon the death of the loveless and self-contracting ego, revealing a destiny beyond death, beyond suffering, beyond space and time and tears and terror, and hence found to be right here, right now, in the timeless moment in which all reality comes to be.

In other words, the altered-state experience will be interpreted, in part, according to the stage that one is at. There is a magic Christ, a mythic Christ, a rational Christ, a pluralistic Christ, an integral and super-integral Christ, and so on. This, of course, is true of any experience, but it becomes particularly important with spiritual and religious experiences. (Wilber 2007: 142–145)

Richard Rohr, an American Franciscan who founded the Centre for Action and Contemplation in Albuquerque, gives a Christian insider's analysis of Wilber's levels in an audio CD called *Where You Are Is Where I'll Meet You* (Rohr 2009). Although his examples and my discussion here are mainly Christian, such an analysis could be useful for understanding many different traditions. What follows is Rohr's application of Wilber, and some additional reflections of my own. Where I have added my own zone 4 comments to Rohr's, mainly zone 1 and 3 analysis, it should be clear. Rohr's summary statements are given in italics:

- Level 1 – *I am my body and self image.* There is a strong need to protect this.
- Level 2 – *My external behaviour and the group I belong to is who I am.* This is "religion as a belonging system, religion as group think, religion as group loyalty, religion as outer authority that holds us together" (disc 1, track 7). Rohr says that religious and political conservatives find great security and safety at this level but there is a shadow side – anyone who doesn't do what I do is inevitably misguided and wrong, may well be a threat and a corrupting influence, and will be punished. This is the mythic level and there are many people at this level. Rohr suggests that much religiously inspired violence can be understood as an expression of this level of consciousness and as to why many biblical prophets faced serious challenges during their ministries.

- Level 3 – *My thoughts and feelings are who I am.* This is the highly individual, liberal and rational stage, with subjective experience feeling like enlightenment. Rohr argues that in the 1940s-1960s many people, benefiting from higher levels of education, moved to this level. I wonder whether the "death of Christian Britain" in the 1960s announced by Callum Brown (2001) reflected a wide-scale move, to Wilber's level 3, with "lower level" forms of Christianity being rejected. I think it would be very useful to use an understanding of these levels to inform discussion of secularization more generally (see for example Davie 1994; Day 2011). Rohr comments that it is very hard for institutions to ever move beyond level 3 and cites, as an example, the way the Anglican church is being torn apart over the issues of women's ministry and homosexuality.
- Level 4 is a major transition stage which arises out of failure, struggle and a sense of things falling apart in the outside world. *My deeper intuitions and the felt knowledge in my body is who I am.* By keeping the head and heart space open, and grounded in the body, there is a real sense of presence. It may be that much New Age practice could be understood to be at this level.[2] Level 4 is pluralistic, very optimistic and positive about human potential and it may seem lovely to stay at this level. However, it is a very individualistic approach concerned with my enlightenment, an absorption with the self, with inner work, instead of any encounter with the other or compassion for others or the earth. Within the study of religion this would make sense of the findings of Paul Heelas and Linda Woodhead concerning the "subjective turn" in the Kendal project (Heelas and Woodhead 2004).
- Level 5 takes seriously a sense of inner unworthiness. *The shadow self is who I am.* It is very hard to face one's needy, self-absorbed reality and raw uninvited emotions. There is anger, false motivation, pride, meanness and so on and this has to be wrestled with. It is described sometimes as the false self or the small self, and the irony at this level is that while the shadow is real, it can't fix itself. This is the beginning of what Christian mystics, including St John of the Cross, have described as the dark night of the senses. Any serious contemplative practice begins to open up the unconscious so we are here beginning to explore aspects of experience accessed through contemplation.
- Level 6 – *I am empty and powerless,*[3] and so open to the transforming love of God. This is "God's waiting room", a time of getting out of the way, learning trust, patience and compassion, learning how to be a conduit for love. Again, St John of the Cross, calls this "the dark night of the soul" and speaks of "luminous darkness".

- At level 7 *I am so much more than I thought I was* because "it is not I who lives but Christ who lives in me" (Galatians 2:20). Ordinary language struggles to express these experiences and silence becomes big enough to "absorb the unsayable". Fully non-dualistic, out of sync with surrounding culture, the person at this level is still partially living in the void, unsure of what is happening.
- At Level 8 *I and the Father are One* (John 10:30). In Christian thought, at this level, Jesus is understood as the first, not the only, one to experience this unity. He doesn't say, "worship me", but "follow me". When people at this level move among us, we are deeply touched, healed and transformed. They are spacious so there is space for us around them. They see the indwelling of God in everyone because they experience it in themselves.
- Finally level 9 is the holy fool – *I am who I am* – just a person, warts and all. All existence is understood as relational – there is no autonomous anything in the cosmos.

Rohr comments, "All sacraments, all bible quotes, all priesthood, all religious rituals ... all spiritual reading are simply to make you and allow you to experience your true self hidden ... with God. They earn you nothing, they awaken everything" (Rohr 2009: disc 2, track 13). Such a judgement comes from a contemplative approach to religion, and from Rohr's "Alternative Orthodoxy" which he describes as being "on the edge of the inside".

Applying integral theory more widely

Just as integral analysis is a useful and interesting way of approaching religions it might also, for example, offer some insights into the growing phenomenon of SBNR – spiritual but not religious.[4] It would enable us to articulate the possibility that some, at least, of the people involved could be categorized within Wilber's framework as experiencing higher *states* of spiritual consciousness (zone 1). Even if they wanted to, they are not able to find equally high *level* (institutional) forms of religion (zone 3) within which such states could be understood and integrated and so religion, as such, is rejected. This might parallel the movement of spiritual seekers in the west towards Eastern spiritual practices throughout the twentieth century because the Western (Christian, Jewish or Muslim) contemplative traditions were so little known.

In *Belief without Borders*, Linda Mercadante (2014) reports on extended interviews with Americans who identified as SBNRs. One of the common themes among the participants is that all religions are the same at their core:

> Their contention that all religions and spiritualties are, at bottom, essentially similar made them comfortable in choosing diverse elements to add to their own spiritual tool-belt of beliefs and practices. This "self-spirituality" made them feel they had the right – and ability – to distinguish those beliefs which derived from deep common wisdom and those which were simply cultural accretions or products of ego. They seemed to see their SBNR posture as a higher platform, as it were, from which to view people and groups they felt were confined within or limited to individual religions. (Mercadante 2014: 85)

Although she does not discuss levels of development in her work, the quotation above can, in fact, be seen as an example of Wilber's pluralistic stage and Rohr's level 4. From the perspective of integral theory it is noteworthy that Mercadante seems to believe that these people *should* be religious – that this would give them access to a better "theology", one that does not revoke religious authority in favour of personal decision. She also suggests that "spirituality may be a smaller, not larger category than religion" (Mercadante 2014: 238) and that (American) society needs the values that come from its religious roots (ibid.: 242). Mercadante's view here can thus be seen as a critique of the SBNRs which weaves together elements of Rohr's two earlier levels promoting the reasonableness of religion and seeing it as the glue that keeps a society together.

Now, to briefly anticipate the second part of this chapter, which explores ways in which the situation of the researcher impacts on their study of religion, let's focus on what she says about herself. Linda Mercadante is quite clear that her own spiritual journey was as a "seeker". She identifies five different types of SBNR – dissenters, casuals, explorers, seekers and immigrants (Mercadante 2014: 50–67). She finally found what she was looking for in mainline Protestantism and became a "religious professional". "I have dedicated my life", she writes in a personal prelude, "to making faith relevant, vital and soul-satisfying" (ibid.: xvi). Her analysis of the situation of those who define as spiritual but not religious is thorough but throughout the discussion she clearly judges them to be in need of conversion – as she was converted to a form of mainstream religion and became fully an insider. Because of this, she pre-judges, which is not a helpful approach to understanding the "other".

Conversion

I think that conversion (or de-conversion) is a very interesting case where the boundaries between insider and outsider are "fuzzy".[5] In previous work I have used the idea of "translation" to suggest that although much changes when someone converts, some things, at least, remain the same (Scholefield 2009). Here, I am arguing that a convert may always remain, to some extent, "on the edge of the inside". I will also speculate about how the process of conversion may stimulate a higher level of consciousness, but that ironically, this may lead to some dissatisfaction with the new tradition unless it offers the potential for a deeper spiritual practice.

An interesting account of the stages of conversion comes from Lewis Rambo (1993). He argues that conversion is always a process and not an event and proposes a stage model that can be used to understand the very complex nature of conversion. Rambo's seven stages are context, crisis, quest, encounter, interaction, commitment and consequences (ibid.: 17) and he sums up the meaning and significance of conversion very well:

> Through conversion an individual may gain some sense of ultimate worth, and may participate in a community of faith that connects him or her to both a rich past and an ordered and exciting present which generates a vision of the future that mobilizes energy and inspires confidence. Affiliating with a group and subscribing to a philosophy may offer nurture, guidance, a focus for loyalty, and a framework for action. Involvement in mythic, ritual and symbolic systems with like-minded people makes it possible to connect with other human beings on deeper intellectual and emotional levels. (Rambo 1993: 2)

This is obviously attractive but the convert is not a local – he or she has come from outside. The Polish Jewish writer Eva Hoffman wrote about her life story in the book *Lost in Translation* (1998). Having settled in Canada, she went to Harvard University and towards the end of the book is reflecting about the differences between herself and her American friends. She could just as well be speaking about the challenge for a convert who does not want to remain "on the edge of the inside" when she writes:

> If I don't want to remain in arid internal exile for the rest of my life, I have to find a way to lose my alienation without losing my self. But how does one bend towards another culture without falling over, how does one strike an elastic balance between rigidity and self-effacement? How does one stop reading the exterior signs of a foreign tribe and *step into their inwardness* [my italics], the viscera of their meanings? ... if I am not to risk mild cultural schizophrenia, I have to make a shift in the innermost ways. I have to translate myself. (Hoffman 1998: 209)

In the Western world, many people are moving from one religious tradition to another and this suggests that the boundaries between religions can, in many cases, be fairly easily crossed, that one person may, at different times in their life, be sincerely and wholeheartedly both *this* religion, and then *that* religion.

I am reminded of the frequently quoted words from John Henry Newman, himself a convert to Roman Catholicism in the nineteenth century, that to live is to change, and to have lived well is to have changed often. Integral theory might suggest that these changes include stages of development of consciousness and spirituality. At a higher level of development it is no surprise to find the claim that there is a universal religious or spiritual impulse which we all share although we understand the details of what is true and holy in different ways. At the lower levels, claims to universality will be understood as claims to exclusivity.

So, for the convert, their level of consciousness is expressed in a new form. Or maybe, and perhaps even more likely, the process of conversion, its traumas and uncertainties, sometimes move someone onto the next stage of development. We can make sense of this in the terms proposed by Daniele Hervieu-Leger (1998) who discusses the way in which religious identity is no longer "given" but has to be constructed. She suggests that this construction uses the symbolic resources to which we have access and that identity "is analysed, in this perspective, as the result (always precarious and likely to be called into question again) of a *trajectory of identification* which realizes itself over the long haul" (ibid.: 218).

She wasn't writing about converts but the relevance of what she says is striking since they are (re)constructing their religious identity in a heightened and more self-conscious way, perhaps, than other religious people. In my research with those who had converted to Islam (Scholefield 2001), often because they were drawn by the spiritual richness in the tradition, several spoke of *"embracing* Islam". This is a very embodied, personal and loving image. High expectations were not always met, though. Samir, one of my informants, told me how he formally converted just before his marriage to a Muslim woman. Although a moving and genuine experience for him, it seemed as if everyone else treated it merely as a formality. When the other men went to pray they did not take Samir with them. This is an example of a very enthusiastic convert who wanted a much fuller and richer Muslim life than he actually found in his new wife's family. A number of converts spoke of how they found it impossible to feel at home in a mosque and several said they had no interest in dressing or eating in what could be understood as a "culturally" Muslim way. Another informant, Safiyya, distinguished clearly between what she saw as the essential and non-essential parts of being a Muslim. She does not buy *halal* meat, for example. She wouldn't eat pork but believes that the Islamic principles are to do with humane treatment of animals and reverence for God as creator. She believes that these principles are put into practice much more seriously by organic meat producers than by Asian butchers.

To use the language of integral theory, these converts were probably operating at the rational or pluralistic level yet found themselves now involved, to some extent, in mythic religion. Although they had insider experience of Islam, they were also aware, to some extent, of its culturally constructed nature (zone 4). I received an email during my research from a source who wished to remain completely anonymous. The email spoke disparagingly of "sad losers...who go native – ostentatious Pakistani clothing or in the case of women, full *niqab* (face covering) etc. Although Islam is universal, these people choose to adopt a foreign culture and do not strip Islam down to its theological basics, unencumbered by centuries of foreign tradition."

Of course, these are specific examples which are not necessarily representative of all converts to Islam or to all converts, but integral theory has given us a way of analysing more fully the experiences of conversion, partly by drawing attention to how both personal and shared experience, can, and needs to, be seen from both the inside (zones 1 and 3) and the outside (zones 2 and 4) if a full account is to be given.

I now want to change the focus to the second part of this chapter which argues that for the person studying religion, their level of consciousness, including, perhaps, a contemplative approach, affects the possibilities for understanding religion. This explores how the student or scholar, whether they, themselves, are religious or not, might "step into their inwardness" (Hoffman 1998: 209) to engage both their own experience and that of those they study.

How does contemplation fit into this?

Wilber, a Buddhist, writes extensively about contemplation – it is an important part of integral theory and of his interests. Contemplative practices lead to higher meditative or contemplative states of consciousness. As we have seen these are zone 1 experiences and always have to be interpreted, and religions (zone 3) teach these practices and traditions. The Franciscan, Richard Rohr, uses Wilber's work extensively in developing his own understanding of religion and spirituality. In his book, *Eager to Love*, he calls contemplation a different way of knowing, that is a distinct epistemological approach. "It is quite simply a higher level of seeing ... consciousness or deep consciousness. It comes down to this: when we see things in a unitive way ... what we see is very different" (Rohr 2014: 62). Rohr borrows a Pauline text from 1 Corinthians 2:13 to express this: "We must know spiritual things spiritually."

This wisdom involves body, mind and heart working together. Rohr writes in a Daily Meditation email:

> it is a way of being – a way of being whole and fully open to a knowing that is more than rational thought alone ... Tilden Edwards, founder of the Shalem Institute, describes the spiritual faculty of heart as "a quality of intuitive awareness ... a sense of inclusive, compassionate, undefended, direct in-touchness" ... This "undefended knowing" allows us to drop beneath the thinking mind, to touch upon real experience, unhindered by ego's sense of self, without fear or agenda. (Rohr, Daily Meditation email, 13 January 2015)

Or, as Tobin Hart, co-founder of the ChildSpirit Institute writes, "Instead of grasping for certainty, wisdom rides the question, lives the question ... When the quest for certainty and control is pushed to the background, the possibility of wonder returns. Wonder provides a gateway to wise insight" (Hart 2009: 12).[6]

Another way of describing contemplative awareness would be as "non dual". James Finley, on the CD *Intimacy: the Divine Ambush*, describes dualism as the "objective fact of otherness, what can be observed as other than ourselves and can be measured and manipulated" (Finley and Rohr 2013: disc 2). But to contemplate is:

> to observe carefully, to pay attention. Sustained in an attentive manner this leads to contemplative experience of oneness with an inherent preciousness of what one is contemplating. In the quietness of the attentive gaze one intimately comes upon a certain value, or depth, or preciousness – a worth for which no words can be found that do it justice – and also recognise ourselves to be one with that intimately recognised preciousness. (Finley and Rohr 2013: disc 2)

The impact of levels of consciousness and contemplative awareness on the study of religion

According to Aquinas, "Quidquid recipitur ad modum recipientis recipitur" ("Whatever is received, is received according to the manner of the receiver"). This section addresses the question of what difference the stage or level of consciousness of the researcher might make to the study of religion. Or to put this another way, how might non-dual thinking affect the study of religion? A contemplative approach to the study of religion encourages the researcher to *get on the edge of the inside of the level of consciousness manifested in the aspect of religion being studied* in order to understand it. So, using Wilber's framework, this means that a researcher at the rational level must not reject or denigrate in advance the magic, mythic or tribal stages, and also it suggests that contemplative work needs to be done to understand the higher levels of consciousness that are manifest in some religious phenomena. It does not mean that someone needs to be religious themselves to understand religion; neither is being religious a handicap to understanding religion. What I am arguing, is that the level of consciousness of the researcher makes a difference to their understanding of religion.

Consider this quotation from E. E. Evans Pritchard, an English anthropologist who undertook extensive fieldwork with the Azande and Nuer communities in central Africa in the 1930s:

> In my own culture, in the climate of thought I was born into and brought up in and have been conditioned by, I rejected, and reject, Zande notions of witchcraft. In their culture, in the set of ideas I then lived in, I accepted them; in a kind of way I believed them ... You cannot have a remunerative, even intelligent, conversation with people about something they take as self-evident if you give them the impression that you regard their belief as an illusion or a delusion ... If one must act as though one believed, one ends in believing, or half-believing as one acts. (Evans-Pritchard 1973: 4)

What he says here is an interesting example of a reflexive approach to fieldwork in the study of religion, and it also hints at some transformation of consciousness in the process. My hunch is that he, maybe, never felt completely at home in either England or Africa; perhaps his experiences meant that he was operating at a non-dual level. He is a very good example of someone studying religion who "became a sign of hope that one could be both a Christian and a pre-eminent anthropologist" (Larsen 2014: 221). In *The Slain God*, Larsen argues that Evans Pritchard is a pivotal figure between early anthropologists of religion like E. B. Tylor and James Frazer and more recent scholars like Mary Douglas and the Turners (ibid.: 222). Tyler and Frazer denied the possibility of being a Christian anthropologist, either through their own personal experience or through polemical argument that anthropology undermined Christianity. For Douglas and the Turners there are clear, two way, interactions between their field experiences and anthropological writing, and their own spiritual experiences and consciousness. Larsen concludes that, "anthropology – befitting its very nature, which lends itself to asking the most basic questions about the contours and meaning of human experience – will always be a site of both deconversions and conversions, gain and loss, doubt and faith ... Perhaps one of the more counterintuitive findings of this study is how much theology not only has been but continues to be a conversation partner for anthropology" (ibid.: 224–225).

In a study of the writings of the English mystic, Julian of Norwich, the feminist philosopher and professor of religion, gender and culture, Grace Jantzen, says that "one's background and intellectual framework forms the perspective for any experience, vitally affecting what the experience will be, as well as its subsequent interpretation" (Jantzen 1987: 99). The questions that one asks and the way in which what is found is analysed depend on the researcher. The English theologian, Sarah Coakley, takes this further in *Powers and Submissions* when she writes:

> It is important to note that this gender-play bespeaks shifts in human epistemological *capacity* [her italics] which *cannot be gained except through painstaking, spiritual growth* [my italics]. If Gregory (of Nyssa) is right about this, there may be different (more or less spiritually mature) ways of discussing the Trinity depending on the spiritual growth of the discussants. (Coakley 2002: 128, n. 67)

The American religious scholar and teacher, Cynthia Bourgeault, argues that contemplatives are able to understand the medieval mystical text *The Cloud of Unknowing* (unknown author, see for example Progoff 1957) better than other scholars. In a discussion of the German mystic, Jacob Boehme, she writes:

> The basic hermeneutic principle when dealing with all visionary mystics, I'm convinced, is encapsulated in that brief one-liner in Psalm 42:7 "One deep calls to another". In the contemplative depths, imaginal reality is readily accessible to every attuned heart. (Bourgeault 2013: 95)

Following Wilber, she defines a phenomenologist as "someone who pays close attention to what goes on, on the inside" (Bourgeault 2009).

Another way of understanding what Bourgeault is suggesting, is what is known as "heart cognition". This might be described as "putting the mind in the heart", deliberately bringing heart and brain into electromagnetic resonance. The Institute of HeartMath was founded in 1991 and, in *The HeartMath Solution*, Childre and Martin (1999: 15–22) claim that "entrainment" reduces stress and enhances perception and intuition. This can be learned and practised as Buhner (2004) suggests in *The Secret Teaching of Plants: The Intelligence of the Heart in the Direct Perception of Nature*. It involves sustained awareness, attention and receptivity to a place, a person or ritual. It means not thinking and not judging, but being present, "sitting with" something, staying connected with it, and slowly letting images and meanings arise. This non-dual practice of heart cognition has been taught within various spiritual traditions but I am recommending it here as an epistemological practice, a contemplative approach to the study of religion which allows the religious outsider to be on the edge of the inside.

Contemplative practice may also enable the insider to achieve deeper scholarly understanding. During the writing of this chapter the news came through of the death of the Buddhist practitioner and scholar of Buddhism, Rita Gross. The following extract from an earlier 2013 post for *Feminism and Religion* was reposted and provides here an excellent example of what I have been arguing. Contemplative practice can lead to higher, more open, levels of development *within* a tradition and also enable the scholar to understand aspects of that tradition more deeply.

> What I am describing is the process of dealing with *kleshas* (mental afflictions) discussed in Mahamudra teachings. One is instructed to focus on troubling emotions, such as grasping or aggression, and to look directly into them without either accepting or rejecting them, thereby liberating their enlightened clarity and energy. The phrase "looking nakedly" is critical in these instructions, which say nothing about acting out on the basis of the emotion, nor do they advise ignoring the whole situation. Unfortunately, fear of acting out on the basis of strong emotions often leads people to be advised to ignore them instead.
>
> I didn't need to conjure up the obstacles of male dominance and my anger with it. They were glaringly omnipresent. Nor could I have ignored them, even if I had thought that was good advice. However, several years of working with these obstacles, using what I now recognize to be *mahamudra vipashyana* (insight meditation practice), yielded surprising results, taming my anger and releasing a great deal of clarity about male dominance, both in Buddhism and in general. I began to write about this process in the early 1980s. This work culminated in *Buddhism after Patriarchy*. Something that occurred shortly after the book was published is instructive. Another male colleague reported to me that a mutual acquaintance who had discussed the book with him noted that I had interpreted many familiar texts in ways that were startlingly new to him. This acquaintance said, "Her interpretations are obviously correct! Why didn't any of us ever see them?" I ached to tell him that it hadn't been in his self-interest to notice how male dominant the conventional interpretations are! Or, as realtors like to say, "Location, location, location!" Painfully, the only person who can unlock the liberating potential of an obstacle is the person who *has* the obstacle. But an obstacle is, by definition, debilitating and extremely difficult to transmute. (Gross 2013)

Some concluding thoughts

The argument of the preceding part of the chapter, then, is that contemplative, non-dual, or meditative practice opens up levels of consciousness, which allow a greater inter-subjectivity which "changes both the subject and the object. The texture of inter-subjectivity brings forth worlds that can be seen and felt neither as merely subjective (and hence merely relative) nor merely objective (and hence merely universal). Herein lies the entire world of the Lower Left quadrant" (Wilber 2006: 157–158). In the study of religion someone is able to see more of the zone 4, "ethnomethodological", outside perspective on religion because higher levels of consciousness give some, limited, edgy, access to the zone 3, insider, hermeneutical perspective. It is also worth noting here that being contemplative does not mean denigrating or rejecting cognitive development. Wilber writes, "developmentalists view cognition as the *capacity to take perspectives* … So cognitive development is defined as an *increase in the number of others with whom you can identify* and an *increase in the number of perspectives you can take*" (ibid.: 113).

My point is that rationality doesn't take us far enough. By advocating a contemplative approach to the study of religion I am agreeing with Graham Harvey who challenges the view of religion as primarily about transcendence and belief. He says that this is "the *scholarly* conceit of attempting to transcend the real world of relatedness and participation that is most deeply damaging to studying religion and other facets of human other-than-human life" (Harvey 2014: 59). Harvey's approach to religion very much includes what doesn't easily fit the rational mould and, interestingly, Harvey also extends this non-dual approach to the non-human person.

I am reminded, by this, of the way in which St Bonaventure in the thirteenth century sees a wholeness in creation where human beings share with vegetation, animals and angels. (Sermon IX in Delio 2013: 193). Wholeness and holiness hang together. Wilber writes:

> There is a Spirit for each and every wave of awareness, since Spirit is that very Awareness appearing in the different levels of its own development, the same Awareness that slumbers in the mineral, stirs in the plant, moves in the animal, revives in the human, and returns to itself in the awakened sage. Most extraordinarily, all of us – including me and you – are invited to become an awakened sage ourselves. (Wilber 2007: 157)

He argues that, uniquely in our age, those people with non-dual thinking can understand all the preceding centuries:

> Knowledge itself is now global. This means that, also for the first time, the sum total of human knowledge is available to us – the knowledge, experience, wisdom, and reflection of all major human civilization – pre-modern, modern, and postmodern – are open to study by anyone. (Wilber 2007: 16)

To ignore all this and to focus only on what can be known from the inside of a religious tradition is to seriously limit one's understanding. Any adequate account of religious or spiritual experience must include zones 2 and 4. Interestingly, in *Integral Spirituality*, Wilber has a final Appendix (III) called "The Myth of the Given Lives On …". He critiques the work of a number of very well-known writers such as Rupert Sheldrake, Deepak Chopra and Daniel Goleman who he says, "have some truly wonderful contributions to make, but they are clearly devoid of any extensive understanding or incorporation of the postmodern revolution that replaced perception with perspective, the myth of the given with intersubjectivity" (Wilber 2007: 275).

What this chapter as a whole is concerned with, are contemplative approaches which move us towards a fuller understanding. This shift can allow scholars to loosen the ties that bind us to one particular way of seeing, From the edge of the inside one can see farther and deeper into things and people and religion, as well as ourselves. There is an openness, a non-judgmental interest and acceptance, a "both and" approach. Of course, I am not suggesting that to understand a religion one needs to belong to it. J. R. R. Tolkien (1964) used the interesting phrase, the "willing suspension of disbelief" in his essay, "On Fairy Stories". This is not meant as an ideal way of appreciating a story. Rather, it indicates that the sense of the real experience of the imagined world has failed and one now looks in, perhaps rather critically, from the outside. As Michael Tomko explains:

> Tolkien identifies the dynamic of suspended disbelief as a remedial state – a modified version of the critical vantage. It arises with a broken illusion and this takes stoic distance as its starting place. What Tolkien clarifies is that the "willing suspension of disbelief" may be the best that one can do to keep going, to bide one's time … but this delimited "going along" can hardly be called, for Tolkien, an idea or a goal. (Tomko 2015: 54–55)

Being on the edge of the inside does not mean procedural agnosticism in the study of religion but a deliberate deepening of our own spiritual awareness and understanding through contemplation. This leads to a re-evaluation of oneself as a knowing subject, to more right-brain awareness, to body knowing and to heart cognition. To return to the question with which this chapter began, what should we now answer? Who are "we"? "We", in the study of religion, are as fully present as possible to religious people and what they say and do, to rituals, texts and material objects. And we might also, in the words of the poem "Black Rook in Rainy Weather" by Sylvia Plath, be open to "a brief respite from fear of total neutrality", inspiration, hallowing and the angel (Plath 1981: 56–57).

About the author

Lynne Scholefield was formerly senior research fellow at St Mary's University, Twickenham, where she was previously programme director for theology and religious studies. Lynne's research interests focus around religious identity in Jewish, Christian and Muslim communities, including in converts between these traditions. Recent publications include *Engaging with Living Religion* (Routledge, 2015 with Stephen E. Gregg), "Memories and Translations in the Stories Told by Converts to Catholicism and Islam", DISKUS Vol 10 (2009) and "Bagels, Schnitzel and McDonalds – 'Fuzzy Frontiers' of Jewish Identity in an English Jewish Secondary School" in *British Journal of Religious Education* 26(3) (2004): 237–248.

Notes

1 A classic example of this would be the term "Orientalism" (Said 1978).
2 Compare this advice from Martha Beck: "Today, look upon your life, your bank account, your family, each person you meet, as a wild horse. If a problem looks difficult, relax. If it looks impossible, relax even more. Then begin encouraging small changes, putting just enough pressure on yourself to move one turtle step forward. Then rest, savor, celebrate. Then step again. You'll find that slow is fast, gentle is powerful, and stillness moves mountains" (from http://marthabeck.com/2013/11/taming-wild-mustangs, accessed 30 January 2018).
3 Interestingly this is very like the first step of the Alcoholics Anonymous Twelve Step programme, and many of the steps echo these higher levels. Step 12 refers to the process as one of "spiritual awakening" (see www.alcoholics-anonymous.org.uk/About-AA/The-12-Steps-of-AA, accessed 30 January 2018).
4 See for example www.pewforum.org/religious-landscape-study/religious-denomination/spiritual-but-not-religious (accessed 8 March 2018).
5 I first got interested in the academic study of conversion because I converted to Roman Catholicism. The integral model helps me understand why I have often felt an outsider, with a worldview and perspective on things that no one seems to share, although this was not necessarily to do with religion. My "conversion" was definitely partly about becoming an "insider" in the Catholic university I work in, a search for a sense of belonging, and I now see it as more of a "dropping in" for a while. For different reasons to him, I am perhaps what Adrian Hastings (1990) called a "Protestant Catholic" and I now worship in my local Church of England parish church.
6 Teaching religious education in a secondary school, it always seemed to me that the students who were "best at RE" were those who could live with uncertainty, who didn't need definite answers to questions and who didn't see things in black and white. Sometimes very able students, who were used to always getting it right in most of their subjects, found it hard dealing with ambiguity, symbolic meaning and more intuitive or poetic religious language.

References

Beck, D. E. and Cowan, C. (1996). *Spiral Dynamics*. Oxford: Blackwell.
Bourgeault, C. (2009). Advent Message November 2009. Retrieved from http://vimeo.com/15606260 (accessed 30 January 2015).
Bourgeault, C. (2013). *The Holy Trinity and the Law of Three*. Boston, MA: Shambhala.
Brown, C. G. (2001). *The Death of Christian Britain*. Abingdon: Routledge.
Buhner, S. H. (2004). *The Secret Teaching of Plants: The Intelligence of the Heart in the Direct Perception of Nature*. Rochester, VT: Bear and Company.
Childre, D. and Martin, H. (1999). *The HeartMath Solution*. New York: HarperCollins.
Coakley, S. (2002). *Powers and Submissions, Spirituality, Philosophy and Gender*. Oxford: Blackwell. https://doi.org/10.1002/9780470693407
Davidman, L. (2002). Truth, Subjectivity and Ethnographic Research. In J. V. Spickard, J. S. Landres and M. B. McGuire (eds), *Personal Knowledge and Beyond: Reshaping the Ethnography of Religion*, 17–26. New York: New York University Press.
Davie, G. (1994). *Religion in Britain since 1945: Believing without Belonging*. Oxford: John Wiley & Sons.
Day, A. (2011). *Believing in Belonging: Belief and Social Identity in the Modern World*. Oxford: Oxford University Press. https://doi.org/10.1093/acprof:oso/9780199577873.001.0001
Delio, I. (2013) *Simply Bonaventure* (2nd edition). New York: New City Press.
Evans-Pritchard, E. E. (1973). Some Reminiscences and Reflection on Fieldwork. *Journal of the Anthropological Society of Oxford* 4: 1–12. Retrieved from www.anthro.ox.ac.uk/fileadmin/ISCA/JASO/JASO_Archive_pdfs/1973_JASO_04.pdf (accessed 11 November 2015).
Finley, J and Rohr, R. (2013). *Intimacy: the Divine Ambush*. CD recording of a conference. Albuquerque, NM: Center for Action and Contemplation.
Fowler, J. (1981). *Stages of Faith*. New York: HarperCollins.
Gilligan, C. (1990). *In a Different Voice*. Cambridge, MA: Harvard University Press.
Gross, R. (2013). Working with Obstacles. Is Female Rebirth an Obstacle? Retrieved from http://feminismandreligion.com/2013/02/06/working-with-obstacles-is-female-rebirth-an-obstacle-by-rita-m-gross (accessed 11 November 2015).
Hart, T. (2009). *From Information to Transformation: Education for the Evolution of Consciousness* (revised edition). New York: Peter Lang.
Harvey, G. (2014). Elsewhere: Seeking Alternatives to European Understandings of "Religion". *Diskus* 16 (3): 57–68. https://doi.org/10.18792/diskus.v16i3.54
Hastings, A. (1990). *The Theology of a Protestant Catholic*. London: SCM Press.
Heelas, P. and Woodhead, L. (2004). *The Spiritual Revolution: Why Religion is Giving Way to Spirituality*. Oxford: John Wiley & Sons.
Hervieu-Leger, D. (1998). The Transmission and Formation of Socio-religious Identities. *International Sociology* 13(2): 213–228. https://doi.org/10.1177/026858098013002005
Hoffman, E. (1998). *Lost in Translation*. London: Vintage.
Jantzen, G. (1987). *Julian of Norwich: Mystic and Theologian*. New York: Paulist Press.

Larsen, T. (2014). *The Slain God*. Oxford: Oxford University Press. https://doi.org/10.1093/acprof:oso/9780199657872.001.0001

Mercadante, L. A. (2014). *Belief without Borders*. Oxford: Oxford University Press. https://doi.org/10.1093/acprof:oso/9780199931002.001.0001

Piaget, J. (2001). *The Language and Thought of the Child*. London: Routledge. Originally published in 1926.

Plath, S. (1981). *Collected Poems* (ed. T. Hughes). New York: Buccaneer Books.

Progoff, I. (ed., trans.) (1957). *The Cloud of Unknowing*. New York: Delta. https://doi.org/10.1007/BF01785303

Rambo, L. (1993). *Understanding Religious Conversion*. New Haven, CT: Yale University Press.

Rohr, R. (2009). *Where You Are is Where I'll Meet You*. CD. Albuquerque, NM: Center for Action and Contemplation.

Rohr, R. (2014). *Eager to Love*. London: Hodder & Stoughton.

Said, E. W. (1978). *Orientalism*. London: Routledge & Kegan Paul.

Scholefield, L. (2001). Becoming a British Muslim: A Critical Study of Some Aspects of the Identity of Converts to Islam in Britain. Unpublished MA thesis, SOAS, University of London.

Scholefield, L. (2009). Memories and Translations in the Stories Told by Converts to Catholicism and Islam. *Diskus* 10.

Smith, P. R. (2011). *Integral Christianity*. St Paul, MN: Paragon House.

Spretnak, C. (2011). Anatomy of a Backlash: Concerning the Work of Marija Gimbutas. *Journal of Archaeomythology* 11: 25–51.

Tolkien, J. R. R. (1964) On Fairy Stories. In his *Tree and Leaf*. London: George Allen & Unwin.

Tomko, M. (2015). *Beyond the Willing Suspension of Disbelief: Poetic Faith from Coleridge to Tolkien*. London: Bloomsbury Academic.

Wilber, K. (2006). *Integral Spirituality: A Startling New Role for Religion in the Modern and Postmodern World*. Boston, MA: Integral Books.

Wilber, K. (2007). *The Integral Vision*. Boston, MA: Shambhala Press.

8

Taking sides

On the (im)possibility of participant observation

Rebecca Moore

It was during the April 2015 reunion of Jonestown survivors – occasions characterized mainly by friendship and warm memories – that the conversation veered dangerously close towards confrontation.

The reunions embody the remnants of Peoples Temple, the religious group that tragically and dramatically ended in a mass murder-suicide of more than 900 men, women, and children on 18 November 1978 at its agricultural project in Jonestown, Guyana. Fewer than 100 members of the Temple living in Guyana survived that day. These include 16 Jonestown residents who had left with a congressman to return to the US; a handful who escaped into the jungle; a half dozen who were on Temple boats or in Venezuela on Temple business; about 45 members who were in the Temple's headquarters in the capital city of Georgetown; and seven who survived in Jonestown itself. Several hundred members who still lived in California and others who had left the organization – or defected, in the Temple's rhetoric – also survived the final cataclysm. Ever since the twenty-fifth anniversary of the deaths, members in each of these categories have gathered together periodically for memorial services, potlucks, and reunions. Although we had never belonged to Peoples Temple, my husband, Fielding McGehee, and I are included in these events.

On this occasion, though, the discussion grew a little tense when one of the survivors claimed that Jonestown survivor Mike Prokes used to criticize the Temple in private conversations with reporters, even as he only praised it in public. In 1972 Prokes, a television newsman, had visited the Temple's facilities in northern California in order to do an exposé on the group, which had already received negative media attention. He joined the Temple instead, impressed with its political vision and action, and became its media adviser (Reiterman and Jacobs 1982: 264). Prokes left Jonestown on 18 November with two other young men, all three carrying suitcases full of cash with orders from Jonestown leaders to deliver them to the Soviet Embassy in Georgetown.

(Full disclosure: Mike was the "husband" of my sister Carolyn in a sham wedding designed to give her illegitimate son a last name.) At a press conference he called four months later in March 1979, Prokes announced that a conspiracy against the Temple had existed and challenged the assembled reporters to investigate it. He then went into a bathroom and fatally shot himself.

I was dubious about the claim that Mike had criticized the Temple to outsiders – especially reporters – and asked the survivor bluntly: "Who said this?" She replied that some had asked her about it, but she did not really answer my query. Although I did not pursue it, my probing indicated my lack of belief in her account.

As the evening progressed, I, too, was questioned about my own assertions that Prokes wanted to declare what he thought was the truth about Peoples Temple and Jonestown. "What was that truth?", someone asked me in a rather hostile tone. A wave of unspoken anger roiled around the table. It subsided a bit, as it always does in these gatherings, because everyone there knows each of them has a different understanding of what is true about Jonestown. In order to maintain camaraderie, it is necessary to give and take, to not fight to the death on principle. That had already happened in Jonestown, and survivors seem to appreciate that some battles are not worth the casualties.

As both an outsider and an insider at these gatherings, I usually back down when things are contested. My older sister, Carolyn Layton, and my younger sister, Annie Moore, died in Jonestown, along with my three-year-old nephew Kimo – one of two illegitimate children fathered by Jim Jones – and hundreds of other people I knew as friends and family of my sisters. Their deaths gave me a type of insider status that I also earned by virtue of establishing Alternative Considerations of Jonestown and Peoples Temple (http://jonestown.sdsu.edu), a website that has served as the demilitarized zone, in the words of one survivor, for the competing and conflicting voices of those affected directly and indirectly by the deaths in Jonestown. Because the website, currently managed by Fielding McGehee, presents a wide variety of opinion – much of which is material with which we personally disagree – survivors view us as fair and open, and see the website as a neutral meeting ground.

But on some occasions at these gatherings, I do take a stand. Several times, for example, I have questioned what survivors mean when they say they were brainwashed. Some have undergone counselling, and their therapists offered brainwashing as the explanation for why they behaved the way they did. Nell Smart, a member of the Los Angeles branch of the Temple who lost four children in Jonestown, along with her mother and uncle, alludes to the discomfort my questioning provoked at the reunion in 2006:

> It was not the matter of brainwashing alone that ruffled feathers, but rather the statement that one must take responsibility for one's own actions. I believe each of us wants to think of ourselves as a good person, so it is hard to admit that any bad deeds done while in PT could have been done by the good person that we think we are. The only way to accept that is to believe that we must have been brainwashed. And if we have to bear the responsibility for our actions, does that not also mean that each of us is in part responsible for what happened on November 18? (Smart 2006)

I had crossed the boundary between remaining a neutral observer and becoming an engaged participant when I talked about personal responsibility, conscience, and agency with the survivors of Jonestown.

The anthropologist Benjamin Paul captures my dilemma when he writes: "Participation implies emotional involvement; observation requires detachment. It is a strain to try to sympathize with others and at the same time strive for scientific objectivity" (Paul 1953: 441). A large body of ethnographic literature has described in great detail the role of the participant observer in the field. A discernible shift from valorizing the detached analyst to lionizing the engaged scholar occurred over the course of the twentieth century. Anthony Forge represents the former viewpoint in an article from 1972:

> It is true that the anthropologist must strive for a certain sort of objectivity but it is the objectivity that comes from analysis rather than the supercilious objectivity of the disinterested observer that must be his aim. If he is getting a real understanding of the workings of the society he is studying, he must be involved without identifying, he must participate in the exotic culture but at all times remain a member of his own. (Forge 1972: 297)

Reneé Fox reflects the newer perspective on engagement and detachment when she writes that

> it is through ongoing interaction and a developing relationship with the individuals and groups who belong to the milieu being explored that the researcher enters ever-more deeply – psychologically and interpersonally, as well as intellectually – into its social structure and culture and the experiences, personae, and lives of those who people it. (Fox 2004: 315)

In a literature review that traces the shifts from monograph to memoir to narrative ethnology, Barbara Tedlock notes that, "What was only a trickle [of first-person accounts] in the 1930s grew into a stream of confessional accounts by the 1960s and became a swollen river of self-revelatory celebration by the 1980s" (Tedlock 1991: 79). She attributes the change to a number of factors, including a wider reading audience for ethnographic material and a democratization of knowledge that embraced indigenous anthropologists. More fundamentally, an "epistemological shift" occurred in anthropological analyses and ethics, and the stigma of "going native" was replaced with the positive task of becoming "bicultural" (ibid. 82).

In this chapter I would like to question whether it is possible to be perfectly bicultural, or if at some point we must make the decision to choose one identity at the expense of the other. The issue of making a choice, of taking sides, would appear to make the classic participant observer – in, but not of, the culture – an impossibility. Anthropologists today emphasize the responsibility that the researcher has for the relationships being established with persons, rather than subjects (Strathern 2006). I wish to go further than the idea of responsibility, however, and raise the issue of commitment. To what extent have we committed ourselves when we as scholars enter into the lives of others? Whose side are we on?

My answer is too ambivalent to be satisfying: I believe we are on both sides, all sides, and no sides. My own experience of being an insider and an outsider within the Peoples Temple survivor community is one of constant negotiation, reflection, empathy, alienation, love, disgust ... and much more. On the one hand, the survivors have become my very family. I have exchanged much more than anecdotes and potlucks with them. On the other, as long as I continue to write about Peoples Temple and Jonestown, I remain locked outside, a place I intentionally choose to be at times. Once I retire for the night during our weekend gatherings, Temple survivors continue to talk for hours, freed of my inhibiting presence. Even a fly on the wall makes a buzz.

What follows is a description of how I came to this understanding of participant observation through my probe of Peoples Temple and interactions with its survivors. I describe a number of ways in which my thinking has changed about the organization and the events of Jonestown. A major part of this transformation is my growing conviction that memory is extremely untrustworthy, which has led to increasing scepticism about whatever survivors relate about the past. Their narratives have become set in stone and thus prove very difficult to dislodge, even when faced with evidence to the contrary. This disjunction between fact and fiction has made me less patient with the old, old stories that are rehashed at every meeting. I should add that I particularly distrust my own memories of anything having to do with Peoples Temple.

My experiences have taught me to interrogate the stories I now hear, especially those that I pick up for the very first time some 35 to 40 years after the events. "What is true" has become "What is true *for them* today." That is not the same as history. The trauma of Jonestown has undeniably affected the memories of survivors, making them unreliable witnesses. While the Jonestown website has offered them a venue for exploring the past and putting their stories into texts that others may utilize to understand Peoples Temple and Jonestown, how much credence can we grant them other than the subjective truth of their own testimony?

I therefore conclude by arguing that we cannot escape taking sides. Even the observer adopts a position: to observe rather than to be absorbed, to remain outside rather than to enter inside all the way. This may explain why I am alive and my sisters are dead.

Observant participation

I have always felt that autoethnography was one of the lowest forms of self-gratification. "If classic ethnography's vice was the slippage from the ideal of detachment to actual indifference, that of present-day reflexivity is the tendency for the self-absorbed Self to lose sight altogether of the culturally different Other," says anthropologist Renato Rosaldo (1993: 3). Max Weber repeatedly emphasizes that the scholar "should keep unconditionally separate" the establishment of facts and his/her own evaluation of the facts, at least in the classroom (Weber 1949: 11). I agree with both Rosaldo and Weber, and consider autoethnography lazy research conducted by individuals too egocentric to be able to enter into the lives of others. Unable or unwilling to engage with people different from oneself in a meaningful encounter, the autoethnographer turns inward to report on her own feelings and anxieties. Even an armchair anthropologist attempts to understand foreign cultures by reading about them. Yet this chapter can only be described as autoethnography, though it is not merely that.

I find the discussion by Barbara Tedlock helpful in this regard. She writes that participant observation has become "observing participation," a method that locates the observer in the narrative, but makes her or him a secondary character in the account, rather than the hero of the story (Tedlock 1991). In this way, the inevitable impact of the presence of an outsider on in-group activities is taken into consideration but does not become central to the plot, as it would in a traditional memoir. It takes ethnography out of the world of abstractions and into the reality of human lives and actions.

I would like to modify Tedlock's model slightly by characterizing my own investigations of the Peoples Temple survivor community as "observant participation," although my studies have been neither systematic nor methodical. My research cannot be classified as the intensive fieldwork of Malinowski, the functional interpretation of Oeser, or the thick description of Geertz. On the contrary, I fell into it by accident as I reflected upon my sisters' deaths. We might call Carolyn and Annie my sponsors into the closed system of the Temple, if we follow the classic fieldwork pattern of entry, maintaining one's position, and exit from the group (Bell 1969). My credibility derived from several sources: their leadership in Peoples Temple, with Carolyn as one of Jim Jones' primary mistresses and Annie as his nurse; the high regard for my parents John and Barbara Moore which Jones cultivated among the wider membership; and the loss experienced in the deaths that I shared with survivors of Jonestown. My position as an observant participant has changed over the years, which I discuss below. Unlike most researchers, however, I have never left the group under observation. We only half-jokingly say that I have been a member of Peoples Temple longer than either of my sisters lived. The difference is that I have written about my participation, and theirs, in a number of different ways that have been altered by time: apologetic, analytical, critical, and, in this chapter, self-reflexive. We could therefore call my research a longitudinal inquiry into the effects of trauma on the members of a high-commitment group, and upon myself.

Initially I saw my role as a mediator or interpreter, the go-between that was neither harshly critical of the "crazy cultists" nor cautiously defensive of the group's actions. In the immediate aftermath of Jonestown, my family's self-appointed task was to humanize those who died, by talking with reporters, friends, and outsiders about my sisters. We tried to describe who they were and what they were trying to do. This effort earned us the sobriquet of cult apologists, and worse, collaborators in the evils of Jim Jones, epithets which can be found on the internet today.

But we also saw ourselves as government watchdogs, monitoring the activities of various local, state, and federal agencies in order to find out what transpired in Peoples Temple and in Jonestown. Given conflicting news stories, discrepancies in the body counts, and the prevalent climate of political paranoia in the 1970s, it was only natural that we sought the truth in much the same way that conspiracy theorists seek it today. This led to our making dozens of Freedom of Information Act requests with government agencies, and to filing three FOIA lawsuits against the government.

Within a year of the deaths, I began transcribing letters which my sisters had written to my parents with the idea of writing a book. This led to publication of five books with Edwin Mellen Press – the only press at that point that would consider a work on Peoples Temple and Jonestown from someone who was neither a scholar nor a journalist. These books had provocative titles, such as *The Need for a Second Look at Jonestown* (Moore and McGehee 1989), *A*

Sympathetic History of Jonestown (Moore 1985), and perhaps most incendiary of all, *In Defense of Peoples Temple* (Moore 1988). These names reflect the apologetic, even defiant, stance I had adopted in the first decade after Jonestown.

The end of the 1980s marked the beginning of a ten-year abandonment of all things relating to Peoples Temple and Jonestown. I donated dozens of boxes of original research and family memorabilia to the California Historical Society. The moratorium continued throughout graduate work in an entirely different area of Religious Studies. This period ended, however, at the twentieth anniversary of the deaths, when I launched Alternative Considerations of Jonestown and Peoples Temple at the University of North Dakota as an educational and informational website. Given the fact that twenty years of scholarship had sharpened understanding of Peoples Temple, and that comparative studies following the 1993 tragedy at Mount Carmel in Waco, Texas had highlighted the flaws in the standard anticult narrative, I wanted the alternative to afford a substitute for apostate accounts. My purpose had become analytical rather than apologetic.

In retrospect, I recognize that I had finally accepted my dharma – or duty – of being an interpreter of the history of Peoples Temple. I did not have to accept this duty, but once I did, I saw my task as a vocation that required total commitment. This allowed me to move into a number of new directions. One path led into the academic examination of New Religions in general and of Peoples Temple in particular, and resulted in having the privilege of serving as a co-editor for *Nova Religio: The Journal of Alternative and Emergent Religions* for ten years.

Another path led to becoming a public scholar through the Alternative Considerations website, which is now the largest digital archive of any New Religious Movement. Hosted by the Special Collections at the San Diego State University Library, and featuring literally thousands of pages of primary source documents, hundreds of digitized audiofiles, photographs, articles, and reviews, Alternative Considerations is the first stop for researchers, writers, documentarians, students, and any casual visitors wanting to understand Peoples Temple and Jonestown. Playing an instrumental role in this accomplishment is Fielding McGehee, who has worked full-time on Peoples Temple research for twenty years, and on the website itself for fifteen. Additionally, the digital archive that is Alternative Considerations would not exist without the whole-hearted support provided by Robert Ray, the Head of SDSU Special Collections.

Yet a third path took us directly into the community of survivors by way of the website and its listing of those who died. Because the deaths in Jonestown were highly stigmatized, the grief that survivors felt was disenfranchised

(Moore 2011b). The guilt and shame that survivors and relatives alike felt over the deaths in Jonestown were exacerbated by their inability to express bereavement publicly. Almost all experienced ostracism – including loss of jobs, housing, and relationships – once their connection to Peoples Temple became known. All felt isolation and shame borne by the expression "drinking the Kool-Aid." And all learned to keep quiet. The presence of Alternative Considerations allowed them to connect with each other and to locate friends and relatives they had not seen since 1978. As a "locus for grief," it empowered survivors to speak up in a safe environment.

In an era before social media, the website actually helped to create the community of survivors. For one thing, they could find each other. For another, outsiders could find them. This led to a wave of documentaries which told the old story in fresh ways. Perhaps most extraordinary was creation of the drama, *The People's Temple* (purposely spelled with an apostrophe), which could not have occurred without relying upon a network of survivors. More than 40 individuals were interviewed for the documentary play, which debuted in 2005.

The contours of the website have changed over the years. Not only is it a repository of primary source material that conveys the story of Peoples Temple in its own voice, it has become an online memorial for those who died. The addition of membership and passport photos literally gave faces to the names; the biographical data on each of the deceased identified them as human; the link for writing memorials gave relatives and friends an outlet for the expression of love and grief. Working with Denice Stephenson at the California Historical Society, and with Laura Johnston Kohl and Don Beck, two Temple survivors, Fielding finalized a roster of everyone who died in Jonestown. If there is an official death list, this is it. In 2011, the Jonestown Memorial Fund – an ad hoc survivor group – relied upon "The Jonestown Memorial List" in the engraving of four plaques placed at Evergreen Cemetery in Oakland, California. And in 2014 the medical examiner's office in the State of Delaware used the register to locate the relatives of Jonestown victims whose cremated remains were found at a defunct funeral home, 36 years after their deaths.

Although both Fielding and I have become participants in the survivor community, we are occasionally reminded that we have not been wholly accepted into the tribe. It was only in 2015, as I was planning to move out of California, that two survivors felt comfortable enough to let me know that they disliked my sister Carolyn. Because she had the ultimate access to power by sleeping with Jim Jones, she was feared and distrusted. She also had a sharp personality and was not easy to like, in contrast to my sister Annie, who was a spontaneous and free-spirited prankster. Another survivor told me that he forgave me for writing, in 1985, that he was a CIA agent; since he has forgiven me many times for this I suspect that I am *not* forgiven.

An exchange between Garry Lambrev, a Temple member and defector, and my husband really brings home our outsider status. Fielding has transcribed hundreds of audiotapes made by Jim Jones and members of the Temple; moreover, he has written all of the tape summaries that appear online. One of these tapes, Q 608, made in 1974, is a telephone conversation between Lambrev, who was desperately suicidal, and Karen Tow Layton, a Temple member whose advice seemed intended to protect the life of Jim Jones rather than that of Garry Lambrev. Fielding tries to remain dispassionate and analytical in his summaries, but on this occasion he let himself offer an editorial comment: "[Layton's] handling of a potential suicide is naïve at best, her response blinded by her loyalty to the Temple. She says some soothing things ... but they are buried under the Temple's party line" (McGehee 2014).

Lambrev responded, both in a phone call and in writing, to Fielding's notes. "This just shows you were never a member of the Temple," he remarked. "You just don't get it." My husband suggested he put his response to the tape and the summary in writing so that it could end up on the site. Lambrev did.

> Though I can understand that someone who was not "there" – in that very complicated, potentially difficult and perceived as "dangerous" context – might regard the part played by Karen as high-handed, inconsiderate and/or manipulative, the truth is that she was navigating very treacherous waters, thinking she knew my fundamental reason for calling but needing to be certain in her conclusions before she reported back to Jones. (Lambrev 2014)

As outsiders looking in, we hear the exchange simply as ordinary people listening to a shocking tape, rather than as insiders speaking a coded language they know very well. The website does allow us to compensate for our outsider status by publishing the insights and reflections of those like Lambrev, whose experience gives them knowledge we would never have.

Observing trauma remembered

Perhaps more descriptive than the concept of observant participant is the idea of observant listener, since any scrutiny of Temple survivors requires being an attentive witness to their testimony as to what they endured. At times this seems to be an exercise in trauma studies. Survivors' experiences in the Temple, as well as their losses in Jonestown, clearly meet the definition of trauma: an event that is life-threatening or capable of producing severe injury, in which one experiences pain, terror, and helplessness, and feels a threat to the integrity of one's self or others (McNally 2003: 79). A threat to integrity: Jones' requiring a young woman to strip naked in front of members of the Temple Planning Commission. A feeling of helplessness: euthanizing all of the pets in Redwood Valley before making the move to Jonestown. An experience of terror: being enveloped by a large snake, or being sent into the jungle where tigers supposedly await.

Audiotapes graphically depict the physical and emotional cruelty members both dispensed and received. Jim Jones and the residents of Jonestown, for example, heap abuse on one young man during a White Night in April 1978, humiliating him, berating him, and probably beating him, since Jones warns people not to tear the man's clothes (Audiotapes Q 635–Q 639 1978). Most of us would consider these examples to be traumatic events, and that is certainly how survivors see them. But can we trust their memories?

Those who study trauma today seem to be divided regarding the accuracy of memories created as the result of catastrophic events. Although Freud can be said to have inaugurated the formal exploration of trauma, the field changed dramatically as a result of the Vietnam War and the post-war flashbacks, intrusive memories, and nightmares that veterans reported. In 1980, the American Psychiatric Association introduced Post Traumatic Stress Disorder into its *Diagnostic and Statistical Manual of Mental Disorders* (DSM-III); subsequent updates of the DSM include as symptoms of the disorder the paradox of having excruciating memories of the initial trauma, and of having an inability to remember the incident (McNally 2003: 10; American Psychiatric Association 1980). Numerous studies of trauma have attempted to deepen our understanding of the impact it has on memory. Some argue that trauma is encoded in the brain differently than other events, leaving, in effect, a hole or gap where the memory should be (van der Kolk et al. 1996; Caruth 1996). They contend that memory does not exist but only the event itself, waiting to be repeated or re-lived, rather than remembered. Others dismiss this view, claiming that while memories of trauma may be more vivid and clear, they are encoded the usual way (Leys 2000; McNally 2003).

Since I am neither a neurobiologist nor a psychologist, I cannot make a judgment on how the brain processes these terrible experiences. But as an observant listener, I can report that survivors' memories are quite imperfect when it comes to remembering some of the things, although not everything, that happened when they were members of Peoples Temple. Studies of Operation Desert Storm war veterans support this ad hoc observation (Southwick et al. 1997), as does the research of Elizabeth Loftus on the distortion and degradation of memory of stressful incidents. Loftus and her colleagues describe the role that "misinformation acceptance" plays in shaping, or rather re-shaping, individuals' memories (Loftus and Hoffman 1989). The phenomenon of misinformation acceptance not only explains why accounts of Temple members change, but also illuminates why it is so difficult to correct the general public's understanding of Jonestown. For example, because initial intelligence reported a changing body count, many continue to believe that hundreds of Jonestown residents escaped into the jungle. A more trivial example is the fact that most people believe that residents of Jonestown "drank the Kool-Aid," whereas in reality they drank a British copy, called "Flavor Aid."

I myself have tried to correct survivors' misperceptions on a number of occasions. I have disputed the belief that massive numbers of guns were smuggled into Jonestown, by providing evidence that only 35 weapons were recovered from the community (McGehee 2013). While it is true that a few dissidents in Jonestown were drugged in order to control them, it is not true that everyone in the community was secretly given tranquilizers. It is unimaginable that they could have accomplished the arduous work that they did under any kind of pharmaceutical influence.

Another factor undermining the accuracy of the survivors' memories is the fact that memories are re-encoded each time we take them out for a viewing. "Recall of memory is a creative process", according to neurobiologist Eric Kandel. "What the brain stores is thought to be only a core memory. Upon recall, this core memory is then elaborated upon and reconstructed, with subtractions, additions, elaborations, and distortions" (Kandel 2006: 281). In other words, remembering is not like viewing a videotape or DVD; instead, it is a reconstruction and reconstitution, with changes and modifications made each time we look back. We revisit the memory, rather than revisiting the past itself. "It is startling to realize that some of our most cherished memories may have never happened," observed the neurologist Oliver Sacks, "or may have happened to someone else" (Sacks 2013).

I have witnessed many instances of the slippage of memory among Temple survivors. One of the most striking was an email exchange from 2006, in which a survivor who had been living in San Francisco in 1978 declared with certainty that Christine Lucientes had not died in Jonestown. He wrote in an email to another survivor that, "Christine didn't die in Jonestown. If she did, I've lost my mind. I could swear I saw her here long after 1978" (James Randolph, personal email correspondence, 2006). And yet there is solid evidence to the contrary. Christine's own brother told us that he had received her remains from Jonestown. Her name also appears on numerous, independently created catalogues of those who died in Jonestown, including the first list produced by the US Department of State (Staff Investigative Group 1979: 120). Another instance of faulty memory: Laura Johnston Kohl does not recall ever being physically harmed as a member of the group. But a tape recorded in Jonestown plainly indicates her being beaten at one of the public gatherings:

> [Rose Shelton]: (striking Laura repeatedly as she speaks to her) How come you can't keep your – keep your mouth shut and do your work? Huh? How come you can't keep your mouth shut and do your work ... (Audiotape Q 734, 1978)

A final case: Thom Bogue, who was wounded at the Port Kaituma airstrip as he attempted to escape from Jonestown on 18 November, distinctly remembers that on one occasion Stephan Jones put a chokehold on him until he passed out, and, on another occasion, pointed a gun at him (Bogue 2012); Stephan Jones, however, had no memory of either incident. Fortunately, Bogue's article on the Alternative Considerations website led to a reconciliation between himself and Stephan.

Yet another factor that leads to the erosion of memory is the contamination – if I may employ a loaded word utilized by psychological researchers – by a number of different sources: counsellors who proffer particular lenses with which to view experiences; the news media that frame the story; competing narratives that offer new facts and alternative theories; and survivors who tell their own stories. In the immediate aftermath of Jonestown, therapists at the Human Freedom Center in Berkeley, California persuaded the few who sought help there that they had been brainwashed. This explanation also satisfied the widespread disbelief engendered by the fact that parents killed their own children. Journalists continually constructed the Jonestown story as a morality tale featuring good guys and bad guys. It has been extremely difficult to eradicate this paradigm, and, through repetition, the framing has tended to stick. Competing narratives provided in numerous books can reinterpret the story, but they simultaneously introduce misinformation. A relatively recent non-fiction book about Peoples Temple and Jonestown describes Jim Jones as pulling people towards the vat of poison, an allegation probably made by Stanley Clayton, who escaped that day (Scheeres 2011: 232). But Clayton is an unreliable witness for a number of tragic reasons; moreover, Temple survivors agree, Jones always had others do the dirty work. Yet this new version of the final day will undoubtedly alter the historical record.

When survivors chronicle their own histories at the reunions, they also affect the perspectives of others. Memories are either confirmed or challenged as people muse about those who died, or about events that occurred in San Francisco, Redwood Valley, Los Angeles, Georgetown or Jonestown.

Some survivors had been insiders and knew a great deal; others had lived on the margins of power, or were too young, to be involved in a number of decisions being made. At the earliest reunions, people asked for forgiveness from those they felt they had wronged; those supposed to give absolution had no memory of the offense that had occurred. While these therapeutic sessions provide opportunities to process traumatic memories, they also alter those memories. Laboratory studies confirm that peripherally disturbing memories can be distorted (Crombag, Wagenaar and van Koppen 1996) and "even traumatic memories are experimentally malleable" (Nourkova, Bernstein and Loftus 2004: 575).

Sometimes interpretation of events, rather than memory of them, may differ. Various survivors can remember the same episode in radically dissimilar ways. Grace Stoen, an apostate survivor, remembers a nightmarish trip on a boat travelling up the Kaituma River to Jonestown, and describes the people on board as being hot, hungry, and exhausted. Laura Johnston Kohl, a loyalist survivor, remembers a wonderful adventure sailing into a tropical paradise with high hopes. They were riding the same boat at the same time. Whom are we to credit?

It is also possible to see development in survivors' narratives. Laura Johnston Kohl's book *Jonestown Survivor* presents Peoples Temple and Jonestown in a positive light (Kohl 2010). She found the hard work meaningful and valued the opportunities available for self-development and personal growth. She especially prized the commitment to inter-racial egalitarianism. Yet over the years I have watched Laura become more critical of Jim Jones, and even modify her explanation of the Jonestown tragedy. Whereas she once described the deaths as mass suicide, she now calls them mass murder, declaring that people would not have killed their children or themselves had not Jones facilitated and encouraged the deaths through his leadership team.

My own understanding has changed as well. Like Laura, I have become more critical of Jones and the dynamics that existed in the Temple. I concede some of this in the essay "American as Cherry Pie" (Moore 2000), although even then my discourse retains an apologetic tone: yes, the Temple was violent, but so was the society in which it grew. A decade later, I was willing to write, "While the last day represented the most shocking, extensive, and visible example of violence in Peoples Temple, members had engaged in increasingly severe forms of brutality for at least a decade" (Moore 2011a: 99). I identified a typology of four types of violence applied in the Temple: discipline, behaviour modification, behaviour control, and terror (Moore 2011a). Learning of my own sisters' roles in planning and executing the mass deaths certainly transformed my views (Moore 2014: 76). Listening to the tapes made in Jonestown is also sobering. And, as I hear the survivors speak for themselves, I have been moved to accept their reality, though not necessarily their historicity.

At the most basic level, though, I no longer believe what survivors and former members say about their experiences in Peoples Temple. Nothing they say is true, although their statements have a truth to them. It is their individual truth, but it is not necessarily true. The survivors of Peoples Temple have told and re-told their sagas so many times that I can mouth the words along with them. So can everyone else. The constant rehearsing of anecdotes for documentaries, plays, TV programmes, books, and news shows not only make survivors' memories less reliable, they tend to make the narrators less believable.

I must confess that my own memory is as fallible as everyone else's. I distinctly recall one survivor telling me she had been asked by the Guyana police to administer mouth-to-mouth resuscitation on someone in the Lamaha Gardens house in Georgetown on 18 November. Liane Harris and her mother had slashed each other's throats in response to the order to commit suicide, but Liane did not die immediately. The survivor I remember telling me this gruesome story, however, had not been in Georgetown or Jonestown that day. The truly sad thing about this admission is that I received this information shortly before writing this chapter.

Taking sides

It is difficult to imagine the possibility of maintaining notions of neutrality and objectivity today, given our postmodern scepticism about them. The oxymoronic participant observer would seem to belong to the modern sensibility of the nineteenth and twentieth centuries. When we attempt to combine the insider and the outsider perspectives – the emic and the etic – we get an emetic, a purgative that leaves us either empty and wasted, or freed of our illusions. Renato Rosaldo's description of the death of his wife in 1981 illuminates this ambiguity.

In a critique of the emphasis given to ritual rather than to human processes in anthropological analyses of death, Rosaldo wrote that the formalism of traditional ethnography "conveniently conceals ... the agonies of the survivors who muddle through shifting, powerful emotional states" (Rosaldo 1993: 13). As outsiders, Renato and Michelle Rosaldo studied the way the Ilongot, an indigenous tribal group on the island of Luzon in the Philippines, assuaged the rage they felt at unexpected deaths by going on headhunting missions. It was not until Michelle slipped and fell 65 feet to her death while doing fieldwork that Renato suddenly understood how anger and grief could be inextricably intertwined. He had moved from simply observing the Ilongot to observing himself, and could feel empathy, rather than sympathy, for the intense emotions that led the Ilongot to murder out of grief. These experiences caused him to re-evaluate and protest the ways in which anthropologists customarily describe mortuary rituals. Nevertheless, empathy is not membership, and Rosaldo did not take up headhunting.

Throughout all of our dealings with Peoples Temple, my family was asked to take sides. Although my parents were never scholarly participant observers, and always remained outside the Temple as far as its members were concerned, their experiences exemplify the quandaries that ethnographers often meet. One such example occurred in 1975, when they explicitly refused to back the Temple. After conducting a hostile interview with my father John in my parents' home in Berkeley, the conservative journalist Lester Kinsolving inadvertently left his briefcase behind. John called my sister Carolyn to let her know, and, in response, Temple leaders asked my parents to bring the briefcase to San Francisco. John and Barbara drove across the bay, leaving the briefcase in their home. Carolyn begged John to give them the briefcase or to destroy it himself. Another Temple leader asked my parents if they would have turned Jews over to the Nazis in Hitler's Germany. Upon returning to Berkeley, John took the unopened briefcase to the Oakland airport, since it bore a luggage tag for United Airlines, and it was returned to the journalist.

For decades afterwards, Kinsolving accused John of leaking the documents to Peoples Temple. It was not until 2007 that we learned that my younger sister Annie had gone to my parents' Berkeley house while John and Barbara were in San Francisco and had taken the papers from the briefcase, photocopied them, and returned them to the briefcase. In this instance, my parents did not choose for Peoples Temple, nor did they take the advice or accede to the entreaty of Temple leaders.

On another occasion, however, they sided with the Temple, refusing a request to join the Concerned Relatives, the oppositional group organized by former Temple members and families of people living in Jonestown. In a meeting with John in spring 1978, Tim Stoen, who had once been an attorney for the Temple and now led the opposition, said that Jones was a devil. "I never believed that Jim [Jones] was God," John later wrote, "nor do I now believe that he is the devil" (Moore 1985: 267).

Benjamin Paul notes the pitfall of factionalism that genuine ethnographers face (Paul 1953). If the researcher favours one party, the other party may reject her or him. And if misfortune strikes, the fieldworker may be blamed. This is exactly what happened to my parents after Jonestown. Because John and Barbara chose to extend unconditional love and support to their daughters and grandson, they were reproached for not opposing Jim Jones. A few months after the deaths, Jeannie Mills, one of the leaders of the Concerned Relatives, accosted my parents at an event, telling them that they could have prevented the deaths in Jonestown. Ten years later, Deborah Layton – an apostate who had fled Jonestown in May 1978 – said to my mother: "You could have stopped Jim Jones." Lester Kinsolving and his children, Tom and Kathleen, continue to rebuke and disparage my father, charging that he abetted Jim Jones. Tom expresses his ire through the blog "Jonestown Apologists Alert", where he calls me "one of the more prominent cult apologists in circulation", and labels Carolyn and Annie mass murderers (Kinsolving 2012).

I consider the ire of the Kinsolvings and others like them to be a badge of honour, proof that in some respects I am indeed an insider. Their abuse of the Moore family scarcely equals that poured upon actual survivors, however. While apostates are praised, those who remained loyalists sustain ongoing vilification. In summer 2015, I was asked to forward the following email to a survivor:

> Sorry douche bag, you should be tried and convicted of the murder of 909 innocent humans. Nearly 40 years later does not absolve you of responsibility. FUCK YOU, YOU PIECE OF SHIT. (Identifying information withheld)

I did not forward this or any other emails like it that we have received over the years. Not all of it is hate mail: sometimes groupies and voyeurs want to make contact with Jonestown celebrities, separated by less than six degrees from the violence of 18 November. And sometimes people are genuinely seeking information, like those who frequently write Stephan Jones to ask if he has forgiven his father, Jim Jones.

I am often asked why I never joined Peoples Temple. My sisters sincerely wanted my parents and me to take up their cause. By not joining, we would forever remain outside the cadre of those willing to put their lives on the line. In fact, Jones called my parents cowards for not living out their political commitments. Why didn't I join? I usually respond by admitting that I am not really a joiner. Crowds make me anxious, groups make me bored, and leaders make me suspicious. Life in the Temple, as revealed by the audiotapes, makes me realize I would not have lasted five minutes under the barrage of the Temple's radical rhetoric and the members' uncritical glorification of their leader. Perhaps it is simply geography that saved me: I lived in Washington DC throughout the 1970s, while the Temple flourished in California.

Which side, or rather, whose side am I on today? If neutrality is no longer an option, is participant observation even conceivable? I believe that it is, to the extent that researchers try to be fair, impartial, and honest to the best of their ability. We are trusting the instincts and integrity of the scholar, a problematic endeavour to be sure. Ethnographers are doing the best that they can.

Ultimately, though, I think it is *not* possible to remain neutral. That does not mean accepting one dogma and rejecting another. Rather, it means being engaged and responding in a human fashion to other humans as individuals. Disagreeing, arguing, challenging, questioning – being real. The way this has affected my relations with Temple survivors is mixed. I am accepted and not accepted: acknowledged as a facilitator of larger cultural conversations about Peoples Temple and an interpreter of the Temple to outsiders; but not received as someone who has suffered the outrages of membership in my person, or more directly, in my body. I did not undergo the terror, joy, shame, or the fundamental life and death undertaking that Temple survivors can boast. That is where they put me.

But where do I put myself? Observant participation and observant listening truly portray the social location of both my husband and myself. Our participation in the Temple is qualitatively different than that of other survivors, despite the deep bonds of love and affection we have in what Fielding calls the "Temple Community". Fielding's credentials as a member of that community are much stronger than mine. He organized the campaign for the early release of Larry Layton from prison; identified all 918 who died on 18 November; raised money to pay for memorial plaques at Evergreen Cemetery; and has edited books, articles, and memoirs by survivors. My own scholarly work has gone largely unnoticed by the survivors, although I always write under the assumption that they will read what has been written. I am also critically aware of whether or not we have profited financially from the losses we have all experienced and am happy to reiterate that our work has not been remunerative in the slightest.

As an observant participant I have decided not to thoroughly identify with the survivors. This gives me the freedom to be honest with myself, and with them, when I disagree with what they are saying. Sometimes diplomacy requires silence: the issue is not worth an argument. Other times, integrity demands voice: the truth is at stake. The tricky part is having the wisdom to know the difference.

About the author

Rebecca Moore is emerita professor of religious studies at San Diego State University. She is currently reviews editor for *Nova Religio: The Journal of Alternative and Emergent*

Religions, published by University of California Press. Her most recent book is *Beyond Brainwashing: Perspectives on Cultic Violence* (Cambridge University Press, 2018).

References

American Psychiatric Association (1980). *Diagnostic and Statistical Manual of Mental Disorders*, 3rd edition [DSM-III]. Washington, DC: American Psychiatric Association.

Audiotape Q 734 (1978). Transcript. Retrieved from http://jonestown.sdsu.edu/?page_id=27567 (accessed 4 June 2019).

Audiotapes Q 635–Q 639 (1978). Tapes Prepared by the Jonestown Institute. Retrieved from http://jonestown.sdsu.edu/?page_id=28703#Jonestown (accessed 4 June 2019).

Bell, Colin (1969). A Note On Participant Observation. *Sociology* 3(3): 417–18. https://doi.org/10.1177/003803856900300309

Bogue, Thom (2012). I Want to Go With You but They Won't Let Me. *the jonestown report* 14. Retrieved from http://jonestown.sdsu.edu/?page_id=34231. accessed 4 June 2019.

Caruth, Cathy (1996). Recapturing the Past: Introduction. In *Trauma: Explorations in Memory*, edited by Cathy Caruth, 151–157. Baltimore, MD: Johns Hopkins University Press.

Crombag, Hans F. M., Willem A. Wagenaar, and Peter J. Van Koppen (1996). Crashing Memories and the Problem of "Source Monitoring". *Applied Cognitive Psychology* 10(2): 95–104. https://doi.org/10.1002/(SICI)1099-0720(199604)10:2<95::AID-ACP366>3.0.CO;2-#

Forge, Anthony (1972). The Lonely Anthropologist. In *Crossing Cultural Boundaries: The Anthropological Experience*, edited by Solon T. Kimball and James B. Watson, 292–304. San Francisco, CA: Chandler.

Fox, Renée C. (2004). Observations and Reflections of a Perpetual Fieldworker. *Annals of the American Academy of Political and Social Science* 595: 209–226. https://doi.org/10.1177/0002716204266635

Kandel, Eric R. (2006). *In Search of Memory: The Emergence of a New Science of Mind*. New York: W. W. Norton.

Kinsolving, Tom (2012). 34th Anniversary Day: People's Temple New Cult of the Faithful Celebrates a Macabre Memorial for Mass Murderers. Retrieved from http://jonestownapologistsalert.blogspot.com/, accessed 4 June 2019.

Kohl, Laura Johnston (2010). *Jonestown Survivor: An Insider's Look*. New York: iUniverse.

Lambrev, Garrett (2014). The Tale of the Tape. Retrieved from http://jonestown.sdsu.edu/?page_id=40178, accessed 4 June 2019.

Leys, Ruth (2000). *Trauma: A Genealogy*. Chicago, IL: University of Chicago.

Loftus, Elizabeth and Hunter G. Hoffman (1989). Misinformation and Memory: The Creation of New Memories. *Journal of Experimental Psychology* 118(1): 100–104. https://doi.org/10.1037//0096-3445.118.1.100

McGehee, Fielding III (2013). Was Jonestown an Armed Camp? Retrieved from http://jonestown.sdsu.edu/?page_id=35354, accessed 4 June 2019.
McGehee, Fielding III (2014). Q 608 Summary. Retrieved from http://jonestown.sdsu.edu/?page_id=28194, accessed 4 June 2019.
McNally, Richard J. (2003). *Remembering Trauma*. Cambridge, MA: Belknap Press. https://doi.org/10.1038/nm1203-1448
Moore, Rebecca (1985). *A Sympathetic History of Jonestown*. Lewiston, NY: Edwin Mellen Press.
Moore, Rebecca (1988). *In Defense of Peoples Temple*. Lewiston, NY: Edwin Mellen Press.
Moore, Rebecca (2000). "American as Cherry Pie": Peoples Temple and Violence in America. In *Millennialism, Persecution, and Violence: Historical Cases*, edited by Catherine Wessinger, 121–137. Syracuse, NY: Syracuse University Press.
Moore, Rebecca (2011a). Narratives of Persecution, Suffering, and Martyrdom: Violence in Peoples Temple and Jonestown. In *Violence and New Religious Movements*, edited by James R. Lewis, 95–111. New York: Oxford University Press.
Moore, Rebecca (2011b). The Stigmatized Deaths in Jonestown: Finding a Locus for Grief. *Death Studies* 35(1): 42–58. https://doi.org/10.1080/07481181003772465
Moore, Rebecca (2014). Rhetoric, Revolution, and Resistance in Jonestown, Guyana. In *Sacred Suicide*, edited by James R. Lewis and Carole M. Cusack, 73–90. Burlington, VT: Ashgate. https://doi.org/10.4324/9781315607382-5
Moore, Rebecca and Fielding McGehee III (1989). *The Need for a Second Look at Jonestown*. Lewiston, NY: Edwin Mellen Press.
Nourkova, Veronika, Daniel M. Bernstein and Elizabeth F. Loftus (2004). Altering Traumatic Memory. In *Emotional Memory Failures*, edited by Ineke Wessel and Daniel B. Wright, 575–585. New York: Taylor and Francis.
Paul, Benjamin D. (1953). Interview Techniques and Field Relationships. In *Anthropology Today: An Encyclopedic Inventory*, edited by A. L. Kroeber, 430–451. Chicago, IL: University of Chicago.
Reiterman, Tim with John Jacobs (1982). *Raven: The Untold Story of the Rev. Jim Jones and his People*. New York: E. P. Dutton.
Rosaldo, Renato (1993). Introduction: Grief and a Headhunter's Rage. In *Culture and Truth: The Remaking of Social Analysis*. Boston, MA: Beacon Press.
Sacks, Oliver (2013). Speak, Memory. *The New York Review of Books*, 21 February. Retrieved from www.nybooks.com/articles/archives/2013/feb/21/speak-memory/, accessed 4 June 2019.
Scheeres, Julia (2011). *A Thousand Lives: The Untold Story of Hope, Deception, and Survival at Jonestown*. New York: The Free Press.
Smart, Nell (2006). Fourth of July Gatherings Provide Safe Environment for Former Members. *the jonestown report* 8. Retrieved from http://jonestown.sdsu.edu/?page_id=32004, accessed 4 June 2019.
Southwick, Steven M., C. Andrew Morgan III, Andreas L. Nicolaou and Dennis S. Charney (1997). Consistency of Memory for Combat-Related Traumatic Events in Veterans of Operation Desert Storm. *The American Journal of Psychiatry* 154(2): 173–177. https://doi.org/10.1176/ajp.154.2.173

Staff Investigative Group (1979). *The Assassination of Representative Leo J. Ryan and the Jonestown, Guyana Tragedy.* Washington, DC: Government Printing Office.

Strathern, Marilyn (2006). Don't Eat Unwashed Lettuce. *American Ethnologist* 33(4): 532–534. https://doi.org/10.1525/ae.2006.33.4.532

Tedlock, Barbara (1991). From Participant Observation to the Observation of Participation: The Emergence of Narrative Ethnography. *Journal of Anthropological Research* 47(1): 69–94. https://doi.org/10.1086/jar.47.1.3630581

Van der Kolk, Bessel A., Alexander C. McFarlane, and Lars Weisaeth (eds) (1996). *Traumatic Stress: The Effects of Overwhelming Experience on Mind, Body, and Society.* New York: Guilford.

Weber, Max (1949). *The Methodology of the Social Sciences.* Translated and edited by Edward A. Shils and Henry A. Finch. New York: Free Press.

9

Who researches? Who changes?

Christian autoethnography and Muslim pupil identity in a Church of England primary school

Tom Wilson

> Research is an active process, in which accounts of the world are produced through selective observation and theoretical interpretation of what is seen, through asking particular questions and interpreting what is said in reply, through writing fieldnotes and transcribing audio- and video-recordings, as well as through writing research reports. (Hammersley and Atkinson 2007: 16)

Between 2010 and 2012, I spent two academic years conducting fieldwork as a stimulus for a theological PhD that examined the experiences of Muslim children in an Anglican Primary School (Wilson 2015). I was not only a researcher in the school, but also chair of governors and curate (assistant minister) at the local Anglican Church, which was closely connected to that school. My position as a researcher was therefore quite complex. This chapter reflects on the questions of truthfulness and change in the context of my research. The chapter begins with some biographical information, outlining the nature of my PhD fieldwork among Muslim pupils in an Anglican primary school, as well as my own faith position as an evangelical Anglican minister. The chapter then discusses how Christians consciously engage in fieldwork before tackling questions of being truthful, forthright and static in turn. The issue of truthfulness relates to how honest a researcher ought to be about personal faith convictions when engaging with those of a very different perspective. The chapter argues that researchers must be honest about their own views if they expect those they are working with to be honest about theirs. The second issue, of being forthright, is related to the first. A distinction is drawn between being truthful about one's own beliefs and being forthright in sharing those beliefs. Examples from fieldwork, including discussion of belief about Christmas and Easter and experience of fasting during Ramadan are used to illustrate the point under discussion. The chapter argues that while researchers must be truthful, there are times when they should not be forthright about their own beliefs. Third, the chapter discusses the author's experience of personal change during his fieldwork, explaining how his beliefs about Islam and practise of Christianity were altered as a result of his fieldwork.

My involvement with the field site

My research was conducted between 2010 and 2012. During those two academic years, I engaged in self-reflexive participant observation fieldwork, written up in a field journal, following the guidance of Emerson (1995) and Walford (2009). I conducted thirty-one focus groups with all pupils in school years four to six (pupils aged 8–11) and ten semi-structured interviews with their teachers. Class teachers arranged the makeup of the focus groups, and they followed a semi-structured group interview format, each group consisting of between two and four pupils. I also taught twelve RE lessons, and analysed relevant official paperwork. The findings were triangulated through a further twenty-eight focus groups, a lesson with a whole class and an additional seven semi-structured interviews with staff.

My research was conducted among friends, and so it was important for me to consciously reflect on my presuppositions, my relationship with those whom I have studied and my role in creating the reality I have reported (Heikkinen et al. 2007). I had what were perhaps best described as "collegiate friendships" with the majority of the staff, established before I began my research, and close personal friendships with a number of staff. By "collegiate friendship" I mean that we were colleagues, engaged in the business of educating children, but we were also friends, able to discuss personal issues in the staff room and during other opportunities for casual conversation. They were typical of the friendships Coffey (1999: 47) describes as originating in fieldwork: strong because of shared understandings and fieldwork objectives, but also fragile because they only had meaning in the specific context of the school. Such close relationships did raise an important ethical dilemma about distinguishing research data from casual comments made to a friend. I resolved that only comments made in an overtly research focused context (such as a focus group or semi-structured interview) would be included. Casual comments might prompt further investigation, but were not data in and of themselves.

Questions of researcher identity: who conducted the research?

Questions of researcher identity have traditionally been framed in terms of a discussion of "outsiders" and "insiders." Anthropologists, striving for a more "scientific" and "objective" stance, questioned the validity of an insider perspective in fieldwork. In religious studies, the debate concerned whether an "outsider" could truly understand a religion and whether an "insider" could be objective enough to engage in academic research on their own faith (Stringer 2002). The debate has now become considerably more sophisticated than this simple dichotomy suggests, viewing insider and outsider as "umbrella terms which embrace variety" (Waterhouse 2002: 72), that is to say, both individual identity and societal structures are considerably more complex than a binary distinction can allow. To say that because I am an Anglican minister who conducted research in an Anglican school, I must therefore have been an insider in the research process is to oversimplify my identity. My identity is more complex than this, and many different factors influence how I was perceived during the research process. While it is true that I was an insider in terms of faith conviction vis-à-vis the school hierarchy, that same faith made me an outsider to the Muslim pupils whom I engaged with. Furthermore, a chair of governors is both an insider to the management of the school, but also an outsider to the teaching staff. My outsider status in this respect was clear from my freedom of movement: I was under no obligation to be in the school from 8:30 a.m. every weekday during term time. Having outlined something of the complexity of my own position, I will now examine further the debate regarding researcher identity in more detail.

As Sen (2006: xii) notes, we can simultaneously be members of many groups, without any contradiction. He suggests the example of a woman who is an American citizen, of Caribbean origin, with African ancestry, a Christian, a liberal, a woman, a long-distance runner, a historian, and his list goes on. If this person were to engage in fieldwork, all these factors could potentially influence the nature of that work. Thus Narayan (1993: 672) states that factors including "education, gender, sexual orientation, class, race or sheer duration of contacts may at different times outweigh the cultural identity we associate with insider or outsider status." Similarly, Bridges (2009: 108) comments that no individual is ever entirely an outsider to a situation, but always has some form of shared identity. At the same time we will never be entirely insiders to another's condition, as the fact of our individuality means there will always be something that sets us apart. We all have elements of both insider and outsider affiliation in any relationship. Longkumer's (2009) discussion of his fieldwork in Assam, northeast India, demonstrates how depending on the context and conversational protagonists he was both an insider and outsider within the same field-site. Likewise Collins (2002) notes the fluidity of his identity as a researcher and Waterhouse (2002) comments that her Buddhist faith made her an insider to her research with Soka Gakkai, but her lack of adherence to this particular sect within Buddhism simultaneously made her an outsider.

In line with the argument of the preceding paragraph, Donovan (1999) correctly argues that observer neutrality is impossible to attain, and even participant neutrality is very difficult to achieve. What is more appropriate is for a researcher to be reflexive, in order to avoid the danger of "romancing the field" (Coffey 1999: 97–113). Rather than define identity in rigid terms, least of all in a binary category, it is imperative that the researcher must recognize and state the issues that arise from his or her own positionality, discussing issues of power and representation of the field of research (Merriam et al. 2001). Self-awareness is of fundamental importance in the research process, since experience is messy, and attempting to provide an ordered account of observed reality is far more complex than it might initially appear (Hufford 1999; Milner 1999; Wolf 1999). While recognizing the limited value of the terms "insider" and "outsider" I will nevertheless continue to use them in order to help clarify my own positionality. I will discuss the opportunities and challenges of a more insider and more outsider perspective, before reflecting on my own position with my research field.

Some scholars argue in favour of a more insider perspective, reasoning that sometimes you must participate in order to understand. Thus Lobetti (2010) discusses fieldwork researching Japanese ascetic practices of fire walking and sword-ladder climbing, suggesting that without experiencing them for himself, he would not have been able to fully appreciate their significance for other participants. Similarly Knibbe et al. (2011) discuss participation in a number of religious rituals, arguing that since ritual involves more than verbal communication, it must be experienced to be properly understood. These could be thought of as particular examples of MacIntyre's (1999) claim that the researcher and his research subject must share religious convictions if true understanding is to be reached, although it is perhaps more accurate to state that experience from an insider perspective is recommended by some scholars as a route to a richer understanding of the significance of ritual in particular and group behaviour in general.

It is certainly true that genuine experience of a field will greatly enhance the researcher's ability to understand that field. But aspiring to an entirely insider perspective can be problematic. I will outline three possible concerns. First, it must be recognized that it is sometimes impossible to genuinely become an insider. Thus Irvine (2010: 224) reflects on his fieldwork in an English Benedictine Monastery, noting that his fieldwork was conducted "as a guest, who learns and leaves" since he was not a monk, nor even a novice but a temporary outsider, welcomed in, but never truly one of the community.

Second, attempts to gain insider status can also result in serious ethical concerns. For example, Mézié (2010) found that as a liberal atheist lesbian woman, her identity precluded any form of insider experience of the evangelical Haitian Christian groups she wished to research. She therefore feigned conversion to Chrisitanity in order to gain insider status. Third, perceived insider status may be problematic for the researcher herself. Trzebiatowska (2010) records the tension which existed between her own recently developed liberal attitudes and echoes of her more conservative upbringing when researching Polish Catholicism, both in her native Poland and in her adopted country of Scotland. For Trzebiatowska, being regarded as an insider by the research participants, whether Polish nuns in Poland, or Polish Catholics now resident in Scotland caused her considerable personal emotional stress. Aspiring to an insider perspective is therefore not necessarily straightforward.

Far fewer scholars of religious studies or theology argue in favour of an entirely outsider perspective. Wiebe (1999: 270) begins to develop the case by suggests that "epistemologically we can conclude that knowledge about religion does not require religious understanding or religious experience." Irvine (2010) argues that he was able to conduct valid research into an English Benedictine Monastery while remaining an outsider. Bridges (2009: 114-116) develops a similar point when he suggests that with patience, persistence and hard work, an outsider can begin to attain insider understanding. A skilled practitioner, working with appropriate tools, suitably employing imagination and empathy can develop a nuanced and sophisticated understanding of others' perceptions and understandings. Bridges (ibid.: 118-121) also outlines some challenges for an outsider perspective, especially the arrogance of claims to understanding on the basis of limited knowledge; the refusal to understand others in their own terms; the risk of outsiders exploiting insiders for personal (academic and professional) gain; undue invasion of privacy and overly reductionist explanations of complex phenomena and people. Being an outsider is no more problem free than being an insider.

My fieldwork was therefore not conducted from the single perspective of either an insider or an outsider. My position had elements of both, and during my fieldwork I oscillated between them depending on the precise context. This is entirely normal: as Marcus (1998: 118) notes, fieldwork inevitably involves being both an insider and an outsider. I will briefly consider seven aspects of my identity and discuss how each might be viewed on the continuum between insider and outsider. I conducted my research as an adult, white, male, Christian, who was vicar, chair of governors and researcher. As an adult, I was an outsider to the children, a figure of power and authority, but an insider to members of staff. As someone who is white British by birth (with

Polish maternal ancestry), I was an outsider to the majority of the pupils and parents I engaged with, not just the Muslims, but an insider to some pupils and staff. The fact that I know a few words of Polish, and my mother is a native speaker, was significant for building relationships with Polish pupils, for example. As a man, I was an outsider to many of those I engaged with, especially for Somali and Yemeni mothers of pupils in the school. As a Christian, I was an outsider to the Muslims, Buddhists, Hindus and atheists in the school, but an insider to those who identified themselves as Christian. As a vicar I was an insider to the official status of the school, but an outsider in the sense that I was not employed by the school. As chair of governors, I was an insider to the management of the school, but an outsider to the staff. As a researcher I was a complete outsider. This mix of identities was always present throughout my research, in a mutually supporting web that could not be separated, although different aspects would be foregrounded depending on the context. Thus when I attempted to engage with parents, it was my gender and my faith that precluded much meaningful contact with Somali and Yemeni mothers. When I conducted an evaluatory whole-class session, it was my identity as a researcher that was at the fore. When I took an assembly, I was present as vicar and as researcher. I was not a singular affiliation or partial identity, but a whole person.

Foregrounding aspects of personal identity

In the section above I have discussed my identity at some length. I turn now to foreground a particular aspect of my identity, namely my Christian faith. My identity is more than this singular affiliation, but nevertheless it was a significant factor in research with those of a different faith tradition, and so merits more detailed examination. Rather than understand researcher positionality in terms of the binary category of insider/outsider, it is more productive to highlight which aspects of personal identity were foregrounded by the research context and elucidate them in order to provide a clearer understanding of the researcher's own position. I will illustrate this point by discussing developments in consciously Christian fieldwork.

The case for a consciously Christian approach to fieldwork is set out at some length by Scharen and Vigen (2011), and also in the approach dubbed "ordinary theology" (Astley 2002; Astley and Francis 2013), which brings sophisticated academic theological reflection into contact with the reflections of committed believers who have undergone no formal or academic study of their faith. It is by no means an easy process. Scharen and Vigen argue that ethnography is a method for honouring and understanding God's handiwork, a way of Christian discipleship that enables practitioners to immerse themselves in the depths and complexities of the suffering present in the world and a means of witnessing to, and expressing solidarity with, those who are in pain or in need (Scharen and Vigen 2011: 73).

Similarly, Swinton and Mowat (2006: 91–94) argue that practical theology should go hand-in-hand with qualitative research. They suggest three Christian practices are central. First, hospitality, understood specifically as hospitality to research methods unfamiliar to the Christian (that is, those of qualitative research). Second, conversion, by which they mean qualitative research be reoriented to include recognition of God's action in the world. Third, critical faithfulness, which

> acknowledges the divine givenness of scripture and the genuine working of the Holy Spirit in the interpretation of what is given, while at the same time taking seriously the interpretative dimensions of the process of understanding revelation and ensuring the faithful practices of individuals and communities. (Swinton and Mowat 2006: 93)

Swinton and Mowat (ibid.: 94–98) outline a four-stage process for the qualitative research that is also a conscious exercise in Christian practical theology. First, recognition of the situation, the pre-reflective phase in which critical issues are identified. Second, the cultural/contextual analysis, whereby a deep understanding of the situation is developed. It is in this stage that qualitative tools are key. Third, theological reflection, where findings are analysed from a consciously theological perspective. Fourth, formulating revised forms of practice that are authentic to the situation but at the same time allow new forms of practice that will transform the situation.

All researchers work on the basis of an assumed epistemology and this section has briefly outlined a consciously Christian approach. The remainder of the chapter examines in greater detail three specific issues that arise from a Christian approach to fieldwork. These relate to truthfulness and the personal identity of the researcher.

How truthful?

The first question is how truthful should one be about one's own religious convictions when engaged in research with those of a different faith from one's own? This is especially relevant in the context of working within ethical witness guidelines. One of Theissen's criteria for ethical witness is the criterion of truthfulness about the religion being advocated (Theissen 2011: 236). I would extrapolate from this an expectation that a Christian engaged in fieldwork must be truthful about personal identity. To ask the question in a different way, how ethical is it to deceive or avoid in order to gain access to research participants, especially if one holds a personal faith conviction that prohibits such behaviour? This question is brought into sharp relief by the reflections of Mézié (2010), who, as noted above, found that as a liberal atheist lesbian woman, her identity precluded any form of insider experience of the evangelical Haitian Christian groups she wished to research. She resorted to lying, claiming conversion to Christianity, and minimizing or avoiding any reference to her own sexuality and areas of her worldview which conflicted with her participants' views.

My own fieldwork ethics were governed by the British Educational Research Association's guidelines (BERA 2011: 5–6), which clearly advocate openness, disclosure of purpose and state that participants always have the voluntary right to withdraw from research. Coming from a background of research with children, issues of power and deceit are brought into sharper relief, and concerns about honesty are perhaps more pressing than research in some complex areas of adult life where covert research is most likely to yield positive results. My fieldwork did not allow space for the type of deception practised by Mézié. But does this mean her approach is invalid?

Not all professional guidelines are as stringent as BERA's. Thus the British Sociological Association's guidelines include a brief section on covert research (BSA 2002: 4). These argue that in certain circumstances covert research may be necessary, as some participants may change their behaviour if they know they are being studied. In these circumstances, every effort must be taken to preserve the anonymity of the research subjects. Moreover, even if one has the best of intentions, it is not always practical to gain explicit informed consent from every participant (Calvey 2008: 908), and this is exacerbated if the research concerns activity that is illegal or socially unacceptable. Pearson notes that a researcher investigating illegal activity will be inevitably find himself in a situation where he is under pressure to commit illegal acts (Pearson 2009: 245). He details his research among football hooligans, explaining where he committed illegal acts in order to facilitate the gathering of "rich" data. Pearson acknowledges the lack of specific guidance in relation to researchers committing criminal acts in the course of research and states he expects this situation to continue because of the complexity of producing such explicit guidance. Perhaps the closest to guidance available are the recommendations of a team engaged in covert research of smoking in public places in Scotland (Petticrew et al. 2007). The specific Christian concern I have about covert research is whether the means justifies the end. Although Christians are discouraged from deceit, there is a rich ethical tradition of justifying deceit in certain circumstances, of which the classic example is a Christian lying about concealing a Jewish friend from the German authorities during the Second World War. At what point do the ends of research output justify the means of deceit about researcher identity and intentions?

Even if one does obtain clearance from the relevant University ethics committee before beginning research, the majority of ethical issues researchers face tend, as Dennis (2010) states, to be raised in the process of doing fieldwork, rather than prior to the work commencing. One's ethical framework is always therefore tested by the fieldwork itself. Furthermore, it is undoubtedly true that when you begin to negotiate access to a field site, you cannot tell the gatekeepers exactly what you want to do for two simple reasons: first you do not want to unduly prejudice your research, and secondly, you may not exactly know. Initial fieldwork discoveries, pragmatic constraints of time, access and developing contacts all influence and direct how a plan for fieldwork develops into the reality of research (Hammersley and Atkinson 2007: 210–212).

But these nuances are very different from Mézié's fabrication of her own identity. I personally do not think it is ethical for researchers to lie about their own identity simply to further their own research interests. As a Christian engaged in fieldwork, while I could justify deceit on the part of a researcher investigating criminal activity in order to inform law enforcement, I would struggle to justify deceit by a researcher solely to further her career. In particular, if the researcher is investigating the religious convictions of others, how ethical it is to lie about your own religious convictions while expecting others to be truthful about theirs? Granted this may preclude particular individuals from gaining access to certain field sites, but this limitation should be recognized and accepted; fieldwork should not be undertaken under such false pretences, especially if the authorizing institution claims some type of Christian identity, as in the case of so called "Cathedral group" universities.

Researchers, especially those operating to tight deadlines, or wishing to establish or advance a career on the basis of their research, might well be tempted to be less than truthful about their own identity when engaging in fieldwork. One could, as Mézié did, even deny one's own identity in order to obtain a degree of insider status with one's research participants. The long-term damage, both to researcher and research participants, is considerable. Mézié's own reflections are those of discomfort, disappointment and frustration, and although her participants are not given a voice in her reflections, I suspect that were they to learn the truth of her identity, they too would experience similar emotions.

Sometimes a researcher is unable to lie to gain access. Gilliat-Ray (2005) reflects on unsuccessful efforts made to negotiate research access to four Deobandi *dar ul-uloom* (Islamic training colleges) in the UK. But as she argues, even this failure to gain access nevertheless counts as a form of fieldwork data, and stimulates informative reflection, potentially impacting public policy and research practice. By remaining truthful about experiencing failure, Gilliat-Ray was able to contribute to an on-going discussion about the nature of fieldwork among a hard to access community, and provide an account that resonates with the experience of others, including, but not limited to those engaged in fieldwork. It is important that one remains truthful, even if this raises problematic issues related to access and progress in fieldwork.

This section concludes with a further example from my fieldwork, namely the interplay between my role as researcher and chair of governors. The presence of the chair of governors at school events, such as an international bring-and-share food event would cause little comment. However the presence of a researcher, questioning parents about their views on the school, is more problematic in this context, especially since a crowded and noisy room is not conducive to explaining the details of a research project to someone who speaks English as their fourth language. My experience of failing to engage with parents from a research perspective at such school events led me to change my fieldwork strategy. Rather than attend with an agenda, I attended simply to observe and participate as best I could, a strategy which proved much more effective for understanding the school and gaining access to have subsequent more detailed conversations in an explicitly research-focused context.

How forthright?

There is, of course, a difference between lying and remaining silent, and it is entirely ethical, and indeed often necessary, for a researcher to remain silent during fieldwork. An example from my fieldwork may illustrate the distinction. When I discussed beliefs about Christmas and Easter with focus groups of pupils aged eight to eleven, there was some confusion evident among some Muslim pupils as to what they should believe in relation to Christmas and Easter, a confusion also reported by Haw (2010: 350) among adult Muslims looking back at their childhood. Although many pupils were able to articulate an orthodox Islamic view of Christmas and Easter, some were much more confused. This is especially evident among a group of eight and nine year old Muslim pupils who told me in focus groups conducted in June 2011 that they didn't believe in the Christmas story, but were quite happy with the Easter story (the opposite of orthodox Islamic doctrine). For example one boy with Somali parents, who self-identified as English, said that for him Christmas was a problem because of "people singing outside your house when you're trying to sleep." He said he liked Easter because you get chocolate eggs. Similarly a girl who self-identified as Somali stated that in relation to Christmas, she did not "believe about the angel going to Mary", but that the events of Easter week were "all true." Another Somali girl said "some Somalis say that Christmas is *haram* but I don't know why", and also stated that she didn't see Easter as a problem at all. In an RE lesson on 12 May 2011, I read *Sura Miriam* to the class, which details the Qur'anic account of Jesus' virgin birth. I did not tell the class the origin of the text, but simply read it to them, and then asked them to tell me the source document. They all suggested it was from the Bible, and were surprised, and the Muslims quite pleased, to discover it was actually from the Qur'an.

The focus group conversations all happened in the context of my being engaged in academic fieldwork in the primary school, and so I did not feel it was appropriate to correct the pupils' misunderstanding at that moment. I was concerned that if I had done so, the pupils might then have become more reluctant to tell me what they actually thought about different topics. Moreover, I was not their teacher and the pupils did not ask my opinion on what they had stated about their beliefs, and so I did not have permission to correct them. This was not lying, but it was not being forthright about religious belief, an important distinction. The more formal setting of a class context did, however offer the opportunity for correcting a factual misunderstanding. But the class context was not always a place to be forthright.

The question of how forthright one should be is of particular relevance when one is discussing areas of doctrinal disagreement. As a Christian minister, the pupils were well aware of my views about the Easter story. Indeed they all attended school assemblies in which I explained the Christian understanding and encouraged them to decide for themselves what they thought about it. But in the context of research, they were also able to tell me about their own differing views. This included discussing whether Easter or Christmas were more problematic for their lived experience, as well as outlining the different Muslim understandings of the events of Easter. During focus groups, pupils were happy to discuss such differences, and we were able to have friendly conversations about them. However, in more public contexts, such as RE lessons, pupils were reluctant to engage with the issues. I suggest that concerns related to group honour and identity precluded individuals from doing anything other than supporting an entirely orthodox position. It was therefore important that I was not forthright in these more public settings in telling pupils what they should believe, especially since they concerned issues of honour and shame.

As Gilmore (1987: 3) notes, honour and shame are reciprocal moral values which represent the integration into or exclusion of individuals from a group. To simplify, honour is public esteem and shame the removal of that esteem. All societies operate with some form of honour and shame, and as was noted above, identity is complex, and no single facet dominates to the exclusion of all others. Nevertheless, it is generally true that many societies in which Islam is the dominant religion operate more in terms of shame than of guilt, and Muslim individuals take notions of honour very seriously. This has a big impact on behaviour, especially in the concept of how an individual's behaviour directly affects the status of the groups to which he belongs (Muller 2000: 46–55). Thus for an individual to engage in shameful behaviour impacts not only himself, but also his extended family and potentially his whole people group (Musk 2005: 67–88). Awareness of this dynamic was important when deciding how forthright to be: in the relatively personal and exclusive setting of a focus group, it was possible to be far more forthright than in the public and inclusive setting of a whole class, but even in focus group settings I had to be circumspect at times, as the following example illustrates.

I conducted a focus group with two ten year old girls, one British born to Somali parents, the other Sri Lankan, both Muslim, who got into a sharp disagreement about music. They were discussing a question I put to them, to the effect that although there is a debate about music within Islam, this is never a problem in their school. The Somali girl agreed, stating that it was *halal* (permitted) for her to learn the guitar now, but that if she were older it would be *haram* (forbidden). I asked her why this was the case, and she said that if she died now she'd go to heaven, so it was okay to learn it. I think by this she meant that she was a child and so could not be held accountable for her actions, but that once she reached puberty and became an adult, she would be, and so should not risk doing something that would get her into trouble. Her Sri Lankan friend didn't understand this at all, and started questioning her, saying that she didn't understand how it could be *halal* now but *haram* when she was older. The Sri Lankan appeared to think that there was no problem at all in learning the guitar and was trying to suggest this. The Somali girl got really irritated at this point, and when she was asked, "Why is it *haram* to learn guitar when you are older?" snapped "Because Allah says so", before turning to me and commenting "She's annoying me now." I decided at this point that things might get out of hand, so we moved on to the next question.

I believe the unstated issue here was the onset of puberty. The Somali girl's Islamic understanding was that, as a child she was permitted to do things, but that once she reached puberty, she would become an adult and so could not act so freely. She did not want to discuss the onset of puberty, a potentially shaming change, in front of a white, male Christian adult, and so expected her friend to realize this. However, the Sri Lankan girl did not pick up any of the hints (spoken or unspoken), leading the Somali girl to become annoyed with her. In this situation, there was no honourable way to explain the issue in a forthright fashion, and my only option was simply to move the discussion on, which I duly did. This was not an issue of insider/outsider status, but of reflexivity, cultural sensitivity and the ability to delicately manage a complex situation. Researchers must learn when to be forthright, truthful, or silent.

The distinction between pupils' willingness to talk in a focus group and reluctance to speak out in a whole-class setting related not just to discussion of orthodoxy but also orthopraxy. Decisions regarding fasting during Ramadan will illustrate the point. In the context of a focus group, Muslim pupils would tell me that they did not fast during Ramadan and that they had been teased as a consequence. But if I questioned a whole class about this, first they would deny such teasing ever happened, and second those who did not fast would not make their own experience public. The issue of teasing those who were not fasting was an instructive one: both myself and the school staff were clear it took place, and challenged pupils over it, but in the context of a whole-class discussion, the pupils themselves denied it took place, stating that to tease a fellow Muslim would invalidate one's own fast. The question in this context for me as the researcher is how forthright should I have been? I decided that in this instance I would have to challenge the pupils, and state that I have seen teasing occur, primarily out of concern for those who had experienced the teasing. Here I moved out of my role as a researcher and into that of vicar and Chair of Governors. This was because I believed that pupils' well-being was more important than my research outcomes, and illustrates the complexity and fluidity of researcher identity in the field site.

The challenge I faced as a Christian researcher was thus to be truthful to my own identity but at the same time to give those I was engaged in research with the space to be truthful to their identities. This meant maintaining a balance of being appropriately forthright while maintaining space for amicable disagreement. This is a markedly different approach to fieldwork to that advocated by Mézié, who invites comparison between an ethnographer and an actor:

> Like the actor, the ethnologist acquires bodily and performance capacities and ordinary faculties of the role he is going to play. He shapes himself, informs himself, trains himself and models himself on the contact with the Other, from which he wants to learn and understand the reasons for actions and beliefs.
> (Mézié 2010: 186)

If one is acting when engaged in fieldwork, then presumably one is not always forthright about what one personally believes, because to do so would compromise the role performed. Mézié recognizes this, but also recognizes the possibility advocated in this paper, whereby forthright statement and action on the basis of a particular belief dramatically shapes the fieldwork. The example she cites is of Florence Brunois, an ethnographer who was active in defending the territorial rights of the Kausa tribe in New Guinea (Mézié 2010: 188).

What must be recognized is that any position relating to truth and forthrightness will automatically set boundaries on the research. My decision to be clear on my Christian identity and to challenge teasing in relation to fasting at Ramadan probably precluded my discovering certain views of some pupils. Mézié notes that her public role of a convert to Christianity precluded her accessing information about voodoo practices (Mézié 2010: 189). The argument of this chapter is therefore not that all researchers must always be truthful and forthright about everything they do, but that any Christian researcher must make decisions about truth and falsehood on the basis of a Christian epistemology, not fieldwork pragmatics. As Swinton and Mowat note, Christian theological reflection does presume the existence of an objective truth, which is to be sought after, in a mutual critical conversation which respects a variety of perspectives and methodologies, but is ultimately grounded in a particular worldview (ibid.: 80–82).

How static?

It is common to observe that researcher identity shapes the research, but it is equally true that the research can shape the researcher. As Astley (2002: 21) notes, learning is change. This was my own experience. The question discussed in this final section is how static should a researcher expect to be? That is to say, should we expect the research we engage in to change our own beliefs and practices? It did change me to some extent. I was never tempted to convert to Islam by any aspect of my research (and indeed did not see any Muslims express any interest in converting to Christianity) but I was nevertheless changed by my research in two main ways.

The first change was my greater appreciation of Islamic beliefs. Lived and doctrinal religion are different things, and it is only after meeting and talking with those of a different religion that one can truly appreciate its teaching. Over the course of my research I have read a number of articulate Muslims scholars but more importantly have talked with well over one hundred convinced Muslims of a variety of ages about what they believe and why they believe it. Twice during my five years of involvement with the school where I did my research, I took an assembly on the wedding at Cana, in which Jesus turns water into wine (John 2:1-11). The second occasion was during my fieldwork, on 17 January 2011, and I realized that for many Muslims, the idea of a Prophet producing alcohol would potentially be deeply offensive, and so ensured I commented on this fact during the assembly. This was motivated by a greater respect for my audience, and a desire to engage with them in a way they could understand. These feelings were a direct result of my fieldwork with them.

The second area of change has been in my own Christian faith. Discussing with Muslims their desire to pray five times a day, even with those Muslims who do not actually realize this desire, has forced me to evaluate my own habits of Christian prayer. I was challenged by reading Tariq Ramadan's arguments about *halal* food, in particular his argument that an organically reared, free range hen slaughtered without any ritual practices, but over whom the formula *"Bismi-Llahi ar Rahman ar Rahim"* is pronounced before consumption may actually be more *halal* than a factory farmed chicken, slaughtered in an approved abattoir, where the formula may simply be played on a recording, or even said endlessly by employees as they kill chickens by the hundred (Ramadan 2009: 249). This forced me think about my own practices of meat consumption, and reflection on a Christian belief about divine-given responsibility to steward creation led me to think that I too should buy organic meat where possible.

Research is an active process and there is a symbiotic relationship between researcher and research topic. The fact that an Anglican Christian is engaged in research with Muslim primary school children does not preclude real changes occurring in the life of the researcher. Researchers should not expect to remain static, but be open to the possibility of being changed by those with whom they are engaged in research.

Concluding reflections

Some people may find it difficult to think of an Anglican minister engaged in ethically rigorous research with Muslim primary school children. However, I believe that I did so, and my reflections above illustrate how this was achieved. The chapter argued that for Christian researchers, truth about personal identity and honesty about intentions in engaging in research are of paramount importance. It developed the notion of how Christian epistemology must take precedence over fieldwork pragmatics, as for a Christian ends may not always justify certain deceitful means. Thus certain approaches to covert research are potentially not available for Christians engaged in fieldwork, although there are circumstances when covert research would be appropriate, for example to facilitate law enforcement. Reflexivity is central to this decision making process. The maintenance of a suitable critical distance between researcher and researched will enable appropriate decisions to be more easily made.

The second main point the chapter made is that being true to one's own identity does not necessarily mean being forthright. The research itself will demand a certain degree of caution about how much of one's own views are expressed, especially if those with whom one is engaged in research do not invite personal reflections from the researcher. Moreover, evasive answers may at times be necessary for the maintenance of good relationships within the field. Thus, while the chapter argued in favour of being truthful, this does not mean always forthright about what one believes.

Third, the chapter argued that researchers might experience personal change as a result of fieldwork. Part of a reflexive approach to fieldwork is an examination of personal motivations and an increase in intellectual knowledge may also translate into changed personal behaviour.

The chapter has argued that it is possible for a consciously Christian epistemology to undergird fieldwork. The decisions a Christian fieldworker makes may or may not be the same as those whose epistemology has a different foundation but the case has been made here for a truthful, but not necessarily forthright, approach to fieldwork that is open to the possibility of personal change.

About the author

Tom Wilson was awarded his PhD from Liverpool Hope University in 2014. He is an Anglican clergyman, and Director of the St Philip's Centre, an interfaith training organisation. He was formerly reviews editor of *Anvil*, an Anglican journal of theology and mission. His publications include *Hospitality and Translation: An Exploration of How Muslim Pupils Translate Their Faith in the Context of an Anglican Primary School* (Cambridge Scholars Press, 2015), and articles in *Fieldwork in Religion* and *Islam and Christian-Muslim Relations*.

References

Astley, J. (2002). *Ordinary Theology: Looking, Listening and Learning in Theology.* Farnham: Ashgate.
Astley, J. and Francis, L. J. (eds) (2013). *Exploring Ordinary Theology: Everyday Christian Believing and the Church.* Farnham: Ashgate.
BERA. (2011). Ethical Guidelines for Educational Research. London: British Educational Research Association.
Bridges, D. (2009). Education and the Possibility of Outsider Understanding. *Ethics and Education* 4(2): 105–123. https://doi.org/10.1080/17449640903326714
BSA. (2002). Statement of Ethical Practice for the British Sociological Association. Durham: British Sociological Association.
Calvey, D. (2008). The Art and Politics of Covert Research: Doing "Situated Ethics" in the Field. *Sociology* 42(5): 905–918. https://doi.org/10.1177/0038038508094569
Coffey, A. (1999). *The Ethnographic Self: Fieldwork and the Representation of Identity.* London: Sage.
Collins, P. (2002). Connecting Anthropology and Quakerism: Transcending the Insider/Outsider Dichotomy. In E. Arweck and M. D. Stringer (eds), *Theorizing Faith: The Insider/Outsider Problem in the Study of Ritual,* 77–96. Birmingham: Birmingham University Press.
Dennis, B. (2010). Ethical Dilemmas in the Field: The Complex Nature of Doing Education Ethnography. *Ethnography and Education* 5(2): 123–127. https://doi.org/10.1080/17457823.2010.493391
Donovan, P. (1999). Neutrality in Religious Studies. In R. T. McCutcheon (ed.), *The Insider/Outsider Problem in the Study of Religion,* 235–247. London: Continuum.
Emerson, R. M. et al. (1995). *Writing Ethnographic Fieldnotes.* Chicago, IL: University of Chicago Press. https://doi.org/10.7208/chicago/9780226206851.001.0001
Gilliat-Ray, S. (2005). Closed Worlds: (Not) Accessing Deobandi *dar ul-uloom* in Britain. *Fieldwork in Religion* 1(1): 7–33. https://doi.org/10.1558/firn.v1i1.7
Gilmore, D. D. (1987). Introduction: The Shame of Dishonor. In D. D. Gilmore (ed.) *Honor and Shame and the Unity of the Mediterranean,* 2–21. Arlington, VA: American Anthropological Association.
Hammersley, M. and Atkinson, P. (2007). *Ethnography: Principles in Practice.* London: Routledge. https://doi.org/10.4324/9780203944769
Haw, K. (2010). Being, Becoming and Belonging: Young Muslim Women in Contemporary Britain. *Journal of Intercultural Studies* 31(4): 345–361. https://doi.org/10.1080/07256868.2010.491273
Heikkinen, H. L. T. et al. (2007). Action Research as Narrative: Five Principles for Validation. *Educational Action Research* 15(1): 5–19. https://doi.org/10.1080/09650790601150709
Hufford, D. J. (1999). The Scholarly Voice and the Personal Voice: Reflexivity in Belief Studies. In R. T. McCutcheon (ed.), *The Insider/Outsider Problem in the Study of Religion,* 294–310. London: Continuum.

Irvine, R. D. G. (2010). The Experience of Ethnographic Fieldwork in an English Benedictine Monastery: Or, Not Playing at Being a Monk. *Fieldwork in Religion* 5(2): 221–235. https://doi.org/10.1558/firn.v5i2.221

Knibbe, K. et al. (2011). Why Participation Matters to Understand Ritual Experience. *Fieldwork in Religion* 6(2): 104–119. https://doi.org/10.1558/firn.v6i2.104

Lobetti, T. (2010). Fieldwork and Pain: Issues in Field Research Methodologies Involving Extreme Field Conditions. *Fieldwork in Religion* 5(2): 144–161. https://doi.org/10.1558/firn.v5i2.144

Longkumer, A. (2009). Exploring the Diversity of Religion: The Geo-political Dimensions of Fieldwork and Identity in the North East of India. *Fieldwork in Religion* 4(1): 46–66. https://doi.org/10.1558/firn.v4i1.46

MacIntyre, A. (1999). Is Understanding Religion Compatible With Believing? In R. T. McCutcheon (ed.), *The Insider/Outsider Problem in the Study of Religion*, 37–49. London: Continuum.

Marcus, G. E. (1998). *Ethnography through Thick and Thin*. Princeton: Princeton University Press.

Merriam, S. B. et al. (2001). Power and Positionality: Negotiating Insider/Outsider Status within and across Cultures. *International Journal of Lifelong Education* 20(5): 405–416. https://doi.org/10.1080/02601370120490

Mézié, N. (2010). "Wi, se kretyènn mwen ye" (Yes, I Am a Christian): Methodological Falsehood in Fieldwork. *Fieldwork in Religion* 5(2): 180–192. https://doi.org/10.1558/firn.v5i2.180

Milner, H. (1999). Body Ritual among the Nacirema. *The Insider/Outsider Problem in the Study of Religion: A Reader*. R. T. McCutcheon. London: Continuum: 23–27.

Muller, R. (2000). *Honor and Shame: Unlocking the Door*. Xlibris.

Musk, B. (2005). *Touching the Soul of Islam*. London: Monarch.

Narayan, K. (1993). How Native is a "Native" Anthropologist? *American Anthropological Association* 95(3): 671–686. https://doi.org/10.1525/aa.1993.95.3.02a00070

Pearson, G. (2009). The Researcher as Hooligan: Where "Participant" Observation Means Breaking the Law. *International Journal of Social Research Methodology* 12(3): 243–255. https://doi.org/10.1080/13645570701804250

Petticrew, M. et al. (2007). Covert Observation in Practice: Lessons from the Evaluation of the Prohibition of Smoking in Public Places in Scotland. *BMC Public Health* 7: 204. https://doi.org/10.1186/1471-2458-7-204

Ramadan, T. (2009). *Radical Reform: Islamic Ethics and Liberation*. Oxford: Oxford University Press. https://doi.org/10.1093/acprof:oso/9780195331714.003.0014

Scharen, C. and Vigen, A. M. (eds). (2011). *Ethnography as Christian Theology and Ethics*. London: Continuum.

Sen, A. (2006). *Identity and Violence*. London: Penguin.

Stringer, M. D. (2002). Introduction: Theorizing Faith. In E. Arweck and M. D. Stringer (eds), *Theorizing Faith: The Insider/Outsider Problem in the Study of Ritual*, 1–20. Birmingham: University of Birmingham Press.

Swinton, J. and Mowat, H. (2006). *Practical Theology and Qualitative Research*. London: SCM Press.

Thiessen, E. (2011). *The Ethics of Evangelism: A Philosophical Defence of Ethical Proselytizing and Persuasion.* Milton Keynes: Paternoster.

Trzebiatowska, M. (2010). When Reflexivity Is Not Enough: Doing Research with Polish Catholics. *Fieldwork in Religion* 5(1): 78–96. https://doi.org/10.1558/firn.v5i1.78

Walford, G. (2009). The Practice of Writing Ethnographic Fieldnotes. *Ethnography and Education* 4(2): 117–130. https://doi.org/10.1080/17457820902972713

Waterhouse, H. (2002). Insider/Outsider Perspectives on Ritual in Soka Gakkai International-UK. In E. Arweck and M. D. Stringer (eds), *Theorizing Faith: The Insider/Outsider Problem in the Study of Ritual*, 57–76. Birmingham: Birmingham University Press.

Wiebe, D. (1999). Does Understanding Religion Require Religious Understanding? In R. T. McCutcheon (ed.), *The Insider/Outsider Problem in the Study of Religion*, 260–273. London: Continuum.

Wilson, T. (2015). *Hospitality and Translation: An Exploration of How Muslim Pupils Translate their Faith in the Context of an Anglican Primary School.* Newcastle-upon-Tyne: Cambridge Scholars Publishing.

Wolf, M. (1999). Writing Ethnography: The Poetics and Politics of Culture. In R. T. McCutcheon (ed.), *The Insider/Outsider Problem in the Study of Religion*, 354–363. London: Continuum.

10

Imported insider/outsider boundaries
The case of contemporary Chinese Christianity researchers

Naomi E. Thurston

Introduction: the Sino-Christian discourse and theology outside the Church[1]

Why did I say that I was not a Church Christian ... ? ... Since I did not belong to any denomination, of course, I was not qualified to argue for my identity as a Church Christian. But why did I again confirm to other people that I was a Christian? Can someone who does not belong to a Church not say that he believes in Christ? (Liu 2015: 109)

In 1992, Liu Xiaofeng (b. 1956), Chinese academic and mediator of Western theology into Chinese discourse, was asked to give a talk at a German seminary about the emergence of so-called "Cultural Christians" in Mainland China at that time. The designation was given to a group of Chinese intellectuals, of whom Liu himself was in fact a prototype, who studied Christianity as a way of understanding Western intellectual history and a variety of social and historical phenomena shaped by Christianity, including Christianity in China. Some studied the Bible, though mostly from the perspective of comparative literature rather than as philologists or traditional theologians, while others delved into the works of medieval theology, Western Enlightenment philosophers, or contemporary thinkers such as John Macquarrie or John Hick. Some studied China's missionary history, which contributed to the early development of Sinology, with the nineteenth-century Scottish China missionary James Legge establishing the first Chair of Chinese Language and Literature at Oxford University. Others were interested in the sociology of religion and went on to pioneer the social scientific study of Chinese Christianity in post-Mao China. Some of these scholars, from diverse disciplinary backgrounds and studying Christianity for different reasons, explored Christian faith as part of their own intellectual journeys and in some instances experienced, as Liu

Xiaofeng writes, "a change in their individual faith". Liu highlighted the fact that, as "these Christians pursue academic studies or are creative artists, the expressions of their faith are not simply actions of daily life but also take the forms of academic and artistic achievements" (Liu 2015: 109).

When asked to comment on this phenomenon of China's "Cultural Christians", Liu himself was nearing the completion of his doctoral degree in theology at the University of Basel with a dissertation on the phenomenology of Max Scheler. While his degree might once have warranted Liu's designation as a theologian, this label would no longer be accurate, as he has since the 1990s shifted his focus from theological studies to promoting liberal arts style education based on the thought of the classicist and political philosopher Leo Strauss (1899–1973). In the early 1990s, however, Liu Xiaofeng was still establishing himself as the pioneer of what he and his Hong Kong academic colleague Daniel Yeung introduced as "Sino-Christian theology", *Hanyu shenxue* (Yeung 2009: 1), which Liu himself wrote about extensively and in novel fashion for the Chinese context.[2] Liu frequently takes up Hegel's judgment on Chinese culture as being "far removed" (*weit entfert*) from the Christian, Western, or European spirit, categories deliberately conflated in a discourse that, in an effort to understand and assess them, has creatively retraced the development of Christian thought. The questions that Sino-Christian theology was asking with some of its early promoters, and which some Chinese scholars in the academy continue to ponder, though most frequently under disciplinary designations other than "theology" as an *independent* discipline, were never primarily questions of Christian apologetics, although today a number of younger scholars professing Christianity hope that their research at some level might address issues of the Christian life and thus serve an audience beyond the academic sphere. But the questions asked by the first generation of Mainland Chinese scholars reentering academic life in the late seventies after the disaster years of the Cultural Revolution were not those of dogma for the sake of discovering what the Church's answer ought to be on given issues from the viewpoint of faith or biblical exegesis. In other words, there was no program among scholars to construct a Chinese theology for the Church, nor was there a concentrated effort here to systematize Chinese theological thought of previous decades, a project for which, as one interviewee explained, contemporary Chinese academics lack any direct professional incentive. What most scholars tended to publish were translations, works on the influence of Christian theology on Western philosophy, or even comparisons between the *dao* and the logos. Sino-Christian theology also pursued an open-ended philosophical inquiry focused on the history of Western thought and bringing a Chinese reading of this into conversation with its counterpart traditions in ancient China. While this may sound like a grand project, it in fact fits neatly into some of the humanities research that is currently receiving funding in the People's Republic of China, which includes a wide array of research projects on Chinese traditional culture and, with this, comparative studies, incentives that complement efforts at a reassessment and strategic celebrating of traditional Chinese culture, or selected elements, that reinforce a shared national and cultural consciousness.

Sino-Christian, or Chinese-language, theology, emerged as a field of scholarly inquiry played out in the Chinese humanities and social sciences and driven by some of these Cultural Christians who had not necessarily studied theology in the Western intellectual tradition, but who were working on Chinese reinterpretations[3] of that tradition (which they had studied "from the outside") from the linguistic and thought perspectives of Chinese experience. The task of Sino-Christian theology includes the translation of Christian theological classics into Chinese, initially somewhat unsystematically, from the early church fathers to Jürgen Moltmann and Hans Küng, which Liu Xiaofeng spearheaded after leaving Europe and co-founding the Hong Kong Institute of Sino-Christian Studies in 1994.

What is of interest about Liu Xiaofeng and the beginnings of this phenomenon, which has also been referred to as a cultural-theological "movement" in recent scholarship (see, for instance, Lai 2012 or Lai and Lam 2010), is not so much the rather unsurprising emergence and reworking of Western disciplines and some discursive paradigms in Sinophone academic discourse, but the ways in which promoters of Christian studies have positioned themselves and, more interestingly, how they have constructed the discourses of Christian theology and the wider field of Christian studies within a Chinese humanities and social sciences habitus. In essence, despite the documented appeal of the exotic and sophisticated and the association of some prominent and widely read intellectuals with the field, the Christian studies discourse according to the descriptions and definitions of its own participants remains a clear outsider vis-à-vis the academic mainstream. Positioning themselves in the margins of the academy, actors in this field claim a fringe position for strategic purposes, including retaining sufficient critical distance from the academic mainstream so as not to be expected to align themselves or their discourse with one of the competing ideologies of the day.[4]

While this choosing of an institutional fringe position might seem removed from the situation of a religiously unaffiliated, "objective" scholar of religion wanting to remain an outsider in order to provide a less biased account of what religious practitioners are up to, the professional anxiety about remaining "outside" so as to ensure a carefully guarded perspective understood to be less skewed is similar in that the outsider's position in both instances is upheld through narrative constructions. In both scenarios, moreover, the scholar-observers are protecting themselves or their critical research from the feared imposition of having to adhere to the internal demands of a system, or its mainstream mechanisms, the understanding of which their work also depends on. In the case of Sino-Christian studies, the scholars I interviewed were both anxious to separate their work from "theology" understood in the sense of service to God or theology as adoration (or any theologizing in the service of the Church), while at the same time identifying with networks of scholars and institutions among whom a number of key figures are actively promoting the development of a Chinese-language theology in academic discourse.[5] Almost all interviewees stressed that, at least in part due to the potential political sensitivity of its content, academic Sino-Christian theology would remain outside the academic mainstream indefinitely. Interestingly, the early Liu Xiaofeng, who explicitly places himself and his writings outside any denominational church context, wrote that "Christian theology is the faith-oriented contemplation and speaking about God's word, and this contemplation and speech as an event of faith happen[s] within a concrete national-historical language experience" (Liu 2015: 128). At the time he was promoting Christian studies, however, Liu also held that "in order to understand the word of God", Chinese-language Christian theology (Liu 2015: 130)

> must implement a kind of deconstruction of Chinese-language thought, and this is the effort of Chinese-language thought when it tries to understand God's word. This is precisely the historical hermeneutical problem of Chinese-language Christian theology – to leave behind one's own original ultimate reality and to turn to the word of God, which in itself is the faith event of believing in Christ. (Liu 2015: 123)

Liu Xiaofeng's particular brand of "Sino-Christian theology" (translated here as "Chinese-language Christian theology") may not be one that scholars in the field of Christian studies in Mainland China are developing today, but his early work on Christianity is widely referred to and thus still worth noting today.[6]

In the rest of this chapter, I turn to a discussion of the particular modes of outsider-ness that today are being discursively constructed by Chinese scholars in the interdisciplinary field of Christian studies within Chinese academic settings. I examine these modes with regard to the status and significance of the discourse itself as well as the positions of the scholars engaging in it. The insider/outsider binary of an institutional mainstream versus marginality warrants some consideration. While Sino-Christian studies are not an area lacking in academic prestige, as both my interview data and the popularity of notable scholarly works on Christianity demonstrate, Christian studies have no privileged space in the structural academic hierarchy, where religious studies itself as a second-tier national discipline is subsidiary to philosophy, and where theology as an independent discipline is studied at seminaries only. Further, while some conferences in recent years have included the disciplinary designation "theology" in their titles, most academic journals, conferences and university course titles avoid the term. In some instances, research centres that are known to focus primarily on Christian culture choose names that include "religion and society" or "Western culture", avoiding the term Christianity (see Starr 2013).

Insider/outsider binaries are also pronounced in researchers' self-reflexive descriptions of their own positions with regard to religious affiliation or religious faith. There is no clear dividing line in stances between professing religious adherents and non-adherents. One observer of the field, an intellectual historian, thinks that only those with religious faith should attempt to engage in Sino-Christian theology (a field not restricted to theologians in Mainland China), while another scholar, a self-professed Christian (unlike the historian), promotes the construction of an academic theological discourse that welcomes input from contributors whose point of departure is not religious faith.

Finally, a distinguishing feature of Sino-Christian theology, or what some prefer to call "theological studies", i.e. studies *on* theology, is the "inside/outside the Church" binary. "Sino-Christian 'theologians'" have been accused by theologians overseas or outside of Mainland China of doing theology outside the Church, a charge that sparked debate between Hong Kong theologians and Mainland Chinese scholars in the 1990s. The fields of Sino-Christian theology and Sino-Christian studies have diversified since then, and with some figures inside the church now researching Christianity at state-run institutions, the debate is still of interest. It certainly differs from debates in the West, where Christianity for centuries enjoyed many forms of institutional protection. Here the discussion has many other components. One is the "Chinese" element of Chinese-language theology. If any cultural construct enjoys institutional privileging apart from Communism or "Socialism with Chinese characteristics", it is the socio-political construction of "Chineseness" in contemporary political rhetoric. Efforts of the present administration to construct and embellish grand narratives that feed on Chinese essentialism, including the "Chinese Dream" and the strategic exploitation of the "excellent" elements of traditional culture, have sometimes encouraged scholarship that sustains narratives of Chinese uniqueness. In this regard, the question of whether or not the Christian religion can overcome its foreign image in China is of continued relevance for the Sino-Christian theological discourse. As one expert writes: "Christianity is often caught in the cleft of being seen as a 'foreign' religion by insiders and as 'Chinese' by outsiders, and having to defend itself against … charges of 'cultural self-colonization'" (Starr 2016).

Research on religion in the post-Mao habitus: from a globalized concept of religion to an inter-disciplinary study of Christian Culture

Sino-Christian theology in post-Mao China begins with the revival of open intellectual engagement, a period of vibrant literary production, reading salons, and the creation of new journals and launching of book series, the "cultural fever" that is ascribed to the intellectual climate of 1980s China. The period also saw the appearance of numerous works on Western philosophy, literature, and, in a decade marked not only by economic but also a cultural Opening and Reform, theology. Further, this is a time when new paradigms emerged for the study of religion, marking what has also been described as the rebirth of religious studies in Mainland China.

Writings in pre-Republican China relating to religion, according to He Guanghu (1950–), a prominent Chinese philosopher of religion, who until his recent retirement was based at Renmin University of China in Beijing, largely focused on the "three teachings" (*sanjiao*), Daoism, Confucianism and Buddhism, in the form of commentaries on religious texts and polemic by representatives of one tradition aimed at one or both of the others. He does not view these approaches as religious studies as the academic discipline is understood today.

Countering the view held by some that little or nothing existed by way of the scientific study of religion (history of religion or comparative religious studies) in China before the resurgence of religion and its study in the post-Mao 1980s, Christian Meyer has traced the development of the field in pre-Communist China, outlining

> how in the 1920s a "Science of Religion" (*zongjiao xue*) as a new discipline was not only discussed and called for by major intellectuals, but actually constituted an integral part of the discursive ways to approach the modern category of "religion" and apply it to the modern Chinese situation. (Meyer 2014: 304)

"Christian Chinese intellectuals" in particular, as Meyer further demonstrates, played an important role in developing the academic study of religion in Republican China and can in a way be seen as some of the pivotal forerunners of Sino-Christian scholars today, as the article also concludes:

> [T]he introduction of the discipline in the Republican period with its relations to public debates is strongly reminiscent of the more recent developments in Mainland China and can even be regarded as a precursor in the Chinese "genealogy of religion". (Meyer 2014: 344)

Further, "globalization of the 'contested category of religion' takes place as an *ongoing* process within a multitude of simultaneous processes and phenomena" (Meyer 2014: 304–305; emphasis mine). Thus, despite the recurring affirmations of religious "revival" or renaissance and the frequent highlighting of renewed and blossoming intellectual interest in religion during the "cultural fever" of the 1980s, it is against this backdrop that the substantive, amassing volume of scholarly research on religion in China today must be understood, that is: the backdrop of continued existence, rather than the supposed death and resurrection of Chinese religious life and, with it, a supposed "brand-new" Chinese study of religion, a field of discourse which in fact dates back to more than one hundred years ago.

It is important however to realize that the 1980s did, after the forced disintegration of intellectual life and extreme isolationism of the Cultural Revolution decade (1966–1976), bring about important reinterpretations of the *role* of religion in society (and with that a new discursive place and potential for the institutional realization of religious studies), a process in which Christian and other intellectuals with an interest in, or sympathetically inclined toward, religion played key roles. As Goossaert and Palmer summarize:

> An important discursive change occurred when, in the early 1980s, scholars were permitted to debate and reinterpret Marx's comments on "religion as the opiate of the masses", claiming that this statement applied to the role of religion in nineteenth-century Germany and not to the essence of religion itself. This opened the way for religion to be depicted as having positive as well negative factors. (Goossaert and Palmer 2011: 323)

Many scholars engaged in Christianity research today recall this era of reinterpretation and reassessment, a time when not only religious studies as an academic discipline but religion itself, as part of a discourse on transcendence, and religious thought and value systems as alternative frameworks and ethical orientations to be mined for Chinese national discourse (attempts, as it were, to think about theology politically within the Chinese context) were well received in Chinese society. New avenues of discourse were opened up not least through the advocacy of Christian thinkers and theologians such as Zhao Fusan (1926–), a Christian scholar and former vice president of the national TSPM Committee, who through his publications in the journal *Zongjiao* (Religion) ignited a debate between "Marxist hardliners" and those advocating a softer line with regard to interpreting Marx's "'religion is opium' dictum". Debates such as this one constituted more than ivory tower discussions. The so-called "Third Opium War", a debate "between the liberal 'Southern School' of religious studies ... and the 'Northern School' of more doctrinaire Marxist theorists" had, as Ryan Dunch points out, "direct policy ramifications". Dunch notes that

> [t]he debate came out of internal-circulation journals and into the open in 1985, when Zhao Fusan used the yearly session of the Chinese People's Political Consultative Conference (CPPCC) as a forum to press for a more liberal attitude toward religion ... Zhao ... was the most prominent Protestant intellectual in China, being at the time a deputy secretary-general in CASS. He pointed out the intimate links between religion and culture in all civilizations, and argued that simply labelling religion "a political tool of the reactionary classes" or "opium" was unscientific and incomplete as a representation of the objective reality of religion in society. His speech reportedly received a standing ovation. (Dunch 2008: 165–166)

The close connection between religion and culture, as noted here by Zhao Fusan at the CPPCC session in 1985 at the time of the cultural fever, is one broadly stressed by Sino-Christian scholars today, a connection lending itself to comparative studies between Western and Chinese cultures, a research agenda which the Chinese government has been actively promoting in line with an intensified focus on cultural diplomacy and soft power engineering (Starr 2014: 379). Culture was also, as Chloë Starr notes, "recalibrated" in the Hu Jintao years through Hu's explicit focus on "the importance of the task of building a culturally strong Socialist state" that sets itself the task of cultural construction ... to enhance the moral quality of the people and the scientific quality of culture itself (ibid.).[7]

Hu's stressing of the progressive and "scientific quality" of culture enabled its promotion to be seen as a continuation both of Deng's emphasis on science and technology and of Jiang Zemin's "Three Represents", particularly Jiang's emphasis on "representing the progressive course of China's advanced culture", which, in a globalized context can only be actualized in cross-cultural dialogue and exchange.

Insiders/outsiders vis-à-vis society: marginal intellectuals and intellectual vocation

Intellectuals have been described as culturally marginal (Billson 2005: 30), having chosen interpretive positions that, as Said (2000) finds, overcome the "logic of the conventional". Cultural marginality, unlike social (socially given) or structural (systemically imposed, institutionally conditioned), refers to a type of marginality that can be explicitly chosen and is not necessarily imposed by systemic forces or social criteria, although in the case of Chinese Christianity, structural marginality can and does play a role, further complicating the position of scholars researching Christianity in the academy. Individuals may choose positions of cultural marginality to deliberately distance themselves from the cultural mainstream of a social context. Examples include artists or contemplatives who may seek seclusion for professional reasons, introspection or self-cultivation.

Said further argues that "to be as marginal and as undomesticated as someone who is in real exile" allows intellectuals to probe more deeply into the issues they have distanced themselves from in some way (ibid.). According to Liu Xiaofeng, Chinese ethical values and means of addressing societal issues were traditionally informed by an "elitist ethics" (Liu 1995), an authority from above. The dominance of elitist-intellectual influence on public ethics has seemingly receded, elitist ethics having first been replaced by "party ethics" only to leave what Liu calls an "ethical vacuum" and give rise to popular ethics. Liu also notes that in contemporary China "groups of intellectuals have attempted to revive elitist ethics". Perhaps there is a middle ground intellectuals can effectively negotiate for themselves as positions of influence between the elitist and the popular. For many intellectuals the tension of such middle ground might best be held in roles of cultural marginality and interpretive positions of metaphorical exile vis-à-vis society.

As highlighted above, scholars in Chinese Christian studies have inherited a program of doing theology outside the Church from Sino-Christian theology's early initiators. The philosopher Wang Xiaochao of Qinghua University in Beijing sees this position as one of the defining characteristics of Sino-Christian theology, the other two being its academic nature and its stance of dialogue and openness (Wang 2005). One scholar in Mainland China told me that should Sino-Christian theology part ways with its current orientations, including its position outside the Church, he would be parting ways with Sino-Christian theology. For him, the academic agenda of the movement is central to its legitimacy as an academic discourse.

It is no surprise then that some of the Chinese scholars interested in Christian theology, who, as mentioned, have been referred to as "Cultural Christians", should look to someone like Simone Weil, who penned the following words, for intellectual and religious inspiration:

> ... I felt definitely and certainly ... that my vocation imposes upon me the necessity of remaining outside the Church, without so much as engaging myself in any way, even implicitly, to her or to the dogmas of Christianity, in any case for as long as I am not quite incapable of intellectual work. And that is that I may serve God and the Christian faith in the realm of intelligence. The degree of intellectual honesty that is obligatory for me, by reason of my particular vocation, demands that my thought should be indifferent to all ideas without exception, including for instance materialism and atheism; it must be equally welcoming and equally reserved with regard to every one of them ... I am under an obligation to be like this; and I could never be like this if I were in the Church. (Weil 2009: 40)

The French-Jewish philosopher and mystic Simone Weil (1909–1943) is of particular interest to scholars in the Sino-Christian intellectual scene. Not only was her writing important for Liu Xiaofeng; she is also cited as an influential figure by some of the younger Chinese Christianity researchers as someone admired for her strength of character and religious sensibility, as well as for her intellect. Further, despite her tireless activism, prompted by a deep sense of social obligation and compassion, Weil is known for her fringe status as someone who wrote about Christianity but remained deliberately outside the Church. She struggled with the issue of baptism. This is a characteristic Weil shares with the Cultural Christians, some of whom found Christian faith but decided to remain outside a Christian community (Lo 1999). Weil's reputation as an outsider has also been explained as an "[intentional choice] never to be an insider, regardless of the intrinsic merits of a given group, because she mistrusted the perspective of the insider" (Frost and Bell-Metereau 1998: 19).

While Sino-Christianity researchers in the course of different interviews repeatedly cast the lack of interaction between church and academy as a drawback, the call for more openness to church voices and a more regular exchange of ideas for many scholars does not mean that Sino-Christian theology is to become a theology of the church: this explicitly is not what is envisioned. Scholars with a clear confessional stance or those more theologically oriented also emphasize the separation of the two spheres. The need to uphold distinctions between the ecclesial and academic realms is emphatically stressed, although how to demarcate the various theologies in Chinese contexts is not a point on which researchers across the board agree.

Zhuo Xinping of the Chinese Academy of Social Sciences in Beijing draws a line between Sino-Christian theology as initiated by Liu Xiaofeng (Zhuo dates this back to the early nineties), and a theology which he calls "academic theology" (*xueshu shenxue*), in his words a "theology of academic inquiry" (Zhuo 2013), which should follow Greek philosophical reasoning without the supposition of the Christian, or any other, G/god. Zhuo also sets ambitious goals for a non-confessional theology in the contemporary Chinese academic context that is open to comparative study, seeks out religious dialogue and, most interestingly, understands itself as continuing a tradition that dates back to pre-Christian Greek philosophers and a time when the word "theology" was introduced to mean "discourse on God", rather than Christian apologetic. Zhuo contrasts this type of theological *inquiry* (Zhuo *does*, in fact, envision a questioning of and into ultimate realities) with non-neutral, faith-based theologies:

> Unlike traditional confessional theology, which inquires into belief in God, academic theology as defined here aims to inquire into knowledge about God, to be academically rigorous, and to take a keen interest in fundamental issues such as ultimacy, authenticity, eternity, supremacy, absoluteness, regularity and truth. It is resolved to ponder these issues deeply, investigate them exhaustively and trace them back to their roots. (Zhuo 2013: 25)

Zhuo thus depicts theology outside the Church and within the academic sphere as divided: one carrying on the legacy of the Cultural Christians and another as a theology of greater openness and religious diversity, resembling rather the study of religions, although a scholar of religions is not necessarily interested in the truth of the traditions investigated (this may not be a given either), while Zhuo's academic theology seeks ultimate truth.

This outsider or fringe position of theology outside the Church is thus an important one for Christianity researchers across the sphere. On the one hand, it recalls and in some ways continues the direction of the Cultural Christians who pioneered Sino-Christian theology with its present academic outlook. Further, it extends to other "brands" of theological thinking which explicitly identify themselves as outside the Church tradition *and* as non-confessional.

One question that can be revisited here is whether or not insiders can serve as objective interpreters or critics of their own cultural, religious and otherwise contextually particular traditions. The question might also be turned around. As Andrew Walls has argued, "[r]eligious commitment" constitutes an important vantage point from which to study religion insofar as it "at least presupposes the reality of the subject matter" (Walls in Cox 2006: 154). Ninian Smart's methodological agnosticism (Smart in Cox 2006: 160) may help solve this dilemma in theory. As concerns an understanding of religious sentiment or feeling, one of my interviewees argues that human experiences, sentiments and sensations connected with religious experience can be understood across religions as part of universal human experience. One need not necessarily accept this generalization to appreciate the implied intellectual effort, which is the humanities or social scientific researcher's honest attempt to identify at some level with the subject matter engaged. The question of being an insider or outsider to the Christian faith remains an issue that scholars in Chinese Christian studies wrestle with. Both scholars who confess Christian faith and those who do not have varying stances on the issue.

The division drawn here by some interviewees is the division between theology and the study of Christian culture. While in fact some scholars identifying as non-Christians are more interested in theological themes while some professing Christian scholars are more interested in other disciplinary approaches, this distinction seems to be a type of categorization that is accepted by a number of scholars as natural. One of my interviewees draws the same distinction when depicting Sino-Christian theology in the narrow sense as a theology constructed by Christian scholars and Sino-Christian theology in the wide sense as the research and translation work of academics who are "non-Christians" "collaborating" with confessing Sino-Christian theologians. Not all scholars, however, follow this distinction. In fact, Wang Xiaochao argues that "[b]oth Christian and non-Christian scholars may engage in this program. I would say that any scholar has the right to do it" (Wang 2005). Wang goes on to specify the position of Sino-Christian theology vis-à-vis the church:

> "Non-ecclesiastic" (or beyond denominational) is the first characteristic of Sino-Christian theology .... All Christian theologians agree that Christian theology should be "from the church", "for the church", and "towards the church". However, from my observation, Sino-Christian theology from its primordial design to its concrete actualization serves the whole society, including the church. It wills to satisfy the spiritual need of all people, regardless of their identities. In this sense, Sino-Christian theology is neither totally from the church nor totally for the church, but it has to face both the people on the inside and outside of the church. This is the key to talk more accurately about the role of Sino-Christian theology in contemporary Chinese society. (Wang 2005)

The tension of marginality and insider/outsider binaries: suspended in interdisciplinary space

Another way to approach insider and outsider positions in Chinese Christian studies is by looking at the field as not being anchored in a particular home discipline, but rather suspended in "interdisciplinary space". An interdisciplinary approach has been central to the work of the Beijing-based scholar of comparative literature and religion Yang Huilin (1954–). He explores topics and themes such as "intellectual dialogue between China and the West" at the time missionaries were translating the Chinese classics into Western languages, translations of Western literature into Chinese by Western missionaries, theology and language, postmodern theology and, over the last decade, "Scriptural Reasoning" in a Chinese discursive context. Yang presents his own approach of critically assembling selected themes in contemporary Western philosophy and relating them to theological problems, or issues of "meaning", in terms of responding to the "necessity" to protect meaning against the incursion of modern scepticism (Yang 2014: 96). He suggests that a "plurality of methods" can prove useful in this process, which is one reason to consult theology as a dialogue partner here. His work is not "religiously" aimed at a sort of a universal consensus. Rather, it emphasizes difference and offers a framework for engaging in dialogue. For Yang, theology is a type of language that any serious student of Western culture must acquire. In my opinion, the reading and teaching of Christian culture in Chinese academia today, despite the marginality ascribed to this field, relates to the much more mainstream concern of understanding, becoming conversant in, and dismantling Western thought.

We might try to place the rationale and basis of Yang's comparative approach in context. While deliberately writing from the "perspective of a non-believer" (Yang 2014: 79), Yang is interested in the Christian spirit, which he deems the shared inheritance of Christianity and the humanities: this explains his efforts to introduce a "theological perspective". For Yang, the history of Christianity as a tradition that questions its own premises and is open to self-examination and renewal, contains insights into the type of wisdom-seeking, intellectual encounters he is trying to promote in which no single discourse is meant to dominate. According to Yang, no participant in cross-cultural, or "cross-discursive", dialogue owns the discourse on God. Thus theology is brought into comparative discourses; but it is simultaneously denied an authoritative voice on its own subject. The tension, however, between speaking and silence is in turn balanced by the interdisciplinary/interfaith/inter-discursive equality that should characterize the exchange.

Effectively, ideally, there is no authoritative last word. As an effective outsider, theology gets to mingle, but it remains both institutionally and culturally on the margins relative to the mainstream academic discourses.

Commenting on the project of "Scriptural Reasoning" with reference to the Chinese classics and the "Westward movement" of Chinese culture (Yang 2014: 181), Yang notes that

> [t]o Chinese scholars, real understanding and interpretation of Western academic studies depends on disclosing the inner motives of those studies, diagnosing their subjects, and dismantling Western discourse. Consequently, the distance between Chinese culture and "other" ideologies and cultures can be highlighted. This, in turn, will help Chinese scholars to realize their own particular standpoints and to raise their own questions. It will ensure the mutually beneficial dialogue between Western studies in the Chinese context and Chinese studies in the Western context …
>
> Therefore, the primary condition for the de-centering of scriptural reasoning is to "let the other be other". (Yang 2010: 181–182)

Yang repeatedly mentions his apprehension with regard to the overemphasis on "seeking common ground", as well as the ethicization of Christianity guided by a paradigm of adaptation to existing ethical systems in Chinese culture. The "ethicization" focus is a method of inculturation that was first used to adapt Christianity to Daoism and Buddhism and later to Confucian teachings, a method that Yang warns runs the risk of negating the core of Christianity itself: a set of ethical values that should complement the context into which they are introduced is preached along with the proclamation of the "rest of the Christian message" and being fashioned as Christianity's central claim to legitimacy in the target culture:

> This assimilative method of making use of existing interpretive frameworks makes it possible [for Christianity], on the one hand, to enter the popular cultural system without too much hindrance. On the other hand, it must constantly activate its own most challenging elements in the course of mutual interpretation of heterogeneous concepts, and not merely obtain a place for itself by "seeking common ground". (Yang 2014: 55)

In this short passage, Yang touches on a paradox in the contemplation of marginality. In adapting to the cultural status quo, what is originally marginal may fashion itself as, and eventually metamorphose into, something with a more mainstream character. It may even become fully adapted, "inculturated" or "contextualized". If, however, in doing so, it loses the essence that originally required its adaptation, the question arises as to the need for its introduction in the first place.

Similarly, if Christian theology's "most challenging elements" are what prompt its introduction into Chinese discourse, then the position of "suspended tension" between and among various disciplines in the humanities may be seen as its "safest" *modus operandi*, should it want to retain and continue to trade in the resources that constitute its unique value. This may be one reason why Yang Huilin keeps returning to theologians like Barth and Bonhoeffer and draws attention to the "marginalization of God" in a "world come of age", a world "without a working hypothesis of God" as described by Bonhoeffer and to the "religionless Christianity" that the German theologian sketched out from his Tegel prison cell between the spring and summer of 1944. The essence of Christianity for which there is apparently real demand becomes neutralized in futile attempts to adapt it to the mainstream. Yet Yang, as already mentioned, explicitly identifies a place for theology in the humanities in light of a string of hypotheses, or, as here, post-modern theories, held out against it:

> In the twentieth century, we indeed see the marginalization of the position of Christianity in the area of secular life; yet in various thoughts of humanities involving "value judgments", theological perspective assumes an increasingly prominent and irreplaceable significance because the pursuit of "value" in secular arenas leads eventually to relativity of all "values". Through the deconstruction of "grand narrative" brought about by postmodern criticisms, Christian theology receives more room for exploration. To a certain extent, this room reveals a similar deep structure of humanities and theology. (Yang 2010: 97)

Conclusion

Interviewing scholars in Chinese Christian studies, I realized that the general willingness among interviewees to identify with a "theological movement" was confined to a small number. With some notable exceptions, scholars do not want to be seen as spokespersons for religious groups, or as public or church theologians. Further, serviceable though a movement would be to public discourse and debate, this is not the route most participants in the Sino-Christian discourse, whether participating in more narrowly defined theological study or not, presently favour.

Sino-Christian theology aims to protect and uphold its academic ethos over any confessional identity or church allegiance. If the movement were publicly known as a platform for confessional theology, it could face the unwanted situation of drawing Church criticism (which in some quarters it already does) rather than eliciting the exchange with disciplines in the humanities and social sciences that it seeks.[8] The field must then negotiate between protecting its unique discourse, and engaging in interdisciplinary dialogue on the one hand, and moving into the public sphere on the other: if indeed it wants to move beyond the academic margins, it needs to explain itself beyond the confines of those margins. How can this be achieved without the forfeiture of critical distance? Essentially, it cannot remain a-political. But what increased engagement would mean for the development of the Sino-Christian discourse, should it move in this direction, remains to be seen.

Beginning with the Republican era, "Chinese nationalism", as Vincent Goossaert recaps, "was built largely without, and even partly against, religion, and indeed, the whole of traditional culture" (Goossaert 2005, referring to Cohen 2005). If Chin Kenpa's assertion is correct though that there is real "hidden dialogue" potential between Sino-Christian theology and the New Left (Chin 2014: 27–52), a dialogue concerned with nationalism, notions of Chineseness, and the contemporary projects of Chinese nation-building, then Sino-Christian scholars could exploit this particular discursive exchange to bring religion back into the national discussion, as was attempted in the early twentieth century, on a more mainstream platform. This move has not yet been realized, as Chin points out, but it constitutes an important potential channel of conducting discourse beyond the fringes or margins along which Sino-Christian theology has in many ways, with notable exceptions such as the public "pro-Christian" stances taken by He Guanghu and other public intellectuals, positioned itself to date.

About the author

Naomi Thurston holds a PhD in religious studies from the University of Wales Trinity Saint David (2015). She is a postdoctoral research fellow at the Yuelu Academy of Hunan University, China, and the author of *Studying Christianity in China: Constructions of an Emerging Discourse* (Brill, 2018), which gives a fuller account of "Sino-Christian theology and Sino-Christian studies.

Acknowledgements

I am deeply grateful to the Institute for the Advanced Study in Asian Cultures and Theologies 2015, Chung Chi Divinity School at the Chinese University of Hong Kong, and the United Board for their generous support of my research in June 2015. In particular, I would like to thank Philip Wickeri and Bonita Aleaz for their constructive criticism in the drafting of this chapter, parts of which are based on Chapter 9 of my recent monograph (Thurston, 2018).

Notes

1 The Hong Kong-based advocates of this movement, whose translation work and theological journal have had some influence in academic Christian studies circles in Mainland China over the past 20 years, use the English translation "Sino-Christian theology" *Hanyu shenxue*, literally, Han-language theology, although "Sino-theology" has also appeared in print as a translation of *Hanyu shenxue*. The Chinese term has, as have some of its English translations, seen some variations, for example in the work of the Finland-based theologian and editor of the *International Journal of Sino-Western Studies*, Paulos Huang (b. 1966), who also uses "Sino-Christian Academic Theology" (*Hanyu xueshu shenxue*). For a recent introduction of the phenomenon of "Sino-Christian theology", see Starr (2014).

2 Initially, Liu offered his vision of a Sino-Christian theology in an article entitled "Sino-Christian Theology in the Modern Context", which appeared in the Chinese-language journal *Logos and Pneuma: Chinese Journal of Theology*, published by the Institute of Sino-Christian Studies in Hong Kong, for which he served as academic director at the time (see Liu 1995). One reason why Liu's Chinese texts on Western theology in the 1980s and early 1990s can be said to represent a "novel" approach in theological thinking is simply their packaging and context: newly founded scholarly journals on philosophical and literary themes that were widely read in the post-Cultural Revolution decade of the so-called "cultural fever". By the 1990s, the intellectual climate had somewhat changed and newly imported knowledge was now being systematized. Some critics point out, however, that translation projects in the field tended to be eclectic.

3 There is debate among Chinese and non-Chinese China scholars whether a field of study can or should properly be labelled "Chinese". If so, what does it mean to call an intellectual endeavor "Chinese"? Does this designate the identity, national or cultural, of the researcher, the language that ideas are communicated in, or a "Chinese" mode of thought or cultural consciousness? For another field, Ralph Weber addresses this problem. See Weber (2013).

4 While some vocal Christian intellectuals in China today are known to support liberal ideals and have been outspoken in human rights debates, including Christian human rights lawyers, academics in Christian studies do not champion one political agenda or even leaning across the board. Liu Xiaofeng for example eschews the label of public intellectual (*gonggong zhishifenzi*), claiming that those who describe themselves as such must openly side with either the Liberals or the New Left, presumably forfeiting a kind of scholarly critical distance.

5 A two-volume *Sino-Christian Theology Reader* published in 2010 introduces Chinese "theological" texts that date all the way back to the seventh-century Nestorian

Stele, through the Ming and Qing dynasties, the 1920s and thirties, and to the People's Republic of China. This collection not only introduces works that have in some way shaped or addressed the development of Chinese-language Christian thought, but also provides impetus for further research and theological work in the field. See He and Yeung (2009).
6   Liu is a prolific intellectual whose work has been criticized from different camps; certainly, there is no unanimous verdict on his intellectual motivations for promoting Christian theology in the Chinese academic world of the 1980s and 1990s. See, as an example of one critical voice, Lu (2014).
7   Starr quotes from Hu's speech given at the 17th Party Congress in October 2011, in which he portrays "soft power" as a defensive mechanism *against* "international hostile forces [and] their imposition of Westernization".
8   It should also be noted here that a number of prominent Chinese dissident intellectuals have converted to Christianity; some of these are now serving as Christian ministers in China or the United States, while others have taken their original careers abroad.

References

Billson, J. M. (2005). No Owner of Soil: Redefining the Concept of Marginality. In R. M. Dennis (ed.), *Marginality, Power and Social Structure: Issues in Race, Class, and Gender Analysis*. Amsterdam: Elsevier.

Chin K. (2014). Hanyu shenxue yu xin zuopai de yinni duihua [The Hidden Dialogue of Sino-Christian Theology with Chinese New Left]. *Logos and Pneuma*, 41 (Autumn): 27–52.

Cohen, M. L. (2005). *Kinship, Contract, Community, and State*. Stanford, CA: Stanford University Press.

Cox, J. L. (2006). *A Guide to the Phenomenology of Religion: Key Figures, Formative Influences and Subsequent Debates*. London: T&T International.

Dunch, R. (2008). Christianity and "Adaptation of Socialism". In M. M. Yang (ed.), *Chinese Religiosities: Afflictions of Modernity and State Formation*. Berkeley, CA: University of California Press.

Frost, C. J. and Bell-Metereau, R. L. (1998). *Simone Weil: On Politics, Religion and Society*. London: Sage.

Goossaert, V. (2005). State and Religion in Modern China: Religious Policies and Scholarly Paradigms. communication au colloque du cinquantenaire de l'Institut d'Histoire Moderne de l'Academia Sinica. Retrieved from halshs.archives-ouvertes.fr/docs/00/10/61/87/PDF/Paradigms.pdf (accessed 12 February 2016).

Goossaert, V. and Palmer, D. A. (2011). *The Religious Question in Modern China*. Chicago, IL: University of Chicago Press. https://doi.org/10.7208/chicago/9780226304182.001.0001

He G. and Yeung, D. (2009). *Hanyu shenxue duben, shang xia ce* [Sino-Christian Theology Reader, Volumes I and II]. Institute of Sino-Christian Studies (Monograph Series 35). Hong Kong: Logos and Pneuma.

Lai P. (2012). Cong Hanyu shenxue dao Hanyu Jidu zongjiao yanjiu: Hanyu shenxue de chuancheng yu fazhan [From Sino-Christian Theology to Sino-Christian Studies: the Inheritance and Development of Sino-Christian Theology]. In D. Yeung, J. Lam and X. Gao (eds), *Inheritance and Development: Essays from the 4th Roundtable Symposium on Sino-Christian Studies*. Hong Kong: Logos and Pneuma.

Lai P. and Lam, J. (2010). Retrospect and Prospect of Sino-Christian Theology: An Introduction. In P. Lai and J. Lam (eds), *Sino-Christian Theology: A Theological Qua Cultural Movement*. Frankfurt am Main: Peter Lang. https://doi.org/10.3726/978-3-653-00165-5

Liu X. (1995). Xiandai yujing zhong de Hanyu Jidu shenxue [Sino-Christian Theology in the Modern Context]. *Logos and Pneuma* 2 (Spring): 9–48.

Liu X. (2015). The "Chinese Language" Problem of Christian Theology. In *Sino-Theology and the Philosophy of History: A Collection of Essays by Liu Xiaofeng* (trans. L. Leeb). Brill: Leiden.

Lo P. (1999). China's "Apolloses" and the 1997 Crisis for Hong Kong's Theologians. In S. D. Ling and S. Bieler (eds), *Chinese Intellectuals and the Gospel*. San Gabriel, CA: China Horizon.

Lu X. (2014). The Crime of Lu Xun, Anti-Enlightenment, and Chinese Modernity: A Critique of Liu Xiaofeng's "Christian Theology". In T. Cao et al. (eds), *Culture and Social Transformations: Theoretical Framework and Chinese Context*. Leiden: Brill.

Meyer, C. (2014). How the "Science of Religion" (*zongjiaoxue*) as a Discipline Globalized "Religion" in Late Qing and Republican China 1890–1949: Global Concepts, Knowledge Transfer, and Local Discourses. In T. Jansen, T. Klein and C. Meyer (eds), *Chinese Religions in the Age of Globalization, 1800–Present: Transnational Religions, Local Agents, and the Study of Religions 1800–Present*. Leiden: Brill.

Said, E. (2000). Intellectual Exile: Expatriates and Marginals. In M. Bayoumi and A. Rubin (eds), *The Edward Said Reader*. New York: Vintage Books.

Starr, C. (2013). Classroom Christianity: How Theology Is Flourishing in China. *Christian Century* 130(3): 28–31. Retrieved from www.christiancentury.org/article/2013-01/classroom-christianity (accessed 22 February 2016).

Starr, C. (2014). Sino-Christian Theology: Treading a Fine Line between Self-Determination and Globalization. In T. Jansen, T. Klein and C. Meyer (eds), *Chinese Religions in the Age of Globalization, 1800–Present: Transnational Religions, Local Agents, and the Study of Religions 1800–Present*. Leiden: Brill.

Starr, C. (2016). *Chinese Theology: Text and Context*. New Haven, CT: Yale University Press. https://doi.org/10.12987/yale/9780300204216.001.0001

Thurston, N. (2018). *Studying Christianity in China: Constructions of an Emerging Discourse*. Leiden: Brill.

Wang X. (2005). Lüelun Hanyu shenxue yanjiu san tezhi [On the Three Characteristics of Sino-Christian Theology]. *ISCS Newsletter* (Spring). Retrieved from www.iscs.org.

hk/Common/Reader/Channel/ShowPage.jsp?Cid=190&Pid=8&Version=0&Charset=iso-8859-1&page=0 (accessed 22 February 2016).
Weber, R. (2013). Why Talk About Chinese Metaphysics? *Frontiers of Philosophy in China* 8(1): 99–119.
Weil, S. (2009). Letter V: Her Intellectual Vocation. In J. M. Perrin (ed.), *Waiting for God*. New York: Harper.
Yang H. (2010). The Value of Theology in the Humanities: Possible Approaches to Sino-Christian Theology. In P. Lai and J. Lam (eds), *Sino-Christian Theology: A Theological Qua Cultural Movement*. Frankfurt am Main: Peter Lang.
Yang H. (2014). *China, Christianity, and the Question of Culture*. Waco, TX: Baylor.
Yeung, D. (2009). Xuyan. Yige bu tingliao de gushi: Hanyu shenxue [Preface. An Unstoppable Story: Sino-Christian Theology]. In G. He and D. Yeung (eds), *Hanyu shenxue duben, shang xia ce* [*Sino-Christian Theology Reader, Volumes I and II*]. Institute of Sino-Christian Studies (Monograph Series 35). Hong Kong: Logos and Pneuma.
Zhuo X. (2013). *Christianity*. Leiden: Brill.

Unpublished sources: interview and survey data

Interviews 1–48. Personal interviews with the author. 18 August 2011 to 16 December 2013. Audio files and transcripts.
Questionnaire Responses. Sent to and collected by the author. August to September 2011. Email correspondence.

PART II
CONTESTED IDENTITIES IN THE STUDY OF RELIGION

11

Close encounters of a guru kind
Ethnographic research as encounters with the cognitive worlds of others

Steven Jacobs

This chapter reflects on my experiences of undertaking fieldwork in religious communities of which I am ostensibly not a member. In other words, this would seem to be a classic case of the "outsider" undertaking ethnographic research in order to gain some understanding of an unfamiliar cultural setting. The specific stimuli for this paper were encounters I had with two Hindu gurus: Swami Divyananda Saraswati – the head of a traditional Hindu lineage – and Sri Sri Ravi Shankar[1] – the founder of a global meditation movement called Art of Living (AOL).

Traditional ethnographic research, or what is sometimes referred to as ethnographic realism, suggests that research involves a linear trajectory in which the outside researcher moves from a state of cultural ignorance, negotiates access to the field, followed by a subjective experience in the field, and finally writing an objective account of the field experiences. Another way of expressing this is that ethnographic accounts entail a movement from outsider to insider and back. The assumed distinction between insider and outsider is inherently implicated with the apparent opposition between subjectivity and objectivity. Subjective experience is critical to ethnographic research, but this subjectivity has to be represented in objective terms. Subjective accounts by outsiders of their field experiences, it is argued by ethnographic realists, are anecdotal and trivial. Similarly, the subjective accounts of insiders, it is suggested, lack critical distance, are merely apologetics for particular religious traditions, and therefore both biased and lack insight.

Traditional ethnographic research suggests that there is a straightforward binary opposition between the insider and the outsider. However, this dichotomy is increasingly being challenged. Sonya Dwyer and Jennifer Buckle (2009: 60) observe "holding membership of a group does not denote complete sameness within that group. Likewise, not being a member of a group does not denote complete difference". Research is interactional and takes place in a third space "a space of paradox, ambiguity, and ambivalence, as well as conjunction and disjunction" (Dwyer and Buckle 2009: 60).

It is often suggested that the critical aspect of ethnographic research is that the outsider must undertake prolonged participation in the world of the other in order to gain any significant understanding of the insider's worldview. My encounters with these two Hindu gurus were both extremely brief – so fleeting in fact that they could be construed as a failure to access the insider's world, and therefore of no ethnographic worth. However, I maintain that a reflection on any interaction in this "third space" – no matter how brief – can lead to significant insight.

I will first briefly describe these two encounters. I use the term "encounter" very deliberately as it has connotations of both meeting with and experiencing difficulties. These two anecdotal accounts are consistent with the narrative of arrival that is a common convention in ethnographic monographs. Narratives of arrival are frequently placed at the beginning of accounts, and give some – often humorous – details of the ethnographer's discomfort on arriving in an unfamiliar cultural context.

Encounter one: the acharya of Kailash Ashram

In 2009 I was in the Hindu pilgrimage town of Rishikesh in northern India. Hindus regard Rishikesh as a particularly sacred place and a vast number of spiritual communities have been established in the area. There is an informal hierarchy among these communities, and by far the most respected institution in the area is Kailash Ashram. This first of the major ashrams in the area was founded in 1880 by Swami Dhanrajgiri (Keemattam 1997: 29). The current head of this ashram, Swami Divyananda Saraswati, is often referred to as *acharya*[2] – a title accorded to the most respected spiritual preceptors and which indicates an individual who is well versed in the Sanskrit texts. For many Hindus the incumbent head of Kailash Ashram is regarded as the most senior religious figure in an area that is swarming with swamis, sadhus, sannyasins and pilgrims.

A local friend who was helping me in my research came to me one day in great excitement, as he had obtained an interview for me with this revered *acharya*. This was quite a coup and could potentially provide some very useful data for the project that I was working on. On the appointed day we went to Kailash Ashram, and were only kept waiting for about half an hour – a relatively short wait for an appointment with a very senior religious figure – before being ushered into Swami Divyananda's august presence. The *acharya* was sitting on a *gaddi* – a large chair, almost like a throne, to which traditionally only very senior religious figures are entitled. We sat on the floor looking up at Divyananda. Once my friend had explained in Hindi who I was and what I wanted, the *acharya* looked imperiously down at me. In my field notes I observe that this encounter felt a bit like being back in kindergarten.

I began by thanking Swami for his time, and asked him: "Can you tell me about Kailash Ashram?" His response was rather abrupt and caught me by surprise: "No", he answered. So I asked him: "Will you tell me about your beliefs?" Again the answer was "No". Clearly this line of questioning was not resonating with Swami Divyananda, so I thought that I would try and ascertain what he considered worth knowing, so I asked him: "What can you tell me Swamiji?"[3] "Nothing, you may go now" was his dismissive response, and we were ushered rapidly away.

Encounter two: His Holiness Sri Sri Ravi Shankar

In August 2011 I was again in India, undertaking fieldwork for a different project. I was staying at the International Centre of the Art of Living (AOL), in Bangalore. To cut a long story short, AOL may be considered as both what Maya Warrier (2005) terms a transnational guru organization, and what elsewhere (Jacobs 2015) I have called a Hindu-derived meditation network. Although different, AOL shares many similarities with Transcendental Meditation. Like Transcendental Meditation, AOL offers a number of courses, and I was in Bangalore to take one of their advanced courses as a participant observer.

One day there was great excitement as it was announced that Sri Sri Ravi Shankar, the founder and spiritual preceptor of AOL would meet all of us who were taking the course. We were duly shown to the part of the ashram where Sri Sri Ravi Shankar held his audiences – or *darshan*. *Darshan* is an important concept in Hindu devotionalism. It translates as "sight". When a Hindu goes to a temple or visits a guru, they often express this as going for *darshan*. This is a two way process in which the devotee both sees and is seen by the sacred, either in the form of an image in the temple or in the human form of their guru. Meeting the guru of this large transnational organization was managed with almost military precision, as so many devotees are always very eager to meet with Sri Sri Ravi Shankar. We were instructed to sit in parallel lines, each line facing one other line. There were about 80 of us in total. There was an air of hushed anticipation. Suddenly everyone strained to see the guru as he entered in his customary white robes and clutching a flower. He walked between the facing lines; six to eight people stood at a time and clustered around Sri Sri Ravi Shankar. Many of the devotees knelt on the floor and touched his feet – a traditional sign of respect. The rest of us remained seated and waited expectantly. Sri Sri Ravi Shankar spent a few minutes exchanging a few words and smiling benevolently with each group before moving on. When Sri Sri Ravi Shankar got to my vicinity we stood up. I was the obvious one who stood out, being the only person who had taken the course from a non-South Asian background.[4] Sri Sri Ravi Shankar asked me about what I had got from participating in the advanced course, to which I had a stock and as truthful a reply as I could muster, and I indicated that I had found it "challenging, but rewarding". Many of the other participants articulated their experience of doing the course as transformative, which I honestly did not. I am not sure how satisfied Sri Sri Ravi Shankar was with my response, and after beaming at me he quickly moved on.

Reflexivity

These two encounters are the starting point for a reflection on some key aspects of ethnographic fieldwork. Charlotte Davis (2002: 4) defines reflexivity as "a turning back on oneself, a process of self-reference". Reflexivity is not simply some sort of navel gazing activity, but is an acknowledgement that all research is situated, and consequently inherently imbricated with issues of subjectivity and objectivity. Research is situated in both the – often unacknowledged – ideological context of the academic discipline and the presuppositions of the researcher. Since the development of standpoint theory in feminist scholarship, the notion of objective knowledge "the separation of the knower from what he knows" (Smith 2004: 24) is no longer tenable. The knower has to be included in any account of what is represented as knowledge. David Hufford (1999: 295) observes that "reflexivity in knowledge-making involves bringing the subject, the "doer" of the knowledge-making, back into the account of knowledge".

Reflexivity is particularly important in ethnographic research as the ethnographer, by definition, is more than any other type of researcher inherently a part of the research context. As ethnographic research is interactional – an interaction between the researcher and those people who inhabit the ethnographic field that the researcher is interested in – the ethnographer cannot be left out of the account of knowledge. Reflexivity involves what Bourdieu (1977) calls a break. In fact reflexivity involves a double break, which involves both critical distance from the religious and cultural group being studied, and also a critical distance from one's own theoretical and personal perspectives.

Bourdieu's call for a double-break requires the ethnographer to creatively imagine that they are a stranger to themselves as well as to others.

Most ethnographers are sceptical of accounts that fail to maintain some critical distance between the researcher and the researched. Producers of these accounts are often rather scathingly categorized as "going native". The failure to create any critical distance between researcher and researched results in an apologetic description and fails to produce any analytical understanding. The outsider ethnographer who has been in effect converted to the worldview of the insider is accused of no longer able to produce a valid and analytical account of the insider's world. The criticism that the ethnographer who has gone native, and cannot produce a critical account, suggests an inverse relationship between outsider academic and insider adherent fails to take into account that insiders and outsiders are not homogenous groups. There is no simple inverse relationship between outsider academic and insider adherent. There are clearly degrees of participation in any particular religious tradition or cultural group (see Jacobs 2015: 148–150). Furthermore, insiders can adopt a critical approach to an analysis of their own traditions. Conversely outsiders are not simply neutral observers, but come with their own perspectives that impact on what and how they observe.

Consequently, the break that Bourdieu calls for is the creation of a critical distance between the researcher and their own personal history and theoretical presuppositions. Bourdieu (1977: 3) argues that this second break "is needed in order to grasp the limits of objectivist knowledge". Mats Alvesson and Kaj Sköldberg (2009: 9) describe this reflection as turning "attention inwards towards the person of the researcher, the relevant research community, society as a whole, intellectual and cultural traditions, as well as the problematic nature of language and narrative in the research context". Alevesson and Sköldberg (ibid.: 9) suggest that reflexivity can be defined as "the interpretation of interpretation".

Reflexivity challenges the ethnographic realist's claim that the observer can give some objective, neutral account of the other. Reflexivity also challenges Malinowski's assertion in his seminal book *Argonauts of the Western Pacific*, first published in 1922, that "the final goal of ethnography is to grasp the native's point of view, his relation to life, to realise *his* vision of *his* world" (Malinowski 1978: 19). I also argue that reflexivity challenges a phenomenological approach to the study of religion. Drawing on the philosophy of Edmund Husserl, phenomenologists of religion appropriate the concepts of *epoche* – bracketing out presuppositions and *eidetic vision* "seeing into the very nature or meaning of what exists in the world" (Cox 1996: 19). James Cox (ibid.: 29) suggests that "the phenomenologist of religion must "get inside" the religion he is studying and view the world, as far as possible, as a believer does" – a view very similar to Malinowski's call to "grasp the native's point of view".

A phenomenological approach to the study of religion is a noble endeavour, and is certainly a necessary corrective to the evaluative accounts of other religions by colonials, missionaries, and other political and religious zealots. However, I would agree with Nancy Scheper-Hughs, who observes:

> Both the danger and *the value* of anthropology lie in the clash and collision of cultures and interpretations as the anthropologist meets her subjects in a spirit of open engagement, frankness and receptivity. (Scheper-Hughs 2000: 172)

Reflexivity contributes to an understanding of one's own position as a researcher in relationship to those being researched. It also contributes to the breaking of what Paul Rabinow (1977: 4) calls the double bind of anthropology in which the significance of ethnographic research is the subjective experience of field work, yet once returning from the field all that is important is "the objective data" that one has gathered.

Many ethnographers try to circumvent this double bind of subjective experience and objective data through what is sometimes called a chapter of arrival. In the opening chapter of an ethnographic monograph the author uses the personal pronoun, often providing an amusing subjective account of their personal experience of trying to fit in with an alien cultural milieu. These narratives of arrival are very similar to the anecdotal accounts of my encounters with the gurus that I recount at the beginning of this chapter. Narratives of arrival emphasize the ethnographic assertion that the research is valid because the researcher was present at the events described. However, for the majority of the ethnographic monograph personal pronouns often disappear and the passive voice is frequently used, which gives an impression that the ethnographer stands above in a privileged and objective relationship to the people with whom s/he is engaged. Narratives of arrival also suggest the possibility of learning other cultures, and the movement from the culturally ignorant outsider to the, to use Morris Freilich's term, "marginal native" (cited in Hammersley and Atkinson 1989: 100). The marginal native, although not necessarily fully incorporated in the new cultural context, are culturally competent – and viewed as an honorary insider as it were.

A good example of a narrative of arrival can be found in Ann Grodzins Gold's (1990) excellent account of Rajasthani pilgrims. In the opening chapter Gold provides an amusing account of how she struggled to find an appropriate mode of dress which was acceptable to all the various demographic groups in the village – Muslims, Rajputs, Brahmins – where she was doing her research (Gold 1990: 13–14). This itself is indicative that there is no simple monolithic insider perspective. After this introduction chapter, Gold predominantly uses the third person in her exposition on the Rajasthani pilgrims. This gives the impression that her book is essentially an objective and neutral account of the lives of Rajasthani pilgrims and not a subjective record of her personal experiences in the ambiguous third-space of ethnographic encounters.

Reflexivity is critical as it elucidates a number of significant and interconnected aspects of ethnographic research. Reflexivity is concerned with the nature of field relationships, and in particular a consideration of access. Reflexivity engages with the epistemological debate of what constitutes valid knowledge, the relationship between subjective and objective knowledge, and in particular the nature of participant observation. Consideration of epistemological issues will also impact on the rhetorical style of writing ethnographic monographs. Reflection therefore can challenge the conventional description of ethnography, which holds that the task for the outsider is "to make the strange familiar" while the challenge for the insider is "to make the familiar strange".

As I have indicated, my brief encounters ostensibly are those of the outsider. However, in the two encounters my outside status was slightly different. We live in complex and overlapping worlds, and the way in which my world intersects with the *acharya* of Kailash Ashram is different to that of Sri Sri Ravi Shankar's and AOL. Kailash Ashram primarily provides young men from the Hindu community the opportunity to study Sanskrit texts. AOL is an international meditation group that promotes a particular breathing technique for overcoming stress (see Jacobs 2015). Consequently, while I share little in common with the demographic group at Kailash ashram, there are a number of ways in which my world intersects with participants in AOL. Participants in AOL are drawn from well beyond the Hindu community, and I encountered many individuals, both in the UK and in other parts of the world, whose demographic and educational background was in many ways similar to mine. Just as the insider group is not homogenous, neither is the world of the academic outsider. Nonetheless, because I was neither particularly interested in the exegesis of Sanskrit texts, nor was my experience of doing the AOL course personally transformative, it could be argued that my encounters with these two worlds was desultory at best, and I could in no way be said to have grasped the "native's point of view". Nonetheless, I argue that the outsider's failure "to grasp the native's point of view" is not an obstacle to ethnographic research, but that reflection on ethnographic encounters – even those as fleeting as my meetings with the two gurus – provides valuable insight into the cognitive world of others. However this insight is always from a particular standpoint grounded in the personal and cultural context of the ethnographer.

Access

One of the main issues for the ethnographer as outsider is the issue of access. The issue of access is frequently articulated in terms of gatekeepers. The term "gatekeeper" is itself problematic, as it suggests that there is some sort of wall that separates the insider's world from that of the outsider's world, and there are very limited ways of accessing the religious and spiritual worlds of others. However, as we tend to inhabit a multiplicity of intersecting worlds, boundaries between the insider and the outsider worlds are much more permeable than the metaphor of the gatekeeper suggests.

The mainstay of ethnographic research is fieldwork. This is defined by Schensul, Schensul and LaCompte (1999: 70) as when researchers "leave their own communities, institutional settings, and familiar behavioural and cognitive patterns to enter another social world – the world in which the research is to be conducted". This points to two types of access, which may be termed practical and cognitive access. Practical access involves the formal permissions required to enter the field, whereas cognitive access is associated with the idea of finding out "what is really going on". One of the questions that I address is: can the outsider achieve cognitive access in any real sense?

It is often assumed that practical access is a necessary, but not sufficient requirement, for cognitive access. However, practical and formal access to the field is in some part also contingent upon cognition. Attila Bruni (2006: 138) observes that "there is no substantial reason for assuming that negotiating access takes place in a dimension unconnected with the actors' everyday logics and practices of action". You have to know something about the social world that you wish to enter in order to identify gatekeepers, and know how to communicate effectively with gatekeepers. Bruni (ibid.: 147) suggests that "the tipping point in the negotiation [for access] often comes when the researcher manages to show that s/he belongs to the same world as the actors". If this tipping point is not reached, does this represent a barrier to ethnographic research? I will argue that lack of practical access is not necessarily an insurmountable obstacle to some degree of cognitive access as "negotiation of access may be an important moment of observation per se" (ibid.: 138). I will also argue that there are severe limitations to cognitive access, yet this itself does not invalidate ethnographic research.

Sophie Gilliat-Ray's paper *Closed Worlds* is an account of how she failed, despite her best efforts, to gain any formal permission to access a number of Islamic Deobandi seminaries in the UK. Gilliat-Ray's paper is not simply methodological musings about the nature of access, but I would agree with her observation that under certain circumstances "lack of access in itself constitutes a form of data" (Gilliat-Ray 2005: 10). Gilliat-Ray explores the ideological and cultural aspects of these communities that are revealed through her failure to gain any formal access. For example, failure to gain access indicated something about the nature of authority within these seminaries. Gilliat-Ray (ibid.: 21) suggests that failure to access one of the seminaries demonstrated "the centralization of Deobandi power in Britain".

My experience with the *acharya* of Kailash ashram could be understood in terms of gaining practical access, but failing to gain any cognitive access. There was clearly almost no communication between Swami Divyananda Saraswati and myself. One way of interpreting this failure of communication is to suggest that my, less than a couple of minutes, encounter was useless. We inhabit different interpretive communities – I failed to comprehend the *acharya*'s world, and therefore did not frame questions in a way that he could relate to. Conversely, for Swami Divyananda Saraswati, the world of the Western academic was equally closed. However, this brief encounter does reveal some useful data about the world of the *acharya*. As Hammersley and Atkinson (1989: 14) observe, "how people respond to the presence of the researcher may be as informative as how they react to other situations". Divyananda's, albeit rather dismissive, response to my presence is informative. While this is not the place to discuss this in any depth, I will very briefly allude to two aspects revealed by this encounter. First, Divyananda's response indicates a great deal about the nature of authority and status of the *acharya* himself. Second, my dismissal provides an indication of what constitutes valid knowledge in Kailash Ashram. In the tradition to which the *acharya* belongs, the ancient Sanskrit compositions known as the Vedas are regarded as the only valid source of knowledge. Consequently, questions that pertain to the exegesis of these texts are considered to be the only productive questions. The ineffectiveness of my questions highlights the central role that the Vedas play in the epistemology of Kailash ashram. I can only speculate, but I hazard that had I asked a question on the *Chandogya Upanishad*, I might well have received a full answer.

Knowledge in many forms of Hinduism is transmitted within a *parampara* or tradition. There is a line of succession, and acquisition of knowledge is contingent upon initiation and a close relationship between the guru and disciple (*chela*) – who himself[5] has to possess certain qualities or characteristics. For example, the great Vedantin philosopher Shankara, the founder of the lineage which Kailash Ashram is associated with, suggested that a disciple must have an intense desire for liberation, which I clearly did not have. Consequently, it is important to reflect upon the question of whether the ethnographer must have an intense desire for liberation, rather than an intense desire for data, to gain access to the cognitive world of Kailash ashram.

The world, goals and concepts of truth and knowledge of the *acharya* are possibly incommensurate with mine as a non-Hindu academic, but a great deal can be learned through that incommensurability and the apparent lack of communication. Consequently, I argue that there are no absolutely closed worlds, and even the apparently firmly shut gate is open a crack. However, is a brief glimpse from the outside through a crack sufficient to gain that all-important understanding of another's world?

Participation: from objective observation to subjective experience

Most ethnographers argue that a brief glimpse is not sufficient and that lengthy fieldwork, which involves participant observation, is the prime method for opening the door on other worlds more widely. After all, the validating principle of ethnographic research is not only, "I was there to observe that", but more importantly "I actively participated in that culture". It is suggested that participation involves a move from the outsider, objective observer to a subjective experience, where it is possible "to grasp "the native's point of view".

Participation in the field raises the issue of the distinction between subjectivity and objectivity, between opinion and fact. The hard sciences are of course founded in the idea of "objective facts". The social sciences informed by Auguste Comte's ideas on positivism and developed by Emile Durkheim in his *Rules of Sociological Method* also suggest that it is possible to discover objective facts about the social world. This conceptualization of knowledge as objective fact has faced a number of challenges. Nietzsche's (in Kaufmann 1968: 267) riposte to positivism in *Will to Power* is that "facts is [sic] precisely what there is not, only interpretations. We cannot establish any fact 'in itself': perhaps it is folly to want to do such a thing".

The tradition of challenging positivism reaches its zenith with postmodernity. While this is not the place for any detailed discussion of postmodernity, there are a couple of significant aspects that challenge the possibility of the ethnographic realist attempt to "grasp the native's point of view" and provide an objective account of that world. The first is that postmodernity challenged the quest of modernity to identify universal explanations, or what Jean-François Lyotard called "grand narratives". Second is the idea that language constructs our world rather than reflects any independent pre-existent reality. The implications of these two interconnected ideas are far-reaching. It suggests that there is no possibility of providing any sort of universally accepted or acceptable account of the role of gurus in the Hindu traditions. Postmodern thought suggests that subjectivity is paramount – all ideas are partial and perspectival. Gayle Letherby (in Letherby, Scott and Williams 2013: 57) observes postmodernity "denies any reality outside the discursive and accepts no narrative as superior. From this perspective, a multitude of standpoints is possible and neither is superior to any other". The logical corollary of this argument is that there are only personal subjective experiences. However radical relativism itself can be challenged by the argument that this thesis itself is relative and perspectival. If this is the case, then it is necessary to question whether the ethnographer's account of their subjective experience is of any more value than any other narrative. Before addressing the issue of the ethnographic narrative, it is necessary to indicate something about the nature of participation.

There is a difference between me sitting and observing the AOL advanced course and actively participating in it. The renowned scholar of religions Ninian Smart (1995: 3) appropriated a Native American aphorism, which suggests that you should never judge another until you have walked a mile in their moccasins. In many ways participation in fieldwork can be considered as form of moccasin walking. What Smart neglects to indicate is that another person's shoes are almost inevitably not going to fit and there is always a degree of discomfort. In other words my experience of walking in your moccasins is not the same as your experience. Nonetheless by taking the Art of Living course at the ashram in Bangalore, I had demonstrated to some extent that I belonged to the same world as the actors – I could count as "a marginal native" – and this facilitated access to Sri Sri Ravi Shankar.

Both before and after my brief encounter with Sri Sri Ravi Shankar I talked to various devotees who said that they had met or knew Sri Sri Ravi Shankar, and I realized that their interaction with him had in most instances been little more than mine had been. Obviously their brief encounters had meant something quite different to these devotees, than it had for me. While I find various aspects of Sri Sri Ravi Shankar, such as the way he presents himself, interesting I cannot say that I have the same reverence for him as many of his devotees. There is therefore some lack of fit between my cognitive world and that of the AOL world. It is precisely this lack of fit and its concomitant discomfort which is where reflexivity comes into play and is the most productive space for understanding another's world. Reflection of the different experiences between myself as a non-believer and the devotees is the space that can provide some cognitive access.

As I mentioned in my account of my second brief encounter, my meeting with Sri Sri Ravi Shankar arose because I had taken active part in an AOL course. AOL, which was founded by Ravi Shankar in 1981, is now a vast transnational network claiming a presence in over 150 countries. People become involved AOL by joining a course in order to learn the basic technique – a rhythmic breathing exercise known as *sudarshan kriya*. My strategy for accessing this group was to join the basic course, which everybody has to do in order to participate in any way in AOL. Taking this introductory course also allows those interested to take further courses. So I decided that the best way to access the AOL International Centre in Bangalore – commonly simply called The Bangalore Ashram – was to join the advanced course. This is not the place to discuss the minutiae of the course, but just to give you a sense of what it entailed. The course lasted four days, three of which were in total silence, when we were instructed that we should not speak at all. The day was long, lasting from 6:00 in the morning to 9:00 or 10:00 at night. The day would start with some yoga, and doing our *sudarshan kriya*. We would be expected to do what is called *seva*, which loosely translates as service, and refers to doing some sort of work, such as cleaning the accommodation. The rest of the day we were taught a variety of yoga techniques, participated in what might be called quasi-psychotherapeutic exercises and did a lot of guided meditation.

My field notes written during and after the course reflect the fact that I did not find much of the experience at all comfortable. I found the long hours of sitting in meditation to be physically uncomfortable. I missed tea and coffee as caffeine is regarded as counteracting the benefits of the yoga exercises. I personally disliked and felt very awkward with some of the quasi-psychotherapeutic exercises, such as complimenting a stranger or recounting to a stranger the things that were bothering you. I felt like an obvious outsider as, although everybody made me extremely welcome on the course, I was the only non-Indian. I felt slightly hypocritical as I was primarily participating in the course for academic research rather than personal transformation. I found it stressful trying to balance being an active participant experiencing the course and the objective observer of what was going on around me.[6]

We were constantly reminded to give a hundred percent to the course, and this of course raises a dilemma for the ethnographer. How is it possible to participate a hundred percent and still undertake the requirements of fieldwork? Conversely if I focus on the fieldwork, then I am not giving a hundred percent to the various course activities and therefore I am not participating in the same way as the other participants. Participant observation is one of the main methodological tools of ethnographic research. One could argue that participant observation is an oxymoron – observation suggesting passiveness, objectivity and cognitive distance; whereas participation indicates active involvement, subjectivity and cognitive proximity. Drawing on the work of Buford Junker, Hammersley and Atkinson (1989: 93-94) suggest a spectrum of emphases, with the complete observer at one pole and the complete participant at the other. Both poles tend to be criticized. The passive observer, will always remain the excluded outsider, and therefore cannot hope to gain any real access to the cognitive world of the other. If I had sat and passively observed the course, and not taken part in any of the activities, could I really have gained any useful insight?

The complete participant is often accused of turning "native". The complete participant, it is suggested, fails to maintain the necessary critical space between him/herself and the cultural group that they are interested in. Failure to maintain critical distance leaves the ethnographer open to an accusation of anecdotalism, and the charge that they will no longer be able to identify and analyse the taken-for-granted cultural assumptions of "natives". The question here is: if I had found the course to be personally transformative and became an active and committed participant of AOL, a convert as it were, would this invalidate my research? To put this another way, if I had moved from being an "outsider" to what Andrew Dawson (2009: 177) calls a "provisional insider" to becoming a "real insider" what impact would this have on the validity of my research? The answer to this question is often articulated in terms of how the fieldwork is written, a subject that I will discuss below. Most ethnographers choose to undertake their research somewhere between the poles of observation and participation. Kim Knott (2010: 266) identifies this midway position as "the observer-as-participant", where the outsider researcher through participation in events and activities hopes to gain some empathetic understanding of the religious world of others.[7] An important aspect of being an observer-as-participant was also to observe my own self in relationship to the experience of doing the AOL course and my close encounters with the gurus. This self-reflection – a turning back on myself – was the process which revealed the lack of fit between my discursive world and that of the participants, and paradoxically at the same time facilitated an understanding of that world.

While there is no absolute agreement among the devotees as to why they took courses and why they continued to actively participate in AOL, there is a fairly consistent narrative from the members of AOL. This narrative suggests that their lives were in some sense unsatisfactory and that by participating in AOL this dissatisfaction was somehow resolved. Many of the active members of AOL talked about how their lives had been transformed, for example feeling less stressed, less angry, more fulfilled and so on. Also many spoke of having very powerful experiences when doing *sudarshan kriya*. Linked to this narrative is a very clear reverence for the person of Sri Sri Ravi Shankar. However, my own personal experience of doing *sudarshan kriya* was not in any sense powerful, nor do I feel that my life has been transformed in any way by being involved in AOL, and I personally do not believe that Sri Sri Ravi Shankar is an enlightened master. So in what sense have I gained any insight into the cognitive world of the active participant? Was my time on the course simply playing at being a participant, which had little more relationship to the cognitive world of the committed participant than the experience of the child playing at being a doctor has to the lived experience of being a doctor? It is impossible to accept the simple idea that participation in a different cultural milieu provides a straightforward understanding of that milieu. Nonetheless, I would argue that an understanding of different cultural worlds is possible. This is where reflexivity is a critical aspect.

Drawing on the insights of Wilhelm Dilthey, Victor Turner (1982: 14) observes that:

> We can know our subjective depths as much by scrutinizing the meaningful objectifications "expressed" by other minds, as by introspection. In complementary fashion self-scrutiny may give us clues to the penetrations of objectifications of life generated from the experiences of others. There is a kind of "hermeneutic circle" involved here, or rather, "spiral", for each turn transcends its predecessor. (Turner 1982: 14)

The investigation of other cultures and religions leads to greater insight about ourselves, conversely the reflexive turn within is a prerequisite for accessing the cultural and social worlds of others. Personal reflection on our experiences and encounters in the field is the space where insight into the cognitive worlds of others can be gained.

There is a dialectic relationship between my beliefs about the world and my experience of the world. No matter how much I immerse myself in another cultural world, my experience of that world will inevitably be influenced by my beliefs, which in turn are reassessed in light of my experience. As my beliefs about the effectiveness of *sudarshan kriya* and the status of Sri Sri Ravi Shankar are not the same as those of devotees, inevitably my encounter with Sri Sri Ravi Shankar and even my experience of active participation in AOL events and courses is fundamentally different to the experiences of the believer, but this does not preclude some access to the insider's cognitive world.

A straightforward binary opposition between insider and outsider is difficult to maintain. Many of the commentators of postmodernity have argued identity must be understood as a discursive process, rather than an essential quality. As Kirin Narayan (1993: 671–672) observes "the loci along which we are aligned with or set apart from those who we study are multiple and in flux. Factors such as education, gender, race or sheer duration of contacts may at different times outweigh the cultural identity we associate with insider or outsider". We all have complex and multiple identities that intersect in multi-faceted ways with others. Consequently there is no single "native's point of view to grasp". In the postmodern context commentators tend to avoid the term "identity", which implies a single unified sense of self, and prefer the term "subject", which implies that senses of self are conditioned by discourses. Indeed, the notion of the insider and outsider are subject positions determined by ethnographic discourse, and the purpose of this book is to deconstruct this discursive process. Research encounters are discursive events that construct, rather than simply reveal, different subjectivities.

Many commentators (see Castells 2009; van Dijk 2012) suggest that the best way of understanding the contemporary world is in terms of networks. The concept of the network society also challenges a binary opposition between insider and outsider. We are all linked into a diverse range of associative networks, not only through demographic and cultural subjectivities, but also through shared interests. These associative networks intersect in a diverse and complex ways.

The Art of Living Foundation can also be understood as an associative network, formed by a variety of links that both unify and divide participants. While, as I have indicated above, I felt a degree of discomfort while I was taking the AOL course, my field notes also indicate how at home I felt on the ashram. Not only was I familiar with the ethos of Indian ashrams, but also because of shared interests or similar life experiences, I had much in common with many of the people that I encountered.

Andrew Dawson (2009: 175) observes ritual participation can be perceived as "the definitive marker of insider-outsider status". Dawson (ibid.: 176) continues "the act of ritual participation results in the participant being ascribed a form of qualified insider status". Certainly I was regarded, having participated in the course, as a member of the group in the *darshan* line waiting to see Sri Sri Ravi Shankar. I was linked into the network of those who had participated in the course, but at the same time I was also linked into a variety of other networks of association – such as the academic community. Consequently, it could be said that I acted as a node that linked these two networks together. Another way of looking at this encounter is that I was simultaneously both an insider and outsider. While in the field the ethnographer is the equivalent to the paradox of Schrödinger's cat. However, the classical view is that once leaving the field, the ethnographer, particularly when writing up the field experience, returns to becoming unambiguously the outsider.

Writing ethnography – back to objectivity?

The traditional model of ethnographic realism suggests that the researcher not only moves from being an objective outsider to the subjective experience of fieldwork, but also on leaving the field the ethnographer creates that critical distance that enables the objective analysis and writing up of the data. However, those of us that have engaged in ethnographic fieldwork in religious or spiritual communities are well aware that the research trajectory is far more complex and convoluted than this linear model – moving from objective outsider to subjective experience and then to becoming the detached and objective author – suggests. Nonetheless the ethnographic author is expected to translate the coherent world of the insider – what Kenneth L. Pike (1999) has termed the emic standpoint, into a description or analysis that is alien to the insider – which Pike terms the etic standpoint.

The complete participant effectively becomes an insider, and may well produce an apologetic rather than analytical account of the group studied. Durkheim (in Lukes 1982: 31) observes that a science of society must not "consist of a mere paraphrase of traditional prejudices". There are certainly a number of apologetic accounts written by committed participants of AOL. For example Michael Fischman's (2011) *Stumbling into Infinity* is a highly personal account of his encounter with Sri Sri Ravi Shankar and his involvement with AOL. Fischman's book is described on the back cover as an "intimate and startling account". While ethnographic authors might wish that their publications to be "startling", they are rarely "intimate". There is a different rhetorical style to insider and outsider accounts that is, at least in part, determined by the classification of these two types of account as distinct genres and their intended readerships.

Mary Lou Pratt (1986: 27) observes there is "a well-established habit among ethnographers of defining ethnographic writing over and against older, less specialised genres, such as travel books". These "less specialised genres" are often characterized in the academic context as anecdotal, personal and intimate. When the ethnographic account becomes too intimate the academic community tends to dismiss these accounts as a failure to maintain the appropriate critical distance, and therefore are not regarded as credible or valid. Genres such as travel writing and memoirs tend to be condemned as trivial and entertaining.

Pratt (1986) provides an interesting account of the controversy about Florinda Donner's 1982 book *Shabono: A True Adventure in the Remote and Magical Heart of the South American Jungle*, based on her supposed experiences[8] among the Yanomama Indians – a remote tribal group in Venezuela. Debra Picchi (cited in Pratt 1986: 30) suggested that Donner's account was too much about her own personal experience and that this "renders the discipline trivial and inconsequential". Donner (1982: viii) herself stated in her author's note at the beginning of the book: "I did not keep the distance and detachment required of objective research". Certainly *Shabono* comes across as a very personal account – the first person is used throughout the book and Donner writes more about her personal experiences and encounters than details of kinship, rituals and so on that are the normal conventions of ethnographic monographs. For example, early on her account as she is being led to the Yanomama village, Donner (ibid.: 28) reflects "I sensed some change within me, as if crossing the river marked the end of a phase, a turning point". This is not the sort of highly personalized statement that the academic community would anticipate from an ethnographic account.

There is, as Pratt (1986: 32) points out, a tension between "the authority that is anchored to a large extent in a subjective, sensuous experience" and the written account of the experience which "is supposed to conform to the norms of a scientific discourse whose authority resides in the absolute effacement of the speaking and experiencing subject". However, since the development of standpoint theory and theories of postmodernity it has been recognized that the ethnographic self can never be effaced. Amanda Coffey (1999: 119) suggests that "all ethnographic writing is to some extent autobiographical. We author texts from a perspective of having been to, and lived in, the field". Certainly some of what I have written and published – including of course this chapter – is not only informed by my subjective encounters in the field, but also by my own personal life story that took me to India in my early twenties in the first place.

The personal experience of the ethnographer can never be effaced, and indeed we are encouraged to write a personal and subjective account alongside the more "objective" data in our field notes. However, this personalized aspect of field notes, until the impact of postmodern critical theory and feminism, was not regarded as apposite for publication. When the raw data – field notes, interview transcripts and so on – are cooked with relevant theoretical perspectives and previous studies to produce a published monograph or article, the emotional and personal tends to be discarded as irrelevant.

It is very telling that Bronislaw Malinowski's personal diary was published posthumously in 1967.[9] Raymond Firth, in the introduction to the second edition of the diary, commented that it received very mixed reviews, and friends and colleagues of Malinowski in particular felt that it should have remained in the private domain. A reviewer in *American Anthroplogist* suggested that "the volume holds no interest for anyone, be he anthropologist, psychologist, student of biography or merely a gossip" (cited by Firth in Malinowski 1989: xxii). Ten years later however, Paul Rabinow (1977) published his *Reflections on Fieldwork in Morocco*, which is a highly personal account of his encounters in the field. As Pierre Bourdieu expresses it in his afterword to Rabinow's (1977: 163) reflections, "the objectification of the knowing subject" marks a "decisive break with the positivist conception of scientific work". This objectification of the knowing subject paradoxically facilitates the acceptance of the personal voice in ethnographic accounts.

Perhaps one of the most interesting examples of the use of the personal voice is *Return to Laughter: An Anthropological Novel.* This book was first published in 1954 by the anthropologist Laura Bohannan. In other words it was published before the decisive break with positivism identified by Bourdieu. It is telling that Bohannan published it using the pseudonym Elenore Smith Bowen and that she describes it in the sub-heading as a novel. *Return to Laughter* is an amusing account of Bohannan's encounters in the field as a neophyte anthropologist undertaking research in Nigeria. However, I agree with David Riesman who indicates in the Foreword to the 1964 edition that you can learn a great deal about not only the lives of the Nigerian villagers, but also about the ethnographic method through reading about these very personal experiences, which Riesman (in Bowen 1964: x) characterizes as "fashioned by the play of imagination upon her diary and field notes".

Since the publication of *Return to Laughter,* influenced by post-structuralism and critiques of the possibility of objective accounts, a trend in what has been called autoethnography has emerged. Autoethnography includes the personal voice and blurs the distinction "between 'fact' and 'fiction' and between 'true' and 'imagined'" (Richardson and St Pierre cited in Denshire 2014: 831). The trend in autoethnographies "invites writers to see themselves and everyone else as human subjects constructed in a tangle of cultural, social and historical situations in contact zones" (Brodkey cited in Denshire 2014: 833). All ethnographic research as relational events occur within particular historical and cultural contexts not only requires reflection but undermines the possibility of objective neutral accounts. Perhaps the rhetorical style of accounts such as *Shabono* are more "truthful", as the subtitle of the book suggests, than the supposed "objective" ethnographic monographs about the Yanomama Indians.

Conclusion

The insider/outsider problem in all ethnographic research, and particularly research into religious and spiritual traditions, is deeply imbricated with issues of subjectivity and objectivity. Ethnographic realism suggests that the outsider enters the field as a cultural stranger, has a subjective experience within the field where they learn to "grasp the native's point of view" and then emerges from the field to write an objective account of that experience. Kenneth L. Pike (1999) suggests the ethnographer is expected to discover the insider world – or as he terms it the emic system, but the analysis and description is undertaken from a position outside that world – from an etic standpoint. However there is no simple dichotomy between the emic and etic standpoint. Pike (ibid.: 32–33) indicates that these two perspectives function like a stereoscopic viewer on the same data resulting in "a kind of "tridimensional understanding" of human behaviour". While I agree that "tridimensional" accounts of the cognitive world of others is contingent on this dual perspective it is far more complex than Pike suggests, as there is neither a single etic nor emic perspective. Neither standpoint is quite as coherent as suggested by the analogy of the stereoscopic viewer. Perhaps a better analogy would be a stereoscopic kaleidoscope – each twist of the viewer providing a new, but equally valid perspective on the cognitive world of others.

Pike (1999: 30) has suggested that any significant cognitive insight is contingent on grasping the cultural (emic) system as a whole. He likens this to understanding "the structural functioning of a particular car as a whole. My brief encounter with Swami Divyananada could not possibly enable me to grasp the emic system as a whole, and therefore I could not, according to Pike's view, gain the all-important "tridimensional understanding" of Kailash Ashram, but merely "a flat etic one". However, I have argued that this brief encounter is much more three dimensional than Pike's view allows. Failure to grasp the system as a whole does not preclude significant insight into insider's worlds, as the encounter takes place in a third space – neither the insider's nor the outsider's. It is the reflection on this ambiguous third space that provides insight and understanding.

Even though my actual encounter with Sri Sri Ravi Shankar was fleeting, it can be suggested that my participation in AOL activities provided a fuller grasp of the insider's world. However, it can be argued that even this active participation in the AOL courses does not facilitate any reliable access to the cognitive world of others, as my experience is contingent upon my beliefs. Consequently, the world of others is always closed. Furthermore, researchers who work within a positivist paradigm often criticize ethnographic research findings as not being verifiable. My encounters are unique and cannot be replicated. A different researcher, or even myself on another occasion, will almost inevitably have a totally different experience, possibly leading to very different conclusions. In other words all ethnographic fieldwork, not just research like that conducted by Florinda Donner as recorded in *Shabono*, is essentially anecdotal. All that is different is the rhetorical style of more respected ethnographers conceals this anecdotal nature of the research in the spurious language of objectivism.

As I have indicated, reflection on the dismissive response by Swami Divyananda can tell us a great deal about his world. The door to the cognitive world of the *acharya* is not fully closed by his brusque engagement. However, no worlds are totally open. Full participation can never fully open cognitive doors. There is inevitably a critical space between the researcher and the researched, and this has to be acknowledged. Critical space is the place where both researcher and the researched can be given "credit", to utilize Scheper-Hughs's (2000: 128) term. It is the domain where ethnography is not reduced to anecdotal trivia or ostensibly objective accounts that are unrecognisable to the subjects of research. Critical space is created through a reflection on the differences between the cognitive world of the outsider and the cognitive world of the researcher. Consequently, I want to reappraise Smart's concept of moccasin walking. Yes, let's make the attempt to walk that mile: the more uncomfortable that mile is the more we are likely to be able to achieve that double break called for by Bourdieu and a dialogue will be entered into with both the native's point of view and with the presuppositions of our own worlds. In other words there has to be a reflexive dialogue with both emic and etic perspectives. It is this reflexive dialogue that enables some access to the other's world and enables the ethnographer to represent the other in a meaningful way. While there is still a place for what might be called traditional ethnographic monographs, the reflective turn of ethnographic research, informed by feminism and postmodernity, has also opened up the possibility of more experimental genres and personal modes of representing other cognitive worlds.

About the author

Stephen Jacobs is senior lecturer in media, religion and culture at the University of Wolverhampton. Specializing in Indian traditions and religion and mass media communication, his recent publications include *Hinduism Today* (Bloomsbury, 2010), "Simulating the Apocalypse: Theology and Structure of the Left Behind Games" Online" in *Heidelberg Journal of Religion and the Internet* (2015) and *Art of Living: Spirituality and Wellbeing in the Global Context* (Ashgate, 2015).

Notes

1 Sri Sri Ravi Shankar must not be confused with the famous sitar player of the same name. It is sometimes suggested that Ravi Shankar adopted the double honorific to distinguish him from the musician (see Jacobs 2015).
2 I have anglicized the spelling for Sanskrit terms and not used the conventions of diacritics.
3 "Ji" is a suffix used to indicate respect.
4 Many of the courses on the ashram in Bangalore are very international, but it just transpired that all the other participants on course that I enrolled on were Indian. However, there was a strong international contingent staying on the ashram while I was there, although these international visitors were not taking the same course.
5 The gender specific term is used here as it is only men who become disciples in this particular tradition.
6 In an initial draft I wrote this paragraph in a more passive and objective voice. For example I had written, "there was the physical discomfort of long hours of meditation". It was as though I was not describing my feelings and distancing myself from the fieldwork experience. However, on reflection I decided that the personal and active voice is more apposite as it was my personal experience that is significant. I expand on this point in the section on writing ethnography.
7 Kim Knott (2010: 267) also identifies the position of the participant-as-observer, where the "insider" produces a critical account of their own religious/spiritual world. Knott citing Jo Pearson's ethnography of British Wicca, suggests that this position can be described as "going native in reverse".
8 Donner has also been accused of faking her account of her stay among the Yanomama Indians (see Pratt 1986). Whether or not Donner's account was entirely made up is not the point. The point is that the accusation represents her account not merely as a travel book or memoir – of little academic merit themselves – but as a work of fiction – a genre even less worthy of academic merit.
9 The decision to publish these diaries was made by his widow Valetta Malinowska "with the deliberate aim of revealing the personality [of Malinowski], and linking up this knowledge with the work left behind" (Valetta Malinowski in the preface to Malinowski 1989: ix).

References

Alvesson, Mats and Kaj Sköldberg (2009). *Reflexive Methodology: New Vistas for Qualitative Research*. London: Sage.

Bourdieu, P. (1977). *Outline of a Theory of Practice*. Cambridge: Cambridge University Press. https://doi.org/10.1017/CBO9780511812507

Bowen, Elenore Smith (1964). *Return to Laughter: An Anthropological Novel*. New York: Anchor Books.

Bruni, A. (2006). Access as Trajectory: Entering the Field in Organizational Ethnography. *M@n@gement* 9(3): 129–144. https://doi.org/10.3917/mana.093.0137

Castells, Manuel (2009). *The Rise of the Network Society*. Oxford: Blackwell. https://doi.org/10.1002/9781444319514

Coffey, Amanda (1999). *The Ethnographic Self: Fieldwork and the Representation of Identity*. London: Sage. https://doi.org/10.4135/9780857020048

Cox, James L. (1996). *Expressing the Sacred: An Introduction to the Phenomenology of Religion*. Harare: University of Zimbabwe Press.

Davies, Charlotte (2002). *Reflexive Ethnography: A Guide to Researching Selves and Others*. London: Routledge.

Dawson, Andrew (2009). Positionality and Role-Identity in a New Religious Context: Participant Observation at Céu do Mapiá. *Religion* 40: 173–181. https://doi.org/10.1016/j.religion.2009.09.007

Denshire, Sally (2014). On Auto-ethnography. *Current Sociology Review* 62(6): 831–850. https://doi.org/10.1177/0011392114533339

Donner, Florinda (1982). *Shabono: A Visit to a Remote and Magical World in the South American Rainforest*. New York: HarperCollins.

Dwyer, Sonya Corbin and Jennifer L. Buckle (2009). The Space Between: On Being an Insider-Outsider in Qualitative Research. *International Journal of Qualitative Methodology* 8(1): 54–63. https://doi.org/10.1177/160940690900800105

Fischman, Michael (2011). *Stumbling Into Infinity: An Ordinary Man in the Sphere of Enlightenment*. New York: Morgan James Publishing.

Gilliat-Ray, Sophie (2005). Closed Worlds: (Not) Accessing Deobandi *da rul-uloom* in Britain. *Fieldwork in Religion* 1(1): 7–33. https://doi.org/10.1558/firn.v1i1.7

Gold, Ann Grodzins (1990). *Fruitful Journeys: The Ways of Rajasthani Pilgrims*. Berkeley, CA: University of California Press.

Hammersley, Martyn and Paul Atkinson (1989). *Ethnography: Principles in Practice*. London: Routledge.

Hufford, David J. (1999). The Scholarly Voice and the Personal Voice: Reflexivity in Belief Studies. In Russell McCutcheon (ed.), *The Insider/Outsider Problem in the Study of Religion*. London: Cassell.

Jacobs, S. (2015). *The Art of Living Foundation: Spirituality and Wellbeing in the Global Context*. Farnham: Ashgate. https://doi.org/10.4324/9781315612621

Kaufmann, Walter (ed.) (1968). *Friedrich Nietzsche: The Will to Power*. New York: Random House.

Keemattam, A. (1997). *The Hermits of Rishikesh: A Sociological Study.* New Delhi: Intercultural Publications.
Knott, K. (2010). Insider/Outsider Prespective. In John Hinnells (ed.), *The Routledge Companion to the Study of Religion.* London: Routledge.
Letherby, Gayle, John Scott and Malcolm Williams (2013). *Objectivity and Subjectivity in Social Research.* London: Sage. https://doi.org/10.4135/9781473913929
Lukes, Steven (ed.) (1982). *Durkheim: The Rules of Sociological Method and Selected Texts on Sociology and its Methods.* New York: Free Press.
Malinowski, Bronislaw (1978). *Argonauts of the Western Pacific.* London: Routledge.
Malinowski, Bronislaw (1989). *A Diary in the Strict Sense of the Term* (2nd edition). London: Athlone Press.
Narayan, Kirin (1993). How Native is a "Native" Anthroplogist? *American Anthroplogist* 95(3): 671–686. https://doi.org/10.1525/aa.1993.95.3.02a00070
Pike, Kenneth L. (1999). Etic and Emic Standpoints for the Description of Behaviour. In Russell McCutcheon (ed.), *The Insider/Outsider Problem in the Study of Religion.* London: Cassell.
Pratt, M. L. (1986). Fieldwork in Common Places. In J. Clifford and G. Marcus (eds), *Writing Culture: The Poetics and Politics of Ethnography.* Berkeley, CA: University of California Press.
Rabinow, Paul (1977). *Reflections on Fieldwork in Morocco.* Berkeley, CA: University of California Press.
Schensul, Stephen, Jean Schensul and Margaret LeCompte (1999). *Essential Ethnographic Methods 2: Observations, Interviews and Questionnaires.* Walnut Creek, CA: AltaMira Press.
Scheper-Hughes, Nancy (2000). Ire in Ireland. *Ethnography* 1(1): 117–140. https://doi.org/10.1177/14661380022230660
Smart, Ninian (1995). *Worldviews: Crosscultural Explorations of Human Beliefs.* Englewood Cliffs, NJ: Prentice Hall.
Smith, Dorothy. E. (2004). Women's Perspective as a Radical Critique of Sociology. In S. Harding (ed.), *The Feminist Standpoint Theory Reader: Intellectual and Political Controversies*, 21–33. London: Routledge.
Turner, Victor (1982). *From Ritual to Theatre: The Human Seriousness of Play.* New York: PAJ Publications.
Van Dijk, Jan (2012). *The Network Society.* London: Sage.
Warrier, M. (2005). *Hindu Selves in a Modern World: Guru Faith in the Mata Amritanandamayi Mission.* London: Routledge. https://doi.org/10.4324/9780203462065

12

Who is a Jew?
New approaches to an old question

Dan Cohn-Sherbok

In recent years a number of books have been published dealing with the concept of insiders and outsiders in Judaism. Studies by authors such as Lawrence Wills (2013), David Baile (1998), Chaim Zimmerman (1979) and Ben-Amy Shilony (1992) explore this issue from a wide range of perspectives. The aim of this chapter is to provide a panoramic overview of this issue and to sketch briefly a new constructive and inclusive approach to the insider/outsider question in modern Jewish life.

The Jewish faith has been in existence for nearly 4,000 years. Yet, paradoxically in modern times it has become increasingly unclear who belongs to the Jewish community, and who does not. Across the religious spectrum, there are conflicting interpretations of the criteria for determining Jewishness. In addition, there currently exist a wide variety of branches of Judaism as well as Jewish groups who hold radically divergent philosophies of the Jewish way of life. This has made it increasingly difficult to determine who is an insider and who is an outsider in the Jewish world and how the Jewish religion should be observed. Given such uncertainty, arguably there is now a need for a new vision of Judaism which would enable individuals to live Jewish lives according to their own personal preferences. Jewish identity, belief and practice would in this way become a matter of individual choice and thereby alleviate the current confusion which exists in the Jewish world.

Jewish status

In the Hebrew Bible, the status of the offspring of mixed marriages was determined patrilineally – Jewishness was inherited from the father. Yet, in the Hellenistic period there was a fundamental change in perception. According to the Mishnah (the first compilation of rabbinic law), the offspring of a mixed marriage is determined matrilineally; in such cases, the status of the child is determined by the mother. This change may have taken place because tannaitic scholars during the Hellenistic period were influenced by Roman law which dictated that when a parent could not contract a legal marriage, the offspring would follow the mother.

Through the centuries, rabbinic law has followed Mishnaic precedent. Hence, according to halakha, to determine a person's Jewish status, one needs to consider the status of both parents. If both parents are Jewish, their child is regarded as Jewish, and the child takes the status of the father (for example, if he is a cohen (priest)). If either parent is subject to a genealogically disability (such as being a *mamzer*), then the child inherits that disability. If one of the parents is not Jewish, the child takes the status of the mother. Thus, if the mother is Jewish, her child is Jewish as well. However, if she is not Jewish, then neither she nor her child is regarded as Jewish. Only if the child is converted, is he or she regarded as a Jew. In such a case (where the child is not regarded as Jewish), a male child is not subject to any disabilities or special status (such as being cohen) to which the father is subject.

Today all branches of Orthodox Judaism (including the Hasidim) as well as Conservative Judaism subscribe to these halakhic rules concerning maternal descent. British Reform and Liberal Judaism, however, do not view the halakhic rules as binding. Instead, they accept a child of either Jewish parent, regardless whether it is the father or mother, as Jewish as long as the parents raise the child as a Jew and encourage the child to have a Jewish identity.

In the United States, Reform rabbis regard a person with one Jewish parent as a Jew if there have been "appropriate and timely public formal acts of identification within the Jewish religion and people". This includes such events as a Jewish naming ceremony, circumcision, and bar and bat mitzvah ceremonies. Individual Reform rabbis interpret these criteria in different ways; hence there is considerable variation in practice. The central principle is that a child should have a Jewish upbringing.

Such a shift away from the traditional understanding of matrilineal descent has created considerable controversy within the Jewish world. Orthodox and Conservative communities do not recognize a person as Jewish if only the father is Jewish. Reform and Liberal Jews, however, regard that person as a born Jew. For such an individual to be accepted as Jewish by an Orthodox or Conservative synagogue requires formal conversion in accordance with Orthodox standards.

Turing to conversion, all mainstream forms of Judaism accept converts. According to rabbinic Judaism, the laws of conversion are based on law codified in the Shulkhan Arukh (Code of Jewish Law). For Orthodox and Conservative Jews, this legislation is authoritative. Traditionally the halakhic requirements for conversion include instruction in the commandments, circumcision for men, immersion in a *mikveh* (ritual bath) before witnesses, and acceptance of the *mitzvot* (commandments). Orthodox authorities demand that conversions take place in accordance with Jewish law and recognize only those conversions that have taken place in the prescribed manner. Converts must accept the binding nature of Jewish law and undertake to follow these prescriptions in their daily life. Orthodox authorities do not accept as valid conversions preformed outside the Orthodox fold. Similarly, Conservative authorities require that conversions are conducted according to the halakha. In general they recognize any conversion done in accordance with the requirements of Jewish law, even if it is done outside the Conservative movement. As a result, in some instances Conservative rabbis accept the validity of Reform conversions as long as Jewish law has been followed.

Reform Judaism, however, has significantly departed from tradition. The Union for Reform Judaism states that people considering conversion are expected to study about Judaism and incorporate Jewish practices into their lives. The length of preparation for conversion varies depending on the rabbi, but in general this takes about a year. The Central Conference of American Rabbis recommends that three rabbis are present at the conversion ceremony. In Israel the Rabbinic Court of the Israel Movement for Progressive Judaism requires an average of a year of study. Following this, converts are required to immerse in a *mikvah*, be circumcised if male, and accept the commandments before a rabbinical court. In general Reform converts are not accepted by the Orthodox establishment.

According to rabbinic law, Jews of maternal descent who convert to another faith are regarded as apostates but remain Jews. Traditionally such individuals have a ban (*cherem*) placed on them, but such communal exclusion does not affect their Jewish status. Traditional Judaism also views as Jewish those who involuntarily converted from Judaism to another religion, and their matrilineal descendants are also considered to be Jewish. Reform Judaism, however, views Jews who convert to or are raised in another religion as non-Jews. Any Jew who leaves Judaism is free to return to the religion at any time, and no formal conversion ceremony is required. All movements welcome the return to Judaism of those who have left, or were raised in another faith. It is expected that such individuals will discard their previous practices and adopt Jewish customs. It should be noted that in addition to those officially affiliate with the major religious denominations, there are millions of ethnic Jews who are Jewish by virtue of descent, but do not actively practice the Jewish religion.

Since the creation of the State of Israel, in 1948, the Law of Return was enacted to grant any Jew the right to immigrate to Israel and become a citizen. However, due to an inability of the lawmakers to agree, this Law did not define who is a Jew. Besides the generally accepted rabbinic definition of who is a Jew based on maternal descent, the Law extended the categories of person who are entitled to immigration and citizenship to the children and grandchildren of Jews, regardless of their present religious affiliation as well as their spouses. Also, converts to Judaism whose conversion was preformed outside the State of Israel, regardless of under whose auspices it took place, are entitled to immigration under the Law. However, any person who has converted to another religion is not entitled to immigration regardless of their halakhic position.

In Israel, anyone who immigrated after 1990 and wishes to marry or divorce through the Jewish tradition must undergo a Judaism test at a rabbinical court. In this test, the person would need to prove their claim to be Jewish beyond a reasonable doubt. This involves presenting original documentation of maternal descent up to their great-grandmother. In addition, they are obliged to provide government documents with nationality/religion shown as Jewish. In the case of those whose original documents have been lost or never existed, it may prove difficult to demonstrate their Jewish status. Halakhic law also applies to burial which is under the jurisdiction of the Israeli Interior Ministry.

Jewish denominations

Alongside the debate concerning the status of individuals within the Jewish community, Jewry is deeply divided about the legitimacy of the various forms of Judaism that have emerged in the modern world. The *Haredim* (which includes Strictly Orthodox Jews and the Hasidim) regard Orthodox Judaism in its various forms as the only authentic Jewish way of life; all other branches are viewed as heretical. Other branches of Judaism, however, view themselves as legitimate interpretations of the faith more suited to modern circumstances. Hence, in the modern Jewish world there is profound disagreement about the fundamental beliefs and practices of the Jewish faith.

Orthodox Judaism

Traditionally Jewish life centred around the observance of the law. It was an article of faith that the Torah was given to Moses in its entirety by God. Therefore it must be true in every detail. In handing down the Torah, Moses acted like a scribe, writing from dictation. Thus the whole Torah is literally the word of God. This conviction has sustained the Jewish community through persecution and disaster, from the loss of the Temple in 70 CE, through the experience of exile and during periods of persecution and massacre. Together with the oneness of God, it has been an essential element of the Jewish creed.

In modern society the findings of biblical criticism and general scepticism have undermined this view of the Torah. Nonetheless, the faithful adhere to doctrine of *Torah MiSinai* (the Torah is from Mount Sinai). The Orthodox define themselves as those who remain true to the doctrine that the Five Books of Moses are from Heaven. This has enormous practical consequence of their day-to-day life since they follow not only the provisions of the Pentateuch, but also all the manifold details of the Oral Law. This means that they must live in a particular area of a city because mechanical transport is forbidden on the Sabbath, and they must walk to synagogue. Many of the men attend synagogue daily, and within the synagogue building, the women sit separately often behind a thick screen.

Birth control is frowned on except for strict medical reasons and a large family is viewed as a blessing. Men and women have clearly demarcated roles. A woman must keep a kosher home, following all the complicated food laws. She should look after and sustain her family and dedicate herself to their nerds. She is excused from the positive time-bound commandments (such as saying prayers three times a day) to enable her to run her household smoothly. Totally faithful to her husband, she must dress modestly and ensure her daughters do the same. The children attend Jewish schools where boys and girls are taught separately and follow different curricula. The boys must study traditional Jewish law, and after they leave school they normally attend a yeshiva (talmudic academy) for several years before earning a living. Young people normally marry in their early twenties and the matches are supervised by their parents. It is common for parents to support the newly wed couple while the husband finishes his education.

Despite this pattern, there are within the Orthodox community a variety of approaches to the Jewish way of life. The Strictly Orthodox are mainly Jews of Eastern European origin who aim to reproduce the lifestyle of their ancestors who lived in Russia, Poland and Lithuania. Large numbers have settled in Israel where they exert considerable influence through their own political parties, but there are also groups in most large European and American cities. In addition, there are Oriental Jews who trace their origins back to the ancient communities of the East. They have their own synagogues and liturgy. Like their Eastern European counterparts, they insist that the Torah was directly given by God to Moses on Mt Sinai, but they have their own specific traditions.

A significant new Orthodox group emerged in the nineteenth century under the leadership of Samson Raphael Hirsch. In his view, it is possible to remain an Orthodox Jew while being fully conversant with modern culture. This view, known as Neo-Orthodoxy promotes strict observance of biblical and rabbinic law; nonetheless, adherents have no hesitation in dressing in modern Western fashion and attending secular universities. The majority of Orthodox synagogues in Britain and the United States are of this type. In some men and women even sit together. Although the Neo-Orthodox often send their children to Jewish schools, girls and boys are educated in the same classroom and follow the same curriculum. Many Neo-Orthodox girls would expect to have their own professional careers, and it is likely that the number of children in the family is planned.

Orthodox Judaism should not be regarded as an organized movement, and there is a certain degree of disagreement among the various groups. Nonetheless, the Orthodox are united in the conviction that the Torah was given directly by God to Moses, and in their unwavering disapproval of the more liberal forms of Judaism. In their view, the various branches of the Judaism (Reform, Conservative, Reconstructionist and Humanistic Judaism) are aberrations of the true faith. Orthodox Judaism in its various forms has an influence far beyond its numerical strength, partly because Orthodox Jews are regarded with a degree of awe by their more secular co-religionists and also because they have control of the religious establishment in the State of Israel (see Sacks 1993).

Hasidism

The most visible group among the Orthodox are the Hasidim. The word *hasidim* means "the pious", and the Hasidim are known for their spiritual devotion. They are immediately recognisable. The men are bearded and wear side-curls which are twisted and tucked behind their ears. They are invariable dressed in black – large black hats worn over small black skull-caps, black jacket, plain black grousers and black shoes and socks. Their shirts are white, buttoned up to the neck and worn without a tie. Issuing forth from the waistband of their trousers are the ritual fringes which are attached to their undergarments. They are generally tucked into trouser pockets. On the Sabbath, the men exchange their weekday jacket for a long black silk coat, and instead of the everyday hat, many wear large fur hats. As with all strictly Orthodox Jews the women follow rules of modesty. Their skirts cover their knees; their sleeves extend over their elbows, and their necklines are high. If women are married, they wear wigs. In general, Hasidic families are large, often with five children or more.

The origins of Hasidism date from the eighteenth century. The founder, Israel ben Eliezer, known as the Baal Shem Tov, emphasized personal piety and mystical worship. As the movement spread throughout Eastern Europe, it centred around the court of various spiritual leaders, known as the *tsaddikim*, who were viewed as possessing extraordinary powers. When a *tsaddik* died, he was succeeded by a prominent disciple, often his own son, son-in-law or grandson. The *tsaddikim* were believed to have a special relationship with God. His prayers protected him and his followers, and in some cases the *tsaddikim* performed miracles. Due to role as spiritual leader of his community, it was regarded as an honour to sit at his Sabbath meal and share in his leftovers. In the courts of the *tsaddikim* it was common for there to be dancing and singing on festivals.

European Hasidic dynasties were subsequently devastated by the Nazi Holocaust. Nonetheless, Hasidism has survived, particularly in the United States and Israel. Today the most prominent groups are the Belz, the Ger, the Satmar and the Lubavitcher Hasidim. The latter is the best known of these groups since their mission is to bring secular Jews back to the tradition. The late *tsaddik*, Menahem Mendel Schneersohn, was viewed by a number of his followers as the long-anticipated Messiah. When he died in 1994, the movement was in disarray since he left no son as his successor. In the past there was considerable friction between the Orthodox establishment and the Hasidim. Traditionalists believed that the movement was excessive in its spiritual orientation. In their view, the Hasidim was disrespectful of their rabbinic establishment. In addition, the veneration of the *tsaddik* was viewed as a form of idolatry. Further, the emphasis of the movement on mystical joy rather than Talmudic study was regarded as heretical. Bills of excommunication were issued against Hasidic groups. Children who joined the movement were disowned, and families were divided. More recently, however, traditional Orthodox Jews have embraced the Hasidim. Even though they have different liturgies and customs, they are united in their adherence to Jewish law and religious belief (see Rabinowicz 1988).

Conservative Judaism

Among religious Jews, the great divide is between the Orthodox and non-Orthodox. Non-Orthodox Judaism emerged in respond to Jewish participation in mainstream civilization. Increasingly Western European Jews became uncomfortable with the traditional service. Many Jews were unable to read Hebrew and some of the traditional doctrines and practices were perceived as irrelevant to modern life. Hymns and prayers were offered in German; choirs were introduced into synagogues; and services were conducted with decorum. Later in the nineteenth century, an attempt was made to study the evolution of the Jewish faith. Adopting some of the advances made in biblical scholarship, reformers maintained that the Torah was a composite work originating during various periods of Jewish history.

Unlike Reform Judaism which adopted a radical approach to the tradition, Conservative Judaism arose in reaction to the policies of nineteenth-century Reformers. Standing midway between Orthodoxy and Reform Judaism, Conservative Judaism seeks to retain the central features of the faith while modifying Jewish belief and practice. The two founders of Conservative Judaism were Zechariah Frankel and Solomon Schechter. Both understood the Jewish tradition in dynamic terms. They believed that Judaism has evolved through the centuries and that the ultimate source of authority must be the Jewish people themselves. In this light, they argued that some aspects of the tradition are permanent, whereas others are only meaningful during certain periods.

Today Conservative Judaism covers a wide variety of beliefs and practices and there are considerable tensions within the movement. Nonetheless, Conservative leaders are agreed about a series of key principles. In various official statements the movement affirms that historical development of the traditions had constantly taken place, and that the tradition continues to develop. Furthermore, Conservative leaders affirm the indispensability of the Halakha [Jewish law] but insist that it needs to change according to contemporary needs. In recent years the Conservative movement has spread beyond the United States. In Israel and Great Britain there are now small Conservative organizations known as the Masorti (traditional).

Reconstructionist Judaism

Alongside Conservative Judaism, a new more radical approach emerged from within the movement. Founded in the 1930s Reconstructionist Judaism is based on the writings of Mordecai Kaplan. According to Kaplan, Judaism should not be understood as a divinely revealed religion. In his view, God is not a supernatural being, but the sum of all the animating, organizing forces and relationships which are forever making a cosmos out of chaos.

In the 1940s and 1950s the leaders of Reconstructionist Judaism insisted they were not attempting to form a new branch of Judaism. Throughout this period, Reconstructionists hoped they would be able to infuse Orthodox,

Conservative and Reform Judaism with its ideas. However, by the end of the 1960s the Reconstructionist movement had become a separate denomination. It had founded a seminary to train rabbis and instituted a congregational structure. Regarding halakha or Jewish law, the Reconstructionist Rabbinical Association issued a statement at its 1980 convention that placed authority in the Jewish people (as opposed to the rabbis) and created a process whereby each congregation would be free to form its own minhag, or "customs". Three year later the Association produced guidelines on intermarriage, encouraging rabbis to welcome mixed coupes (a Jew and non-Jew), permit them to participate in Jewish synagogue life, and recognize their children as Jewish if raised as Jews. In addition, the Association decreed that rabbis could sanctify an intermarriage as long as it was accompanied by civil, rather than a religious, ceremony (see Kaplan 1967).

Reform Judaism

At the end of the eighteenth century such advocates of Jewish enlightenment as Moses Mendelssohn encouraged Jews to integrate into the societies in which they lived. Later early reformers sought to modify Jewish education by widening the traditional curriculum of Jewish schools. During this period a number of Reform temples were opened in Germany with innovations to the liturgy, including prayers and sermons in German as well as choral singing and organ music. The main aim of these reformers was to adapt Jewish worship to contemporary aesthetic standards.

In response to these developments, the Orthodox asserted that any change to the tradition is a violation of the Jewish heritage. For these traditionalists, the Written and Oral Torah constitute an infallible chain of divinely revealed truth. Despite this reaction, some German rabbis began to reevaluate the Jewish heritage. In this endeavour the achievements of Jewish scholars who engaged in the scientific study of Judaism had a profound impact. Eventually a series of Reform synods were held in Germany to formulate the guiding principles of the movement. In England and the United States similar developments took place. Eventually in 1885 at a gathering of Reform rabbis in Pittsburgh, Pennsylvania, a programme of reform was set forth in the Pittsburgh Platform.

Fifty years later, the Jewish world had undergone major changes: America had become the centre of the diaspora; Zionism had become a vital force in Jewish life; Hitler was in power. In 1937 The Columbus Platform reflected a new approach to liberal Judaism. In later years the Reform movement underwent further change. In the 1960s new liturgies were used, and in the 1970s a new Reform prayer book was published. Two years later the first woman rabbi was ordained, and by the early 1980s more than 75 women had entered the rabbinate. In 1976 the Reform movement produced the San Francisco Platform; more recently another platform was issued by the Central Conference of American Rabbis. At the onset of the twenty-first century, this rabbinic body set out a new statement that affirmed the central tenets of Judaism – God, Torah and Israel – while acknowledging the diversity of Reform Jewish belief and practice (see Meyer 1988).

Humanistic Judaism

Like Reconstructionist Judaism, Humanistic Judaism offers a non-theistic interpretation of the Jewish faith. Originating in the 1960s in Detroit under the leadership of Sherwin Wine, Humanistic Judaism now numbers about 40,000 members in the United States, Israel, Europe and elsewhere. The movement originated in 1965 when the Birmingham Temple in a suburb of Detroit began to publicize its philosophy of Judaism. Eventually a magazine, *Humanistic Judaism*, was created. Later two new Humanistic congregations were established in Illinois and Connecticut. In 1969 the Society for Humanistic Judaism was founded to provide a basis for cooperation among Humanistic Jews. During the next ten years new congregations were established in Boston, Toronto, Los Angeles, Washington, Miami, Long Beach and Huntington, New York. In subsequent years Secular Humanistic Judaism became an international movement with supporters on five continents.

In 1986 The Federation of the movement issued a proclamation stating its ideology and aims. According to this document, Humanistic Jews value human reason and the reality of the world which reason discloses. In their view, the natural universe stands on its own, requiring no supernatural intervention. In this light, Humanists believe in the value of human existence and in the power of human beings to solve their problems individually and collectively. Life, the movement maintains, should be directed to the satisfaction of human needs. In their view, Judaism, is a human creation – it embraces all manifestations of Jewish existence.

The Jewish people, Humanists insist, is a world with a pluralistic culture and civilization all its own. Judaism as the culture of the Jews, is thus more than theological content. It encompasses many languages, a vast body of literature, historical memories and ethical values. Yet, unlike other modern movements, Humanistic Judaism seeks to welcome all people who wish to identify with Jewish culture and destiny. Hence, Humanists have redefined the notion of Jewishness. A Jew, they state, is a person of Jewish descent or any person who declares himself or herself to be a Jew, and who identifies with the history, ethical values, culture, civilization and community of the Jewish nation (see Wine 1985).

Reformulating Jewishness

As we have noted, there is considerable debate in Jewish circles about the definition of Jewishness. Across the Jewish spectrum there are a wide range of views about Jewish heredity and conversion. As a consequence, in the modern world there are serious differences of opinion about what makes a person Jewish. In addition, there is considerable confusion about how Judaism is to be practised. Is there any solution to this profound dilemma? In the light of the wide variety of interpretations of the Jewish faith, it is clear that the absolutism of the past has been superseded by a new understanding of Judaism. Given the multiplicity of views about Jewish belief and practice, arguably Jews who belong to the various movements should no longer regard their interpretations of the tradition as absolute and binding. Rather they should accept that Orthodox, Conservative, Reform, Reconstructionist and Humanistic Jews make personal choices about how Judaism is to be observed based on subjective interpretations of the Jewish heritage.

Such openness offers a new orientation to the current perplexities regarding Jewish identity. A solution to this problem is to apply a non-dogmatic interpretation of religious doctrine to the issue of Jewishness. Given such a view, there is no reason to regard the traditional halakhic understanding of Jewishness as absolute and binding. Instead, Jewish identity could be redefined along the lines suggested by Humanistic Judaism. As we have seen, Humanistic Jews are anxious to avoid any form of racism in their definition of Jewishness. Nor do they seek to impose a religious test on converts. Rather, they desire to accept within the Jewish fold all those who wish to identify themselves with the Jewish people regardless of birth.

Similarly an open approach to Judaism – with its emphasis on personal autonomy – could offer a similar definition of Jewishness. Distancing itself from either biological descent or correct belief and practice, such a stance would welcome as Jews all those, regardless of ancestry, who desire to be identified in this fashion. On this basis, Jewish identity would be solely a matter of individual choice. In other words, Jewishness would be construed as an optional identification rather than the result of matrilineal or patrilineal descent or religious conviction formally accepted by a rabbinic body. Being a Jew would then be an option open to all. Although such a reinterpretation of Jewish status would not be acceptable to the major branches of Judaism, it would eliminate the uncertainty surrounding the question: Who is a Jew? The simple answer would be: all those who wish to adopt such an identification.

Such openness also challenges dogmatism about Jewish belief. Within this framework the theological systems of the various branches of contemporary Judaism should be viewed as subjective religious assumptions. The implications of this shift from the absolutism of the past to a new understanding of Judaism are radical and far reaching. The various branches of modern Judaism including non-theistic movements have advanced absolute, universal truth claims about the nature of God and the world. Yet, it should be accepted that there can be no way of attaining complete certainty about these beliefs. A cardinal aspect of this new way of viewing the various branches of Judaism is the appropriateness of modifying the tradition according to personal needs. This signifies that all theological concepts should be amenable to change. Hence the modifications to traditional Orthodox teaching proposed by Reform, Conservative, Reconstructionist and Humanistic rabbis should be regarded as admissible. Moreover, there should be no compulsion for such altered notions to be accepted by all members of the community.

Such openness similarly offers a new foundation for dealing with Jewish practice. Advancing the principle of personal autonomy, it celebrates freedom of choice as a cardinal virtue. What is crucial is the freedom such a view gives to individuals to determine for themselves which Jewish practices they find spiritually significant. At its core is its advocacy of freedom of choice in selecting those mitzvot which the person wishes to include in his or her religious observance. Unlike the past where centralized religious coercion dominated Jewish life, it is the individual who is ultimately responsible for determining how to live as a modern Jew.

Conclusion

Today, as we have seen, the Jewish community is deeply divided over questions of Jewish identity as well as belief and practice. To meet the challenge of such diversity, it has been suggested that Jews adopt a liberal stance of toleration. It might be assumed that such openness is at odds with the nature of modern Jewish life: the various movements we have surveyed embrace varying systems of belief and practice and appear unwilling to tolerate variant interpretations of the tradition. Nonetheless, it is undeniable that Jews worldwide

– other than the strictly Orthodox – choose which aspects of the Jewish faith they wish to embrace. In all cases this is a personal decision determined by subjective criteria. There has thus been a fundamental shift in orientation from the past. Prior to the emancipation of Jewry in the eighteenth and nineteenth centuries, the rabbinic establishment dominated Jewish existence. Rabbinic authorities were thus able to impose their own religious demands on the community. In contemporary society, this is no longer the case. Instead there is a widespread recognition and acceptance of the subjective character of Jewish existence – such diversity of approach should be perceived as a non-authoritative answer to the question: who is a Jew?

About the author

Dan Cohn-Sherbok is professor emeritus of Judaism at the University of Wales. He has previously taught at the University of Kent, and has been a visiting fellow at Wolfson College, Cambridge and Harris Manchester College, Oxford. He has been a visiting professor in numerous universities around the world. The author and editor of over 90 books, his works have been translated into fifteen languages.

References

Biale, David (1998). *Insider/Outsider: American Jews and Multiculturalism.* Berkeley, CA: University of California Press.
Kaplan, Mordecai (1967). *Judaism as a Civilisation: Toward a Reconstruction of American-Jewish Life.* New York: Schocken Books.
Meyer, M. (1988). *Response to Modernity: A History of the Reform Movement in Judaism.* Oxford: Oxford University Press.
Rabinowicz, H. (1988). *Hasidism: The Movement and its Masters.* Northvale NJ: Jason Aaronson.
Sacks, J. (1993). *One People? Tradition, Modernity and Jewish Unity.* London: Littman Library of Jewish Civilization. https://doi.org/10.2307/j.ctv36zr1g
Shilony, Ben-Amy (1992). *The Jews and the Japanese: The Successful Outsiders.* Rutland VT: Tuttle.
Wills, Lawrence (2013). *Not God's People: Insiders and Outsiders in the Biblical World.* Lanham, MD: Rowman and Littlefield.
Wine, S. (1985). *Judaism beyond God.* Hoboken, NJ: KTAV Publishing House.
Zimmerman, Chaim (1979). *Torah and Reason: Insiders and Outsiders of Torah.* Jerusalem: He'd Press.

13

Between institutional oppression and spiritual liberation

The female ordination movement in the Catholic Church and its utilization of social media

Lyndel Spence

Religion is necessarily a highly enigmatic and elusive issue within contemporary sociology that "places quite special demands on the sociological imagination" (Giddens 2009: 677). This assertion is especially accurate when attempting to conceptualize how individuals and groups can occupy seemingly liminal positions in institutional religious settings. Within religion in particular, groups and individuals are habitually categorized as being either *inside*, namely compliant, devout and faithful, or *outside*, namely dissenting, secular, heretical, or even anti-religious. This inside/outside binary has plagued sociological accounts of religion, often with the unintended corollary of applying a reductionist logic to the study of religious social movements which belies the complexity and reflexivity of religiosity within late modernity. This chapter will seek to problematize this set binary and will proffer the dualism of oppression and liberation as a more apposite and dynamic mode of interrogating how individuals and groups can simultaneously occupy positions of inclusion and exclusion within a religious context. This dualism extends upon traditional views of religious membership, which define an individual's status in a linear and essentialist manner. Further, this dualism embraces an appreciation for individual agency and self-determinism in faith, and the ability of faith believers to liberate themselves from repressive religious doctrines, dogmas and exegeses.

The female ordination movement within the Catholic Church is a dynamic and forceful example of the paradoxical binary of institutional oppression and individual liberation operating within the contemporary religious sphere. Amidst the entrenched patriarchy and misogyny of the Roman Catholic Church, women have been relegated to an inferior position of submissiveness and subjugation, cut off from full membership and participation in the

Church. The ideology of ecclesial patriarchy thus has severe consequences for the agency and self-determinism of women, with women being confined to the outsider position of "men's other" (de Beauvoir 2009[1949]) within the Catholic Church. As a result of this intense gendered exclusion, women have experienced acute forms of alienation and marginalization. Members of this intersectional feminist movement are seeking emancipation from these rigid forms of kyriarchy which dominate Roman Catholicism, and are seeking justice and gender equality in the face of the systematic patriarchal oppression of women. This radical and pioneering international movement is struggling for recognition as a legitimate religious formation as it campaigns for a more inclusive and accountable Catholic Church. The female ordination movement thereby provides a fertile conduit for examining how religion can both oppress individual freedoms and also be used to mobilize political, social and spiritual liberation from institutional disempowerment.

This chapter will utilize critical discourse analysis of various social media outlets and webpages to elaborate on the institutional oppression and spiritual liberation which lies at the heart of this religious group. Information Communication Technology (ICT) has come to occupy a central role within religious communities in the ever-escalating "network society" (Castells 2000) of the late modern age. For as Shirkey expands, "we are witnessing the rise of new ways of coordinating action that take advantage of that change ... we are living in the middle of a remarkable increase in our ability to share, to cooperate with one another, and to take collective action, all outside of the framework of traditional institutions and organisations" (Shirky 2008: 20–21). ICT has been used by both the institutional Catholic Church, and by the female ordination movement with differing aims and intentions. This chapter will first assess ways in which the Roman Catholic Church has been able to utilize online media platforms to entrench the institutional repression of women within the Church. Subsequently, this chapter will draw upon feminist theology and Heidi Campbell's (2010) "religious-social shaping approach", to explore the effectiveness of social media in connecting women across the world who are facing institutional religious repression and who are seeking support from likeminded faith believers. Through critical discourse analysis, this chapter will find that the Roman Catholic Church has been able to promulgate ideologies and doctrines which serve to peripheralize and suppress the participation of women in the Catholic Church. While social media are used by groups involved in the female ordination movement such as the Catholic Network for Women's Equality (CNWE), Women's Ordination Worldwide (WOW) and the Women's Alliance for Theology, Ethics and Ritual (WATER), to subvert the dominant attitudes towards women within the Catholic Church and to provide an alternative form of religious expression for disaffected Catholic women. These groups are thereby able to mobilize women into a solidary international religious formation which empowers women who have experienced suppression or subjugation from the Roman Catholic Church. Given that women's religious experiences have been noticeably absent from the androcentric history of the Catholic tradition, the inclusion of their voices constitutes an important contribution to scholarly inquiries that seek to shed more comprehensive light on the complexities of people's spiritually oriented and religiously based realities (Chittister 2004; Johnson 2002; Schneiders 2004). In this way this study will seek to illuminate and empower the narratives of women, who have for so long been consigned to an outside position within the Catholic imaginary and consciousness.

Positioning the movement: historical and ideological context of the female ordination movement

This transformative movement for reform and renewal in the Church remains a relatively under-researched and tragically misunderstood example of feminist activism within a conservative religious institution. The core impetus of this movement is to advance equality and justice in the Church, through the ordination of women and the creation of intersectionally inclusive worshipping communities. Historically, the leadership of the Roman Catholic Church has been dominated by men – a hierarchical fact which has manifested into a heavily ingrained patriarchalism within the Church. The Church's prohibition of the ordination of women is justified by the androcentric assumptions ensconced within the Doctrine of Apostolic Succession, which holds that only men may be ordained, and therefore that only men can be the Church's authentic teachers of faith and morals (Bourgeois 2013). Kelley has argued that this doctrine "puts women in both a position of dependence and subordination that ultimately maintains the patriarchal structure of Catholic Christianity" (2011: 1218–1219).

The women whom I studied routinely discussed an acute sense of alienation and atomization from the Church community, as a result of this entrenched patriarchalism inside the Catholic Church. Unwilling to confine themselves to the margins of Church life, these women have attempted to overcome their liminal position in two key ways; first through the creation of supportive communities united around a shared feminist ethos and progressive outlook on Catholic spirituality, and second through the formation of religious solidarities that practise this feminist vision through reimagined acts of collective worship and activism. The members of this movement are thereby placed in a precarious condition of both being excluded from the institutional Catholic Church, and belonging to a renewed, yet institutionally unrecognized Catholic community. This movement thereby finds itself on the nexus of being simultaneously inside and outside, as its members seek liberation from patriarchal oppression within the Church.

The female ordination movement is indisputably transnational in nature and is constituted by members and communities in Europe, Canada, America, South Africa, Colombia and Mexico. Although the movement began in earnest in Europe, the epicentre of the movement now lies in North America with over seventy-five inclusive communities. The organization of this movement is structured around two key groups; Roman Catholic Womenpriests (RCWP) and the Association of Roman Catholic Womenpriests (ARCWP). While both are committed to gender equality and social justice within the Church, RCWP and ARCWP each have their own administrative structure and unique approach to governance. The core function of RCWP and ARCWP is not centred on control or regulation of the constituent Church communities, but rather the function of these groups is to provide support for women who have a vocational calling to the Catholic priesthood. RCWP and ARCWP have developed rigorous models of spiritual formation and discernment for prospective women priests, which requires candidates to complete postgraduate level studies in theology or divinity, as well as continuing study with courses specifically designed by RCWP and ARCWP. These organizations conduct and oversee the ordination process, and provide a source of ongoing support and direction for women priests. As of September 2015, internationally there were 155 ordained women priests, 33 deacons, 21 candidates and 7 deceased members.

This movement began in 2002 when a cluster of renegade male clerics ordained the seven females as the first women priests aboard a boat on the River Danube. The ordinations took place on an international waterway, so as to prevent Vatican sanctions against a particular nation or diocese, and were shrouded in clandestine secrecy so as to prevent Vatican attempts to thwart this historic event. The group was heralded as "the Danube Seven"; a nickname which highlights the infamy and distinction surrounding this affair. Like other Catholics, these women believed in Apostolic Succession, the idea that priestly ordinations are valid if the bishop who performs the rites can trace his ecclesiastical lineage back 2,000 years to the original 12 apostles. Accordingly, the women were ordained by Bishop Rómulo Antonio Braschi, an Independent Catholic bishop who was staunchly opposed to the prohibition of female ordination. The bishop used the same rites that are used for male candidates, and the women took the same vows, prostrating themselves as men do when they are being ordained (Loh 2013). It appears as somewhat contradictory that these women would seek to actively apply the doctrine and ordination practices which had for so long ensured their oppression and exclusion within the Church. However, the women of the ordination movement have sought to utilize Apostolic Succession as a tool of authenticity, to signal that their ordinations are valid and should be recognized as legitimate by the Church. For as woman priest Jane Via affirms, "if we want to make change, *real* change within the Church, we have to follow and *then* subvert the traditional structures and ways of the Church" (interview with author, 4 April 2014). However, in the eyes of the institutional Church these ordinations were declared to be "invalid and null" (Meehan 2010: 47) and were considered as an act of heretical heterodoxy. The Vatican has responded to the plight of women priests in quite a caustic and punitive fashion – excommunicating women who have been ordained as priests, excommunicating men and women who have publically supported the ordination of women priests, and excommunicating male priests who have advocated or aided this movement.

Despite this institutional chastisement of the movement, female priests and their supporters, continue to serve the church in renewed ministry by welcoming all to celebrate the sacraments in inclusive, Christ-centred, Spirit-empowered communities. Roman Catholic women priests are at the forefront of a model of service that offers Catholics a renewed priestly ministry in vibrant grassroots communities, as well as ministering in the areas of hospital and hospice chaplaincy, homeless ministries, social work programs, social justice and peace advocacy, prison ministry, interfaith ministry, as well as publicizing the movement through a variety of media forms. The specific charism of the female ordination movement is to live Gospel equality and justice for all, and they "work in solidarity with the poor, exploited and marginalized for structural and transformative justice in partnership with all believers", as they state on their website (https://arcwp.org). Consequently the movement is founded upon a democratic approach to governance, in which they "act as a community of equals in decision-making both as an organization and within [their] faith communities" (ibid.). These communities have embraced the mantle of "intersectionality" (Crenshaw 1991) and acknowledge the overlapping and intersecting systems of oppression operating within the Church. As such the movement is concerned with overturning the myriad forms of domination in the Church, including homophobia, racism, classism, clerical authoritarianism and the discrimination of the disabled, and moving towards a truly inclusive and liberatory vision of Catholicism.

Overcoming outsider status: the individualization of religion

In order to contextualize this study it is also necessary to briefly consider the landscape of contemporary late-modern religion. It is this study's key contention that the potential of personal liberation from oppressive institutional religious structures is only possible amidst the pervasive detraditionalization and personalization of religion within late-modernity. The potential for individual agency and self-determinism in faith is a theme which has been addressed through the body of theory referred to as the Individualization Thesis. Proponents of the Individualization Thesis conceptualize dynamic processes such as "de-secularization" (Berger 1999), "de-communalization" (Casanova 1994), "re-spiritualization" (Horx 1993) or "the return of the religions" (Riesebrodt 2000) as dominating the religious landscape of the modern era. Further, Beck (2010: 26) advances the "revitalization of religiosity and spirituality in the twenty-first century" predicated on "exemplary religious individualism" (ibid.: 11) as the unassailable development of modern religiosity. The Individualization Thesis therefore contends that amidst the extensive individuation of modern society, institutional religion has become detraditionalized as individual believers have usurped authority in the construction of what Beck terms a "God of One's Own" (ibid.). Thus Hervieu-Léger (2003: 172) identifies a schism "between the official forms of religion and individually accepted religious perceptions and behaviours", as "individuals are more and more freed from established religious authorities and thus enabled to autonomously determine their belief systems" (ibid.: 175).

Beck affirms that the key to the revitalization of religiosity, within Giddens's framework of "reflexive modernity", is the "decoupling of (institutional) religion and (subjective) faith" (Giddens 2009: 26). Thus, for Beck, the detraditionalizing processes of cosmopolitanization and individualization have severed the seemingly inextricable bond between personal religious belief and the organized structures of the church. This process of detraditionalization, according to Heelas (1996: 2), "involves a shift from 'without' to 'within'", as the authority or "'voice' is displaced from established sources, coming to rest with the individualized self". This rise in autonomy for individual faith believers is crucial for the liberation of people from oppressive religious structures. Given the agency to determine their own spiritual trajectory and their own vision of faith enables individuals to make the transition from being trapped inside oppressive religious traditions to embracing emancipatory renderings of their faith outside of institutional control. Such individualized patterns of religiosity have been avidly pursued by faith believers who hold strong objections to their church's official stance towards various issues such as homosexuality, the ordination of female priests, sexual ethics and the role of women within the hierarchy of the church. These individuals are able to confront and contest the orthodoxy of institutional religions in order to forge personally meaningful and fulfilling systems of faith.

Virtualized religion: the role of the internet and social media

Within the context of this rise of self-inscribed and de-institutionalized religiosity, the internet and social media have become vital tools in the enactment of faith, and in the formation of alternative religious formations which resist the orthodoxy of traditional religious institutions. As scholars such as Lundby (2011), Cowan (2012), Campbell (2010), and Lochhead (1997) aver, religions have been transformed by adopting new media technologies ever since the invention of the printing press. Now at the beginning of the twenty-first century, we are witnessing the proliferation of new web applications that provide more opportunities for interaction, collaboration, participation and content creation than traditional, static websites. Described by the term "Web 2.0" (DiNucci 1999) these new kinds of interactive sites include blogs, wikis, photo and video sharing and social network sites, and have reinvigorated the political potential of the internet as a medium for information dissemination and group mobilization. Amid the democratizing effects of the Web 2.0 revolution, public religion is confronted by the adjustment to new technologies, styles and formats. Religious organizations, leaders, groups and individuals have taken on the challenge to create and introduce new ways of conducting religious rituals and community practices online, and believers are similarly looking to the internet and virtual forms of religion to satiate their desires for religious self-fulfilment and actualization.

This optimistic and constructive view of the efficacy of online and digitized forms of religion, however, has not always dominated discourse surrounding religion and the internet. For many religious groups and individuals there is an insistent assumption that media and religion are distinct cultural domains; one sacred and the other secular. These groups have held a dominant ideology that the internet serves as a source of corruption and moral pollution (Golan and Campbell 2015) and is therein an adversary of religion and religious authority in the contemporary era. Proponents of this view of the internet, such as Tal Brooke and the conservative Christian think tank the Spiritual Counterfeits Project, argued against Christian use of the internet, contending that "cyberspace is a breeding ground for delusion ... creating the worst kind of alienation – from reality and from God" (Brooke 1997: 176). Further, Douglas Groothuis, a professor from an evangelical seminary, voiced the concern that "technology has taken the place of the deity and people worship it instead of God" (1997: 15). Such scholars and religious figures or groups have exhibited a distinct distrust, fear and aversion towards the internet. For them, the internet is to be viewed as a severely atomizing and oppressive force for the continuity of traditional religious orthodoxy.

For the preponderance of religious groups and scholars, however, the internet and its ancillary forms of social media have been viewed as a "hybrid technology ... that serve[s] as a digital playground of new opportunities for sharing and experimentation" (Campbell 2010: 19). The internet has thus been viewed as a tool that can be used to promote religion and religious practice. Chama was able to encapsulate this sense of the profound implications for the use of online media for religion in her 1996 article in *Time Magazine*, entitled "Finding God on the Web". Here Chama astutely surmised that:

> For many signing on to the web is a transformative act. In their eyes, the web is more than just a global tapestry of personal computers. It is a vast cathedral of the mind, a place where ideas about God and religion can resonate, where faith can be shaped and defined by a collective spirit. (Chama 1996: 57)

In the age of deinstitutionalized and highly individualized religion, faith believers are able to engage in a process of "bricolage" (Lévi-Strauss 1966), as they retrieve information from these online sources and construct a personally meaningful "God of one's own" (Beck 2010). However, even more significantly, they are also given the ability to join with other believers in a transnational space of worship and spiritual exploration, through their performance of what Helland (2005) terms "online religion". Campbell (2010) attests to the innate potential of the internet for religious life, and has developed a model of the ways in which religious individuals employ the internet: first as a "spiritual network" – a place where spiritual encounters are being made; second as a "worship space" – the internet provides a space in which religious rituals or activities are able to be conducted; third as a "missionary tool" – the internet has become used as a way of promoting a religion's message and beliefs; and lastly as a "religious identity" affirmer – the internet is used for individuals to find out more about their own religion and theology which helps them build their own religious identity. These are opportunities which social media and internet offer apply to faith believers and by extension to religious groups and organizations alike. These functions of the internet for religion have been appropriated by a range of religious groups, as they seek to cultivate both traditional and non-traditional forms of religion in a new media context.

Through this discussion of the stances taken by religious groups towards the intersection of internet-based media in contemporary forms of religion and religious practice, two competing views are palpable. First, the internet is viewed as a social evil which generates moral corruption and contamination, and second, the internet is viewed as a transformative source of religious empowerment in the late-modern age. Thus, we can observe that the internet is seen to possess the potential for both the oppression and liberation of religious groups. Therefore, the paradox of oppression and liberation extends not only to the case study of the female ordination movement, but also on to the medium by which they are seeking to attain spiritual emancipation.

Campbell's social-shaping approach

The critical discourse analysis of this study has been framed by Heidi Campbell's (2010) "religious-social shaping approach to technology". This is a conceptual framework that acknowledges how a religious community's historical life practice, interpretive tradition and the contemporary outworking of their values informs their choices about the adoption and adaptation of technology (ibid.: 41). This approach takes into account the factors informing a religious community's responses to new media – their relationship to community, authority and text – and combines it with a social shaping approach that highlights the practices surrounding technology evaluation. Within this framework, "technology is seen as a social process and the possibility is recognized that social groups may shape technologies towards their own ends, rather than the character of the technology determining use and outcomes" (ibid.: 50). Of particular interest are the special qualities and constraints of religious communities which mediate their use of media-based technology. Thus, a unique element of the religious-social shaping of technology is that it seeks to explore in more detail how spiritual, moral, and theological codes of practice guide technological negotiation (ibid.: 59). Thus, this framework calls for a deeper awareness of the role which history and tradition play in religious communities' process of negotiation (ibid.). The result is a four-part model which identifies the following four aspects: history and tradition, core beliefs and patterns, the negotiation process and communal framing and discourse, as the framework for studying religious communities' media engagement. These criteria will form the basis for the critical discourse analysis of the use of internet-based media forms and social media by both the Roman

Catholic Church and various female ordination groups, in relation to the position of women within the Church.

A noteworthy caveat to this approach is that "it is important to consider not only the tradition a religious community comes from, but also the particular characteristics and lived practice of the specific group when reflecting on media use" (Campbell 2010: 20). It will therefore be elucidated that the Roman Catholic Church and the female ordination movement have utilized these media forms in strikingly dissimilar ways. For the female ordination movement, internet-based media have been employed to mobilize likeminded believers around a shared set of feminist ideals and to create a sense of solidarity for those who have felt excluded by the wider Catholic Church. While, for the Roman Catholic Church, their conservative and literalist interpretation of the Bible's teachings has impelled them to use the internet to entrench and propagate their religious and ideological position on the issue of female participation and ministry within the Church.

History and tradition

The Roman Catholic Church, despite its early reservations about the corruptive influence of the internet, has come to embrace the internet and its digital ancillaries as a tool to accomplish its evangelizing mission in the late modern era. In his 1990 World Communication Day messages, the late Pope John Paul II urged for the Church to embrace the opportunities offered by computers and telecommunication technology to fulfil its mission. As he stated, "in the new 'computer culture', the Church can more readily inform the world of her beliefs and explain the reasons for her stance on any given issue or event" (PCSC 1990). The Pope's stamp of approval on the internet as "a new forum for proclaiming the gospel" (PCSC 2002) has allowed for the Catholic use and appropriation of internet-based media to flourish. This is an important fact to consider, as the official sanctioning of official-Church based media forms by the Pontiff bestows upon these webpages a high degree of credibility and authority, and thereby ensures their high exposure and popularity within Roman Catholic communities.

The internet-based media forms of the Roman Catholic Church, namely in the form of webpages at both the Vatican and Sydney archdiocese levels, draw upon the prestige, history and tradition of the Catholic Church in order to lay emphasis to their institutional authority. To this end, the graphic formatting and layout of the official Vatican webpage (www.vatican.va), right down to the inclusion of Pope Francis's official crest on the banner and an abstract image of the imposing edifice of the Vatican, evokes this sense of tradition and gravitas. Further, the webpage provides a chronology of past Popes, as well as a chronicle of the history of the Catholic Church, dating back some 2000 years. This accumulation of heritage ensconces a sense of the legitimacy and authority which the Church holds. Subsequently, the teachings and doctrines which they espouse are given a dogmatic ascendancy and prestige. This fact is echoed in this webpage, in which the images of high-ranking members of the clerical hierarchy are exalted as figures of power. Again, the official crest, as well as the ethereal image of St. Peter's Basilica, is vestigial of the enduring legacy and credo of the Church. This positioning and affirmation of the Vatican as a traditional source of religious supremacy imbues the content of its webpage, including outlines of church and canon law, church doctrine and teachings, and spiritual reflections, with authority and credo. For "religious surfers" (Helland 2005), the information and ideology outlined on these webpages would therefore be taken to be the official and legitimate stance of the Catholic tradition.

In contrast, the Female Ordination groups, in particular the RCWP, Women-Church Convergence, WATER and Mary Magdalene Apostolic Catholic Community (MMACC), seek to establish their history in opposition to the legacy of the Papacy and the Vatican. For example, WATER explains in detail the development of the female ordination movement in relation to the sanctions, condemnations and excommunications handed down to members of the movement, by the Roman Catholic Church (see www.waterwomensalliance.org). The inclusion of these historical details serves to malign the Roman Catholic Church and elucidate the historical trajectory and reality of the marginalization of women within the Church. This fact would appeal to women who may be experiencing similar forms of alienation or coercion in their own Catholic parishes and who similarly perceive themselves to be othered outsiders in the Church. Overall, the webpages of these female ordination groups serve to construct the origins and tradition of this movement in opposition to that of the Roman Catholic Church. Further, each of these websites features detailed histories of the emergence and development of these ordination groups. Each of the webpages contains information and references to the revisionist historical, archaeological, and theological evidence of women's ministry throughout the ages, in an effort to dismiss the Church's justification for prohibiting female priests on the grounds of tradition. The movement seeks to draw upon the historic lineage of female ordination in the Church to legitimate their mission, as proclaimed on their website (http://romancatholicwomenpriests.org), to "reclaim their ancient spiritual heritage and re-shape a more inclusive, Christ-centered Church for the 21st century", based upon "a new model of priestly ministry united with the people with whom [they] serve".

The movement therein seeks to counter the tradition and historical antiquity of the official Vatican webpages by positioning themselves as a resistance to traditional patterns of Catholicism, and as a progressive and reformist religious formation. The typefaces and colour patterns of these webpages, as typified by the RCWP webpage, feature a vibrant mosaic of colours, which conjures images of the vitality and vigour of this religious community. The website is not shrouded in the stiff and ceremonial pomp of the Vatican or Archdiocese webpage and has more of an accessible and convivial air. These webpages thereby seek to counteract the transcendence of the official Roman Catholic Church. For as the vision statement on the MMACC website affirms, "we have a vision of a new way to be Roman Catholic, a new way of making Roman Catholicism relevant" (see www.mmacc.org). The insinuation that they are seeking to make Catholicism relevant positions this group in direct opposition to the institutional orthodoxy of the Roman Catholic Church, and would attract those who feel embittered by the Catholic Church, or those who are seeking a more contemporary and modern rendering of Catholicism.

Core beliefs and patterns

The Roman Catholic Church uses internet-based media to promulgate and operationalize its beliefs on the rightful place of women within Catholicism and Catholic practices. The official church stance towards the issue of female ordination is grounded in the Doctrine of Apostolic Succession. The doctrine holds that Jesus Christ, understood in Christianity as God incarnate, conferred full sacramental authority upon his apostles, in effect naming them the full bishops of the church (Kelley 2011). The official and institutionalized beliefs of the church in relation to the position of women are echoed in their use of online media as a space for ritual engagement. Recent scholarship has extolled the potential of the internet to offer interaction and new processes of communication in the context of rituals (Campbell 2011; Casey 2006; Radde-Antweiler 2006). The Roman Catholic Church has begun to employ internet technology to perform rituals such as the Daily Mass. The CatholicTV.org website, for example, enables faith believers to instantaneously access daily Mass from the privacy and comfort of their own homes. The enactment and performance of ritual rites is a formative element of the Catholic faith, and must be understood as being constituted by the beliefs and teachings of the Church. It is unsurprising therefore that the Masses available on media platforms such as CatholicTV.org, are rituals which are dominated by men – men lead the Mass, whether it be the Pope, the Bishop or the Priest, men carry out other sacramental duties – acolytes, altar services, ministers of communion, and men even read the Gospel and sing in the choir. Men, according to this image, can have it all! But what about the place of women? Through this online rendering of Catholic religious practice, which mirrors and cements patterns in real life Catholicism, women are placed on the margins of Catholic rituals thereby reflecting and reinforcing their subordinate position within the Church.

These beliefs and views surrounding the participation of women in the church have also filtered down into the construction of gender-specific roles for women in the Catholic Church. In the ground-breaking second wave feminist text *The Feminine Mystique* (1963), Betty Friedan's reference to "the problem that has no name" calls attention to the limiting effects of patriarchal gender roles. Feminist scholars such as Basow (1992) explain that gender stereotypes are constructed by socializing agents and forces within society, through the construction of socially shared descriptive norms and prescriptive norms (Eagly et al. 2004) that perpetuate the demarcation of gender roles. Father Wojciech Giertych, head theologian to Pope Benedict XVI, explains that "women don't need the priesthood, because their mission is so beautiful in the Church already" (Rocca 2013). So let us examine the nature of this beautiful mission and the gender roles demarcated for women, as defined by the Roman Catholic Church. The website of the Catholic Office for the Participation of Women (OPW) provides the most constructive platform by which to assess the Church's prototype for appropriate female involvement (see www.opw.catholic.org.au). This webpage has a section entitled "Women Matter". From this tool bar one can select profiles of individuals whom OPW defines as "inspirational women". The women represented in this section conform to patriarchal gender norms. For example, there is a nun, a nurse, a foster parent, a grandmother, a carer for disabled children and a volunteer. While these women are no doubt inspirational, it is interesting to note that the Catholic Church in this webpage advances a definition of being an "inspirational woman" in terms of her ability to nurture and care for others in a submissive role. There is a condescending undertone to this webpage that these subservient gender-specific roles are all that women can aspire to in the realms of Catholicism. It is evident therefore that the Roman Catholic Church utilizes internet-based forms of media to disseminate its beliefs and theological convictions surrounding the limitations which should be imposed upon women's participation and agency. This ideology has thereby suffused its attitudes towards the role of women within the Church, peripheralizing women into a position of inferiority within the Catholic Church.

If we look to the female ordination movement's utilization of internet-based media a similar ethic of proselytization can be observed; however, the underlying beliefs and practices are starkly different. For the female ordination groups, the internet is not a space for performing religion and enacting religious ritual, but rather the platforms of the internet provides a forum to disseminate a political message and to provide alternative forms of religiosity for those who have become disillusioned by the orthodox belief systems and practices of the Roman Catholic Church. The female ordination movement thereby embarks on a mission of information dissemination, as its members seek to subvert dominant church teachings and practices, through their proselytization of a new form of faith rooted in egalitarianism. I term this form of preaching "fem-evangelization", as it is founded on a holistic integration of feminist principles and feminist theology with mainstream Catholic values. According to this model, the female ordination movement is equally committed to disseminating both its faith and its feminist political project: Catholicism and feminism must be conceptualized as concomitant and mutually reinforcing ideologies for the members of this movement. In this way, members of the ordination movement are able to oppose the inherent gender-based oppression within the Catholic Church and thereby attain liberated forms of spiritual actualization.

Through fem-evangelization these nontraditional religious formations are able to disseminate a progressive and alternative belief system which draws upon feminist theology to complement traditional Catholic teachings and beliefs. Feminist theology, in the words of eminent theologian Rosemary Radford Ruether (1985: 704), is "engaged in a critique of the androcentrism and misogyny of patriarchal theology, and is positioned as a contestation of kyriarchy. Kyriarchy is a neologism developed by eminent feminist theologian Elisabeth Schussler-Fiorenza (2009) to describe interconnected, interacting and self-extending systems of domination and submission. It is an intersectional extension of the idea of patriarchy beyond gender, to encompass sexism, racism, economic forms of injustice, and other forms of dominating hierarchy in which subordination is internalized and institutionalized. Feminist theology therein seeks to confront and overcome kyriarchal structures and practices within religion.

Each of the female ordination movement groups studied emphasized the importance of feminist theology to the movement and to the construction of their faith. Therefore, each of the groups have links to publications, media releases, theological journals, theological blogs and books which can educate individuals on the theological basis of this religious formation. WATER, for example, was actually founded by Diane Neu and Mary Hunt, two eminent scholars in the field of feminist theology, and this webpage provides access to a myriad of theological resources, as well as online conferences, discussion boards and online forums, which allow individuals to engage on both a conceptual and interactive level. Various Web 2.0 technologies such as blog posts, interactive discussion forums, chat rooms and annual online conferences on the webpages of RCWP, WATER and Women–Church Convergence all offer an alternative critical view of canonical Catholic teachings, and a space for people to learn and dialogue on such ideas. The inclusion of these resources on the webpages of these groups serves to verify the theological legitimacy of their religious formation, and allows a space for the dissemination of this renewed vision of Catholic theology.

This vision of faith is emphasized in the mission statements of these religious communities, available on their websites, and Facebook and Twitter pages. For example, the second line of the MMACC mission statement explains that its mission is to "dedicate ourselves to living the Gospel values, especially those of compassion, peace and social justice, as taught and exemplified by Jesus the Christ, while also committing ourselves to the full equality of women and men in a transformed Roman Catholic Church and world" (www.mmacc.org). In order to further embed these beliefs into the faith lives of their followers, as an active process of fem-evangelization, the websites of the ordination movements have access to prayers, spiritual reflections, hymns, meditations, homilies and other devotional resources which reflect their beliefs and practices, and which encourage others to pursue these progressive forms of religiosity. For example, MMACC offers hyperlinks to a range of prayers, including their Profession of Faith, which they recite at Mass each week. This prayer is a reinterpretation of the same prayer which is used in Roman Catholic Masses, but has been revised to incorporate more inclusive language and rhetoric. Phrases such as "Amen to the partnership of *women and men* in God's plan" replace the traditional nomenclature of phrases such as "For us *men* and for our salvation, *He* came down from heaven" evoking a sense of the egalitarianism upon which their form of faith is based. By granting online access to these spiritual resources, groups such as the MMACC are able to spread the core message of their belief system, while also inviting people outside of their parish to engage in more inclusive and progressive forms of Catholic faith.

The negotiation process

Having established the ways in which both the Roman Catholic Church and the various female ordination groups have been able to utilize internet media forms, in terms of both their history and traditions and their core beliefs and practices, it is necessary now to consider how these groups negotiate online media technologies. The Roman Catholic Church has predominantly relied upon the webpages at the Vatican and archdiocese level, as well as the webpages of its associated offices and associations, such as the Office for the Participation of Women, to disseminate information in an online format. As previously mentioned, the Church has also pioneered new forms of online visual material, such as Masstv.com and the Vatican's own YouTube channel (www.youtube.com/user/vatican).

However, it is this study's position that the female ordination movement has been able to use a more diverse range of online technologies in a more inspired and resourceful manner than the Catholic Church. In addition to the official webpages of these groups, there are accompanying blogs, YouTube clips, multimedia slideshows, documentaries, discussion forums, online conferences, interactive prayer request forums, weekly email newsletters, and Twitter and Facebook pages which have been integrated into the interface of these sites. These social networking sites have allowed for a further reach of audience and have allowed for a more regular and visible presence of these groups in the lives of its followers.

The most illustrative example of the creativity and dynamism embedded within the female ordination movement's utilization of the internet is the Facebook page "Pope Vicky's People" (www.facebook.com/Pope-Vickys-People-204610439560743). This is a page which has created a satirical character called Pope Vicky, who is essentially a Barbie doll irreverently dressed in the ceremonial garb of the Catholic clergy. This doll has then been inserted into scenes with religious figures such as Pope Francis and into images which bear captions such as "Barbie's had over a hundred careers. Now she's added Pope." Now, while this may have the impression of triviality, these images, and this appropriation of the pop-culture icon of Barbie, have been utilized by the page's creator to convey a significant message and socio-cultural meaning. The juxtaposition of hyper-feminized form of Barbie with the exclusively masculine role of Pope or Bishop problematizes the gendered divisions and exclusions which have suffused the Catholic hierarchy. It is this appropriation of cultural forms on online media platforms which typify how the female ordination movement has been able to combine serious theological debate with more light-hearted and contemporary rhetoric in order to appeal to a wider range of people and in order to counter the rigidity of institutional orthodox elements of Catholicism. Its negotiation of media forms has also allowed for a more interactive and collaborative experience than the Roman Catholic Church. This has enhanced the efficacy of these media forms both for proselytization and for engaging faith believers.

Communal framing

Finally, it is necessary to evaluate the communal framing of these religious groups' use of internet-based media, and how they are able to utilize these online technologies in the creation of what functionalist sociologists such as Émile Durkheim (1955) would term religious solidarity. While the Roman Catholic Church is an exemplary example of an international religious formation, from this modest discourse analysis it is clear that their utilization of media has been only partially effective in creating a sense of communalism or collectivism among its adherents. The purpose of their use of online media must be considered here, as these websites serve more as a source of sacramental information, edification, and clarification, rather than as the basis for the formation of religious communities.

The female ordination movement groups, however, are able to galvanize members around a shared commitment to ideals and belief, and engender meaningful transnational solidarities through their aforementioned interactive online activities. Again, the purpose of these groups must be considered. MMACC succinctly encapsulates the impetus of this movement in the first line of its mission statement, which is on the home page of its website. This mission statement says that "[its] mission is to welcome all, and reach out to those across the world who feel marginalized by the traditional Roman Catholic Church" (www.mmacc.org). Further, the Women–Church Convergence acknowledges on its website's homepage that it is "a coalition of autonomous Catholic-rooted organizations/groups raising a feminist voice and committed to an ekklesia of women which is participative, egalitarian and self-governing" (Women–Church Convergence 2013). Here, the Women–Church Convergence has appropriated Elisabeth Schüssler Fiorenza's (1993) concept of "ekklesia-ology", and the creation of a "discipleship of equals". This concept is highly constructive here, as the female ordination group movement has been able to utilize internet-based media to enact and to sustain dynamic forms of "virtual ekklesia" (Howard 2010) based on the premise of a discipleship of equals, in which "women would no longer feel estranged from the Church" (Collins 1999: 48).

In defiance of the institutional power of the Roman Catholic Church, this movement mobilizes women around their shared faith and their mutual desire for an expression of faith which is completely inclusive and which does not discriminate on the basis of gender, race, or sexuality. This movement aims to welcome in those who have felt marginalized by the Catholic Church and to liberate them from institutional religious repression. Communalization and the creation of solidarities thereby stand as an imperative mode of empowerment for women who have been alienated from the institutional Church. As Audre Lorde affirms, "without community there is no liberation, only the most temporary armistice between an individual and her oppression" (Lorde 1984: 112). These online communities provide a space for women who have been continually placed on the outside of the Church to be welcomed in and to be given the freedom to celebrate their faith and their spiritual identity without constraints or constrictions. The online media technologies, such as webpages, social media pages, blogs and discussion forums, used by the female ordination groups thereby act as a conduit to the galvanization of transnational religious communities, united in their quest for liberation from the patriarchal oppression of institutional Catholicism.

Conclusion: the Holy Trinity Framework

It is thus this study's contention that the female ordination movement has been able to utilize online media forms in a manner which has empowered its vision of faith and which has provided an apparatus for women worldwide to be able to liberate themselves from kyriarchal oppression. By way of conclusion and in order to draw together the analysis of this chapter, I would like to propose a model for the manner in which the female ordination movement has been able to utilize online media forms in pursuit of liberation from patriarchal and institutional repression. This three-part model has sardonically been labelled the Holy Trinity Framework. The Holy Trinity Framework holds that the main ways in which these groups are able to utilize online media are: resistance, communalization, and fem-evangelization.

In this way, members of the female ordination movement are able to use forms of social media to subvert the dominant attitudes towards women in the Catholic Church and to provide an alternative form of religious expression for disaffected women and men within the Catholic Church. These groups are thereby able to mobilize women into a solidary international formation which empowers women who have experienced subjugation or oppression from the Roman Catholic Church. In so doing, members of the female ordination movement are able to liberate themselves from the oppressive structures which have placed them on the outside of Church practice and the Catholic imaginary. This case study therein attests to and emblematizes the profound and emancipatory potential of ICT and the internet for religious social movements within the highly individuated milieu of late modern society. As online forms of communication and communalization continue to expand and intensify, the mediatization of religion offers infinite opportunities for the formation of transformative and liberatory religious solidarities.

About the author

Lyndel Spence teaches international global studies at the University of Sydney. From 2008 to 2010 Lyndel completed a Bachelor of International Global Studies at the University of Sydney, majoring in sociology and winning the Raewyn Connell Prize in Social Theory. She received her PhD, titled "Breaking the Stained Glass Ceiling: Intersectionality and the Female Ordination Movement in the Roman Catholic Church", in 2016. Her core research interests are religion, community, resistance, globalization, social justice, human rights, identity and gender and she maintains a keen interest in both classical and contemporary social theory. Lyndel has collaborated on the creation of a new sociology textbook with Pearson Education Australia, and currently has several journal articles in the process of being published. She also has a dedication for social justice, and is currently the Secretary of the NSW Amnesty International Women's Network.

References

Basow, S. A. (1992). *Gender: Stereotypes and Roles*. Belmont, CA: Thomson Brooks/Cole Publishing.
Beck, U. (2010). *A God of One's Own: Religion's Capacity for Peace and Potential for Violence*. Cambridge: Polity Press.
Berger, P. (1999). *The Desecularization of the World: Resurgent Religion and World Politics*. Washington: Ethics and Public Policy Center.
Bourgeois, R. (2013). *My Journey from Silence to Solidarity*. Yellow Springs, Ohio: fxBear.
Brooke, T. (1997). *Virtual Gods*. Eugene, OR: Harvest House.
Campbell, H. A. (2010). *When Religion Meets New Media*. New York: Routledge. https://doi.org/10.4324/9780203695371
Campbell, H. A. (2011). Understanding the Relationship between Religion Online and Offline in a Networked Society. *Journal of the American Academy of Religion* 80(1): 64-93. https://doi.org/10.1093/jaarel/lfr074
Casanova, J. (1994). *Public Religions in the Modern World*. Chicago, IL: University of Chicago Press. https://doi.org/10.7208/chicago/9780226190204.001.0001
Casey, C.A. (2006). Virtual Ritual, Real Faith: The Revirtualization of Religious Ritual in Cyberspace. *Journal of Religions on the Internet* 2(1): 72-90.
Castells, M. (2000). *The Rise of the Network Society* (2nd edition). Malden, MA: Blackwell Publishing.
Chama, J. C. (1996). Finding God on the Web. *Time Magazine*, December: 54-59.
Chittister, J. (2004). *Called to Question: A Spiritual Memoir*. Oxford: Sheed & Ward.
Collins, J. N. (1999). Does Equality of Discipleship Add Up to Church? A Critique of Feminist Ekklesia-ology. *New Theology Review* 12(3): 48-57.
Cowan, E. (2012). New Religious Movements and the Evolving Internet. In O. Hammer and M. Rothstein (eds), *The Cambridge Companion to New Religious Movements*. Cambridge: Cambridge University Press.

Crenshaw, K. (1991). Mapping the Margins: Intersectionality, Identity Politics, and Violence Against Women of Color. *Stanford Law Review* 43(6): 1241–1299. https://doi.org/10.2307/1229039

De Beauvoir, S. (2009[1949]). *The Second Sex* (trans. C. Borde and S. Malovany-Chevallier). New York: Random House.

DiNucci, D. (1999). Fragmented Future. *Print* 53(4): 32–44.

Durkheim, É. (1955). *The Elementary Forms of Religious Life: The Totemic System in Australia* (trans. K. E. Fields). New York: Free Press.

Eagly, A. H., R. M. Barron, and V. L. Hamilton, Prejudice: Toward a More Inclusive Understanding. In A. H. Eagly, R. M. Barron and V. L. Hamilton (eds), *The Social Psychology of Group Identity and Social Conflict: Theory, Application, and Practice*. Washington, DC: American Psychological Association.

Friedan, B. (1963). *The Feminine Mystique*. New York: W. W. Norton.

Giddens, A. (2009). *Sociology*. Cambridge: Polity Press.

Golan, O. and H. Campbell (2015). Strategic Management of Religious Websites: The case of Israel's Orthodox Communities. *Journal of Computer-Mediated Communication* 20(4): 467–486. https://doi.org/10.1111/jcc4.12118

Groothuis, D. R. (1997). *The Soul in Cyberspace*. Grand Rapids: Baker Books.

Heelas, P. (1996). *Detraditionalization: Critical Reflections on Authority and Identity*. Malden, MA: Blackwell.

Helland, C. (2005). Online Religion as Lived Religion: Methodological Issues in the Study of Religious Participation on the Internet. *Heidelberg Journal of Religions on the Internet* 1(1): 1–16.

Hervieu-Léger, D. (2003). Individualism, The Validation of Faith and the Social Nature of Religion in Modernity. In R. K. Fern (ed.), *The Blackwell Companion to Sociology of Religion*. Oxford: Blackwell Publishing.

Horx, M. (1993). *Trendbuch, Bd 1: Der Erste Große Deutsche Trendreprt*. Munich: Econ.

Howard, R. G. (2010). Enacting a Virtual "Ekklesia": Online Christian Fundamentalism as Vernacular Religion. *New Media and Society* 12(5): 729–744. https://doi.org/10.1177/1461444809342765

Johnson, E. (2002). *She Who Is: The Mystery of God in Feminist Theological Discourse*. New York: Crossroad.

Kelley, K. S. (2011). Women In Religion. In M. Zeiss Stange, C. K. Oyster and J. E. Sloan (eds), *Encyclopedia of Women In Today's World*. Thousand Oaks, CA: Sage.

Lévi-Strauss, C. (1966). *The Savage Mind* (trans. G. Weidenfield) Chicago, IL: University of Chicago Press.

Lochhead, D. (1997). *Shifting realities: Information Technology and the Church*. Geneva: World Council of Churches.

Loh, S. T. (2013). Priests. *More Magazine*, May: 112–117.

Lorde, A. (1984). *Sister Outsider: Essays and Speeches*. New York: Ten Speed Press.

Lundby, K. (2011). Mediatizing Faith: Digital Storytelling on the Unspoken. In M. Bailey and G. Redden (eds), *Mediating Faiths: Religion and Socio-cultural Change in the 21st Century*. London: Ashgate.

Meehan, B. M. (2010). *Living Gospel Equality Now: Loving in the Heart of God: A Roman Catholic Woman Priest Story*. College Station, TX: Virtual Bookworm Publishing.

PSCS (1990). The Christian Message in a Computer Culture. Retrieved from http://w2.vatican.va/content/john-paul-ii/en/messages/communications/documents/hf_jp-ii_mes_24011990_world-communications-day.html (9 November 2015).

PSCS (2002). Ethics in Communications. Retrieved from http://www.vatican.va/roman_curia/pontifical_councils/pccs/documents/rc_pc_pccs_doc_20000530_ethics-communications_en.html (10 November 2015).

Radde-Antweiler, K. (2006). Rituals Online: Transferring and Designing Rituals. *Journal of Religions on the Internet* 2(1): 54–72.

Ruether, R. R. (1985). The Future of Feminist Theology in the Academy. *Journal of the American Academy of Religion* 53(4): 703–713. https://doi.org/10.1093/jaarel/LIII.4.703

Riesebrodt, M. (2000). *Die Rückkehr der Religionen: Fundamentalismus und der Kampf der Kulturen*. Munich: Beck.

Rocca, Francis X. (2013). Why Not Women Priests? The Papal Theologian Explains. *National Catholic Reporter*, 5 February. Retrieved from www.ncronline.org/news/theology/why-not-women-priests-papal-theologian-explains (accessed 9 May 2019).

Schneiders, S. (2004). *Beyond Patching: Faith and Feminism in the Catholic Church*. Mahwah, NJ: Paulist Press.

Schussler Fiorenza, E. (1993). *Discipleship of Equals: A Critical Feminist Ekklesialogy of Liberation*. New York: Crossroad.

Schussler Fiorenza, E. (2009). Introduction: Exploring the Intersections of Race, Gender, Status and Ethnicity in Early Christian Studies. In L. Nasrallah and E. Schüssler Fiorenza (eds), *Prejudice and Christian Beginnings: Investigating Race, Gender, and Ethnicity in Early Christian Studies*. Minneapolis, MN: Fortress Press.

Shirky, C. (2008). *Here Comes Everybody: The Power of Organizing Without Organizations*. London: Allen Lane.

Women–Church Convergence (2015). Women–Church Convergence Amplifies Diverse, Feminist, Faith-Filled Voices. Retrieved from www.women-churchconvergence.org (5 December 2015).

14
Navigating multiplicity in a binary world
A Javanese example of complex religious identity

Katherine C. Rand

Introduction

This chapter explores the spiritual practice, identity, and commitments of a small group of study participants from fieldwork conducted in and around Yogyakarta in Central Java, Indonesia, in 2013, looking specifically at their experience with multiple religious traditions. I approach this subject as a practical theologian and a spiritual care provider. In order to give some sense of where my disciplinary commitments lie, I reference the words of Kathleen Greider (2011), who writes in "Multiplicity and the Care of Souls":

> Practical and pastoral theology begin with the study of lived religion: our primary commitment is to learn from the ways in which persons and communities navigate the interplay between religion/spirituality and the living of their lives. One way to illustrate how this prioritization functions is to note that there is debate among some scholars of religion (perhaps especially Christianity) about whether religious multiplicity is, from the point of view of doctrine and church authority, possible. *In practical and pastoral theology, we start with the reality that persons and communities say that religious multiplicity is an aspect of their lives, and seek to learn from these persons and communities how religious multiplicity is, in fact, possible.* Pastoral theology is a form of constructive theology in which care is the orienting value and evaluative standard.
> (Greider 2011: 120; my emphasis)

Following Greider's definition, as a practical theologian concerned primarily with the lived experience of religion and/or spirituality, instead of asking how the subjects in this study *can* integrate different religions, I accept the fact that *they already do*. As such, the participant's own voices shed light on their experience as people who are influenced by multiple religious and cultural traditions. As a person who also considers herself religiously plural, I have in some small way an insider status, since we share this mixed aspect of our identity. So, at the same time, my own voice and interpretations influence the voices of the participants, as theirs do mine, and there is a process of mutual transformation.

The subject of religious hybridity or, what I prefer to call in the individual context, complex religious identity, has not been explored at great length in the theological literature. What few texts we have generally do not come from a spiritual care perspective. Three of the more significant monographs addressing this issue are Catherine Cornille's *Many Mansions? Multiple Religious Belonging and Christian Identity* (2002), Gideon Goosen's *Hyphenated Christians* (2011) and Rose Drew's *Buddhist and Christian?* (2011). Goosen, Drew and Cornille's contributors largely respond to the question of how an individual can reconcile two different belief systems. Always, this is from the primary perspective of Christianity, and frequently it is in relation to Buddhism.

Although I too am an Anglophone and of European heritage, and have been influenced by the two traditions most often explored to date, I will demonstrate that this particular location does not prevent me from offering a unique perspective. The question of reconciliation is a non-issue for me because, while I am influenced culturally by Christianity, I do not subscribe to the tenets and doctrines of the Christian faith. In a similar vein, my interview participants are not concerned with how they can reconcile different belief systems because they are not necessarily coming at this issue from a place of belief. In this chapter, I also attempt to privilege their voices over mine. Most of my research participants would be described as nominal or cultural Muslims (or, in some cases, Catholics) who have incorporated or unconsciously inherited traditional Javanese rituals, and/or who practice meditation informed by one or more tradition. If the issue of reconciling competing truth claims is not a question for my participants, then it will not be my concern either, quite independent of the emphasis given to this aspect in the existing literature on dual belonging.

Methodology

While striving to present the authenticity and reliability of qualitative research, it is important to also recognize the subjective nature of relating with other human beings – our research participants – and subsequent research data. As individuals, we come to this work with a particular frame of reference, one that influences the research questions we ask, the conversations we have, and the overall interpretation and presentation of our data.

I am interested in relationships of power and the ways in which institutional forms of religion marginalize people who we might call spiritually independent or religiously complex. In this sense, I see qualitative inquiry in general and my particular research as belonging to the tradition of critical theory. Further, as a pastoral theologian, I am always relating to my subjects and data with a particular interest in the implications for the provision of spiritual care.

Although the methodological approach I have taken with this research is largely phenomenological in nature – in that I attempt to describe, through narrative, the phenomenon of having multiple religious and cultural influences on one's spiritual belief, practice and expression – it does not assume that I as researcher can entirely "bracket out" my own experiences. Instead, viewed with a more hermeneutical lens, this research seeks to uncover hidden meanings embedded in the psychospiritual experience of both the researcher and the participants. In the context of discussing *epoché* (the bracketing of one's own beliefs, values, opinions, etc.), which he says is an impossibility, Ramon Panikkar (1978) argues that "interreligious dialogue demands a mutual confrontation of everything we are, believe and believe we are, in order to establish that deeper human fellowship without prejudicing the results, without precluding any possible transformation of our personal religiousness" (ibid.: 44). In this case, what Panikkar says about interreligious dialogue can apply equally well to cross-cultural qualitative research. Ultimately, I came to this research with a deeply personal interest in the experience of plurality within the individual, and that shapes how the research was conducted and interpreted.

I have also incorporated elements of ethnography in this research. During the course of my field work, I conducted 18 formal in-depth interviews with 16 informants (14 individuals and one couple), had numerous informal conversations with the same participants and with other individuals, and also spent time in the company of the participants in social settings. Although it was potentially boundary-crossing to engage the research participants in more informal ways, being entirely new to Indonesia, it was important for me to take advantage of the opportunity to get to know the culture through these social engagements, and to strengthen my access to and knowledge of the sub-culture I was researching in this way.

I recruited participants using a combination of convenience and snowball sampling. My initial informants came from one of three main locations:

- a spiritual retreat for advanced meditators at a *vihara* (Theravada Buddhist temple) with monks in residence;

- a local *vihara* in the city run by laypeople, where local people gathered weekly for meditation practice; and
- the Indonesian Consortium for Religious Studies and the Center for Religious and Cross-Cultural Studies (ICRS/CRCS) at the University of Gadjah Madah.

In the first instance, I was not a retreatant but had gone to meet with the meditation instructor for the day, and then met some of the participants in the retreat who in initial conversations revealed themselves to be good candidates for my research and, when asked, were amenable to participating at a later date. In the second context, I was a sporadic participant in the weekly meditation gatherings and discussions that followed (primarily in Bahasa Indonesian, though people graciously translated for me), and was able to recruit participants at that time. And in the third case, I was hosted as an international researcher by ICRS/CRCS and was actively involved in classes and activities that were part of the program, allowing for conversations that led to gaining additional participants. I therefore had varying levels of access and time in the field with each of the three populations, and acted to varying degrees as observer and participant observer.

The first contact I made within the community of advanced meditators became my key informant and gatekeeper from that point forward. She introduced me to participants who were either (1) part of the community of students who work with this particular meditation teacher, or (2) the "adopted children" or students of her two mentors from the Javanese indigenous tradition (*kejawen*). While I interviewed both the meditation teacher and the *kejawen* mentors, I chose to focus on a small subset of my participants for the purposes of this paper, which does not include the teachers. I chose these three participants because in many ways they are representative of the entire sample while, specifically, they have a shared spiritual community, practice, and vernacular, which together provided a point of connection with the researcher as well. The quasi-"insider" status I as the researcher was able to achieve with this subset of participants is both a liability and an asset. It was an asset in that I was able to build rapport and trust with the participants, which led to rich conversations; it was a liability in that I may have engaged in more leading questions and influenced the language choice of the participants during our conversations. Given that my intention, working from a place of critical hermeneutics, is to understand and interpret, and to challenge norms and power structures, assuming that this influence went both ways, this could be a desirable outcome. However, it is important to note that this was not an entirely reciprocal exchange. Beyond the power relationship inherent in my being a researcher, the interviews were conducted in English, and my participants' native language was Bahasa Indonesia and/or cara Jawa (Javanese). This, combined with my relative inexperience with qualitative research, meant there were ample opportunities to impose my view when words did not come easily for them.

I also drew from the tradition of grounded theory in order to analyse my data. After transcribing the interviews verbatim, I went through an initial open coding process in which the data was coded line-by-line, focusing on actions and processes (Charmaz 2006). I compared the codes across interviews and made modifications to the in vivo codes in each of the transcripts accordingly. I then analysed the most prominent themes in the interviews and identified categories that represented the most frequently occurring codes. The process was inductive and iterative; however, this was somewhat limited by timeline and scope of a semester-long graduate-level directed study. The themes that I chose to highlight are representative of the particular research questions I asked going into this project and they are representative of the relationships that I was able to foster with the individual participants while in the field. Any number of other interpretations could be made and would be made by another researcher or, had I approached the research with a different interpretive lens or had I had the opportunity to dig even deeper into the data. Suffice it to say, this is only one possible interpretation of a small subset of the data.

The context: religion in Indonesia

Research was conducted in Yogyakarta, Central Java, Indonesia, during a nine-week period between May and July 2013. Yogyakarta is a city of slightly under 400,000, which is part of a metro region of nearly 2.5 million. The majority of its residents are ethnically Javanese though, due to a large number of universities in the city, there are also students who come from other parts of Indonesia as well as from foreign countries. While the overall population in Indonesia has approximately an 87 per cent Muslim majority, in Yogyakarta the estimates are over 90 per cent. Although in recent decades more and more practice a strict (or "pure") form of Islam that approximates the traditions of the Middle East, many practice what is referred to as "popular Islam". This latter form is an outgrowth of the Javanese folk traditions (which I will refer to generically as my participants did, as *kejawen*), which have absorbed Hindu, Buddhist, and Muslim – particularly Sufi – influences over the centuries. In discussing the indigenous religion of Java, Mesach Krisetya (2007) explains that it is not doctrinal, but of the 300 or more forms, there are shared assumptions rooted in concepts of unity and interdependence, the divine nature of the human being, the need for spiritual and intellectual development of the human being, and shared ritual (*slametan*) which symbolizes the social and mystical unity of its participants (ibid.: 209–210).

In 1947, after Indonesia gained independence from Dutch colonial rule and a brief Japanese takeover, the philosophical foundation of *pancasila* (lit: five principles) was implemented by President Sukarno. First among the principles was citizens' required belief in the divinity of God (the word *Tahun* replaced the original *Allah* to placate non-Muslims). *Pancasila* is understood to have been a sort of compromise between various factions within the new Indonesian government and, in order for the majority that did not want Sharia Law, to avoid its implementation. Soon after, six official religions – reduced to five during the long Suharto era (1967–1998) – were named and Indonesia's citizens were required to claim one, which would be listed on the individual's government-issued identification card.[1] Officially, indigenous religion is characterized as a belief system (*kepercayaan*) or worldview, instead of a religion (*agama*),[2] so for those that primarily identified with *kejawen* or other traditional belief systems, a primary religion among the approved traditions had to be named instead. In some cases, individuals chose Buddhism or Hinduism as more accommodating than the monotheistic traditions of Christianity, Catholicism, and Islam.[3] At the same time, with the increasing Islamization of Indonesia, it became more and more attractive to claim one's religion as Muslim, and we can assume that some people who are officially Muslim are more *kejawen* in heart. While a law was passed in 2006 allowing citizens to leave the religion section of their identification card blank, in practice this is hardly ever used, either because the local bureaucrat issuing the ID is not aware of the law or does not want to implement it, or because citizens themselves fear the consequence of claiming no religion.[4]

Also of note is the 1974 Marriage Law, which has been widely interpreted as prohibiting interreligious marriage in Indonesia, largely because a civil marriage ceremony would no longer be recognized and only one done in accordance with one of the six official religions could be registered with the State (Buchanan 2012). Since 1974, couples choosing to marry across religious traditions have either had to perform their ceremonies overseas or had one individual convert to the other tradition.

Voices of the spiritually independent: the participants

The three participants used for this discussion, for which I am using pseudonyms, are all students of the meditation teacher whom I will call Pak (Father)

Wahyu. Mas (Brother) Buana is a 30-year-old man who is officially Muslim, and works as a freelance environmental researcher. He is the middle of three children. Mbak (Sister) Indah, also officially Muslim, is the only child of a Christian father and a Muslim mother, who were married before 1974. Indah is 27, has a bachelor's degree in communication, and is an entrepreneur. Romo (Priest) Wibisono is 45, is the eighth of eleven children, and is a Jesuit priest trained in philosophy and theology. I would consider each of the three to have a complex religious identity, in that they depart from the mainstream interpretations and doctrines of their traditions and, in that they are influenced by and engage in multiple religious traditions and spiritual practices. We could also call them spiritually independent. While the characteristics they share – making them representative of the participant sample and of the larger population I am interested in understanding better – are related to spiritual and intellectual independence, as well as mystical conceptions of the sacred, each has their own way of talking about their religious identity and different strategies for responding to the cultural and "legal" or practical obligation as Indonesians to both claim a religious identity among the six available, and to believe in God.

Rejecting authority

All three participants grew up with a strong religious family culture. In both Buana and Indah's case, there was a strong negative connotation to religious rituals, particularly *solat* or formal prayer, which ideally occurs five times a day, and a resultant questioning and ultimate rejection of religious authority and doctrine. Buana describes his questioning spirit and his desire to understand the meaning of the rituals he engaged in:

> [U]ntil now, even until I got to college, I still feel searching in myself, I feel searching: "Why should I do solat, why should I read Qur'an?" Even after I have many teachings from my teachers, my parents, and imam or someone else. They always talk about, if you don't do your solat you'll go to hell. Things like that. It's not about something human. I mean, what about, my question is always, "This will happen in the future, if I don't do solat, in the future I'll go to hell. But, what's the implication if I do this now, or I don't do it now? What's the real implication in human life? In my life?" And I don't feel the difference until I realize once I go to Bali [meditation retreat, 2011], I join the meditation, I start to understand that there is something more than doing solat. There's something more. I got the knowledge of seeing inside me, seeing the depth of my soul maybe? If I can use that word.

Buana is not interested in a punishing theology or an obligatory ritual, and he wants the religious rituals and teachings to speak to his daily life and experience. He finds meaning internally, which is helped through the experience of meditation. It is not that there is something inherent to meditation which prayer could not provide and still meet Buana's spiritual needs, but it is the appeal to direct experiential knowledge, as opposed to obedience and faith in the knowledge of others, that he gets from the meditation retreat which revives his connectedness to the sacred. Having to say prayers in Arabic, a language unintelligible to Buana, did not help make him feel that formal prayer was transcendent. As it was at the time of the interview, Buana was not doing *solat*.

Indah's experience growing up is that she felt very much responsible for her parent's salvation, understanding both the Christian and Muslim doctrines presented to her as saying that each of her parents would go to hell if she were not of his or her faith. However, understandably, given the cultural context and the doctrinal interpretations, Indah never considered it a possibility to be both Christian *and* Muslim, and so she faced an insufferable predicament. She would secretly go to church with her father, and secretly pray with her mother, all the while fearing for her parents' souls. Indah recounts a particularly impactful memory of the secrecy and the confusion that came from competing truth claims in her own family. She says:

> When I was five, my father know that when me and my mom, we were praying, we were *solat maghrib*, in the evening, 6:00 when my father noticed and he was very mad and he just throw my *mukenah* [prayer shawl] in the garbage and then, since then I have big trauma with *solat*. When I did *solat*, I always got afraid.

Despite this difficult experience, at an early age, Indah identified as Muslim. Religious education is part of the public education curriculum in Indonesia, and there are separate classrooms and teachers for Christian, Catholic, and Muslim students, though not often for the other traditions. Indah explains:

> Yeah. I must choose Islam because I grew up in the Islamic tradition of education. I mean, in the school I have to study Islam, in my junior high school I have to study Islam also, so then I just put Islam on my ID.

Presumably, associating her father's religion with one that is punishing not just in the hereafter, but in the here and now, would also have affected Indah's religious identification, but when asked for clarification, Indah said that her mother was similarly angry when she found out that Indah had attended church services with her father. She couldn't win:

> For some time I believed that doctrine. I did believe [that my mother would burn in hell if I wasn't a Muslim; that my father would burn in hell if I wasn't a Christian]. Doctrine. That's doctrine. It's just the same. Even when you go to Buddhism, they will call it karma. Punishment is karma. You will get bad karma. Yeah, every doctrine is just the same.

As her words convey strongly, formal religion ends up leaving Indah dissatisfied. She is compelled to continue searching for something that resonates, however, and diligently attends to the spiritual life from childhood on.

Curiosity about other religions

Unlike Indah and Buana, Romo Wibisono, whose parents were both converts from *kejawen* to devout Catholicism, experiences prayer as an important family time marking the beginning and ending of each day. He was drawn to the priesthood from an early age, moved by his older brother's ordination ceremony, and inspired by local priests, both of which he encountered as a teenager. Part of what attracted Romo Wibisono to the Society of Jesus was the service orientation of the priests in his village. After he entered the priesthood he says, "We worked for the empowerment of poor people in Jakarta, urban-based NGO, but also we were involved in advocacy for political violence, for political rights." Wibisono did this for seven years, and he got burned out, disillusioned that anything could ever change. Unlike the experience of his younger spiritual friends, Buana and Indah, Wibisono found something personally resonant and rewarding in his given tradition, but it led to compassion fatigue when he encountered a larger world that did not share the same values.[5]

Being interested in both the intellectual and contemplative aspects of the Jesuit tradition as well, Wibisono ventured to Sri Lanka to spend some time on spiritual retreat. There he encountered Buddhist forms of meditation, which added to his knowledge of the Catholic contemplative practices he already engaged in but was not totally satisfied with. In India, Wibisono went on retreat with a Jesuit priest and Zen master who taught him meditation in the Zen tradition. This teacher asked Wibisono to "drop all the concepts, all the theology, all the spiritual experiences". Later, Wibisono would read the teachings of Jiddu Krishnamurti and he said, at that time, he was "still imprisoned by dogmas and doctrines, so many concepts". After continuing to read Krishnamurti and going on retreat with Pak Wahyu, Wibisono said, "Step by step, I see the truth. And, I do agree [with Krishnamurti] that there is no ... way to the real truth, to the Absolute Truth, there is no way. And we have go beyond all the doctrine, all the concept." Wibisono refers to the form of meditation that he, Buana, and Indah practice under the guidance of Pak Wahyu as a kind of pure *vipassanā* (lit: insight, a form of meditation prevalent in the Southern or Theravada school of Buddhism), or what he says may be better termed "post-vipassana", one free of dogma, doctrine, and concepts, and thus, one ostensibly compatible with other religious practices. Wibisono, as a priest and religious leader, faces challenges the others do not have, in that he still has to operate within the structure of the church. He explains, "the problem comes from community, because I live and work in community, I'm still doing ritual [providing the Eucharist] everyday to these people. So I have to talk about [doctrine, by giving a homily] ... so it gives me tension."

Buana was aware of religious diversity from a young age, seeing friends in school who were Catholic and Christian and, in particular, engaging with a non-Muslim family that his entire family was close to. Buana began to have questions early on, because of seeing what he called inconsistencies in the teachings he received and in people's actions. Buana, in remembering his growing up, was startled to hear other children talking about how so and so would go to heaven and so and so would not, just because they were from a different religion. Buana recognized and affirmed difference and wondered how anyone could say, "we are the right ones" or "we have the true faith". After 9/11, he saw an even greater religiosity among Muslims in Indonesia, and he felt even more that this was not the Islam he knew. Buana's parents also became increasingly more strict Muslims as he grew older and, as he heard his father talk about *kejawen* customs as now forbidden, he started to have questions. Buana began to read the Bible, in secret, because he was curious. As he read parts of the Bible, the Qur'an, and the Barnabas Bible, the latter of which his father okayed, Buana said comparison helped him to understand. He says he realized about Christians, "They are not wrong, because they have it as I have Qur'an. Their parents give them Bibles, just like my parents give me Qur'an. And that's not wrong." Beginning in his adolescence, Buana also was influenced by an older cousin who would go both to church and the mosque and modelled good relations with many different kinds of people. This family member also connected Buana with his ancestral tradition, with *kejawen*.

Indah's interreligious education was even more explicit than Buana's, being pulled on a regular basis between her parents' faiths, and having both Christian and Muslim extended family. Early on she became interested in exploring Christianity and Buddhism, but she also wanted to strengthen her understanding of Islam. In college, Indah joined a Shia discussion group because she was attracted to the more intellectual approach of that tradition as compared to the Sunni tradition she grew up in, which is also the majority in Indonesia. Indah admits that she was also influenced by secular values, largely instilled by her father, who she said encouraged her liberal and feminist ways of thinking and being in the world.

A mystical understanding of God

Indah shared with me on several occasions how she walked her own path. Talking about her conception of God, and how others made her feel "weird" because of it, she explains:

> I believe in God, but not the God in the book, in the holy book, Holy Bible ... God is inside my heart, inside my body, inside my gut. Everywhere ... When I was a teenager, I understood that. I have a personal relationship experience with God ... And when I was around 12 or 13, I feel like I want to find my own way, my own religion, my own God, and at that moment ... I feel like when I talk to myself, I talk to God. But my Islam teacher, my private Islam teacher told me "No!" And my classmates told me that I'm a weirdo because at that time, my perspective of God was very different from theirs ... [W]hen doctrine came, every doctrine came, just made me feel God's far away from here. God is over there, God is in the sky, above the sky. God is not close here ["here" said pointing to chest].

This idea of God as inside, close by, and also something unknown or inexpressible, was shared by all three respondents. Both Buana and Indah found comfort in their internal monologues, as a way of being close to God. Buana, who suffered chronic physical abuse growing up, says he's agnostic about God. He feels that he knows that which people call God from his meditation experience and, as he realized during the course of our conversation, also from the times that he sat alone in his room as a child, talking to himself and wondering why a loving God would allow his father to hit him. He says:

> Because in the teachings I've received before, they always said God is up there, is out there. And after meditation, I start to realize that God is inside. It's so close to me, it's not out there. So if you want to ask something to God, just ask to yourself. Not praying to something out there that we don't know. [A]nd why I still believe in that is that there is something inside me that I still cannot explain. I found something and I don't know what to call this entity, but somehow when I do meditation there's still other power inside that I cannot explain. I only see my mind, my soul, and this other thing. And, yeah, I cannot explain it ...

Romo Wibisono speaks at two different levels when he discusses God. He understands God in a more typically Christian way as love, but he says that he also understands God as a concept, a symbol expressing that which cannot truly be expressed. He says:

> God for me is no different from God before I know this kind of [awareness or meditation] practice, yeah. God is, now is, something unknown. You know? So, yeah, when we talk about God, I think when we talk about God as God, I think we can talk just in the level of intellect ... [W]e cannot talk about God, you know? Yeah, we know that there is something beyond, something unknown, something like Krishnamurti said, immeasurable. God is love, love that is not love we know.

So for Wibisono, God is fundamentally a concept. And this is what he teaches when he leads people in retreat – people who identify as atheist, agnostic, Catholic, Muslim, you name it – in his blog writing and published books, and perhaps even more surprising, it is also what he teaches during his homilies.

Identifying religiously

Indah explained to me that she does not intend to tell her parents much about the changes she has experienced in her religious practice and spiritual life. While they know that she meditates, they do not know that she has stopped observing Islamic rituals. Even though her Christian father already had to accept her choice to identify as Muslim when she first got an identity card at age 17, to tell them that she no longer identifies with Islam, she feels would only hurt them. Moreover, surrendering her claim to Islam would be impractical. Indah explains her identity like this:

> I'm now in a God religion, where, yeah, that's the religion of God. Not Islam, not Christianity, not Buddhism, not Hinduism, just God's religion. It's just God and me. Yeah ... [I]f I don't choose [my official religion on my state ID], I will get difficulties. If I can choose by myself, I can write it down, I will choose God. Or just leave it blank. So what I can say about me is I'm a religious person, but I don't have any religion. But I'm religious.

Indah has already explained that the God she knows is not the God of the Bible or of the Qur'an. Her understanding of the kind of religion that is meaningful to her is that it is one that transcends sectarian and philosophical boundaries, thus "God's religion". Her relationship with God is personal, and it is shaped by both her awareness practice with Pak Wahyu and the silent meditation combined with ancestor devotion that she practices with her *kejawen* community, the latter of which is undoubtedly also a deeply, perhaps largely unconscious, transgenerational influence on most Javanese people.

Speaking to the multiple influences on Indah's spirituality which leads her to claim the rather uniform "religion of God", Michael von Brück writes, "identity is a construct in multiple relationships which are to be interpreted in a host of multiple or plural parameters ... we cannot avoid facing reality as a pluriform and pluralistic field of references" (von Brück 2007: 182). And Greider writes, "the notion that religious purity is possible...makes it difficult for us to recognize how persons are themselves often religiously plural" (Greider 2010: 296). Not surprisingly, Indah's identity does not fit neatly in a box, although she checks one to ensure that law enforcement doesn't give her any trouble, as well as to avoid uncomfortable conversations with acquaintances. For many people, though, Indah's explanation that she is religious *and* that she doesn't have religion would not compute.

In the United States, terms like "spiritual but not religious" (SBNR) – or even the "nones" – attempt to corral these kinds of people into some "known" category, but such categorization is not likely to be terribly meaningful. Like Indah, I consider myself deeply religious though not identified with a particular religion. I prefer the term religious to spiritual in this sense, because the idea of someone being spiritual is something that I think is indisputable. As a spiritual caregiver, I recognize that the spiritual realm is inherent to all human beings. Being religious, however, is particular to *some* people and, as a term, it is imprecise in that it could refer either to those who focus on the interior or contemplative life or to those who are more concerned with the externals – the going to church, the doctrines, etc. Or, of course, to someone who appreciates both. Traditionally in the Western world, religion is more often associated with belief, and particularly belief in God, than it is with other aspects of religion such as practices, rituals, community, action/service, ethics, etc. However, this obviously limits what it means to be religious a great deal.

Buana is a little bit more comfortable with his Muslim identity than is Indah. Initially, it was difficult for him to accept that he could incorporate aspects of Buddhism or *kejawen* into his spiritual life. When he first started meditating, he had a hard time walking into the *vihara* because he thought it was *haram* (forbidden). Now he has resolved that for himself. In fact he feels like his awareness practice may be even more authentic prayer than the traditional *solat*.[6] Regarding his identity, Buana says,

> I'm not leaving Islamic faith, because I still have Islamic faith, but I'm not doing what I used to or what my teacher or my parents said to me ... I'm not

doing what most Muslims do, but I think I still have influence from Islamic ways. In that way, I think I haven't "left" Islam because I'm still [guided by] their values, their teachings. The difference is just that I'm not doing what they used to do ... [W]hat I'm doing, and what religion or what practice I like to choose, this is my personal things, and what my parents have to know is just that I become myself, I do what I want to do. It's not their right anymore to rule me. Yeah. About telling them? Mmm, if it's, I think, when it's time. When it's necessary I would tell them.

Buana expresses here what it means to be culturally or nominally Muslim, given that he accepts that being Muslim is just a fact for him. It's an important thread in his relationship to his parents. Buana has been shaped by Islam at home, in school, and by the larger society and though he may have a different interpretation of the teachings than that of others, he does not feel a need to abandon his identification as Muslim. However, the rituals – fasting during the month of Ramadan, *solat*, reading the Qur'an, do not hold as much meaning for him now as does meditation or exploring the *kejawen* tradition.

We can see in Buana what Goosen (2011) argues, that in instances of complex religious identity, "the main religion remains, so there is nothing that remotely resembles a movement which involves an abandonment of religion A to embrace religion B [typical conversion], or a movement from unbelief to belief ... There is a movement or development but it is more the use of religious symbols, insights and rituals from another tradition which are able to speak to us of the transcendent" (ibid.: 146). One of the more powerful comments that Buana made during our conversations was that this inner journey had really provided a confidence in his inner moral compass. He says:

I usually, after meditation, I usually ask my heart, my inside, that's what I have to trust because I cannot trust the teaching from others. Because, I don't know where they get those teachings from or if they're good for my way of life. I don't know. I only trust myself, my inside. That's when I disconnected from the teaching, the teaching in my past.

Wibisono who, early on in giving sermons that departed from traditional doctrine was disciplined by church leadership, says that his congregants have slowly come to understand the teachings he is trying to share. He knows not everyone will understand, but he has learned how to use the language of the church to convey the messages that he believes are crucial. He explains, ultimately that he is "beyond religion", saying:

[F]or me, belief system is not a big thing now ... Except that this is important tools to talk about, and because I have a congregation, to help people through these kind of concepts. But, personally, this is not a big deal. It's not an important thing. [F]or the sake of ... you know, for practical reasons, I can express I am a Catholic. But, deeply, I am beyond Catholic. No religion, yeah.

As they describe their religious identity, we can see the intellectual influence of Krishnamurti (see Appendix) – also a key source for Pak Wahyu's teachings – on all three participants, a reliance on direct experience, and a redefining of what it means to be religious, as well as what the concept of God points to.

Discussion: what these voices reflect about complex religious identity

Often complex religious identity is spoken of in negative terms. Cornille writes of those who no longer accept every aspect of a religion as taking "a more piecemeal approach to doctrine, symbols, and practices governed by personal judgment and taste" (Cornille 2002: 3). The "cafeteria" or *bricolage* style which people associate with New Age, and the use of the word "piecemeal" and "personal taste" here specifically, are characteristic of the way that religious syncretism in general has been discussed in the academy. Goosen (2011: 14) contends that what keeps a religiously plural person from falling into this "unholy bricolage" is having a "sound religious base" or "sound understanding of at least one tradition". Although the participants chosen for this discussion do have a sound base in their respective traditions, nothing in their presentation suggests that this is a requirement for their authentic experience of being religious people. Cornille further argues "the experience of profound identification with one religion without losing one's attachment and commitment to another seems to be more often than not deeply confusing and spiritually unsettling" (Cornille 2002:4). My participants' narratives certainly challenge this perspective. They have approached the spiritual practices learned from both Buddhism and *kejawen* not as belief systems, but as ways of being. Any sense of conflict around their incorporation of different spiritual systems stems not from internal confusion, but from the external expectations of others: parents, bishops, teachers and the society at large. Like Buana, wondering if it was *haram* for him to meditate, Indah has struggled with questions along the way as to whether or not she was a "good Muslim". But by and large, the participants have resisted the norms imposed on them in conventional interpretations of their traditions – with varying results in terms of their willingness to identify with their respective birth religions.

The idea of being hybrid, as in Buddhist-Christian or Muslim American, whether hyphenated or not, points to something akin to being bilingual or multiracial, where depending on the context one is in, one identity might be more predominant than the other. We see aspects of our identity becoming more salient when it is appropriate for them to be so, depending on whom we are with. Of course this assumes that, in the above examples, being Muslim and being American are somehow mutually exclusive, which is not a fair assumption at all. There is the related phenomenon of "code-switching" in which one fluidly alternates between one form of speaking (dialect, language) and another (Burke 2009: 70). This does not appear to be what is happening for my participants; they are not Catholic one day and Buddhist the next. They are not Muslim in some, and *kejawen* in other company. Their identities are more integrated than that. They have not converted, nor have they abandoned their religious frame of reference, (often referred to as like "clothing" by my participants, or by Wibisono as like "family", community). Instead, they have sought a more authentic expression of their identities through the exploration of the more universal aspects of the various religions and cultures influencing their spirituality.

Retsikas's (2012) ethnography of the people of Probolinggo, on the north coast of East Java, where people are often of mixed ancestry, offers another perspective on hybridity. Retsikas refers to the *diaphoron* person, whom he says, "is to be understood not as the site and source of a pre-given identity but as an unstable and shifting subject permeated by and constituted by means of difference" (ibid.: xxii). Retsikas further explains that:

> The idea of mixing refers to the collapse of "pure" and "original" categories of people...and asserts that their personhood is composite and plural rather than elemental and singular ... *To be a mixed person means to be of different kinds of people simultaneously, emphasizing the innovative and novel character of the persons involved* ... The self of mixed persons is both part of and yet different from the other to the extent that it consists of several others; it is marked by multiplicity, its presence is excessive. (Retsikas 2012: 40; author's italics)

This idea of simultaneity (as opposed to switching) does seem to be more representative of not only my participants' experience of their religious identities, but also of how many multiracial American individuals express their experience, e.g., "I am 100 per cent Korean *and* 100 per cent Black." Not half and half. Also, Retsikas's reference to the innovative and novel character of these people is refreshing when set aside the more frequently cited voices on religious multiplicity.

Spiritual care implications and conclusion

Although these findings are suggestive rather than conclusive, they do point to an experience of plurality in the individual, which is something that could be celebrated as opposed to maligned. As teachers, friends, caregivers, therapists and others in relationship with people who have complex religious identities, we can honour the different sources of wisdom that make these individuals who they are, and we can explore ways of connecting to their spirituality independent of doctrinal interpretations and scriptural references. We can accept individuals' right to self-identify religiously and spiritually speaking. Far more research needs to be done in order to understand exactly who are the "nones" and the "SBNRs" in America today. Although the Javanese experience is clearly unique, what it shares with the American context is that Islam, like Christianity here, is a predominant cultural force, even though we both live in an ostensibly secular nation and one that is obviously culturally and religiously diverse. Although Americans have more religious freedom than do Indonesians, since we do not have to state our religion on our identity cards, nor do we receive religious education in public school, we are still significantly shaped by the larger religio-cultural norms. Further, the idea of being something other than one of the conventionally accepted and clearly delineated religious traditions is no more acceptable in the US than it is in Java – although this expectation does not generally become explicit until we are in religious contexts. These similarities would suggest that the experience of complex religious identity may be more common than we realize here in America. Also, the experience of being culturally Christian, a phenomenon that has been explored qualitatively in Denmark from an atheist and sociological perspective (Zimmerman 2010), but has not been explored from a pastoral theological point of view, may be significant.

Insight into the phenomenon of complex religious identity and more generally the lived experience of religion will not be realized primarily through surveys or experimental means, but will be best explored through qualitative research. I hope to inspire others to conduct this research and to contribute to such scholarship myself for years to come. Hermeneutical inquiry appears to be an appropriate methodology to use in exploring the subject of complex religious identity from a spiritual care perspective as well:

> Hermeneutics suggests that the fusion of horizons is more like a posture, a style, a way of living, or a way of conducting oneself than it is a way of knowing. It involves the willingness to open oneself to the standpoint of another in such a way that we genuinely let the standpoint of another speak to us, and in

such a way that we are willing to be influenced by the perspective of another.
(Thompson 1990: 246)

This is similar to the experience that a hospital chaplain might have in a spiritual care encounter – one in which ideally there is transformation on the part of the caregiver and perhaps, on that of the care receiver as well.

How did my participants transform the way that I understand the phenomenon of complex religious identity? In many ways but, perhaps most significantly, in the ease with which they have navigated their spiritual journeys, and the independence with which they have explored their authentic spiritual selves, I am inspired. These individuals have challenged the existing characterizations of complex religious identity, and demonstrate that terms like dual or multiple religious belonging may be insufficient in describing this experience. For one, belonging may not be at the heart of the identification with one tradition or another. In other words, one may not feel that she or he *belongs* to a community of believers, to a congregation or mosque, or to a shared set of doctrines. This is the reason that I prefer to use the term identity to describe this phenomenon.

Further, as the Greider reference used earlier highlights, the myth of religious (as in racial) purity belies the reality of plurality that exists not only within individuals, within communities and within religious traditions, but also the plurality of responses in which complex religious identity can emerge. An individual does not have to convert, become an apostate, or practice/worship/congregate in more than one tradition in order to fit the criteria for complex religious identity. People do not have to check one box, no box, two or more boxes – spiritual independence takes many different expressions and may not be able to be categorized so neatly. Goosen writes:

> Perhaps one hundred percent belonging to two religions is not possible because it is not possible to be fully acculturated into a new religious culture. This presumes one is only enculturated once in one's life, and that attempts at a second (religious) culture will always be less than one hundred percent.
> (Goosen 2011: 143)

Clearly this presumption does not fit the Javanese context, and it may in fact reflect the American context no more adeptly. The assumption that there is a chronological adoption of religious norms and values does not represent the experience of people who are raised in multireligious households, nor does it reflect the experience of people who are shaped simultaneously by cultural traditions that may have a spiritual aspect, and religious rituals or practices, which of course may derive from traditions that number greater than two. Again, bilingual, bicultural and multiracial people and families provide an analogy for the kinds of experience that can produce individuals with complex religious identity.

These narratives begin to bring light to a phenomenon that while enlarged by the Javanese context is certainly not unique to people living in Java. Complex religious identity is a universal phenomenon, one made even more likely by the intersection of cultures brought on by colonization, globalization, immigration, and the subsequent plural environments in which many of the world's people now live. It is time that we take a more nuanced approach to this subject and privilege the religious voices of those who identify in less mainstream ways, and from all walks of life.

Appendix: Krishnamurti (1970) on religion

Sir, what is religion? Actually, what is religion? First of all to find out what is religion we must negate what it is not. What it is not; then it is. It's like seeing what is not love. Love is not hate, love is not jealousy, love is not ambition, love is not violence. When you negate all that, the other is, which is compassion. In the same way if you negate what is not religion then you find out what is true religion; that is, what is the truly religious mind. Belief is not religion, and the authority which the churches, the organized religions assume, is not religion. In that there is all the sense of obedience, conformity, acceptance, the hierarchical approach to life. The division between the Protestant, the Catholic, the Hindu, the Moslem, that's not religion. When you negate all that, which means you are no longer a Hindu, no longer a Catholic, no longer belonging to any sectarian outlook, then your mind questions, asks what is true religion? This is free from their ritual, without their masters, without their Saviour; all that is not religion. When the mind discards that, intelligently, because it has seen that it's not religion, then it can ask what is religion. Religion is not what I think, but religion is the sense of comprehension of the totality of existence, in which there is no division between you and me. Then if there is that quality of goodness which is virtue, real virtue not the phony virtue of society, but real virtue, then the mind can go beyond and find out, through meditation, through a deep, quiet silence, if there is such a thing as reality. Therefore a religious mind is a mind that is constantly aware, sensitive, attentive, so that it goes beyond itself into a dimension where there is no time at all.

About the author

Katherine C. Rand, PhD is an independent spiritual care scholar practitioner with a particular interest in reflective practice, narrative methods, and relational research. When pushed to label herself, Katherine will identify as religiously plural, spiritually fluid, or as having a complex religious identity. More specifically, she has been formed significantly within the Christian tradition – both culturally and academically – has humanistic and sceptical leanings, has engaged in a long practice and study of Buddhism and is an ordained Buddhist lay minister and trained healthcare chaplain. Katherine rejects the a/theist binary and hopes to assist those working in clinical, educational and congregational contexts to better understand and support individuals shaped by more than one religious tradition, including those who might be termed "spiritual-but-not-religious" and "nones". Through her work, she hopes to expand the boundaries of chaplaincy to include the moral and spiritual life of organizations and systems (while, of course, supporting the individuals within them), and to help heal structural wounds in the process.

Notes

1 The official religions are Christianity, Catholicism, Hinduism, Islam, Buddhism, and the one not allowed under Suharto, Confucianism.
2 Religion is defined officially, by the Ministry of Religious Affairs, as something that has a) sacred texts, b) a prophet, and c) is recognized the world over.
3 Today, there are communities throughout the Indonesian archipelago advocating for the right to identify themselves by their indigenous religion, without having to call it by another name.
4 This information was shared informally with the researcher by her Indonesian informants and confirmed by the US State Department in their International Religious Freedom Report (Department of State 2010).
5 I am referring to Wibisono's family culture and the religious tradition he was acculturated with as "given". However, it's important to note that Wibisono is a minority Catholic in a Muslim world, and he is also the child of parents who converted from the *kejawen* tradition and, despite their commitment to Catholicism, are likely still very much shaped by their inherited belief system. Therefore he is necessarily plural, although as a Jesuit priest his primary frame of reference may be Catholic.
6 Buana says, "After I understand that yeah, we can do *solat* everywhere, anywhere, what is most important thing is, do you really want to do that? Do you really need to do that? And what, uh, what motive [intention] you have in doing this. Is it the right motive or not? Yeah, that's what I have been learning in *vihara*, not in mosque. Something like that, and that's changed my view on how religion works. That's really changed me a lot".

References

Buchanan, K. (2012). Indonesia: Inter-Religious Marriage. Law Library of Congress, 30 April. Retrieved from www.loc.gov/law/help/religious-marriage.php (accessed 20 December 2013).

Burke, P. (2009). *Cultural Hybridity*. Cambridge: Polity Press.

Charmaz, K. (2006). *Constructing Grounded Theory*. Thousand Oaks, CA: Sage.

Cornille, C. (2002). *Many Mansions? Multiple Religious Belonging and Christian Identity*. Eugene, OR: Wipf & Stock.

Department of State (2010). *Indonesia*. Retrieved from www.state.gov/j/drl/rls/irf/2010/148869.htm (accessed 20 December 2013).

Drew, R. (2011). *Buddhist and Christian? An Exploration of Dual Belonging* (1st edition). New York: Routledge.

Goosen, G. (2011). *Hyphenated Christians: Towards a Better Understanding of Dual Religious Belonging*. Bern, Switzerland: Peter Lang Publishing. https://doi.org/10.3726/978-3-0353-0151-9

Greider, K. J. (2010). Soul Care amid Religious Plurality: Excavating an Emerging Dimension of Multicultural Challenge and Competence. In J. Stevenson-Moessner and T. Snorton (eds), *Women Out of Order*, 293–313. Minneapolis, MN: Fortress Press.

Greider, K. J. (2011). Multiplicity and Care of Souls. In I. Noth, C. Morgenthaler and K. J. Greider (eds), *Pastoralpsychologie und Religionspsychologie im Dialog [Pastoral Psychology and Psychology of Religion in Dialogue]*, 119–135. Stuttgart: Kohlhammer.

Krisetya, M. (2007). Pastoral Care and Counseling in Cultural Context – Religion and Culture: Understanding Javanese Indigenous Religion and its Implications for a Ministry of Pastoral Care in Java. In D. S. Schipani (ed.), *Mennonite Perspectives on Pastoral Counseling*, 207–224. Elkhart, IN: Institute of Mennonite Studies; Herald Press.

Krishnamurti, J. (1970). ABC Television Interview, Sydney, Australia, 20 November. Retrieved from www.jiddu-krishnamurti.net/en/1970/1970-11-20-jiddu-krishnamurti-abc-television-interview

Panikkar, R. (1978). *The Intrareligious Dialogue*. New York: Paulist Press.

Retsikas, K. (2012). *Becoming: An Anthropological Approach to Understandings of the Person in Java*. New York: Anthem Press.

Von Brück, M. (2007). A Theology of Multiple Religious Identity. In J. D'Arcy May (ed.), *Converging Ways?: Conversion and Belonging in Buddhism and Christianity*, 181–206. St. Ottilien, Germany: EOS Verlag.

Zuckerman, P. (2010). *Society without God: What the Least Religious Nations Can Tell Us about Contentment*. New York: New York University Press.

15

When it gets crowded under the umbrella

An examination of scholarly categorization of Buddhist communities in the United States

Claire Miller Skriletz

Introduction

In November 2011 I was fortunate enough to be in San Francisco at the right time to attend a special service at the main temple of the Buddhist Churches of America temple on Octavia Street. On a cold, rainy winter day I received a warm welcome from the assembled community gathered at the temple for a memorial service dedicated to Eshinni and Kakushinni, Shinran's wife and daughter, and women of the BCA more generally.[1] It was a moving tribute to the women of the BCA, past and present. Most of the service was in English, or alternated between Japanese and English. The one exception was an impassioned recollection in Japanese by one of the participants. Translation, though, wasn't necessary to see the depth of her feelings, nor that of some of the other people in the temple.

The Buddhist Churches of America has been held up by many scholars as the quintessential "ethnic" Buddhist institution in the United States. My experience at the temple on Octavia Street, and subsequent research about the BCA, reveals a much more complex situation than the scholarly literature represents. After my visit to the main BCA temple, and reading the existing scholarship, I became conscious of how often scholars of Buddhism rely on the perceived ethnicity of community members to categorize and generalize about Buddhist communities in the United States. This scholarly trend started in the 1970s and has continued in various forms through recent publications.

In this chapter, I examine the persistent scholarly reliance on the binaries of ethnic/convert, Asian/white, and immigrant/established resident to describe, divide, and explain Buddhist communities in the United States. I will argue there is an approach that does not depend on the perceived or claimed identity of the community members. This approach, which I call the *dynamic-contextual* approach, looks at a number of factors relating to the identity of the community and its practitioners. This approach to the study of Buddhisms in the United States emphasizes the identities the practitioners claim for themselves (both as individuals and as a community) as well as the sociocultural and geographic origins of the community. The end goal of this approach is to create a way for scholars to organize, arrange, categorize, or classify religious communities in the United States which fully accounts for the people involved and the communities of which they are part. In creating this approach, I have been influenced not only by work in the field of religious studies, but scholarship in the fields of anthropology, feminism and gender studies, history, and racial and ethnic studies.

In the first section I briefly review the debate that has taken place among scholars of Buddhism regarding how Buddhist groups in the United States are categorized. Due to space constraints, this is not an exhaustive literature review. I have selected pieces of the debate that are the most relevant to my overall discussion; the endnotes and bibliography contain additional sources.

In the second section, I discuss key terms in this debate, including *ethnic*, *ethnicity*, and *race*, as well as the troublesome concepts of Buddhism and American Buddhism. As with the first section, the second section is not intended as a comprehensive examination of the notions of ethnicity, race, or racism. Rather, I attempt to offer an understanding of each term for the purposes of this study.

In the third part of this chapter, I present the *dynamic-contextual* approach, using the Buddhist Churches of America as a case study. I also discuss the self-location of researchers studying contemporary religious communities in the United States. The chapter concludes with a reflection on the notions of *insiders* and *outsiders* in the academic study of religion as it relates to the *dynamic-contextual* approach I have presented here.

Background

Three works were published in the late 1970s that this chapter considers the starting point for the categorization of Buddhist communities in the United States: *Buddhism in America* (1976) by Emma McCloy Layman, *Buddhism in America: The Social Organization of an Ethnic Religious Institution* (1977) by Tetsuden Kashima, and *American Buddhism* (1979) by Charles Prebish. Layman's work offered a general overview of the major Buddhist traditions that existed in the United States at the time, whereas Kashima's work focused on the Buddhist Churches of America. Prebish's *American Buddhism* presented two types of Buddhism, and is often credited with laying the foundation for the ongoing debate over classification models. Prebish divides Buddhist groups into those that are established, tradition-oriented religious groups, which place an emphasis on doctrines shared across the various Buddhist traditions and "solid religious practice (Prebish 1979: 51). Prebish characterizes these Buddhist communities as "slow to develop, conservative in nature, and remarkably stable in growth, activity, and teaching" (ibid.). In contrast, Prebish's second type encompasses communities that more closely resemble what would now be called new religions or new religious movements. Characteristics of groups of the second type are that they emerge in response to "radical social movements", gathering as members those who have been disenchanted by recent social upheaval, and are organized around a charismatic figure (ibid.). Groups of the second type view the first type of group as old-fashioned, backwards, and out of touch with a modern audience. Prebish views the second type as inherently unstable, and does not see their success as guaranteed. After providing this basic division, Prebish presents an overview of Buddhist traditions in the United States.

The conversation regarding classification methods was dormant until the 1990s, as a debate emerged over Helen Tworkov's editorial in the Buddhist magazine *Tricycle* in which she wrote, "the spokespeople for Buddhism in America have been, almost exclusively, educated members of the white middle class" and that Asian Americans "so far ... have not figured prominently in the development of something called American Buddhism" (quoted in Nattier 1998: 190).[2] In the wake of Tworkov's comments, the issues surrounding how to define the idea of American Buddhism drew a fair amount of attention among scholars and practitioners. The ideas of *ethnicity* and *ethnic Buddhism* are central to this debate, as one of the types of Buddhism is nearly always a model of non-English speaking, Asian immigrant practitioners. This grouping of Buddhists, generally made without any distinction between the geographic region of origin and tradition of Buddhism practised, is contrasted with English-speaking, middle-class Americans of Western European descent who practice various types of adapted Buddhist meditation that is neither lay nor monastic. The second group became known as *convert Buddhists*. These two types of Buddhism share more than a passing resemblance to Prebish's typology from 1979, drawing dichotomies between traditional and modern, unchanging and updated, and backward and progressive.

In response to critiques of her editorial, Tworkov "held her ground, contending that her statements were not at all racist ... but simply made 'an accurate distinction between Buddhism in America and American Buddhism'" (quoted in Nattier 1998: 191).³ Tworkov's dichotomy equates American Buddhism with the practices and communities of Euro-Americans, practices that have been modified to suit a Western audience; Buddhism in America refers to everything else, everything that isn't American Buddhism. American Buddhism is presented as progressive, adaptive, and modern, in contrast to the ungainly category of anything that is not American Buddhism, that is, ethnic Buddhism. This is uncomfortably similar to the Orientalist approach described by Edward Said in which Asia was presented as unchanging, while the West is dynamic, progressive, and above all, modern (Said 2004). Tworkov's model is especially troublesome given the diversity of attitudes, styles, and practices contained within these groupings.

It is not possible in this chapter to review all published materials regarding Buddhist traditions in the United States. However, it is necessary to present a brief summary of key models introduced by scholars since the debate emerged in the 1990s in order to place the *dynamic-contextual* approach in context.⁴ What follows is a short discussion of the strengths and limitations of existing classification models.

The first scholarly publications of note are Prebish's 1993 publication in the *Buddhist Studies Review*, "Two Buddhisms Reconsidered" (Prebish 1993), and *The Faces of Buddhism in America* (1998), a collection of essays drawn from a 1994 lecture series at the Institute for Buddhist Studies titled "Buddhisms in America: An Expanding Frontier" (Prebish 1999: 87). In "Two Buddhisms Reconsidered" (and again in *Luminous Passage*), Prebish highlights Peter Williams tri-fold model of ethnic religions (those practised by Asian immigrants and potentially their descendants), export religions (those popular among well-educated, intellectual Americans), and new religions (those which develop as "revolutionary outgrowths" of the other two types.) (Prebish 1993: 192–193). Prebish infers from Williams' remarks that the "on-going success of ethnic religions" may be evaluated based on the "degree to which they make the transition from past to present" and therefore by "their ability to become Americanised" (ibid.: 193). It is the last piece – becoming "Americanised" or acculturated – which forms a key criterion for evaluation of Buddhist communities in the United States. The arbitrary, and often rigid, division between ethnic and convert groups supported by Prebish and Tworkov depended upon a judgment of racial and ethnic characteristics by the researcher.

Several other approaches are gathered in *The Faces of Buddhism in America*, including Jan Nattier's tri-fold model of import, export, and baggage Buddhism, which focuses on the mechanisms by which Buddhism is transmitted to the United States.⁵ Nattier's model was a step in the right direction, as it accounts for transnational movement. Unfortunately Nattier's explanation of each type of Buddhism displayed similar thinking to that of Prebish and Williams, and ultimately relies on ethnicity as one of the defining features (Nattier 1998).

Two essays by Rick Fields, "Confessions of a White Buddhist" (Fields 1994) and "Divided Dharma: White Buddhists, Ethnic Buddhists, and Racism" (Fields 1998), are important for how Fields approaches the topic rather than for presenting a new approach. In his "Confessions of a White Buddhist", Fields writes from his perspective as a Euro-American convert to Buddhism. He supports the "two Buddhisms" division, believing it to have theoretical merit as well as seeing it reflected in the real world of practising communities. The true value of Fields' essays, though, is his recognition of the racist attitudes often present in the conversation over ethnic and convert Buddhism. Fields notes that part – a very large part – of who and where you are in society is defined by what colour you are:

> A deeper and perhaps equally powerful aspect of racism, however, is the power to define, always the paramount power in a racist society. It's hardly surprising, then, that in the ongoing discussion about the meaning of an emergent "American Buddhism", it is mainly white Buddhists who are busy doing the defining. Nor is it surprising that they're defining it in their own image. (Fields 1994: 54)

In the article, Fields observes that white Buddhists are missing out on something vital, something fundamentally Buddhist by shunning the devotional practices that are seen as a defining characteristic of *ethnic Buddhism*.[6] The contradictions present in the essays by Fields and Nattier are noteworthy: both scholars express concern over the scholarly trend to focus on ethnicity – and the racist overtones of that trend – while simultaneously promoting classification schemes which, at their core, divide communities along racial or ethnic lines.

The lived complexity is acknowledged by Fields in his essay in *The Faces of Buddhism in America*, "Divided Dharma: White Buddhists, Ethnic Buddhists, and Racism". Fields writes about his research on Buddhism:

> [It] revealed a landscape of complex and bewildering variety: what might be called American Tibetan Buddhists, American Japanese Zen Buddhists, American Korean Buddhists, American Burmese (or Vipassana) Buddhists on one side; and immigrant Asian Buddhists and their often native-born bicultural children: Japanese American Buddhists, Korean American Buddhists, Vietnamese American Buddhists, Burmese American Buddhists on the other. (Fields 1998: 197)

Note that in order to make the distinction between the two types of Buddhism – convert and ethnic – Fields moves the placement of "American". For convert communities, "American" is placed ahead of the geographic region of origin; for immigrant communities, the country of origin (or the nationality of the practitioners) is placed first, then "American" is added. As a way of prefacing his argument for the merits of the white Buddhism model, Fields notes that his classification is "problematic", citing the Buddhist Churches of America as an example. At the time Fields was writing, the BCA communities included "thoroughly acculturated fourth-generation Japanese Americans, as well as at least a scattering of white Americans. In fact, five out of sixty BCA ministers are white Americans" (Fields 1998: 197). Fields wonders how, then, can this be considered an ethnic or immigrant Buddhism?

Despite acknowledging the conflicting nature of the categorization of ethnic Buddhism, Fields suggests the categorization of *white Buddhism* (also based on race and ethnicity!) as a way out of his "definitional frustration". White Buddhism is not lacking in problems, but Fields believes it to highlight a facet of Buddhism in the United States that is often overlooked: "the fact that the so-called missionary or Euro-American Buddhism, in all its bewildering variety, is largely white and middle class" (Fields 1998: 197). Fields further sets out six defining traits of white Buddhism as: (1) a lay movement; (2) based on a "strenuous practice" of seated meditation derived from Zen or vipassana; (3) Western psychology is a "valid and useful" addition; (4) significantly influenced by "feminist insights and critiques"; (5) social justice action is encouraged; and (6) has also been influenced by "democratic" and "antiauthoritarian or antihierarchical sentiments" (Fields 1998: 202). These traits agree with Prebish's remarks about Euro-American convert Buddhism in *Luminous Passage* and Nattier's Elite Buddhism typology. It appears that while the naming schemes of the categories shift depending on the model under discussion, progress away from ethnic Buddhism is not achieved – one constant throughout these models is the concept of Buddhist communities based entirely on the ethnicity of the membership, whether that is Euro-American or Asian.

Kenneth Tanaka's observations in the Epilogue to *The Faces of Buddhism in America* and his essay "Issues of Ethnicity in the Buddhist Churches of America" (Tanaka 1998: 287–298) appear to be the only serious challenge to the application of ethnic to the BCA communities, although not necessarily a challenge of the overall *ethnic Buddhism* category. Tanaka observes that the scholarly division between convert and ethnic Buddhist communities cannot be "denied completely", rather, that the "reality is not as serious as reported" (ibid.: 288). Tanaka views the separation between the two types of communities ("camps") as a "natural tendency to gravitate to those with shared background and interests" and that enclaves of immigrant Buddhists in the United States may be for practical, rather than ideological, reasons (ibid.). Tanaka's perspective is reminiscent of Paul Numrich's model of parallel congregations, which attempts to account for instances of the same physical building house two separate Buddhist communities, one made up of practitioners recently arrived in the United States, and another comprised of Euro-American (or non-immigrant) converts (Numrich 1989; citation via Hickey 2010). Tanaka also suggests that scholars may need to rethink the accuracy of "the sharp dichotomy drawn between the two camps [ethnic and convert], for the membership patterns along racial lines are much more ambiguous and fluid within some Buddhist communities" such as Soka Gakkai and Chinese Buddhist communities (Tanaka 1998: 288).

Stuart Chandler's essay, "Chinese Buddhism in America: Identity and Practice", provides the only significant departure from the ethnic/convert dichotomy (Chandler 1998: 13–30). Chandler's is a compelling classification scheme for its practicality, versatility, and understanding that the nationality of origin of a Buddhist tradition is distinct from the socio-cultural identities of its members. Chandler's model, as well as his remarks about the issues surrounding studying "Chinese" Buddhism, is vital for moving the conversation about classification away from the ethnicity (perceived or actual) of Buddhists in the United States towards one that is more nuanced and adaptable as the community itself changes. The purpose of his study, Chandler explains, is to examine "the highly complex issue of the interrelationship between the adjectives *Buddhist, Chinese,* and *American*" (ibid.: 22; emphasis in original).

Chandler observes that not all Chinese immigrants to the United States bring Buddhism with them as part of their "cultural baggage"; in fact, many first generation immigrants come to Buddhism after entering the United States.[7] This contests Nattier's formulation of Baggage Buddhism as well as the *convert* category. The important difference for Chandler, in the case of Chinese immigrants, is that they are not "maintaining a directly inherited identity so much as reconstructing one", unlike many immigrants in the late 19th and early 20th centuries (Chandler 1998: 23–24). Chandler notes, "the current trend suggests that instead of exaggerating their American citizenship over their Chinese ancestry, they may increasingly regard themselves first and foremost as Buddhists, averring that the universal message of Buddhism transcends all cultural or ethnic dualism" (ibid.: 24). In Chandler's essay we begin to see that it is not only the category of *ethnic Buddhism* which falls short of fully representing a community's identity, but that *convert Buddhism* lacks nuance as well.

These observations lead Chandler to a model that allows for multiple, shifting identities, which he refers to as *constellations of identity*. Chandler's model functions by arranging identifiers – Chinese, Buddhist, American in his case study – in the way most significant to the person or group. For example, arranging the identifiers as American Chinese Buddhist is indicative of someone who first and foremost identifies as a resident of America (an "American" both culturally and geographically); the remaining two identities can either be separate – a person of Chinese ancestry who practices Buddhism, or a person, of any heritage, who is a member of a Chinese Buddhist temple. Likewise, a person who considers their Buddhist identity more important than cultural or ethnic designation would place the Buddhist identifier first, and then American or Chinese to round out the constellation. Each permutation would therefore create a suitable constellation.

The benefit of this model is its broad applicability; it can be tailored to suit a range of identities. However in Chandler's formulation, there is an inherent lack of specificity. Using the constellations of identity model and a different example, "American Japanese Buddhist" could indicate any number of Buddhist traditions originating in Japan (assuming the constellations are not interpreted as an American of Japanese heritage who is Buddhist), which undermines the utility of the model. While Chandler's constellations remove the immediate divide between ethnic and convert Buddhists, it still relies on words that can be interpreted as either ethnic signifiers or geographic location, such as Japanese, Chinese, or Tibetan.

In her 2010 article, "Two Buddhisms, Three Buddhisms, and Racism", Wakoh Shannon Hickey observes that while Numrich's model (mentioned above) has value since it highlights the differences for "first-generation immigrants and refugees" and converts, "this model also points to the realities of race dynamics in the US, where Asian and white Buddhists may not interact very much, and where whites have more power and access to resources than recent Asian immigrants ... These differing needs and race-based disparities or power and access are real and important, and Numrich is right to stress them" (Hickey 2010: 2). Numrich and Hickey remind us that what is being debated is not just nomenclature, but the power structure behind the ethnic and convert division of Buddhist communities.[8]

It is disappointing to see more recent works on Buddhist communities in the United States continue to rely on the dualistic, ethnic/convert model. Joseph Cheah's uncritical use of Prebish's ethnic/convert, immigrant/ Euro-American dichotomies in his 2011 publication, *Race and Religion in American Buddhism: White Supremacy and Immigrant Adaptation* is one example (Cheah 2011). Cheah has a perfect opportunity to deconstruct the idea of *ethnic Buddhism* through his experiences studying a Burmese Buddhist community in California. Instead, Cheah uses the notion of ethnic, immigrant Buddhism as a frame for his arguments regarding white supremacist attitudes towards non-Euro-American Buddhists. While his study is interesting overall, and an important contribution to the literature, Cheah's study falls short of dismantling (or challenging) the way white supremacist and racist attitudes have shaped the ways in which scholars research and write about Buddhisms in the United States.

In sum, *ethnic or immigrant Buddhism* has been characterized by scholars of Buddhism as a Buddhism that is: traditional, static, and slow to change; practised by recent arrivals from the non-Western world (generally Asia), and therefore, in a non-English language; and practices are devotional and ritualistic. This is contrasted with "American Buddhism" which is modern, focused on meditational practices, and has communities made up of white, Western converts to Buddhism. The discussion among scholars is likely to continue for some time. The approach I outline below is not intended to be anything more than one contribution to the conversation, and as such, is not designed to be the ultimate solution. I do not believe there is a single, satisfactory approach that will apply to all situations, there is no "one size fits all" theory for Buddhisms, especially in the complex reality of twenty-first-century North America.

What are race and ethnicity?

As the previous section demonstrated, *ethnic* and *ethnicity* have been used by scholars of Buddhism in the United States for decades to indicate a range of diverse ideas, and I would like to begin by considering the distinctions between *ethnicity* and *race*. In contemporary scholarship it is hardly unusual to note the socially constructed nature of both *ethnicity* and *race*. And yet, it bears mentioning when discussing other constructs, such as scholarly classification models, and imposed boundaries.

Scholars of ethnicity and ethnic studies complicate the question of describing a religious tradition as *ethnic* when religion is one of a set of criteria used to determine an individual's (or group's) ethnicity. In other words, how can scholars of religion describe a Buddhist group as *ethnic Buddhism*, when Buddhism is used to define that very ethnicity? Is it a symbiotic relation, then, between the constructs of religion and ethnicity? Or, does it come down to scholars in separate fields (religious studies and ethnic or race studies) using the same terms with subtly different meanings? It is these questions that led me to the work of Philip Q. Yang, Michael Emerson, George Yancey, John Solomos and Patricia Hill Collins (e.g. Yang 2000; Collins and Solomos 2010; Emerson and Yancey 2011). The fields of ethnic studies and race studies are hardly uniform, nor are there uniform definitions of *ethnic*, *ethnicity*, and *race*. However, becoming acquainted with the work of scholars in those fields has highlighted that the terms cannot be used by scholars of religious studies without critical reflection, or without communicating their reflections to their audience.

It is in the spirit of critical reflection that I offer my perspectives on the terms *ethnic*, *ethnicity*, and *race*, which has subsequently shaped the approach presented later in this chapter. First, we must separate *ethnicity* and *race* in order to be clear what each represents. The meanings of the two terms have some similarities in that both are socially constructed identities that may be claimed by a group or assigned by a dominant group to a minority group. Denton and Deane express it best when they write:

> Fundamental to understanding methodological issues surrounding race and ethnicity in social research is recognising that not only do the meanings of race and ethnicity vary across countries, their meanings have also changed over time, can change over the life course of an individual and continue to evolve in an era of global migration and accelerating rates of intermarriage. (Denton and Deane 2010: 68)

A common distinction among scholars is that *ethnicity* is culturally and geographically located, while *race* indicates physical traits such as the colour of one's eyes, hair and skin (Yang 2000: 9; Denton and Deane 2010: 69–70). Yang (ibid.), referencing Feagin and Feagin (1993), writes that a "narrow" definition of an ethnic group is as a group that is "socially distinguished, by others or by itself, on the basis of its unique culture or national origin". A broad definition of ethnic group, according to Yang, is a group which distinguishes itself on the basis of "racial or physical characteristics", using those characteristics as "determining factors" of insider and outsider (Yang 2000: 11).

Scholars such as Feagin and O'Brien offer another valuable perspective on the idea of *race* – as a colonizing tactic by white, Western imperialists as a way to rationalize "oppressive exploits" (Feagin and O'Brien 2010: 43–66).[9] The power dynamic reflected in this conception of race is pertinent to this discussion in that, historically, the construct of race is used to separate the hegemonic group (such as "white") from minority or marginalized groups based on appearance and perceived biological differences (such as "black" or "yellow"). Perceived or assigned ethnicity has been used for discriminatory purposes as well, such as against Irish and Polish immigrants to the United States in the 19th century.

Although ultimately less than fully satisfactory, these understandings of *ethnicity* and *race* provide us a starting point for the rest of this discussion. Where the question of Buddhist groups in the United States are concerned, we may ask if the idea of *ethnic Buddhism* was used for descriptive purposes, discriminatory purposes, or both. As with the concept of *ethnicity* itself, the answer depends on the context in which it was put to use. When the notion of *ethnic Buddhism* was introduced, it allowed some scholars to think and write about Buddhism in the United States as a more complex phenomenon than previously represented in the literature. The next logical step should have been a deconstruction of "two" Buddhisms into "many" Buddhisms, and a questioning of the continued use of racial or ethnic characteristics as identifying markers for Buddhist communities. What appeared instead was a conversation in which non-White Buddhist communities were continually Othered by language, cultural origins, racial assignment, and type of "practice". Why did scholars choose to focus on the assumed cultural and racial origins of groups rather than categorize the "type" of Buddhism in which the group participated?

In sum, *ethnicity* broadly encompasses many aspects of life, coming together within a group to form an identity. Religion is often used as one of the defining features of a particular ethnicity. The boundaries separating one ethnic group from another change in response to migration, and cultural or socio-political pressures. Furthermore, it is possible for individuals to separate themselves from a previous ethnic identity. The concept of *race*, however, has historically been connected to physical characteristics (the colour of one's hair, skin, and eyes, facial features, and hair texture) and has been assigned by the group in power to a minority or less powerful group. An individual's assigned race is therefore that much harder to put aside. On a systemic level, *race* is used as a means of granting privileges to one group (e.g. whites) while denying those same services or opportunities to others (e.g. blacks). Discrimination based on ethnicity, race, and/or gender is distressingly common in the United States; scholars, academic institutions, and religious organizations are as culpable in this regard as governmental and non-religious organizations. Therefore scholars must be aware of – and fully represent – not only their own identities, but those of the group(s) being studied.

Dynamic-contextual approach

My interest in the Buddhist Churches of America as both an organization and as individual communities provided the inspiration for the *dynamic-contextual* approach. The BCA has a long, rich history in North America, starting with immigrants from Japan arriving at Hawai'i in the nineteenth century, then putting down roots in the mainland United States, Canada, and Mexico. The communities in each of those locations has its own distinct expression of the Jodo Shu and Jodo Shinshu traditions. Moreover, while the Buddhist Churches of America is a national organization, communities in California are different from communities in New Jersey or Virginia.[10]

It seems simplistic to say that location matters, and yet, it also seems that location is too often disregarded by scholars studying Buddhisms in the United States. I'm not referring to merely geographical location. Emplacement – the physical location of a community in time and space – is crucial. However, previous emplacements and the socio-cultural locations of the community's members are equally important to a full understanding of Buddhisms.

While I can appreciate the necessities of teaching and scholarship that reduced the religious traditions of the world into large categories such as "Christianity", "Judaism", and "Buddhism", it also feels like a terrible disservice to the plethora of beliefs, practices, rituals and behaviours exhibited by "Buddhists" or "Christians". It is beyond the scope of this chapter to undertake a critique of the "World Religions" paradigm, a discussion that fortunately is underway in religious studies at this time. It is for this reason, and the assortment of "locations" of Buddhists and their communities, that I confine my remarks to the United States, in the late twentieth and early twenty-first centuries, and use the plural "Buddhisms" rather than "Buddhism" or "American Buddhism".

The *dynamic-contextual* approach seeks to encourage scholars of religion to represent the tradition of Buddhism and its origins alongside the representation of the community's members. There are several terms that can describe a community's history – lineage, heritage, origin, and tradition – as well as nature metaphors, such as branch, stream, or constellation. All of these terms come with critiques and baggage. My inclination is to use "tradition" and "branch", with the understanding that both concepts have limitations to which other scholars may object. However, a "tradition" captures the sense of the present informed or shaped by the past. The past may include oppression based on the beliefs, practices, or identities of the group's members, relocation, cultural adaptation, and major shifts in thinking about or presentation of the religion. Previous iterations of the tradition and its current expression(s) will always have markers indicative of the group's location in time and space, and each will be unique. It is this uniqueness that I have observed seems to get lost in scholarly discourse; for example, the BCA of immediately post-Second World War is somehow the same as the BCA in the twenty-first century, and can be categorized the same way. The *dynamic-contextual* approach encourages paying equal attention to a group's past and present.

There are two key parts to the *dynamic-contextual* approach: first is a mindset, a mental approach taken by scholars. Second is how scholars represent their research subject to the larger community, academic or general. The *dynamic-contextual* approach encourages scholars to divest themselves of their assumptions about a community or tradition before research begins. This requires a degree of awareness of their own racial, ethnic, religious, gender, socioeconomic, and educational locations, as well as how those identities shape their view of the research subject. Additionally, religious studies scholars need to have a conscious awareness of how they were trained in the study of religions, and view that training with critical eyes. This is clearly an ongoing process of self-awareness and discovery, one that unfortunately cannot be reduced to a tidy "things to do before starting a research project" checklist. However, the following questions demonstrate the type of self-awareness to which this approach aspires: from what privileges do I benefit as a researcher? What is my relationship to the religious organization(s) I intend to study? Am I fully conversant with the history of the tradition as a whole, as well as the history of the community? Is my chosen methodological or theoretical approach the best fit for researching a living community of people? Does my research preparation include reading in disciplines beyond my own?

Throughout this chapter I have mentioned the Buddhist Churches of America, a Buddhist tradition and religious organization that has undergone a number of visible changes since its arrival in Hawai'i and the mainland United States in the nineteenth century. The BCA serves as a particularly apt example of the second part of the *dynamic-contextual* approach, which encourages communicating a longer and wider view of a religious organization or community. I selected the BCA not just for the alterations made by the group, but the reasons for those alterations. Chinese and Japanese immigrants to the United States experienced severe discrimination and prejudice based on their origins and appearance (which fits the definition of racism offered above). Adaptation to Christian America by Japanese Jodo Shinshu Buddhists was more a survival skill than voluntary: the "Buddhist Mission to North America" became the "Buddhist Churches of America" in 1944, services were altered to fit a Protestant structure, Protestant hymns were sung with Buddhist words, and some temples were constructed to resemble Christian churches. Japanese internment during World War II prompted additional Christianizing measures in the name of fitting into American society.[11] In short, when writing about the Buddhist Churches of America, scholars must be precise about the where and when, and how those locations impact the scholar's conclusions.

The *dynamic-contextual* approach, in addition to shaping the scholar's approach to research, encourages a more complete representation of the community's – and tradition's – history. For example, the Buddhist Churches of America could be referenced in the following way:

> Buddhist Churches of America[A] (Buddhist[B]; Jodo Shinshu[C]; Jap 13th C[D]; U.S. 20th C[E])

The first part [A] is the name of the organization, group, or community. Next, [B] is the top-order lineage, although the use of Buddhist rather than Buddhism is a deliberate attempt to maintain the focus on the people in the community and how they identify rather than ascribing a "world religion" to the group. Part [C] identifies the specific Buddhist lineage of the community. The last two parts reference when the lineage was founded [D], and when it established in the current location [E]. For the purposes of this example I've used arbitrary abbreviations for the regions of origin and current location, and have chosen to use modern state names for each geographical region rather than terminology from the time period. As this is an approach under development, in practice I might alter that depending on the context or audience.

The parenthetical information only needs to be used once per essay to provide the reader with a bare-bones overview of the group's history. It can also be more specific if talking about multiple individual communities within the same larger organization:

> Tri-State Denver Buddhist Temple (Buddhist Churches of America; Buddhist; Jodo Shinshu; Jap 13th C; Denver 1916)

There is at least one obvious drawback to the *dynamic-contextual* approach I've presented in this section: by its very nature of being specific, it is also cumbersome. I acknowledge that as a concern, and yet, I can't help but think that it forces us to re-think the conventions we currently use. What are we sacrificing by always looking for a shorter, quicker way to refer to a tradition?

While I would like the *dynamic-contextual* approach to be used beyond the study of Buddhism in the United States, I must also acknowledge that it will work better for some traditions than others. For instance, scholars can trace a clear path from the Buddhist Churches of America back through the centuries to the founding of the Jodo Shinshu tradition in medieval Japan. A tradition such as Shinto, however, cannot be as neatly dated. Furthermore, who decides the location or date of origin to use, scholars or members of the tradition? The approach I've presented would allow scholars a relatively easy way distinguish between individual communities, such as a Shinto community in Hawai'i and a Shinto shrine in Japan.

The *dynamic-contextual* approach requires scholars to blend their knowledge, which may have been gained through personal experience as a member of the tradition or through academic study, with the voices of the community. When disjunctions occur – and they are sure to happen – feminist scholars and ethnographers have acknowledged the difference of opinion or interpretation and presented both. This seems the best solution to represent multiple viewpoints. It also has the convenient side effect of avoiding sweeping generalizations from a single perspective.

Beyond insiders and outsiders

Studying feminism has introduced me to several useful methods, one of which is establishing my location, as a person and scholar, related to my research subject. Acknowledging location – education, socioeconomic status, identification with a religious group, and privilege – is key to strong scholarship. I would be remiss if I did not discuss my locations as they influence my approach to studying Buddhisms in the United States, and in relation to this volume dedicated to exploring the question of "insiders" and "outsiders" in the study of religion.

I am a white, middle-class woman with an advanced degree in the academic study of religions. While I was raised Catholic, I consider myself now to be somewhere in the grey area between "agnostic" and "atheist". My interest in religious studies, and the religions of East Asia which have come to the United States, is obviously informed by my life experiences as a white woman. This perspective has been further influenced by my decision, as an embodied woman, to no longer willingly participate in any religious organization that discriminates against women and those who identify as LGBTIA+. Therefore, I am a non-Buddhist, non-religious feminist studying Buddhisms in the United States. I have encountered scholars with the opinion that because I am not Buddhist (or religious at all) I should not be writing about Buddhism. My lack of the "insider" perspective, they maintain, will substantially limit my writing to the point where it will not be useful. (To be clear, I have encountered many scholars who do not hold this opinion.) I am also aware that if I decided to become Buddhist, I would fall into the white, "American" Buddhist category, and that it might be an apt categorization in many ways.

It is my contention that "outsiders" can bring a different perspective to the study of religions, and that this perspective is no less valid or useful than that of an "insider". Additionally, were I still a practicing Catholic studying Buddhism, that would be yet another perspective that could make valuable contributions to the study of religions. My locations and identities provide me with a viewpoint that other scholars may or may not have. To dismiss my scholarship because I am an "outsider" to Buddhism seems short-sighted. To overlook any scholarship due to the scholar's background rather than evaluate it on the basis of its scholarly merits is short-sighted.

The *dynamic-contextual* approach I outlined above is a direct result of coming to the study of Buddhisms as an "outsider". Learning of the stunning array of communities highlights the inaccuracy of writing about "Buddhism" as a monolithic tradition, or to write about the BCA as if it has not changed in the last half-century. I would argue the same for any religious group in the United States.

Conclusion

The very nature of this study places me as an insider and outsider, not just to the topics under examination, but as a scholar as well. I am trained in religious studies, an insider to a single academic discipline. However, I have not made an extensive study of the theory of religious studies (i.e. religious studies as a field) or of the category of religion. As that is a sub-field all to itself, I am more or less an outsider. My Western European heritage and upbringing in the United States, combined with my non-theism, places me solidly outside of either Japanese or Buddhist identities. My heritage also indicates my privilege as a White person and my status as an outsider to issues of race and racism. I therefore have to ask myself: if I am an outsider to Buddhist communities, to persons of colour and to persons of Japanese descent, what is my justification as a scholar for undertaking this research? To put it differently, what locations or perspectives can I claim to justify the analysis presented here? It's a trick question. My position as an outsider provides me with a different perspective than insiders offer. I am aware of the dangers of writing as an outsider, particularly on matters of race. I hope it is clear that I am not attempting to speak for anyone else; rather, my intent is to propose a method for the study of Buddhist communities in the United States that allows the voices of the communities – and individuals within the communities – to be heard and respected.

It is my intention that the *dynamic-contextual* approach I've outlined here provides outsiders like myself, and researchers who occupy the complicated location of scholar-practitioner, a method of analysis for Buddhist communities in a way that neither diminishes nor over-emphasizes the cultural heritage of the tradition. My thinking in this regard owes much to feminist methodologies which encourage collaboration between scholar and community, and the awareness of self-location that feminism encourages in general.

Notes

1. Shinran Shonin (1173-1263) founder of Jodo Shinshu Buddhism. Eshinni was Shinran's wife, and Kakushinni was his youngest daughter. For a brief biography, see http://buddhistchurchesofamerica.org/shinran-shonin.
2. The original editorial by Tworkov was published in *Tricycle* 1(2) (Winter 1991): 4.
3. The citation provided by Nattier for the quote is: Letter of 14 May 1992, reprinted in *The Sangha Newsletter*, 9.
4. For a more detailed discussion of the debate, see Miller Skriletz (2012).
5. In a slightly earlier publication, Nattier (1997) indicated that her intention was to "go beyond race and ethnicity" in order to understand the "landscape of Buddhist America".
6. I do not advocate for using the phrase "white Buddhists" or "white Buddhism". I am using Fields's term to demonstrate the different ways scholars refer to Buddhists in the United States.
7. The phrase "cultural baggage" is from Will Herberg's model, and the quote from Chandler above is part of his discussion of Herberg's approach (see Chandler 1998: 22-23).
8. I have chosen not to discuss Numrich's model at length since it is quite dissimilar to my case study, the Buddhist Churches of America, and is therefore of limited applicability to the model I will be presenting.
9. Feagin and O'Brien (2010: 45) cite T. W. Allen's 1994 *The Invention of the White Race, Volume I* for this concept of race.
10. Jeff Wilson further considers the idea of regional Buddhism(s) in *Dixie Dharma: Inside a Buddhist Temple in the American South* (Wilson 2012).
11. For more information on the effects of the Second World War on the BCA, consult Kikuchi (1991) and Williams (2002: 191-200).

About the author

Claire Miller Skriletz has an undergraduate degree from Drew University (2002) and a Master's degree in Religious Studies from the University of Colorado Boulder (2012). Claire's research interests are broad and multi-disciplinary, including gender and feminist studies of religion, religions in/of Japan, the ethnographic study of religious communities in the United States, and Buddhist communities in the West. Her MA thesis examined the insufficiency of existing theoretical models for the study of Buddhism in the United States, particularly as it applies to the Buddhist Churches of America. She has presented papers looking at gender and representation in *The Book of Margery Kempe* (Rocky Mountain-Great Plains Regional AAR, 2013), and considering gender and ethics in the *Dhammapada Commentary*, a collection of early Buddhist morality tales (International Jain Conference, 2013). Her publications also include reviews of Reiko Ohnuma's *Ties That Bind: Maternal Imagery and Discourse in Indian Buddhism* in Religion and Gender 4:1 (2014), and Joseph Cheah's *Race and Religion in American Buddhism: White Supremacy and Immigrant Adaptation* in Nova Religio 18:1 (August 2014).

References

Chandler, Stuart (1998). Chinese Buddhism in America: Identity and Practice. In Charles Prebish and Kenneth Tanaka (eds), *The Faces of Buddhism in America*, 13–30. Berkeley, CA: University of California Press.

Cheah, Joseph (2011). *Race and Religion in American Buddhism: White Supremacy and Immigrant Adaptation*. Oxford: Oxford University Press, https://doi.org/10.1093/acprof:oso/9780199756285.001.0001

Collins, Patricia Hill, and John Solomos (eds). (2010). *The Sage Handbook of Race and Ethnic Studies*. Thousand Oaks, CA: Sage.

Denton, Nancy A., and Glenn D. Deane (2010). Researching Race and Ethnicity: Methodological Issues. *The Sage Handbook of Race and Ethnic Studies*, 67–89. Thousand Oaks, CA: Sage. https://doi.org/10.4135/9781446200902.n5

Emerson, Michael O., and George Yancey (2011). *Transcending Racial Barriers: Toward a Mutual Obligations Approach*. Oxford: Oxford University Press. https://doi.org/10.1093/acprof:oso/9780199742684.001.0001

Feagin, Joe R., and Eileen O'Brien (2010). Studying "Race" and Ethnicity: Dominant and Marginalised Discourses in the Critical North American Case. In Patricia Hill Collins and John Solomos (eds), *The Sage Handbook of Race and Ethnic Studies*, 43–66. Thousand Oaks, CA: Sage. https://doi.org/10.4135/9781446200902.n4

Fields, Rick (1994). Confessions of a White Buddhist. *Tricycle* 4(1): 54–56.

Fields, Rick (1998). Divided Dharma: White Buddhists, Ethnic Buddhists, and Racism. In Charles Prebish and Kenneth Tanaka (eds), *The Faces of Buddhism in America*, 196–206. Berkeley, CA: University of California Press.

Hickey, Wakoh Shannon (2010). Two Buddhisms, Three Buddhisms, and Racism. *Journal of Global Buddhism* 11: 1–25.

Kashima, T. (1977). *Buddhism in America: The Social Organization of an Ethnic Religious Institution*. Westport CT: Greenwood Press.

Kikuchi, Shigeo (1991). *Memoirs of a Buddhist Woman Missionary in Hawaii*. Honolulu, HI: Buddhist Study Center Press.

Layman, Emma McCloy (1976). *Buddhism in America: The Social Organization of an Ethnic Religious Institution*. Chicago, IL: Nelson-Hall.

Miller Skriletz, Claire (2012). Wisteria, Cherry Trees, and Mountains. MA thesis, University of Colorado, Boulder, CO. Available through ProQuest.

Nattier, Jan (1997). Buddhism Comes to Main Street. *The Wilson Quarterly* 21(2) (Spring): 72–80.

Nattier, Jan (1998). Who is Buddhist? Charting the Landscape of Buddhist America. In Charles Prebish and Kenneth Tanaka (eds), *The Faces of Buddhism in America*, 183–195. Berkeley, CA: University of California Press.

Numrich, Paul (1989). How the Swans Came to Lake Michigan: the Social Organization of Buddhist Chicago. *Journal for the Scientific Study of Religion* 39(2): 189–203. https://doi.org/10.1111/0021-8294.00015

Prebish, Charles (1979). *American Buddhism*. North Scituate, MA: Duxbury Press.

Prebish, Charles (1993). Two Buddhisms Reconsidered. *Buddhist Studies Review* 10(2): 187–206.

Prebish, Charles (1999). *Luminous Passage: The Practice and Study of Buddhism in America*. Berkeley, CA: University of California Press.

Said, Edward (2004). *Orientalism*, 25th anniversary edition. New York: Vintage Books.

Tanaka, Kenneth (1998). Epilogue: The Colors and Contours of American Buddhism. In Charles Prebish and Kenneth Tanaka (eds), *The Faces of Buddhism in America*, 287–298. Berkeley, CA: University of California Press.

Williams, Duncan Ryuken (2002). Camp Dharma. In Charles Prebish and Martin Baumann (eds), *Westward Dharma: Buddhism Beyond Asia*, 191–200. Berkeley, CA: University of CA Press.

Wilson, Jeff (2012). *Dixie Dharma: Inside a Buddhist Temple in the American South*. Chapel Hill, NC: University of North Carolina Press. https://doi.org/10.5149/9780807869970_wilson

Yang, Philip Q. (2000). *Ethnic Studies: Issues and Approaches*. Albany, NY: SUNY Press.

16
Being Catholic since Vatican II
Challenges and opportunities in secular times

Andrew P. Lynch

Introduction

The transformations in Catholicism after Vatican II are noted by a number of analysts as the catalyst for a widespread sense of uncertainty about what it means to be Catholic in modern times (McSweeney 1980; Steinfels 2004; Greeley 2004; Collins 2008; O'Malley 2008). This sense of dis-ease in Catholic identity following the council has been exacerbated by widespread social and cultural changes that have beset industrialized societies since the 1960s. Post-industrialism, the onset of globalization, and technological developments have all played their part in creating a social milieu of unceasing social change and innovation. This situation of constant change has raised questions about its limits or usefulness. A number of theorists have attempted to understand this situation as the onset of late modernity (Giddens 1990; Smart 1992), or the shift towards a postmodern form of social life (Harvey 1990; Lyotard 1993). At the same time, since the 1960s new forms of political and personal individualism have coalesced around issues of identity politics and the rights of individuals from social minorities (Wagner 1994; Isserman and Kazin 2000). From the civil rights movement and the emergence of second wave feminism in the 1960s have come a number of emancipatory projects that seek to widen the social space in which people from a diverse range of ethnic, sexual, and religious minorities are able to live their lives more fully (Wagner 2002, 2008). The Catholic Church, embedded as it is within specific social contexts, is impacted by these transformations and the social movements which they have instigated.

Moreover, how Catholics understand their own faith and identity as Christians has become the subject of reappraisal in the light of these changes. In many respects Catholic identity is today influenced to a large extent by these two, dual influences; namely, Vatican II and the emancipatory identity politics of the 1960s. What it means to be Catholic, and what constitutes membership in the Church, are prominent issues as it grapples with increased individualism and social diversity. Up to now, the Church has upheld its moral teaching by instructing practising Catholics through works such as the *Catechism*. For Catholics who have fallen away from the faith, this text and others like it outline the teachings that they need to align themselves with in order to achieve full communion with the Church. This situation promotes a binary opposition within the Catholic community, of those who are inside the Church and those who are outside.

This chapter argues that notions of insider/outsider status in the Church are being contested, and this is largely coming from a new vision of church that is being promoted by the pontificate of Pope Francis. In what follows we will address this through an analysis of the Church's recent Synod on the Family (taking place 2014–2015), and the Jubilee Year of Mercy (December 2015–November 2016) announced by Pope Francis. These two events exemplify an attempt by the Church to, in sociological terms, enhance a culture of inclusion, specifically by attempting to decrease the barriers to faith and Catholic practice that some Catholics feel, as a result of the clash between Church teachings and secular values. This does not mean that the Church will suddenly jettison the moral teachings it has upheld for centuries, or that Pope Francis has an agenda to liberalize the Church. Rather, the Pope's vision is for a Church that promotes mercy and which creates more avenues for those who have left the Church to re-enter it. However, as we shall also examine, the Pope's attempts to enact reform has met with resistance from those in the Church who are resistant to change.

The Synod on the Family involved meetings of almost 300 bishops and Church leaders who came to the Vatican to discuss how changes in social attitudes towards relationships, marriage, and sexuality are influencing the lifestyles of Catholics, and to establish ways in which the Church's teachings on these issues can be better, if at all, reconciled with a secular social agenda in many countries that emphasizes individual freedom.[1] Also on the agenda for discussion was the pressure on family life from economic concerns. Homosexuality and same-sex relationships were also discussed, especially in the wake of same-sex marriage being legalized in a number of countries. Lay Catholics were invited and some were asked to deliver presentations to the bishops about issues relevant to the family, providing personal experiences. The agenda also included divorce and remarriage for Catholics, and cohabitation. Many of these issues have been high on the agenda for those Catholics who believe that the Church, especially in the post-conciliar period, should embrace change. Other Catholics, however, have expressed greater circumspection about the issues which the Synod chose to deliberate on.

The bishops gathered at the Synod represented these two viewpoints, some encouraging change, while others advocated caution. The 2015–2016 Jubilee Year of Mercy is also relevant to these issues. The announcement of the Jubilee by Pope Francis is inspired, it shall be argued, by similar concerns to those that motivated the Synod, including the desire for a more inclusive Church. As stated, achieving greater levels of inclusion in the Church is a central concern of Pope Francis, and the theme of mercy is an important aspect of this. Mercy is a key theme in Francis's pontificate (Cool 2013; Kasper 2015: 31). The Jubilee is an opportunity for the Church to invite Catholics who may have strayed from the practice of their faith to reengage with the Church. In this way, the Jubilee contests notions of insider/outsider statuses in relation to what it means to be Catholic. We shall examine the Synod and the Jubilee in greater detail below. Before doing so, however, the next section will briefly discuss interpretations of Vatican II. As will be made evident later, the Synod and the Jubilee, and the controversy's which the Synod in particular has sparked, cannot be adequately understood without appreciating Vatican II's impact on the contemporary Church and the issues which it is currently grappling with. This overview on debates about Vatican II will include a brief discussion of the social changes of the 1960s in the context of modern social change in (post) modern, secular conditions, particularly as they impact on religion. The council took place within specific historical and cultural contexts, and these should not be underestimated in coming to grips with its legacy as a formative event in Catholic history. As I have argued elsewhere, the social changes taking place in the 1960s during Vatican II have influenced how the council has been received and interpreted (Lynch 2009).

Interpreting Vatican II in the context of modernity: revolution or continuity?

Although the Synod on the Family is an important event for the Church and an opportunity to discuss a number of social and cultural changes impacting on the family, it is dwarfed by the Church's most important recent gathering of leaders, which took place during the Second Vatican Council. 2012 marked the fiftieth anniversary since the opening of Vatican II. Since the council closed in 1965, after four sessions of intense debate, how it is to be interpreted has been the subject of debate. Overall, two broad interpretations are evident, and these views compete with one another as the hermeneutical key for understanding the council's significance to Catholicism in late modernity. The first of these is what can be called the Revolution school, which understands Vatican II as a key event, revolutionary in its potential to change the Church, and which set out an agenda for widespread change that is yet to be fully implemented (Greeley 2004; Alberigo 2006; O'Malley 2008). The other major interpretation is that which can be called the Reform school, which understands Vatican II as one council among many which ushered in a number of key reforms, but which draws on Church tradition and alters nothing in terms of doctrine (Lamb and Levering 2008). The first interpretation, therefore, sees the council as a "new Pentecost", with the potential to renew the Church and prepare it for the twenty-first century and beyond, and to be, in the words of Karl Rahner, a world Church (Rahner 1979: 717). The second is critical of what it calls a "hermeneutics of rupture", accusing the Revolution school of advocating a wholesale transformation of the Church, instead arguing that Vatican II sought to reform the Church in form rather than substance, and address the concerns of the times. Benedict XVI, in an address at the Vatican, warned that interpreting the council as a revolution, or a new beginning for the Church, jeopardized the traditions that the Church considers authoritative and which stretch back to the early Church. At worst it risks creating "a split between the pre-conciliar Church and the post-conciliar Church" (Benedict XVI 2005). In reply, those who understand the council in revolutionary terms emphasize that it did not try to change doctrine, but rather the style in which the Church conveys its teaching (O'Malley 2008: 11–12). There are other interpretations of the council, but these two have drawn the most attention from theorists and theologians.

The council took place in a decade of significant social change, especially in industrialized countries. A number of social issues came to the fore in the 1960s that had an impact on the Church as it implemented Vatican II. These included calls for greater social equality from minority groups, and the sometimes violent protests that these demands gave rise to. The civil rights campaign in the United States is a case in point, as was the feminist and gay liberation movements. Student protests directed to ending the war in Vietnam, along with a desire for greater personal freedom from youth, and new forms of popular culture expressed through music and art, meant that after the 1960s youth as a social category had a much greater voice than before the decade, achieving in Axel Honneth's (1995) terms, "recognition" as a social group.

A number of theorists have attempted to account for these structural transformations of society which came to a head in the 1960s. Theorists of post-industrialism reveal that many industrialized countries have shifted from a focus on production to economies based to a much greater extent on services and the creation of knowledge (Bell 1974; Castells 1997). As Smart

(1992: 33) points out, this transition is the outcome of advances in science and technological developments. Such a shift has had large scale implications for work and family life, with jobs in heavy industry and manufacturing being superseded by work in the services sector, work that is often less secure and less well paid (Touraine 1970; Sweet and Meiksins 2013). Similarly, Anthony Giddens (1990) writes that innovations in production and new modes of consumption from about the late twentieth-century constitute "high modernity". High modernity is based on higher levels of risk and trust in society. As systems of production and administration become more complex, and as risk increases because more can go wrong, social actors must place greater trust in anonymous experts and the bureaucratic institutions that they administer. Giddens gives the example of taking a flight – although the majority of passengers do not understand the complexities of aviation, we place our trust in those who do and are confident that we will reach our destination safely (Giddens 1990: 28–29). Concomitant with these shifts is the focus on postmodernity which gained credence in the 1980s–1990s. Lyotard discusses new forms of knowledge as being critical to the emergence of postmodernity. Knowledge becomes compartmentalized and, more importantly, commercialized (Lyotard 1993: 5). Grand narratives, such as Marxism and religious understandings of the cosmos, are the casualties of forms of thinking where local, particular knowledge that is relative to specific historical periods and markets is considered to have greater legitimacy. Similarly, David Harvey (1990) examines modernity and the cultural changes underpinning postmodernity as they are evident in the design of cities and other lived spaces and built environments, paying particular attention to the way in which postmodern architecture uses pastiche and the mixing of ancient and modern design in the creation of urban space. Such spaces have a reflexive relationship to modern life, reflecting postmodern attitudes and creating the conditions for increased superficiality and plasticity. Postmodernity's impact on religion is acute. As Chryssides and Greaves (2007: 59-60) point out, postmodernity is hostile towards all "overarching truth discourses", leading to increased levels of uncertainty, anxiety and doubt. Attempts to understand modernity and its impact on the present continue, and Bauman has suggested that we are living in a time of liquid modernity, in which constant change and innovation makes social life appear fluid and unstable, with the result that social agents find it difficult to find solid foundations on which to understand the world and build productive lives and relationships (Bauman 2000). For Bauman, relationships today lack the necessary bonds due to the vagaries of modern careers, insecurity, and subsequent feelings of anxiety, all of which make long-term bonding difficult (Bauman 2003).

Cutting across these issues, and making things more complex still, is the increased levels of political secularism and social secularization that has arisen in modern times (Bruce 1996). For Habermas (1985: 9), the "project of modernity" is based on objective science, universal law, and autonomous art, all of which were promoted during the Enlightenment. As Habermas stresses, modernity "revolts against the normalizing functions of tradition; modernity lives on the experience of rebelling against all that is normative" (Habermas 1985: 5). This conflicts with religious understandings of reality. But some scholars challenge the idea that we are living in a time of decreased spiritual awareness. Charles Taylor (2007) argues that today more options are available to social agents for how they choose to understand the cosmos, which undermines the monopoly that organized religion once had in explaining reality. Grace Davie claims that the religious landscape has been transformed, so that many people continue to believe in the supernatural, but without adhering to the discipline of a particular church, a phenomenon she calls "believing without belonging" (Davie 1994). However, the reality remains that religion has been buffeted by scientific theories about the creation of the universe and the origins of life on earth, and the development of new technologies with the power to create human life in laboratory settings. Secularism's impact on religion has been acute in the industrialized North, and the Catholic Church has responded by promoting evangelisation through events such as World Youth Day, and the establishment of the Pontifical Council for the Promotion of the New Evangelization. In many respects, Vatican II was also prompted by these developments, and sought to create a platform from which the Church could better understand modern social life so as to evangelize it.

Debates about Vatican II, therefore, and the transformations that industrialized nations have undergone since the 1960s, constitute a double-edged shock for Catholics and how they understand both their Church and the wider world. Catholics in many nations have been placed in the difficult position of having to negotiate widespread change in both their Church and in the societies in which they live. How they have done so can be glimpsed in a number of studies from a range of agencies examining Catholic attitudes about everything from Church doctrine through to Church attendance and attitudes to issues including contraception, the role of women in the Church, and Catholic education (for example see Greeley 2004; Gray 2015a, 2015b). Much more research on these topics needs to be done. In the following sections we will examine how the Church is responding to these issues, in both the Synod on the Family which has set itself the goal of discussing social change and its impact on Catholics' attitudes to family life, reproduction and relationships; and the Jubilee Year of Mercy, which is a pastoral plan put forward by the

Church to create a space for wider deliberation by Catholics about how they understand the diversity of views in modern society. We will begin with the Synod on the Family.

The Synod on the family

Prior to the announcement of a synod to discuss the family, Pope Francis made a number of public statements to do with married life and sexuality in which he sought to illustrate his position of mercy as opposed to judgement towards those struggling to live up to the Church's moral teachings on these issues (see Francis 2015a). During his opening address at the Synod, the Pope reminded the bishops gathered that a synod is not a legislative chamber where policy is formed through deal making and concessions (Francis 2015b). Rather, synods are mechanisms through which the Church can analyse a particular issue, raise questions and seek answers, and make decisions about how the Church will proceed. In keeping with this understanding of the purpose of a synod, the Pope encouraged all those present to embark on the discussions by presenting their views freely, based on Church doctrine and theology.

The discussions undertaken during the Synod were based on the Church's understanding of the family as the primary social unit. For the Church, the family is the model social unit, one which best illustrates the relationship between God and the Church, and which mirrors the relationship between the Church and the Christian. Furthermore, the Church sees in the family the ideal social unit where Christian virtues such as piety, prayer and obedience can be encouraged under the guiding hand of parental control. The family is understood as a domestic church (Kasper 2014a: 20). The Church is suspicious, at one extreme, of the individualism that is an important ingredient of modernity. Individualism, Church teaching argues, breaks down communities and authority, and threatens tradition and doctrine through encouraging independent thought and action. At the other extreme, the Church holds reservations about the ability of large scale social institutions to order human life in meaningful ways, without falling into the alienation and dehumanization that has accompanied secular ideologies such as National Socialism, communism, and capitalism. Regarding the former two, John Paul II (2005) referred to them as "ideologies of evil", and Pope Francis has delivered some trenchant criticisms of capitalism, based on his own experiences of pastoral work in some of the world's poorest communities (Moynihan 2013: 59). Furthermore, the family is at the centre of Catholic thinking on social justice. Many of the social encyclicals published by the popes in the modern era have focused on social developments and innovations that threaten the harmony, or stability, of family life, from Leo XIII's *Rerum Novarum* (On the Condition of the Working Classes, 1891), which called for fairness in employment conditions and pay for those providing for their families, through to Francis's *Laudate Si'* (On Care for Our Common Home, 2015), which outlines the impact of climate change and rampant capitalism on, among other things, the family. The documents of Vatican II are also vocal about the impact of modern developments on the family, particularly new technologies of war which destroy not only military targets, but civilian ones as well, including domestic settings where families reside (Flannery 1981: 989–990).

The Synod was particularly interested in getting to grips with a number of social and cultural developments which put Catholic teaching at odds with social norms. An example here is cohabitation among Catholic couples, which the Church teaches is sinful. Although Church leaders at the Synod were not seeking to rework doctrine to make this practice licit, discussions focused on a change in pastoral policy towards those living in this state. The Synod's discussions drew on issues of cultural relativism to reformulate its pastoral policy. The Synod's working document, around which Church leaders discussed key points, highlights that in some cultures living together before being married is an accepted practice, while another view is that poverty forces couples into this arrangement because a wedding cannot be paid for due to the daily struggle to make a living (*Instrumentum Laboris* 2015: §100). The Synod's concluding views on this issue will be released in a forthcoming Apostolic Exhortation by Pope Francis. What the debate reveals, however, is that the Church is willing to acknowledge to a greater extent that social dynamics are worth examining as causal factors contributing to decisions made by Catholics that are contrary to the Church's teaching. This highlights a shift in how the Church approaches such cases, as prior to the council they would have been anathematized, whereas now there is a keener desire to understand why Catholics make the decisions that they do.

At the Synod, Pope Francis stressed the importance of the social and cultural diversity the Church faces by being located in so many different societies. The importance of diversity in relation to discussions about family life was a realisation that became evident to the gathered bishops: "Cultures are in fact quite diverse ... and every general principle needs to be inculturated [sic], if it is to be respected and applied" (Francis 2015c: 16). This awareness of diversity is not novel for the Church, but unlike some pronouncements from popes that have at times overlooked diversity in an effort to apply doctrine uniformly, the Synod was forced to acknowledge diversity in this instance, and concede that family life in different locations is beset by unique challenges which are often contextually and culturally specific. The Synod's acknowledgement of cultural diversity and its impact on families highlights the social pressures faced by families in locations around the world. In the United States, research on Catholic families has revealed the impact of secularism. This includes individualism, which according to scholars has led to higher levels of private decision making on issues to do with faith and morals, rather than a reliance on Church teaching (Rotondaro 2015). Further to this, American Catholic families reveal openness towards homosexual relationships, in contrast to the delegates at the Synod who were unable to come to agreement about the place of such relationships in the Church. As more and more societies legalize same-sex unions, including the United States, this issue will be one which the Church will no doubt need to face again in the future. However, research also shows that American Catholic families are beset by concerns beyond secularization and secularism, including daily financial pressures, employment, and housing costs (Gray 2015b). Economic pressures on the family were raised at the Synod, and the discussants were particularly concerned with "the burden of reckless economic policies and insensitive social policies" as they impact on families, in countries rich and poor (*Instrumentum Laboris* 2015: §9). Such discussion is evidence of the Synod's understanding that Catholics' identity and sense of belonging in the Church are sometimes contingent on wider societal trends and their bearing on coping with life in modern times. Just as many Catholics after Vatican II were caught up in both the reforms introduced by the council and the outcomes of the 1960s decade, today Catholics must navigate a fine line between living up to the teachings of the Church while at the same time coping with rapid social change at both the cultural and economic level in a world of increased diversity and insecurity.

The Synod was not without controversy, which began well before discussions got underway. Central to Pope Francis's vision of the Synod's significance is the idea of mercy, which as we shall see below, underscores the Church's Jubilee Year of Mercy beginning in late 2015. The theme of mercy is the subject of writings by Cardinal Walter Kasper (2014b), who was invited by Pope Francis to give the keynote address to the College of Cardinals at a Vatican session on the family in February 2014, as a prelude to the Synod. During this speech, Kasper gave as an example of the application of mercy the issue of allowing divorced Catholics who have remarried outside of the Church to receive the sacrament of communion. The Church discourages Catholics from divorce, and disallows them to remarry in a Catholic ceremony even if a legal divorce has been granted by the state. For the Church, marriages can only be dissolved if they are annulled, which is a lengthy process that aims to determine whether or not the marriage was technically valid in the first instance, and there are strict criteria for what constitutes a valid marriage. Because many divorced Catholics are not eligible for an annulment and cannot therefore be married again by the Church, some have remarried in civil services. For many divorced and remarried Catholics, these issues were a test of their faith and many left the Church. Others, however, expressed a desire to remain practising Catholics, and the Church has been for some time under pressure to develop better policies to help Catholics in this situation. During his speech to Vatican cardinals and other officials, Kasper drew attention to this dilemma, advocating that greater mercy needed to be shown to people in this situation, and that the issue should be up for discussion and reform at the Synod. In particular, Kasper put forward the principle of *oikonomia*, the idea that a second marriage after divorce can be tolerated by a church community in certain cases; a practice that is accepted in the Eastern Orthodox Church (Kasper 2014a: 50–51). Overall, Kasper suggests that the issue of divorced and civilly remarried Catholics and their access to the sacrament of communion should be assessed on a case by case basis: "The answer can only be a nuanced one. For the situations are very different and must be carefully differentiated" (ibid.: 27). However, reaction to his lecture was mixed among the gathered cardinals.

Among respondents to Kasper's proposal on how to create better pastoral programmes for divorced and civilly remarried Catholics who want to receive communion was a strong conservative reaction that saw any attempt to soften the Church's stance on the issue as a potential attack on tradition and current Church teaching. A group of five cardinals organized a book length refutation of Kasper's views. Under the title *Remaining in the Truth of Christ* (Dodaro 2014), these cardinals and other scholars put forward a selection of essays that stressed that established Catholic teaching determined that full communion back into the Church for the divorced and remarried was not possible, because their previous marriage (if not annulled) was deemed still in effect by the Church. Similarly, a separate book also published in response to Kasper's talk argues that modifying the Church's teaching on this issue gives into the culture of sexual permissiveness in modern secular society (Pérez-Soba and Kampowski 2014). On the other hand, Pope Francis gave Kasper his full support, and has promoted his work on the theme of mercy. Kasper expressed disappointment at the reaction of conservative cardinals and bishops, but expressed little surprise that his views should be attacked. He has likened the Synod, and the controversy that it has raised, to the debates generated by Vatican II: "It happened also at the Second Vatican Council. Then there were people against the aggiornamento of John XXIII and Paul VI, though perhaps not in this organized way" (Kasper, quoted in O'Connell 2014). Although the Synod aimed to discuss a greater array of issues than only the case of divorced and remarried Catholics, the controversy that ensued after Kasper's lecture provides a poignant insight into the challenges that the Church, and the Pope, faces in attempts to reform how it determines social issues. This in turn raises questions about how it will achieve greater levels of inclusion for those Catholics who have discontinued Catholic practice because of a feeling of disconnection between Church teaching and their lifestyle choices. Pope Francis, however, has foreseen this challenge. Therefore, as well as commissioning the Synod to re-evaluate Church discipline for a range of social issues, he has launched a Jubilee Year of Mercy aimed at the pastoral level, to instil in Catholics a greater sense of the importance of mercy, including the acceptance of others from diverse backgrounds and lifestyles. It is to an analysis of the Jubilee Year that we now turn.

The Jubilee Year of Mercy

Jubilee Years, also called Holy Years, are times of pardon and remission of sins, and usually involve opportunities for penance and pilgrimage. Pope Francis announced a Jubilee Year of Mercy to take place from 8 December 2015 through to 20 November 2016, in his Bull of Indiction *Misericordiae Vultus* (Francis 2015d). The purpose of this Jubilee is to instil in Catholics the importance of mercy as a core component of the Gospel and the responsibility of all Christians. As the Pope states, "We need constantly to contemplate the mystery of mercy. It is a wellspring of joy, serenity, and peace. Our salvation depends on it" (ibid.: 11). The Jubilee is a pastoral programme aimed at encouraging everyone in the Church to develop a greater sense of mercy so as to avoid passing judgement on others. It is in some ways a practical application of the purposes behind the Synod, encouraging Catholics around the world to consider many of the issues raised and discussed at the Synod, such as creating a culture of greater acceptance of others and their faults, rather than an attitude of reproach.

The motivation behind the Jubilee of Year of Mercy is for greater inclusion in the Church, especially for those who have fallen away from practising their faith, or who have left the Church and sought to worship at other venues, or not at all. During the Jubilee Year Catholics can participate by making a pilgrimage to their local cathedral or designated parish church, and approach a "door of mercy" that will be set up there, where they can pray for forgiveness for themselves and others. These doors of mercy will also be set up in St. Peter's Basilica and other church's around Rome, for those able to make a pilgrimage there. Furthermore, the Jubilee is an opportunity to enhance the equality of all Catholics, breaking down distinctions between different groups of Catholics who may occupy different positions along an axis of orthodoxy or progressiveness. Also at stake is reaching out to Catholics no longer in the Church. Pope Francis, in his letter to Archbishop Fisichella, the President of the Pontifical Council for the Promotion of the New Evangelization, the Vatican body charged with the task of organizing the Jubilee, makes reference to those who have been excommunicated because of procuring an abortion, and to those attending Masses offered by the Society of Saint Pius X (SSPX; see Francis 2015d: 39–40). Both of these examples illustrate the desire for greater social inclusion in the Church, and the Vatican's call for the equality of all Catholics.

Under the Church's Code of Canon Law the procurement of an abortion by a Catholic woman leads to automatic excommunication from the Church, which means that she cannot receive the sacraments, and her membership from the Church is suspended. This situation can only be rectified if the woman in question approaches her local bishop to be reconciled to the Church. In his Letter to Archbishop Fisichella, Pope Francis has provided all priests during the Jubilee Year with the capacity to reconcile women who have had an abortion through the sacrament of reconciliation (confession), therefore restoring their status as practising Catholics without the complicated process of putting their case to a bishop (Francis 2015d: 40). The Pope's motivation here is to break down barriers to full membership in the Church, and to overcome an insider/outsider dichotomy that places some Catholics outside of the Church because of past actions. He wishes to emphasis a vision of the Church as an institution of acceptance in line with Gospel values, rather than one based on judgement: "Faced with a vision of justice as the mere observance of the law that judges people simply by dividing them into two groups – the just and sinners – Jesus is bent on revealing the great gift of mercy that searches out sinners and offers them pardon and salvation" (ibid.: 30).

Regarding the SSPX, this society was founded by Archbishop Marcel Lefebvre after Vatican II. A detailed analysis of the Society is outside the scope of this chapter, but briefly put, Lefebvre was a participant at Vatican II who questioned the decisions being made, feeling that they were a rejection of the Church's traditional teachings, and which contradicted the preaching of many of the popes. He felt that the council was aligning the Church too closely to modern innovations in culture and society, and established the SSPX to maintain the Latin Mass and other traditional forms of worship that the council sought to reform. Relations between his Society and the Vatican broke down in 1988 when Lefebvre consecrated new bishops without permission from Vatican authorities, resulting in the Society's excommunication from the Church. The excommunication was subsequently lifted, but the Society remains outside of the administrative structures of the Church. Its priests can perform valid Masses and other sacraments, but they do not have the authority to forgive sins in the rite of reconciliation. Popes John Paul II and Benedict XVI made repeated attempts to have the Society return to full communion with the Church, but these were thwarted by the Society's demands in negotiations, such as abandoning key reforms made at the council. Pope Francis, for the duration of the Jubilee Year, is reinstating the Society's authority, which in turn brings it into a closer relationship with the Church. This is an expression of the Pope's hope for a more inclusive Church made up of a diverse array of rites that conform to the Vatican's influence. By bringing the Society closer to the Church, their outsider status is nullified, and their members can consider themselves full members again, a situation which may lead to a successful future rapprochement.

What is at stake for both the Synod and the Jubilee Year of Mercy, therefore, is a reconsideration of the Catholic religious identity, as well as a reconsideration of the notion of what it means to be a Catholic. Rather than reinforce notions of being "inside or outside" the Church, because of sin or allegiance to a particular rite, the Synod, and especially the Jubilee, creates the conditions for recasting the notion of being "a good Catholic" by expanding notions of Catholic belongingness and identity. This harkens back to Vatican II and its call in *Lumen Gentium* (Dogmatic Constitution on the Church) for the Church to remember that all its members are united as pilgrims on a journey of faith (see Flannery 1981: 410). The Jubilee and Vatican II are carefully linked. As Pope Francis explains, the issues raised at the council remain central to the Church's work of evangelisation today, and the Jubilee, its theme of mercy, and its symbolism, are intricately connected to the outcomes of the council: "I will open the Holy Door [to begin the Jubilee Year of Mercy] on the fiftieth anniversary of the closing of the Second Vatican Ecumenical Council. The Church feels a great need to keep this event alive. ... The walls which too long had made the Church a kind of fortress were torn down and the time had come to proclaim the Gospel in a new way" (Francis 2015d: 13). This reference to fortress-Catholicism emphasizes the model of church which the Pope wants to distance himself from, as do many others in the Church's hierarchy. As McSweeney (1980) argues, fortress-Catholicism was a reaction to modernity, and underpinned the positions of those popes who sought to resist modern innovations, inspiring texts such as the *Syllabus of Errors* (1864) of Pope Pius IX. It also created the conditions for the development of ghetto-Catholicism in a number of countries, such as the United States, where Catholics understood themselves as at odds with the social norms of the nation in which they lived.

As we have seen, the Synod and the Jubilee can be interpreted as parts of a wider vision about the Church and Catholic identity, a vision which puts the values of inclusion and equality at the forefront of future reform. In doing so, Pope Francis and like-minded Vatican officials are trying to overcome an understanding of being Catholic that is based on the idea of being inside or outside of the Church depending on one's moral state or way of life. The next section will offer some more detailed remarks about how the holding of the Synod and the Jubilee helps to break down this insider/outsider binary in Catholicism, as well as the significance of Vatican II and social change after the 1960s for such a project.

Council, Synod and Jubilee: Catholicism and the politics of belonging

Above we have discussed the Synod on the Family held from 2014 to 2015 and the efforts of Church leaders gathered at that event to understand social changes impacting on families in the twenty-first century. As we saw, social theorists have ascertained that there are indeed a number of pressures on individuals and families today, many arising from financial and employment issues that go back to the onset of post-industrialism, as well as changes in cultural and social expectations that are particular to specific social contexts, illustrated by theories of "late" or "post-" modernity. Furthermore, we have examined the Church's Jubilee Year of Mercy. As discussed, the Jubilee allows the Catholic faithful at large to consider issues raised at the Synod, which have their roots in debates held at the Second Vatican Council, and is an invitation to Catholics to reconsider notions of belonging in the Church, and Catholic identification, so as to encourage a greater sense of openness about what it means to be Catholic, and a greater compassion towards others. These events each seek to contest notions of being inside or outside of the Church, and to overcome an "us and them" mentality that bedevilled the Church in the decades before Vatican II, most noticeably in what scholars have called ghetto-Catholicism. Both the Synod and the Jubilee confirm that the Church remains committed to an engagement with secular modernity, and that it is conscious of the influence of modern social trends on the lives of individuals, including the challenges that secular modernity presents to living out faith. Prior to Vatican II the Church was satisfied to admonish modern social norms that conflicted with its teaching. But after the council this reactive stand is no longer plausible or useful, and the Church must constantly find new ways to assist Catholics with navigating modern society while living out their faith at the same time. The easier the Church can make this, the more success it will have in retaining its relevance.

Both the Synod and the Jubilee seek to fulfil the criteria of making faith less difficult in modern times. Through debate about contemporary pressures on Catholic families, the Church is able to develop a pastoral plan that bridges the divide between Catholic moral teaching and the individualism of secular society. Although this gap will probably never be completely spanned, the Synod allows the Church to put the realities of this issue on the table and use them to develop guidelines to assist Catholics in their everyday lives. Kasper's call for the Church to find a resolution to the issue of divorced and civilly remarried Catholics, for example, may not come to fruition in the near term if the reaction of others in the Vatican is any guide, but by putting the topic into the spotlight the Synod has highlighted the urgency of this and similar issues, which the Church will continue to grapple with in the years ahead. Similarly, the Jubilee brings to the fore the issue of inclusion in the Church, and what it means to be a Catholic in full communion. By picking out two issues in particular, abortion and the SSPX, Pope Francis has sent a clear message that attitudes of reproach and judgement will not go any way towards building an inclusive Church. Rather, through mercy, the acceptance of diversity, and the recognition that Gospel values are difficult to live up to in the real world, the Pope has put into practice a pastoral event which will give the Church the opportunity to make progress in its continued evangelisation of the modern world that it began at the council.

These issues are all intricately connected to the council and the social transformations of the 1960s. Peter Wagner's understanding of modernity and the events of the 1960s as a "project of emancipation" goes some way in explaining attitudes that appear antithetical to religion, such as individualism and a distrust of authority. Social agents have much more autonomy and freedom in decision making in modern life (Wagner 2008: 12), which undermines the authority of churches to determine what and how people should think. The sexual revolution of the 1960s, furthermore, has been the catalyst for widespread acceptance of artificial contraception, same-sex relationships, cohabitation and higher levels of divorce. These have had an influence not only on society at large in the countries affected, but on Catholic communities as well. The Church has had to negotiate these issues for some time, with mixed outcomes. As Greeley (2004: 192) has pointed out, Vatican II was able to bring the Church into a position of dialogue with modern social institutions, but a number of issues were left unresolved, including artificial contraception which has been an area of contestation between the Vatican hierarchy and the laity since Pope Paul VI's encyclical *Humanae Vitae* (On the Regulation of Birth, 1968). The holding of the Synod and the Jubilee reveals that the Pope and his supporters are taking seriously the impact that these sorts of issues are having on Catholics. Specifically, many in the Vatican are expressing a desire, revealed at the Synod and in preparations for the Jubilee, to open the Church's doors wider so that more Catholics feel that they are committed members of the Church, rather than holding onto the status of lapsed Catholics, or outsiders. As a result of these attitudes within the hierarchy, the insider/outsider status of Church membership may in the future become much more blurred.

However, the controversy that surrounds the Synod highlights how a shift towards greater inclusion in the Church is being resisted. Although it is important not to oversimplify the categories of liberal and conservative in the Church, most commentators agree that these categories do exist and are consequential for how changes to Church teaching are understood. Those who resist change have mobilized against the Pope, as Kasper reveals, stressing the way in which insider/outsider status in the Church is subject to intense debate. Further to this, the often misunderstood notion that change in the Church entails a change in doctrine means that there is much resistance to innovation, making it more difficult for the kinds of reforms that Pope Francis and his supporters hope to initiate. The outcomes of these struggles for reform will only be discernible in the long term.

Conclusion

This chapter has argued that in modern Catholicism, the notion of insider/outsider status in the Church is being contested, and this is coming largely from a new vision of church that is being promoted by the pontificate of Pope Francis. Francis's inspiration, it can be argued, derives from the Second Vatican Council, which scholars have agreed is a watershed moment in Catholic history, regardless of whether they interpret it as a revolution or a series of important reforms. As we saw above, that the Synod on the Family and the Jubilee Year of Mercy have both taken place during the fiftieth anniversary of Vatican II is hardly coincidental. The Synod on the Family is an attempt to scrutinize the Church's position on a number of social issues that are at the forefront of public debate in many nations. These include cohabitation, divorce, same-sex relationships, and the pressures on the family from unfettered capitalism. At the root of the Synod is a desire by the Pope for a more inclusive Church that is open to all, rather than condemning those who fall short of the moral standards that the Church prescribes. The Jubilee Year of Mercy is a Church wide application of the ideas that motivated the Synod, directed at all Catholics, and encouraging them to reconsider their attitude towards those Catholics, and others in the world, who are outside of the Church's doors. Under the rubric of mercy, and using the symbolism of doors of mercy, the Pope has presented a carefully designed set of parameters through which Catholics can reflect on the lives of those who are outside of the Church, and on their own failings and shortcomings, and in doing so contest a narrow definition of what it means to be inside or outside, through showing greater understanding towards others and questioning their own attitudes against the Gospel message of forgiveness.

The success of the Synod on the Family and the Jubilee Year of Mercy is yet to be determined. The final report of the Synod will be released in due time, and further research on this and the outcomes of the Jubilee will be useful to gauge the Church's engagement with social issues under the leadership of Pope Francis. However Pope Francis's reforms play out, the reality is that, as acknowledged at Vatican II, the Church is situated in diverse and ever changing social and cultural contexts which have a substantial influence on the ability of Catholics to live out their faith and to retain a strong sense of belonging and identification with the Church. Moreover, secular modernity since the 1960s has placed a number of pressures on Catholics who are trying to reconcile life under modern conditions, and the autonomy it entails, with a faith tradition that is critical of a number of the innovations in social life that modernity has created. The Synod and the Jubilee reveal that Pope Francis is aware of the tensions engendered by this, and that Catholicism will continue to seek out new ways of reconciling an ancient faith with a brave new world, rather than shy away from it.

About the author

Andrew P. Lynch teaches sociology at the University of Sydney, Australia, and Education at the University of Western Sydney. His PhD was awarded in 2010 for a dissertation titled *Vatican II and the 1960s: Contesting Theories of Church Reform and the Impact of Modernity*. He researches in the areas of the sociology of religion and social theory. Recent publications include *Taylor and Politics: A Critical Introduction* (2018, Edinburgh University Press, with Craig Browne) and *Interreligious Dialogue: From Religion to Geopolitics* (2019, Brill, with Giuseppe Giordan).

Note

1 As well as 279 voting members of the Synod, there were approximately 90 non-voting auditors present, made up of experts, lay people, and representatives from other Christian denominations

References

Alberigo, Giuseppe (2006). *A Brief History of Vatican II*. New York: Orbis.
Bauman, Zygmunt (2000). *Liquid Modernity*. Cambridge: Polity.
Bauman, Zygmunt (2003). *Liquid Love: On the Frailty of Human Bonds*. Cambridge: Polity.
Bell, Daniel (1974). *The Coming of the Post-Industrial Society: A Venture in Social Forecasting*. London: Heinemann.
Benedict XVI (2005). Christmas Address. Retrieved from https://w2.vatican.va/content/benedict-xvi/en/speeches/2005/december/documents/hf_ben_xvi_spe_20051222_roman-curia.html.
Bruce, Steve (1996). *Religion in the Modern World: From Cathedrals to Cults*. Oxford: Oxford University Press.
Castells, Manuel (1997). *The Rise of the Network Society*. Oxford: Blackwell.
Chryssides, George D. and Ron Greaves (2007). *The Study of Religion: An Introduction to Key Ideas and Methods*. London: Continuum.
Collins, Paul (2008). *Believers: Does Australian Catholicism Have a Future?* Sydney: University of New South Wales Press.
Cool, Michel (2013). *Francis: A New World Pope*. Grand Rapids, MI: William B. Eerdmans.
Davie, Grace (1994). *Religion in Britain since 1945: Believing without Belonging*. Oxford: Blackwell.
Dodaro, Robert (ed.) (2014). *Remaining in the Truth of Christ: Marriage and Communion in the Catholic Church*. San Francisco, CA: Ignatius Press.
Flannery, Austin (1981). *Vatican II Council: The Conciliar and Post Conciliar Documents*. Collegeville, MN: Liturgical Press.
Francis (2015a). *Pope Francis and the Family*. London: CTS.
Francis (2015b). Introductory Remarks by His Holiness Pope Francis. October 5. Retrieved from www.vatican.va/roman_curia/synod/index.htm.
Francis (2015c). The Synod on the Family shows vitality of the Church. *Catholic Outlook* 18 (November; Sydney: Diocese of Parramatta): 16.
Francis (2015d). *Misericordiae Vultus: Special Edition*. Sydney: St Pauls Publications.
Giddens, Anthony (1990). *The Consequences of Modernity*. Cambridge: Polity.
Gray, Mark M. (2015a). *The Catholic Family: 21st Century Challenges in the United States*. Center for Applied Research in the Apostolate: Georgetown University.
Gray, Mark M. (2015b). *The U.S Catholic Family: Demographics*. Washington, DC: Center for Applied Research in the Apostolate, Georgetown University.

Greeley, Andrew (2004). *The Catholic Revolution: New Wine, Old Wineskins, and the Second Vatican Council.* Berkeley, CA: University of California Press. https://doi.org/10.1525/california/9780520238176.001.0001

Habermas, Jürgen (1985). Modernity: An Incomplete Project. In Hal Foster (ed.), *Postmodern Culture*, 3–15. London: Pluto Press.

Harvey, David (1990). *The Condition of Postmodernity: An Enquiry into the Origins of Cultural Change.* Oxford: Blackwell.

Honneth, Axel (1995). *The Struggle for Recognition: The Moral Grammar of Social Conflicts.* Trans. Joel Anderson. Cambridge: Polity Press.

Instrumentum Laboris (2015). Retrieved from www.vatican.va/roman_curia/synod/documents/rc_synod_doc_20150623_instrumentum-xiv-assembly_en.html.

Isserman, Maurice and Michael Kazin (2000). *America Divided: The Civil War of the 1960s.* New York: Oxford University Press.

John Paul II (2005). *Memory & Identity: Personal Reflections.* London: Weidenfeld & Nicolson.

Kasper, Walter (2014a). *The Gospel of the Family.* New York: Paulist Press.

Kasper, Walter (2014b). *Mercy: The Essence of the Gospel and the Key to Christian Life.* New York: Paulist Press.

Kasper, Walter (2015). *Pope Francis' Revolution of Tenderness and Love: Theological and Pastoral Perspectives.* New York: Paulist Press.

Lamb, Matthew L. and Matthew Levering (2008). *Vatican II: Renewal within Tradition.* New York: Oxford University Press.

Lynch, Andrew P. (2009). Vatican II and the 1960s: Contesting Theories of Church Reform and the Impact of Modernity. PhD thesis, University of Sydney, Australia.

Lyotard, Jean-François (1993). *The Postmodern Condition: A Report on Knowledge.* Minneapolis, MN: University of Minnesota Press.

McSweeney, Bill (1980). *Roman Catholicism: The Search for Relevance.* Oxford: Blackwell.

Moynihan, Robert (2013). *Pray for Me: The Life and Spiritual Vision of Pope Francis.* London: Rider.

O'Connell, Gerard (2014). Listen to the Spirit: Cardinal Kasper on the Synod on the Family. *America* (20 October). Retrieved from www.americamagazine.org/issue/listen-spirit

O'Malley, John W. (2008). *What Happened at Vatican II.* Cambridge, MA: Harvard University Press.

Pérez-Soba, Juan José and Stephan Kampowski (2014). *The Gospel of the Family: Going Beyond Cardinal Kasper's Proposal in the Debate on Marriage, Civil Re-Marriage, and Communion in the Church.* San Francisco, CA: Ignatius Press.

Rahner, Karl (1979). Towards a Fundamental Theological Interpretation of Vatican II. *Theological Studies* 40 (2): 716–727. https://doi.org/10.1177/004056397904000404

Rotondaro, Vinnie (2015). Reality is messy for US Catholic Families. *National Catholic Reporter* (29 September). Retrieved from www.ncronline.org/news/people/reality-messy-us-catholic-families

Smart, Barry (1992). *Modern Conditions, Postmodern Controversies.* London: Routledge.

Steinfels, Peter (2004). *A People Adrift: The Crisis of the Roman Catholic Church in America.* New York: Simon & Schuster.

Sweet, Stephen and Peter Meiksins (2013). *Changing Contours of Work: Jobs and Opportunities in the New Economy.* Los Angeles, CA: Sage.

Taylor, Charles (2007). *A Secular Age.* Cambridge, MA: Harvard University Press.

Touraine, Alain (1970). *The Post-Industrial Society: Tomorrow's Social History: Classes, Conflicts and Culture in the Programmed Society.* New York: Random House.

Wagner, Peter (1994). *A Sociology of Modernity: Liberty and Discipline.* London: Routledge.

Wagner, Peter (2002). The Project of Emancipation and the Possibility of Politics, Or, What's Wrong with Post-1968 Individualism? *Thesis Eleven* 68: 31–45. https://doi.org/10.1177/0725513602068001003

Wagner, Peter (2008). *Modernity as Experience and Interpretation: A New Sociology of Modernity.* Cambridge: Polity Press.

17

Reflexive and holistic switchers
Older women/newer commitments

Janet B. Eccles

Overview: the changing religio-spiritual landscape

In the closing chapter of their book *Gone for Good? Church Leaving and Returning in the 21st Century* (2007), Francis and Richter propose that one way back into a Christian community for discontented disaffiliates is to consider joining one perceived to be more in tune with their notion of what a good religious community should be. Over the course of a longish life my own relationship with religious communities has followed a somewhat up and down trajectory sometimes "in" and sometimes "out" in my own search for such a community. What happens when one changes affiliation or leaves off altogether? Does one then become a complete outsider as far as former allegiances are concerned? Or does a rather more complex process take place where boundaries between insiders and outsiders remain less clear-cut?

We live in times of considerable religious change (Woodhead and Catto 2012; Woodhead 2012; Eccles 2012b; Lynch 2007; Lynch 2012; Stringer 2008; Brown and Lynch 2012; Droogers and van Harskamp 2014b; Davie 2015). At the start of the new millennium, Callum Brown (2003) argued that religious statistics, derived by quantitative methods, which many sociologists of religion have relied on extensively in the past for determining religiosity, do not begin to say all there is to say about valid expressions of personal faith. He wonders if they can indeed be measured at all since religion cannot be reduced to "bipolarities", the churchgoers and the non-churchgoers, the baptized and the unbaptized. Droogers (2014c: 39; Droogers and van Harskamp 2014a: 4) makes a similar point, going further indeed in asserting that not only is the religiosity of many people composed of characteristics and categories which are not that easily quantifiable but that they are continuously variable, depending on a number of factors, including the role of the researcher and her/his personality in constructing the account of that religiosity. Informants, moreover, argues Droogers (2014c: 39), are often able to make calculated or "correct" use of available meanings and of questions and answers depending on the context they find themselves in. When asked by an interviewer, informants may "appear to cherish a certain opinion, while at the back of their mind an antithetical view is more strongly held." Questions of power also come into play "since both religious and secular worldviews contain mechanisms and constellations of power." Moreover, for various reasons, virtually all followers deviate from their chosen path at times. Nobody lives a religious life in a "pure" unadulterated form and possibly nobody ever did (Bowman 2015: 304).

"Lived religion": collapsing boundaries

Stringer (2008: 16, 51) and other recent writers (Morgan 2010; McDannell 1995; Lynch 2010; McGuire 2007, 2008), focus on ordinary people's "lived religion", finding it more profitable to study the "non-empirical" meaning "that which cannot be proved through any accepted methodology, in the thought and actions of a wide range of very different people." They may hold "situational beliefs", something that "fits" a particular situation for a particular time and which may be quite inconsistent with other beliefs or those of official orthodoxy. Those who are marginalized in society may well see religion as a way of coping with life's considerable vicissitudes (Stringer 2008: 76, 80–82), not a once-and-for-all conversion or transformative experience, as traditional theology might suggest.

These and numerous other changes, suggest Droogers and van Harskamp (2014b), call for new ways of conceptualizing what we may mean by religion and the sacred and how we as researchers approach our subjects who may straddle a number of boundaries between the secular, the sacred and religious and/or spiritual at any given time – as may we ourselves. We are not "single entities" or single selves and what Droogers and van Harskamp (2014a: 4) refer to as "a mixed bag of views" may well be contained in the same person. In modern Western society we often have the freedom to fulfil an expanded range of social roles from a whole range of options and alternatives. In the course of a day we come into contact with a range of diverse contexts, at home, at work, as consumers or as people with leisure time (Droogers 2014c: 36).

Reporting in an earlier article (Droogers 2007: 86), and as I found in my own research (Eccles 2010), Droogers comments that new forms of religiosity such as New Age have found their way into churches without being identified as such, regular churchgoers reporting their belief in reincarnation, for example. A presupposed "linear and irreversible process of change from religion to spirituality" (or for that matter from religion to secular views) does not reflect the degree of unpredictability in individualized unique subjects. Subjects may at one time put large parts of their more traditional repertoire to rest and yet activate them again when the situation seems to demand their renewed application (Droogers 2007: 95). People "play" with their possibilities, adapting to the demands of the contexts they find themselves in at a particular moment or place. Contradictions can then be accommodated, simply because a repertoire is never activated in its totality. We might more usefully conceptualize contemporary times as being those where processes of mixing and melding within individuals and groups are taking place, rather than adherence to fixed boundaries, since on "either side of the supposed boundary there may be coalescence of ideas and practices" (Droogers 2014c: 27). Such a process may occur between religious and secular stances in a category Droogers and van Harskamp (2014b) simply choose to call "worldview". People may have recourse to "repertoires of contradictory meanings"(Droogers 2014c: 19) in forming their worldviews and meaning-making, which may or may not be the result of rational thought processes, while these worldviews are certainly influenced by our experiences, behaviours and emotions (Riis and Woodhead 2010; Eccles 2012a).

The new spirituality and its practitioners

Before describing the methods employed for the study, of which this chapter forms a part, and discussing my own insider/outsider status, it will be useful to review Lynch's work (2007)on "the new spirituality" as the conceptual frame for analysing the particular women's lives discussed here. New spirituality practitioners range from those seeking new forms of Christian expression within the church, on the one hand, to those who have taken up new forms of spirituality outside the church, on the other. Christian progressives are seeking new more liberal forms of religion and spirituality within the Quaker meeting, a Sea of Faith group (www.sofn.org.uk) or the Progressive Christian Network Britain (Lynch 2007: 75, 83), for example. The holistic spiritual at the other end of the spectrum have rejected many of the traditional forms of Christian doctrine and the institution of the Church, favouring practices such as yoga, reiki, meditation and alternative healing, for example, or may belong to specifically female – but also mixed – spirituality groups (Heelas and Woodhead 2005). Lynch characterizes new spirituality practitioners as looking to answer one or more of four different perceived requirements: the need for a credible religion for a modern age; the need for religion which is truly liberating and beneficial to women; the need to reconnect religion with scientific knowledge and the need for a spirituality that can respond to the impending ecological crisis (Lynch 2007: 22). While I did find women who fitted these criteria when looking across the breadth of the whole study (of women churchgoers and leavers) (Eccles 2010), the women I describe here are more likely to be looking for the first two in particular.

Lynch (2007) argues the "Christian" practitioners do not often "meet" the "holistic" practitioners en bloc, although they may as individuals; each tends to know those from the same traditions as themselves, the progressives in the Abrahamic faiths, for example, might collaborate or those in the Pagan milieu, but the priorities of both extremes may be different and they wish to maintain their own distinct identity. However, the women described in this chapter float in and out of both Christian and holistic/Pagan circles, although possibly assuming somewhat different identities in each. As Droogers (2007) claims, contexts change and new demands are made on us from time to time. Qualitative methods: unstructured interviews, participant observation and case studies are particularly effective in showing such variations, given that individual difference, rather than homogeneity of views, is such a striking characteristic of the new world of worldviews (Droogers 2014b: 44). Lynch (2007: 40), too, warns against assuming that any one group of new spiritual followers will espouse uniform sets of beliefs and practices: "'religions' may be more useful to people as a source of relationships and resources that they can use in different ways, depending upon their particular needs and circumstances".

Context and methods

This chapter, then, considers the changing religio-spiritual lives of two groups of women whom I spoke to between 2004 and 2006 to determine their religious and value commitments. They were part of a larger study (Eccles 2010) to determine what differences there might be between Christian affiliated women and disaffiliates who had lived through the 1960s. I began with the assumption there would be a clear boundary between them but this proved not to be the case. Rather, the various women I spoke to could be placed on a spectrum running from the fully committed churchgoers at one end to the secularists at the other (Eccles 2008). The women described here fall somewhere between the two ends.

Seventy women in total, living across South Lakeland, agreed to act as my informants, speaking to me in semi-structured interviews which lasted up to two hours, sometimes in my home, sometimes in theirs. I invited them to "tell me something of your religious and/or spiritual and/or secular journey through life to this point", with minimum interference from me, in an attempt to let them choose the direction the narrative would take. This finally resulted in my drawing up a sixfold typology of affiliates and disaffiliates (Eccles 2012b) which tries to represent this spectrum. The two groups on which this chapter is based I have designated reflexive switchers (affiliates) and holistic switchers (disaffiliates). The former have switched from one form of Christian church to another more liberal type of congregation (or various others), as Francis and Richter (2007) suggest the discontented might do, with the disaffiliates mixing formal Christian practices, to lesser or greater degrees, with holistic spiritualities.

All the women had lived through that period of turbulent cultural, social and religious change, the cultural revolution of the 1960s (Brown 2001; Brown 2006; Marwick 1999; McLeod 2007; Hobsbawm 1995) and informants were gathered through various networks and groups I belonged to, as well as the snowball method. These included a Churches Together local group which provided contacts across various denominations; through my work as a lay preacher, at the time, in the United Reformed Church (URC); involvement in holistic spiritualities groups; leisure activities such as yoga and serving on a couple of charitable committees in the area of South Lakeland where I live. I have kept in touch with several of my subjects who were (or became) my friends (Droogers 2014b: 51) and I have spoken again to the informants in this chapter more recently to determine to what extent, if any, their life has changed since the first interview. I was also engaged, and in some cases still am, in participant observation and observant participation of their activities. This work covers, therefore, a span of roughly ten years.

My role as researcher: insider or outsider?

My own association with the Christian church extends to more than 60 years. As a child born during the Second World War, I attended Sunday School pretty faithfully right up to my teenage years which then moved seamlessly into Sunday evening worship, attending as a matter of course rather than conviction, with no parental pressure, contra a number of the women I spoke to. I married in the Congregational church of my childhood, but then disaffiliated completely for a dozen or so years, not through a conscious attempt to break free of stifling religious conventions (contra Brown 2001, 2006), but more as an example of disaffiliation through the pursuit of McLeod's (2007) "companionate marriage". Young couples of my generation were more focused on putting their new home together, buying a car and going out in their free time, rather than attending church. I had not "lost faith" at this point, but was simply distracted, because when my children were born, I was drawn back into joining an Anglican Mothers' Union group, even though not an Anglican, and becoming a regular Methodist church attender and even a lay preacher. Major disagreements in the local church sent me back to the Congregational church (now URC).

Moving to a new area in the late 1990s and still a churchgoer, I became secretary of the local Churches Together group and involved in the life of the town's URC and across South Lakeland as a lay preacher. However, starting my doctoral work introduced me to new ideas about the function of religion for women and the possibility of religion itself being nothing more than a social construction, varying in expression according to the geographical location in which it surfaces. I "defected" to the Quakers with its more liberal expression of Christian belief and doctrine, finding silent worship more in tune with my new stance. I also learnt about forms of spirituality which seemed to favour more individual experience, without demanding any particular affiliation, and which did indeed *seem* to have more to offer women (Woodhead 2007, 2008). However, the groups I joined, although largely composed of women, disappointingly, were not particularly focused on women's experiences, somewhat contra Woodhead. I still continue attending one holistic spiritual group but, having embarked as research associate on a project on atheism among young people(Catto and Eccles 2013; Eccles and Catto 2015), I became interested in humanism. This seemed open to all genders and orientations, not to mention its being a good way of having "commitments" without the need for supernatural belief. So my trajectory has certainly followed that of some church leavers described by Francis and Richter (Richter and Francis 1998; Francis and Richter 2007). More lately, still very much a professional "religion", or perhaps more accurately, "worldview" watcher, I would not like to say what I am other than inclining to humanism, although contemplating and writing about others' worldviews on an almost daily basis and still very much fascinated by individuals' meaning making processes.

So, do others switch in and out of religious/spiritual/secular institutions for a whole variety of reasons? Droogers (2007) would suggest they do. And does that make me (and them) an insider or an outsider when speaking with those whose allegiances have shifted and changed over time? I would argue that my own perambulations through and flirtations with various forms of Christian religious life and none, have certainly been helpful in being able to enter into dialogue with those of varying persuasions and commitments, a process Droogers (2014a) characterizes as methodological ludism, playing the "game", however individual players choose to set up the playing field and devise the rules of engagement. And did my informants appear to "cherish a certain opinion, while at the back of their mind holding an antithetical view" (ibid.: 39)? To what extent were "constellations of power" at work in my interviews? Both the reflexive and holistic switchers were middle class and a number knew me. It seems likely therefore that the issues of power were less acute, although researchers, simply because they ask the questions, almost inevitably have more control of the situation than the informant. Was a different view held by my informants than the one I actually heard and have recorded and transcribed? Given my participant observation of these women, thus as insider and outsider simultaneously in various milieux, and my willingness to "play the game" as nearly as possible, I would contend that such instances were minimized. Moreover, a number of informants expressed a sense of gratitude that they had been able to share their stories for the first time in their lives. Turning now to actual informants, I begin with reflexive switchers: Bronwen, Anna and Carla. All names are pseudonyms and no location is described in detail in the interest of protecting confidentiality.

Reflexive switchers

Bronwen was born and brought up in Anglicanism, recounting bitter memories of her life as a daughter of the vicarage when her overbearing clergyman father tyrannized the whole household. She took the first opportunity to leave home, applying and being accepted to read sociology at university.

> And that was like going to heaven really. I could be myself and I suppose from a religious point of view I felt I wanted to leave anything to do with organized Christianity behind. But actually I didn't leave it completely behind. I went to the university church and I couldn't really subscribe to the sort of views I was expected to subscribe to, so I left after about six months. But throughout my religious and spiritual history there is this, on the one hand, the rejection of traditionally organized Christianity which very much relates to my family experience and on the other hand, if I do reject it completely, something important is missing ... and that would seem to be the theme throughout. So really I then went into psychiatric social work because I felt I wanted to do something worthwhile. So there was a sense of moral values which has always been important to me. And my sense of what I "ought" to do goes back to my earliest experiences and is obviously something quite strong, although at times it has been quite a handicap really.

She described herself as having "very strong intertwinings" between "personal history and religion." These continued when Bronwen found herself attracted to a man about to be ordained. Despite misgivings on her part that she would be tied to the very church she determined to escape, they eventually married but Bronwen was intent on ensuring that hers would be a much more "symmetrical marriage" than her parents'. After his first post in a northern industrial inner city parish her husband entered sector ministry, allowing Bronwen time and space to develop her own considerable career in psychiatric social work. When she participated in the parish life in his first post she had to "find a way of managing the role of being vicar's wife in that situation". She effectively functioned as a social worker for the congregation, being comfortable as a "facilitator". Years later, approaching retirement, they knew they did not want to be connected to the Church of England any longer, although Bronwen had existed on its margins most of her married life. "And yet I do have quite a strong spiritual sense ... and I felt I wanted to be somewhere where I could do something for other people but that could also be nurtured in me." She became a member of Sea of Faith and "that's really my orientation. We cover a spectrum from people who go to some sort of religious place of worship and others who are agnostic bordering on atheism, I would say." In addition, Bronwen has joined the liberal-Liberal Quakers (Dandelion 2007), where she has found a similar agreeably broad range of views. When I spoke to her recently, she had become very heavily involved, thus fulfilling her strong moral sense that she must be committed to the good of others but she also attends a holistic spiritual group looking at a broad range of alternative therapies and practices, many focusing on work on the self.

Anna, born and brought up a Catholic, was so incensed by what she regarded as the irrational aspects of belief and ritual in her church, excluding people for apparently petty reasons, that she switched denominations in her thirties to become an Anglican. She remembers what should have been her first communion as a child of seven. She was supposed to fast beforehand, but in helping to prepare Sunday lunch she had eaten a single pea. "So I couldn't make my first communion. There was a huge fuss and I was mortified at seven. And left out really. I mean it was fairly awful, looking back."

She continued going, however, married an Anglican in a Catholic church at age 25, although not able to have full nuptial mass, but she refused to make a commitment to bring up any children from the union as Catholics. She trained as a teacher, and even taught in a Catholic secondary school, but her doubts began to be more pressing towards the end of the 1970s. "I started reflecting, you know, on the indoctrination at school in the infants and how things had happened over the years." Eventually she spoke to a "very good Church of

England minister" in an area near where they lived and as a result became an Anglican. The new minister didn't have confessions; he had "chats": "And it was sort of working round how you thought and what you thought. And I thought this is more about a faith as it should be."

However, Anna, seemingly committed as secretary of the Parochial Church Council (PCC), concluded our conversation by saying that she found "the actual institution" annoying and bureaucratic "and I don't think, actually at this stage, now I'm this age, I don't think you need to go to church to be a Christian". Interestingly, however, she thought she simply needed to go to church to receive communion. She did not want "all the worship, the actual ceremony. I would be quite happy if it was in a field somewhere and it was just straight communion". When asked to explain, it transpired that "communion" was not to be understood in the traditional Catholic sense of the mass, the meal from which she was disbarred as a child for eating a pea, but "to link with whatever you want to call the creator, God, the universe, it is just a linking for me with that whole creation, the whole thing. I'm part of it. I think I should have been a Buddhist really. I can see that, you know, everything to me is part of the same thing, inanimate objects even." As a practitioner of reiki, she found that "it works, because one side of me can see that everything is the same spiritual energy coming from a greater universe, or God, and you need to channel that to let it go through you. And going to church, since I've actually practised reiki has actually been better. So I suppose I am pulled away from the dogma of Christianity, but left with the spiritual." Ten years ago, she felt that having been in the Anglican church for a number of years she was no longer convinced they do things any differently from the Catholics, "and now probably I wouldn't move, I would just do my own thing, which is what I've done". Ten years later, meeting up with Anna again, I expected to find her on the margins of the church, if there at all. Not so, Anna is now serving a four year curacy in a nearby Anglican parish. She had given up her teaching job, had then become a carer "as something to do", eventually obtaining employment in a Catholic nursing home, run by a religious order of nuns. At the same time she undertook the Anglican lay reader's certificate, although adamant she would not become a priest. Somehow she was persuaded and accepted for non-stipendiary ministerial training. When I expressed some surprise at the turnaround in her thinking, she insisted that she had always seen "God outside the box" and, her curacy completed, she intended to work outside the traditional institution of the church.

Carla, a retired teacher and progressive faced with many choices regarding religious practice and belonging, seems unable to opt for one in particular, not knowing if she really wants any. Although currently attending an ancient priory church, she is sure she would "easily fall into the hypocrite category." In our conversation ten years ago, she explained that there was little commitment to any form of worship when she was growing up until she became a student and fell in with an evangelical and then charismatic evangelical group. She was "completely frightened off after an exorcism which led to a murder and I gave up religion". She married an atheist in a registry office wedding but then her mother died quite young. The birth of her son four months later somehow prompted her to have him christened. She left again, moved house and returned to church again, largely, this time, she says, to have an hour's peace and quiet from her growing family on a Sunday morning. She was then baptized in a charismatic evangelical church, "total commitment", as she described it, but she got "fed up" and went to the Quakers, followed by the Orthodox where she "was chrismated". On moving to the village with the priory church, where she lives now, she attended to be able to sing in the choir. "I am a complete religious mongrel and a hypocrite, thinking of giving the whole thing up. The minute I join something I want to leave it!" When asked why she doesn't, it appears she goes to church because she likes some of the people that do go and she likes to "be with people who are asking questions." She also belonged to a small nucleus of people, as I did at the time of our first interview, who formed part of an informal progressive Christian discussion group. Carla listened to what was going on, I observed, but seemed a rather reluctant and hesitant participant, perhaps because there were two or three very vocal, well informed men who usually "led" the discussion.

Ten years on, she is not sure she has any beliefs to speak of; she just likes "commonsense, down to earth practical people". She can't "see the point of the prayers [in church services]. Who are we talking to exactly? And what is the creed all about?" Beliefs are "something we aspire to – an indulgence for the comfortable but which fly out of the window at moments of crisis like ante-natal advice at the moment of childbirth." Then, however, she somewhat retracts this by saying, "in an anxious time this week I found comfort in the Orthodox reading and prayer for that day. Perhaps it's a bit like an anaesthetic. I go along with it all and I don't feel any the worse for it." But she's sure she doesn't really believe because she would have taught her children Bible stories or how to pray and she hasn't done either. She concluded by saying she thought that "we have resources within ourselves to cope with life and we discover them when we need them". She is still a member of the choir at the priory church but she had arrived at the crossroads in her village the previous Sunday morning and it was several minutes before she turned towards the priory rather than in the other direction to the Quaker meeting. She concluded that she is still trying "to find some sort of internal integrity – a way of unifying all the different bits of one's personality to make a coherent whole and something to work with. So there's always something there that keeps me hanging on, always looking."

I turn next to Lily, Denise and Phoebe, three examples of holistic switchers who, to varying degrees, have revisited earlier parts of their life's experience, in returning to a traditional church in the midst of their holistic activities.

Holistic switchers

The early part of Lily's interview ten years ago suggested that religion served as "an assumed backdrop for the drama of everyday life" (Lynch 2007: 113) as she was growing up in the 1940s and 1950s. She was taken regularly to church by her parents, because "it was the thing to do" although she was always "free to question". As a child she was interested in fossils but this left her perplexed when she encountered those who held a literalist view of the bible and its teachings on the supposed age of the earth. She married in church, although her husband was Pagan, and had her children christened "because, I think it's part of custom, even if you don't have orthodox religious beliefs. I think it's part of accepted custom and so, you know, you do it to keep the family happy."

They ceased regular churchgoing on marriage, neither of them having what Lily referred to as "orthodox beliefs" but the children went to Sunday school. Lily attended the re-baptism of her son by full immersion as a teenager and went occasionally. Through the course of her 71 years Lily has decided: "I can't say I fit into any one bracket and personally it doesn't matter to me. I mean, my husband's more in one slot than I am." She does incline somewhat to her husband's Paganism, particularly its emphasis on the interconnectedness of all nature, saying, "I don't know what I would call myself. For those who are Christian I suppose I would be a Pagan but for the Pagans I would seem more Christian. But I think I'm somewhere more in the middle," although it is not entirely clear "in the middle" of what exactly. She describes her beliefs as "a mixture of commonsense, how can anybody possibly believe [in the truth of the bible], because it doesn't make sense? And then I go off at a tangent and I think, well, there are ghosts. What they are, I'm not entirely sure but there are spirits, things like that."

More recently, Lily started attending a Methodist church – although irregularly. Her (now) son-in-law wanted to be married to Lily's daughter in a church so they decided on the Methodists. Lily was "rather embarrassed about this" but the "lady vicar", as she describes the minister, was "very kind", so "we do go every now and again, go down there". She and her husband are also

Companions of the Chalice Well in Glastonbury and she is impressed by the volunteers from a number of different holistic communities who act as guardians. "I suppose that is what a church might be, if there were that kind of church, where people mix and I suppose there are places, like the Unitarians, but it is quite a long way for me to go from where I live." She, in common with a number of women I spoke to, sees the church (in general) as very anti-women and "a lot of the bible has been removed before it became known as a bible because it didn't fit in with the early church leaders' views". She's impressed by the colour, music and spectacle of the local Catholic church "and that is very important in people's lives" but, again in common with a number of women, sees it as an institution exercising the type of control best avoided by free spirits like herself. However, Lily does believe quite firmly in an afterlife, although realizes there may be inconsistency here between such a belief and her reliance on "commonsense". "You can't join it all up because there are so many imponderable things between everything. I do think, yes, I do think we'll meet the relatives up in heaven, whether we come down or … or we're reincarnated but that's it. I find it a difficult concept" and she has to admit that it is "all completely at odds probably with things I've said or seem to believe or not believe in". But then she wonders, are all forms of religion and spirituality "one of the needs as the brain develops through time for something religious? Or is the notion of heaven no more than a human construct?" Ten years on, Lily is still a Companion of the Chalice Well but has not attended church much recently, preferring the more holistic forms of practice and belief found in Paganism.

Coming from a less conventional background, retired art teacher, Phoebe, born of an artistic mother, was allowed "pretty much free reign" to follow her own inclinations, whether that was "covering the house with painting and drawing" or choosing not to attend Sunday school. She was married at 18 and "because I'd been brought up in a church school I was happy to have a church wedding, nice chap, the clergyman". She quickly had two children but her mother died of cancer when they were still very young and she found it hard to cope with the death process "because everything I had ever come across, including the Christian upbringing, didn't touch [how to deal with it]".

She couldn't exactly think what she believed when the children were growing up, because "my beliefs have changed so much since then, but I think I believed that I was powerless. Humans had no power at all, just buffeted around by life and a big God out there. I wasn't sure about the patriarchal thing but I knew there was this big supreme you know, God-like energy." However, she loved the sacred choral traditions, church art and architecture, singing regularly in a choir which performed many sacred works. Otherwise,

Phoebe only attended the occasional offices. "I was very comfortable in that setting because of my junior [church] school upbringing but I didn't question liturgy, not just then." Her first marriage was dissolved and she remarried but her second husband's health broke down soon after. Then, quite out of the blue, her daughter committed suicide at the age of 21. Phoebe was left "on the floor", feeling even more powerless to cope. Having been introduced by a friend to Eastern philosophy and meditation techniques, she visited a guru in India and "learnt so much" that, after many long months of reflecting upon her traumatic experiences, she began to accept what had happened, not through anything she had learned from Christian beliefs and practices, but through her understanding of Hindu dharma and belief in reincarnation. However, in common with a number of holistic practitioners, "I just take and dip into things" and she "can go in any religious place and talk with anybody". In common with other holistic practitioners, she is sure that "spirituality is part of life", but "it's all at such odds with the church".

I had expected at this point that Phoebe would terminate our encounter, and I would note her down as a fully paid up member of the holistic spirituality movement, with any form of Christian engagement firmly written out of the script. However, she continued the conversation by recounting her husband's conversion to Roman Catholicism, his love of and devotion to the church and her own frequent visits, accompanying him to mass. It is perhaps unsurprising, however, given Phoebe's feminist stance, that "the liturgy makes my hair curl, because it's taking power from the people. The church is in control [not ordinary people]."

Phoebe's own worldview, echoed by many in the holistic movement: "the whole universe is within us; I just believe we're so connected to everything that is" has been arrived at "through a long journey". Phoebe's emotional attachment to (and connection with) her husband whose health has been so poor, demanded a different form of allegiance on Sunday morning, however, at that time. Ten years on, Phoebe's husband is now in a nursing home. I spoke to her briefly to discover her devotion continues, no longer including churchgoing, but certainly involving a demanding schedule of daily visiting.

Lastly, I turn to Denise whom I have known for nearly 40 years. As she said of churchgoing in her youthful years, when I spoke to her in 2004, "Got a lot out of it when I went. I enjoyed good preachers especially when they were in touch with what was going on. You learned something. The service gave me a spiritual dimension which you don't get any other way. I miss it in some ways." She trained as a nurse and continued working after she married and had children which meant she could not go every Sunday. In addition she cared for her parents when both were ill.

> I was virtually running two households, two children, house needed quite a lot of work. I just decided you can't do everything. I did what I absolutely needed to do and looked after Mum and Dad. I think I wanted to "live" my Christianity not go on Sunday rather than look as if you're doing it. You either go and do it properly or you do it outside ... I couldn't put anything back because I'm too busy but then I think it's more important to do than just be spiritually renewed. It's not just a question of going to a service, it takes a lot of commitment. To combine the whole lot is impossible.

When Denise moved to a different part of the country, she became friends with a woman who was a professional astrologer and another who practised druidry. They in turn introduced her to a number of others in the holistic milieu, including Phoebe, above, and the holistic spirituality group attended by Bronwen. Rather like Phoebe she thought the church does not "do" spirituality very well. "So you access spirituality in other ways." In addition she had become disillusioned with the church.

> Well it's the people in it. They're self-righteous, well, not everybody, other people are very good, but I do not like the evangelical aspect of things, ramming it down your throat. I am looking for something spiritual but not church. Some very good things can be taken from other religions [but] I just want to do my good works in a secular setting. I don't want to limit what I do to work with Christians. The evangelicals mention Jesus in every other sentence. They're always wanting to tell you and it's not always borne out by what they do. Have you read *The Poisonwood Bible*? That shows you people taking themselves so seriously, like Alan at St Matthew's [a neighbour].

At the time of our 2004 conversation Denise's daughter was suffering a number of mental health problems about which Denise consulted a number of holistic practitioners including the ones who had befriended her. After several years her difficulties began to be resolved and her daughter, who had two children by this stage, met and married a man whose mother was very prominent in the very evangelical church which Denise had castigated. In an attempt to be as supportive to her daughter and her in-laws, as possible, Denise became a regular attender and volunteered for various church-related activities. This lasted a couple of years or so but at the time of writing, more than ten years after our first conversation, Denise has quit the evangelical church to attend an ancient Anglican priory which is "more in tune with what I really think" and much more like the church she attended in her youth.

Reflexive and holistic switchers: insiders or outsiders?

Taking the life stories of the women here, would we argue for their being insiders or outsiders of those institutions that they have left behind and those they subsequently (and sometimes multiply) espouse? Perhaps they are both, depending on the particular context they find themselves in. A better way to conceive of their religiosity/worldview might be in terms of "lived religio-spirituality" (Ammerman 2007; McGuire 2007, 2008), the beliefs, values and practices of which McGuire characterizes as being multifaceted, diverse and malleable. Such diversity and malleability, she argues, are what make up many, perhaps most, persons' own religions (see also Lynch 2007: 40–42; Droogers and van Harskamp 2014b).

There are times when large parts of individual repertoires are put to rest. Despite claiming to be holistically spiritual and possibly Christian, Lily wonders if heaven is not just some human construct, while Denise has decided twice in her faith journey that the evangelical churchgoers take themselves "too seriously" and presently opts for a more mainstream Anglicanism. We have seen Anna "play with possibilities", changing tack in different situations and contexts, veering to the more holistic/spiritual, reiki and Buddhist practices on the one hand, ten years ago, combined with being secretary of the PCC, and now choosing to be ordained but determined to work with a "God outside the box". Carla has flitted in and out of various forms of Christianity and veers from attending (to sing in the church choir) to "giving it up altogether." But occasions do arise, usually driven by emotional attachments to those close to them, a spouse, daughter or son, for example, which cause dormant parts of the repertoire to be re-activated. Although Denise attends an Anglican mainstream church currently, her emotional commitment to care for her parents and pursue her nursing career meant no time for churchgoing at one stage in her life. In an attempt to help heal her daughter she has also ventured at another stage into the realm of holistic practice. In an attempt to show solidarity with her son-in-law's immediate family she joined their evangelical church for a while. Bronwen talked of wanting "a symmetrical marriage" but wanted to support her husband in his first parish, framing this role as "facilitator" rather than vicar's wife, but supporting him nonetheless. She chose a caring profession because, having a strong sense of moral values, she wanted to "do something worthwhile" but wanted to pursue this outside the church. Phoebe had very little sympathy with the patriarchal and hierarchical Catholic Church as a mature adult, but devotion to her husband ensured her regular committed attendance as long as he needed her, while a holistic spiritual worldview has helped her to come to terms with the devastating loss of a daughter.

Conclusion

We could argue that how these women live their religio-spiritual-secular lives *is* their "religion" but perhaps we should talk more inclusively and more accurately as its being their worldview (Droogers and van Harskamp 2014a; Droogers 2014c), which combines the traditionally religious with the spiritual and the secular. This may sometimes mean adopting what perhaps might be more accurately styled "situational practices", rather than Stringer's (2008: 51) situational beliefs where actual beliefs may be at odds with those practices. However, no matter how "contradictory" they may appear from a more "orthodox" viewpoint, such beliefs, practices and belongings are how these women negotiate and survive the considerable vicissitudes which life has thrown up. They provide as Lynch (2007: 40) contends, sources of resources and relationships, which they use in different ways, depending on their particular needs. Coping strategies, then, as Stringer (2008) suggests, not the once-and-for-all conversion of traditional theology.

Alternative spiritualities have often been disparaged as "pick-and-mix" religion, "bricolage", "religion-lite", hence incoherent, narcissistic, relativistic, lacking moral grounds (Bruce 2002; Bellah et al. 1985; Voas and Bruce 2007; Carrette and King 2005), as well as being "an uncritical expression of the cultural assumptions of late capitalism" (Lynch 2007: 65). There seems little that is narcissistic or lacking in moral grounds, nor, for that matter, incoherent, in the secular-religio-spirituality of these women's lives, if we adopt the viewpoint advocated here. Such lives have involved considerable emotional investment (Eccles 2012a; Riis and Woodhead 2010) in dealing with traumatic family experiences and attitudes, and it is how some women, maybe many, live their lives, sometimes inside certain "hallowed" boundaries, sometimes out. These forms of worldview are valid and meaningful, if we agree with Bowman (2015: 304) that no-one lives a life that is religiously "pure": these faith lives are not the result of women somehow getting religion "wrong".

Focusing specifically on the way a contemporary emphasis on the spiritual has changed perceptions, Huss (2014: 51) argues that it creates novel taxonomies and shapes new lifestyles, social practices and cultural artefacts. He sees these as blurring and undermining the modernist distinction between not just the religious and the spiritual but between the religious and the secular. "These practices and products constitute a different social and cultural realm that cannot easily be defined inside the boundaries of either religious or secular culture." On this basis, Huss (ibid.: 58) contends that we must explore the historical and social significance of these new cultural formations and social practices and question the familiar and entrenched suppositions and categories that they challenge, particularly in terms of what does and does not constitute "religion".

About the author

Janet B. Eccles gained her PhD in 2010 in the sociology of religion as a mature student at Lancaster University, UK. She then spent 18 months as research associate on the Young Atheist Project, based at Lancaster. Currently she is a part-time adult education tutor in religious studies in Cumbria and an independent researcher. Her research interests cover women and religion, forms of non-religion, chaplaincy studies and, more recently, religion and social class and Anglican monasticism. She has published on women, Christian affiliation and disaffiliation, alternative spiritualities and forms of non-religion in the *Journal of Contemporary Religion, Temenos* and the *Journal of Belief and Values*, among others, and on multi-faith chaplaincy in the *Journal for Pastoral Care and Counseling*. She has a chapter, "Speaking Personally: Women Making Meaning through Subjectivised Belief", in A. Day (ed.), *Religion and the Individual: Belief, Practice, Identity* (2008).

References

Ammerman, N. (2007). *Everyday Religion: Observing Modern Religious Lives*. Oxford: Oxford University Press. https://doi.org/10.1093/acprof:oso/9780195305418.001.0001

Bellah, R. N., Madsden, R., Sullivan W. N. et al. (1985). *Habits of the Heart: Individualism and Commitment in American Life*. Berkeley, CA: University of California Press.

Bowman, M. (2015). Christianity, Plurality and Vernacular Religion in Early Twentieth-Century Glastonbury: A Sign of Things to Come? In C. Methuen, A. Spicer and J. Wolffe (eds), *Christianity and Religious Plurality: Volume 51: Studies in Church History*, 302-321. Woodbridge: Boydell. https://doi.org/10.1017/S0424208400050257

Brown, C. G. (2001). *The Death of Christian Britain: Understanding Secularization 1800-2000*. New York: Routledge.

Brown, C. G. (2003). The Secularization Decade: What the 1960s Have Done to the Study of Religious History. In H. McLeod (ed.), *The Decline of Christianity in Western Europe, 1750-2000*, 29-46. Cambridge: Cambridge University Press. https://doi.org/10.1017/CBO9780511496783.003

Brown, C. G. (2006). *Religion and Society in Twentieth-Century Britain*. Harlow: Pearson Education Ltd.

Brown, C. G and Lynch, G. (2012). Cultural Perspectives. In L. Woodhead and R. Catto (eds), *Religion and Change in Modern Britain*, 329–351. New York: Routledge.

Bruce, S. (2002). *God is Dead: Secularization in the West*. Oxford: Blackwell.

Carrette J. and King, R. (2005). *Selling Spirituality: The Silent Takeover of Religion*. London: Routledge. https://doi.org/10.4324/9780203494875

Catto, R. and Eccles, J. B. (2013). (Dis)Believing and Belonging: Investigating the Narratives of Young British Atheists. *Temenos: Nordic Journal of Comparative Religion* 49: 37–63.

Dandelion, P. (2007). *An Introduction to Quakerism*. Cambridge: Cambridge University Press.

Davie, G. (2015). *Religion in Britain: A Persistent Paradox*. Chichester: Wiley Blackwell.

Droogers, A. (2007). Beyond Secularisation versus Sacralisation: Lessons from a Study of the Dutch Case. In K. Flanagan and P. Jupp (eds), *A Sociology of Spirituality*, 81–99. Burlington, VT: Ashgate.

Droogers, A. (2014a). Playing with Perspectives. In A. Droogers and A. van Harskamp (eds), *Methods for the Study of Religious Change: From Religious Studies to Worldview Studies*, 61–79. Sheffield: Equinox.

Droogers, A. (2014b). Quantitative and Qualitative Approaches Compared. In A. Droogers and A. van Harskamp (eds), *Methods for the Study of Religious Change: From Religious Studies to Worldview Studies*, 43–60. Sheffield: Equinox.

Droogers, A. (2014c). The World of Worldviews. In A. Droogers and A. van Harskamp (eds), *Methods for the Study of Religious Change: From Religious Studies to Worldview Studies*, 17–42. Sheffield: Equinox.

Droogers, A and van Harskamp, A. (2014a). Introduction. In A. Droogers and A. van Harskamp (eds), *Methods for the Study of Religious Change: From Religious Studies to Worldview Studies*, 1–15. Sheffield: Equinox.

Droogers, A and van Harskamp, A. (2014b). *Methods for the Study of Religious Change: From Religious Studies to Worldview Studies*. Sheffield: Equinox.

Eccles, J. B. (2008). Speaking Personally: Women Making Meaning through Subjectivised Belief. In A. Day (ed.), *Religion and the Individual: Belief, Practice, Identity*, 19–32. Burlington, VT: Ashgate.

Eccles, J. B. (2010). How Have Preboomer and Boomer Women Raised in Christianity Who Have Lived through the "Sixties Revolution" Been Affected in Terms of Their Religious and Value Commitments? An Interview-Based Study with Informants from South Cumbria. Lancaster: Lancaster University.

Eccles, J. B. (2012a). Changing "Emotional Regimes": Their Impact on Beliefs and Values in Some Older Women. *Journal of Beliefs and Values: Studies in Religion and Education* 33: 11–21. https://doi.org/10.1080/13617672.2012.650026

Eccles, J. B. (2012b). The Religious and Non-Religious Commitments of Older Women in the UK: Towards a New Typology. *Journal of Contemporary Religion* 27: 469–484. https://doi.org/10.1080/13537903.2012.722296

Eccles, J. B. and Catto, R. (2015). Espousing Apostasy and Feminism? Older and Younger British Female Apostates Compared. *Secularism and Nonreligion* 4: 1–12. https://doi.org/10.5334/snr.ax

Francis, L. J. and Richter, P. (2007). *Gone for Good? Church-Leaving and Returning in the Twenty-First Century*. Peterborough: Epworth.

Heelas, P. and Woodhead, L. (2005). *The Spiritual Revolution: Why Religion is Giving Way to Spirituality*. Oxford: Blackwell.

Hobsbawm, E. (1995). *Age of Extremes: The Short Twentieth Century 1914-1991*, London: Abacus.

Huss B. (2014). Spirituality: The Emergence of a New Cultural Category and its Challenge to ,the Religious and the Secular. *Journal of Contemporary Religion* 29: 47–60. https://doi.org/10.1080/13537903.2014.864803

Lynch, G. (2007). *The New Spirituality: An Introduction to Progressive Belief in the Twenty-First Century*. London: I B Tauris.

Lynch, G. (2010). Object Theory: Toward an Intersubjective, Mediated and Dynamic Theory of Religion. In D. Morgan (ed.), *Religion and Material Culture: The Matter of Belief*, 40–54. New York: Routledge.

Lynch, G. (2012). *The Sacred in the Modern World: A Cultural Sociological Approach*. Oxford: Oxford University Press. https://doi.org/10.1093/acprof:oso/9780199557011.001.0001

Marwick, A. (1999). *The Sixties: Cultural Revolution in Britain, France, Italy and the United States. c1958-c1974*. Oxford: Oxford University Press.

McDannell, C. (1995). *Material Christianity: Religion and Popular Culture in America*. New Haven, CT: Yale University Press.

McGuire, M. B. (2007). Embodied Practices: Negotiation and Resistance. In N. Ammerman (ed.), *Everyday Religion: Observing Modern Religious Lives*, 187–200. Oxford: Oxford University Press. https://doi.org/10.1093/acprof:oso/9780195305418.003.0011

McGuire, M. B. (2008). *Lived Religion: Faith and Practice in Everyday Life*. Oxford: Oxford University Press. https://doi.org/10.1093/acprof:oso/9780195172621.001.0001

McLeod, H. (2007). *The Religious Crisis of the 1960s*. Oxford: Oxford University Press. https://doi.org/10.1093/acprof:oso/9780199298259.001.0001

Morgan, D. (2010). *Religion and Material Culture: The Matter of Belief*. London: Routledge.

Richter, P. and Francis, L. J. (1998). *Gone but Not Forgotten: Church Leaving and Returning*. London: Darton, Longman and Todd.

Riis, O. and Woodhead, L. (2010). *A Sociology of Religious Emotion*. Oxford: Oxford University Press. https://doi.org/10.1093/acprof:oso/9780199567607.001.0001

Stringer, M. D. (2008). *Contemporary Western Ethnography and the Definition of Religion*. London and New York: Continuum.

Voas, D. and Bruce, S. (2007). The Spiritual Revolution: Another False Dawn for the Sacred. In K. Flanagan and P. Jupp (eds), *A Sociology of Spirituality*, 43–61. Burlington, VT: Ashgate.

Woodhead, L. (2007). Why so Many Women in Holistic Spirituality? A Puzzle Revisited. In K. Flanagan and P. Jupp (eds), *A Sociology of Spirituality*, 115–125. Aldershot: Ashgate.

Woodhead, L. (2008). "Because I'm Worth It": Religion and Women's Changing Lives in the West. In Aune K, Sharma S and Vincett G (eds). *Women and Religion in the West: Challenging Secularization.* Burlington, VT: Ashgate, 147–161.

Woodhead, L. (2012). Introduction. In L. Woodhead and R. Catto (eds), *Religion and Change in Modern Britain*, 1–33. Abingdon: Routledge. https://doi.org/10.4324/9780203130643

Woodhead, L. and Catto, R. (2012). *Religion and Change in Modern Britain.* Abingdon: Routledge. https://doi.org/10.4324/9780203130643

18

Scientology inside out
Complex religious belonging in the Church of Scientology and the Free Zone

Stephen E. Gregg and Aled J. L. Thomas

Despite the intention of L. Ron Hubbard to establish Scientology as a practice conducted within his institution of the Church of Scientology (CoS), the past thirty years have demonstrated an increasing number of individuals, many of whom identify themselves as Scientologists, practising Hubbard's technology away from the Church. Those who identify themselves as Scientologists with no involvement with the Church of Scientology, whether they practise Hubbard's teachings as a part of a community or individually, are collectively known as the Free Zone. This divide has prompted heated disagreement within Scientologist communities with regard to conceptions of inside/outside and religious identity and belonging. Akin to many "majority" religious establishments within wider traditions, the CoS does not consider those who practise Scientology away from the Church to be Scientologists, while, akin to many schismatic groups, members of the Free Zone often argue that their vision of Scientology possesses a greater relation to Hubbard's original purpose for his technology. Yet, despite this contrast between the CoS and Free Zone, the distinction between those who practise Scientology in the Free Zone is more nuanced than it appears on face value. Individual Free Zone groups have emerged in recent years, creating clear distinctions between different types of Free Zone Scientologists. Similarly, clear identity markers between Dianetical practice and Scientology practice *within* the CoS, in addition to the hierarchical nature of Scientology teaching systems and membership, means that conceptions of religious belonging are contested and complicated not only between the Free Zone/CoS but also within these identity labels.

Research in this area is particularly pertinent in the academic study of Scientology, as discourse on Scientology, both public and academic,[1] has invariably conflated Scientology with the CoS. Indeed, this is the desire of the CoS themselves, whose approach to the texts and practices of Scientology may best be summed up as *"extra ordo, nulla salus"*, but this does not reflect the lived reality of everyday practitioners – experiences beyond the "official line" of the CoS need to be understood more fully (or indeed, at all) if we are to understand the legacy and impact of Hubbard's teachings for diverse communities in diverse contexts.

The relationship between those that practise in the Free Zone, and CoS parishioners is further complicated by the different departure points and dynamic changes within the history of the CoS, and by association, the effect this has had on movement of individuals to Free Zone activities. Changes in the leadership of the CoS, editing of texts/scripture and changes of membership category over the last several decades have all impacted upon the internal and external identities of religious adherents who identify as Scientologists. This is particularly important as, with the dominance of attention on the CoS, addressing questions of identity "outside" the CoS necessarily asks questions as fundamental as "who Scientologists are" and "what Scientology is" that previous generations of scholars have not investigated. This is especially pertinent in the light of emerging methodologies in the wider Study of Religion, which reject accepted "World Religions Paradigm" approaches to religious traditions (see Chapter 1, this volume) which preferenced institution, scripture and hierarchical authority, and instead start from the "bottom-up", responding to the embodied everyday practice of devotees – often in relation to institution and hierarchy, but not emergent from them.

In light of these new approaches, this chapter explores the tensions between the Church of Scientology and independent Scientologists, while considering how Scientology can be practised in the "unregulated" environment of the Free Zone. This will then be contextualized within a "relational continuum of identity" approach to the insider/outsider issue, to produce a nuanced understanding of religious belonging and identity within Scientology/Scientologies.

History of Free Zone Scientology

The roots of Scientology lie in L. Ron Hubbard's work on the human mind and its treatment through the auditing process.[2] Despite its religious significance in Scientology, Hubbard initially promoted auditing as an ostensibly secular practice through the publication of *Dianetics: The Modern Science of Mental Health* in 1950. *Dianetics* became an instant bestseller, with Dianetic groups being formed by supporters and Hubbard becoming a highly popular public speaker for his presentations on auditing and Dianetic theory (Bromley 2009). The purpose of auditing and Dianetic theory is to allow a trained auditor to remove "engrams" (Scientologist nomenclature for the presence of anxieties and psychoses in the human mind that negatively affect the individual) stored in a part of the mind known as the "reactive mind" (Melton 2009; Harley and Kieffer 2009). Beginning their auditing sessions at the stage of "Preclear" (PC), Scientologists aim to reach the goal of "Clear" through the removal of their engrams. An individual that achieves this state becomes "the optimum individual; no longer possessed of any engrams" (Hubbard 1950: 494), and is referred to as "a Clear". This initial secular form of auditing is frequently referred to as Book One auditing (Harley and Kieffer 2009), yet as Hubbard's work on auditing developed, a distinctly religious element became present in its practice, including the concept of the "thetan" (the Scientologist understanding of the soul) and the exploration of past lives during auditing sessions (Rothstein 2009; Hubbard 1960).

These examples demonstrate the important distinction between *Dianetic auditing* and *Scientology auditing*; Dianetic auditing treats the mind, while Scientology auditing treats the thetan in its spiritual development, particularly through the use of the E-Meter, a device used to assist in the detection and removal of engrams (Chryssides 1999). The goal of Dianetic auditing is to achieve the state of Clear, and while this is also true of Scientology auditing, Clears will continue their spiritual practice beyond Clear and into the Operating Thetan Levels, progressing on Hubbard's "Bridge to Total Freedom", a series of hierarchically organized spiritual study and practice levels. Applying the teachings of these esoteric levels is believed by Scientologists to develop the spiritual abilities of the thetan to command the physical universe, overcoming the need for a physical body (Church of Scientology International 1998; Bromley 2009).

Through turning his attention to the religious aspects of auditing, Hubbard established the Church of Scientology as a religious organization in 1951 (Melton 2000; Lewis 2009). Despite this rise in popularity, the Church of Scientology was faced with considerable criticism very soon after its initial foundation, such as the Food and Drug Association's condemnation of the E-Meter's alleged abilities to cure medical conditions through auditing (Young 1972).[3] Yet conflict for the Church of Scientology was not limited to "outsiders", as several members of the Church began to leave the institution, particularly in the early 1980s, citing disagreements over issues such as the management of the Church and application of Hubbard's spiritual technology [see below]. Many of these individuals continued practising Scientology outside the Church of Scientology, and have become collectively known as the Free Zone (Grossman 2004).

One of the most immediately noticeable aspects of the Free Zone is its distancing of itself from the institutionalized Church of Scientology, keen to promote a difference between "Scientology" as a system of beliefs and practices, and the organizational "Church of Scientology" from which the Free Zone is entirely separate (Independent Scientology n.d.a). However, to simply summarize the Free Zone as being a movement that is separate from the Church of Scientology would be a great error, as the unregulated environment of the Free Zone results in a large range of Scientologists that often both interpret and practise Hubbard's tech in different ways. Unlike the Church of Scientology's Orgs, the Free Zone typically lacks fixed locations and staff to maintain a regulated application of Scientology. Consequently, groups of Free Zone Scientologists have emerged to create their own schisms of Scientology – such as the notably named Ron's Org, which this chapter will address – resulting in new Scientology groups with their own guidelines and practices. In a contrast to this, other Freezoners simply practise Scientology independently, allowing for interpretations and development of Hubbard's work to occur, ranging from Freezoners that create their own E-Meters and adopt new auditing techniques, to auditors that conduct their auditing sessions online to overcome the challenge of auditing Freezoners around the world. It is important to note that the category of the "Free Zone" is popularly used in both scholarship and public discourse to describe all Scientologists that practise Scientology outside the Church of Scientology (Ex-Scientology Kids n.d.). We, however, argue that the term "Free Zone" is widely debated in independent Scientologist communities, which leads to a variety of complicated and contested Free Zone notions of identity.

The inception of Free Zone Scientology is often attributed to Captain Bill Robertson, who became an influential figure in the initial major schism in Scientology. Robertson shared a close friendship with Hubbard, as demonstrated by his promotion to the rank of Captain in the Scientology Sea Org,[4] giving him a considerable level of authority among Scientologists. The origins of Robertson's involvement with the Free Zone is unclear due to contradictory accounts. Robertson is alleged to have confidentially met with Hubbard in the 1970s and was informed that, should other agents gain control of Scientology and the tech, he should "start the game anew outside" (Ron's Org Committee n.d.b; see also Hellesøy 2013). During the early 1980s Hubbard withdrew from public life and managerial roles of the Church of Scientology to concentrate on his writing. This resulted in his successors' establishment of the Church of Scientology International (CSI) to coordinate Church affairs (Rigal-Cellard 2009). Following Hubbard's alleged disappearance from the Church, Robertson is said to have discovered evidence[5] to support his working theory that the Church "had been infiltrated and taken over by government agents" (Ron's Org Committee n.d.a), soon leading to his disassociation from the Church. Robertson, believing that core Scientology beliefs and practices could be found in the books and lectures of Hubbard, insisted that the government's involvement with the Church of Scientology would eventually result in the suppression of the tech for practising Scientologists. He urged those leaving the Church to create a safe collection of Hubbard's written work or recordings, before the government does a "Ray Bradbury Fahrenheit 451 on everyone they can; that means burn your books" (Robertson 1983).

Robertson's Free Zone work became heavily involved with cosmology and narrative mythology known within Scientology as "space opera". His exploration of this area was both influenced by and in-line with Hubbard's work on the Operating Thetan (OT) levels. The most publicly known aspect of Hubbard's cosmology is OT III, which concerns the Xenu mythology. The OT III narrative outlines how Lord Xenu, head of the Galactic Federation, attempted to solve an overpopulation problem by sending thetans to the planet Teegeeack (Earth). This subsequently resulted in thetans becoming both attached to physical bodies and trapped in the physical universe (Rothstein 2009). Expanding on this, it is believed among some Freezoners that Robertson received an "Official Decree" from the Galactic Grand Council, stating that Earth is free from the interference of "any non-planetary agency or power", and is therefore a "Free Zone" (Galactic Patrol n.d.). Expanding on the cosmological aspects of Scientology was evidently important to Robertson, yet it is clear that his close personal relationship with Hubbard was the dominant factor in establishing a role of authority with other disillusioned members of the Church of Scientology. Using his influence among these disillusioned members to gather a group of followers, Robertson was able to establish Ron's Org in 1984, a schism of Scientology that aims to preserve and deliver Hubbard's tech while distancing itself from all other forms of Scientology (Ron's Org Bern n.d.).

Understandably, relations between the Church of Scientology and the Free Zone are turbulent. The Church has often adopted controversial attempts to respond to criticisms, such as their "fair game" policy, which states that any critic of Scientology is a "suppressive person" (SP) and is therefore open to be "tricked, sued or lied to or destroyed" (Lewis 2012: 140; Hubbard 1967). James R. Lewis notes that the fair game policy has simply attracted further criticism aimed towards the Church, arguing, for example, that the Church draws further public attention to critical books on Scientology by campaigning against their publication. Lewis notes that Hubbard abandoned the fair game policy in 1968, stating that it resulted in "bad public relations" (Lewis 2012: 140; Hubbard 1968), yet this distancing from the fair game policy seems to be in name only. Controversial responses towards former Scientologists by Church of Scientology members remains a persistent issue, with certain incidents of harassment being highly publicized in media accounts. For example, media reports were circulated in 2011 regarding Marty Rathbun's harassment from the "Squirrel Busters", a group of alleged Church of Scientology members that harassed Rathbun outside his home accusing him of "squirrelling" – "practising the technology of Hubbard outside the sanctioned remit of the Religious Technology Centre" (Gregg and Chryssides 2017: 26). Videos of the incident are also widely available online, and were keenly reported on by the tabloid press (Hartley-Parkinson 2011; Scientology Shock Squad 2011). Harriet Whitehead (1987) argues that such conflicts and controversies involving the Church of Scientology simply escalate any hostile responses from critics, rather than diffusing the situation.

Alongside the fair game policy, the Church of Scientology has also attracted criticism for its highly controversial disconnection policy, in which members of the Church are urged to "disconnect" (end all contact and communications) with individuals declared an SP. Lewis argues that this policy provokes "many otherwise neutral to moderately critical ex-members [becoming] devoted enemies of the Church" (Lewis 2012: 141), and as a result could somewhat explain the rising popularity of Free Zone Scientology, which is often openly critical of the Church's management and practices.

The development of the Free Zone, therefore, raises particular questions and issues regarding religious identity, and the projection of this identity, for religious actors across the spectrum of Scientological practice, both within and without the CoS. Issues of authority, authenticity, leadership, practice and continuity percolate the nuanced and relational bricolaged identities of individual Scientologists, which will be explored further below.

Relational identities in Free Zone Scientology

At first glance, the primary concern of Free Zone Scientologists appears to be the protection of Hubbard's spiritual technology, and preventing it from falling into corruption. Some Free Zone practitioners accuse the current leader of the Church of Scientology, David Miscavige, of changing the organization to a detrimental extent, including placing all Scientologist missions under Sea Org management (Independent Scientology n.d.b). The Free Zone promotes auditing as a part of the "Standard Tech", which categorizes teachings from Hubbard that are unaffected by any development from third parties, including the Church of Scientology itself (Independent Scientology n.d.a). This is relevant to Free Zone identity, often promoted as more true to Hubbard's original intentions, due to the numerous shifts in policy from the CoS over the decades – in particular the continued editing of Hubbard's published works (Christensen 2009: 414), and changes to practice; in particular New Era Dianetics, launched in 1978, and the Golden Age of Technology, launched in 1996, both of which sought to re-emphasize and retain authority and efficacy of Scientology practice and tradition within the CoS. As we will see, actions such as these both consolidated and ring-fenced Scientology identities within the CoS, but also caused insiders to leave the CoS, citing the desire to stay true to Hubbard's original teachings and practices.

Lewis (2013) writes that the Free Zone sports a diverse range of elements and methods for Scientologist practice. The lack of an organizational aspect to a large amount of the Free Zone results in many Scientologists finding their own methods of practising auditing and other forms of Scientologist teaching. As auditing remains a crucial practice and ritual in Scientology, a concern for Free Zone Scientologists is ensuring that independent Scientologists have access to auditing of a high standard. This has prompted many experienced Free Zone auditors to promote their services online, and resulted in the formation of Free Zone organizations, such as the Association of Professional Independent Scientologists (APIS) that specialize in promoting and preserving L. Ron Hubbard's teachings and tech. The APIS aims to assist in practising Scientology in the Free Zone, and provides a worldwide auditing directory of groups, organizations, and individuals that can be contacted for auditing assistance (International Freezone Association n.d.a, n.d.b).

While the APIS could be viewed as a directory of various independent Scientologist practitioners, Ron's Org serves as an example of an organized Free Zone community, and conducts auditing sessions through a network of groups that "are not hierarchically organized" (Ron's Org Bern n.d.: 16). Those who wish to practise auditing, or train to become professional auditors themselves, are able to contact a number of Ron's Org groups that practise auditing in a way they view as specific to the teachings of Hubbard. They are highly critical of the fees charged by the Church of Scientology for their auditing services, claiming that the Church has lost sight of the true goal of auditing, and now focuses on using the tech "against people, to gain power over them and get the maximum money out of their pockets" (Ron's Org Bern n.d.: 17).

Ron's Org is the most notable demonstration of a Free Zone group that has developed into its own organization, distinct from the Church of Scientology, yet with its own clear guidelines on how Scientology should be practised. Yet, as Lewis (2013) observes, Ron's Org provides a fluidity for Free Zone groups, by allowing unaffiliated Free Zone auditors the opportunity to conduct auditing sessions at their centres. However, this organizational approach is not adopted by all Free Zone groups, with many Scientology auditors operating entirely independently. The internet has become an invaluable tool for these auditors, allowing them not only the ability to publicly promote a vision of Hubbard's work that is unconnected to the Church of Scientology, but also giving them the opportunity to advertise their services online through Free Zone websites (International Freezone Association n.d.b; Freezone Auditors n.d.).

Much of the Free Zone presence on the internet presents many testimonies of a perceived increase in effectiveness in Hubbard's tech; yet not all these testimonies provide positive accounts of Free Zone auditing. In a response to the online Free Zone presence, former Free Zone Scientologists (that have now returned to practising auditing within the Church of Scientology) are using online blogs to document their experiences of what they deem to be inadequate and ineffective forms of independent auditing. A notable account on the Free Zone Survivors Association blog from "J", a former Free Zone practitioner, found independent auditing to be more destructive than beneficial. J outlines several examples of different forms of auditing practised in the Free Zone. These include a type of auditing developed by a Free Zone auditor that is delivered by telephone. During these sessions, J experienced issues regarding ARC[6] breaks – emotional upsets that disrupt the auditing session. Another issue for J was the lack of a Case Supervisor in these sessions, an individual trained to ensure that auditing is conducted correctly and appropriately (Free Zone Earth n.d.).

Soon J ended their own practice of auditing in the Free Zone, emphasizing the importance of the Hubbard's *Auditor's Code*, a series of guidelines that must be adhered to throughout auditing sessions (Hubbard 1950). J sums up their experience of Free Zone auditing and the independent Scientologist practice by stating that:

> There is no "Central Control" in the Freezone [sic] to ensure services are delivered standardly or mistakes repaired both for PC and auditor. So all these "out" actions continue unaddressed. PCs wander away broken-spirited & Auditors continue to deliver incorrect services. (J 2007)

J's argument that the Church of Scientology adopts a more systematic approach to auditing highlights the interaction between the perceived "inside" Church Scientologists and "outside" Free Zone Scientologists, with particular reference to the correct application of Scientologists' beliefs. However, the practice of auditing in the Free Zone is far too nuanced to be simply viewed in these terms. As our case study will show, Free Zone auditing is not only varied, but presents divisions in the independent Scientologist community itself.

Case study

To demonstrate the nuanced nature of Free Zone identities, this case study will explore the responses of Free Zone Scientologists in first hand interviews. It is worthy of note that all the Freezoners involved in this study are former members of the Church of Scientology. This is not intentional; all participants were gathered via a snowballing methodology, yet none initially became Scientologists through the Free Zone. This is important as the stage of entry into an organization, for example entry as a birth insider or conversion at different life-stages, affects the nuanced relational identity of the adherent; indeed, in this case where all informants are ex-members of the CoS, they will retain a relational form of identity which constantly refers to notions of outsideness (in regard to the CoS) and insideness (both to their new community, and to their conception of remaining true to Hubbard's original intentions). These independent Scientologists do not belong to one specific Free Zone organization, but cover a range of Free Zone groups or individuals who practise Scientology outside the Church of Scientology. This plethora of groups leads to a distortion of boundaries between different Free Zone identities. Despite this fluidity, some binaries are still apparent, particularly with regard to Free Zone approaches to the relationship between Scientologists and L. Ron Hubbard, and the notion of the "true" tech. Throughout Free Zone discourse, it is highly common for Free Zone Scientologists to accuse the Church of Scientology of distorting the work of Hubbard, yet the nature of the Free Zone has allowed some Freezoners to alter or develop their own versions of Scientologist tech to their own preference, resulting in debate among Freezoners on the importance of Hubbard's original writings in the application of Scientology. This case study will demonstrate and explore the complex nature of Free Zone identities that emerge as a result of these issues.

An immediate distinction between different Free Zone groups and individuals is the issue of self-identity, particularly pertaining to the term "Free Zone". These interviews demonstrate that a number of Scientologists who have left the Church of Scientology in recent years that view the Free Zone as a specific group of independent Scientologists from the 1980s, particularly those who followed the work of Captain Bill Robertson. "James", an independent Scientologist and auditor, outlined his view of Free Zone Scientology accordingly:

> [The Free Zone is] a particular group that left the Church much earlier than I did and had some ideological differences. Not necessarily a great many, but it's sort of stuck in the 70s and 80s in terms of what Scientology is. (James, cited in Thomas 2018)

Expanding on this issue of identity, James describes himself as an "independent, independent Scientologist" or "Indie" (cited in Thomas 2018), and claims that Scientology was continuously developed under the supervision of Hubbard until his death in 1986, resulting in the "Free Zone" practising a dated form of Scientology. Further demonstrating the nuanced nature of Free Zone identity, James will often identify as Buddhist when speaking to outsiders, based on his view of Scientology as technological Buddhism:[7]

> If somebody asks me in the street what I believe, I say I'm a Buddhist. I don't have to say the word "Scientologist" as really it is Buddhism. We believe in reincarnation, we believe in karma (Scientology has something very similar to karma). And even Hubbard said in many lectures that the problem with Buddhism for him (and I have to agree) is that sitting on a mountaintop didn't really do much for most people. A small percentage might reach a higher plane, but most people get cold and lose weight – that's all that happens. All that Scientology really does is the auditing side of things, which builds a way of going from a lower awareness level to a higher awareness level. They're spiritual techniques that basically don't require you to go and live in a cave (James, cited in Thomas 2018).

This quotation further complicates the notions of insideness and outsideness regarding Scientologist identity in the Free Zone, and the wider field of religion. By observing crossovers between Scientologist and Buddhist faith (rebirth, karma, spiritual development), James is able to identify as Buddhist, particularly when engaging with "outsiders" less familiar with Scientology, while still practising Scientology and making use of Hubbard's tech. Here, then, we can see an example of a projection of relational "represented" religion that critiques paradigms of religious membership based on outdated unilateral categories of participation, by focusing on lived experience (Sharma 2008; Harvey 2013; Gregg and Scholefield 2015). Despite considering himself an independent Scientologist, James does not belong to an organized independent group, believing that many independent Scientologists still follow "Church of Scientology type" practices, which he argues are mistakes made by L. Ron Hubbard to protect the security of Scientology. Such a criticism of Hubbard's work is a stark contrast to how he is typically viewed by Church of Scientology members, who often refer to Hubbard as "Source", in relation to his role as the founder of Scientology its spiritual knowledge and philosophy (Atack n.d.).

In comparison to James's identity as an Indie Scientologist, Tracy, a Free Zone auditor who left the Church of Scientology during Captain Bill Robertson's establishment of the Free Zone, believes that Indie Scientologists practise a squirrel form of Scientology that is currently practised by the Church of Scientology, claiming that "Indies think all of the Free Zone is squirrel, but some of the RTC (Religious Technology Centre) training and methodology they were trained in is squirrel" (cited in Thomas 2018).[8] Despite distancing himself from what he views as the Free Zone community of the 1980s, James holds an inclusive view of the Free Zone, stating: "I'm not against the Free Zone, I'm just not a Free Zone member" (cited in Thomas 2018), yet this division can cause disagreement on the correct application of Hubbard's tech, and what "true" Scientology entails as a result. Another independent Scientologist, Chris, views the Free Zone in a highly negative light due to what he perceives as Freezoners straying from Hubbard's original work:

> I prefer the term "Field" or "Independent Field". "Free Zone" has come to be a tainted term, since the Free Zone contains a lot of people who are "squirrelling" and/or highly critical of the Founder. Apparently, "Free Zone" used to be a more neutral term, but that was before I came to be part of the Independent Field. (Chris, cited in Thomas 2018)

Chris's statement highlights the predominant factor that distorts the boundaries between Free Zone groups – the relationship between Scientologists and L. Ron Hubbard, and claims of authenticity based upon this. Taking a highly critical stance of any Scientologist who develops or changes any aspect of Hubbard's work, Chris views a distinction between two types of Free Zone Scientologist, those "with-LRH" or "not-with-LRH":

> There are the people who are "with-LRH". And the people who are not. The "with-LRH" people are often the most trained and educated in the subject. They insist on precision of application of the technology, and adherence to the policies laid down by Ron in relation to the technology. ...
> "What is Scientology" is a very narrow thing, and very precisely laid out by what LRH wrote and said. There is little or no room for "interpretation". (Chris, cited in Thomas 2018)

Indeed, Chris's view here is demonstrative of a central complicating factor in the dynamics of identity for "what Scientology is", which raises questions of what it means to be an "insider" or "outsider". Put simply, we here find a situation where both insiders and outsiders to the CoS, the Free Zone in general, and Chris's sub-demarcation of the Free Zone into "with-LRH" and "not-with-LRH", are negotiating identities which claim authenticity, provenance and efficacy of practice in direct relation to other communities or identities within the meta-term Scientology. Their identities are not binary insider/outsider (for one could be an insider to LRH's teaching but an outsider to the CoS and other Free Zone communities, for example) but are negotiated *relational* identities that cross the boundaries of externally observed or set identity markers. They are defined as much by what they are not, as by what they are.

Chris's criticism of innovation and development of Hubbard's work in the practice of Scientology is a strong contrast with the view of James, who views the true distinction between Scientology in the Church and the Free Zone as being institutional, allowing Freezoners access to an uncostly Scientology that is free from strict regulation. He states that:

> There are few differences in the way the "technology" is delivered, though I'm sure some will say "we have the one true tech" because I have heard such claims, but they are false. The real difference is in the atmosphere and spirit in which it is delivered in the indie field, much less draconian, much less emphasis on having to donate endless sums of money, disconnect[ed] from nay-sayers etc. ...
>
> Others believe that Captain Bill Robertson had a posthumous line to Hubbard and that Hubbard dictated new materials to him ... I beg to differ. Robertson was a trained auditor himself and has simply continued and developed new materials, but if he doesn't say they are Hubbard's then they won't be followed, which is crazy because Hubbard encouraged highly trained people to develop new tech. (James, cited in Thomas 2018)

These two opposing statements, both from Scientologists that identify as independent Scientologists, demonstrate a facet of the wide spectrum of attitudes to the sanctity of Hubbard's tech in the Free Zone, and the range of Free Zone identities that can emerge as a result. Chris acts as an example of an independent Scientologist that lays claim to an authentic form of Scientology, purely dictated by Hubbard and unchanged by any outsiders, while James promotes a view of a fluid Scientology, open to interpretation and development.

This case study demonstrates the wide variety of groups and identities in the Free Zone, often caused by perceptions of L. Ron Hubbard's authority and tech. While the Free Zone's identity is largely based on its opposition to the Church of Scientology, there is little unity in the independent Scientologist community regarding core Scientologist principles, and views of its founder. There are now accusations of "squirrelling" among the "squirrels", and thus the Free Zone cannot be merely defined as a unified "outsider" group, rather a large collection of Scientologist groups outside the institutionalized Church of Scientology, with different stances on belonging, practice and belief.

Complex religious belonging in Scientology

In this chapter, we have sought to explore the complexity of Scientologist identities beyond inherited monolithic categorizations which limit the use of the terms Scientology and Scientologist within the remit of, or in direct association with, the CoS. While our main case study has been to demonstrate complexity of identity and diversity of experience within the Free Zone, this section will offer further critiques of binary notions of "insideness" and "outsideness" both within the CoS, the Free Zone, and also of related religious identities from actors who do not self-identify as Scientologists. To do so, we will relate to aspects of everyday religious practice which inform and relate to identity formation, noting how these problematize binary notions of insider/outsider wherever relevant.

Perhaps the most clear-cut dynamic which affects a person's identity is their joining or leaving a community. Much scholarship has previously focused upon points of entry or departure (conversion and disengagement) and, while these are important factors which we will explore, it must be remembered that religious identities are constantly re-negotiated between individuals and their host groups, meaning that an individual's identity will change while they are within a group, as well as when they are entering or leaving it. With this caveat in mind, it is still relevant to explore some of these "identity staging posts" that have led to change and schism (perhaps with a small "s") that altered and produced a great diversity of Scientological identities both *within* the CoS and also within diverse Free Zone groups.

The first such staging post is the point of arrival into a group or culture, and it is interesting to note that all of the informants in our Free Zone case study were prior converts to the CoS, rather than birth insiders to either group. This means that their identity as a Free Zoner is still, in large part, informed by their relation to the CoS, and this is clear from the statements of informants, who consistently refer to the practices or actions of the CoS, particularly with regard to interpretations of Hubbard's wishes or intentions for ritual practice. This places such informants' identities on a liminal stage – while they actively self-identify as ex-members of the CoS, their continual re-negotiation of religious identity can only be fully understood in relation to their past membership of, and continuing relationship with, the CoS, which colours, or informs, their present religious actions. This can be viewed on a group, rather than individual scale, when we consider the exit points of many members of the Free Zone – indeed, most major breakaway groups date from the 1980s, and can be seen in large part to be responses to changes in the leadership of the CoS and their initiatives. The Mission Holders' Conference in 1982,[9] as has been noted by Hellesøy (2013), is a clear example of an event which caused disaffection within the membership, and particularly those who had previously managed Orgs, and who were now essentially being disenfranchised by the central management of the CoS, led by David Miscavige, who would go on officially to replace Hubbard after his death, and who were effectively running the CoS at this time. Similar to this was the introduction of the Golden Age of Technology, introduced in two stages by Miscavige in 1996 and 2012, which radically altered auditor training and practice from Hubbard's original work.

Such events, while on the one hand acting as very obvious departure points for ex-members and break-away groups, also complicate notions of insideness and outsideness; when many members left at these junctures, they continued to argue (as we have seen in our informant testimonies) that they have remained more true to Hubbard's original teachings than the CoS, despite the Church holding legal copyright of texts and practices. This highlights a particular issue in the insider-outsider debate, which is the dynamic relationship between an individual adherent and an institution which changes policy, leaving a person or group of persons, who had previously identified as insiders, outside their community, not through their own change of viewpoint, but because the institution has changed its position. Those who are on the inside may be ejected by the institution and become nominal outsiders, but their identity may still be predicated on the understanding that they remain "inside" the original worldview of their spiritual authority (for example, Chris, above).

Such moves from "insider" to "outsider" status can also be seen with regard to policy decisions of the CoS, but again this should be understood beyond inherited binary notions. One high profile apostate from Scientology in recent years has been Paul Haggis, the Academy Award-winning Director and Screenwriter, who left very publicly in 2009. Haggis's split from the CoS was centred on his perception of a lack of action by CoS authorities, and the then official spokesperson of the CoS in particular, Tommy Davis, in opposing a group of California-based Scientologists from supporting "Prop 8" (a piece of legislation which sought to deny marriage rights to same sex couples in the State of California). This was a very personal mission for Haggis, whose daughter is gay.[10] Haggis's movement away from the CoS is interesting, for his actions were predicated upon a social policy disagreement (see Jolly 2016) rather than, for example, Jason Beghe's claims of financial control, Aimee Scobie's claims of physical abuse, or Mike Rinder's claims of family disconnection.[11] Indeed, each of these ex-members can claim to be a different type of "outsider", as their religious identity external to the CoS will be conditioned by their experiences inside the community, and are still relational to the CoS in their public projection. Indeed, when one examines recent apostates such as Leah Remini, Mike Rinder and Marty Rathbun, we find that their continued public religious identity is either projected entirely in relation to the CoS (Remini and Rinder) or that they continued to practise Hubbard's Tech independently after leaving (Rathbun), making their inside/outside status at best liminal, or at the very least relational.

This outside-but-still-linked-to-the-inside status also affects many ex-Scientologists who have family members still within the CoS. The controversial practice of disconnection, outlined above, affects many families, but perhaps none so more publically than Jenna Miscavige-Hill, niece of the current leader David Miscavige. Founder of "Ex-Scientology Kids", a support and information group for adults who grew up as children in the CoS, Miscavige-Hill is a vocal opponent of the current CoS leadership (Miscavige-Hill 2013). As such, to understand her status as a binary outsider cannot be nuanced enough; she engages publicly with a projected religious identity in direct relation to the CoS, which is often used to validate her current writing on Scientology, and has a unique insight into the leadership, including the split between her father, who also left the CoS, and his brother, who remains as leader. Put simply, she remains relational (in both senses of the word) to the CoS, despite being an "outsider". Miscavige-Hill also brings us to our final issue in this chapter – that of the complexity of membership, rank and knowledge both within and without the CoS, which further complicates and contests binary notions of insideness or outsideness in Scientology religious identities.

In a commentary piece on her website, Miscavige-Hill addresses the oft-publicized issue of the Space Opera creation narrative, often referred to as the Xenu event (Rothstein 2009), and which is often used by critics of Scientology to ridicule or demean the community. In the piece (Miscavige-Hill n.d.) Miscavige-Hill notes how, due to the hierarchical training programme of the "Bridge to Total Freedom" used by CoS practitioners, many members will not be familiar with this esoteric OTIII document, which is only shared with devotees at a relatively late stage of their religious training and initiation – often many years after joining, and often not at all for members who do not proceed that far up the Bridge. Miscavige-Hill's particular focus is in asking why CoS officials often deny the existence of these materials – a position which is at odds with the fact that the OT Levels, in Hubbard's own distinctive handwriting, have been in the public domain since the mid-1990s when they were leaked onto the internet, and have become a major tranche of public (mis)understanding of Scientology beliefs and practices. Of course, for the purposes of our current investigation, this highlights the fact that there are different types of insider in the CoS; members will have different levels of knowledge regarding Hubbard's Dianetic practices and techniques, but also different levels of knowledge regarding Hubbard's meta-narrative of humanity's place in existence.

Of course, it would also be true to say that Cardinals in the Roman Catholic Church, who participate in conclave and produce policy for the Vatican, will have a different form of "insideness" from a regular parishioner, but this is amplified within the CoS due to the hierarchical and strictly-enforced esotericism of the religious knowledge contained at different stages of the Bridge. Miscavige-Hill's conclusion as to one of the reasons why Scientologists often deny the existence of the Xenu materials is that they honestly do not know about their existence as they have not yet reached that stage of the Bridge. This therefore offers another example of the complexity of inside/outside relational identities within Scientology; put simply, there is a common occurrence wherein people on the outside of the CoS may have knowledge that people on the inside do not possess. If one possesses knowledge, does that make one a form of insider, or is it only relevant what one does with that information? If the latter, then there is an intriguing, if a little playful, possibility of linking a group of discordant outsiders (Gregg and Chryssides 2017) with a relational form of identity with Scientology, and that is organized protesters – best known in the form of the internet collective Anonymous, famous for their Guy Fawkes mask-wearing protests against CoS premises around the world.

Now, of course, it is not the suggestion that such protesters should be classified as Scientologists in any meaningful way, but it is apparent that their publicly projected identities with regard to religious institutions and practices only make sense when understood in relation to the CoS; indeed, the protesters often focus directly on their interpretation of Xenu cosmology, making their view of the CoS, as "outsiders" directly reliant on "inside information" that not all "insiders" will necessarily be familiar with. What is particularly interesting is that, despite Anonymous's original mass protest (codenamed Operation Chanology) started in 2008 as a direct action against the CoS, recent updates on their website (Anonymous n.d.) contain specific updates on "Independent Scientology", suggesting that, for these "outsiders", both the CoS and Free Zone Scientology are viewed within a bell curve of Scientological identity, and therefore are linked together as "insiders".

In conclusion, this chapter has sought to highlight the diverse forms of Scientology identities, both in the CoS and Free Zone groups, to move scholarship away from previous conflation of Scientology and the CoS, and to highlight the diversity of different forms of insideness and outsideness that occur within all of these communities. Through applying new approaches to understanding religious identity as a relational dynamic, it is possible to move beyond binary-based frameworks of belonging of previous generations of scholarship. This is necessary to understand the everyday lives and practices of Scientologists from the bottom-up, rather than the top-down projections of "what Scientology is" and "what Scientologists do". These top-down projections have emanated from scholarship which previously privileged hierarchical institutional voices, and gave rise to a monolithic understanding of authority in Scientological practice. As this chapter has sought to demonstrate, however, this is far from the lived reality of Scientology adherents.

About the authors

Stephen E. Gregg is senior lecturer in religious studies at the University of Wolverhampton, and honorary secretary of the British Association for the Study of Religions. He studied at the University of Wales, Lampeter, and has previously taught at the University of Wales, and Liverpool Hope University. His work focuses upon minority communities and muted voices in contemporary religion, and method and theory in the study of religion. Recent and in-press books include *Jesus Beyond Christianity* (Oxford University Press, 2010 with Gregory A. Barker) *Engaging with Living Religion* (Routledge, 2015 with Lynne Scholefield), *A Universal Advaita: Swami Vivekananda and Non-Hindu Traditions* (Routledge, 2019) and *The Bloomsbury Handbook to Studying Christians* (Bloomsbury, 2019 with George D. Chryssides).

Aled J. Ll. Thomas is a PhD candidate at the Open University. His thesis focuses on the contemporary practice of auditing across a variety of Scientologies, particularly in the Free Zone. He also holds an MA from the University of Wales: Trinity Saint David, and has presented papers on his research at conferences in the USA and Belgium, and across the UK.

Notes

1 The first major academic publication on Scientology (Lewis 2009) remains a vital source, but should more accurately have been titled "The Church of Scientology", as all 22 chapters deal exclusively with Scientology *inside* the Church.
2 A form of religious practice in the style of counselling involving intensive application of Hubbard's texts and practices, usually involving one-to-one sessions with a mentor.
3 A piece of religious apparatus that practitioners use during Auditing to measure the individual's emotional or spiritual response to the particular task being undertaken.

4   The monastic element of Scientology, where members sign up to serve the Church in this lifetime and all future lifetimes.
5   Details of this evidence are unclear.
6   ARC stands for Affinity, Reality, Communication and is a method of ensuring effective communication in Hubbard's teachings.
7   This line has also been taken by scholars seeking to categorize Scientology within existing religious categorization paradigms. See, in particular, Flinn (2009) and Kent (1996).
8   The RTC is the central management organization of the CoS – popular scholarship often equates it with the place of the Vatican in the Roman Catholic Church.
9   The Mission Holders' Conference saw the end of Org's being run effectively as franchises and brought control of these centres back into the body of the CoS, consolidating authority.
10 The CoS's position on diverse adult sexualities is a contested and complicated issue among current and former Scientologists. While Hubbard clearly categorized homosexuality (including lesbianism) as a "deviation" and representative of people who are "actually quite ill physically" (Hubbard 1950: 125) later policy documents of the Church do not condemn people for being homosexual, and in lectures in the later 1950s, Hubbard expressed concern that people should be judged on their sexuality. There is, however, much apostate testimony of Miscavige highlighting members's sexuality, including aggressive treatment of gay Scientologists, but this should be understood in the wider context of the careful treatment and analysis required of all apostate testimonies. See comments discussion of Rathbun (2009).
11 It is important to note that the CoS has rejected each and every one of these claims in multiple media outlets.

References

Anonymous (n.d.). Independent Scientology. Retrieved from whyweprotest.net/forums/independent-scientology.225 (accessed 20 August 2018)

Atack, J. (n.d.). Possible Origins for Dianetics and Scientology. Retrieved from www.spaink.net/cos/essays/atack_origin.html (Accessed 29 November, 2017).

Bromley, D. (2009). Making Sense of Scientology: Prophetic, Contractual Religion. In J. R. Lewis (ed.), *Scientology*. New York: Oxford University Press. https://doi.org/10.1093/acprof:oso/9780195331493.003.0005

Christensen, D. R. (2009). Sources for the Study of Scientology: Presentations and Reflections. In Lewis (ed.) *Scientology*, Oxford: Oxford University Press. https://doi.org/10.1093/acprof:oso/9780195331493.003.0022

Chryssides, G. D. (1999). *Exploring New Religions*, London: Continuum.

Church of Scientology International (1998). *What is Scientology?*, California: Bridge Publications.

Ex-Scientology Kids (n.d.). The Freezone/Independent Scientology. Retrieved from http://exscientologykids.com/freezone (accessed 20 August 2018).

Flinn, Frank K. (2009). "Scientology as Technological Buddhism" in Lewis (ed.) *Scientology*, Oxford: Oxford University Press. https://doi.org/10.1093/acprof:oso/9780195331493.003.0011

Free Zone Earth (n.d.). Solo-Auditing. Retrieved from www.freezoneearth.org/Prometheus04/otOne/preot1/solo_audit.htm (accessed 20 August 2018).

Freezone Auditors (n.d.). Auditor List. Retrieved from www.freezoneauditors.org/auditor (accessed 20 August 2018).

Galactic Patrol (n.d.). The Free Zone Decree. Retrieved from www.galac-patra.org (accessed 20 August 2018).

Gregg, S. E. and Chryssides, G. D. (2017). "The Silent Majority?" Understanding Apostate Testimony Beyond "Insider/Outsider" Binaries in the Study of New Religions. In E. V. Gallagher (ed.), *Visioning New and Minority Religions: Projecting the Future*, 20–32. Abingdon: Routledge.

Gregg, S. E. and Scholefield, L. (2015). *Engaging with Living Religion*. New York: Routledge. https://doi.org/10.4324/9781315716671

Grossman, W. M. (2004). alt.scientology.war. Retrieved from www.wired.com/wired/archive/3.12/alt.scientology.war_pr.html (accessed 20 August 2018).

Harley, G. M. and Kieffer, J. (2009). The Development and Reality of Auditing. In J. R. Lewis (ed.), *Scientology*. New York: Oxford University Press. https://doi.org/10.1093/acprof:oso/9780195331493.003.0010

Hartley-Parkinson, R. (2011). Meet the Scientologist "Squirrel Busters": How Teams With Cameras Fixed to their Hats "Stalk" Church Defectors. *Daily Mail*, 21 April. Retrieved from www.dailymail.co.uk/news/article-1379274/Scientologist-Squirrel-busters-stalk-church-defector.html (accessed 20 August 2018).

Harvey, G. (2013). *Food, Sex & Strangers: Understanding Religion as Everyday Life*. Durham: Acumen. https://doi.org/10.4324/9781315729572

Hellesøy, K. (2013). Scientology Schisms and the Mission Holders' Conference of 1982. *Alternative Spirituality and Religion Review* 4(2): 216–227. https://doi.org/10.5840/asrr2013423

Hubbard, L. R. (1950). *Dianetics: The Modern Science of Mental Health*. Copenhagen: New Era Publications (this edition 2007).

Hubbard, L. R. (1960). *Have You Lived Before This Life?* Copenhagen: New Era Publications (this edition 1989).

Hubbard, L. R. (1967). HCO Policy Letter of 18 October 1967, Issue IV: Penalties for Lower Conditions. *Operation Clambake*, 18 October. Retrieved from www.xenu.net/fairgame-e.html (accessed 20 August 2018).

Hubbard, L. R. (1968). HCO Policy Letter of 21 October 1968: Cancellation of Fair Game. *Operation Clambake*, 21 October. Retrieved from www.xenu.net/fairgame-e.html (accessed 20 August 2018).

Independent Scientology (n.d.a). Beliefs of Independent Scientology. Retrieved from www.iscientology.org/about-us/beliefs (accessed 20 August 2018).

Independent Scientology (n.d.b). Management of Independent Scientology. Retrieved from www.iscientology.org/about-us/management (accessed 20 August 2018).
International Freezone Association Inc. (n.d.a). Association of Professional Independent Scientologists Purposes. Retrieved from http://internationalfreezone.net/Purposes.shtml (accessed 20 August 2018).
International Freezone Association Inc. (n.d.b). Member Auditor & Group Directory. Retrieved from http://internationalfreezone.net/auditor-directory.shtml (accessed 20 August 2018).
J (2007). My Experience of the Freezone. July. Retrieved from www.fzsurvivors.com/case-histories/my-experience-of-the-freezone (Accessed 7 November 2015).
Jolly, D. (2016). Sexuality in Three Ex-Scientology Narratives. In J. R. Lewis and K. Hellesøy (eds), *Handbook of Scientology*, 411–420. Leiden: Brill. https://doi.org/10.1163/9789004330542_019
Kent, S. A. (1996). Scientology's Relationship With Eastern Religious Traditions. *Journal of Contemporary Religion* 11(1): 21–36. https://doi.org/10.1080/13537909608580753
Lewis, J. R. (2009). Introduction. In J. R. Lewis (ed.), *Scientology*. New York: Oxford University Press. https://doi.org/10.1093/acprof:oso/9780195331493.001.0001
Lewis, J. (2012). Scientology: Up Stat, Down Stat. In O. Hammer and M. Rothstein (eds), *The Cambridge Companion to New Religious Movements*. Cambridge: Cambridge University Press.
Lewis, J. (2013). Free Zone Scientology and Other Movement Milieus: A Preliminary Characterization. *Temenos: Nordic Journal of Comparative Religion* 49(2): 255–276.
Melton, J. G. (2000). *Studies in Contemporary Religion: The Church of Scientology*. New York: Signature Books.
Melton, J. G. (2009). Birth of a Religion. In J. R. Lewis (ed.), *Scientology*. New York: Oxford University Press. https://doi.org/10.1093/acprof:oso/9780195331493.003.0002
Miscavige-Hill, J. (n.d.). OTIII Materials. Retrieved from http://exscientologykids.com/ot3 (accessed 20 August 2018)
Miscavige-Hill, J. with Pulitzer, L (2013). *Beyond Belief: My Secret Life inside Scientology and My Harrowing Escape*. New York: HarperCollins.
Rathbun, M. (2009). Paul Haggis Letter. Retrieved from https://markrathbun.blog/2009/10/24/a-very-important-letter-finale (accessed 20 August 2018)
Rigal-Cellard, B. (2009). Scientology Missions International (SMI): An Immutable Model of Technological Missionary Activity. In J. R. Lewis (ed.), *Scientology*, New York: Oxford University Press. https://doi.org/10.1093/acprof:oso/9780195331493.003.0017
Robertson, B. (1983). Captain Bill Robertson at Crown Hotel Meeting 1983 East Grinstead Scientology.avi. Retrieved from www.youtube.com/watch?v=tvfioivtY6c (accessed 20 August 2018).
Ron's Org Bern (n.d.). The Movement of Alternative Scientology. Retrieved from https://ronsorg.com/wp-content/uploads/2017/06/ronsorgengl.pdf (accessed 20 August 2018).
Ron's Org Committee (n.d.a). Bill Robertson. Retrieved from https://ronsorg.com/bill-robertson/ (accessed 20 August 2018).

Ron's Org Committee (n.d.b). Myths and Facts about Captain Bill Robertson. Retrieved from http://ronsorg.com/roc/english/mythaboutcbr.html (accessed 20 August 2018).

Rothstein, M. (2009). "His Name was Xenu. He Used Renegades ...": Aspects of Scientology's Founding Myth. In J. R. Lewis (ed.), *Scientology*. New York: Oxford University Press. https://doi.org/10.1093/acprof:oso/9780195331493.003.0020

Scientology Shock Squad (2011). Scientology Shock Squad Hits Casablanca. Retrieved from www.youtube.com/watch?v=OBwJ5RypLfI (accessed 29 October 2015).

Sharma, A. (2008). The Hermeneutics of the Word "Religion" and Its Implications for the World of Indian Religions. In R. D. Sherma and A. Sharma (eds), *Hermeneutics and Hindu Thought: Toward a Fusion of Horizons*. London: Springer. https://doi.org/10.1007/978-1-4020-8192-7

Thomas, A. (2018). Auditing in Contemporary Scientologies: The Self, Authenticity, and Material Culture. PhD thesis, Open University: Milton Keynes.

Whitehead, H. (1987). *Renunciation and Reformulation: A Study of Conversion in an American Sect*. Ithaca, NY: Cornell University Press.

Young, J. H. (1972). The Persistence of Medical Quackery in America: Some Reflections on the Complex and Subtle Interrelationship Among Three Parties: the Citizen as Patient, the Orthodox Practitioner, the Quack Himself. *American Scientist* 60(3): 318–326.

19

Moving out

Disengagement and ex-membership in new religious movements

George D. Chryssides

The study of religion tends to focus on the insider. Insiders are relatively easy to locate, and scholarly research tends to examine what individuals and communities believe and practise, rather than those who do not share their worldview and lifestyle. In this chapter I wish to focus on ex-members, with particular reference to new religious movements (NRMs), and I wish to explore a number of questions. What factors can cause disengagement? How have those who disengage been affected by their period of belonging? How reliable is their testimony? What problems do ex-members of NRMs face, and what support might they need?

The stereotypical picture of the ex-member, propagated by the media and the anticult movement (ACM), is that the ex-member has been "recruited" into joining, abandoning family and friends, and undergoing brainwashing by a charismatic leader who exploits members for cheap labour to finance the movement and to evangelize. The anticult rhetoric additionally incorporates words like "destructive", "bizarre" and "dangerous", describing "children" (rather than young adults) as being "lost to the cult", and portraying members as "victims" who need to be "rescued" and "rehabilitated".

Researching ex-members poses obvious difficulties. Where does one find them? It is relatively easy to locate the premises in which a form of spirituality is practised, and to ascertain what the attendees do. Finding those who are no longer there, having once belonged, is harder. There are, of course, ex-members who have written substantially on their experiences, and there are organizations and support groups, whose membership is substantially composed of former members. Such groups are not without interest to the researcher, but their members tend to be hostile to the organization they have left, and one must ask how representative their accounts are. Elsewhere, Gregg and Chryssides have suggested that the membership of the UK's most prominent NRM-monitoring organization is unlikely to consist of more than 0.23 per cent of those who have left an NRM (Gregg and Chryssides 2017: 23).

Another approach, adopted by Heinz Streib (2012), is to advertise for informants but, as Streib acknowledges, this creates an obvious bias, since it is likely to attract a disproportion of the more vociferous ex-members, and those who have left an organization through lack of interest are less likely to have retained sufficient motivation to respond to a call for volunteers. In his study of the New Acropolis in France, Massimo Introvigne (1999) successfully persuaded the organization to release names and addresses of former members, and his team of researchers were able to send out questionnaires by post. Such an approach is problematic, as Introvigne acknowledges; not only does it incur significant expense and a team of assistants, but the researchers inevitably discovered that a sizeable proportion of mailings were undeliverable, since the destined recipients had changed address, and it was not easy to distinguish between addressees who had not received the researchers' mailing, and those who were simply unwilling to respond. These problems and limitations do not mean, of course, that such research is worthless, but merely that one has to take such factors into account when interpreting one's findings.

The stereotype of the NRM members and ex-members has tended to be that of the seeker who joins a full-time community, thus suggesting a rather sharp contrast between "inside" and "outside". Intentional communities[1] have little place for the waverer: either one is a resident, or one is not, and if one decides to join such a community, one has made the decision to live outside of conventional society, and inside an organization which may be regarded as deviant. Community living was characteristic of the early years of certain NRMs in the West – principally the Unification Church, the Children of God (now The Family International), and the International Society for Krishna Consciousness (ISKCON – the Hare Krishna movement), as well as a number of others. Such lifestyles gained media prominence from the 1960s until around the 1980s, but it was by no means a requirement, and community living as an aspect of NRM membership has since declined. However, notwithstanding the changes that NRMs have undergone in the past decades, the ACM continues to portray NRM membership in terms of parents and acquaintances "losing" friends and family to "the cults". One fairly recent publication depicts on its front cover a father, mother and young daughter, sitting at a dining table with a vacant chair in the foreground, portraying the missing child (who would need to be at least 16 years old, in all probability) as "outside" the family domicile, and now "inside the cult" (Chaytor 2011).

Problems of ex-member testimony

In contrast to the ACM portrayal, academic scholars have been wary of privileging the ex-member's testimony, preferring to accept the believer's account of affairs. "The believer is always right" has been a maxim that has typically been applied to traditional religions, stemming from W. Cantwell Smith's belief that any account of a traditional religion should be recognized by the religious community itself (Smith 1959: 42).

Ex-member testimony tends to receive privileged credence by the media and the ACM, no doubt for a number of reasons. By being vociferous, such ex-members have been able to make their voices heard. Those who do not have a particularly interesting story to tell, or who do not feel negative, are unlikely to take the initiative in recounting their experiences. The "atrocity tale" inevitably makes a better story for the media than an account from someone whose interest has simply waned. Further, the apostate can claim to have seen both sides of the coin – "inside" and "outside" – in contrast to the rest of society, who have never been tempted to join. By returning to a conventional lifestyle, the apostate can also claim that he or she is now able to see matters aright, unlike those who remain inside, and are supposedly under the control of the movement.

As with all evidence, however, the researcher must evaluate ex-member testimony. Opinion is divided as to how much credence the ex-member deserves. Sociologist Bryan Wilson gives a very negative evaluation of ex-member testimony, when he writes:

> The apostate is generally in need of self-justification. He seeks to reconstruct his own past, to excuse his former affiliation, and to blame those who were formerly his closest associates. Not uncommonly the apostate learns to rehearse an "atrocity story" to explain how, by manipulation, trickery, coercion, or deceit, he was induced to join or remain within an organization that he now forswears and condemns. Apostates, sensationalized by the press, have sometimes sought to make a profit from accounts of their experiences in stories sold to newspapers or produced as books ... Neither the objective sociological researcher nor the court of law can readily regard the apostate as a credible or reliable source of evidence. He must always be seen as one whose personal history predisposes him to bias with respect to both his previous religious commitment and to his former associates. (Wilson 1994: 19)

Lonnie D. Kliever (1995) suggests that apostate ex-members can devise a scenario to account for their conversion, sojourn within the movement and eventual exit. Belonging to an NRM tends to carry a social stigma, and hence there is an incentive for an ex-member to explain that he or she was not responsible for joining or remaining. Encouraged by the media and the ACM, ex-members can enhance, or even create, a version of their experiences that fits their expectations. From the point of view of the ACM and the media, the apostate has a better story than the seeker who falls by the wayside at an early stage. Apostates can often recount an extended period within the organization, sometimes with colourful incidents, and can claim to know more about the organization than the average outsider, being able to add a personal dimension that outsiders have not experienced for themselves. Depending on the status apostates have gained within the movement, they can provide insider information, sometimes purporting to divulge secrets ("what they don't want you to know"), giving themselves an air of importance through superior and privileged knowledge. Being vociferous, this 0.23 per cent are thus taken to be representative of the typical insider, when in reality they are stereotypical. Daniel Carson Johnson goes so far as to claim the existence of "apostates who never were", citing instances of fictitious identities. The proliferation of works of fiction around ex-members – a phenomenon that is particularly found in connection with Jehovah's Witnesses – serves to blur the distinction between fiction and fact. A well-crafted work of fiction must build on genuine details about the organization under discussion, and hence should not merely be dismissed as pure story; similarly, ex-member material – much of which is written autobiographically – can be coloured by false memories, bias and creative licence. There is certainly scope for further research on the relationship between truth-claiming accounts of experiences within NRMs and works of fiction built around them.

Introvigne's (1999) investigation of ex-members of New Acropolis is therefore a salutary corrective to ACM portrayals. As mentioned above, his team obtained addresses of 530 former members who had decided not to renew their subscriptions to the organization during the period 1986–1997. All of these ex-members were sent a questionnaire, which sought to elicit demographic information, their evaluation of New Acropolis, and the reasons for leaving. A total of 294 questionnaires were completed and returned. Explaining their reasons for leaving, 65 per cent of respondents stated that New Acropolis "while interesting, had lasted long enough"; 10.2 per cent attributed changes in the organization's ethos as factors affecting their decision to quit; 8.5 per cent had moved away; 7.6 per cent left for "ideological" reasons; while 6.8 per cent mentioned negative media publicity, and 1.7 per cent negative judgements by friends and family. Asked if the ACM played a role in the decision to leave, 7.5 per cent mentioned ADFI (Association for the Defence of Families and the Individual), which is France's largest NRM-monitoring organization;

no respondents mentioned CCMM (Center Against Mental Manipulations);[2] and 0.8 per cent cited another unspecified organization. The research team analysed the responses of those who mentioned anti-cult involvement in the decision to leave, comparing their perceptions of New Acropolis with the total sample. The results are shown in Table 19.1.

Table 19.1   Reasons for leaving New Acropolis (derived from Introvigne 1999).

	Total respondents (%)	Anti-cult (%)
Believed New Acropolis to be a religion	3.4	20
Influenced by hostile media	6.8	30
Regarded New Acropolis as a "dangerous cult"	10.3	90
Brainwashing used by NA	6.7	80
Leaders of NA intolerant	7.6	70
Money stolen by fraud	5	50
NA extremist/Nazi/fascist	5.1	30
NA racist	7.6	70
Respondent married	35.3	70

These findings do more than make the obvious point that those involved in the ACM are more hostile to New Acropolis than those who are not. What is important is that those for whom the ACM played a role in the disengagement constitute a mere 8.3 per cent of the total respondents. It is also worth noting that the left-hand column represents the total respondents, and not the non-ACM ones; if the results had compared non-ACM with ACM, the statistics on the left-hand column would have been in even sharper contrast. In short, the substantial majority of leavers did not believe that New Acropolis was a dangerous cult, that it used brainwashing techniques, that its leaders were intolerant and misappropriated funds, and so on.

Of course, the relationship between negative evaluations of New Acropolis and involvement with the ACM does not establish which is the cause and which is the effect, or whether the relationship is a symbiotic one. It might also be pointed out that New Acropolis is atypical of new religions more widely: it makes no claim to be a religion; it offers lectures and courses rather than forms of worship. Unlike some of the more controversial new religions, its members do not live in communities, and hence their disengagement was somewhat different from those of intentional communities. Nonetheless, the ACM regards it as an organization falling within its remit, and the Belgian parliamentary commission listed it as a *secte* in 1997,[3] as did the 1999 French parliamentary commission report (Chambre des Représentants de Belgique 1997; Assemblé Nationale 1999). Introvigne's findings indicate that, at least in this case study, only a small minority of ex-members were allied to ACM groups, thus indicating that those involved in the ACM by no means speak on behalf of the more typical leaver.

Types of ex-member

If the vociferous NRM ex-member is not typical of ex-members more widely, it may be useful to look at the variety of modes of leave-taking. Several scholars have suggested typologies of ex-members. Streib's six-fold categorization is based is on their destination after exit, and is as follows: (1) secularizing exiters; (2) oppositional exiters; (3) religious switchers; (4) integrating exiters; (5) privatizing exiters; (6) heretical exiters. The first category (secularizing exiters) consists of those who lose faith altogether. The second group are those who have exited in favour of an oppositional group or a religious organization whose beliefs and practices contrast markedly with the leaver's previous allegiance. This category contains, although is not confined to ex-members who join an anticult organization.

"Religious switchers" are those who disaffiliate in favour of an organization with very similar beliefs and practices, and where the switch only requires marginal reintegration. An example might be someone who moved house and decided to join the nearest church, which happened to be a part of a different denomination. This might be done for convenience rather than from conviction. The fourth category – integrating exiters – includes spiritual seekers, who sample a variety of spiritual groups; they may be spiritual nomads who never find a permanent spiritual home, or they may eventually settle within a movement that satisfies their needs. These are often adolescents or young adults. It is not uncommon for those who finally discover a suitable religious organization to reported that they previously belonged briefly to an organization that was similar, but did not completely provide what the seeker was looking for.

The last two types (privatizing and heretical) include those who gradually withdraw from a spiritual group without finding a subsequent organization. Streib and Keller (2004) stated that these categories form part of Luckman's concept of "invisible religion". In the former case, the privatizing exiter continues with his or her previous beliefs and practices as an individual rather than within a community, while heretical exiters come to hold different religious beliefs or take up different spiritual practices in private.

Whereas Streib's categorization is based on where the ex-member goes, David Bromley (1998) suggests a three-fold typology, based on the method of one's departure. In many cases, exiting a religious organization is unproblematic, and Bromley describes such scenarios as "simple leave-taking". Examples might be the member who moves house, or a situation where religious premises relocate, and it is no longer feasible for a member to attend. Simple leave-takers also include erstwhile members simply lose interest and decide to withdraw. Such scenarios occur frequently – although not exclusively – in mainstream churches, temples and mosques; no controversy or stigma surrounds the person's departure, and little or no negotiation is needed. (In a few organizations the member may need to request a certificate of membership or a letter of introduction to a new congregation, but this is usually easy enough.)

Other forms of leaving are more problematic. Bromley suggests that one's method of "leave taking" is directly related to the type of organization from which one exits, depending on whether it is "allegiant", "contestant", or "subversive". These three categories are in descending order of "legitimacy": an example of an allegiant organization is a mainstream church, which advocates a lifestyle that is largely consistent with that of the dominant culture; the contestant organization is at least to some degree controversial, having a legitimate agenda, but opponents; while the subversive organization stands in substantial conflict with society, advocating a different lifestyle and challenging societal values. Bromley labels those who leave these categories of organization respectively as the defector, the whistleblower and the apostate. These categories are "ideal types", in Weber's sense, and many examples of leave-taking will display features of more than one.

The defector is someone who negotiates his or her exit from the organization, and who leaves with the agreement, although not the approval, of the hierarchy. Bromley cites the example of a monk or a nun leaving holy orders. They have made a life-long vow, which they are now breaking, but their superiors will allow the departure, taking steps to make it possible. If there has been any misconduct on the part of either party, such conflict will be suppressed, ensuring that those both inside and outside the organization find out as little as possible about controversy.

The second category – the whistleblower – is somewhat more difficult to understand, and Bromley says that it is uncommon. He mentions the involvement of regulatory agencies, citing the example of the Worldwide Church of God, in which a major controversy caused a group of dissidents to resign, and to bring a civil lawsuit against the organization. In this connection Bromley also cites conservative Christian organizations, which seek to maintain their own preferred version of the Christian faith; he names the Christian Research Institute, the Moody Bible Institute, Christian Apologetics and Information Service, and the Spiritual Counterfeits Project. These examples seem somewhat at variance with Bromley's analysis, since they are not regulatory bodies to which one can appeal in the event of a dispute involving leave-taking; however, they serve to make the point that such bodies can draw attention both to ideas they regard as unduly liberal (such as higher criticism of the Bible), or to organizations that lie outside Christian orthodoxy – he names Jehovah's Witnesses, Mormons and Seventh-day Adventists in this connection. Reference to these conservative Christian bodies also highlights the fact that entire Christian or Christian-derived groups can be treated as outsiders and, at least conceptually, can be placed beyond the boundaries of the Christian faith. In this connection, mention could be made of umbrella organizations to which denominations can affiliate, for example denominational federations, and national Councils of Churches. To give examples, the Bugbrooke Jesus Fellowship (subsequently the Jesus Fellowship Church) was expelled by the Baptist Union in 1986, and the Unification Church has consistently failed to gain entry to national Councils of Churches. Interestingly, the Jesus Fellowship Church resigned from the Evangelical Alliance in 1985 because other groups threatened to pull out if they remained in: placing oneself as an insider can depend on who else is in or out.

Bromley's third category – the apostate – is connected with the subversive. New religious movements – at least those that are publicized by the media and the ACM – run counter to the norms of the dominant culture. Their lifestyle may be different: some NRMs have created intentional communities; some value their form of spirituality over education and career aspirations; some require unconventional dress; some call into question the conventional mores relating to sex and marriage; and others may propagate ideas that appear eccentric to most, for instance that the world is about to end, or that the gods are extra-terrestrials. Such beliefs and practices put them in conflict with conventional members of society, who can often view them as dangerous, or at least threatening. It is therefore important to a subversive organization that its members stand firm in a struggle against the norms that it challenges. For this reason, a member who succumbs to the pressures of conventional society is perceived as a traitor – someone who is incapable of maintaining the struggle, and who has weakened in the face of opposition. The term "apostate" therefore tends to carry pejorative connotations and is seldom, if ever, used as a self-description, but rather tends to be applied by others, particularly those who remain within the community, having demonstrated faith maintenance.

Apostasy must therefore be differentiated from falling away or backsliding, these being manifestations of dwindling commitment, through apathy or competing interests. It is also to be differentiated from heresy, which is doctrine that deviates significantly and disturbingly from that which is officially taught within the community. In many cases the heretic has wished to remain within the community, but is either compelled to recant or, perhaps more usually, is forced out by the application of sanctions. The apostate is not simply an ex-member: although apostates have once belonged to the organization they have quit, they do more than simply stand outside. They have changed sides, aligning themselves with opponents, either having given in to pressure in the face of opposition, or having made the conscious decision now to work against their previous faith, rebelling against it or attacking it. For this reason they are perceived as malevolent, and have frequently been subject to serious sanctions, ranging from execution in some Islamic states, to confiscation of property, annulment of marriage and investigation by authorities. Penalties may be enforced by the state, or else by the religious community itself, which may have its own judicial procedures: the best known are probably Jehovah's Witnesses, where "disfellowshipping" (exclusion) involves shunning. In the case of the Witnesses, any communication or table fellowship with an apostate could incur the sanction of being disfellowshipped oneself.[4]

The notion of standing outside need not simply be applied to individual leave-takers: indeed, the term "apostasy" has been applied collectively to large sections of the Christian Church. Jehovah's Witnesses, for example, not only describe those who have left the organization as apostates, but describe the entirety of post-apostolic Christendom as apostate, on the grounds that it allegedly abandoned the original teachings and practices of the earliest apostles, and appropriated "pagan" ideas, particularly from Greek philosophy and its notion of the soul's immortality, and the adoption of non-Christian festivals such as Christmas and Easter, in addition to many new features which the Watch Tower Bible and Tract Society of Pennsylvania came to regard as unwelcome. Some Seventh-day Adventist groups have regarded Christian apostasy as being more recent, objecting to phenomena such as the ecumenical and interfaith movements, the conformity of colleges to secular pressures, modern trends in Christian theology, and an increasing reluctance to proselytize. Some groups have regarded such apostasy as a sign of the last days, heralding Christ's Second Advent.

Another way of examining ex-membership comes from Stuart A. Wright. Wright identifies the positive features of belonging, and considers disengagement in terms of the erstwhile member's benefits being withdrawn. As Wright contends, "we cannot really explain why people leave unless we explain why they stay" (Wright 1987: 21). There may be no single answer to this question, but Wright suggests that one should look at the factors that create a coherent organization and foster faith maintenance. Wright suggests five factors which he regards as important:

1. *Insulation from wider society* serves to promote faith maintenance. Community living plays an important role in achieving this. This factor particularly applies to intentional communities. An organization that offers communal living may insist on a number of ways of asserting their followers' identity, for example a particular dress code, rules governing behaviour which are at times unconventional, and perhaps even a change of name. Unconventional forms of dress can be found among Hare Krishna devotees, in Buddhist monastic groups, and in Christian organizations like the Salvation Army and the Jesus Army. Even where one's dress is not societally unconventional, failure to conform to expectations can readily mark the visitor as an outsider. In Western society Jehovah's Witnesses, for example, expect men to wear suits and ties, and women to wear dresses that cover the knees. To dress casually, or for a woman to attend a meeting wearing trousers rather than a skirt, is an indication that one is an outsider.
2. *Control of two-person intimacy* is a second factor which Wright identifies. Conventionally, sexual practices are regarded as private and not subject to wider discussion; hence, when members allow such intimate aspects of one's life to be subjected to such control, they are signalling a deep level of commitment. Control of one's sexual practices may involve vows of celibacy at one extreme, or it may involve greater permissiveness, as exemplified by The Family International's practice of "sharing" sexual partners. The Unification Movement is well known for its unconventional methods of creating marriage partnerships, and its Blessing Ceremony (popularly known as the "mass marriage") is bounded by rules relating to sexual practice, including periods of "separation" and detailed instructions for consummating the partnership. As Wright points out, such rules about bonding reinforce the concept of "dyadic exclusivity", as he labels it: one is bonded not merely to a sexual partner, but to the movement itself. This notion can be reinforced by theological ideas such as the Church as being the "bride of Christ" and the Roman Catholic and Eastern Orthodox notions that the taking of monastic vows is an alternative sacrament to the sacrament of marriage.
3. *A sense of urgency* is likely to increase commitment. Religions typically place humankind at the end of time, frequently suggesting that the overthrow of the present system of affairs is imminent. Hence there is a need to make

personal sacrifices, which will be more than compensated by the successful ushering in of the new age. If striving for the movement's goals is onerous, one's efforts will be more than compensated in the imminent utopia.

4 *Fulfilling one's affective needs* is a further necessity for creating and maintaining a community. Overtly, religious communities purport to fulfil members' spiritual needs – what Blaise Pascal called the "God-shaped blank" that needs to be filled. However, although a religious community views the fulfilment of members' spiritual needs as its main purpose, human beings have a variety of needs that need to be met, and arguably are prerequisites for spiritual attainment. Readers will no doubt be familiar with Abraham Maslow's hierarchy of needs, which includes – in ascending order – physiological needs, the need for safety and security, the need for love and belonging, the need for esteem, and finally self-realization. It may be argued that religious communities constitute exceptions: followers may undertake periods of fasting, thus forgoing physiological needs, or they may risk safety and security in the name of their faith. Nonetheless, such basic needs must be met at least to some minimal degree, otherwise a community will be unsustainable. Members need at least some basic form of shelter and sufficient sustenance to maintain the level of activity that is expected of them. Religious communities are at least in theory committed to being loving and, as Wright notes, they often act as surrogate families: terms like "brother", "sister" and "family" are frequently employed within spiritual groups, as well as – particularly in the Unification Movement – terms like "spiritual parent", "True Parents", and so on.

5 *The role of an exemplary leader* is the final condition that Wright suggests for retaining members. New religious movements typically have a founder-leader who is accorded superhuman status. He or (not so frequently) she is "charismatic": while charisma may also depend on the recognition of those qualities by followers, the NRM leader carries an authority that does not depend on institutional status. He or she does not have students, but disciples, giving teachings rather than facilitating discussion and divergence of opinion. It is not unusual for a hagiography to develop around the leader, sometimes emanating from the leader's own self-dramatized account of his or her earlier life.

Disengagement occurs when one or more of Wright's conditions of group cohesiveness fails to be satisfied. Where a member has become isolated from the group, and brought back into wider society, this has been instrumental in the decision to defect. Wright cites examples of Unification Church members who have accidentally separated from the group; this has had obvious repercussions in the member's lack of ability to evangelize, fundraise and participate in the community's spiritual life. In some cases, the intervention of deprogrammers has isolated the member from the group, although it success rate is contested. An isolated member may still feel bonded in spirit to the group, and regard his or her ordeal as a test of faith, thus resulting in faith maintenance rather than defection.

Where the sense of urgency is undermined, drop off may occur. The history of Jehovah's Witnesses bears this out: the years 1925 and 1975 in particular, when their end-time expectations failed to materialize, resulted in substantial withdrawal. However, Leon Festinger et al. (1956), in their famous study of Sananda, discovered that commitment was actually higher in the wake of Dorothy Martin's prophetic failures. Much depends on whether a community can maintain its momentum in the wake of disappointed expectations.

Regarding affective needs, it is not uncommon for a member to experience some trauma, only to find that the group is less than supportive. Another scenario is when a second-generation arrives: in one instance the couple had been allocated a single room in the group's headquarters, and the organization refused to provide them with larger premises to accommodate their three children. They moved out and, although they did not leave the organization immediately, the transition from full-time membership to ordinary home-based membership heralded a gradual withdrawal.

The role of two-person intimacy, where strict rules for marital and sexual relationships are expected, can have the effect of making departure more difficult. A husband and wife may not necessarily both experience similar negative attitudes to a spiritual group; consequently, a decision to leave the group may also entail a decision to leave one's spouse, thus providing a major disincentive for disengagement. The scenario becomes complicated when family relationships are firmly bound up with belonging. In the case of the Unification Church there was a period in which members were told that parents were expected to conduct the marriages of their own children. This proved problematic for one family known to the author, when the husband was becoming disillusioned with the organization and his wife wavering, while their children, then in their teens, continued to feel positive about the organization, having become involved in its youth programme, and having established friendships.

Wright's fifth factor is the exemplary leader. Numerous religious leaders have been the target of scandals reported in the media, and are often remarkably resilient to them. This is understandable, since holding someone in high esteem inevitably makes one disbelieve the evidence against him or her. One can readily assume that the leader has been the victim of injustice or distorted media reports, or that opposition is to be expected from the outside world, who do not understand the group's mission. However, as evidence builds up, defending one's leader becomes increasingly difficult, as with Sun Myung Moon. From the very inception of the movement there were allegations against him, but his past prison sentences were easily dismissed by his followers as examples of injustice and victimization. They could even be seen as vindication of Moon's teachings, since *Divine Principle* states that the Lord of the Second Advent will be persecuted and condemned as a heretic (Eu 1997: 407). In the 1990s, however, events occurred that were more difficult to dismiss, and a number of members have been unconvinced by the organization's explanations for his conduct, and decided to withdraw. Some of Moon's supposedly sinless children exhibited behaviour that was difficult to reconcile with their purported status, including adultery and addictions to drugs, gambling and alcohol. Investigations into Moon's own history revealed that he had at least one illegitimate son, and that he had committed adultery on several occasions. This proved too much for a number of members, who became disillusioned and left.

Further exiting scenarios

There are other exiting scenarios that have not been covered by Streib, Bromley or Wright, and which deserve some comment. One important category is the schismatical leaver. With schisms, which can be found in both major and minor traditions, members of the parent organization generally secede *en masse*, usually because they feel unable to accept changes within the movement. This sometimes follows the death of a leader, accompanied by various factions contesting the succession, as in the case of the Unification Movement, where a number of different family members have claimed the right to lead the organization following the death of founder-leader Sun Myung Moon in 2012. Other examples include (Roman Catholic) Sedavacantist groups, most of whom contended that Pope John XXIII had forfeited his right to the Holy See on account of his reforms; similar schisms in the Continuing Anglican tradition arise from issues such as women's ordination, liturgical innovations, and attitudes to sexual morality – particularly homosexuality. Such organizations tend not to attract the attention of the anticult movement, no doubt for a variety of reasons, but they are nonetheless minority groups outside the mainstream that have come into being in recent times.

Where schism is brought about by the death of the founder-leader, the successor may be judged to be unacceptable by certain sectors of the movement.

There may be a dispute about who has the right to succeed – a matter that is currently being bitterly disputed within the Unification Movement – or there may be questioning as to whether the new leader is being faithful to the old leader's teachings. Some members may resent doctrinally or organizational innovations that the new leader may wish to bring about. Examples are not hard to find. At the time of writing there is bitter dissent as to which of Sun Myung Moon's surviving family ought to lead. In 2008 Moon formally handed over the leadership to his youngest son Hyung Jin, but after his death in 2012 his wife Hak Ja Han Moon, supported by the eldest son Hyun Jin, took the helm, with ownership of most of the Church's assets. Describing his mother as a demon, Hyung Jin formed his own Sanctuary Church, together with numerous supporters. In the International Society for Krishna Consciousness (ISKCON), founder leader Prabhupada's death raised ambiguities regarding the powers of the Governing Body Committee of initiating gurus, causing some followers to split off, reverting to the name Gaudia Math – the name of the movement in which Prabhupada was initiated – and circulating a magazine entitled *Back to Prabhupada*. Scientology also is rife with schism, as a number of former Scientologists have moved out of the Church of Scientology, forming their own organizations that continue to use the "tech" of L. Ron Hubbard. Over half a century previously, many of Charles Taze Russell's Bible Students could not agree to Joseph Franklin Rutherford's insistence on uniformity within the organization, and withdrew to form independent organizations, some of which continue to exist today.

The phenomenon of schism is particularly interesting for a number of reasons. Those insiders who follow the schism are in one sense ex-members and outsiders of the continuing organization, but on the other hand they would contended that it is the organization, not themselves, that has fallen away and has become disloyal to its original teachings and purpose. In the case of Scientology, there is no effective difference between the schismatical outsider and the orthodox insider: the schismatic simply wants the right to practise independently of the main organization. If loyalty to a tradition is the hallmark of the true insider, then often the schismatic has a better claim to be an upholder of an organization's original objectives. Is the true insider the one who is resilient to change, or is it the one who can accept new leadership and organizational innovation? Ultimately, in event of a schism, the question of who are insiders and who are outsiders is often determined by legal and financial matters such as property ownership. In the case of Anglican and Roman Catholic traditions, which do not employ a congregational form of governance, the church buildings of dissenting congregations are owned by the wider organization and not the congregation, and hence the schismatics are obliged to move out and acquire independent funding for their dissenting convictions. Whatever the outcomes of any legal settlements, the effect of a schism is to create two or more circles of allegiance and forms of "insideness".

Schismatics generally have convictions, but the converse phenomenon involves those who have never become fully committed. Not every adherent actually joined in the first place. Many followers of NRMs are second or third generation members, and have belonged from birth, having been brought up in the organization by their parents. In some cases a member's child may not have gone through the relevant initiation process: for example, many Jehovah's Witness children have attended meetings and engaged in house-to-house evangelism, but have never put themselves forward for baptism, which is regarded as the true gateway into full commitment, indicating that one has accepted "the truth". They may simply have lost interest; they may have started to reason independently, and concluded that the truth was not to be found in the Watch Tower organization; they may have found tensions at school, making friends with non-believing children, and been introduced to a different lifestyle from the semi-closed community of the Kingdom Hall. According to one estimate, two out of three children decide to leave the Watch Tower organization (Kistler and Munger 2009).

If there are those whose membership or partial membership is involuntary, there are also those who have left without having chosen to do so. Ex-membership can arise through expulsion ("disfellowshipping" in the terminology of Adventists, Christadelphians, and notably Jehovah's Witnesses). In the eyes of Jehovah's Witnesses, offending members have already put themselves outside of Jehovah's organization by actions such as sexual impropriety or accepting a blood transfusion. Some members have been brought out forcibly from their organization: the phenomenon of "deprogramming" was particularly publicized in the 1970s and the 1980s. Deprogramming involved forcible abduction, usually commissioned by a member's parents, and involved luring the member into an apparently safe environment in which they could be kidnapped and taken to a "safe house" in which they were physically confined, and in which the deprogrammers endeavoured to reverse the alleged indoctrination that had caused the member to join in the first place. While the deprogrammers' degree of success remains contested, there is no doubt that some members exited from NRMs in this way, and indeed were grateful for their "rescue" (Heftmann 1982: 271).

A further phenomenon involves members who have not taken the trouble to offer a formal resignation. This can be for a variety of reasons. The outgoing member simply may not like to tell the organization's office bearers that he or she is leaving, or the backslider may want to keep his or her options open, viewing return as a possibility. In this category is the – perhaps rather curious – phenomenon of those who remain insiders and maintain contact and even attendance, but affiliate with some other religious group that may not be compatible. Sometimes they continue to maintain a keen interest in the organization from which they are exiting. One such example known to the author is a member of the Unification Church, who has become disillusioned, no longer accepts Unificationist teachings, does not attend meetings, and effectively behaves as an outsider. However, he has not handed in any resignation. This somewhat ambiguous role, however, gives him access to information which he shares – mainly online – with other apostates, in the hope that a substantial publication will emerge, portraying the organization in a very different light from its official history. Another scenario is the member who maintains a physical presence, but has mentally detached himself or herself from the organization's beliefs and practices. One case reported to the author was of a Jehovah's Witness elder who continues to fulfil his role, but only remains in the congregation in order to maintain family relationships. The fact that there is much "leaked" information about Jehovah's Witnesses to be found on the internet indicates that there are insiders who are not fully committed – indeed quite the reverse – who use their insider position in order to undermine the Watch Tower organization's work.

When ex-membership is impossible

There are other situations where those who remain as insiders do so from necessity. As new religions become older, their members do so also, and contemplating life outside the organization becomes increasingly difficult. How does someone get a job if he or she is now 50 or 60 years old, and lacking a convincing CV? How does one acquire sufficient money and possessions to resume a conventional lifestyle outside the organization, if much of one's assets have been shared by the group? The remainer may decide simply to ignore the evidence against the leader, or other problems he or she has encountered. As one member said to me when I asked what he thought of the allegations against Sun Myung Moon, "Well, I guess I keep struggling on in faith." Others continue to deny the allegations, whereas a group of Unificationist leaders has engaged in theological reflection about what a "sinless child" means. At the other extreme, there are those who have left and have become so embittered that they continue to monitor events and issues in the organization, publicizing fresh evidence and reflections online. In fact, their interest in the organization is probably greater than that of the lukewarm member who is involved sporadically or half-heartedly. Their interest in the movement is effectively as great as that of many insiders.

On occasions, leave-takers have felt the need to intimate the departure to the organization to which they have belonged. There was a period in the Watch Tower organization's history when those who joined the organization were encouraged to write "letters of withdrawal" to mainstream clergy, in order to make the decision to leave clear. More recently, the Raelian movement has encouraged "de-baptism": being opposed to mainstream Christianity, founder-leader Raël urges members to renounce their baptism by writing to the member of the clergy who baptized them or, if that is not possible, to the Bishop of the diocese or someone with a key position in the appropriate Christian denomination's hierarchy. However, the notion of de-baptism is problematic from the standpoint of mainstream Christianity, since baptism is a once-and-for-all rite, which is normally unrepeatable. If someone were to reverse their commitment to the Raelian movement and seek reinstatement in a Christian denomination, re-baptism would not be required. God's grace, conferred upon baptism, would be judged to remain with the leaver, since the commitment at baptism is "until one's life's end". The Roman Catholic Church has taught that any priest who is involved in a second baptism can himself be declared apostate. There is therefore a sense in which any baptized Christian always remains an "insider", at least of sorts, and many pious Christians would aver that, however far one strays, the backslider always remains within Christ's love. The lost sheep in Jesus' parable (Luke 15:3-7) still belongs to the fold: it merely needs to be brought back.

There is a view held in some evangelical Protestant circles that, once someone has made a commitment to Jesus Christ, his or her salvation is assured for all time, and, whatever happens in the subsequent life, they are guaranteed a place in Christ's kingdom eternally. Some Christians have gone so far less to speculate that Judas Iscariot, generally regarded as the traitor who had a key role in Jesus' arrest, will nonetheless have a place in heaven. Jesus regarded him as a member of "the twelve" at the Last Supper, and the Bible records that he repented and handed back the blood money to the Jewish authorities (Matthew 27:3). Having had a key role in Jesus death, he consequently had a key role in Christ's attainment of the world's salvation. Pope Benedict XVI went as far as to say, "His betrayal led to the death of Jesus, who transformed this tremendous torment into a space of salvific love by consigning himself to the Father (cf. Gal 2:20; Eph 5:2, 25)." (Pope Benedict XVI 2006; see also All About God 2018). However, unlike Peter, who denied his insider status when challenged in the high priest's courtyard (Mark 14:66-72), he was never reinstated to the ranks of the apostles, so was he an "insider" or "outsider"?

In this context it may also be worth mentioning those who employ a theological rationale for even wider inclusivity. Universalists hold that ultimately all will achieve the final spiritual goal, and hence are ultimately "insiders". The doctrine takes various forms. It is particularly associated with the Christian tradition, in which Universalists teach that all will ultimately be brought to salvation, either directly after death, or through intermediary states such as hell or purgatory, which have a purifying rather than a punitive role. Universalists who base their beliefs on the Bible can cite texts such as "For as in Adam all die, so in Christ all will be made alive" (1 Corinthians 15:22). Universalism thus contrasts with the ultra-Calvinist position that Christ died only for the elect, and that God decreed from the moment of creation that a large proportion of humankind were irredeemably damned – in our terminology, irretrievable outsiders. The Unification Church teaches that there are various levels in the spirit world in which men and women will find themselves after death, according to their degree of purity, and all will be enabled to progress in accordance with the amount of "indemnity" (the Unificationist term for compensation) they pay for past sin, until finally they may enter the Kingdom of Heaven. All will therefore be insiders in the end, even Satan himself, who is finally expected to repent. Universalism can also be found within the Hindu and Buddhist traditions, in which it is taught that liberation will ultimately be achieved by all sentient beings, although this may take a large number of successive rebirths. Those who remain outside the faith, or who wilfully abandon it, are only be outsiders temporarily, and can expect finally to be brought inside.

What support does the ex-member need?

Much of my argument has been directed against the ACM's perception of the ex-member. However, ex-member organizations have several functions. Many of the anticult organizations act as pressure groups, providing information and spokespersons to the media, and acting as a source of information about NRMs to the public and to politicians. A number of pieces of legislation in Europe have resulted from anticult pressure. Whether this is desirable may be disputed; there are undoubtedly malpractices within new religious movements (although this is also true of some mainstream religious communities), but the ACM can be accused of undue scaremongering and giving rise to discriminatory treatment against unpopular organizations.

A further function that is served by ACM groups is the provision of a community to the ex-member. Leaving a religious community is no easy matter, since a large proportion of one's time and interests are bound up with the organization, and indeed one's entire worldview. The religious organization has provided a community of friends, like-minded people and regular activities. Abandoning one's faith therefore involves more than a questioning of one's beliefs. Inevitably there will be a loss of most, if not all, of one's friends, who will continue to invest their time and efforts into the movement, while the leaver has now become the outsider to all of this. Particularly if one has been disfellowshipped, Jehovah's Witnesses are particularly well known for severing all social contacts with the erring member, to the extent of even ignoring that person if they should pass them in the street. The friends with whom the ex-member associated before joining the religious organization may well have left the area, have defined their own social circles, and feel they have little in common with someone who has "gone religious" and who may in any case feel embarrassed about one's time in the organization and having to explain the circumstances of entry and exit. Particularly, too, if one has belonged to a religious community with a highly structured daily schedule, leavers can experience problems about what to do with their time, especially in the interim period in which they have not found secular employment. One former member known to the author, who left a contemplative order of nuns, found herself saying the daily office on her own, at home, at the prescribed hours, being unable to devise any other profitable way of spending her time. NRM-monitoring and ex-member organizations therefore provide an alternative community that is ready to receive the new outsider. Particularly if they are NRM-specific, the offer of ready-made community of people with a common background and set of interests, and where the need be no embarrassment about identifying oneself as an ex-member. The advent of the internet has made it easier to locate such groups and to organize meetings in physical space as well as online.

Conclusions

A number of conclusions emerge from this study of ex-members. First, people move out of religious communities for a variety of reasons and in different ways. The various typologies that I have considered are not mutually exclusive, but suggest a wide – but not exhaustive – variety of scenarios relating to disengagement. Second, ex-member testimony should not be disregarded, but it should not be privileged either and, in particular, the vociferous hostile ex-member should not be regarded as speaking on behalf of all who leave that organization. Scholars need to "manage" their informants, as is customary with all research data, evaluating the available evidence. In the case of ex-members, some of their accounts bear interesting unwitting testimony – details about life in the community that tend not to be explicitly mentioned, either in the organization's own literature or in scholarly writing. Analysing ex-members' narratives, increasingly expressed in novels – sometimes fictional and sometimes autobiographical – may well be a fruitful area of future research, which has hitherto been largely ignored. Finally, it is unfortunate that there is such polarization between the majority of academic writers and the ACM. As I have argued, ex-member organizations serve an important purpose, although sheer hostility can frequently militate against good information and reconciliation. At any rate, those who are not present within an organization can be just as interesting as those who remain insiders, and should certainly not be ignored in the study of religion.

About the author

George D. Chryssides studied philosophy and theology at the University of Glasgow, and gained his doctorate from the University of Oxford. He taught philosophy and religious studies at various British universities, and was head of religious studies at the University of Wolverhampton, England from 2001 to 2008. He is currently honorary research fellow at York St John University. He has published extensively, principally on new religious movements, and recent publications include *The A to Z of Jehovah's Witnesses* (2009); *Heaven's Gate: Postmodernity and Popular Culture in a Suicide Group* (2011); *Christians in the Twenty-First Century* (with Margaret Z. Wilkins, 2011); *Historical Dictionary of New Religious Movements* (2012) and *Jehovah's Witnesses: Continuity and Change* (2016). He has co-edited (with Benjamin E. Zeller) *The Bloomsbury Companion to New Religious Movements* (2014), *The Bloomsbury Handbook to Studying Christians* (2019), edited with Stephen E. Gregg.

Notes

1 An intentional community is a group of people who deliberately choose to live together, often as a religious body.
2 Centre de documentation, d'éducation et d'action contre les manipulations mentales (Documentation Centre for Education and Action against Mind Control), founded in 1981 to assist ex-members of "sectarian" movements.
3 The term "*secte*" in French is the equivalent of the English "cult", having similar pejorative connotations.
4 A disfellowshipped member is one who is formally declared to be no longer a Jehovah's Witnesses. He or she may continue to attend meetings, but may not

converse with other attendees. The disfellowshipped member may seek reinstatement, once the elders are satisfied of his or her genuine repentance.

References

All About God (2018). Once Saved, Always Saved. Retrieved from www.allaboutgod.com/once-saved-always-saved.htm (accessed 26 August 2018).

Assemblé Nationale (1999). *Rapport fait au nom de la Commission d'Enquête sur la situation financière, patrimoniale et fiscale des sectes, ainsi que sur leurs activités économiques et leurs relations avec les milieux économiques et financiers.* Document no. 1687. Paris: Les Documents d'Information de l'Assemblee Nationale.

Bromley, David G. (1998). The Social Construction of Contested Exit Roles: Defectors, Whistleblowers, and Apostates. In David G. Bromley (ed.), *The Politics of Religious Apostasy: The Role of Apostates in the Transformation of Religious Movements.* Westport, CT: Praeger:

Chambre des Représentants de Belgique (1997). *Enquête Parlementaire visant à élaborer une politique en vue de lutter contre les pratiques illégales des sectes et le danger qu'elles représentent pour la société et pour les personnes, particulièrement les mineurs d'âge.* Brussels: Chambre des Représentants de Belgique. Retrieved from www.dekamer.be/kvvcr/pdf_sections/publications/sectes/sectes.pdf (accessed 28 August 2018).

Chaytor, Audrey (2011). *Cults: Who is Vulnerable?* Middlesbrough: Quoin Publishing.

Eu, Hyo Won (1997). *Exposition of the Divine Principle.* New York: The Holy Spirit Association for the Unification of World Christianity.

Festinger, Leon, Henry W. Riecken and Stanley Schachter. (1956). *When Prophecy Fails.* New York: Harper-Torchbooks. https://doi.org/10.1037/10030-000

Gregg, S. E. and Chryssides, George D. (2017). "The Silent Majority?" Understanding Apostate Testimony beyond "Insider/Outsider" Binaries in the Study of New Religions. In Eugene V. Gallagher (ed.), *Visioning New and Minority Religions: Projecting the Future,* 20–32. London: Routledge.

Heftmann, Erica (1982). *Dark Side of the Moonies.* Harmondsworth: Penguin.

Introvigne, Massimo (1999) Defectors, Ordinary Leave-takers, and Apostates: A Quantitative Study of Former Members of New Acropolis in France. *Nova Religio: The Journal of Alternative and Emergent Religions* 3(1) (October): 83–99. https://doi.org/10.1525/nr.1999.3.1.83

Kistler, Jenn and Munger, Kel (2009). Growing up J.W. Retrieved from www.newsreview.com/sacramento/growing-up-j-w/content?oid=974916 (accessed 27 August 2018).

Kliever, Lonnie D. (1995). *The Reliability of Apostate Testimony about New Religious Movements.* Los Angeles, CA: Freedom Publishing.

Pope Benedict XVI (2006). Judas Iscariot and Matthias. Saint Peter's Square, 18 October. Retrieved from https://w2.vatican.va/content/benedict-xvi/en/audiences/2006/documents/hf_ben-xvi_aud_20061018.pdf (accessed 26 August 2016).

Smith, W. Cantwell (1959). Comparative Religion: Whither and Why? In Mircea Eliade and J. M. Kitagawa (eds), *The History of Religions; Essays in Methodology*, 31–58. Chicago, IL: University of Chicago Press.

Streib, Heinz (2012). Deconversion. In L. R. Rambo & C. E. Farhadian (eds) (2012). *Oxford Handbook on Religious Conversion*. Oxford: Oxford University Press.

Streib, Heinz and Keller, Barbara (2004). The Variety of Deconversion Experiences: Contours of a Concept in respect to Empirical Research. *Archiv für Religionspsychologie/Archive for the Psychology of Religion* 26: 181–200. https://doi.org/10.1163/0084672053598030

Wilson, B. (1994). Apostates and New Religious Movements. Retrieved from www.scientologyreligion.org/religious-expertises/apostates-and-new-religious-movements/page1.html (accessed 27 August 2018).

Wright, Stuart A. (1987). *Leaving Cults: The Dynamics of Defection*. Washington, DC: Society for the Scientific Study of Religion.

20

Both outside and inside
"Ex-members" of new religions and spiritualities and the maintenance of community and identity on the internet

Carole M. Cusack

Introduction

Early scholarly studies of conversion and apostasy in new religious movements (NRMs) tended to draw clear boundaries between the pre- and post-conversion identity of those involved, and to presume that apostasy, "leaving the fold" and de-conversion (all fairly clumsy terms for the experience of no longer belonging) were similarly unproblematic. Like much of the scholarship on NRMs, this model was drawn from studies of Christianity (Richardson 1985: 165). Conversion to NRMs was usually not accorded the theological weight or positive social value as conversion to Christianity, described as being "born again" or "saved" (ibid.). This was, in part, because NRMs were thought not to be "real religions" but "cults" or other types of social movements (Richardson 1993: 352–354); conversion to such groups was termed "recruitment" and apostasy viewed as a minor matter, except in cases when "brainwashing" was invoked and when there was recourse to deprogrammers (Melton 2004: 232–235).

Since the 1990s the study of conversion and apostasy has become more nuanced, and it is increasingly evident that distinguishing an "insider" from an "outsider" is not only difficult, but often impossible given that individuals and communities typically inhabit multiple roles and realities (Gleig 2012; Haddon 2013). The subfield of conversion and apostasy studies is linked to two other areas in the study of religion. These are: the methodological debate commonly termed "the insider/ outsider problem in the study of religion", which is also important in anthropology, and which often focuses on researchers and the groups they are studying (McCutcheon 1999); and the recent prominent debate about "believing" and "belonging", and all potential interactions of these two positions (Davie 1994; Day 2012) in the context of the substantially secularized West (Demerath 2007).

This chapter considers two "ex-member" communities with extensive websites regarding the groups to which they once belonged. These are Kerista Commune (www.kerista.com) and the School of Economic Science (SES) Forums (www.ses-forums.org).[1] The constituents of these communities are "ex-members" in only one, strict, sense. Kerista disbanded in 1991, thus it is no longer possible to be a member (Anapol 2010: 58). The Kerista Commune site is a place where members and associates post essays that record memories and honour deceased members, in a spirit of warmth and support, to facilitate open communication, with the aim of healing those who feel injured by the group and of continuing mutually sustaining friendships between those who are at peace with their history in the group. In stark contrast, the SES Forums site is largely populated by ex-members who perceive themselves to have been harmed by the SES (a Gurdjieff splinter group that now teaches a form of Advaita Vedanta), an organization that still exists (Petsche 2015). These people sometimes left of their own accord, or were expelled for various infringements of group's rules. Other crucial factors that affect the respective tone of these online ex-member groups include the fact that, whereas "New Tribe" Kerista was a local, San Francisco phenomenon, the School of Economic Science has a global reach under a variety of names. Kerista ex-members tend to have known each other in the "meat world", where SES ex-members did not, except for in specific local groups. The mood and tone of the two online communities differs, but the common theme encountered is that when people physically "leave" new religions and spiritualities, they very often remain deeply engaged with the group's teachings and practice, and the reasons why they left (Rubin 2011; Dyason and Doherty 2015). Thus to identify as an ex-member and to find community with other ex-members is an almost infallible sign of being both inside and outside the group, paradoxically belonging without belonging.

Insider/outsider, conversion/apostasy and believing/belonging

The academic study of religion emerged in nineteenth century Europe, in part as a reaction against theological understandings of Christianity as the true and only religion, and in part as a response to the colonial experience of the New World, India, China, and the myriad cultures and religions encountered by Europeans since the sixteenth century. Initially, identifying "insiders" and "outsiders" was seemingly unproblematic; European scholars learned Sanskrit, Chinese, Avestan and Japanese, and one of the founders of religious studies, Max Müller (1823–1900), initiated the Sacred Books of the East series of translated religious texts published by Oxford University Press from 1879 to 1910 (Girardot 2002). It was not imagined that scholars would become converts to the religions they studied. The emergence of sociology and anthropology as important methods in the study of religion reinforced the impression that scholars were "outsiders" working with people of different beliefs, values and practices for periods of time, and whose own culture and community were other than that which they researched. Fieldwork among indigenous peoples and migrant communities occasionally resulted in "going native", an experience akin to conversion in which the student took on the perspective and values of the studied (Gesch 2001). In research areas like NRMs and Western Esotericism, the need for initiation or special access made scholars dependent on participant observation (which may result in joining the group, either temporarily or permanently), or relying on information from ex-members (Knott 2005: 254).

Conversely, in some groups, the view that only an insider could authentically speak prevailed, and members of some religious communities expressed hostile criticism towards Western scholarly assessments of their traditions (Knott 2005: 243–244; Bado 2013). This is because religious studies proposes naturalistic (historical, cultural, political, psychological, and so on) explanations for religious phenomena, rather than accepting theological verities. This instance of outsider perspectives confronting insider understandings goes deeper than just outsiders studying insiders, or insiders studying insiders, might indicate. The historical trajectory of religious studies according to Ingvild Sælid Gilhus and Lisbeth Mikaelsson, has a first phase characterized by evolutionary models, a second phase by the phenomenological method, and a third, current phase that is characterized by cultural approaches (Gilhus and Mikaelsson 2001). According to this schema, scholars searched first for "origins" of religion among "primitive" peoples, a stance that was abandoned when the phenomenological method came to the fore. Phenomenologists of religion argued that religious phenomena were unique and irreducible, but "capable of understanding by means of empathy, that is, by reliving in one's own experience that which appears to be alien" (Knott 2005: 245). This meant that scholars themselves were encouraged to privilege the insider approach, to view religions as adherents did. The terms "etic" and "emic" (introduced by linguist Kenneth Pike) have often been used to mean "outsider" and "insider" in the study of religion, though this is a fundamental misunderstanding of Pike's distinction. As Jeppe Sinding Jensen argues, "-etic denotes the construction of systems by the analyst from the -emic material in relation to specific theorizing and a specific theoretical object" (Jensen 1993: 124). This means that for the scholar of religion the emic aspect is the data from the religious tradition or community, and the etic aspect is the theoretical model or models that are derived from, or applied to, this data.

The "cultural approaches" hailed as the third phase of the disciplinary history of religious studies emerged as the phenomenological approach was being decried as untenable by a host of scholars (Gilhus and Mikaelsson 2001). This cultural phase encourages critical approaches to religion that reject the obligation to understand religion, to be empathetic or sympathetic to it, and rather affirms the scientific assessment of religious phenomena, or at the least discursive analysis that interrogates issues of power and authority, personal autonomy, and the gulf between official and popular religion. This methodological complexity reveals a landscape that is vastly more nuanced than the simple opposition of theology and religious studies found in the nineteenth and early twentieth centuries. In the twenty-first century, even cases of complicated boundaries such as described above no longer appear compelling, as the multiple worlds individuals inhabit, and the selves that they perform in different circumstances, make it difficult to posit a clear dividing line between insider and outsider. In fact, Jensen asserts that "the insider–outsider" distinction is a "pseudo-problem". He categorically rejects the notion that certain special people have privileged information, which is an essentialist assertion that fails to perceive that the insider/outsider divide "at best demonstrates the plain reality that knowledge is unevenly distributed across subjects" (Jensen 2011: 30).

In Gilhus and Mikaelsson's first and second phases, scholarly definitions of religion involved an element of essentialism, the claim that religion was *sui generis*, special and not susceptible to explanation in terms of other phenomena (psychology, sociology, politics, and so on). This reflected the Christian heritage of religious studies, which is also observable in the terminology of conversion and apostasy. For example, Arthur Darby Nock's seminal work *Conversion* (1933) emphasized the profundity of the conversion experience, which "involves moral judgements ... within the psyche of the individual" (Cusack 1996: 2). The social dimensions of religious conversion were ignored by Nock, who argued that in the ancient world only Christianity demanded "true" conversion, the "reorienting of the soul of an individual, his deliberate turning from indifference or from an earlier form of piety, to another, a turning which implies that a great change is involved, that the old was wrong and the new is right" (quoted in Cusack 1996: 2). From the 1960s, new religious movements emerged in the West and scholars studied them from various perspectives: as deviant phenomena, as groups that gave insights into the origins of religions, and so on. The language used to describe joining and leaving such movements was corporate rather than theological; recruitment and exiting were preferred to conversion and apostasy. Over time this changed, with models of conversion developed by scholars that worked with NRMs invoking "motifs" like intellectual, mystical, experimental, affectional and coercive, as factors in the self-motivated spiritual journey of seekers (Lofland and Skonovd 1981: 375). These models of conversion decisively abandoned the theologically inflected, revelatory "transformation", of earlier scholarship.

The final methodological issue that is relevant to this study of ex-members of Kerista and the SES is the "believing without belonging" debate heralded by the publication of Grace Davie's *Religion in Britain since 1945: Believing without Belonging* in 1994. Davie took issue with the traditional secularization thesis, which predicted the inevitable decline and even death of religion in the modern West, and argued that while institutional church affiliation was undeniably in decline, people continued to affirm that they believed in God, and to identify as Christian (Davie 1994). The census in Britain included a question about religion for the first time in 2001, and 72 per cent of the population nominated Christianity as their religious affiliation. However, in the fifteen years since 2001, the religious landscape has shifted, and Davie's affirmation of continuing belief in the face of institutional disillusionment no longer convinces. The rise of "New Atheism" from 2005 onwards, and the mainstreaming of the "no religion" option, has resulted in 48.5 per cent of the population of England and Wales affirming that they had no religion in 2014, and 52 per cent of respondents in a 2016 Scottish Social Attitudes Survey doing likewise (Sherwood 2016). Davie's "believing without belonging" now seems the wishful thinking of religious institutions and functionaries that want to affirm the continued relevance of Christianity in the face of empty churches and changed social *mores*. Other scholars suggested that the real state of affairs likely was "belonging without believing" or perhaps "believing in belonging" (Marchisio and Pisati 1999; Day 2012). This chapter suggests that a further permutation, "belonging without belonging", is also a possible position.

Just as conversion has gradually come to be understood not as an instantaneous transformation like that of Paul on the road to Damascus, but rather a gradual process that is ongoing (Rambo 1993), identity is no longer regarded as fixed and unchanging, but "flexible, amenable to infinite reshaping according to mood, whim, desire and imagination" (Lyon 2002: 92). This is part of a larger epistemological shift in the study of religion (and more generally humanities and social science fields) from essentialism to constructionism

(Engler 2004). The insider-outsider distinction may have ceased to be useful in terms of delimiting a hard and fast boundary between the insider and the outsider, but it is arguable that it has mutated into a condition that may be experienced simultaneously by individuals and communities, and is thus no longer a philosophical problem (if it ever was), but is rather part of a religious and spiritual landscape in the late capitalist West that is complicated, contentious and constantly changing.

Kerista

The two case studies in this chapter are movements that might not be considered religions or even "religious" by many. Kerista, in both its "Old" and "New" Tribes is best classified as an "intentional community" (Miller 2013: 1) which voluntarily banded together in the desire to live communally according to a philosophy that challenged the values of mainstream society (Hall 1978). Kerista began with John ("Brother Jud") Presmont, formerly Jake Peltz (c.1923–2009), who in 1956 had a vision in which he was charged to establish a utopian, sexually experimental commune that he sought to realize from that day onward. Until 1971, "Old Tribe" Kerista (defined as groups from 1956 to 1970) involved small groups of fellow-travellers founding communes in the United States and in various other places, including Ibiza, Dominica and Roatan (Kerista 2002–2015). Major figures from that era included Dau (Leonard Freitag) and E.Z. (pronounced "Easy"). The communes practised nudism, free love and drug-taking as a spiritual practice (Gruen 1966). Journalist, speculative fiction writer and occultist Robert Anton Wilson wrote an article about the Greenwich Village communal house in 1965. Wilson reported that after a 1962 vision "in which he spotted Buddhas dwelling on an island called Kerista, containing a mammoth mountain, Presmont now spoke of the religion of Kerista ... a religion of freedom and joy, a religion without dogma or restriction, and a religion of ecstasy" (Cottrell 2015: 240).

The Keristans told Wilson that: they chose their names using a Ouija board; the community lived and preached a gospel of sex and love; and Jud speculated about founding a political party aimed at liberalizing American society. Wilson noted that Jud had begun writing a type of creed for Kerista, known as the "69 Positions" (echoing the 10 Commandments of the Old Testament and the 39 Articles of the Anglican church, but with a sexual spin), which he regarded as "common sense". From a vantage point in the twenty-first century, some of these principles appear self-evident, while others remain deeply strange:

> Legalize group marriage. Legalize indecent exposure. Legalize trial marriage. Legalize abortion. Legalize miscegenation. Legalize religious intermarriage. Legalize marijuana. Legalize narcotics. Legalize cunnilinctus [sic]. Legalize transvestitism. Legalize pornography. Legalize obscene language. Legalize sexual intercourse. Legalize group sex. Legalize sodomy. Legalize fellatio. Legalize prostitution. Legalize incest. Legalize birth control. Legalize Lesbianism. Legalize polygamy. Legalize polyandry. Legalize polygyny. Legalize homosexuality. Legalize voluntary flagellation. (Wilson 1965)

During Wilson's visit to the New York household he met nine members, all of whom agreed that Kerista had no leader, although Jud was acknowledged as a prophet. Yet some members disagreed with Presmont's classification of Kerista as a religion, and viewed it rather as a revolutionary social movement.

In the 1960s Kerista crossed paths with both Kerry Thornley (1938–1998), the co-founder of Discordianism, and Tim Zell (b. 1942), the co-founder of the Church of All Worlds (CAW), two of the most important modern religions that draw inspiration from fiction and popular culture (Cusack 2010). Margot Adler credits Thornley with the first use of the term "Pagan" to describe ancient and contemporary nature religions. In 1966 Thornley joined the southern Californian branch of Kerista. That year he wrote:

> Kerista is a religion and the mood of Kerista is one of holiness, Do not, however, look for a profusion of rituals, dogmas, doctrines and scriptures. Kerista is too sacred for that. It is more akin to the religions of the East and, also, the so-called pagan religions of the pre-Christian West. Its fount of being is the religious experience and … Kerista, like those religions of olden times, is life affirming. (Quoted in Adler 1986: 294)

In October 1966 the science fiction author Robert A. Heinlein, whose *Stranger in a Strange Land* (1961) was the inspiration for the formation of CAW, wrote to his publisher Lurton Blassingame that he had been offered $100 to address the Los Angeles branch of Kerista, which he termed "far-out cult". He had been invited because the group regarded his novel "the 'New Testament' – and compulsory reading" (Heinlein 1989: 236). He refused the invitation. It is interesting to speculate on these alternative spiritual connections between Kerista, CAW and Discordianism, and to wonder if Kerry Thornley sent Heinlein that invitation (he and his wife lived in Watts, Los Angeles, in 1966), as he was a lifelong science fiction fan.

The "New Tribe" dates from the meeting of Brother Jud and Eve (formerly Susan) Furchgott (known in Kerista as "Even Eve") in the Haight-Ashbury district of San Francisco in February 1971. With Eve's friend Eva (Bluejay) Way they formed the "Living School Residence Group", that was later known as a "superfamily, then as a PCG (polyfidelitous closed group), then as a BFIC (Best Friend Identity Cluster)" (Kerista 2002–2015). This commune was small, with around forty official members, though others passed through over the years. Keristans practised "polyfidelity", defined by Even Eve as a group of adults united by elective affinity, in which members are "non-monogamous, relating to all their partners without a hierarchy of preference", and in which no member has sexual relationships outside of the family (Even Eve, "Polyfidelity", in Kerista 2002–2015). This resulted in sleeping schedules to make sex equally available to all, and Keristans coined the term "compersion" to refer to "the opposite of jealousy, positive feelings about your partner's *other* intimacies" (Kerista 2002–2015). BFICs ("beefics") of four to fifteen people were formed, and had names like the Purple Submarine and Sanity Mix (Kerista 2002–2015).

Despite its idealistic identity and commitments, Kerista was not without tensions and early on, in the New York commune of the mid-1960s conflicts developed between Jud and other members. Dau's lengthy 1984 essay, reproduced on the *Kerista Commune* site, notes that Jud supported the Vietnam War, got the group expelled from Belize when he attacked "the Bible and championed wild sex to local Christians", and was "greedy for women and for money" (Dau, "History of the Communal Utopian Spiritual Movement", in Kerista 2002–2015). Memories of the group posted online in essay format generally focus on meeting and/or joining Kerista, the impact that polyfidelity had on members, tensions between Jud and other members, and the final phase in which, in spite of the group's successful Apple computing business and twenty year anniversary, a majority of members split from Jud in November 1991 (Miller 1995: 425). He left to form the World Academy of Keristan Education. According to Even Eve, whose six-person marriage group (named Mariah) had spearheaded the split, by the end of 1992 "the economic, social, and ideological union that had formed the Kerista Commune was dissolved ... One way to see it is that, basically, most of us had just grown up and were ready for a different set of challenges in life" (Even Eve, "Afterword: What Happened to Kerista?", in Kerista 2002–2015).

For this chapter, the webpage menu "Real Peoples' Stories" (subdivided into "Ex-Keristans Speak" and Non-Keristans Speak") is the most important repository. The ex-Keristans include Kip, whose "My Long Slow Road to Monogamy" is typical of many of the spiritual and personal autobiographies from Kerista. He ruefully opens with:

> My fantasy life does have me involved with many beautiful intelligent woman who hang on my every word and anticipate ALL my sexual needs, but I am

actually a 43-year-old bald guy with a adult-sized belly who really needs to clean my room, untangle my checking account, mow my estate, talk to my wife, learn to partner dance, run every day, lose some weight, wash the car, get a good night's sleep every night, keep my job, have some fun with friends regularly, get into the ocean as much as possible, and keep myself sane. I don't really have the time or energy for more lovers in my life ...

I also think non-monogamy is a wonderful idea and I sort of wish it had worked out in my life, but it didn't. During and after Kerista, when I was non-monogamous: I ended up depressed, out-of-shape, exhausted, and emotionally and spiritually drained. It took me years to get myself to where I felt good again. I don't blame the women for this, they were doing the best they could to love me. I blame the structure for not giving me what I needed in the long run. (Kip, "My Long Slow Road to Monogamy", in Kerista 2002–2015)

Kip's sentiments are echoed by Even Eve (to whom he is now married in a monogamous relationship), who says that with six people Mariah was a balanced and viable unit for a time, but that attempting to build a group marriage of over thirty people now seems inconceivable. The constrictions of polyfidelity and the steadfast commitment to treating all lovers equally is noted by Delv, who identifies as still believing in Kerista's philosophy, but notes that the dogmatic enforcement of that ideal meant that "we only discovered what people really believed after they left the commune!" (Delv, "One USec [Utopian Second?] On the Sleeping Schedule", in Kerista 2002–2015).

Many of the postings are brief greetings and expressions of pleasure that the site offers the possibility to catch up with old friends. Kap posted "Thanks for putting the website together", while Ora wrote, "I appreciate the Kerista documentary of sorts you've put up. I especially like the chuckles I get out of the phrases you published. Thanks" (Kerista 2002–2015). The posts from non-Keristans often emphasize the importance that the community had in San Francisco, from the "rap groups" and newspapers that it produced as outreach, and meetings with certain members. Aries Rising says "I read your newspaper for years and met a couple of Keristans during the few months I lived in the Bay Area", and goes on to criticize the fact that when s/he wrote questioning letters to the commune in the 1980s they were answered by different people on a rota, which gave Aries Rising the impression that "the Keristans I corresponded with were intellectually out to lunch" and "didn't read much about philosophy, culture or politics, and didn't form individual (and therefore diverse) opinions" (Aries Rising, "10/17/03 From Aries Rising", in Kerista 2002–2015). A more hostile post from Roger Knull, a former employee who had been a musician and drug addict, ends with his praise of Way's insight and sympathetic conversation, and a humorous reference to

"Joan Jett, the once adopted Matron Saint of Kerista" (Roger Knull, "My Brief Encounter With Kerista: An Outsider's Account", in Kerista 2002–2015).

The palpable sense of Kerista Commune being a "safe place" where ex-members and passers-by can reminisce about the positive and negative aspects of being part of the group is nowhere more evident than in the memories of the late Jud Presmont. He is acknowledged to have been a difficult character, who constantly harangued members and non-members alike (the Kerista term for this activity was "gestalt"). Nu Luv's lengthy essay "The Dark Side of Community" traces his participation in the group over the last eleven years of its existence, using the Jungian imagery of light and shadow. He affirms the lightness and joy of joining in 1981, and the positive experience of the first six years, despite Jud's "intensely negative comments that he often introduced during gestalt encounters" (Nu Luv, "The Dark Side of Community: Hidden Limits to Lasting Groups", in Kerista 2002–2015). Nu Luv chronicles the last five years as the triumph of the shadow, and he identifies traps that Kerista unwittingly fell into: the Harmony Trap, the Equality Trap, and the failure to recognize or deal with Hidden Agendas and Power Plays. This reflects Even Eve's observation, "only the most courageous Keristans dared to openly disagree with Jud", that over time he "became increasingly aggressive and difficult to deal with", and her realization, later on, that "Kerista was in many ways a cult with a charismatic leader" (Even Eve, "Afterword: What Happened to Kerista?", in Kerista 2002–2015). The realization of Jud's controlling personality, need to dominate and negative impact on many members does not prevent ex-Keristans and non-Keristans from celebrating his achievements, such as they were, and honouring his distinctive, uncompromisingly countercultural, vision.

The Kerista Commune site is an online continuation of both the "Old Tribe" and the "New Tribe" communes, in which friendships are maintained and renewed, a form of therapeutic conversation about the experience of polyfidelity and group life is conducted, and a large number of participants are strongly positive about the experience of being a Keristan, and what it brought to their lives. This holds whether the ex-members are now in monogamous, group, or no relationships at the time of posting. The creed of freedom and defiance of convention preached by Jud Presmont continues to inspire many, who see the problems leading to the group's eventual demise as failure to realize an ideal, rather than pursuing a flawed ideal in the first place (Miller 1992: 83). The psychologists Ayala Pines and Elliot Aronson studied Kerista in the 1980s, and "found no vestiges of sexual jealousy" (cited in Wolfe 2003: 67). Leanna Wolfe observes that, "the high social demands of the community and that the groups [sic] social-sexual units were not pair-bonded" probably assisted the group to "achieve this rarified state" (Wolfe 2003: 68). The acrimony of its final days has all but disappeared, and both tribes are comfortable with their status as still (in some sense) belonging to a group that no longer exists in the real world as an institution. Ex-members continue to "believe" to a certain degree, but the sense that they still belong is stronger.

The School of Economic Science

The School of Economic Science (SES) was founded by Leonardo da Vinci (Leon) MacLaren (1910–1994) in 1937 as the Henry George School of Economics. The American economist Henry George (1839–1897), author of *Progress and Poverty* (1879) and several other works, campaigned for social justice, chiefly advocating a "single tax" on land (Hooper 2008). MacLaren changed the name to the School of Economic Science in 1942, as he moved away from George's ideas. In the late 1940s MacLaren became influenced by the ideas of the Russian philosopher and esotericist P. D. Ouspensky (1878–1947), an important pupil of G. I. Gurdjieff (c.1866–1949). He then incorporated philosophical and religio-spiritual ideas from the Fourth Way in his teaching at the SES (Petsche 2015: 198). In 1953 MacLaren met Dr Francis C. Roles (1901–1982), a pupil of Ouspensky who had established The Study Society in 1951 to continue the teaching of the Fourth Way. Johanna Petsche states that from that meeting MacLaren's teaching was integrated "with Gurdjieffian principles as taught by Ouspensky, and it was this influence that enabled the SES to ... forge an identity and gain momentum as a spiritual group" (Petsche 2015: 198). Roles and MacLaren were eager to discover the source of the Fourth Way teaching, and began to practise Transcendental Meditation after meeting Maharishi Mahesh Yogi (1918–2008), who came to Britain to teach in 1960. In 1961 Roles and MacLaren went to India and became followers of Swami Shantananda Saraswati, "who had been a disciple, with the Maharishi, of the previous Shankacharya [of the North], Swami Brahmananda Saraswati (who died in 1953)" (Rawlinson 1997: 425).

From then on the SES taught a form of Advaita Vedanta (Adago 2014: 43–45, 88–93). Roles and MacLaren parted ways in the mid-1960s after the SES was registered as an educational charity by MacLaren in 1964. The SES went on to establish branches, under a variety of names, in the Netherlands, the United States, Australia, New Zealand, Canada, Ireland, and sundry other countries (Hounam and Hogg 1985: 58). There is little academic research on the SES, with publications being mostly short entries in encyclopaedias or compendia of spiritual groups and NRMs. The most notable are by Andrew Rawlinson

(1997) and David V. Barrett (2001). In 2008 Dorine Tolley (née van Oyen), MacLaren's personal assistant from 1973 to his death in 1994, published a memoir of her time with MacLaren, and in 2010 Brian Hodgkinson, a teacher at the SES St James School in London, wrote *In Search of Truth: The Story of the School of Economic Science* (Tolley 2008; Hodgkinson 2010). Hodgkinson's wholly positive account, has been criticized by the ex-member community, though some sympathy has been expressed regarding Tolley's book (SES Forums 2004–2014). One prominent former member, the English actress Clara Salaman, who was raised in the SES, published a novel, *Shame on You* (2009), in which the SES is called "The Organization", and her experiences of SES schooling, religious teaching, diet, and discipline of the group, are presented in harrowing detail. In 1984 Peter Hounam and Andrew Hogg, two journalists on the staff of the *Evening Standard*, published *Secret Cult*, a politically motivated exposé revealing that "the chairman of the Liberal Party and several Liberal parliamentary candidates were involved with the SES" (Barrett 2001: 269). It transpired that David Boddy, an adviser to Conservative Prime Minister Margaret Thatcher was also a member. Hounam and Hogg's negative account is supplemented by William Shaw's more neutral chapter in *Spying in Guru Land*, an entertaining and informative book detailing a year in which he participated in a range of Britain's "cults", including the Emin, the Jesus Army and the SES (Shaw 1995). Until recently it was difficult to obtain copies of MacLaren's lectures and teachings, though second hand copies of books like *The Nature of Society and Other Essays* (MacLaren 1943) are now occasionally available on the internet.

Ex-member accounts are biased (negatively) and member testimonies also are biased (positively). Benjamin Zablocki distinguished three groups in research into religions; "believers", "apostates" and "ethnographers". He established that "there is very little difference between the *reliability* (that is, stability across time) of accounts from believers and ex-believers (or apostates)" (cited in Carter 1998: 222). The *validity* of the accounts is harder to establish, given that the believer focuses on positives while the apostate focuses on the negatives. The academic "ethnographer" can use both of these accounts, and supplement them with personal analysis and information from external sources. Nevertheless, ex-member testimonies contain information that is "sometimes quite specific and subsequently verifiable; this is especially true of financial records, incorporation papers, court cases, and other kinds of documentary evidence" (Carter 1998: 222). Here reminiscences from the SES Forums site are compared with positive publications from prominent SES members, and with journalistic and scholarly sources, to establish a coherent picture of the SES.

Shaw's account of classes in the "London headquarters of the School of Economic Science, a beautiful pair of white regency buildings in South Kensington" notes: the conservative clothing and opinions of the teachers and members; the curious notion of "philosophy" that is taught, which is not about intellectual enquiry, but rather Hindu doctrines and meditation; and the hostility to and suppression of sexuality, which chiefly manifested in restrictions on women in the group (Shaw 1995: 123–129). Shaw lists the writers that the SES approves of (Kahlil Gibran, William Shakespeare, Plato, Gurdjieff, Ouspensky) and discusses the St James School, where corporal punishment is still practised and the curriculum is focused on "the Upanishads and Socrates, Sanskrit and Greek ... Mozart and 'lots of Shakespeare'" (ibid.: 139). Rawlinson describes the SES idea of "Measure" (which he equates with *dharma*), and how it manifests in the group: a vegetarian (largely raw food) diet; long skirts and long sleeves worn by women and suits by men; teaching "Sanskrit, Vedic mathematics and 'traditional' Hindu history and geography" (Rawlinson 1997: 427); and the pursuit of *sattva*, purity, lightness, and truth. Hodgkinson confirms this approach, arguing for a view of the self as illusory (as in Indian traditions) and a focus on "identification", that in the Gurdjieff teaching is a strong force that keeps people "asleep" (Hodgkinson 2010: 69). Hodgkinson and Tolley confirm the importance of the Gurdjieffian laws of Three and Seven,[2] and the severity of the diet, and discipline that members were subjected to. This included "residential" times at sundry country properties the SES rented or purchased, most notably Waterperry (Oxfordshire), in which hard physical labour was employed, as it was at Gurdjieff's own Institute at the Prieuré des Basses Loges, south of Paris (Petsche 2015: 209). Gurdjieff pupils including Ouspensky, John Godolphin Bennett, Maurice Nicol, and others, all perpetuated this tradition of residential workshops in the country, which were understood to be a vital part of the Work (Cusack 2015; Coates 2013).

Tolley's experience as MacLaren's companion makes for uncomfortable reading. It is clear that she believed Leon MacLaren to be a great man, and a charismatic spiritual teacher. Her parents had been pupils of Ouspensky from 1936 onwards, and later of both Francis Roles and MacLaren. They were in charge of in the SES in the Netherlands, the School voor Filosofie, which was later led by Tolley's brother Paul van Oyen (Petsche 2015: 200–201). Tolley met MacLaren as a guest of her parents in their home in Amsterdam in 1961, at the age of fourteen. Ten years later this highly educated, academically successful, musically gifted young woman gave up her own life to serve the master, in what amounted to a celibate, "unofficial" marriage, "for better or for worse", as MacLaren himself said (Tolley 2008: 107). This involved sleeping on the floor in his room for several years, as MacLaren suffered from sundry ailments, attending to his every wish, accompanying him on trips, driving him in London and the countryside, and abandoning hopes of marriage and children while he lived, which she admits was a great sacrifice (ibid.: 121–123, 269–270). She records that: MacLaren permitted her to ride a horse if she "would ride side saddle and wear a long skirt" (this is the 1970s); notes an occasion when he hit her for expressing a desire to go home for Christmas rather than spend it at the residential site of Stanhill; observes that at Stanhill the sexes were segregated, even married couples; and details how she was charged with home-schooling teenage girls, leading ladies' groups, and various other tasks, while doing all his secretarial work, and helping to realize sundry musical and artistic plans of the SES (ibid.: 157, 212, 147–148, and *passim*).

It is interesting that the SES Forums site, which has some postings removed and is now closed, though it continues to exist as an archive of ex-member stories, contains a brief discussion of Tolley's book. Ahamty2 in Australia first expresses personal liking for Tolley, "I found Dorine van Oyen a relief when she came with LM, her close relationship with LM made it more relaxed and not so tense", but then remarks that her memoir of a "very close and intimate relationship at such a young age, a father substitute, almost a sugar daddy view of LM" cannot excuse MacLaren's harshness within the SES, particularly in the case of the St James School (Ahamty2, SES Forums 2004–2014). As many of the posts on the site are complaints about physical and psychological ill-treatment, it is appropriate here to mention James Townend's document, *St Vedast/ St James Inquiry: Report of a Private Independent Inquiry Commissioned by the Governors of St James Independent Schools and Held in London Between 20 June–6 October 2005*, which was the result of complaints by former pupils and parents of current pupils, and bad publicity regarding the SES as a result of the allegations, which had been building since Hounam and Hogg's *Secret Cult* was published in 1984. Claims of physical violence (despite corporal punishment being illegal in the United Kingdom from 1986 in government schools), and what Townend termed "rough handling, physical and mental mistreatment" resulted in reform of the schools that relaxed the discipline to an extent (Townend 2005; SES Forums 2004–2014).

Such harsh discipline was experienced in all levels of the SES, including primary and secondary schools, day care centres, and residential retreats for adult members. Tolley's memoir contains the following passage:

> I had heard that some serious problems had arisen with regards to children exposed to harsh treatments in a day care centre in one of the overseas schools. While having lunch with him I raised the issue, urging him to look

into it. To my horror he would not listen, even when amidst tears of anger I shouted at him that the Truth was being violated and the children's welfare was at stake if he did not take any action. I said that he had always upheld justice and truthfulness and it was as if he had abandoned both. He left the room and said nothing more about it. But that same evening, as if it were the most natural thing in the world, he told the members of his group what he had heard and that he would take appropriate measures to protect the children. It was his way. In the end Justice and Truth always gained the upper hand. (Tolley 2008: 212–213)

It may be that Tolley's recollections are accurate regarding Maclaren's attitude to the discipline of children and that he may not have authorized the punishments that were experienced. However, many posts on the SES Forums site are by ex-St James and St Vedast pupils, and also former pupils of the schools established by the SES around the world. Discussion of Tolley's memoir, and that passage in particular, include assertions that MacLaren "an almost god-like status within the cult" and that "most of the long-term staff of the schools show themselves as unwilling to recognise the environment they helped cultivate" (Tom Grubb and Bonsai, SES Forums 2004–2014).

The extent of the violence and systemic abuse within international SES groups is particularly clear in the case of the School of Philosophy (SOP) in Australia during the time it was run by a married couple, the Mavros. Michael and Nina Mavro were pupils of MacLaren in London, and he charged them with setting up the School of Philosophy in Australia in 1967 (Hounam and Hogg 1985: 68). The Mavros, who were expelled from the SES by MacLaren on account of the brutality of their regime, remain a focus of anger and pain for ex-members. This was apparent in Hounam and Hogg's book, as they had interviewed Anthony and Celia Ravesi, who left the Sydney SOP in 1980. Anthony stated that, "according to Mr MacLaren and Mr Mavro we in Australia are the scum and dregs of Europe ... It is the work of the school here to change that and become the aristocrats of Australia" (ibid.: 68–69). Celia stated that MacLaren believed that Australian Indigenous people "should be allowed to die out" and there were no Maoris in the New Zealand SES because "they are not sufficiently intelligent" (ibid.: 269).

Celia also spoke of the back-breaking physical labour members did on the country property the Sydney SOP owned at the beautiful and exclusive Blue Mountains heritage village, Mount Wilson, which is a frequent topic on the SES Forums site. For example, Ahamty2 wrote:

Especially in the early days of Mt W, when it was nearly all virgin Australian bush land. Can you imagine them at Waterperry meeting five of the world's most deadly venomous snake sunbaking in their path while they tended to its pristine grounds. It was common to meet an eastern brown, tiger snake, copper head, death adder or a red bellied black with death just minutes away from you. Then there were the funnel web spiders whose habitat was continually disturbed by us, crawling into your sleeping bag or running across your face at night, one bite or two, that's it. The leeches on your legs and arms became so bloated with your blood they just dropped off, leaving you covered with irritated sites all over you. Mt W was real blood, real toil and real sweat!

At Mt W, MM came into his own, he would push everyone to their physical and psychological limit and sometimes beyond. It made training for the SAS Commando Unit child's play. Then in the evenings you would be struggling to stay awake, having to give your observations of the working surface. No wonder some of the most ridiculous delusional comments were made at Mt W and MM would latch onto them for hours. The penal colony all over again, in the late 20th century, at the direction of our British masters, all on the sacred land of the indigenous people of this great country. (Ahamty2, SES Forums 2004–2014)

There are many other postings discussing Nina Mavro's advocacy of physical violence against children who expressed dissent or even questioned the Mavros' *diktats*, and other humiliations and sufferings that group members endured. Ahmaty2 linked the sacking of the Mavros from the Sydney SOP with the fact that in the 1980s the Wellington school in New Zealand (which was the largest SES organization in the southern hemisphere) exited the SES as a body and went over to Francis Roles' Study Society. Ahmaty2 claims that MacLaren sacked the Mavros, who promptly founded a near-identical body called the School for Self Knowledge, rather than lose the Sydney SOP, which was likely to go the same way as Wellington, and opt for the Study Society (SES Forums 2004–2014).

The creator and moderator of the SES Forums, Daffy, closed the site on 1 January 2014. The archive is extensive, and is interesting to compare to the Kerista site. The sheer number of "house-keeping" announcements in which Daffy explains that posters' accounts have been closed or people have been banned for trolling, and the lengthy, hostile exchanges between current SES members from various countries and the ex-members are evidence of an atmosphere that could not be more different than the supportive and positive ex-member community that Kerista Commune has fostered. (For example, a whole thread concerning Michael Mavro's actual name has been censored, so the postings are visible but empty, presumably for legal reasons). Many members are resigned; they have made their peace with staying in a less than ideal organization when they were aware of the need to leave. A constant question is "Why did you join/stay?" and the commonest answers are that involvement in the SES or one of its daughter schools began innocuously, and that members participated in the "reality" that they were taught, and often did not perceive harm for many years. Tootsie reflects that, "it sounds silly now but alt the work was done as service to the absolute. By putting school first in all our activities we were overcoming our own personal desires and working for humanity and the world" (Tootsie, SES Forums 2004–2014). Ahamty2 agrees:

> Why didn't I leave earlier? Why did I give the best years of my young adult life in an organization such as the SES [sic] ... Free and Tootsie have given some aspects of the reasons ... Jo-Anne, you asked why we didn't just leave, rather than put up with it all. Our "ego" wouldn't let us leave. There is the sense of failure, turning our back on the truth, and worst of all, not serving the Absolute, whatever that is in reality. The impossible dream: fighting windmills and "marching into hell for the heaven above" says the words of the song. (Ahmaty2, SES Forums 2004–2014)

This post reveals that the ideal of the SES was presented as both valuable and attractive, but for the ex-members participating in the forum, the ideal failed. In contrast to ex-Keristans, ex-SES members did not just lose faith in the institution, they lost faith in the philosophy, coming to see it as empty and a sham, not just something that was unachievable.

Conclusion

This chapter has examined only a fraction of the testimonies and conversations that are available for scholarly consideration on the Kerista Commune and SES Forums sites. It has been argued that the ex-members participating in these online communities are only ex-members in the strict sense that they no longer belong to the organization formally. For Kerista, this is because it ceased to exist in 1991, and for the SES because the members were either expelled for breaches of the rules, or left once they perceived that they had been ill-used by the group and its leaders. David G. Bromley has suggested that, "most individuals exiting religious movements labeled subversive are not hostile to the groups with which they were formerly affiliated" (Bromley 1998: 7). There is some evidence that this is the case; recent empirical research indicates that some former Scientology members are still practising the religion outside of Church structures (Rubin 2011), and an assessment of the psychological state of ex-members of various groups suggests they are still positively disposed to spiritual and religious ideals (Buxant and Saroglou 2008). The key issues seem to be whether the ex-members still uphold the teaching or the ideal (as is the case with Free Zone Scientologists and ex-Keristans) but have either lost confidence in the organizational structures and official "leaders", or that structure has ceased to exist. In these cases to speak of de-conversion or apostasy is simply incorrect, and to classify these people as "outsiders" is also misconceived. They remain in many important ways "insiders" of the teaching they have followed, and continue to belong to it despite no longer belonging in any official sense. To take this argument a step further, Free Zone Scientologists and Kerista Commune online have chosen not to re-create the group they exited from, but have built a different (yet perhaps substitutionary) community without the problems. Ex-Keristans online no longer have to live according to a sleeping schedule or be "gestalted" by Jud; Free Zone Scientologists are liberated from David Miscavige, and the structures of the Church of Scientology. Both groups are also free to remember their deceased "charismatic leader", be it Jud Presmont or L. Ron Hubbard, without the negative traits that they manifested when alive.

Ex-members of the SES, however, defy the positive forecast of lack of hostility toward the group they left, and positive assessments of the orientation toward spirituality of "apostates". In some cases, ex-members on SES Forums have indicated that they have found help and solace in some other spiritual or religious teachings. Yet, overwhelmingly, they demonstrate hostility to the SES organization, and lack of faith in the leadership, while maintaining interest in their belonging to the SES and its associated organizations and raking over the coals of every detail of what that belonging involved. Clara Salaman's *Shame on You*, mentioned above, is a fictionalized account, but it is teeming with details of daily life in the SES, and suggests that even those who escaped the SES when young, and have built successful careers as adults, find it difficult to escape its shadow (Salaman 2009). The SES ex-members remain deeply engaged with the institution that dictated the pattern that their lives took for so long. Both ex-Keristans and ex-SES testify to the difficulty of identifying a conversion moment, or an exit/ apostasy moment, and they blur the categories of "insider" and "outsider" so thoroughly that it may be that they are irrelevant to the discussion in this chapter. A scholarly examination of these two ex-member communities demands the recognition that believing, belonging, outsideness and insideness, are inextricably connected, rather than clean and separable states.

About the author

Carole M. Cusack is professor of religious studies at the University of Sydney. She trained as a medievalist and her doctorate was published as *Conversion among the Germanic Peoples* (Cassell, 1998). She researches contemporary religious trends and Western esotericism. Her books include (with Katharine Buljan) *Anime, Religion and Spirituality: Profane and Sacred Worlds in Contemporary Japan* (Equinox, 2015), *Invented Religions: Imagination, Fiction and Faith* (Ashgate, 2010), and *The Sacred Tree: Ancient and Medieval Manifestations* (Cambridge Scholars Publishing, 2011). She has published widely in edited volumes and journals, and is the editor (with Christopher Hartney) of *Religion and Retributive Logic: Essays in Honour of Garry W. Trompf* (Brill 2010) and (with Alex Norman) of *Handbook of New Religions and Cultural Production* (Brill 2012). With Rachelle Scott (University of Tennessee, Knoxville) she is editor of *Fieldwork in Religion* (Equinox). She is editor of *Literature & Aesthetics* (the journal of the Sydney Society of Literature and Aesthetics).

Acknowledgements

Thanks are due to Johanna Petsche, Venetia Robertson, Zoe Alderton and Elisha McIntyre, who have been my research assistants over the years, and have contributed to my thinking on this subject. I am grateful also to Donald Barrett, whose support and interest have contributed in no small way to my work for two decades.

Notes

1 When both the Kerista Commune and SES Forums sites are referenced in the text of this chapter, the name of the author and the title of their essay will be given, if it is available. However, the sites are given as a single bibliographical listing.
2 In Gurdjieff's system there are two fundamental laws, the Law of Three (*Triamazikamno*) and the Law of Seven (*Heptaparaparshinokh*). The first rejects dualistic understandings, through positing three forces, positive, negative and reconciling (rather than just positive and negative), "[t]he higher blends with the lower to actualize the middle, which becomes higher or the preceding lower and lower for the succeeding higher" (Gurdjieff 1999: 751). These are called the affirming, denying, and reconciling forces. The Law of Seven applies to multiple aspects of the teaching: there are seven levels of energy, seven different cosmoses, and the Ray of Creation diagram has seven emanations (Moore 1991: 45).

References

Adago, John (2014). *East Meets West: The Stories of the Remarkable Men and Women From the East and the West Who Built a Bridge Across a Cultural Divide and Introduced Meditation and Eastern Philosophy to the West*. London: Shepheard-Walwyn.

Adler, Margot (1986). *Drawing Down the Moon: Witches, Druids, Goddess Worshippers, and Other Pagan in America Today*, 2nd edition. Boston, MA: Beacon Press.

Anapol, Deborah (2010). *Polyamory in the Twenty-First Century: Love and Intimacy with Multiple Partners*. Lanham, MD: Rowman and Littlefield.

Bado, Nikki (2013). Dancing in a Universe of Light and Shadows. *The Pomegranate: The International Journal of Pagan Studies* 15(1-2): 122-135. https://doi.org/10.1558/pome.v15i1-2.122

Barrett, David V. (2001). *The New Believers: A Survey of Sects, Cults and Alternative Religions*. London: Cassell & Co.

Bromley, David G. (1998). Sociological Perspectives on Apostasy: An Overview. In *The Politics of Religious Apostasy*, ed. David G. Bromley, 3-16. Westport, CT: Praeger.

Buxant, Coralie and Vassilis Saroglou (2008). Joining and Leaving a New Religious Movement: A Study of Ex-Members' Mental Health. *Mental Health, Religion & Culture* 11(3): 251-271. https://doi.org/10.1080/13674670701247528

Carter, Lewis F. (1998). Carriers of Tales: On Assessing Credibility of Apostate and Other Outsider Accounts of Religious Practices. In *The Politics of Religious Apostasy: The Role of Apostates in the Transformation of Religious Movements*, ed. David G. Bromley, 221-237. Westport, CT: Greenwood Publishing.

Coates, Chris (2013). How Many Arks Does It Take? In *Spiritual and Visionary Communities: Out to Save the World*, ed. Timothy Miller, 176-189. Farnham: Ashgate.

Cottrell, Robert C. (2015). *Sex, Drugs, and Rock 'n' Roll: The Rise of America's 1960s Counterculture*. Lanham, MD: Rowman and Littlefield.

Cusack, Carole M. (1996). Towards a General Theory of Conversion. *Religious Change, Conversion and Culture*, ed. Lynette Olson, 1-22. Sydney: Sydney Studies in Society and Culture.

Cusack, Carole M. (2010). *Invented Religions: Imagination, Fiction, and Faith*. Farnham: Ashgate.

Cusack, Carole M. (2015). Intentional Communities in the Gurdjieff Teaching. *International Journal for the Study of New Religions* 6(2): 159-178. https://doi.org/10.1558/ijsnr.v6i2.28875

Davie, Grace (1994). *Religion in Britain since 1945: Believing Without Belonging*. Oxford: Blackwell.

Day, Abby (2012). *Believing in Belonging: Belief and Social Identity in the Modern World*. Oxford: Oxford University Press.

Demerath, N. J. (2007). Secularization and Sacralization Deconstructed and Reconstructed. In *The Sage Handbook of the Sociology of Religion*, ed. James A. Beckford and N. J. Demerath, III, 57-80. London: Sage Publications. https://doi.org/10.4135/9781848607965.n4

Dyason, Laura and Bernard Doherty (2015). The Modern Hydra: The Exclusive Brethren's Online Critics. A Case Study of Cult Awareness Activity and Community Formation in Cyberspace. *St Mark's Review* 233: 116–134.

Engler, Steven (2004). Constructionism versus What? *Religion* 34: 291–313. https://doi.org/10.1016/j.religion.2004.09.001

George, Henry (1879). *Progress and Poverty: An Inquiry into the Cause of Industrial Depressions and of Increase of Want with Increase of Wealth: The Remedy.* New York: B. Appleton and Company.

Gesch, Patrick (2001). On Conversion from the Global to the Local: Going Beyond One's Best Understanding in. Sepik Initiation. In *The End of Religions? Religion in an Age of Globalisation*, ed. Carole M. Cusack and Peter Oldmeadow, 3–20. Sydney: Sydney Studies in Religion.

Gilhus, Ingvild Sælid and Lisbeth Mikaelsson (2001). *Nytt blikk pa religion: Studiet av religion i dag.* Oslo: Pax.

Girardot, N. J. (2002). Max Müller's Sacred Books and the Nineteenth Century Production of the Comparative Science of Religions. *History of Religions* 41(3): 213–250. https://doi.org/10.1086/463683

Gleig, Ann (2012). Researching New Religious Movements From the Inside Out and the Outside In: Methodological Reflections from Collaborative and Participatory Perspectives. *Nova Religio: The Journal of Alternative and Emergent Religions* 16(1): 88–103. https://doi.org/10.1525/nr.2012.16.1.88

Gruen, John (1966). *The New Bohemia.* Pennington, NJ: A Capella Press.

Gurdjieff, George Ivanovitch (1999). *Beelzebub's Tales to His Grandson.* New York: Penguin Arkana. First published in 1950.

Haddon, Malcolm (2013). Anthropological Proselytism: Reflexive Questions for a Hare Krishna Ethnography. *The Australian Journal of Anthropology* 24: 250–269. https://doi.org/10.1111/taja.12050

Hall, John R. (1978). *The Ways Out: Utopian Communal Groups in an Age of Babylon.* London: Routledge and Kegan Paul.

Heinlein, Robert (1961). *Stranger in a Strange Land.* New York: G. P. Putnam's Sons.

Heinlein, Robert A. (1989). *Grumbles From The Grave*, ed. Virginia Heinlein. New York: Ballantine Books.

Hodgkinson, Brian (2010). *In Search of Truth: The Story of the School of Economic Science.* London: Shepheard Walwyn Publishers.

Hooper, Charles L. (2008). Henry George (1839–1897). *The Concise Encyclopedia of Economics*, 2nd edition. Retrieved from www.econlib.org/library/Enc/bios/George.html (accessed 23 May 2016).

Hounam, Peter and Andrew Hogg (1985). *Secret Cult.* Tring: Lion Books.

Jensen, Jeppe Sinding (1993). Is a Phenomenology of Religion Possible? On the Ideas of a Human and Social Science of Religion. *Method and Theory in the Study of Religion* 5(2): 109–133. https://doi.org/10.1163/157006893X00092

Jensen, Jeppe Sinding (2011). Revisiting the Insider-Outsider Debate: Dismantling a Pseudo-Problem in the Study of Religion. *Method and Theory in the Study of Religion* 23(1): 23–47. https://doi.org/10.1163/157006811X549689

Kerista (2002–2015). Kerista Commune: We Didn't Save the World. We Didn't Even Try. We Talked About It A Lot. Retrieved from www.kerista.com (accessed 20 May 2016).

Knott, Kim (2005). Insider/Outsider Perspectives. In *The Routledge Companion to the Study of Religion*, ed. John R. Hinnells, 243–258. New York: Routledge.

Lofland, John and Norman Skonovd (1981). Conversion Motifs. *Journal for the Scientific Study of Religion* 20(1): 373–385. https://doi.org/10.2307/1386185

Lyon, David (2002). *Jesus in Disneyland: Religion in Postmodern Times*. Oxford: Polity.

MacLaren, Leon (1943). *Nature of Society and Other Essays*. London: School of Economic Science.

Marchisio, Roberto and Maurizio Pisati (1999). Belonging Without Believing: Catholics in Italy. *Journal of Modern Italian Studies* 4(2): 236–255. https://doi.org/10.1080/13545719908455008

McCutcheon, Russell T. (ed.) (1999). *The Insider/Outsider Problem in the Study of Religion: A Reader*. London: Continuum.

Melton, J. Gordon (2004). The Fate of NRMs and Their Detractors in Twenty-First Century America. In *New Religious Movements in the Twenty-First Century: Legal, Political, and Social Challenges in Global Perspective*, ed. Phillip Charles Lucas and Thomas Robbins, 229–240. New York: Routledge.

Miller, Timothy (1992). The Roots of the 1960s Communal Revival. *American Studies* 33(2): 79–93.

Miller, Timothy (1995). Kerista. In *America's Alternative Religions*, ed. Timothy Miller, 425. New York: State University of New York Press.

Miller, Timothy (2013). Introduction. Persistence Over Millennia: The Perennial Presence of Intentional Communities. In *Spiritual and Visionary Communities: Out to Save the World*, ed. Timothy Miller, 1–14. Farnham: Ashgate.

Moore, James (1991). *Gurdjieff: The Anatomy of a Myth*. Rockport, MA: Element.

Nock, Arthur Darby (1933). *Conversion*. Oxford: Oxford University Press.

Petsche, Johanna J. M. (2015). Gurdjieffian Overtones in Leon MacLaren's School of Economic Science. *International Journal for the Study of New Religions* 6(2): 195–216. https://doi.org/10.1558/ijsnr.v6i2.28443

Rambo, Lewis (1993). *Understanding Religious Conversion*. New Haven, CT: Yale University Press.

Rawlinson, Andrew (1997). *The Book of Enlightened Masters: Western Teachers in Eastern Traditions*. Chicago, IL: Open Court.

Richardson, James T. (1985). The Active vs. Passive Convert: Paradigm Conflict in Conversion/Recruitment Research. *Journal for the Scientific Study of Religion* 24(2): 119–236. https://doi.org/10.2307/1386340

Richardson, James T. (1993). Definitions of Cult: From Sociological-Technical to Popular-Negative. *Review of Religious Research* 34(4): 348–356. https://doi.org/10.2307/3511972

Rubin, Elisabeth Tuxen (2011). Disaffiliation Among Scientologists: A Sociological Study of Post Apostasy Behaviour and Attitudes. *International Journal for the Study of New Religions* 2(2): 201–224. https://doi.org/10.1558/ijsnr.v2i2.201

Salaman, Clara (2009). *Shame On You*. London: Penguin.
SES Forums (2004–2014). SES Forums: Forums for the Discussion of the School of Economic Science and its Satellite Schools Around the World. Retrieved from www.ses-forums.org/viewtopic.php?f=31&p=12067#p12067 (accessed 20 May 2016).
Shaw, William (1995). *Spying in Guru Land: Inside Britain's Cults*. London: Fourth Estate.
Sherwood, Harriet (2016). People of No Religion Outnumber Christians in England and Wales – Study. *The Guardian*, 24 May. Retrieved from www.theguardian.com/world/2016/may/23/no-religion-outnumber-christians-england-wales-study (accessed 23 May 2016).
Tolley, Dorine (2008). *The Power Within: Leon MacLaren. A Memoir of His Life and Work*. Sydney: author.
Townend, James (2005). *St Vedast/ St James Inquiry: Report of a Private Independent Inquiry Commissioned by the Governors of St James Independent Schools and Held in London Between 20 June-6 October 2005*. Retrieved from http://reference.ses-forums.org/wp-content/uploads/townend-report.pdf (accessed 20 May 2016).
Wilson, Robert Anton (1965). The Religion of Kerista and Its 69 Positions. *Fact* 2(4): 23–29. Retrieved from https://theanarchistlibrary.org/library/robert-anton-wilson-the-religion-of-kerista-and-its–69-positions (accessed 20 May 2016).
Wolfe, Leanna Phyllis (2003). Jealousy and Transformation in Polyamorous Relationships. PhD, Institute for Advanced Study of Human Sexuality, San Francisco, CA.

Index

abortion 48, 321, 324, 399
access 15–6, 32, 61, 74, 118, 178–80, 220–1, 272–3, 298, 395
Advaita Vedanta 394, 403
affiliation 3, 19, 173, 176, 239, 330, 335, 373, 397
agnosticism 8, 10, 280–1, 305, 337
Ahmed, Farah 66-7
Alfred, Randall 81–2
Alvesson, Mats 217
Amerindians 15, 19, 114–5, 125
Ammerman, N. 17, 344
Anglicanism 19, 136, 171, 185, 337–8, 344, 383, 384, 379, 388
animism 6, 12, 13, 24, 127
Anonymous 24, 365
Anthony, Dick 78–9
anthropology 34, 59, 66, 112, 120–1, 143, 218, 393, 395
anticult movement (ACM) 157, 371–6, 383, 378, 388–9
apostasy 8, 21, 287, 363, 367, 373–9, 387, 394–7, 404
apostolic succession 251–3, 260
Art of Living (AOL) 213, 215, 219, 223- 7
Atay, Tayfun 76. 79
atheism 8, 10, 21, 47, 175, 199, 286, 335, 337, 397

Bailey, Alice 41, 45
baptism 3, 10, 199, 340, 385, 387–8
  de-baptism 387–8
Barker, Eileen 17, 75–6
Beck, U 254, 256
Benedict XVI, Pope 261, 313, 322, 387
Bhaskar, Roy 113, 124, 127
Bible 4, 9, 48, 60, 137, 181, 190, 236, 279, 340–1, 378, 388, 400
birth control 11, 240, 315, 324, 399
Bohannan, Laura 230
Bourdieu, Pierre 216–7, 230, 232
Bourgeault, Cynthia 144
Bowie, Fiona 59, 126,

Bowman, Marion 16, 63, 331, 345
brainwashing 152-3, 371, 162, 375, 393
British Association for the Study of Religions 26, 47, 66, 366
Bromley, David G. 70, 351, 377, 383, 409
Brooke, Tal 255–6
Brown, Callum 136, 330
Brown, Karen McCarthy 15, 77–8
Brown, Mick 43
Bruni, Attila 220
Buddhism 9, 12–13, 145, 203, 271, 275, 284, 291–306, 359, 388
  Buddhist Churches of America 291–3, 296, 301–4
  and ethnicity 292–306
  Jodo Shinshu 302–4
  meditation 13, 145, 278–9, 293, 296
  missionary 296
  Soka Gakkai 173
  Western 13–4, 145, 293–6, 299
  Zen 278, 295–6

Callaway, Helen 59
Calley, Malcolm 73–4, 81
Calvinism 388
Campbell, Colin 44
capitalism 12, 111, 316–7, 325, 345
censuses 3, 17, 397
Chama, J.C. 256
Chandler, Stuart 297–8
Cheah, Joseph 298–9
Children of God, *see* The Family International
Christianity 3–4, 9–11, 65, 135–7, 143, 172, 176–86, 271, 377–8, 396–7
  in China 190-205
  as exclusive 4, 11–12, 275
  influence on the study of religion 5–7, 14, 396
Christmas 10, 171, 180–1, 379, 406
Chin Kenpa 205
Church of Satan 82
Coakley, Sarah 144

Coffey, Amanda 172, 174, 229
Confucianism 12, 195, 203, 289
contemplation 131, 134, 136, 141-5, 146, 193
conversion 78-80, 138-21, 177-8, 237-9, 331, 345, 362, 393-7, 410
Cornille, Catherine 271, 284
Cottee, S. 21
covert research 72-5, 77, 81-2, 85, 178, 186; *see also* ethics
Cox, James 57, 217
Crenshaw, Kimberle 90, 96, 253
cults, *see* new religious movements
Cumbey, Constance 41-2
Cunningham, Claire 18

Daoism 12, 45, 195, 203
Davie, Grace 136, 315, 397
Davis, Charlotte 216
Davis, Tommy 363
Dawson, Andrew 225, 227
Deoband 61-3, 180, 221
Dianetics 351, 356
disfellowshipping 379, 385, 388, 390
diversity 21, 91, 95, 134, 200, 247-8, 279, 294, 317-8, 344
divorce 239, 311, 318-9, 324
Donner, Florinda 229, 232, 233
Droogers, A. 330-6, 345
Druidry 13, 343
Dunch. Ryan 197
Durkheim, Émile 222, 228, 265

Easter 10, 171, 180-1, 379
embodiment 18, 98, 101-2, 104
Enlightenment 111, 133, 190, 244, 315
ethics 53, 63, 67, 70-84, 154, 178, 198
ethnicity 66, 113, 291-301
evangelicals 4, 79, 171, 175, 256, 339, 343-4, 387
Evans-Pritchard, E.E. 124, 143
ex-members 355, 358, 362-3, 371-90, 393-411

Family International, The (Children of God) 77, 372, 380
family issues 20. 276-8, 311-2, 315-8, 325, 364
Favret-Saada, Jeanne 112, 116-21, 124-5
feminism 229, 232, 250-1, 261-2, 292,296, 305, 307, 310, 313
    feminist scholarship 62, 88-104, 216, 261, 305-6

Festinger, Leon 73, 382
Fields, Rick 295-6
Finley, James 142
Fischman, Michael 228
Fitzgerald, Timothy 56-7
Forge, Anthony 153
Fox, Kate 112
Fox, Renee 153
Francis, Pope 264, 311-2, 316-26
Free Zone 350-66, 410

gatekeepers, *see* access
Geertz, Clifford 22, 47, 156
gender 15, 18, 25, 98, 250, 262, 301
    issues 61-2, 94, 96, 98, 101-2, 176
    roles 61, 240, 261
Giddens, Anthony 254, 314
Gilhus, Ingvild 395-6
Gilliat-Ray, Sophie 61-2, 180, 221
Gleig, Ann 84
Gold, Ann Grodzins 218-9
Goosen, G. 271, 283, 284, 287
Gordon, D.F. 72, 78
Graeber, David 113, 123-5
Greeley, Andrew 310, 315, 324
Greider, Kathleen 270, 282, 287
Gross, Rita 94, 145

Habermas, Jürgen 315
Haggis, Paul 363
halakha 237-9, 243, 244, 246
Haraway, Donna 92, 104
Harris, Marvin 30-1, 34, 37-41, 46, 48
Hart, Tobin 142
Harvey, Graham 15, 16, 19, 62, 64, 146
Hasidim 237, 241-2
Heelas, Paul 48, 136, 254
Hegel, G.W. F. 92, 191
He Guanghu 195, 205
Heinlein, Robert A. 399
heretics 20, 239, 242, 249, 253, 376, 379, 383
Hervieu-Leger, Daniele 140, 254
Hinduism 6, 7, 9, 17, 213-9, 342, 388, 405
Hoffman, Eva 139
holistic issues 35, 39, 59, 133, 262, 332-7, 340-5
Homan, R. 81
homosexuality 136, 255, 311, 318, 367, 383
Hubbard, L. Ron 350-62, 367, 384, 410
Hufford, David 62, 113, 121-2, 123, 216

humanism 47, 335
  Humanistic Judaism 245–6
Husserl, Edmund 5, 217

indigenous religion 9, 57, 164, 273, 274–5
International Society for Krishna Consciousness (ISKCON) 372, 380, 384
internet 24, 156, 255–66, 357, 365, 386, 389, 404
intersectionality 90. 96–9, 104, 250, 253, 262
Introvigne, Massimo 372, 375
Islam 6–7, 21, 53–4, 67, 140–1, 171–86
  Deobandi 61–3, 180, 221
  in Java 274–88
  Sufism 6, 76, 79, 274
  Wahhabis 7

Jantzen, Grace 143–4
Jehovah's Witnesses 3, 11, 374, 378–80, 382, 385–6, 388–9
Jensen, Jeppe 32–3, 126, 395–6
Jesus 4, 10, 24, 134–5, 137, 181, 260, 231, 387–8
Jesus Fellowship Church (formerly Jesus Army) 378, 380, 404
Jodo Shinshu 302–4
John XVIII, Pope 319, 383
John Paul II, Pope 258, 316, 322
Johnson, Daniel Carson 374
Jones, Jim 152, 156, 158–60, 162–3, 165–6
Jones, Kathy 45
Jones, Stephan 162, 166
Jonestown 151–167
Jubilee Year of Mercy 311–2, 320–6
Juche 9
Judaism 236–48
  conversion to 237–9, 246
  denominations within 239–48
  identity 236, 237, 246–7
  status 237–9

Kailash Ashram 214–5, 219, 221–2, 231
Kandel, Eric 161
Kasper, Walter 318–9, 325
kejawen 273–5, 278–9, 282–5, 289
Kerista 394, 398–403, 408–10
Kinsolving, Lester 165–6
Kliever, Lonnie D. 373
Kohl, Laura Johnston 158, 162, 163
Krishnamurti, Jiddu 278, 281,284, 288
kyriarchy 250, 262

Lambrev, Garry 159
Larsen, T. 143
Latter-day Saints 11, 15, 24, 378
Lauder, M. A. 74, 82
Layton, Carolyn 152, 156, 158, 165, 166
Leatham, M.C. 80
Lewis, Philip 61
Lewis, James R. 354–6
Liu Xiaofeng 190–3, 198–200, 206–7
Loftus, Elizabeth 160–1

Mackian, Sara 43–4
MacLaren, Leon 403–8
Malinowski, Bronislaw 155, 217, 230, 233
McCutcheon, Russell 35, 47
McGehee, Fielding 151, 152, 157
McLeod, W.H. 60
marriage 236–7, 275, 311, 318–9, 337, 378–80, 400–1
  remarriage 319
  same-sex 311, 363
Marrs, Texe 42
Marxism 93, 196–7, 314
Mavro, Michael and Nina 406–7
Mead, G.R.S. 42
meditation 13, 145, 215, 219, 224, 273–81, 283, 296, 342, 405
mediumship 110–1, 125
Mercadante, Linda 137–8
Merton, Robert 32
Meyer, Christian 195–6
Mézié, N. 175, 178–9, 183–4
Mikaelssson, Lisbeth 395
Miscavige, David 355, 363–4, 367, 410
Miscavige-Hill, Jenna 364–5
Mishnah 236
missionaries 4, 6, 9, 115, 190, 202, 218
Moon, Sun Myung 383–4, 386
Moore, Annie 152, 156, 158, 165, 166
Moore, John and Barbara 156, 165, 166
Mormons *see* Latter-day Saints
Muslims, *see* Islam
Muslims in Britain Research Network 52–4

Narayan, Kirin 173, 227
Nattier, Jan 293–5
near-death experience 112, 122
Neitz, Mary Jo 80–1
New Acropolis 372, 374–5

New Age 33, 41–2, 60, 136, 284, 331, 381
neutrality 58, 90, 94, 147, 164, 166, 174
Nielsen, Jorgen 54
Nock, A. D. 396
Numrich. Paul 297–8

ontological turn 111, 113, 115, 123, 127
Open University 43, 55, 60
ordination (of women) 249–66, 383
Orthodox
    Christianity 319, 339, 380
    Judaism 237–42, 244, 247–8
Orsi, Robert 17, 62
Ouspensky, P.D. 403, 405

Paganism 35, 95, 333, 340, 341, 379, 399
Palmer, Susan 74–6
Panikkar, Ramon 272
participant observation 14, 63, 71, 153–67,
    172, 215, 219, 222, 225–6, 273, 333–4,
    336, 395
patriarchy 91, 93, 145, 249–52, 261–2, 266, 341,
    344
Paul, Benjamin 153, 165
Peace Mission 83
Pentecostalism 10, 72, 73–4, 81
Peoples Temple 152–8, 162–7
Pew Research Center 20
phenomenology 5–6, 13, 56–57, 113, 125, 127,
    132, 191, 218, 272, 395–6
Phillips, D.Z. 7–8
phonetics 35
Pike, Kenneth 30–1, 34–7, 46, 228, 231, 395
postmodernism 59, 133, 147, 164, 202, 223, 229,
    310, 314
Post Traumatic Stress Disorder 160
Pratt, Mary Lou 228–9
prayer 63, 66, 82, 185, 263, 264, 276–8, 282, 339
Prebish, Charles 292–5
Presmont, Jud 398, 402, 410
Primiano, L.N. 16–7
Prokes, Mike 151–2
proselytism 78–9, 262, 264
Protestantism 4, 11–2, 17, 62, 134, 393, 387
Pryce, Ken 72–3

Quakers 10, 332, 335, 337, 339
queer issues 18, 94, 98
Qur'an 9, 21, 60, 63, 67, 181, 276, 279, 281, 283

Rabinow, Paul 218, 230
race 95–8. 104, 173, 227, 265, 292, 296, 298–301,
    306
racism 246, 253, 262, 292, 285, 303, 306
Raelians 24, 387
Rahner, Karl 313
Ramadan 171, 183, 283
Ramadan, Tariq 185
Rambo, Lewis 139, 397
Rathbun, Marty 355, 364
reflexivity 63, 58–60, 62, 90, 99–104, 183, 186,
    216–9, 226, 249
reiki 332, 338, 344
relativism 111, 223, 317
Retsikas, K. 285
Rinder, Mike 363–4
ritual 24, 81, 98, 111, 138, 144, 174, 227, 279
    in Roman Catholicism 260, 262, 337
    in Scientology 24, 356, 362
Robertson, Bill 353–4, 358, 361
Rohr, Richard 135–7, 141–2
Roles, Francis 403, 405, 408
Roman Catholicism 10, 20, 175, 249–53, 258–67,
    278, 310–26, 365, 380; *see also* Vatican
Ron's Org 353–4, 356
Rosaldo, Renato 155, 164–5
Rose, S. 43
Ruether, Rosemary Radford 262

Salaman, Clara 404, 410
Saraswati, Sri Divyananda 213–5, 221
School of Ecomomic Science 394, 403–10
Schussler Fiorenza, Elisabeth 262
science 113, 124, 125, 127, 197, 314, 315
Scientology 24, 77, 350–66, 384, 409–10
scriptures 7, 9, 177, 351, 399; *see also* Bible,
    Qur'an
Sea of Faith 332, 337
secularism 315, 318
secularization 45, 136, 315, 318, 376, 394, 397
Sedevacantists 383
seekers 43–5, 55, 60, 73, 80, 137–8, 372, 374, 376,
    397
Segal, Robert 56–7
Seventh-day Adventists 378–9, 385
sexuality 17–8, 25, 35, 94, 130, 178, 265, 316, 405
Shaffir, W. 74, 82–3
Shankar, Sri Sri Ravi 215–6, 223–4, 226–8, 231
Sharma, A. 17

Shaw, William 404–5
Sikhism 6–7, 9, 60, 65
Skőldberg, Kaj 217
Smart, Ninian 5, 56, 57, 200, 223
Smith, Paul 131
Smith, Wilfred Cantwell 5, 19, 373
Snow, D.A. 84
social media 158, 250, 255–7, 263–6
Society of St Pius X 9, 321, 324
Soka Gakkai 173, 297
Spicker, P. 72
spirit possession 110–1, 123
spirituality
  as a category 42–3, 45, 138
  Catholic 251
  differing forms of 4, 6, 10, 12–3, 133, 140–1, 254, 371, 378
  holistic 342, 345
  individual 270, 282, 285, 286, 332, 332–3, 341–5, 410
Spretnak, Charlene 131
Sri Lanka 9, 12, 182, 278
Strauss, Leo 191
Streib, Heinz 372, 376–7, 383
Stringer, Martin 31–2, 331, 345
Sufism 6, 76, 79, 274
suicide 151, 159, 164, 342
Synod on the Family 311, 326

Tanaka, Kenneth 296–7
technology 37, 187, 250, 255–8, 260, 263–4, 310, 314, 359
  as Scientology term 350, 352, 355–6, 360–1, 384
Tedlock, Barbara 153, 155
theology 32, 57, 65, 143, 175–7, 252, 256, 379, 396
  in China 190–205
  feminist 250, 262
  pastoral 270
  traditional 316, 331, 345
Theosophy 42
Thornley, Kerry 399
Timol, Riyaz 64–5
Tolley, Dorine 404–7
Tomko, Michael 147
Torah 239–45
Transcendental Meditation 215, 403
Tremlett, Paul-Francois 56–7
Turner, Edith 120
Turner, Victor 226

Tutu, Desmond 22, 24
Tworkov, Helen 293–4

UFO groups 41, 73
Unification Church 3, 76, 372, 378, 380–4, 386, 388
Universalism 388

Valk, Ulo 16, 63
Van Zandt, D.E. 77
Vatican 24, 252–3, 258–60, 311, 321, 323–5
  Second Vatican Council 310, 312–3, 315, 317–9, 321–3, 325–6
Vivieiros de Castro, Eduardo 114–5, 123, 127
Vodou 15, 77, 184
voodoo, *see* Vodou

Waco 157
Wafer, James 77–8
Wagner, Peter 310, 324
Wallis, R. 77
Wang Xiaochao 198, 201
Wansbrough, John 60
Weber, Max 41, 155, 377
Weber, Ralph 206
Weil, Simone 199
Whaling, Frank 56, 64
Wicca 80, 233; *see also* witchcraft
Wilber, Ken 131–5, 141, 144, 146–7
Wilcox, M.M. 71
Wilson, Bryan 373
Wilson, Robert Anton 398–9
witchcraft 116–20, 122, 124, 143
Wittgenstein, Ludwig 8
Woodhead, Linda 136, 330, 335, 345
World Council of Churches 11
Wright, Stuart A. 379–81, 383

Yang Huilin 202–4
Yang, Philip Q. 300
Yeung, Daniel 191
Yinger, J.M 32–3, 45
Yip Tuck, A. 18
yoga 12, 224, 332, 334

Zell, Tim 399
Zen 278, 295–6
Zhao Fusan 197
Zhuo Xinping 200
Zionism 244

www.ingramcontent.com/pod-product-compliance
Lightning Source LLC
Chambersburg PA
CBHW070057020526
44112CB00034B/1430